a.handbook of

# Personnel
# Management
# Practice

# About the Author

Michael Armstrong is an honours graduate in economics from the London School of Economics, a Fellow of the Institute of Personnel and Development and a Fellow of the Institute of Management Consultants. He is also Chief Examiner (Employee Reward) for the Institute of Personnel and Development.

This book is largely based on Michael Armstrong's hands-on experience as a personnel practitioner, initially in the engineering industry, specialising in industrial relations, and then in the engineering and food industries as an employee development specialist.

For twelve years he was an executive director with responsibility for personnel in a large publishing firm and for a further ten years he headed up the HR consultancy division of Coopers & Lybrand. He now practices as an independent consultant. This experience has been supplemented recently by a number of research projects carried out on behalf of the Institute of Personnel and Development. These covered the personnel function's contribution to the bottom line, strategic HRM, incentive pay, job evaluation, team rewards and broad-banded pay structures.

His publications for Kogan Page include *Reward Management, Performance Management, How to Be an Even Better Manager, A Handbook of Management Techniques, Improving Organisational Effectiveness* and *HRM: Strategy and Action.*

a handbook of

# Personnel
# Management
## Practice

## Michael
## Armstrong

SIXTH EDITION

KOGAN
PAGE

## YOURS TO HAVE AND TO HOLD

### BUT NOT TO COPY

First published in 1977
Second edition 1984
Third Edition 1988
Fourth Edition 1991
Fifth Edition 1995
Reprinted in 1996
Sixth edition 1996
Reprinted 1996
Reprinted 1997

Kogan Page Limited
120 Pentonville Road
London N1 9JN

© Michael Armstrong, 1977, 1984, 1988, 1991, 1995, 1996

**British Library Cataloguing in Publication Data**

A CIP record for this book is available from the British Library.

ISBN 0 7494 2028 6

Typeset by DP Photosetting, Aylesbury, Bucks
Printed in England by Clays Ltd, St Ives plc

# Contents

List of figures and tables      **17**

List of tables      **19**

Foreword      **21**

**Part I      Personnel and Development Management — An Overview**      **25**

**1   The Basis and Evolution of Personnel and Development Management**      **27**

Key purpose and concerns 27; Key activities 28; Key requirements 30; Stages in the evolution of personnel management 32; Influences on personnel management 34

**2   The Context of Personnel and Development Management**      **36**

Introduction 36; Environmental factors 37; Contingency theory 37; Technology 39; Competitive pressure 39; The role of the government in setting the agenda for personnel management 42; The European context 46; The global context 50

**3   The Personnel and Development Function**      **52**

Overall role of the function 52; The roles of personnel and development practitioners 53; Changes in the role of the personnel function 55; Models of personnel management 59; Organizing the personnel function 62

**4  The Practice of Personnel and Development Management**      **65**

The key roles of personnel practitioners 65; The internal
consultancy role 66; Outsourcing personnel work 69; Using
management consultants 71; Integrating the personnel and
development contribution 74; Innovations and interventions 78;
Marketing the personnel function 82; Preparing, justifying and
protecting the personnel budget 84; Gaining support and
commitment 85; Personnel and line management 88; Ambiguities
in the personnel contribution 90; Conflict in the personnel and
development contribution 92; Ethics in personnel and
development 93; How to be an effective personnel practitioner
97; Competence in personnel management 100; The contribution
of the Institute of Personnel and Development 102

**5  The Contribution of the Personnel Function to**
**Organizational Success**      **104**

Organizational success 104; The managerial factors which create
organizational success 105; The people factors which create
organizational success 105; To what extent does the personnel
function contribute to organizational success? 106; How does the
personnel function contribute to organizational success 108;
Contribution to added value 108; Contribution to competitive
advantage 109; In what areas does the personnel function
contribute to organizational success? 110; The personnel
function's contribution to change management 111; The
personnel function's contribution to continuous improvement
112; The personnel function's contribution to quality
management 113

**6  Evaluating the Personnel Function Contribution**      **117**

Approaches to evaluation 117; Overall methods of evaluation
118; Types of performance measures 119; Evaluation criteria 119;
Practical methods of evaluation 120; Preferred approach 128

**7  International Personnel Management**      **129**

International personnel management defined 129; The challenge
of international personnel management 129; Characteristics of
international personnel management 130; International
employment and development strategies 131; Recruitment across
international boundaries 133; International employee
development 134; Managing expatriates 136

# Contents

**Part II        Human Resource Management**                    **139**

**8   The Concept of Human Resource Management**                **141**

Development of the HRM concept — the US models 142; UK
versions of the HRM model 144; Characteristics of HRM 147;
Reservations about HRM 148; HRM and personnel management
152; The take-up of HRM 154; Conclusions 155

**9   Strategic Human Resource Management**                     **157**

Strategic HRM defined 157; The aims of strategic HRM 158;
Strategic management 158; Origins of the concept of strategic
HRM 161; The rationale for strategic HRM 162; The meaning of
strategic HRM 162; Strategic integration: integrating business
and HR strategies 163; The requirements for strategic HRM 168;
Conclusions 168

**Part III        Personnel Processes and Activities**          **169**

**10   Personnel Strategies, Policies and Procedures**          **171**

Personnel strategies – nature and content 171; Approaches to the
formulation of personnel strategies 174; Personnel policies 178;
Formulating personnel policies 185; Personnel procedures 187

**11   Competence-related Personnel Management**                **188**

The concept of competence 189; Types of competences 190; The
meaning of competence 192; The constituents of competence 194;
Using the concept 195; Describing competences 195; Competence
lists 196; Differentiating competences 199; Applications of
competence 200

**12   Job and Competence Analysis**                           **204**

Definitions 204; Job analysis 206; Role analysis 216; Skills analysis
216; Competence analysis 219; Job descriptions 225; Role
definitions 230

**13   Performance Management**                                 **232**

Purpose 232; Background to performance management 234;
Principles of performance management 235; The process of
performance management 235; Performance management
activities 236; Performance agreements 237; Performance plans

242; Managing performance throughout the year 243;
Performance reviews 248; Performance rating 252;
Documentation 257; Introducing performance management 258;
Monitoring and evaluating performance management 260


**Part IV     Organizational Behaviour**                                    **263**

**14   The Individual at Work**                                            **265**

Individual differences 265; The nature of skilled performance
and competence 270; What happens to people over time 270;
Sources of social influences on individuals 273; Attribution
theory — how we make judgements about people 274; Behaviour
at work 275; Orientation to work 278; Roles 280; Implications for
personnel specialists 281

**15   The Nature of Work, the Employment Relationship and the
Psychological Contract**                                                  **284**

The nature of work 284; The nature of the employment
relationship 286; The psychological contract defined 288; The
basic nature of the psychological contract 289; The changing
nature of the psychological contract 290; How psychological
contracts develop 291; The significance of the psychological
contract 292; Managing the employment relationship 293

**16   Motivation**                                                        **295**

Definition of motivation 296; The process of motivation 296;
Intrinsic and extrinsic motivation 299; Motivation theories 299;
Instrumentality theory 300; Needs (content) theory 301;
Herzberg's two-factor model 304; Process theory 306;
Behavioural theory 310; Social learning theory 310; Attribution
theory 311; Role modelling 311; The key messages of motivation
theory 311; The relationship between motivation and
performance 313; Motivation and money 314; Motivation
strategies 315; Conclusions 318

**17   Commitment**                                                        **319**

The meaning of organizational commitment 319; The significance
of commitment 319; Problems with the concept of commitment
321; Creating a commitment strategy 324; Commitment and
mutuality 327

# Contents

**18  How Organizations Function**    **329**

Basic considerations 329; The classical school 330; The human relations school 331; The behavioural science school 332; The bureaucratic model 335; The systems school 336; The contingency school 337; The modernists 339; Organizational structure 342; Organizational processes 343; Types of organization 357

**19  Organizational Culture**    **361**

Definition 361; The importance of culture to organizations 361; Components of organizational culture 362; Development of culture 366; Varieties of culture 367; Culture management 368

**20  Organization Design**    **372**

The process of organizing 372; Aim 373; Conducting organization reviews 374; Organization analysis 374; Organization diagnosis 375; Organization planning 377; Who does the work? 378

**21  Job Design**    **379**

What is job design? 379; The process of intrinsic motivation 380; Characteristics of task structure 381; Motivating characteristics of jobs 381; Approaches to job design 382; Job enrichment 384; Empowerment 385; Self-managing teams 388; A quality of working life strategy 388

**22  Organizational Development**    **390**

What is organizational development? 390; Basis of organizational development 390; Methods of organizational development 391; Change management 395; Conflict resolution 400; Educational activities in organizational development 401; The role of the OD practitioner 401; Where has OD got to? 402

**Part V    Employee Resourcing**    **403**

**23  Human Resource Planning**    **405**

Definition 405; The labour market 405; Aims 406; Achieving the aims 407; Employee resourcing strategy 409; Turning broad strategies into action plans 410; Demand forecasting 411; Supply forecasting 416; Analysing existing human resources 416;

Employee turnover or wastage 417; Analysing the effect of promotions and transfers 422; Assessing changes in conditions of work and absenteeism 423; Analysing sources of supply 423; Forecasting human resource requirements 424; Flexibility arrangements 427; Productivity and costs 430; Action planning 431; Overall plan 431; The human resource development plan 432; The recruitment plan 432; The retention plan 433; The flexibility plan 436; The productivity plan 440; The downsizing plan 441; Control 441

**24  Recruitment and Selection**                                                      **443**

The recruitment and selection process 443; Defining requirements 446; Attracting candidates 451; Advertising 453; Using recruitment agencies 457; Using recruitment consultants 457; Using executive search consultants 458; Educational and training establishments 458; Sifting applications 459; Types of interview 462; Assessment centres 463; Interviewing arrangements 464; Interviewing 465; Selection tests 472; Improving the effectiveness of recruitment and selection 478; Evaluating the recruitment process 479; The legal framework 480; The ethical framework 480; References and offers 481; Induction and follow-up arrangements 483

**25  Release from the Organization**                                                  **486**

General considerations 486; Redundancy 489; Outplacement 493; Dismissal 495; Voluntary leavers 501; References 503; Retirement 503

**Part VI      Employee Development**                                                  **505**

**26  The Basis of Employee Development**                                              **507**

Definition of employee development 507; Aims 507; Employee development activities 507; Employee development strategy 508; The context of employee development 510; Marketing employee development 511; Evaluating the employee development contribution 512

**27  Learning and Development**                                                       **513**

How people learn 513; Learning theory 516; Conditions for effective learning 520; The learning organization 521; Continuous development 524; Self-managed learning 525; Personal development plans 526

# Contents

**28  Training**      **529**

Definition 529; Aim 529; Benefits 530; Understanding training 530; Training philosophy 531; The process of training 533; Identifying learning and training needs 536; Planning training programmes 540; Training techniques 543; Conducting training programmes 544; Team building training 550; Meeting the training needs of special groups 552; Responsibility for training 552; Evaluation of training 553

**29  Management Development**      **556**

What is management development? 556; Management development as a business-led process 556; The impact of management development 557; The processes of management development 558; The nature of management development 559; Management development strategy 560; Responsibility for management development 560; The basis of management development 564; Approaches to management development 565; An integrated approach to management development 567; Competence-based management development 568; Development centres 569

**30  Career Management – Management Succession and Career Planning**      **571**

Definitions 571; Overall aims 571; The process of career management 572; Career management policies 576; Demand and supply forecasts 578; Succession planning 580; Performance and potential assessment 580; Recruitment 582; Career planning 582; Career management in delayered organizations 586

**Part VII    Employee Reward**      **587**

**31  Employee Reward Systems**      **589**

Introduction 589; The employee reward system 589; The elements of employee reward 590; General factors determining pay levels 593; Economic factors affecting pay levels 593; Aims of employee reward — the organization's requirements 597; Reward aims from the employee's point of view 598; Achieving the aims 598; The new pay 599; Reward strategy 600; Reward policy 601; Developments in the reward management scene 603

**32  Evaluating and Pricing Jobs**                                605

Job evaluation — definition and purpose 605; The key features of job evaluation 606; Basic methodology 607; Job evaluation schemes 607; Job ranking 609; Job classification 609; Internal benchmarking 610; Point-factor rating 610; Skill-based evaluation 616; Competence-based evaluation 617; Market pricing 617; Pros and cons of formal job-centred evaluation 618; Is job evaluation necessary? 620; Introducing job evaluation 620; Developing a point-factor scheme 622; Conducting the job evaluation exercise 625; Equal value 629; Establishing market rates 630

**33  Pay Structures**                                            636

Definition 636; Purpose 636; Criteria for pay structures 637; Number of pay structures 637; The basis of pay structures 638; Graded pay structures 640; Broad-banded pay structures 645; Individual job ranges 648; Job family structures 648; Pay curves 649; Spot rate structures 652; Pay spines 652; Pay structures for manual workers 653; Integrated pay structures 655; Rate for age scales 655; Choice of structure 655

**34  Paying for Individual Performance, Skill and Competence**   657

Paying for performance 657; Criteria for success 660; Performance related pay 661; Executive bonus and incentive schemes 666; Shop floor incentive schemes 667; Skill-based pay 672; Competence-related pay 674

**35  Paying for Team and Organizational Performance**            675

Team rewards 675; Relating rewards to organizational performance 678

**36  Employee Benefits, Pensions and Allowances**               681

Employee benefits 681; Occupational pension schemes 683; Allowances and other payments to employees 685

**37  Rewarding Special Groups — Sales Staff, International Staff and Directors**                                              687

Sales staff 687; International pay and expatriate's rewards 690; Rewards for directors and senior executives 692

# Contents

**38  Managing Employee Reward**                                    **696**

Reward budgets and forecasts 696; Evaluating the reward system 697; Pay reviews 699; Control 700; Reward procedures 701; Responsibility for reward 703; Communicating to employees 704


**Part VIII    Employee Relations**                                **707**

**39  The Employee Relations Framework**                            **711**

The elements of employee relations 711; Industrial relations as a system of rules 712; Collective bargaining 714; The unitary and pluralist views 716; Individualism and collectivism 717; Voluntarism and its decline 717; The HRM approach to employee relations 718; The context of employee relations 721; Developments in industrial relations 722; The current industrial relations scene 725; The parties to industrial relations 729; The trade unions 730; The Trades Union Congress (TUC) 732; International union organizations 733; Staff associations 733; The role of management 733; Employers' organizations 734; The Confederation of British Industry (CBI) 734; Institutions, agencies and officers 735

**40  Employee Relations — Processes and Outcomes**                **737**

Employee relations policies 738; Employee relations objectives 741; Employee relations strategies 742; Employee relations climate 743; Union recognition and derecognition 745; Collective bargaining arrangements 748; Informal employee relations processes 751; Other features of the industrial relations scene 752; Employee relations outcomes 754; Harmonization 757; Managing with trade unions 758; Managing without trade unions 761

**41  Negotiating and Bargaining**                                  **763**

The nature of negotiating and bargaining 763; Negotiations 764; Negotiating and bargaining skills 772

**42  Involvement, Participation and Communications**              **774**

Definitions 775; Aims of employee involvement and participation 776; Forms of employee involvement and participation 778; Varieties of employee involvement and participation 779; Attitude surveys 782; Quality circles 784; Suggestion schemes 786; Joist consultation 788; Works councils 790; Worker directors 790; Incidence of involvement and

13

participation 791; Requirements for successful employee
involvement and participation 791; Planning for involvement
and participation 792; Communications 793; Communication
systems 798


### Part IX    Health, Safety and Welfare    803

### 43  Occupational Health and Safety    805

Factors affecting health and safety 806; Principles of health and
safety management 806; Occupational health and safety
programmes 807; Analysis of health and safety performance 808;
Occupational health and safety policies 809; Health and safety
organization 811; Occupational health programmes 813;
Accident prevention 815; Measuring safety performance 817;
Health and safety training 819; Conclusions 820

### 44  Welfare Services    821

Why provide welfare services? 821; What sort of welfare
services? 823; Individual services 824; Group welfare services
827; Provision of employee welfare services 828; Internal
counselling services 828; Employee assistance programmes 828


### Part X    Employment and Personnel Services    831

### 45  Employment Practices and Procedures    833

Terms and conditions and contracts of employment 833; Mobility
clauses 835; Grievances 835; Transfer procedures 836; Promotion
procedures 838; Attendance management 838; Equal opportunity
840; Ethnic monitoring 841; Managing diversity 842; Age and
employment 843; Sexual harassment 843; Smoking 846;
Substance abuse at work 846; AIDS 848

### 46  Personnel Information and Record Systems    849

Introduction 849; Benefits of a computerized personnel
information system (CPIS) 850; Information technology strategy
for a CPIS 850; Developing a CPIS 853; Examples of CPIS
applications 856; Manual records 863

# Contents

## Appendices                                                    865

**Appendix A Personnel job descriptions**                         867

Personnel director 867; Personnel manager 868; Personnel officer
870

**Appendix B Generic role definitions**                           874

Managers 874; Team leaders 874

**Appendix C Personnel forms**                                    877

Application form 877; Performance management forms 881;
Personnel record forms 888

**Appendix D Training techniques**                                892

On-the-job training techniques 892; On- or off-the-job training
techniques 894; Off-the-job training techniques 898

**Appendix E Personnel procedures**                               904

Grievance procedure 904; Disciplinary procedure 905;
Redundancy procedure 906; Promotion policy and procedure
909

**References**                                                    910

**Subject Index**                                                 928

**Author Index**                                                  956

# List of Figures

| | | |
|---|---|---|
| 1.1 | Personnel activities — interrelationships | 31 |
| 2.1 | Deterministic contingency model | 38 |
| 2.2 | Action theory contingency model | 38 |
| 4.1 | Personnel competence map | 101 |
| 10.1 | Personnel strategy model | 175 |
| 11.1 | Competence-based integrated personnel management | 201 |
| 13.1 | Performance management as an integrating force | 234 |
| 13.2 | The performance management cycle | 236 |
| 13.3 | Managing performance throughout the year | 244 |
| 16.1 | The process of motivation | 296 |
| 16.2 | Approaches to motivation | 318 |
| 18.1 | Channels of communication within groups | 348 |
| 23.1 | The process of human resource planning | 412 |
| 23.2 | Forecast form | 414 |
| 23.3 | Analysis of age distribution | 417 |
| 23.4 | A survival curve | 421 |
| 23.5 | A human resource system | 425 |
| 23.6 | Stocks and flows data schedule | 426 |
| 24.1 | Recruitment flowchart — preliminary stages | 444 |
| 24.2 | Recruitment flowchart — interviewing | 445 |
| 24.3 | Staff requisition form | 447 |
| 24.4(a) | Job and person specification form | 450 |
| 24.4(b) | Job and person specification form | 451 |
| 24.5 | Recruitment control sheet | 460 |
| 24.6 | A normal curve | 474 |
| 27.1 | A standard learning curve | 514 |
| 27.2 | Different rates of learning | 515 |
| 27.3 | A stepped learning curve | 516 |
| 27.4 | The Kolb learning cycle | 519 |
| 28.1 | The process of planned training | 535 |

17

| | | |
|---|---|---|
| 28.2 | The training gap | 537 |
| 28.3 | Training needs analysis — areas and methods | 537 |
| 28.4 | Team building as an influence on attitudes and behaviour | 551 |
| 29.1 | The strategic impact of management development | 557 |
| 30.1 | The process of career management | 573 |
| 30.2 | Career progression curves | 574 |
| 30.3 | Progress analysis | 574 |
| 30.4 | Demand and supply models | 579 |
| 30.5 | Management succession schedule | 581 |
| 30.6 | Competence-based career progression curves | 584 |
| 31.1 | Reward management — strategy and processes | 594 |
| 32.1 | Example of the definition of a factor and its levels | 613 |
| 32.2 | Job evaluation programme | 624 |
| 33.1 | A typical graded pay structure | 640 |
| 33.2 | A job family pay curve | 651 |
| 34.1 | Performance-related variable progression | 662 |
| 34.2 | A PRP matrix | 664 |
| 41.1 | Negotiating range with a negotiating gap | 767 |
| 41.2 | Negotiating range with settlement range | 768 |
| 41.3 | Stages of a negotiation | 769 |
| 42.1 | Scale of participation | 781 |
| 43.1 | Health and safety programmes | 808 |
| 43.2 | The role of health and safety policies | 809 |
| 43.3 | Safety audit form | 817 |
| 43.4 | Safety sample inspection form | 817 |
| 43.5 | Team leader's daily check list | 818 |
| 43.6 | Accident report form | 818 |

# List of Tables

| | | |
|---|---|---|
| 2.1 | National differences in the perception of hierarchical organizational systems | 49 |
| 12.1 | Example of a job analysis rating scale | 212 |
| 12.2 | Position analysis questionnaire | 213 |
| 23.1 | Analysis of leavers by length of service | 420 |
| 23.2 | Survival rates analysis | 421 |
| 24.1 | Dos and don'ts of interviewing | 471 |
| 29.1 | Management development benchmark statements | 561 |
| 32.1 | A factor plan | 614 |
| 32.2 | Example of a job evaluation score | 615 |
| 42.1 | Communication areas and objectives | 796 |

# Foreword

This sixth edition is aligned to the Institute of Personnel and Development's professional standards which were introduced in July 1996. It incorporates new chapters on the context of personnel and development management, the contribution of personnel and development to organizational success, international personnel management, the nature of work, the employment relationship and the psychological contract, release from the organization and managing rewards for special groups. There are also substantial additions to other chapters, especially to those dealing with the practice of personnel management and employee relations. Much other new material has been introduced based on IPD and other research projects into personnel and the line, job evaluation and team reward.

## Nomenclature

This book is essentially about the management of people. Whether this process should be called personnel management, personnel and development management or human resource management is not regarded as being crucially important; so, for the sake of continuity, the title used in the first five editions has been retained. Throughout the handbook the approach has been to incorporate references to the latest thinking and best practices in the field of people management whether they have been developed under the heading of HRM or personnel management. However, the philosophy of human resource management is different from the philosophy underpinning many traditional personnel management practices. This is why the HRM concept is examined in depth in Part II.

The word 'personnel' is therefore used throughout the handbook to describe all approaches to personnel and development management, including those referred to as human resource management. No value judgement is intended by the use of this particular word.

The word 'business' in this handbook refers to all types of organizations whether they are in the public, private or voluntary sectors, on the grounds that they all have to be businesslike. IPD is used as the acronym for the Institute of Personnel and Development.

## Plan of the handbook

The handbook is structured as follows:

- *Part I* provides an overview of personnel and development management and the role of the personnel function.
- *Part II* examines the concept of human resource management and how it differs, if at all, from personnel management.
- *Part III* covers the basic processes of personnel management. These either provide a foundation for personnel activities (strategy, policy and procedures) or they consist of approaches and techniques which are used in many aspects of the practice of personnel management, underpin a number of other processes and provide means for achieving coherence and integration. These processes consist of competence analysis, job analysis and performance management.
- *Part IV* provides the theoretical and conceptual background to the practice of personnel and development management as defined in Part I. It therefore covers all aspects of organizational and individual behaviour which need to be taken into account in the practice of personnel management as considered in the remaining six parts of the handbook. It also considers the application of these concepts and the general approach to organization design and development.
- *Part V* looks at the basic resourcing activities — human resource planning, recruitment and selection and release from the organization. The term human resource planning is used instead of manpower planning for obvious reasons.
- *Plan VI* covers the whole field of employee development (human resource development) with an emphasis on the process of learning, especially self-managed learning.
- *Part VII* deals with all aspects of employee reward.
- *Part VIII* is concerned with employee relations.

- *Part IX* covers occupational health, safety and welfare services.
- *Part X* deals with employment practices and procedures and personnel information systems.

# Part I
# Personnel and Development Management — An Overview

*Part I provides an overall view of the basis, context, functions and practice of personnel and development management. It examines how the personnel function can contribute to organizational success and how its work can be evaluated.*

*Personnel and development management is considered as an integral part of the overall process of management for which all managers as well as personnel specialists are responsible. Personnel management processes are analysed from the point of view of the objectives, activities, strategies and policies needed to meet organizational requirements. The special area of international personnel management is then dealt with.*

1

# The Basis and Evolution of Personnel and Development Management

### Key purpose and concerns

The key purpose of personnel management was defined by the Personnel Standards Lead Body (1993) as being to 'enable management to enhance the individual and collective contributions of people to the short and long-term success of the enterprise.' The PSLB also stated that personnel is concerned with:

- creating an environment which enables management to recruit, train and motivate the people they need for today's and tomorrow's jobs
- the continuous development of people's potential and the creation of a climate in which all are motivated to meet the objectives of the enterprise
- helping the organization to balance and adapt to the diverse interests of its stakeholders — ie its shareholders, employees, customers, suppliers, national and local government, and the communities in which the enterprise operates
- the fostering of mutual interests and the encouragement of teamwork within and across the enterprise
- monitoring international, national and local movements impacting on employment practices and interpreting their implications on the business strategy
- the management of change: at times it must take a leading role in promoting change; at other times it must provide a stabilizing force

- providing, directly or indirectly, a range of services to support operational processes.

Personnel management is essentially about the management of people in a way that improves organizational effectiveness. As such, it is the concern of all managers and team leaders, although personnel specialists are there to make major contributions to this process, and this will include innovating and intervening as well as the provision of advice, help and services.

## Key activities

The key activities of personnel management as carried out by both line managers and personnel professionals are:

## *Organization*

- *Organization design* — developing an organization which caters for all the activities required, groups them together in a way which encourages integration and co-operation, operates flexibly in response to change, and provides for effective communication and decision making.
- *Job design* — deciding on the content of jobs and roles — their duties and responsibilities, and the relationships that exist between job or role holders and other people in the organization.
- *Organization effectiveness* — stimulating, planning and implementing programmes designed to improve the effectiveness with which the organization functions and adapts to change.

## *Employee resourcing*

- *Human resource planning* — assessing future people requirements in terms both of numbers and of levels of skill and competence, formulating and implementing plans to meet those requirements through recruitment, training, development or, if necessary, downsizing (reducing 'head counts'), taking steps to improve productivity and retention levels and to promote flexibility in the employment of people.
- *Recruitment and selection* — obtaining the number and type of people the organization needs.

## Performance management

Getting better results from the organization, teams and individuals by measuring and managing performance within agreed frameworks of objectives and competence requirements; assessing and improving performance.

## Employee development

- *Development and training* — systematically developing and implementing learning activities to enhance knowledge, skills and competences and to prepare individuals to perform a wider or more demanding range of tasks now and in the future.
- *Management development* — ensuring that the organization has the effective managers it requires to meet its present and future needs.
- *Career management* — planning and developing the careers of people with potential.

## Employee reward

- *Job evaluation* — assessing the relative worth of jobs as a basis for determining relativities.
- *Pay* — developing and administering pay structures and systems.
- *Paying for performance* — relating rewards to effort and results.
- *Employee benefits* — providing benefits in addition to pay, which cater for personal security and personal needs, etc.

## Employee relations

- *Industrial relations* — managing and maintaining formal and informal relationships with trade unions and their members.
- *Employee involvement and participation* — sharing information with employees and involving them in decision making on matters of mutual interest.
- *Communications* — creating and transmitting information of interest to employees.

## Health, safety and welfare services

- *Health and safety* — developing and administering health and safety programmes.
- *Welfare services* — providing welfare services and helping with personal problems.

## Employment and personnel administration

- *Employment practices and procedures* — conditions of service; dealing with promotions, transfers, discipline, grievances and redundancy; implementing policies on such matters as equal opportunity, managing diversity, sexual harassment, racial relations (including ethnic monitoring), age, substance abuse, smoking and AIDS; generally ensuring that the legal and social obligations of the organization are fulfilled.
- *Personnel information systems* — setting up and managing computerized personnel information systems and other records to provide a database and to assist in decision making.

The interdependent nature of these activities is illustrated in Figure 1.1.

### Key requirements

The personnel activities set out in the previous section must emphasize and be aligned to the following key requirements:

- releasing and developing the inherent capacities of people
  - developing processes that maximize their contributions
  - enabling those with potential to obtain an organizational and management perspective early in their careers
  - embedding continuous learning and development for everyone throughout the enterprise as an accepted feature of working life
  - designing, implementing and managing systems to ensure access to relevant experience
  - providing specific skills training
- recruiting, developing and training people with the right combination of specialist know-how and the broader skills and attitudes needed to match the changing demands of the business
- managing an increasingly diverse workforce with different career patterns, career aspirations and loyalties

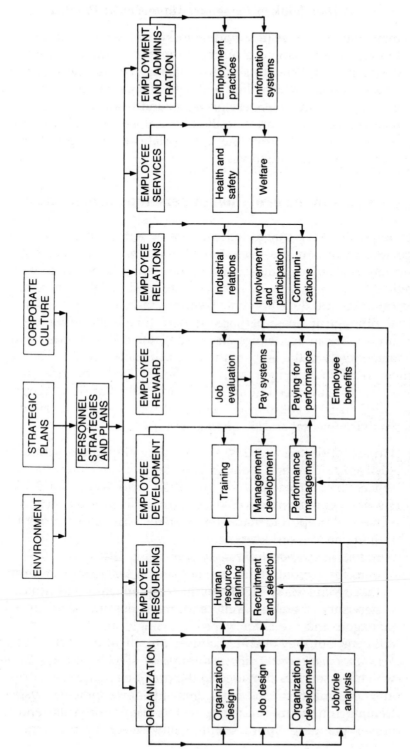

**Figure 1.1** Personnel activities — interrelationships

- managing employee (and wider workforce) relations, collective and individual, retaining commitment through times of change
- designing, implementing and managing reward and performance review systems which align and motivate people, individually and in teams, towards business priorities and results
- maintaining and improving the physical and mental well-being of the workforce by providing appropriate working conditions and health and safety initiatives.

## Stages in the evolution of personnel management

Berridge (1992) has suggested that the evolution of personnel management in Britain has been a haphazard process, occurring in an uneven, unplanned, almost random fashion, and owing more to the environmental forces in industry, business and society than to rational, logical or central development. There is much to be said for this analysis, although it does, perhaps, underestimate the influence of the mainly American academics and management gurus who have contributed largely to the body of thought which produced the concept of human resource management (HRM) and indeed influenced many of the practices introduced in the 1960s and 1970s. Various stages can be identified in the evolution of personnel management as affected by these environmental and people factors:

1.  *Welfare* (c1915 to the 1920s) — providing employees with facilities such as canteens and looking after their personal interests. Welfare officers first appeared in the munition factories of World War I.
2.  *Personnel administration* (1930s) — providing, in addition to welfare, personnel support to management in the form of recruitment, basic training and record keeping.
3.  *Personnel management, the developing phase* (1940s and 1950s) — in which the whole range of personnel services was provided including, in addition to recruitment and record keeping, craft and supervisory training. Welfare officers became staff or labour managers and the latter were increasingly involved in industrial relations, but they operated almost entirely at the tactical level.
4.  *Personnel management, the mature phase* (1960s and 1970s) — in which the services provided in the previous phase were extended into organization and management development, systematic training (under the influence of the training boards) and manpower planning. More sophisticated selection, training, salary

administration and appraisal (management by objectives) techniques were used. Under the influence of the behavioural scientists, some businesses went in for organization development (OD) programmes and job enrichment. Industrial relations were a major preoccupation and the period saw formal productivity bargaining come and go. Personnel or industrial relations directors appeared more frequently on boards, although in most cases the extent to which they were really involved in business strategy was limited. The increase in the amount of employment legislation placed greater onus on personnel professionals to become employment law experts. Personnel managers took on a more professional role.

5. *Human resource management, phase one* (1980s). The concept of HRM emerged from the writings of American academics and was taken up during the entrepreneurial 1980s when personnel specialists found themselves having to adjust to the enterprise culture and the market economy. Major concerns included how personnel or HR management could make an impact on the bottom line, and the development of strategic HRM approaches that integrated HR and business strategy. Personnel management became more business- and management-orientated and the decade saw the rise of performance-related pay as (so it was assumed) a major motivating force. It also witnessed the development of performance management systems. Industrial relations became far less significant as the power of the trade unions declined, more for structural reasons than because of constraining legislation, although the HRM philosophy was sometimes invoked as a means of marginalizing the unions. The personnel director was expected to act as a 'business partner' rather than as a specialist taking an even-handed stance on the needs of the organization and its employees.

6. *Human resource management, phase two* (the 1990s). The 1990s began with a reaction against the more egregious features of the enterprise culture with its emphasis on greed and individualism. The virtues of teamwork, empowerment and continuous development in 'the learning organization' were extolled and the role of HR in total quality initiatives became more important. The language of competences began to be used extensively and more sophisticated approaches were developed to such processes as culture management, performance and reward management, performance-related pay and management development. The recession, however, increased the emphasis on leaner, more

flexible and delayered organizations and the concept of a 'job for life' was no longer the norm. Personnel directors often found themselves involved in major redundancy or 'downsizing' exercises or managing the aftermath of a business process re-engineering study. The importance of being 'strategic' and developing cohesive personnel policies was stressed and personnel specialists often took on the role of internal consultant and became concerned with 'benchmarking' in order to identify and emulate 'best practice'. More personnel work was 'outsourced' and greater use was made of service providers such as recruitment and training consultants.

## Influences on personnel management

The main influences on current thinking in personnel and HR management have come from the following writers and commentators:

- *The human relations school* represented by academics such as Elton Mayo (1933) who emphasized people's social needs and believed that productivity was directly related to job satisfaction.
- *The behavioural science movement* represented by such writers as Maslow (1954), Argyris (1957), Herzberg (1957) and Likert (1961) who underlined the importance of integration and involvement and highlighted the idea that management should accept as a basic value the need to increase the quality of working life as a means of securing improved motivation and better results.
- *The organization development movement* sponsored by academics such as Bennis (1960), Schein (1965; 1969) and Beckhard (1969). This movement was closely associated with the concepts of the behavioural scientists and concentrated on overall organizational effectiveness, especially with regard to 'process' — ie how people behave in situations in which they are constantly interacting with one another.
- *The excellence school* consisting of writers such as Pascale and Athos (1981), and Peters and Waterman (1982) who produced lists of the attributes which they claimed characterized successful companies. These popular writers have strongly influenced management thinking about the need for strong cultures and commitment.
- *The human resource management school* comprising American academics such as Beer et al (1984), Fombrun et al (1984) and Walton (1985a). They popularized the concept of HRM as a strategic

and coherent management-orientated approach to managing people and gaining their commitment in the interests of the organization.

2

# The Context of Personnel and Development Management

## Introduction

The description of the basis of personnel and development management given in the previous chapter was schematic. It was no more than a generalized concept of what are generally regarded as the common elements of personnel management. But there is no such thing as a typical approach to personnel management just as there are no typical organizations. Organizations function in a myriad different forms and so does personnel management, the practice of which will be largely influenced by the internal environment of the organization in which it is practised. Personnel policies and practices will also, of course, be affected by the external environment of the organization. And that will impact on organizations in different ways depending on the nature of the internal environment.

The contextual factors and how they affect personnel management are considered in this chapter under the following headings:

- The environments within which the organization operates as a system.
- Contingency theory — how organizations respond to environmental factors.
- The impact of technology on the internal environment (other internal environmental factors concerned with the employment relationship and organizational structure, culture and behaviour are dealt with in Part IV).
- The external environment in the shape of the impact of competition,

the role of the government and the European and global contexts (the influence of trade unions and employers' associations is examined in Chapter 40).

## Environmental factors

Organizations can be regarded as systems. As such, their effectiveness in the process of transforming inputs to outputs is achieved by integrating the various parts of the system within the organization's internal environment and by developing a fit with its external environment.

### The internal environment

The internal environment of an organization consists of its social system (the ways in which work groups are organized and the processes of interaction that take place) and its technical system (the ways in which the work is organized and carried out to deliver products or services to customers). The internal environment is increasingly being shaped by the use of technology as discussed later in this chapter. System theory and the associated socio-technical model are described in more detail in Chapter 18.

### The external environment

The external environment impacts on organizations through the forces of competition in national, European and global markets. Organizations are also affected by economic and social trends, developments in new technology and government interventions. The external environment is constantly changing and may be turbulent, even chaotic. It imposes change and, often, turbulent conditions on the internal environment.

## Contingency theory

Contingency theory was developed originally in sociology under the name of structural functionalism (Gluckman, 1964). The empirical studies carried out by the various academics as described in chapter 18 applied the theory to work organizations.

In its crude, deterministic form, contingency theory implies that the internal structure and its system are a direct function of the environment, as illustrated in Figure 2.1. This model has been criticized as being simplistic, and Silverman (1970) offered his more sophisticated 'action theory' approach. This suggests a much more complex set of relationships between the contingent factors, which might be external (market, economic), or internal (technical, cultural) and management plans and actions. This is illustrated in Figure 2.2.

Contingency theory tells us that definitions of aims, policies and strategies, lists of activities, and analyses of the role of the personnel department are valid only if they are related to the circumstances of the organization. Descriptions in textbooks such as this can only be generalizations which suggest approaches and provide guidelines for

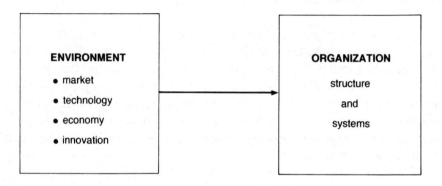

**Figure 2.1** Deterministic contingency model

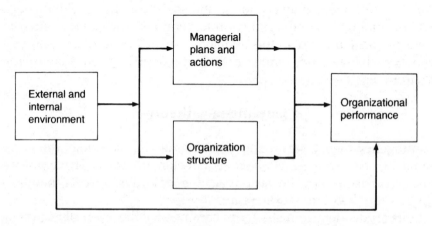

**Figure 2.2** Action theory contingency model

action; they cannot be prescriptive in the sense of laying down what should be done.

There is, however, a risk of simply perpetuating the *status quo* if contingency theory is applied so rigidly that nothing is done unless it conforms to the demands of the existing situation. Organizations have sometimes to 'break the mould'; to change structures, cultures, technologies, policies and practices to respond to a crisis or an entirely new situation. What is to be done will indeed be contingent on these new requirements but it may have nothing to do with the past. Moreover, there can be a tension between the aims of achieving 'best fit' in accordance with contingency theory and implementing 'best practice' — the latter may have to be developed incrementally in accordance with the capacity of the organization and its management to absorb and to manage change.

## Technology

The technology of the business exerts a major influence on the internal environment — how work is organized, managed and carried out. The introduction of new technology may result in considerable changes to systems and processes. Different skills are required, new methods of working are developed. The result may be an extension of the skills base of the organization and its employees, including multiskilling (ensuring that people have a range of skills which enable them to work flexibly on a variety of tasks, often within a teamworking environment). But it could result in deskilling and a reduction in the number of jobs (downsizing). New technology can therefore present a considerable threat to employees.

Knowledge workers and technicians are now operating computerised offices and computer integrated manufacturing systems and they may have to be managed quite differently from the clerks or machine operators they displace.

## Competitive pressures

Global competition in mature production and service sectors is increasing through the multi-nationals and the industrialization of the Pacific rim countries. This is assisted by easily transferable technology and reductions in international trade barriers. Customers are demanding more as new standards are reached through international competition.

## How organizations are responding

Organizations are reacting to this competition by becoming 'customer led', speeding up response times, emphasising quality and continuous improvement, accelerating the introduction of new technology, operating more flexibly and 'losing cost'. The pressure has been for businesses to become 'lean and mean', cutting out layers of management and supervision. They are reducing permanent staff to a core of essential workers and increasing the use of peripheral workers (subcontractors, temporary staff) and 'outsourcing' work to external service providers, thus reducing employment costs and enabling the enterprise easily to increase or reduce the numbers available for work in response to fluctuations in the level of business activity. They become the so-called 'flexible firms'. The ultimate development of this process is the 'virtual' firm or corporation, where through the extensive use of information technology, a high proportion of marketing and professional staff mainly work from home, only coming into the office on special occasions, and spending more time with their customers or clients.

## World class performance

The aim of organizations competing globally is to attain world class performance. This happens when what the organization does and how it does it are as good as, if not better than the world leaders in the sector in which the organization operates. The means by which world class performance can be achieved include:

- benchmarking to establish world class standards
- creating an environment dedicated to continuous improvement and quality
- an unending thrust for innovation (product and process development and new technology)
- determined attacks on costs to achieve cost leadership
- the pursuit of employee resourcing and development goals aimed at creating superior levels of individual and team competence and delivered performance.

The need to achieve world class standards to achieve competitive advantage on a global basis has focused the attention of many organizations on the importance of investing in people and building a high quality, flexible, well-motivated and committed workforce.

## Business process re-engineering

Another popular response to competitive pressures is business process re-engineering (BPR). This is essentially about business *processes* which can be defined as 'the activities that take one or more kinds of input and create an output that is of value to the customer'.

Business process re-engineering does not look at related functions as separate entities. Instead it examines the process that contains and links those functions together from initiation to completion. It looks at processes in organizations horizontally to establish how they can be integrated more effectively as well as streamlined. It can therefore form the basis for an organizational re-design exercise. From a personnel point of view, the outcome of a BPR exercise may well be the need to attract or develop people with new skills as well as pressure for the improvement of teamworking. It also emphasizes the importance of an integrated — a coherent — approach to the development and imple-mentation of personnel policies and employment practices.

Re-engineering often promises more than it achieves and the human aspects are sometimes neglected, insufficient attention having been given to the management of change and re-training staff.

## How is intense competition affecting people?

In *People Make the Difference* the Institute of Personnel and Development (1994) suggested that the driving forces of competition were affecting the way in which people are organized and managed as follows:

- decentralization and devolvement of decision-making
- slimmer and flatter organization structures
- total quality and lean organization initiatives
- fewer specialists directly employed
- the development of a flexible workforce
- more project-based and cross-functional initiatives and team working
- empowered rather than command structures
- greater self-management and responsibility for individuals and teams
- openness, fairness and partnership in employment relations
- greater need for managers to develop their interpersonal, team leadership and motivational skills when carrying out their facil-itating and coordinating roles

- pressure for everyone to become more customer-orientated
- emphasis on continuous development to achieve competitive advantage through people.

## The role of the government in setting the agenda for personnel management

The government contributes to setting the agenda for personnel management by:

- its policies and programmes for economic management
- employment legislation and regulations
- trade union legislation
- setting up services, executives, commissions and agencies such as the Advisory, Conciliation and Arbitration Service (ACAS) and the Health and Safety Executive
- developing the national vocational education and training framework and initiatives such as Investors in People (IIP)
- in its capacity as an employer, acting as an 'exemplar', encouraging the practice of new approaches to personnel management in government departments and agencies, while also reflecting best employment practices.

### Economic management

The economic environment in which organizations operate will be strongly influenced by government policies and programmes designed to counter recession, accelerate growth, control inflation and generally increase productivity and competitiveness. Fiscal policies affect the provision of employee benefits and pensions and encourage profit sharing, share ownership and the development of profit-related pay schemes.

### Employment legislation and regulations

Over the last 30 years an entirely new framework of employment legislation and regulations has been created covering many aspects of employment such as contracts of employment, dismissal, redundancy, discrimination, equal pay, maternity rights, health and safety and data protection and employee rights following mergers and takeovers (transfer of undertakings). Some important aspects of employment, such as contracts, are still governed by common law more than by legislation but the employment legislation programme of successive governments has transformed the context within which people are employed.

## Trade union legislation

Between 1980 and 1993 a legal framework was devised which meant that the government comprehensively intervened in the traditional 'voluntarist' system of industrial relations in the UK. The conduct of industrial relations is now tightly regulated by legislative requirements.

## Government services and agencies

The services and agencies set up by the government include:

- *ACAS*, which provides arbitration and conciliation services. It also publishes codes of practice and advice on particular aspects of personnel management such as performance pay.
- *The Equal Opportunities Commission*, which conducts research and produces guidelines and advice on all aspects of equal opportunity, including equal pay and sex discrimination. It will support individuals in making claims that they have been discriminated against where the case is thought to be particularly significant.
- *The Race Commission*, which provides guidelines and advice aimed at preventing racial discrimination.
- *The Health and Safety Executive*, which promotes healthy and safe practices at work, monitors through its inspectorate the health and safety performance of organizations and initiates legal action against businesses which have contravened the Health and Safety at Work Act and other regulations concerning occupational health and safety.

## Vocational education and training

Government arrangements for vocational education and training frequently change but currently they are based on the National Vocational Education and Training Framework, which is:

- locally based
- an employer-led partnership

- an integrated approach to training, vocational education and enterprise development, focused on economic growth.

The three most important elements of the vocational education and training strategy are the Training and Enterprise Councils (TECs, LFCs in Scotland), the National Vocational Qualifications system (NVQs, SNVQs in Scotland) and Investors in People.

*Training and Enterprise Councils*
TECs or LFCs operate under government contracts, are employer led and are concerned with four programme heads: opportunities for young people, opportunities for the unemployed, promoting training for the employed, and business growth.

*National Vocational Qualifications*
The NVQ and SNVQ systems provide for certificates to be awarded to individuals who are assessed in the workplace as having reached a specified standard of performance at different levels. An NVQ or SNVQ qualification is a statement of competence which, as defined in 1988 by the Training Services Agency, incorporates specified standards 'in the ability to perform in a range of work-related activities and the skills, knowledge and understanding which underpin such performance'. An NVQ consists of a number of units of competence, each of which is separately achievable and certificated. It can be gained by a process of credit accumulation.

The system is controlled by The National Council for Vocational Qualifications in England and Wales and *Scotvec* in Scotland. Industry lead bodies have the overall responsibility for developing standards and NVQs within their sector, but the actual development must be undertaken by the industry itself. Awarding or certification bodies such as City and Guilds and BTEC issue NVQ certificates.

*Investors in People*
Investors in People (IIP) is a national standard based on the practical experiences of successful organizations in developing people to meet the business goals that have been set and communicated. It was developed by the Employment Department and is administered by TECs in England and Wales and LECs in Scotland. The standard consists of four parts which in summary are:

- Making a public commitment from the top to develop all employees to achieve business objectives, including having a written business plan, and ensuring that employees understand their role in achieving this.

- Reviewing regularly the training and development needs of all employees.
- Training and developing employees, beginning with their induction and carrying on throughout their career. This should enable them to meet the objectives and targets of the job, and their own development needs.
- Evaluating the investment in training and development to assess whether it has contributed to the achievement of the organization's goals and targets.

There are clear assessment indicators for each part of the standard to help organizations and managers to identify those areas where they are already meeting the standards, and those on which they need to take further action.

## The state as employer

As an employer the state has traditionally had both an exemplar and a reflective role. The traditional exemplar role of the state was to act as a 'model' employer, adopting progressive employment practices such as offering job security, trade union recognition, jointly agreed employee relations procedures with a strong emphasis on joint consultation, fair wages, equal opportunities and equal pay, occupational pensions, training and the employment of disadvantaged workers. Pressures to reduce the cost and size of the Civil Service and the transfer of government work to agencies which are empowered to develop their own employment policies means that the state is no longer in the same situation as an exemplar as it was before the 1980s.

In its reflective or 'best practice' role the state adopts what it believed to be progressive personnel policies and practices from the private sector. The government toyed with management-by-objectives and analytical job evaluation for civil servants in the 1970s and enthusiastically introduced performance-related pay (PRP) in the 1980s. To a degree, these initiatives were politically motivated and were often based on a naive belief in the techniques as panaceas which would transform the public sector culture to a performance-orientated market-led culture overnight. Many government departments and agencies, for example, have found it difficult to assimilate PRP.

## The European context

Europe is a diverse continent but the European Union (EU) of 15 countries (as at June 1996) has helped it to become one of the most important economic forces in the world (the others are North America and the Pacific Rim countries). Through its social policies as expressed in the Social Charter the EU aims to create a 'social dimension' to the mainly economic measures of the Single European Act. The four main principles of European Social Policy have been expressed as follows:

- employment is the key to social and economic integration
- competitiveness and social progress are two sides of the same coin
- convergence which respects diversity
- a level playing field of common standards.

### EU Directives

The main impact of the EU on personnel policies and practices is made through its directives to which the UK has to adhere, although, through the Social Protocol Agreement, the British government opted out of the Maastricht treaty Social Chapter provisions for the acceleration of the harmonization of employment law. The main EU directives as at June 1996 were:

- *Equal pay for men and women* implements Article 119 of the Treaty and provides for equal pay for same work or work to which equal value is attributed.
- *Collective redundancies* requires prior consultation and notification in the event of proposed collective redundancies.
- *Equality of treatment* prohibits sex discrimination as regards access to employment, vocational training, promotion and employment conditions.
- *Transfer of undertakings* safeguards employees' acquired rights when an undertaking established within the EEC transfers to or merges with another business, and establishes consultation procedures to protect against dismissal.
- *Equal treatment of men and women in social security matters* prohibits discrimination regarding access and entitlement to pay of statutory social security benefits received in respect of unemployment, sickness, disability, old age, industrial accidents and diseases.
- *Protection of employees in event of employer's insolvency* requires the establishment of insolvency funds to meet outstanding employee

claims in respect of wages, sickness, holidays, and retirement benefits, provided claims are made before insolvency.

- *Equal treatment in occupational social security schemes* prohibits sex/ marital discrimination in occupational social security schemes providing coverage for sickness, disability, old age, early retirement, industrial accidents and diseases and unemployment. It requires equality of treatment in schemes in terms of coverage, eligibility, calculation and payment of contributions, and rights to benefits, but not in retirement ages until state schemes are also changed.
- *Mutual recognition of higher-education diplomas* establishes a general system for recognition of higher education diplomas on completion of professional education and training of at least three years' duration to enable diploma holders to exercise their profession in a member state other than the one where the qualifications are gained.
- *Measures to encourage improvement in health and safety at the workplace*
- *Maternity rights* — this provides for a minimum of 14 weeks continuous maternity leave irrespective of the length of service; maternity payment equivalent to statutory sick pay; dismissals protection; assessment of health risks of pregnant women; the right of pregnant women to refuse night work.
- *European Works Councils* involves setting up works councils in European undertakings or groups of undertakings as a means of informing or consulting with employees.

One of the most important impacts of these directives on the UK is that the British nationals can and do appeal direct to the European Court of Justice when they think their treatment has not been in accordance with European law.

## EU institutions

The principal institutions of the EU are:
- *The Council*, which is the decision-making body of the EU.
- *The European Commission*, which proposes measures for discussion by the Council and for implementing its decisions.
- *The European Parliament*, which is a consultative rather than a legislative body.
- *The European Court of Justice*, which rules on the interpretation and application of European law.

## European diversity

The EU accepts that there is always likely to be diversity in cultures and legal systems between member countries and that this fact must be taken into account when developing convergent policies. It has also had to accept, albeit unwillingly, that there are different approaches to employee relations within the EU, especially within the UK (hence the Social Protocol Agreement). In general, the West European traditional approach to employment legislation has been to concentrate on the individual rights of workers. In the UK, the focus has recently been on legislation to curb the trade unions. UK companies operating in Europe, or UK subsidiaries of European companies, have to remember the significant cultural and legal differences when recruiting across national boundaries and employing and training people of different nationalities.

### Cultural diversity

Research conducted by Laurent (1986) revealed significant national differences in the perceptions about organizations in European countries (with the US included for comparison purposes) as set out in Table 2.1. And even if the behaviour of, say, Britons, French, Germans and Italians is often stereotyped, there are noticeable differences in their approaches to work and methods of handling the employment relationship.

### Diversity in social and political philosophies

The EU aim of harmonizing employment protection has been underpinned by European mainland socialist and social democrat traditions which are in conflict with the free market individualistic ideology adopted by UK Conservative governments.

### Diversity in legal regulation of employment

The original six member states of the EU have the Roman-German legal system in which the State plays a central role in industrial relations and there is comprehensive labour market regulation. In contrast, the UK has a more voluntarist tradition based on free collective bargaining.

### Industrial relations

In Germany, Belgium, Holland and Denmark the approach to industrial relations is essentially consensual and there are high levels of common values and beliefs amongst employers, unions and the government.

**Table 2.1** National differences in the perception of hierarchical organizational systems

|  | Belgium | Denmark | France | Germany | Holland | Italy | Sweden | UK | US |
|---|---|---|---|---|---|---|---|---|---|
| *Sample size* | 45 | 54 | 219 | 72 | 42 | 32 | 50 | 190 | 50 |
| *% agreement with* | 27 | 19 | 24 | 16 | 17 | 41 | 4 | 13 | 6 |
| Most organisations would be better off if conflict could be eliminated for ever. |  |  |  |  |  |  |  |  |  |
| *% agreement with* | 44 | 23 | 53 | 46 | 17 | 66 | 10 | 27 | 18 |
| It is important for a manager to have at hand precise answers to most of the questions that his/her subordinates might raise about their work. |  |  |  |  |  |  |  |  |  |
| *% agreement with* | 42 | 37 | 42 | 46 | 39 | 75 | 22 | 31 | 32 |
| In order to have efficient work relationships, it is often necessary to bypass the hierarchical line. |  |  |  |  |  |  |  |  |  |
| *% agreement with* | 84 | 69 | 83 | 79 | 60 | 81 | 64 | 74 | 54 |
| An organizational structure in which certain subordinates have two direct bosses should be avoided at all costs. |  |  |  |  |  |  |  |  |  |

In Sweden, Norway and Austria the approach is less consensual, the various industrial relations parties seeing themselves as having distinctive interests.

In Britain and Italy the industrial relations system is essentially adversarial, in which the ideology of 'them' and 'us' has tended to prevail (although perhaps this characteristic is becoming less pronounced).

## A European approach to personnel management

A European approach to personnel management has to be underpinned by an understanding of cultural diversity factors and the different approaches to employment legislation and industrial relations. It clearly must also be governed by EU social policies and directives, for example the European Works Council Directive 1994 which lays down requirements on information disclosure and consultation in prescribed multinational companies.

A uniform approach to employment policies across Europe is unlikely to be practicable or appropriate. National cultures will influence the employment relationship in each European country. Some Euro-organizations devolve responsibility for personnel matters entirely to their separate European companies and do not attempt to develop common policies. Others aim to achieve the integration of some key policies such as employee and career development and performance management. Their objective may be to develop a cadre of 'Euro-managers' who are at least bi-lingual and can work effectively in any of the corporation's European sites. This policy may be based on the joint recruitment of graduates, especially those from European schools of management such as INSEAD.

## The global context

Global competition is gathering force. The business world is more and more marked by the increasing internationalization of markets and firms. Competitive economies are emerging in areas such as the Pacific rim with high annual rates of growth and strong export performance. Globalization has led to the continuing rise of the multinationals. They have existed for a long time, of course, but accelerating global expansion, takeovers, and mergers have become an increasingly important feature of the industrial and commercial scene as international companies move into the UK, while British firms expand overseas. This 'globalization' of the economy brings into contact business practices from different cultural, national and managerial backgrounds.

The globalization of products and markets has led to 'strategic alliances' between separate firms who act in partnership or as joint ventures to develop and market new products. For example, IBM, Toshiba and Siemens got together on the principle of 'if you can't beat them, join them'. This meant pooling financial, technological and human resources to develop memory chips 16 times more powerful than any currently available.

A truly global organization treats the whole world as if it were one company. But the approach many adopt, as expressed by Torrington (1994) is to act locally, but to plan globally. Effective multinationals recognize that, while a global strategy is necessary, it can only be implemented locally in the light of the prevailing economic, social and legal circumstances of the country concerned.

The global trends noted by the CBI (1990) are:

- an increase in world trade which is ahead of the rate of economic growth
- changes in the structure of world trade as 'new entrant' economies develop outside the traditional industrialized world
- the development of new technologies which facilitate international operation
- rising aspirations and standards around the globe
- the international spread and global reach of a more innovative and enterprising culture.

These business practices are conducted by people, and while it is relatively easy to move finance and technology round the world, moving people presents many difficulties, simply because they are working away from home in new environments and within different cultures. At the same time, deeply rooted cultural differences make it difficult, in fact potentially dangerous, to attempt the imposition of a common approach throughout the world. Hence the importance of adopting specific policies for international personnel management, as considered in chapter 7.

# 3

# The Personnel and Development Function

Personnel and development functions are concerned with any or all of the areas of personnel and development management described in Chapter 1, namely, organization design and development, resourcing (human resource planning and recruitment), employee development, employee reward, employee relations, health and safety, welfare, personnel administration, fulfilment of statutory requirements, equal opportunity issues and other matters concerned with the employment relationship.

The aim of this chapter is to review the role and organization of the function and its members. There are a great variety of roles carried out by personnel departments depending on the structure, technology, internal environment and culture (values and management style) of the organization. So this chapter simply offers a broad analytical framework as a basis for understanding how different approaches to personnel and development management can take place within organizations under the following headings:

- the overall role of the function
- the roles of personnel and development practitioners
- changes in the roles
- models of personnel management
- organization of the personnel function.

## Overall role of the function

The overall role of the personnel and development function is to enable the organization to achieve its objectives by taking initiatives, making interventions and providing guidance and support on all matters relating to its employees. The basic aim is to ensure that management deals effectively with everything concerning the employment and development of people and the relationships that exist between management and the workforce. A further key role for the personnel function is to play a major part in the creation of an environment which enables people to make the best use of their capacities and to realize their potential to the benefit of both the organization and themselves.

As the Personnel Standards Lead Body (1993) stated:

> Personnel is exercised as part of the full business management process and cannot be viewed in isolation. Although a support activity it must be pro-active. It must promote business solutions that take advantage of opportunities stemming from business issues just as it must find solutions to apparent constraints. Practitioners need to work as part of the management team, adopting, in a personal sense, the appropriate role from leader to facilitator that will gain the right end result for the enterprise; that is the result that takes proper account of the personnel issues, balancing the short and long-term considerations. They play a particularly active role in forming aspects of business strategy and ensuring that personnel policy is implemented.

## The roles of personnel and development practitioners

Personnel and development practitioners can have a number of roles within the overall framework described above. The extent to which any individual personnel or HR director, manager or officer will play any of these roles will be dependent partly on the type and structure of the organization, its culture and the environment in which it exists. As Legge (1978) comments:

> Different organizational and environmental considerations will necessitate a transformation of general prescription into concrete strategy adapted to the situation in which it is to operate.

In other words, what personnel specialists do and how they interact with others — their roles — will be contingent on the situation in which they find themselves. The influence they exercise and the contribution they make will depend to a very great extent on *how* they play these various parts. The position they are given in the organization, the receptiveness of management to their suggestions, and the authorities they are allocated will, of course, affect their scope to exercise influence and function effectively. Ultimately, however, what personnel specialists achieve will depend on their credibility to top management and their colleagues. And they will be credible if they can demonstrate their expertise and competence by making a real contribution to organizational effectiveness, and by providing managers with the people they need and any guidance or help they want in managing them.

The various roles that personnel practitioners can play are listed below:

- *business partners* — sharing responsibility with their line management colleagues for the success of the enterprise
- *strategists* — contributing to the development of business strategies and formulating integrated personnel strategies which support the achievement of corporate strategic plans
- *problem solvers* — defining the nature of personnel and organizational problems, analysing the circumstances contributing to the problems, diagnosing the reasons for the problem and deciding on what course of action should be taken
- *innovators* — assessing the needs of the organization and devising and recommending new or revised policies and processes which will meet those needs
- *interventionists* — understanding crucial personnel issues and pressure points on organizational processes and stepping in selectively with proposals on how to deal with them
- *enablers* — helping other people to do things about human resource issues rather than doing things themselves; *empowering* line managers to take full responsibility for managing their human resources and acting as *coaches* to help them develop the human resource management skills they need; acting as *change agents*
- *internal consultants* — advising their clients (line managers) on personnel policies and practices and helping to implement new personnel processes
- *service providers* — providing efficient and cost-effective services to line managers in the fields of resourcing, employee development, reward, employee relations, health and safety and other employee services, personnel information services, and advice and help in handling employment problems to do with discipline, grievances, redundancy, equal opportunity and any other aspects of employment law — personnel specialists have to recognize that their line management colleagues are their clients and

their internal customers and therefore require high levels of service

- *consistency monitors* — overseeing activities to ensure that personnel policies and procedures are implemented and administrated consistently and fairly, that the provisions of employment, equal opportunity and health and safety legislation are put into effect and the organization avoids getting into difficulties on legal matters
- *guardians of the organization's values concerning people* — advising management on the values it should adopt in dealing with its employees and other stakeholders and pointing out when existing behaviour is conflicting with those values or where proposed actions will be inconsistent with them. This role of acting as the 'conscience' of management is perhaps the most difficult one of all to play and it is the one that personnel specialists can too easily neglect in their anxiety to be regarded as business partners.

The three key roles of personnel practitioners as strategists, service providers and internal consultants are considered more fully in Chapter 4.

## Changes in the role of the personnel function

### Changes in scope

The 1990 Workshop Industrial Relations Survey of 2061 workplaces (WIRS3, Millward *et al* 1992) found some evidence of a widening in the scope of the activities of managers responsible for personnel. There was a substantial increase in the proportion of personnel specialists stating that they dealt with procedures for grievances, discipline and disputes, with settling and negotiating terms of employment and job evaluation (the increase in responsibility for pay determination has arisen mainly because of the decentralization of collective bargaining which has taken place over the last decade).

The WIRS3 also showed that a move towards the 'balkanization' (using Tyson's 1987 term) or fragmentation of the personnel function has been taking place. As Sisson (1995) notes, many key personnel activities are being undertaken by non-specialists or by other groups such as training departments. Specialist personnel managers are being left with relatively routine systems maintenance functions, such as recruitment and selection and pay determination. But the WIRS3 also indicated that there has been no change between 1984 and 1990 in the involvement of personnel management at the highest level in organizations (ie as members of the executive board). Sisson comments that: 'If personnel specialists are not even present when key decisions are taken, this effectively means that personnel issues will almost inevitably be condemned to second-order status'. Strategic personnel or HR management and the chances of developing coherent and consistent policies are therefore pretty slim.

## Externalization

The Recruitment and Development Report (1991) based on a survey of nearly 100 large organizations provided further information on changes to the role and activities of the personnel function. Adams (1991) has identified the following four approaches to the traditional department, each of which can be seen as representing a 'kind of scale of increasing degrees of externalization, understood as the application of market forces to the delivery of personnel activities'.

1. The *in-house agency*, in which the personnel department, or any of its activities, such as graduate recruitment, is seen as a cost-centre and the activities are cross-charged to other departments or divisions.
2. The *internal consultancy*, in which the personnel department sells its services to internal customers (line managers), the implication being that managers have some freedom to go elsewhere if they are not happy with the service that is being provided.
3. The *business within a business*, in which some of the activities of the function are formed into a quasi-independent organization which may trade not only with organizational units but also externally.
4. *External consultancy*, in which the organizational units go outside to completely independent businesses for help and advice.

The common feature of all these approaches is that the services delivered are charged for in some form of contract which may incorporate a service level agreement (see Chapter 6).

## What is happening to the personnel function?

As Sisson (1995) remarks:

> The reality of the personnel function in the UK has always been in strong contrast to the picture which appears in the textbooks and practitioner.... The latter has been dominated by what Torrington (1989),

drawing on a medical analogy, has termed the 'general practitioner model, ie personnel managers are (and, by implication, should be) 'professionals' involved in a wide range of activities. In practice, things have been very different.

Sisson points out that in the early 1980s:

- large numbers of personnel specialists — more than half — did not belong to the IPM (as it then was) and were not 'qualified'
- personnel management was not a single homogeneous occupation — it involved a variety of roles and activities which differed from one organization to another and from one level to another in the same organization
- personnel management was highly 'balkanized' — not only was there a variety of roles and activities but these tended to be relatively self-centred, with little movement between them.
- personnel management was structured on gender lines — women made up the great majority of personnel managers, yet they tended to be employed in lower-level and less well-paid jobs than their male counterparts, which helped to reinforce the 'cinderella' image of the function as a whole.

The evidence provided by the WIRS3 as reported by Millward *et al* (1992) and other surveys, has not suggested that there have been significant changes since the 1980s in spite of the emphasis on human resource management (HRM), professionalism and the personnel manager as a business partner. The key findings of the survey were that:

- there does not appear to have been much of a move to include 'human resource' in job titles — the number of specialists calling themselves 'human resource managers' turned out to be less than 1 per cent
- the number of workplaces with a specialist personnel manager remains very small (17 per cent overall compared with 15 per cent in 1980) — as might be expected, the greater the size of the establishment the greater the probability of there being a designated personnel manager (87 per cent in 1990 compared with 88 per cent in 1980)
- only 12 per cent of personnel managers were educated to degree level and only 7 per cent had a degree or postgraduate diploma in personnel/industrial relations/trade union studies

- an increasing number of line managers are spending a large part of their time on personnel matters but, significantly, 28 per cent had academic and/or professional qualifications
- the ratio of corporate personnel staff to employees in 1985 was 1:1250 and 1:352 for UK-owned and foreign-owned companies respectively; in 1992 it was 1:1800 overall (Margerison *et al* 1993)
- there has been a greater division of labour between the various personnel and development activities (ie 'balkanization')
- the proportion of organizations with specialist representation on the board has declined slightly from 43 per cent in 1984 to 40 per cent in 1990.

The *Recruitment and Development Report* (1991) confirmed that there has been a significant shift away from the traditional methods of managing personnel functions in the direction of outsourcing and the use of external consultancies. These aspects of the practice of personnel management and the adoption of an 'internal consultant' role by personnel specialists are discussed in the next chapter.

## Variations in the practice of personnel and development in different organizations

The practice of personnel and development will vary hugely between different organizations because of the influence of such factors as:

- the values and beliefs of top management about the need for a specialist personnel function and the extent to which it will make a contribution to the 'bottom line'
- the organization's business strategy and critical success factors and the degree to which top management believes that strategic goals are more likely to be attained and critical success factors given the attention they deserve if there is a specialist personnel function.
- the structure of the organization, for example, centralized or decentralized, homogeneous or divisionalized, hierarchical or delayered — in Chandler's (1962) phrase, structure follows strategy, and although he was thinking of the business as a whole, this equally applies to the personnel function's structure.
- the culture of the organization generally — if 'the way we do things around here' takes little notice of the ethics and values implicit in a humanistic approach to personnel management that focuses on human needs, then clearly this will diminish the importance attached to the role of the personnel function, which could be left

with routine administrative duties and staffed by Storey's (1992) so-called 'handmaidens'
- the technology and core activities and competences of the organization, which might indicate that a key performance 'driver' is the level of people employed and their skills, motivation and commitment — in these circumstances the need for internal professional advice and consultancy services is more likely to be recognized
- the extent to which there is a thrust to devolve the responsibility for personnel matters to line managers
- the degree to which management believes that it is necessary to have a function or people in the organization whose role is to develop 'best practice' in personnel policies and/or are there to ensure that they are implemented consistently
- the traditional structure and power of the personnel function
- the professional and business expertise, credibility and political strengths of the head of the personnel function.

## Models of personnel management

There is, of course, an immense diversity in personnel roles which is directly related to the immense diversity in organizations and in the people who run them. A universal model for personnel management does not, indeed cannot, exist. It is dangerous to assume that model A is better than model B. However, a number of different models have been suggested, and these are described below.

### The Karen Legge models

Karen Legge (1978) distinguishes between two models of personnel managers:

- *Conformist innovators* who go along with their organization's ends and adjust their means to achieve them. Their expertise is used as a source of professional power to improve the position of their departments.
- *Deviant innovators* who attempt to change this means/ends relationship by gaining acceptance for a different set of criteria for the evaluation of organizational success and their contribution to it.

### The Shaun Tyson models

These models were established by Tyson (1985) following research which identified three approaches to personnel management in the United Kingdom:

1. *The administrative/support model* in which personnel officers concentrate on the basics of a routine activity.
2. *The systems/reactive model* which exists in more sophisticated industrial relations environments where the main sphere of influence is on the creation and maintenance of the rules of the work, through policies and procedures.
3. *The business manager model* where the main characteristics of the personnel specialists are that they:

— integrate their activities closely with top management and ensure that they serve a long-term strategic purpose
— have the capacity to identify business opportunities, to see the broad picture and to see how their personnel role can help to achieve the company's business objectives.

## The Shaun Tyson and Alan Fell models

Perhaps the best known models are those developed by Tyson and Fell (1986). These were derived from the former's initial (1985) version. Tyson and Fell's three personnel management models are:

1. *The clerk of works model* — in this model all authority for action is vested in line managers. Personnel policies are formed or created after the actions which created the need. Policies are not integral to the business and are short-term and ad hoc. Authority is vested in line managers and personnel activities are largely routine — employment and day-to-day administration.
2. *The contracts manager model* — in this model policies are well established, often implicit, with a heavy industrial relations emphasis, possibly derived from an employers' association. The personnel department will use fairly sophisticated systems, especially in the field of employee relations. The personnel manager is likely to be a professional or very experienced in industrial relations. He or she will not be on the board, and although having some authority to 'police' the implementation of policies, acts mainly in an interpretive, not a creative or innovative, role.
3. *The architect model* — in this model explicit personnel policies exist as part of the corporate strategy. Human resource planning and development are important concepts and a long-term view is

taken. Systems tend to be sophisticated. The head of the personnel function is probably on the board and his or her power is derived from professionalism and a perceived contribution to the business.

The 'contracts manager' model is probably less common now since the relative decline in the importance of the industrial relations aspects of the personnel manager's work.

## Kathleen Monks

Kathleen Monks' (1992) survey of personnel practices in 97 organizations in Ireland identified four models which extend the Legge/Tyson and Fell concepts:

1. *Traditional/administrative* — this applied to about one-third of the organizations. The personnel department in this model is very much a support function with a focus on administrative matters, record keeping and the adherence to rules and regulations. Few initiatives were taken by these personnel departments.
2. *Traditional/industrial relations* — these organizations (20 of the sample) concentrated on industrial relations and had elaborate manuals and procedures to deal with industrial relations (IR) matters. But other personnel matters such as recruitment and selection were not given high priority. Personnel managers could meet company expectations if they 'kept the show on the road'. This model corresponds broadly with Tyson and Fell's (1986) 'contracts manager' model.
3. *Innovative/professional* — 35 organizations were defined as 'innovative/professional'. The approach of the personnel specialists in these firms was professional and expert. They were concerned to dismantle the problematic elements of traditional practices with the expectation that whatever emerged had to be better than the existing system. Their firms had well-established activities in such areas as manpower planning, remuneration, training and development, with computerized record systems.
4. *Innovative/sophisticated* — in these mainly high-tech or finance sector organizations (only nine out of the 97, eight of which were foreign owned) personnel issues were integrated into strategic plans, personnel was represented on the board and was recognized as an important function within the organization. Commitment was sought by the intensive use of recruitment and selection practices involving a wide range of tests and several interviews to get the

'right' type of people. The manufacturing firms in this category had implemented programmes such as multi-skilling and job rotation and there was some use of autonomous work groups. Investment in employees involved spending a lot of money on training.

## John Storey

Storey's (1992a) model suggests a two dimensional map: interventionary/non-interventionary and strategic/tactical. From this he identifies four roles:

1.  *Change makers* (interventionary/strategic) which is close to the HRM model.
2.  *Advisers* (non-interventionary/strategic) who act as internal consultants, leaving much of HR practice to the line managers.
3.  *Regulators* (interventionary/tactical) who are 'managers of discontent' concerned with formulating and monitoring employment rules.
4.  *Handmaidens* (non-interventionary/tactical) who merely provide a service to meet the demands of line managers.

## Organizing the personnel function

The organization and staffing of the personnel function clearly depends on the size of the business, the extent to which operations are decentralized, the type of work carried out, the kind of people employed and the role assigned to personnel and development.

There is no standard ratio for the number of personnel specialists to the number of employees. It can vary from 1 to 80, to 1 to 1000 or more. This ratio is affected by all the factors mentioned above and can only be decided empirically by analysing what personnel services are required and then deciding on the extent to which they are provided by full-time professional staff or can be purchased (outsourced) from external agencies or consultants.

There is no blueprint for organizing the personnel function, but current practice suggests that the following guidelines should be taken into account:

●   The head of the function should report directly to the chief executive and should be on the board, or at least on the management committee, in order to contribute to the formulation of corporate strategies and play a full part in the formulation and integration of personnel strategies and policies.

- In a decentralized organization, subsidiary companies, divisions, or operational units should be responsible for their own personnel management affairs within the framework of broad strategic and policy guidelines from the centre.
- The central personnel function in a decentralized organization should be 'slimmed down' to the minimum required to develop group human resource strategies and policies.
- The personnel function has to be capable of delivering the level of advice and services required by the organization. Delivery may be achieved by the direct provision of services but, increasingly, businesses are outsourcing their personnel services.
- The function will be organized in accordance with the level of support and services it is required to give and the range of activities which need to be catered for.

The most important principle to bear in mind about the organization of the personnel function is that it should fit the needs of the business. Against that background, there will always be choice about the best structure to adopt, but this choice should be made on the basis of an analysis of what the organization wants in the way of personnel and development management guidance and services.

## Alternative forms of organization

The many alternative forms of organization include:

- A small but powerful corporate function headed by a board director dealing with strategy, matters concerning the senior management resources of the organization (recruitment, development, career planning and remuneration) and centralized negotiations in the relatively uncommon situations where these still take place. In this type of structure, divisions or strategic business units may be allowed to manage their own personnel affairs, possibly within the framework of some broad corporate policies.
- A large stand-alone company with a personnel director on the board controlling a number of specialist personnel functions such as recruitment, training, health and safety and pay.
- A large- to medium-sized organization with a 'director of personnel' or personnel manager who is not on the board. She or he may report to another specialized board member (often finance) and act

as a generalist with assistance, the scale of which depends on the size and type of the organization and the extent to which management 'believes' in the importance of the personnel function. The support may also be generalist (a personnel officer) or could be a specialist, typically a training officer. Some personnel activities may be outsourced.

● A medium- to small-sized organization with a personnel manager or personnel officer responsible to a senior manager or director for fairly routine personnel activities such as recruitment.

Examples of job descriptions for personnel specialists are given in Appendix A.

4

# The Practice of Personnel and Development Management

## The key roles of personnel practitioners

Although the roles of personnel and development practitioners will vary immensely, the following are the three main roles which they may carry out in different ways, if at all:

1. *Strategists* — addressing major strategic issues concerning the management and development of people and the employment relationship. As strategists they influence and are influenced by the business plans of the organization . They formulate policies, provide levers for change and help to manage change processes. However, many personnel practitioners are hardly involved in this role, especially if they are not part of the top management team. Strategic approaches to personnel and development are associated with the human resource management (HRM) movement and the concept of strategic HRM as examined in Part II. The ways in which personnel practitioners can integrate personnel policies and practices by adopting a strategic perspective are considered later in this chapter (pages 75 to 78).

2. *Internal service providers* — delivering efficient personnel services which meet the needs of the organization, line managers and employees generally. This is the basic personnel role and it involves the development and application of the personnel and development processes, systems and procedures described in Parts V to X of this book.

3. *Internal consultants* — providing advice and guidance to management on handling personnel issues, developing new employment practices, intervening where necessary and enabling and facilitating better employment practices generally. This role is becoming increas-

ingly important and is dealt with in the next section of this chapter (pages 66 to 69).

Personnel practitioners are outsourcing more of their activities and making more use of external help from management consultants. These aspects of personnel management in practice are reviewed in the third and fourth sections of this chapter (pages 69 to 74).

The remaining sections of this chapter examine the following key aspects of the practice of personnel management:

- integrating the personnel and development contribution
- the personnel practitioner as an innovator and an interventionist
- marketing the personnel department
- preparing, justifying and protecting the personnel budget
- gaining the support and commitment of line managers and employees to personnel interventions
- personnel and line management
- ambiguities in the personnel contribution
- conflict in the personnel contribution
- values, ethics and professionalism in personnel and development management
- how to be an effective personnel practitioner.

## The internal consultancy role

As internal consultants, personnel professionals operate like external management consultants, working alongside their clients to identify the need for new or improved approaches in the fields of policy, organization, procedures and methods. They investigate problems, prepare proposals and help to implement agreed recommendations. But like all good consultants they are not there simply to solve other people's problems. Their aim is to build consensus and commitment to action and to facilitate learning so that their clients can operate independently and handle their own affairs without further guidance.

External consultants bring to their clients subject expertise, analytical and diagnostic skills, knowledge of other organizations, independence and objectivity. Internal consultants may have just as much expertise, although as employees it may be more difficult for them to be — or to be seen to be — as independent as those from outside the organization. They have therefore to demonstrate that they are able to deliver truly objective advice. But they have the advantage over external consultants of knowing the organization — its culture, people and politics.

## Methods of operation

Internal personnel consultants can operate in three main areas:

1. *Systems development* — the introduction or amendment of systems such as those for reward, performance management and continuous development.
2. *Service provision* — internal HR consultants can provide the same sort of recruitment, selection and training services as external consultants.
3. *Process consulting* — internal consultants can provide advice and help in process areas such as organization, team building, planning, objective setting, performance and reward management, quality management, conflict resolution and, importantly, change management. This is perhaps the most rewarding but also the most challenging field in which internal consultants can work. Rewarding because they can be involved in the heart of the business, influencing the things that govern its success. Challenging because it requires considerable skill and credibility, and because their lack of independence, as perceived by their clients, may work against them.

## Conducting internal consultancy projects

In carrying out internal consultancy projects the most important thing to remember is that managers do not want ready made products. They value access to expertise, help in problem solving, an independent point of view and support in managing change, but reject pat solutions. Internal consultants must therefore try their hardest to understand what managers want as well as what they need. The art of consultancy is that of bringing together wants and needs.

Internal consultants should be well placed to identify needs as they arise. They do not have to wait to be asked, as do external consultants. They should have a clear understanding of the strategic imperatives of the organization, its business plans, the changing environment in which it has to operate, its culture and its dynamics. Their advice must be embedded in this understanding.

A typical internal consultancy project dealing with a new personnel system will be conducted on exactly the same lines as an external project — ie it will consist of the following phases: contact, contract (deliverables and costs), data collection, analysis, diagnosis, feedback, discussion and agreement of recommendations, and implementation.

A service delivery project will be similar; it will be a simpler affair of defining terms of reference, agreeing programmes and procedures, conducting the assignment and reviewing results.

Process consulting will be more complex and demanding. It is essentially a collaborative approach in which consultants are involved with their clients in gathering information, analyzing and diagnosing needs and problems, obtaining agreement to courses of action and commitment to change.

## Internal consultancy skills

Like all management consultants, internal consultants need analytical ability, diagnostic and interactive skills and the ability to communicate clearly and persuasively.

They have to be able to understand their internal client's situation and problems and work with them in developing solutions. At the same time, they have to remain independent and be capable of taking an objective point of view. Their job is not simply to act in a service role, satisfying the expressed needs of their clients. They must act as 'experts' when required as well as 'helpers'. They have to be able to add value, helping their clients to take a wider view and to look at different approaches to problem resolution. This can be more difficult for internal consultants who may not be perceived by managers as having the expertise, range of experience, knowledge of good practice and ability to remain detached which external consultants are said to possess. Internal consultants need to establish their credibility by demonstrating that they have all those qualities *as well as* a better understanding of the culture and needs of the organization and the political climate in which interventions and innovations take place.

Importantly, internal consultants must be capable of ensuring that their internal clients will be able to implement their proposals. They have to ensure that their clients 'own' the solutions and they must transfer their expertise in dealing with particular problems and requirements to the managers they advise.

Overriding all these skills is the requirement to be alert and responsive to expressed or implicit needs. If a business issue with personnel implications arises at a board meeting (and many do), the personnel director must react immediately with a positive contribution. The same principle applies at all levels in the personnel function. Internal consultants have to be opportunists in the best sense of the word. They must be sensitive to key business and associated human resourcing issues so that they can speedily intervene or exert influence.

## Outsourcing personnel work

Increasingly, personnel services which would previously have been regarded as a business's own responsibility to manage are now routinely being purchased from external suppliers. Managements are facing Tom Peters' (1988) challenge: 'prove it can't be subcontracted'. The formal policy of a major global corporation quoted by Wheatley (1994) reads: 'Manufacture only those items — and internally source only those support services — that directly contribute to, or help to maintain, our competitive advantage'.

The personnel function is well positioned to outsource some of its activities to management consultancies and other agencies or firms which act as service providers in such fields as recruitment, executive search, training, occupational health and welfare. Personnel functions which have been given responsibility for other miscellaneous activities such as catering, car fleet management, facilities management and security (because there is nowhere else to put them) may gladly outsource them to specialist firms.

### The case for outsourcing

There are three reasons for outsourcing:

1. *Cost saving* — personnel costs are reduced because the services are cheaper and the size of the function can be cut back.
2. *Concentration of personnel effort* — members of the function are not diverted from the key tasks which add value.
3. *Obtaining expertise* — knowhow and experience can be purchased which is unavailable in the organization.

### Deciding to outsource

Any of the above reasons may justify a decision to outsource. Consideration of the case for outsourcing starts with making clear distinctions between the function's various activities such as recruitment, training and development, pay, welfare and fulfilment of statutory requirements. This is necessary to assess each area so as to determine whether it can and should be outsourced and exactly what such outsourcing is intended to achieve. The questions to be answered include: Is the activity a core one or peripheral? How efficiently is it run at present? What contribution does it make to the qualitative and financial well-being of the organization? This is an opportunity to re-engineer the personnel function, subjecting each activity to critical examination to establish whether the services can be provided from within or outside the organization, if at all. Clearly, outsourcing will be worthwhile if it can deliver a better service for a better price. But it should still be considered if it can deliver a better service for the same price, or the same service for a better price.

The decision to outsource should be based on rigorous analysis and benchmarking to establish how other organizations manage their personnel activities. This will define the level of service required. The cost of providing the existing service internally should also be measured. This will be easier if an activity-based costing system is used in the organization.

### Selecting service providers

Potential service providers should be required to present tenders in response to a brief. Three or four providers should be approached so that a choice can be made. The tender should set out how the brief will be met and how much it will cost. Selection should take into account the degree to which the tender meets the specification, the quality and reputation of the firm and the cost (this is an important consideration but not the only one — the level of service which will be provided is critical). References should be obtained before a contract is drawn up and agreed. The contract should be very clear about services, costs and the basis upon which it can be terminated.

### Managerial and legal implications of outsourcing

Service providers need to be managed just as carefully — if not more so — than internal services. Service standards and budgets should be reviewed and agreed regularly and management information systems should be set up so that performance can be monitored. Swift corrective action should be taken if things go wrong and the contract terminated if there is a serious shortcoming.

The legal implications of outsourcing are that it will be based on a service contract and the purchaser of the services has the right to insist that the terms of the contract are fulfilled. Purchasers also have the duty to fulfil their side of the contract, for example, providing agreed facilities, meeting the leasing terms set out in a car fleet management contract and paying for the services as required by the contract.

## Using management consultants

Management consultants act as service providers in such fields as recruitment, executive search and training. They also provide outside help and guidance to their clients by advising on the introduction of new systems or procedures or by going through processes of analysis and diagnosis in order to produce recommendations on solutions to problems or to assist generally in the improvement of organizational performance.

Their role is to provide expertise and resources to assist in development and change. Their range and nature include acting as:

- *experts* — providing help and guidance on the basis of knowhow and experience in given fields
- *resource consultants* — mobilising additional resources to help get things done, including the service provision role
- *process consultants* — helping to improve organizational effectiveness by intervention in such areas as organization development (OD), organization design, interpersonal relationships, change management, team work, leadership and conflict resolution. In this capacity, they act as facilitators, helping organizations to reach their own conclusions, rather than as prescribers of cures or solutions.

### The steps required to select and use consultants effectively

1. *Define the need* — the need for consultancy help may arise for a variety of reasons, including a significant change in the circumstances or technology of the organization, a major problem in the employment or development of people or in employee relations, or the perceived requirement for a new approach or innovation in some aspect of personnel management. It is at this stage that the benefits of satisfying the need in such terms as improved performance, better relationships or cost-reductions need to be spelt out. An initial definition can take the form of a one-sentence action statement beginning: 'We want to ...' For example, if it is felt that the job evaluation scheme is out of date and the pay structure is inequitable and uncompetitive, an action statement could read:

We want to introduce an analytical job evaluation scheme which will provide a consistent basis for assessing and managing relativities. We also want to establish the extent to which our pay levels are competitive. On the basis of job evaluation and a market survey, we want to design an equitable and competitive pay structure which, in association with our current performance management and variable pay initiatives, will improve our ability to attract, retain and motivate high quality staff thus making considerable improvements to organizational performance. It is believed that, combined, these will contribute to a reduction in time-to-market which it is estimated will increase sales turnover by about x per cent at a cost of y per cent — a significant increase in added value.

This sort of action statement can be used as the basis for assessing the need for external consultants, defining the work to be done and setting out terms of reference. An attempt should always be made to quantify costs and benefits even when they are hard to estimate.

2. *Justify the use of external consultants* — if the need has been established in cost-benefit terms the use of external consultants rather than internal resources has to be justified. Consultants can:

- provide expertise and resources not available in the organization
- provide an independent, objective and disinterested perspective
- make available the time and resources required to concentrate on the matter in hand
- offer experience in project management and in helping their clients to reach sensible conclusions and to implement recommendations
- act as an 'extra pair of hands'.

Ultimately the only justification for using external consultants is that they will add value. Account must therefore be taken of how much they will cost — consultants can be very expensive. Further information on estimating costs is given in Armstrong (1994) on pages 35–38.

3. *Select the consultants* — if the use of consultants is justified and agreed the following actions are required to select them:

- define the objectives and terms of reference of the assignment and prepare briefing documents
- source the consultants — preferably those known to be effective or those who have been strongly recommended (the Institute of Personnel and Development's consultancy service can provide names)
- invite three or four firms or independent consultants to submit proposals on how they would meet the terms of reference in the light of an oral or written brief (even if a potentially suitable firm is

already known it is still worthwhile to get alternative proposals for comparison purposes) — the proposals should set out deliverables, a programme of work, who will carry out the assignment, the expertise of the firm *and* the consultants who would be assigned to the project, costs of fees *and* expenses and standard contract terms

- select the preferred consultants on the basis of their proposal and an interview (a 'beauty contest') — the criteria should be the degree to which the consultants understand the need, the relevance and acceptability of their proposed deliverables and programme of work, the capacity of the firm and the particular consultants to deliver, whether the consultants will be able to adopt to the culture and management style of the organization, the extent to which they are likely to be acceptable to the people with whom they will work, and the cost (a consideration but, as for service providers, not the ultimate consideration)
- always take up references before confirming the appointment
- agree and sign a contract — this should always be in writing and should set out deliverables, timing and costs, methods of payment and arrangements for termination.

4. *Agree detailed project programme* — the work to be done, who does it, timings, responsibility for project management and arrangements for reviewing progress ('milestone meetings'). When preparing the programme it is necessary to agree the contribution which will be made by members of the personnel function. Consideration should also be given to seeking contributions from line managers, employees and employee representatives (for example, as members of project teams) not only to obtain the benefit of their ideas but also so that they 'own' the outcome of the assignment.

5. *Monitor or control* — monitor the progress of the assignment carefully without unduly interfering in the day-to-day work of the consultants. The consultants may be responsible for managing the project in detail but the client is accountable for the outcome and must therefore exercise overall control.

6. *Evaluate the outcomes* — subject the consultants' interim and final recommendations to a critical examination to ensure that they:

- are based on a thorough analysis and logical diagnosis of what the organization needs and are not solutions reached down from the shelf
- fully meet the terms of reference
- are capable of being implemented by the organization at a reason-

able cost, without the need for an excessive allocation of additional resources and, of course, to the satisfaction of all concerned — so far as that is possible.

*7. Prepare and execute an implementation programme* — this should indicate what needs to be done, who will be responsible for it, the cost budget, timings and the communication and training processes required.

## If things go wrong

If, as does sometimes happen, consultancy assignments go wrong it is because proper attention by both the consultant and the client has not been given to each of the stages described above.

## Legal implications

If there is a serious problem a consultancy assignment can be cancelled if either party has clearly failed to meet the terms of the contract (whether this is a formal contract or simply an exchange of letters). Clients can also sue consultants for professional negligence if they believe that their advice or actions have caused financial or some other form of measurable loss. Professional negligence is, however, not always easy to prove, especially in personnel assignments. Consultants can always claim that their advice was perfectly good but that it has been used incorrectly by the client (this may also be difficult to prove). Suing consultants can be a messy business and should only be undertaken when it is felt that they (or their insurers) should pay for their mistakes and thus help to recoup the client's losses. It should also be remembered that independent consultants and even some small firms may not have taken out professional liability insurance. If that is the case, all the aggrieved client who sues would do is to bankrupt them, which may give the client some satisfaction but could be a somewhat pointless exercise. The latter problem can be overcome if the client only selects consultants who are insured.

## Integrating the personnel and development contribution

Two of the key aims of strategic HRM as described in Chapter 9 are to achieve strategic integration and coherence in the development and operation of personnel policies and employment practices. Strategic integration could be described as vertical integration — the process of ensuring that personnel or HR strategies are integrated with or 'fit' business strategies. The concept of coherence could be defined as horizontal integration — the development of a mutually reinforcing and interrelated set of personnel, employment and development policies and practices.

## Vertical integration — strategic fit

The overall approach to vertical integration could ideally be provided by the strategic HRM model as described in chapter 9. But, as noted there, this is not easy. The problems include the diversity and complexity of strategic processes, the frequent absence of articulated business strategies and the qualitative nature of personnel issues which means that they may be difficult to express in the common business language of financial targets and measures.

Strategic or vertical integration may be chiefly about ensuring that the organization has the skilled, committed and well-motivated work force it needs to achieve its business objectives. It can also be attained by linking personnel strategies to basic competitive strategies. As defined by Porter (1985) these are innovation, quality-enhancement and cost leadership (cost reduction).

Linking personnel strategies to foster innovation means:

- selecting and developing highly skilled people
- giving them more discretion — using minimal controls
- providing more resources for experimentation
- allowing occasional failure
- appraising performance on the basis of its potential long-term contribution.

An integrated strategy for quality enhancement requires the development of a quality-orientated culture by:

- driving through quality initiatives
- appraising and rewarding people in line with their performance in upholding organizational values for quality and for achieving quality targets
- facilitating the achievement of high quality through recruitment and selection, induction training, continuous improvement programmes, organization (for example, self-managing teams), and, of course, communicating the need for high quality and the expectations of the organization about quality performance.

The achievement of cost leadership can be supported by analysing the cost drivers and, as necessary:

- taking cost out of the business by developing a leaner, fitter organization — this will include identifying the scope for reducing head counts without disrupting key organizational activities, and managing the process in a way which is both humane and minimizes disruption
- productivity planning — generally considering any means of increasing productivity in terms of cost per unit of output through reorganization, training or reward practices and the introduction of new technology
- new technology introduction — helping with the introduction of new technology by identifying the necessary competences, finding and developing the skilled people required, providing training or retraining, getting those affected involved in the development process and consulting with employees and their union representatives on any employment implications.

## Horizontal integration

Horizontal integration is accomplished by developing a coherent — a well-knit — range of interconnected and mutually reinforcing personnel policies and practices. This may be achieved by the use of shared processes such as competence analysis which provide a common frame of reference. Integration is also more likely to take place if shared values exist between line managers and personnel managers on how personnel policies should be implemented.

Achieving integration is also about ensuring when planning any innovation that its implications on other aspects of personnel policies and practice are fully considered and that further thought is given on how it could support those policies or practices.

The following realistic comments on the practicality of achieving coherence have been made by Stevens (1995):

People management practices and styles are sometimes very consciously coherent. Equally often, they are an amalgam of conscious decision, pragmatic development and compromise between 'what is' and 'what is to be desired'. Different approaches may be taken with different groups of employees. The consistency of policies for reward, training and development, job security and industrial relations may not be obvious to the outside observer; however, the apparent inconsistencies may be the result of subtle decisions made to fit in with the particular requirements of a particular organization at one point in time.

This is a good description of what actually happens. Conceptually, however, it can be argued that an appropriate measure of coherence is most likely to be attained if personnel strategies, policies and processes are clearly based on a powerful and well articulated vision of where the business is going and the part that should be played by its human resources in getting it there. This may be expressed as an overriding strategic imperative or driving force such as quality, performance or the need to develop skills and competences. Coherence and the integration of personnel initiatives is most likely to be achieved if this declaration of intent initiates various processes and policies which are designed to link together and operate in concert to deliver certain defined results. One approach to achieving coherence is to start from an all-embracing objective — for example, 'to develop a well-motivated, committed, skilled and flexible workforce'. Proposals for achieving that objective could be prepared by a strategy development process which would involve considering each of the key strategic components in turn, exploring the relationships between them and ensuring that they are mutually supportive. The strategic areas could, for example, include motivation, commitment, resourcing, employee development (human resource development) and flexibility. A further area for consideration might be the achievement of a cooperative climate of employee relations.

The 'glue' required to join up these separate elements of strategy could be provided by the development of interrelated processes which could affect the practice of personnel management across a number of the key strategic areas. The choice of which processes or combination of processes to use should be based on consideration of the critical success factors or driving forces which govern business performance. If, for example, the driving force is to improve performance, competence profiling techniques could be used to specify recruitment standards, identify learning and development needs and indicate the standards of behaviour or performance required. The competence frameworks could be used as the basis for human resource planning and in assessment and development centres. They could also be incorporated into a performance management system in which the aims are primarily developmental, and competences are used as criteria for reviewing behaviour and assessing learning and development needs. Job evaluation could be based on levels of competence, and competence-based pay systems (pay curves) could be introduced. Performance management processes as described in Part VII can also be used to integrate a number of different aspects of personnel management such as motivation, reward, learning and development.

It may be difficult to implement a 'grand design' which can be put into immediate effect, and it may have to be developed progressively. In fact, an attempt to impose some instant and comprehensive forms of coherent policies and practices would be doomed to failure, except in a green-site situation. What should be done is to ensure that no initiative is pursued without assessing initially how it is going to fit current policies and practices; and no initiative should be implemented until steps have been taken to ensure that congruence exists between it and existing processes.

## Innovations and interventions

To those whose aim is to build up the significance of the personnel function the cry is that personnel professionals should be pro-active. They should not simply do what they are told or asked to do. They should innovate and intervene. This sounds like a good idea, but is there a danger of innovating because it is fashionable and image enhancing rather than necessary? And is it possible that interventions could be made which are no more than interruptions to established and satisfactory ways of doing things? A critical examination of precepts for innovation and interventions is necessary before they are too easily accepted as what personnel management today is all about.

### Innovation

The point is well made by Marchington (1995) that many management gurus implicitly assume that 'all can be improved by a wave of the magic wand and the slaying of a few evil characters along the way', whereas reality is much more complex. He asserts that while new employment practices such as employee involvement and empowerment are widely embraced as beneficial to employer and employee alike, new approaches such as HRM do not necessarily signal the end of 'macho management' techniques which have led in the past to the harsh treatment of employees, discrimination and victimization.

Marchington believes that there are fundamental methodological and theoretical shortcomings in much of the literature including:

- problems of definition — empowerment, for example, may mean little more than giving employees the opportunity to make suggestions for change
- methodological problems may exist in case-study articles in practitioner magazines which tend to be one-dimensional accounts, written from a managerial and anecdotal perspective, and which may gloss over deep-seated conflicts in organizations
- in many accounts of change there is an implicit assumption that organizations are a-political, with all employees striving towards the same goal, and those who, for some reason, oppose the introduction of new employment practices are characterised as 'dinosaurs' or 'troublemakers'
- the principal reason for introducing new employment practices is to benefit the organization, and any benefits to employees may be incidental or not as great as suggested in the literature — indeed they may even represent a worsening of conditions as employees 'are further incorporated into supporting the organization as a whole, as opposed to defending or improving their own working conditions'.

The danger, according to Marchington, is that managers go in for 'impression management', which is the process of making an impact on superiors and colleagues through publicising high-profile innovations. Personnel specialists who aim to draw attention to themselves simply by promoting current 'flavours of the month' (which more often than not are a re-mix of last month's flavour), are falling into the trap which Drucker (1955) described anticipating Marchington by 40 years, as follows:

> The constant worry of all personnel administrators is their inability to prove that they are making a contribution to the enterprise. Their preoccupation is with the search for a 'gimmick' which will impress their management colleagues.

Of course, what personnel specialists have to be careful about is not innovation *per se* but innovation for innovation's sake or innovating as part of an 'impression management' campaign. Clearly, effective personnel managers will continually analyse the situation the organization is in and produce diagnoses of where improvements are likely to be beneficial *and* cost-effective. If it is believed that these improvements will be best achieved through new employment practices it is necessary to research what they really involve, what benefits they will produce and how much they will cost. The research should involve reading the literature (but taking the claims with large doses of salt), attending conferences (ditto) and benchmarking (finding out what other companies are doing). The aim may be to establish 'best practice' but it is essential to remember that what is good practice in one organization will not necessarily be good practice in another; 'best-fit' is also important.

In finding out what other people are doing it is important not only to listen to glowing accounts about how well it works but also to probe in order to establish costs as well as benefits, problems met in introducing and maintaining the process, and how well it has been received and implemented by line managers, team leaders and employees generally. Any analysis of the potential value of an innovation must take account of this sort of information and it must examine with great care the extent to which it is likely to transfer *well* and how it might best be introduced. It is at this stage that the benefits *and* the costs need to be spelt out prior to persuading management and anyone else concerned that the innovation deserves their support.

There are other dangers and potential problems which need to be considered before launching the innovation. First, there is the risk of pursuing will-o'-the-wisp innovations too eagerly and thus adopting a piecemeal approach which means that new employment practices lack coherence — they are not properly integrated with existing processes. Second, the vigorous pursuit of innovation can lead to neglecting the consolidation and improvement of existing processes. Third, it is easy to underestimate the cost of developing and maintaining the innovation in terms of both money and time. Finally, innovators can slide into the assumption that because they like the idea (not least because it will enhance their image) and because they can persuade top management to take it on board (not always so difficult — chief executives often like to feel that they are being progressive) everyone else will welcome it. They therefore ignore active or passive opposition. Trade unions may object strongly to quality circles because they see them as a device to suborn workers and to by-pass the union. Middle managers and team leaders or supervisors may resist fashionable concepts like empowerment because they see their job as being to get things done (they are told that often enough) and this means telling other people to do things, not going soft on them.

## Interventions

Personnel and development practitioners, often in their role as internal consultants, can usefully intervene in organizational processes involving the management of people, which means most, if not all, processes. To intervene is to modify the course or result of events, and an intervention is an action or an event in itself which is intended to achieve this purpose.

As described in Chapter 22, organizational development (OD) programmes use OD or process consultants (external or internal) to 'intervene' in organizational processes such as interactions between departments and people, team work and change in order to facilitate new ways of managing or conducting those processes. Personnel specialists are in a good position to observe and analyse what is happening in the organization, for example, the introduction of new technology, a business process re-engineering exercise, a change in work methods such as just-in-time (JIT) manufacturing or a total quality management (TQM) programme. They should be capable of understanding the people implications of these organizational innovations and 'intervene' to ensure that proper provision is made to review human resource plans, restructure teams, redesign jobs, involve the people affected, communicate intentions, plans and effects, analyse the new competences required and provide the necessary training and re-training through training interventions.

Personnel professionals can also intervene where they feel that existing people management processes need to be improved or changed. They can observe high levels of employee turnover, a multiplicity of grievances and unfair dismissal cases and then establish causes and make suggestions about what needs to be done about them. This could, for example, be a review of the pay system if it is believed that it is uncompetitive or inequitable and is therefore contributing to high levels of turnover or grievances. Or it might be a training intervention or taking on the role of 'coach' to managers or team leaders who would benefit from one-to-one guidance.

Similarly, personnel people can observe problems of performance or productivity and intervene with ideas about how these might be improved through, for example, performance management processes or training and development programmes.

A senior personnel executive in an international organization as reported in Armstrong (1989) expressed the following views about what he termed 'selective intervention':

You intervene in different ways in different situations and it is an opportunistic business. You have to start with an overview of where the pressure points are within an organization and where you can make a useful intervention. But the opportunity to intervene can come at the most unexpected times.

But intervention should not be allowed to become interference or to be perceived as interference. The interventionist role has to be carried out delicately. An over-enthusiastic personnel manager who proceeds like a bull at a gate will get nowhere. The result is likely to be resentment, rejection or indifference. To intervene effectively it is first necessary to be certain that there is a good case for it. It is then necessary to take people along gently, progressively, but firmly, helping them to understand the problem and to develop solutions which they will implement, with personnel guidance and assistance as required.

## Marketing the personnel function

Theodore Levitt (1983) summed up the marketing concept when he wrote 'The organization must learn to think of itself not as producing goods or services but as *buying customers*, as doing the things that will make people *want* to do business with it'. This principle applies just as forcibly to the internal market within which HR practitioners operate. Top management and line managers generally are the customers whose wants and needs the personnel and development function must identify and meet. How can this be done?

First, it is necessary to understand the needs of the business and its critical success factors — where the business is going, how it intends to get there and what are the things that are going to make the difference between success and failure.

Having ascertained the business needs it is next necessary to find out what managers want to satisfy these needs — starting at the top. This means identifying the people issues that they believe to be important in the areas of resourcing, motivation and reward, gaining commitment, employee development and training, and employee relations. This market research is conducted partly by 'being there', listening to and, importantly, joining in discussions on business issues and establishing the people element in those issues. This is the best reason why heads of HR functions should be members of the executive board. Their role on the board is not just to defend their corners. They are there to take an active part in business discussions because only by doing so will they truly understand the issues and, by making a positive contribution, gain the respect of their colleagues. However, market research is not simply a matter of sitting on boards and committees. Personnel practitioners should be in the business of talking and listening to people at all levels in the organization to find out what they want.

Market research data needs to be converted into marketing plans for the development of products and services to meet ascertained needs — of the business and its managers and employees. If, for example, the need is to raise the skill base or increase levels of competence, attention can be focused on such initiatives and interventions as skill-based or competence-based pay, performance management processes and continuous development programmes with an emphasis on self-development. The marketing plan should establish the costs of introducing and maintaining these initiatives and the benefits that will be obtained from them. Every effort must be made to quantify these benefits in financial terms. If the 'product' were skill-based pay then the costs of pay increases, additional training and accreditation will have to be calculated. Estimates will need to be made of the financial gains that will be achieved through increased productivity and the better use of labour through multi-skilling. Any savings in cost can also be assessed by, for example, the use of better trained employees in a JIT environment to achieve a continuous flow of production to meet demand or supply requirements without delay or waste. If the 'product' were a programme for sub-contracting work the costs of procuring and employing the people required would be assessed against the savings resulting from a reduction in the size of the permanent labour force.

The next step in the marketing process is to persuade management that this is a product or service the business needs. This means spelling out its costs and benefits, covering the financial and human resources required to develop, introduce and maintain it and the impact it will make on the performance of the business. Convincing management that a product or service is worthwhile will be easier if the initial customer research and product development activities have been carried out thoroughly. Credibility is vital. This will be achieved if the proposal for expenditure is credible in itself, but the track record of the HR function in delivering what it proposes to do is equally important. The approach is akin to 'branding' in product planning. This identifies the product or service, spells out the benefits it provides and differentiates it from other services, thus bringing it to the attention of customers. Presentation is important through logos and distinctive brochures. Some personnel departments brand products with an immediately identifiable name such as 'gauge' or 'gemini'. It is particularly important to market employee development as described in chapter 26.

## Preparing, justifying and protecting the personnel budget

### *Preparation*

Personnel budgets are prepared like any other functional department budget in the following stages:

1. Define functional objectives and plans.
2. Forecast the activity levels required to achieve objectives and plans in the light of company budget guidelines and assumptions on future business activity levels and any targets for reducing overheads or for maintaining them at the same level.
3. Assess the resources (people and finance) required to enable the activity levels to be achieved.
4. Cost each activity area — the sum of these costs will be the total budget.

### *Justification*

Justifying budgets means:

- ensuring in advance that objectives and plans are generally agreed — there should be no surprises in a budget submitted to top management
- taking care to prepare a cast-iron case to support the forecast levels of activity in each area
- being rigorous about following budget guidelines, only deviating from them after getting prior agreement on the basis of the case made for the forecast activity levels — again, this adjustment should be agreed in advance if at all possible, it is too late when the budget is reviewed by the board (the writer speaks from long experience)
- meeting targets for reducing overheads or at least maintaining them at the same level by prioritizing activities and cutting back key essential ones — this course is followed if it is the only way to reach the target and if a special case cannot be made to treat the personnel function as an exception (an unlikely event if all the other functions are subject to the same guidelines).

### *Protection*

Although zero-base budgeting may not have become a universally applied technique the concept remains valid. Businesses are no longer prepared to perpetuate commitments that had their origins in the past. They are increasingly requiring managers to re-evaluate all their activities completely in order to establish whether they should be funded at a reduced, similar or increased level, or even whether they should be eliminated altogether. And personnel, as a service function which does not directly generate income, is particularly vulnerable to attacks on its budget. These attacks may come from doubters who question investment in areas like training during times of continuing instability (training budgets are often the first to be cut), or they may originate from jealous rivals in other functions who are competing for scarce financial resources and feel that HR is exerting too much influence in affairs which are primarily their concern. Other issues which are raising questions about the size of personnel budgets include the pressure for devolving responsibility for personnel matters to line managers, the tendency for personnel people to become internal consultants rather than service providers, the focus on 'self-managed learning' and the move towards outsourcing which may not involve the HR function at all.

The best way to protect a budget is to provide in advance a rationale for each area of expenditure which proves that it is necessary and will justify the costs involved. The worst thing that can happen is to be forced onto the defensive. If service delivery standards (service level agreements) are agreed and achieved these will provide a further basis for protecting the budget.

## Gaining support and commitment

Personnel practitioners mainly get results by exerting influence and as Guest and Hoque (1994) note: 'By exerting influence, personnel managers help to shape the framework of personnel policy and practice.' Although line managers may make the day-to-day decisions, influencing skills are therefore necessary for personnel specialists. But there is a constant danger of personnel professionals being so overcome by the beauty and truth of their bright idea that they expect everyone else — management and employees alike — to fall for it immediately. This is not how it is. Management and employees can create blockages and barriers and the support and commitment needs to be gained which is not always easy.

### Blockages and barriers within management

Managers will block or erect barriers to what the personnel function believes to be progress if they are not persuaded that it will benefit both the organization and themselves at an acceptable cost (money and their time and trouble).

## Blockages and barriers from employees

Employees will block or set up barriers to 'progress' or innovations if they feel they conflict with their own interests. They are likely, with reason, to be cynical about protestations that what is good for the organization will always be good for them.

## Getting support from top management

The support of top management is achievable by processes of marketing the personnel function and persuasion. Boards and senior managers, like anyone else, are more likely to be persuaded to take a course of action if:

- it can be demonstrated that it will meet both the needs of the organization and their own personal needs
- the proposal realistically spells out the benefits and the costs and, as far as possible, is justified in added value terms (ie the income generated by the proposal will significantly exceed the cost of implementing it)
- there is proof that the innovation has already worked well within the organization (perhaps as a pilot scheme) or represents 'best practice' which is likely to be transferable to the organization
- it can be shown that in some way the proposal will increase the business' competitive edge; for example enlarging the skill base or multiskilling to ensure that it can achieve competitive advantage through innovation and/or reducing time-to-market
- it can be implemented without too much trouble; for example not taking up a lot of their time, or not meeting with strong opposition from line management, employees or trade unions (it is as well to check the likely reaction before launching a proposal)
- it will add to the reputation of the company by showing that it is a 'world class' organization, ie what it does is as good as, if not better than, the world leaders in the sector in which the business operates (a promise that publicity will be achieved through articles in professional journals, press releases and conference presentations, will help)

- the proposal is brief, to the point and well argued — it should take no more than five minutes to present orally and should be summarised in writing on the proverbial one side of one sheet of paper (supplementary details can be included in appendices).

## Gaining the support and commitment of line management

This can sometimes be more difficult than gaining the support of top management. Line managers can be cynical or realistic about innovation — they have seen it all before and/or they believe it won't work (sometimes with good reason). Innovations pushed down from the top can easily fail.

Gaining line management support requires providing an answer to the question 'what's in it for me'? in terms of how will the innovation help them to achieve better results without imposing unacceptable additional burdens on them. New employment practices which take up precious time and involve paper work will be treated with particular suspicion. Many line managers, often from bitter experience, resent the bureaucracy which can surround and, indeed, engulf systems favoured by personnel people, such as performance appraisal.

Gaining support requires market research and networking — getting around to talk to managers about their needs and testing new ideas to obtain reactions. The aim is to build up a body of information which will indicate approaches which are likely to be most acceptable, and therefore will most probably work, or at least to suggest areas where particular efforts will need to be made to persuade and educate line management. It is also useful to form 'strategic alliances' with influential managers who are enthusiastic about the innovation and will not only lend it vocal support but will also cooperate in pilot-testing it.

On the principle that 'nothing succeeds like success' support for new personnel practices can often be achieved by demonstrating that it has worked well elsewhere in the organization.

Gaining commitment will be easier if managers know that they have been consulted and that their opinions have been listened to and acted upon. It is even better to involve them as members of project teams or task forces in developing the new process or system. This is the way to achieve ownership and therefore commitment.

## Gaining the support and commitment of employees

When it comes to new employment practices employees generally react in exactly the same way as managers, they want to know 'what's in it for us?' They also want to know the hidden agenda — 'Why is the company really wanting to introduce a performance management process? Will it simply be used as a means of gaining evidence for disciplinary proceedings? Or is it even going to provide the information required to select people for redundancy?' As far as possible this kind of question needs to be answered in advance.

Sounding out employee opinion can be conducted through attitude surveys or, even better, focus groups. The latter method involves getting groups of people together to discuss (to 'focus' on) various issues and propositions. A well-run focus group can generate valid information on employees' feelings about and reaction to an initiative.

Employee commitment is also more likely if they participate in the development of the new employment practice and if they know that their contributions have been welcomed and acted upon.

## Personnel and line management

It has been the accepted dogma of personnel management for some time that personnel specialists are there to provide support and services to line managers, not to usurp the latter's role of 'getting things done through people' — their responsibility for managing their own personnel affairs. In practice, the personnel function has frequently had the role of ensuring that personnel policies are implemented consistently as well as the more recent onerous responsibility for ensuring that both the letter and the spirit of employment law is applied throughout the organization. The latter responsibility has often been seen as a process of ensuring that the organization does not get involved in tedious, time-wasting and often expensive industrial tribunal proceedings.

Carrying out this role has often led to the personnel function 'policing' line management, which can be a cause of tension and ambiguity. To avoid this result, personnel specialists may have to adopt a reasonably light touch: providing advice rather than issuing dicta, except when a manager is clearly contravening the law or when his or her actions are likely to lead to an avoidable dispute or an industrial tribunal case which the organization will probably lose.

It has also frequently been the case that, in spite of paying lip service to the principle that 'line managers must manage', personnel departments have usurped the line managers' true role of being involved in key decisions concerning the recruitment, development and remuneration of their people, thus diminishing the managers' capacity to manage their key resource effectively. This situation has arisen most frequently in large bureaucratic organizations and/or those with a powerful centralized personnel function. It still exists in some quarters, but as decentralization and devolution increases and organizations are finding that they are having to operate more flexibly, it is becoming less common.

A delicate balance has to be struck between the personnel specialist's role of achieving the consistent application of policies and acting as the guardian of the organization's values concerning people and the role of providing services, support and, as necessary, guidance to managers without issuing commands or relieving them of their responsibilities. However, the distinction between giving advice and telling people what to do, or between providing help and taking over can be blurred, and the relationship is one that has to be developed and nurtured with great care. The most appropriate line for personnel specialists to take is that of emphasizing that they are there to help line managers achieve their objectives through their people not to do their job for them.

The philosophy of human resource management is, of course, very much that of stressing that the management of human resources is the responsibility of line managers. But personnel professionals are not there simply to support their line manager colleagues. They should be capable of showing the way — taking the lead in pointing out where innovatory personnel practices can increase organizational effectiveness; providing guidance on how line managers can improve their approaches to managing their human resources and acting as business partners in creating added value.

In practice, however, some line managers may be only too glad to let the personnel department do its people management job for them, especially the less pleasant aspects like handling discipline and grievance problems. A delicate balance has therefore to be achieved between providing help and advice when it is clearly needed and creating a 'dependency culture' which discourages managers from thinking and acting for themselves on people matters for which they are responsible. Managers will not learn about dealing with people if they are over-dependent on personnel specialists. The latter therefore have to stand off sometimes and say, in effect, 'that's your problem'.

Research conducted by the IPD (Hutchinson and Wood, 1995) produced the following findings:

- Most organizations reported a trend over the last five years towards greater line management responsibility for personnel management without it causing any significant tension between personnel and the line.

- Devolution offered positive opportunities to the personnel function to become involved in strategic, proactive and internal consultancy roles because they were less involved in day-to-day operational personnel activities.
- Both personnel and line management were involved in operational personnel activities. Line managers were more heavily involved in recruitment, selection and training decisions and in handling discipline issues and grievances. Personnel were still largely responsible for such matters as analysing training needs, running internal courses and pay and benefits.
- There is an underlying concern that line managers are not sufficiently competent to carry out their new roles. This may be for a number of reasons including lack of training, pressures of work, because managers have been promoted for their technical rather than managerial skills, or because they are used to referring certain issues to the personnel department.
- Some personnel specialists also have difficulty in adopting their new roles because they do not have the right skills (such as an understanding of the business) or because they see devolution as a threat to their own job security.
- Other problems over devolution include uncertainty on the part of line managers about the role of the personnel function, lack of commitment by line managers to performing their new roles, and achieving the right balance between providing line managers with as much freedom as possible and the need to retain core controls and direction.

The conclusion reached by the researchers were that:

> If line managers are to take an effective greater responsibility for personnel management activities then, from the outset, the rules and responsibilities of personnel and line managers must be clearly defined and understood. Support is needed from the personnel department in terms of providing a procedural framework, advice and guidance on all personnel management matters, and in terms of training line managers so they have the appropriate skills and knowledge to carry out their new duties.

## Ambiguities in the personnel contribution

Personnel managers, in Thurley's (1981) words, are 'specialists in ambiguity'. This arises partly because of the often equivocal nature of the attitudes of line managers to personnel specialists and the relationships between them but also because the latter are often unsure about where they stand. Ambiguity in the role of the personnel function can result in confusion between ideals and reality. A 'humanistic' approach to personnel management which focuses on the needs of employees may clash with the business needs to which management will give priority.

This ambiguity is reflected in the comments about the role of the personnel function made by writers on personnel management. For example, Mackay and Torrington (1986) suggest that:

> Personnel management is never identified with management interests, as it becomes ineffective when not able to understand and articulate the aspirations of the work force.

In complete contrast, Tyson and Fell (1986) believe that:

> Classical personnel management has not been granted a position in decision-making circles because it has frequently not earned one. It has not been concerned with the totality of the organization but often with issues which have not only been parochial but esoteric to boot.

The debate on human resource management (HRM) versus personnel management has been generated by, but has also contributed to, this ambiguity. HRM is management-orientated, and sees people as a key resource to be used to further the objectives of the business. Traditional personnel management, however, has tended to be more people-orientated ('humanistic'), taking the view that if their needs are satisfied, the organization as well as its members will benefit. Personnel professionals can sometimes find themselves being pulled in both directions. It does not make their life any easier.

One of the questions personnel practitioners have to ask themselves is 'who is the client — the company or the employee?' Personnel professionals may sometimes have to walk a fine line between serving the company that pays their salary and serving individual employees. They may be involved in counselling employees over work problems. This can only be carried out successfully if the employee trusts the personnel specialist to maintain confidentiality. But something might be revealed which is of interest to management and that places the personnel counsellor in a dilemma — to betray or not to betray the trust? There is no pat answer to this question, but the existence of a code of professional conduct and a company ethical code (see pages 94 to 95 of this chapter) can provide guidance.

# Conflict in the personnel and development contribution

Personnel specialists, as Thurley (1981) put it, often 'work against the grain'. Their values may be different from those of line managers and this is a potential cause of conflict. But conflict is inevitable in organizations which are pluralistic societies, the members of which have different frames of reference and interests, particularly self-interest. Management may have their own priorities: 'increase shareholder value', 'keep the City happy', 'innovate', 'get the work done'. Employees might have a completely different set: 'pay me well and equitably', 'give me security', 'provide good working conditions', 'treat me fairly'. Personnel specialists, as noted above, may find themselves somewhere in the middle.

Conflicts in the personnel contribution can arise in the following ways:

- *A clash of values* — line managers may simply regard their workers as factors of production to be used, exploited and dispensed with in accordance with organizational imperatives.
- *Different priorities* — management's priority may be to add value — make more out of less — and if this involves getting rid of people that's too bad. Personnel may recognise the need to add value but not at the expense of employees.
- *Freedom versus control* — line managers may want the freedom to get on with things their own way, interpreting company policies to meet their needs, and the thrust for devolution has encouraged such feelings. But personnel specialists will be concerned about the achievement of a consistent and equitable approach to managing people and implementing personnel policies. They will also be concerned with the attainment of a proper degree of compliance to employment and health and safety law. They may be given the responsibility for exercising control, and conflict is likely if they use this authority too rigidly.
- *Disputes* — if unions are recognized personnel specialists may be involved in conflict during the process of resolution. Even when there are no unions, there may be conflict with individuals or groups of employees about the settlement of grievances.

As Mary Parker Follett (1924) wrote, there is the possibility that conflict can be creative if an integrative approach is used to settle it. This means clarifying priorities, policies and roles, using agreed procedures to deal with grievances and disputes, bringing differences of interpretation out into the open and achieving consensus through a solution which recognises the interests of both parties — a win–win process. Resolving conflict by the sheer exercise of power (win–lose) will only lead to further conflict. Resolving conflict by compromise may lead to both parties being dissatisfied (lose–lose).

## Ethics in personnel and development

Personnel specialists are concerned with ethical standards in two ways: their conduct as professionals and the ethical standards of their firms.

### *Professional conduct*

The IPD's Code of Professional Conduct (1993) states that members must respect the following standards of conduct.

- *Accuracy* — personnel practitioners must maintain high standards of accuracy in the information and advice they provide to employers and employees.
- *Confidentiality* — personnel practitioners must respect their employer's legitimate needs for confidentiality and ensure that all personal information (including information about current, past and prospective employees) remains private.
- *Counselling* — personnel practitioners with the relevant skills must be prepared to act as counsellors to individual employees, pensioners and dependants or to refer them, where appropriate, to other professionals or helping agencies.
- *Developing others* — personnel practitioners must encourage self-development and seek to achieve the fullest possible development of employees in the service of present and future organization needs.
- *Equal opportunities* — personnel practitioners must promote fair, non-discriminatory employment practices.
- *Fair dealing* — personnel practitioners must maintain fair and reasonable standards in their treatment of individuals.
- *Self-development* — personnel practitioners must seek continuously to improve their performance and update their skills and knowledge.

### *Values in personnel and development management*

Personnel professionals are part of management. They are there to further the objectives of the business and not to act as surrogate representatives of the interests of employees. But this does not mean that there may not be occasions when in their professional capacity personnel specialists should not speak out and oppose plans or actions which are clearly at variance with the values of the organization. They must not tolerate injustice or inequality of opportunity. If redundancies are inevitable as a result of business-led 'slimming down' or 'taking costs out of the business' processes, they must ensure that the organization takes whatever steps it can to mitigate detrimental effects by, for example, relying primarily on natural wastage and voluntary redundancy or, if people have to go involuntarily, doing whatever they can to help them find other jobs (outplacement).

Personnel specialists may often find themselves acting within a support function in a hard-nosed, entrepreneurial environment. But this does not mean that they can remain unconcerned about developing and helping to uphold the core values of the organization in line with their own values on how people should be managed. These may not always be reconcilable, and if this is strongly the case, the personnel manager may have to make a choice on whether he or she can remain with the organization.

## Ethical standards in the firm

More and more companies are, rightly, developing and publishing value statements and codes of ethics. The focus on such codes was encouraged by the Cadbury Report on corporate governance which in 1992 recommended that companies should adopt one. The Institute of Business Ethics states that more than a third of major companies had ethics codes in 1995 compared with 18 per cent in 1987.

Ethics codes may include the guiding principles the organization follows in conducting its business and relating to its stakeholders — employees, customers, shareholders (or other providers of finance), suppliers, and society in general. A code will also summarise the ethical standards expected of employees. These may include conflicts of interest, the giving and receiving of gifts, confidentiality, environmental pollution, health and safety, equal opportunities, sexual harassment, moonlighting and political activity. More rarely they may, as at NatWest and Lucas Aerospace have confidential 'ethics hotlines' for employees to report and discuss concerns.

As suggested by Pickard (1995) personnel can contribute to enhancing awareness of ethical issues by:

- deploying professional expertise to develop and communicate an ethics policy and field the response to it, holding training sessions to help people think through the issues and monitoring the policy
- contributing to the formation of company strategy, especially touching on mission and values
- setting an example through professional conduct, on issues such as fairness, equal treatment and confidentiality.

To ensure that a code of ethics is understood and implemented it is important to communicate it properly to employees and to educate and train employees about its meaning and implications. The objectives of an ethics training and development programme could be to:

- increase awareness of the ethical principles and values behind everyday business decisions
- increase awareness of the company's standards of conduct and their application
- identify key ethics issues facing employees in different divisions and functional areas
- increase awareness of pressures that may lead to unethical conduct
- alert employees to the importance of avoiding ethical misconduct and the need to report unethical practices.

## Professionalism

If the term is used loosely, personnel specialists are professional because they display expertise in doing their work. A professional occupation such as medicine or law could, however, be defined as one which gives members of its association exclusive rights to practise their profession. A profession is not so much an occupation as a means of controlling an occupation. Personnel management is obviously not in this category.

Perhaps the nature of professional work was best defined by the Hayes Committee (1972) as follows:

Work done by the professional is usually distinguished by its reference to a framework of fundamental concepts linked with experience rather than by impromptu reaction to events or the application of laid down procedures. Such a high level of distinctive competence reflects the skilful application of specialized education, training and experience. This should be accompanied by a sense of responsibility and an acceptance of recognized standards.

A 'profession' may be identified on the basis of the following criteria:

- skills based on theoretical knowledge; the provision of training and education
- a test of the competence of members administered by a professional body
- a formal professional organization which has the power to regulate entry to the profession
- a professional code of conduct.

By these standards an institution such as the Institute of Personnel and Development carries out all the functions of a professional body.

Another approach to the definition of a profession is to emphasize the service ethic — the professional person is there to serve others. This, however, leads to confusion when applied to personnel specialists. Whom do they serve? The organization and its values, or the people in the organization and their needs? (organizational values and personal needs do not necessarily coincide). As Tyson and Fell (1986) have commented:

> In recent years the personnel manager seems to be encouraged to make the line manager his (sic) client, while trying simultaneously to represent wider social standards, and to possess a sense of service to employees. This results in confusion and difficulty for the personnel executive.

In the face of this difficulty, the question has to be asked, why bother? The answer was suggested by Watson (1977), who asserted that the adoption of a professional image by personnel managers is a strategic response by personnel specialists to their felt lack of authority. They are in an ambiguous situation and sometimes feel they need all the help they can get to clarify and, indeed, strengthen their authority and influence.

If a profession is defined rigidly as a body of people who possess a particular area of competence, who control entry so that only members of the association can practise in that area, who unequivocally adopt the 'service ethic' and who are recognized by themselves and others as belonging to a profession, then personnel management is not a profession. This is the case even when a professional institution like the Institute of Personnel and Development exists with the objective of acting as a professional body in the full sense of the word, an aim which it does its best to fulfil.

On the basis of their research, Guest and Horwood (1981) expressed their doubts about the professional model of personnel management.

The (research) data also highlights the range of career types in personnel management. Given the diversity of personnel roles and organizational contexts, this is surely something to be welcomed. It is tempting but wrong to view personnel managers as homogeneous. Their different backgrounds and fields of operations raise doubts about the value of a professional model and of any attempt to view personnel problems as amenable to solution through a primary focus on professionalism.

However, a broader definition of professionalism as the practice of specific skills based upon a defined body of knowledge in accordance with recognized standards of behaviour would entitle personnel and development management to be regarded as a profession.

The debate continues, but it is an academic one. What matters is that personnel 'professionals' need expertise and have to use it responsibly. In other words, they should act professionally but do not have to be members of a professional association to do that. Such associations, however, have an important part to play in setting and improving professional standards.

If this proposition is accepted, then those who do practise specific personnel management skills based upon a defined body of knowledge in accordance with recognized standards of behaviour can be regarded as members of a profession.

## How to be an effective personnel practitioner

Effective personnel and development practitioners:

- Operate strategically — they have the ability to take, and implement, a strategic and coherent view of the complete range of personnel policies, processes and practices in relation to the business as a whole.
- Ensure that their innovations and services are aligned to business needs and priorities, while taking account of the needs of employees and other shareholders.
- Understand the culture of the organization and have the capability to facilitate change, initiating it when necessary and acting as a stabilizing force in situations where change would be damaging.
- Appreciate organizational and individual needs. Against a background of their knowledge of organizational behaviour, they understand how organizations function and the factors affecting

individual motivation and commitment, they are capable of analysing and diagnosing the people requirements of the organization and proposing and implementing appropriate action.

- Understand personnel systems and techniques — if they are specialists, they have a thorough knowledge of relevant best practice and how to apply it. If they are generalists, their knowledge may be more broadly based, but they will be capable of identifying the need for a specific approach and, with expert help, of putting it to use. In either case, they are careful to ensure that the process or system fits the organization's particular circumstances and needs. Personnel specialists should take a broad overall view of the business and they are ideally placed to do this. They need to know about the correlation between business success and progressive personnel policies.

- Are value driven — they have a well-developed set of broadly humanistic values and ethical standards relating to the management of people and how they carry out their work; and they measure what they propose to do against these values and standards. But they have to be able to cope with the possibility that some of the values they espouse, such as equal opportunity, may not be seen as so important by the managers they advise.

- Are business-like — if they are in the private sector, they are fully aware of the needs of the business as a commercial, market-orientated and profit-making enterprise and are equally aware of how they can help to fulfil these needs. They have to demonstrate that they can make value-added contributions which will increase shareholder value in a public company. They must justify and evaluate their activities on a return on investment basis. In the public or not-for-profit sectors, personnel specialists have to adopt an equally business-like approach. In any sector, they have to demonstrate their efficiency as administrators as well as their effectiveness in an enabling role.

- Get involved — they get involved in the business and with the people who run the business. They must know what is going on. Perhaps the most practical of all personnel techniques is PMBWA: personnel management by walking about. Adopting this approach means that they can find out what people as well as the business need and want. Using their antennae, they can spot symptoms and, using their diagnostic skills (an important attribute), they can identify causes and solutions. If they want to get anything done they know that managers must 'own' both the problem and its solution.

Close involvement means that personnel people can become adept at transferring ownership.

- Are good at networking — they form alliances and identify 'champions of change'.
- Are careful to test their ideas before moving too quickly in a direction which will fail to interest their line management colleagues or even provoke their hostility.
- Recognize that 'nothing succeeds like success'. In other words, if they want to innovate, they may, if there is no urgent requirement for general action, start in one part of the organization (where there is support for the idea) and, having proved that it works well, point out the benefits to managers elsewhere in the organization. It can then be extended progressively. An incremental approach to change on the basis of successful accomplishment can be more effective than a 'big bang' approach.
- Intervene effectively — personnel specialists have to use their knowledge and awareness of business needs to select the right place and time to intervene.
- Are persuasive — they present the proposals and recommendations emerging from their interventions persuasively.
- Are realistic — they recognize what Mary Parker Follett (1924) described as 'the law of the situation' — the logic of facts and events. This means that ideas for improvement or innovation are thoroughly tested against an analysis of the characteristics and true needs of the organization.
- Sell ideas to management on the basis of the practical and, wherever possible, measurable benefits that will result from their implementation (it is not the idea itself that is saleable but the result it can achieve). The proposals are costed and presented with great care to managers so that they demonstrate that they will provide direct help to them in running the business or their department more effectively than before and that the benefits more than justify the cost.
- Provide unobtrusive assistance, guidance and encouragement in implementing new processes and systems — not from the stance of a would-be professional who knows it all, but from the point of view of a colleague who can give practical help in achieving something worthwhile.

## Personnel directors

Personnel directors or heads of personnel functions need to be able to do all the things mentioned above. But there is a particular need for them to be:

- very much part of the top management team
- involved in business planning and the integration of human resource plans with business plans
- well placed to exert influence on the way in which the business is organized, managed and staffed — all with a view to helping it achieve its strategic objectives
- dependent as much if not more on business awareness and skills and credibility as a business partner as on professional competence in personnel techniques
- involved heavily in resourcing at top and senior levels and in so doing are in a strong position to improve organizational effectiveness and, therefore, bottom-line performance
- concerned with the management of change and with shaping corporate culture and values
- fully aware of the needs to develop a vision of what the personnel function exists to do, to define its mission, to provide leadership and guidance to the members of the function (without getting involved in day-to-day personnel matters) and to maintain the quality of the support the function provides to line managers
- essentially enablers but ones who are well placed to make a significant contribution to end results.

## Competence in personnel management

The requirements for effective personnel management set out above can be summed up by the use of the language of competences. This may be done by developing a 'competence map' as illustrated in Figure 4.1. This defines seven competence areas and gives instances of competent behaviour in each of those areas. A map of this nature can be used for the appraisal and development of personnel specialists.

### The Personnel Standards Lead Body

A more exhaustive route to the definition of personnel competences was pursued by the Personnel Standards Lead Body. The Lead Body explained that the standards and qualifications will recognize the need for:

- proper exercise of business and managerial skills as a primary requirement

**Figure 4.1** Personnel Competence Map

| Competence | Indicators |
|---|---|
| **Strategic Capability** | Seeks involvement in strategy formulation and contributes to the development of business strategies. • Understands the critical success factors of the business and the contribution personnel strategy can make in responding to them. • Considers personnel issues and problems in the broad context of the organization's environment and its strategic plans. • Develops and implements coherent and integrated personnel strategies in support of business plans. |
| **Business Awareness** | Understands the activities, processes and technology of the business. • Aware of the implications of the inter-relationships between technological and people factors. • Identifies opportunities to contribute to creating added value and enhancing competitive advantage, and intervenes as necessary. • Adapts activities and behaviour to match the needs of different functions and business units. |
| **Professional Development and Understanding** | Continually improves and extends professional knowledge and skills. • Maintains awareness of recent developments and best practice in the profession and adapts and applies new and appropriate ideas. • Demonstrates understanding of the personnel practices which are the most relevant to organizational needs. • Ensures that line management colleagues understand the significance and relevance of new developments and 'own' any new or changed processes. |
| **Internal Consultancy** | Systematically analyzes and diagnoses organizational and people issues to produce practical ideas for improvements or solutions. • Adapts intervention style to client requirements; acts as catalyst, facilitator or expert depending on circumstances. • Uses process consultancy approaches to help in the analysis, diagnosis and resolution of organizational and people issues. • Coaches internal clients in identifying people issues and implementing new processes; transfers skills. |
| **Organizational Effectiveness** | Understands the key factors which contribute to organizational effectiveness and develops improvement plans and programmes. • Contributes to the implementation of change. • Facilitates team building. • Contributes to the development of a high quality, committed and flexible workforce. |
| **Quality** | Demonstrates total quality approach in own work. • Promotes a total quality approach by all members of the personnel function. • Contributes to the development and implementation of a total quality approach throughout the organization. |
| **Service Delivery** | Responds promptly and efficiently to requests for help and advice. • Identifies, defines and meets client/customer requirements, responding quickly to their needs. • Provides cost-effective services in each of the main areas of personnel management. • Anticipates requirements and sets up or adapts personnel services to meet them. • Empowers line managers to run their own personnel affairs, generating a real sense of ownership of personnel solutions; but provides advice and guidance as required. |

- successful use of a significant body of specialist concepts, theories and principles essential to the full exercise of personnel management
- awareness of current and impending employment legislation and other changes in the UK, Europe and key operating countries
- continuous appraisal of developments in the personnel field and their appropriate application to the situation and needs of the enterprise.

## Requirements for senior personnel professionals

The Lead Body has suggested that to be respected members of the top management team senior personnel professionals must:

- demonstrate to all their colleagues a real contribution to business processes, customer requirements, general management and operation of the business
- 'read the organization' for the chief executive and provide assistance in developing team and individual performance among the top group to achieve corporate objectives
- exercise judgement in supporting or opposing executive actions — provide a balancing and opposing force when the action may be cost-effective in the short term but damaging to morale and productivity at the time or in the longer term.

## The contribution of the Institute of Personnel and Development (IPD)

The mission of the IPD is to be the professional body for all those responsible for the optimum use of human resources to the mutual benefit of the enterprise, each person and the community at large. It:

1. Sets, maintains and promulgates standards and ethics in professional conduct and effective practice.
2. Instigates and evaluates research to update the information resource and to develop the profession.
3. Communicates with members, government and other national organizations and the community.
4. Provides opportunities for members and others to exchange information and ideas for the benefit of the profession.
5. Promotes systems to educate and train for personnel work and the continuous development of its members.

6. Provides a range of services to members to help them maintain and improve their professional performance.
7. Undertakes a range of commercial activities to disseminate knowledge and training, and to contribute towards the operation of the Institute.
8. Plays a part in the rest of Europe and the world wide community.
9. Maintains a structure democratically controlled by the members which directs the internal affairs of the Institute and oversees the profession.

## Continuing professional development

The concept of continuing professional development (CPD) is an important aspect of the work of the Institute in improving professional standards. The CPD philosophy is that personnel professionals should systematically plan their development throughout their career. This is to maintain their professional competence by extending their knowledge and skills, learning from experience and keeping up to date with new personnel practices and the social, political and economic factors which affect their work. CPD involves Institute members in recording their development activities. It is recognised that the learning needed for continuing development can be acquired in a number of different ways, for example, the implementation of a new personnel procedure or process or involvement in a company or relevant external project as well as specific learning events and activities. The outcome of the learning as well as the activities and experiences need to be recorded. Supporting documentation may be provided when appropriate. CPD is a requirement for all corporate members and evidence of CPD is required when applying to upgrade membership.

# 5

# The Contribution of the Personnel Function to Organizational Success

## Organizational success

A business has been defined by Peter Drucker (1995) as an 'organization that adds value and creates wealth'. A successful organization can broadly be defined as one that successfully achieves these objectives while also meeting its responsibilities to its stakeholders. These stakeholders consist of:

1. The owners, shareholders, public authorities or trustees who direct or fund the organization.
2. The employees who run the organization.
3. The customers, clients or members of the public for whom the organization provides goods or services.
4. The third parties through whom the organization does business.
5. The community in which the organization operates.

### The balanced score card

The 'balanced score card', a concept developed by Kaplan and Norton (1992), is a means of measuring organizational success. It enables managers to take a balanced look at the business from four key perspectives:

1. How do customers see us? (customer perspective).
2. What must we excel at? (internal perspective).
3. Can we continue to improve and create value? (innovation and learning perspective).

4.   How do we look to shareholders? (financial perspective).

Kaplan and Norton make the point that 'what you measure is what you get' — the organization's measurement system strongly affects the behaviour of managers. This is the argument for using a simple but well balanced set of criteria as the components of the 'scorecard'. Some organizations are incorporatingthe balance score card approach into their processes for reviewing the contributions of managers — the four headings in the scorecard being used as the main criteria for appraising and rewarding performance.

## The managerial factors which create organizational success

The managerial factors which create organizational success are:

- strong visionary leadership from the top
- a clearly defined and well communicated sense of purpose expressed as a mission
- a value system upheld throughout the organization which emphasizes performance, quality and the responsibilities of the organization to its stakeholders
- the strategic capability at senior management level to develop long-range plans for the accomplishment of the organization's mission within the framework of its core values
- a thrust led by the top, but pervading the organization, to achieve world class levels of performance by processes of benchmarking, continuous improvement and, as necessary, re-engineering the business.

## The people factors which create organizational success

But organizational effectiveness is also highly dependent on the quality of the people in the organization and how well they are managed. It has frequently been argued that 'people make the difference'. The IPD (1993) asserted that organisational success depends on people management practices which stimulate and focus:

- initiative
- creativity
- motivation
- judgement
- capability
- adaptability
- business orientation
- responsibility
- willing contributors

It is certainly the case that organisational success is largely dependent on having the right resources and making the best use of them. Cappelli and Singh (1993) suggest that competitive advantage arises from 'firm-specific, valuable resources which are difficult to imitate'. A study by Hall (1992) of UK chief executive officers found that:

> All CEOs rated company reputation, product reputation, and employee knowhow as the most important contributors to organizational success ... (these) were also identified as the resources which would take longest to replace if they had to be replaced from scratch.

And, as reported by Armstrong and Long (1994) the Managing Director of Boots the Chemist is clear that 'money is easy to get hold of, good people are not'. These matters are the responsibility of all managers in their human resource management role but, of course, they particularly concern the personnel function.

The people factors which contribute to organizational success relate to the development of:

- a powerful management team
- a well-motivated, committed, skilled and flexible workforce
- stable and cooperative relationships with employees
- an overall quality of working life strategy.

The purpose of this chapter is to provide answers to three questions:

1. To what extent does the personnel function contribute to organisation success?
2. How does it generally make that contribution?
3. What are the most important areas in which the contribution is made?

## To what extent does the personnel function contribute to organizational success?

It is generally agreed that the personnel function can make a significant contribution but that it is an indirect one, as the conclusions from two recent studies show. A survey conducted by Tyson *et al* (1995) came to the conclusion that:

> It is difficult to establish the linkage between the activities of the personnel department and the organization's business performance. In the survey there was little support for the notion that there is a direct link, although two strong sources of influence on business strategy were observed. First, employee skills, abilities and competences are seen to be

sources of competitive advantage. Second, the personnel function's contribution to development of these competences is perceived at the 'tactical' level of recruitment, training, and development practices.

Guest and Hoque (1995) in an analysis of the 1990 Workplace Industrial Relations Survey (WIRS3) commented that:

> The personnel role is inevitably somewhat ambiguous and the influence on most outcomes is likely to be indirect. It is worth asking whether we would expect personnel managers to have a direct impact on employee relations climate and on reflection, the answer is probably, no. We know that personnel managers help to formulate personnel policy and practices; they often administer it and thus deal with a wide range of contingencies. However, on a day-to-day basis most personnel decisions are taken by line managers and that is why the concept of partnership is an appropriate one.

They explained in an earlier article (Guest and Hoque, 1994) what they meant by 'indirect influence'.

> It is more useful to take a realistic view of what the personnel department can do. We know that it can help to formulate policy and practice. To take a simple example, personnel departments can set up a sound appraisal system, develop the documentation and procedures and provide training. They can monitor the system. But the actual appraisals must be completed by line managers and the impact of the system ultimately depends on their willingness to do this seriously and competently. Personnel departments should have a direct influence on the appraisal system, but only an indirect influence on its impact.

But there are other views about how much personnel practitioners contribute. For example, Fernie, Metcalf and Woodland (1994) made a notorious attack on the value of personnel specialists. They claimed that their analysis of the WIRS3 reveals that the presence of a personnel manager is associated with a poorer climate of employee relations. However, rather less publicity has been given to their findings that a number of personnel practices are associated with a variety of positive outcomes.

Guest and Hoque's (1995) replication and extension of this analysis used a more cautious three-point measure of employee relations climate rather than the somewhat controversial five point scale on which Fernie *et al* based their analysis. As a result, Guest and Hoque found that there was no longer a significant negative association between the presence of a personnel specialist and the employee relations climate. But they warned that 'the logic in looking for a direct link between personnel management and outcomes is dubious'.

Their conclusion (Guest and Hoque 1994) is that the research evidence shows that the presence of specialist personnel managers is associated with more HR policies and practices, including what would be widely regarded as 'good' practices. But, as they point out:

> The link between practices and outcomes is more tenuous. The key is strategic integration. What this means is the personnel strategy must fit the business strategy, the personnel policies must be fully integrated with one another and the values of the line managers must be sufficiently aligned with the personnel philosophy to ensure that they will implement the personnel policy and practice.

## How does the personnel function contribute to organizational success?

Although the personnel function may not make a direct contribution to the bottom line it can make a considerable indirect contribution to the creation of added value and competitive advantage.

## Contribution to added value

In accounting language, added value is the difference between the income of the business arising from sales (output) and the amount spent on materials and other purchased goods and services (input). In more general terms, it is the development and use of any resource in a way which ensures that it yields a substantial and sustainable higher return on whatever has been invested in it. Added value often means the creation of more out of less, and an increasingly popular index of overall organizational performance is added value per £ of employment costs.

Added value is created by people: people at various levels in organizations who create visions, define values and missions, set goals, develop strategic plans, and implement those plans in accordance with the underpinning values. Added value will be enhanced by anything that is done to obtain and develop the right sort of people, to motivate and manage them effectively, to gain their commitment to organizational values, to build and maintain stable relationships with them, to develop the right sort of organization structure, and to deploy them effectively and productively in that structure.

## Contribution of Personnel and Development

The personnel function contributes to the creation of added value by ensuring that people with the required competences and levels of motivation are available and by helping to create a culture and environment which stimulates quality performance.

An added value approach to personnel will be directed positively to improve employee motivation, commitment, skill, performance and contribution. This approach can aim to get better value for money from personnel expenditure in such areas as training, reward and employee benefits.

There are four ways in which the personnel function can take the lead and make the most of its opportunity to add value:

- by facilitating change, proposing strategies and programmes for developing a more positive quality and performance-orientated culture and helping with their implementation
- by making specific contributions in the areas of human resource planning, resourcing, training and development, performance management, reward and employee relations
- by ensuring that any HR initiatives in such fields as training and development are treated as investments on which a proper return will be obtained which will increase added value
- by delivering cost-effective personnel services, ie providing value for money.

## Contribution to competitive advantage

The concept of sustainable competitive advantage as formulated by Porter (1985) arises when a firm creates value for its customers, selects markets in which it can excel and presents a moving target to its competitors by continually improving its position. According to Porter, three of the most important factors are innovation, quality and cost leadership but he also recognizes that all these depend on the quality of an organization's human resources. The ability to gain and retain competitive advantage is crucial to a business' growth and prosperity.

Unique talents among employees, including superior performance, high productivity, flexibility, innovation, and the ability to deliver high levels of personal customer service are ways in which people provide a critical ingredient in developing an organization's competitive position. People also provide the key to managing the pivotal inter-dependencies across functional activities and the important external relationships. It can be argued that one of the clear benefits arising from competitive advantage based on the effective management of people is that such an advantage is hard to imitate. An organization's personnel strategies, policies and practices are a unique blend of processes, procedures, personalities, styles, capabilities and organizational culture. One of the keys to competitive advantage is the ability to differentiate what the business supplies to its customers from those supplied by its competitors. Such differentiation can be achieved by having higher quality people than those competitors.

Research conducted recently by the European Association for Personnel Management and the International Institute for Management Development (Brooklyn Derr *et al*, 1993) revealed that competitive advantage is achieved by developing core competences in the workforce through traditional services (recruitment, reward, career pathing, employee development), and by dealing effectively with macro concerns such as corporate culture, management development and organizational structure.

The IBM/Towers Perrin (1992) world-wide survey of 2,961 firms established that the top five initiatives for gaining competitive advantage as assessed by line managers and HR executives were as follows:

|                                              | Line | HR |
| -------------------------------------------- | ---- | -- |
| ● Identify high-potential employees early    | 1    | 4  |
| ● Communicate directions, plans, problems    | 2    | 1  |
| ● Reward innovation and creativity           | 3    | 5  |
| ● Reward customer service and quality        | 4    | 2  |
| ● Reward business and/or productivity gains  | 5    | 3  |

## In what areas does the personnel function contribute to organizational success?

The main areas in which the personnel function can contribute to organizational success are by helping to:

● build a well-motivated, committed, skilled and flexible workforce by developing strategies, policies and employment practices in the areas of motivation, commitment, resourcing, employee development and employee reward (these are discussed elsewhere in this book under these headings)

● create and develop effective organizations as described in Chapters 20, 21 and 22

● maintain a good climate of employee relations as discussed in Part VIII

- focus on the 'drivers' of organisational performance, providing levers for change, taking part in change management programmes and supporting continuous improvement and total quality management initiatives.

## The personnel function's contribution to change management

### Providing levers for change

Levers for change which can be provided by interventions advocated or at least facilitated by the personnel function are:

- performance management processes which contribute to the better integration of corporate, team and individual objectives and an increased awareness of the standards of performance required
- performance-related pay which, even if it does not necessarily act as an effective motivator, can be used as a means for delivering messages about the expectations of the organization and its performance priorities
- competence profiling which spells out competence requirements and provides the basis for competence-related personnel management in such areas as recruitment, employee development and employee reward
- continuous development programmes which provide opportunities for learning and career progression
- organization development programmes which are concerned with improving the effectiveness with which an organization functions and responds to change

### The role of the personnel specialist as change agent

Personnel specialists are constantly involved in change management processes and it could be argued that their role as change agents is one of the most important contributions they can make to improving organizational effectiveness.

Personnel specialists, particularly if they are part of the top management team and have the ear of the chief executive, can exert a major influence on change. Their influence will be strongest if they have an understanding of the processes, systems, interventions, media and interactions which are the levers for change, and can relate this understanding to an appreciation of the culture and the key business and people issues and critical success factors affecting the organization.

They can facilitate the process of change management if they:

- intervene to point out where change is required
- help in the articulation of an agenda for change which takes account of all contextual considerations, especially their human aspects
- analyze how people might react to change
- advise on how the change agenda should be communicated in a way which will minimize resistance to change
- facilitate workshops and other means of getting people involved in analyzing the reasons for change, deciding what changes should take place and discussing how it should be implemented
- advise on and manage the education and training programmes required to ensure that employees have the knowledge and skills needed to introduce change and operate new systems.

## The personnel function's contribution to continuous improvement

The concept of continuous improvement is based on the assumption that continually striving to reach higher and higher standards in every part of the organization will provide a series of incremental gains that will build superior performance. In Japan the process is called *kaizen* which is a composite of the word 'kai' meaning change, and 'zen' meaning good or for the better. It consists of the organization creating an environment in which *all* employees can contribute to improving performance and overall effectiveness as a normal and continuing part of their job.

In an environment dedicated to continuous improvement, managers and team leaders have as a prime objective the bringing out of new ideas and concepts from their staff. Their task is to create an environment in which new thinking is encouraged and welcomed.

The role of the personnel function in helping to develop an environment dedicated to continuous improvement is to:

- provide facilities for identifying, reviewing and developing ideas for continuous improvement, eg improvement groups, team meetings, suggestion schemes
- provide training in developing and implementing ideas
- develop performance measures which enable progress to be monitored and assist in determining priorities for future developments

- ensure that good ideas are recognised — the recognition need not necessarily be financial
- communicate to everyone the aims of continuous improvement, how they are expected to contribute and what has been achieved.

## The personnel function's contribution to quality management

### *What quality management is about*

Quality is achieved through people. It is not a system or programme which is lifted down from a consultant's shelf, installed by manufacturing or quality control, and then forgotten. It is not a fad, here today and gone tomorrow, leaving the people concerned (and everyone *is* concerned) bemused about the part they should play in quality management now that the company has taken up business process re-engineering or 360-degree feedback or whatever.

Quality is a race without a finish in which everyone in the organization takes part. It is a race against tough competitors to achieve and sustain world class standards of performance. Quality differentiates companies from those competitors. The aim is to deliver customer satisfaction — the only real measure of the quality of a product or service. Total quality empowers customers to define the service they want, measures the service they get and provides performance feedback to suppliers. And meeting today's requirements is not enough. Businesses and the people in them must be sufficiently flexible and adaptable to continue meeting these requirements as they change and develop in the future.

Total quality (often referred to as TQM — total quality management) is a process which involves everyone in satisfying the needs of both external and internal customers. Quality should be a way of life, deeply rooted in the culture and values of the business and dependent on the attitudes, behaviours and competences of people as individuals or in teams. In quality orientated companies such as Nissan and Rover Group, quality is the centrepiece of their philosophy, with commitment at every level. Quality is achieved through culture change, behaviour modification and skills provision. To achieve total quality it is necessary to:

- incorporate quality objectives into strategic plans
- build accountabilities for quality into every job and into all related processes, eg performance management

- obtain demonstrable commitment from everyone in the organization, starting at the top
- form quality orientated teams which are integrated top to bottom and bottom to top, as well as laterally to include suppliers and customers
- build skills through training
- recognise and reward quality improvement.

## Why the personnel function can contribute to quality management

The personnel function is ideally placed to make a major contribution to total quality improvement. Members of the function have, or should have, non-substitutable expertise in the key aspects of making quality management work through people. They can bring to bear all their creativity in their role as internal consultants and service providers in the fields of culture management, the management of change, team-building, communications, the management of learning, approaches to gaining commitment and modifying behaviour.

## The personnel function's roles

An IPD research project (1993) established four separate roles for personnel in quality management:

- *Hidden persuader*, in which personnel operates at a strategic level, promoting the cause of quality management with top management and advising them on how a total quality culture can be developed and sustained. The personnel function may be much less visible to line managers in this role but can play a significant part behind the scenes in generating new ideas and developing total quality strategies.
- *Change agent*, in which the personnel function plays a major part in driving quality management and managing the change processes required to develop a quality orientated culture.
- *Facilitator*, providing hands-on support to line managers through such activities as training or publicising achievements.
- *Internal contractor*, in which the personnel function draws up and publishes its own targets and standards for providing quality services to its internal customers, including how it can help in improving quality standards generally.

## Carrying out the role

The function can play a major role in quality management strategically, operationally and through support processes.

*Strategically*, personnel practitioners can analyse the culture and climate of the organization and advise on its readiness to change in the direction of a quality approach to all aspects of the business. They can also contribute by assessing the skill base required for total quality and how these skills can be developed.

*Operationally*, personnel can play a major part in the learning programmes which are at the heart of the development of total quality. These will include training in quality awareness, approaches to achieving quality, problem and fault correction techniques, teamworking and the acquisition of new skills as part of a multiskilling process. The function can also manage communications. But exhortation is not enough. People do not become quality conscious by being told to be quality conscious. What can be done is to ensure that everyone is aware of the quality initiatives and achievements of the business and the part people are playing in them.

Operational initiatives are not simply about setting up quality circles. The aim should be to get every work team to recognise that collectively all its members are accountable for quality and that they will be encouraged to make or recommend quality improvements for which they will be recognised and rewarded.

The personnel function can also help total quality to succeed by providing *support processes* in the areas of:

- *Change management* which is the key to continuous quality improvement. Some personnel functions have the process consultancy skills to do it themselves but many are getting help from external advisers, implementation consultants and training providers in handling change processes.
- *Skills provision* — ensuring that recruitment, development and training processes reflect the likely new needs for skill required in a total quality management environment.
- *Training and development* — facilitating continuous improvement and learning in the management and career development process.
- *Reward management* — ensuring that quality and teamworking to achieve quality are rewarded as well as hitting output or sales targets.
- *Performance management* — providing for values such as quality and

customer service to be key factors in setting objectives and reviewing performance, and using performance management processes as the basis for continuous improvement and self-managed learning.

## Demands on the personnel function

Carrying out these roles makes considerable demands on personnel. Members of the function need to be:

- fully aware of the business and operational imperatives of the organization and how competitive advantage can be achieved through quality — this includes an appreciation of the particular factors which contribute to quality performance in their organization
- able to translate this understanding into convincing proposals to top management on what needs to be done to develop a quality culture and how to manage the required change programme
- experts in approaches to behaviour modification, teambuilding, the management of learning and communications
- committed to running the personnel function as a total quality unit in itself — they must act as a role model by demonstrating an ability to deliver quality services to their internal customers.

6

# Evaluating the Personnel Function Contribution

The potential for the personnel function to play a significant, even if indirect, role in increasing added value and achieving competitive advantage may be considerable, as suggested in the last chapter. But how can the effectiveness of the function be measured at both the strategic level and at the level of support and service provision? Such measurements have to be made to ensure that a value-added contribution is being made and to indicate where improvements or changes in direction are needed.

## Approaches to evaluation

The research conducted by Armstrong and Long (1994) established from discussions with chief executives and other directors that the most popular basis for evaluation was their judgement related to factors such as:

- understanding of the organization — its mission, values, critical success factors, product-marketing strategies, technology or method of operation and distinctive competences
- effectiveness of contributions to top management team decision-making on corporate/business issues
- the extent to which innovatory, realistic and persuasive proposals were made on HR strategies, policies and programmes
- the capacity to deliver as promised
- the quality of the advice and services they provided, assessed mainly in subjective terms — eg, it is practical, it meets my needs, it

solves my problem, they (the services) are efficient, they respond quickly to requests for help or advice

- the ability to build and maintain stable and cooperative relationships with trade unions
- the ability to handle difficult situations such as downsizing
- in very general terms, the contribution they make to developing the corporate culture, their influence on management style and their abilities as facilitators and managers of change
- their overall credibility and ability to work as a full member of the top management team.

These largely subjective evaluations were supplemented by the analysis of key employment ratios such as turnover, absenteeism, suggestions received and acted upon, health and safety statistics and the outcome of customer satisfaction surveys.

In some organizations formal surveys were made of the opinions of line managers about the services they received from the personnel function, and employee attitude surveys were also used as a means of evaluation.

But this problem should not deter anyone from making a determined attempt to measure personnel effectiveness, and there are a number of approaches which can be adopted as discussed below.

## Overall methods of evaluation

An important distinction is made by Tsui and Gomez-Mejia (1988) between:

- *process criteria* — how well things are done; and
- *output criteria* — the impact made by the process on organizational and operational performance, ie the effectiveness of the end-result.

This is broadly the old (Peter Drucker, 1967) distinction between efficiency and effectiveness — ie doing things right in terms of *what* you do (efficiency) rather than doing the right things in terms of the results you achieve (effectiveness). In terms of personnel effectiveness, it means determining the extent to which personnel policies, programmes and practices and the advice and support provided by the personnel function enable line managers to achieve business objectives and meet operational requirements.

When deciding on how the personnel function should be evaluated it is also necessary to distinguish between quantitative criteria such as turnover or absenteeism figures, and qualitative criteria such as line managers' opinions of the personnel function or the outcome of employee attitude surveys.

## Types of performance measures

The types of performance measures which can be used to evaluate the personnel function are:

- *Money measures* which include maximizing income, minimizing expenditure and improving rates of return.
- *Time measures* express performance against work timetables, the amount of backlog and speed of activity or response.
- *Measures of effect* include attainment of a standard, changes in behaviour (of colleagues, staff, clients or customers), physical completion of the work and the level of take-up of a service.
- *Reaction* indicates how others judge the function or its members and is therefore a less objective measure. Reaction can be measured by peer assessments, performance ratings by internal or external clients or customers or the analysis of comments and complaints.

## Evaluation criteria

It has been suggested by Guest and Peccei (1994) that the effectiveness of HRM can be measured by reference to:

- *organizational effectiveness* — but it may not be possible to separate HR and organizational effectiveness, which will be affected by external events, and this approach does not provide a base for decisions about HR policy and practice
- *specified goals* — this is a plausible method, if good measures of goal attainment can be used and if allowance is made for unanticipated events
- *specified quantified measures* — labour costs, turnover and pro-ductivity have high credibility but may be difficult to interpret and can be affected by non-HRM factors and are insufficient on their own
- *stakeholder perspective* — this uses the subjective views of key interest groups, eg the board, on personnel effectiveness, and is probably the most satisfactory method.

## Practical methods of evaluation

The approaches that in practice are adopted by organizations to evaluate personnel effectiveness are:

- *quantitative — macro* (organizational)
- *quantitative — micro* (specified aspects of employee behaviour or reaction)
- *quantitative/qualitative* — achievement of specified goals
- *quantitative/qualitative* — achievement of standards set in service level agreements
- *qualitative — macro* — an overall and largely subjective assessment of the personnel function
- *qualitative* — client satisfaction ie 'stakeholder perspective'
- *qualitative* — employee satisfaction, also 'stakeholder perspective'
- *utility analysis*
- *benchmarking.*

### Organizational quantitative criteria

At organizational level, the quantitative criteria which can be used include:

- added value per employee
- profit per employee
- sales value per employee
- costs per employee
- added value per £ of employment costs.

Added value per £ of employment costs was used in two of the organizations covered by the Armstrong and Long (1994) research (Pilkington Optronics and Rover Group) and has the advantage of bringing together both benefits (added value) and costs (of employment).

Another reason for using quantified macro-measures as pointed out by Tyson (1985), is that

> ... the business objectives become 'sold' as part of the personnel policies. The discipline of sitting down to look at training objectives, for example in terms of sales value or added value, brings out what *can* be assessed and raises the useful question of why we are proposing this programme, if we are unable to relate it to the business.

## *Specific quantified criteria*

Specified quantified criteria can be classified into two categories: those relating to measurable aspects of employee behaviours and those relating to the type, level and costs of the services provided by the personnel department to its clients.

### *Employee behaviour criteria*
Employee behaviour criteria include:

- employee retention and turnover rates
- absenteeism rate
- ratio of suggestions received to number of employees
- number of usable proposals from quality circles or improvement groups
- cost savings arising from suggestions and/or quality circle recommendations
- frequency/severity rate of accidents
- ratio of grievances to number of employees
- time lost through disputes
- number of references to industrial tribunals on unfair dismissal, equal opportunity, equal pay, harassment, racial discrimination issues etc and the outcome of such references.

In some of these areas, for example, employee retention and absenteeism rates, the personnel function cannot be held entirely accountable. But it *is* a shared responsibility and the measures will indicate problem areas which may be related to the quality of the advice or services provided by the function.

### *Personnel department service-level criteria*
The quantifiable criteria available to measure the level and value of service provision by the personnel function include:

- average time to fill vacancies
- time to respond to applicants
- ratio of acceptance to offers made
- cost of advertisements per reply/engagement
- training hours/days per employee
- time to respond to and settle grievances
- cost of induction training per employee
- cost of benefits per employee

- measurable improvements in productivity as a direct result of training
- measurable improvements in individual and organizational performance as a direct result of the operation of performance-related pay and performance management schemes
- ratio of personnel department costs to profit, sales turnover or added value
- personnel costs in relation to budget
- ratio of personnel staff to employees.

The usefulness of those measures is variable, as is the practicality of collecting reliable information. Figures on training days per employee do not mean much in themselves unless there is some measure of the relevance and impact of that training. To rely on this measure would be like rewarding sales representatives on the basis of the sales volume they generate rather than the contribution their sales make to profit and fixed costs.

It is also possible that the costs of collecting and analysing some sorts of information may not be justified by the benefits which they could theoretically produce in the shape of improved performance. It is a matter of judgement to select the criteria which are likely to be the most relevant, and this will depend on the circumstances of the organization and the particular pressures to which it and its personnel function is being subjected. It may be appropriate to highlight some criteria for a period and then, if the problem has been resolved, focus attention on other areas.

## Achievement of specified goals

This approach involves measuring achievements against agreed objectives — it could be the final outcome or a measure of progress towards a goal as indicated by the extent to which specified 'milestones' have been reached.

The specified objectives could be expressed in terms such as:

- all employees to have received training on the implementation of equal opportunities policies by 1 June
- an agreement with the various trade unions to setting up single table bargaining to be reached by the end of the year
- the competence analysis programme to be completed within 12 months

- salary surveys to be conducted and a report on the implications on salary scales to be submitted by 1 September
- the new performance management system to be fully operational within the next six months.

'Project' objectives set along these lines should include some indication of the standard of achievement expected, for example:

The effectiveness of the performance management system will be judged on:

(a)  an evaluation of user reactions (managers and individuals)
(b)  an assessment of the quality of the performance review processes
(c)  an analysis of the outputs of the system in terms of development and improvement plans
(d)  the number of upheld appeals on assessments
(e)  the impact the scheme is making on motivation, performance and commitment (as measured by a structured questionnaire to managers and individuals).

## Service level agreements

A service level agreement (SLA) is an agreement between the provider of a service and the customers who use the service. It quantifies the level of service required to meet the business needs. SLAs are most commonly found in the public sector but the principles of such agreements could apply equally well in other sectors. The starting point in drawing up a SLA is to clarify precisely what the customer's needs are and which elements are most important. The aim in setting service targets is that they should be stretching but achievable — although the approach adopted by some service providers is to under-promise so that they can appear to over-achieve.

A service level agreement sets out:

- the nature of the function or service provided
- the volumes and quality to be achieved for each of these services
- the response times to be achieved by the provider when receiving requests for help.

For a personnel function, service level standards could be drawn up for such activities as:

- response to requests for help or guidance in specific areas, eg recruitment, training, handling discipline cases and grievances and health and safety

- the time taken to prepare job descriptions, fill vacancies or conduct a job evaluation
- the amount of lost time through absenteeism or work-related sickness or accidents
- the proportion of discipline and grievance issues settled at the time of the first involvement of personnel
- the number of appeals (successful and unsuccessful) against job evaluation decisions
- the results of evaluations by participants of training provided by the function.

Organizations which charge out the services of the personnel function to users (and this is happening increasingly in local authorities) may set standards in terms of the costs of providing recruitment, training and other services. This could take such forms as a unit charge for each person recruited, a *per capita* charge for each training day, a fixed price sum for undertaking projects such as a pay review, a daily or hourly consultancy rate for work done on an occasional basis, or a lump sum retainer fee for maintaining a general availability to provide advice or services.

To make service level agreements work as a basis for evaluation it is essential that they should be agreed by both providers and customers (purchasers). They should be reasonably simple, especially to begin with (not too many headings), and it should be possible to measure performance against the standards fairly easily — an over-bureaucratic system is likely to defeat the purpose of the agreement. If these requirements can be satisfied a service level agreement can provide a good basis for evaluation.

## Subjective overall evaluation

Perhaps the most common method of evaluating the HR function is a subjective assessment by the chief executive or the board which will be related to such general factors as:

- the quality of the advice and services provided as observed or experienced directly by the evaluator
- the degree to which members of the function are proactive rather than reactive (if that is what the management wants, which is not always the case)
- feedback from line managers obtained in a haphazard basis as to

whether or not they think personnel is 'a good thing' and is 'doing a good job'.

The dangers of relying on subjective and *ad hoc* measures like these are obvious but they are much used.

## User reaction measures

Rather than relying on haphazard and highly subjective assessments this approach involves identifying the key criteria for measuring the degree to which clients of the personnel function in the shape of directors, managers and team leaders are satisfied with the quality of advice and services they provide.

Areas in which the quality of services provided by the personnel function can be assessed include:

- understanding of strategic business imperatives
- anticipation of business and management needs
- ability to function as a 'business partner' in the team
- quality of advice given in terms of its relevance to the problem or issue, the clarity and conviction with which the advice is given, the practicality of the recommendations
- the quality of the back-up advice and services offered to implement recommendations, the extent to which ultimately the proposals worked
- speed of response to requests for advice or services
- promptness in dealing with grievances and appeals
- help to managers in identifying and meeting training needs
- extent to which training and development programmes meet company/individual needs
- delivery of advice and services which make a significant impact on improving the quality and performance of staff
- development of programmes and processes which address short and long-term business needs, which are 'owned' by line managers, and which produce the anticipated impact on motivation, commitment and performance.

Assessments of the contribution of the personnel function in areas such as those listed above can be made by conducting surveys of client opinion.

## Employee satisfaction measures

The degree to which the employee stakeholders are satisfied with personnel policies and practices as they affect them can be measured by attitude surveys which obtain opinions and perceptions of employees on:

- the extent to which they believe promotion, job evaluation, performance appraisal, performance-related pay and grievance processes and procedures operate fairly
- the degree to which they are satisfied with pay and benefits
- the extent to which they feel they are involved in decisions that affect them
- how well they feel they are kept informed on matters of importance to them
- the consistency with which personnel policies concerning pay, equal opportunity, etc are applied
- the opportunities available to them for training and development
- the degree to which their work makes the best use of their skills and abilities
- the extent to which they are clear about what is expected of them
- the support and guidance they receive from their managers and team leaders
- their working environment from the point of view of health and safety, and the general conditions under which they work
- the facilities (restaurant, car parking etc) with which they are provided
- generally, the climate and management style of the organization.

## Individual evaluation

The evaluation approaches listed above are directed at both the personnel function as a whole and its individual members. But it is also necessary specifically to agree the overall objectives and standards of performance expected from members of the function as a basis for assessment.

An example of a list of standards of performance agreed for a personnel manager is given in Appendix A.

## Utility analysis

Utility analysis provides a decision support framework that explicitly considers the costs and benefits of personnel decisions. The aim is to

126

predict, explain and improve the utility or 'usefulness' of those decisions. It focuses on personnel programmes, ie sets of activities or procedures that affect personnel value.

Utility analysis as described by Boudreau (1988) requires:

- a *problem* — a gap between what is desired and what is currently being achieved
- a set of *alternatives* to address the problem
- a set of *attributes* — the variables that describe the important characteristics of the alternatives (such as effects on productivity, costs and employee attitudes)
- a *utility function*, or a system to combine the attributes into an overall judgement of each alternative's usefulness.

Utility analysis focuses on:

- *quantity* — the effect of work behaviours over time
- *quality* — the production of large improvements or the avoidance of large reductions in the quality of those work behaviours
- *cost* — the minimization of the costs of developing, implementing and maintaining programmes.

These are, rightly, in line with the factors used by any other function. It is accepted that all the variables to be assessed may not be capable of being measured precisely, but uncertainty of this kind takes place in all aspects of management (eg measuring consumer preferences).

Utility analysis depends on good management information and the possible limitations of such information and the costs of collecting it should be recognized. Detailed management information will only prove useful if it serves the following purposes:

- it is likely to correct decisions that otherwise would have been incorrect
- the corrections are important and produce large benefits
- the cost of conducting the information does not outweigh the expected benefit of corrected decisions.

## Benchmarking

The methods of measuring personnel effectiveness listed above all rely on collecting and analysing internal data and opinions. But it is also desirable to 'benchmark', ie compare what the personnel function is doing within the organization with what is happening elsewhere. This will involve gaining information on 'best practice' which, even if it is not transferable in total to the organization conducting the survey, should at least provide information on areas for development or improvement.

## Preferred approach

Every organization will develop its own approach to evaluating the effectiveness of the personnel function and its members. There are no standard measures.

Perhaps, as Guest and Peccei (1994) suggest:

> The most sensible and the most important indicator of HRM effectiveness will be the judgements of key stakeholders.... The political, stakeholder, perspective on effectiveness in organizations acknowledges that it is the interpretation placed on quantified results and the attributions of credit and blame that are derived from them that matter most in judging effectiveness. In other words, at the end of the day, it is always the qualitative interpretation by those in positions of power that matter most.

But they recognized 'the desirability of also developing clearly specified goals and quantitative indicators, together with financial criteria'.

# 7

# International Personnel Management

## International personnel management defined

International personnel management is the process of employing and developing people in international organizations which operate in Europe or globally. It means working across national boundaries to formulate and implement resourcing, development, career management and remuneration strategies, policies and practices which can be applied to an international work force. This may include parent country nationals working for long periods as expatriates or on short-term assignments, local country nationals, or third country nationals who work for the corporation in a local country but are not parent country nationals (eg a German working in West Africa for a British owned company).

## The challenge of international personnel management

International personnel management is likely to be more demanding than management within the boundaries of one country for three reasons. The first is likely to be managing the complexity of the workforce mix. For example, wholly-owned subsidiary companies may employ both host and parent-country people together with third country nationals. This may create problems with employment practices as well as remuneration. A joint venture or strategic alliance may have an even more complex workforce consisting of expatriates of the joint venture company, host country nationals, third country nationals and experts from any of the partners who are 'parachuted' in to deal with special problems or to provide consultancy services. Some of the specific people problems arising in joint ventures as noted by Kanter (1989) and others include divided loyalties between the parent company and the joint venture consortium and the difficulties managers may face when trying to be both sensitive to local conditions and aware of the demands made by the consortium or their own parent company.

The second challenge is that of managing diversity — between cultures, social systems and legal requirements. International personnel managers are not in the business of controlling uniformity — if they tried, they would fail.

The third challenge of managing people spread around Europe or the globe is an obvious one, but this does not make it any easier. Even the most sophisticated electronic communication system may not be an adequate substitute for face-to-face contacts.

## Characteristics of international personnel management

It has been suggested by Torrington (1994) that international personnel management is not just about copying practices from the Americans, Japanese, Germans and so on which will not necessarily translate culturally. Neither is it simply a matter of learning the culture of every country and suitably modifying behaviour in each of them, which is an impossible ideal because of the robust and subtle nature of national cultures. He believes that international personnel management is best defined by reference to the following '7cs' characteristics:

- *Cosmopolitan* — people tend to be either members of a high-flying multi-lingual elite who are involved in high level coordination and are constantly on the move, or expatriates who may relocate after periods of several years and can have significant problems on repatriation.
- *Culture* — major differences in cultural backgrounds
- *Compensation* — special requirements for the determination of the pay and benefits of expatriates and host country nationals
- *Communication* — maintaining good communication between all parts of the organization, worldwide
- *Consultancy* — greater need to bring in expertise to deal with local needs
- *Competence* — developing a wider range of competences for people who have to work across political, cultural and organizational boundaries.
- *Coordination* — devising formal and informal methods of getting the different parts of the international business to work closer together.

It has been argued by Torrington that international personnel management is in may ways simply personnel management on a larger scale, albeit more complex, more varied and involving more coordination across national boundaries. Certainly the same basic techniques of recruitment and training may be used but these have to be adapted to fit different cultures and local requirements. And the management and remuneration of expatriates can present particular difficulties.

There are no universal prescriptions for international personnel management and the rest of this chapter deals only with the general considerations to be taken into account when developing approaches in the areas of employment and development strategies, recruitment, employee development and the management of expatriates (international pay is dealt with in Chapter 37).

# International employment and development strategies

International employment and development strategies have to address three main issues: centralisation, staffing management posts and management development.

## Centralization strategy

The centralization strategy has to consider the extent to which employment policies should be developed and controlled from corporate headquarters. This could mean that staffing, employee development, career move and remuneration decisions for people in managerial, professional and technical jobs would be made at the centre. The organization would then be well-placed to plan for management succession and to secure the availability of high quality staff to exploit new opportunities as well as to manage existing operations. Individuals could become more committed because they know that a systematic and world-wide approach exists for developing their potential, managing their careers and rewarding them in accordance with their contribution. But there is a possibility that this could tend to impose the corporate culture throughout the world, which could lead to local tensions.

## Staffing management posts

There are three possible approaches:

1. *Fill all key positions with parent country nationals.* This policy is often adopted in the early stages of internalisation or when overseas

operations are being started in new countries. Parent country nationals will be qualified to transfer the organization's knowhow to the overseas company or plant, but there are a number of potential problems. They might find it difficult to adjust to different conditions, cultures and methods of management. Managing the careers of expatriates is never easy. And there could be inequities between the remuneration of expatriates and local managers who could also be frustrated by the lack of career opportunities.

2. *Appoint home country nationals to manage subsidiaries.* This gets over some or even all of the difficulties mentioned above but there may still be problems inherent in the relationships between the parent country managers who remain in overall control and the local managers. These may arise from cultural differences, conflicting loyalties and language barriers. Furthermore, as noted by Scullion (1995), home country managers will have limited scope to gain experience outside their own country while parent country managers will gain little hands-on international experience, thus potentially reducing the effectiveness of the organization as a global competitor.

3. *Appoint the best people regardless of nationality to manage subsidiaries.* This enables the organization to develop a truly international cadre of managers and avoids the parochial approach which might be adopted if only local nationals are appointed. But this can be a difficult strategy to implement and it does require a fair degree of centralized control.

The third, hybrid, approach is often favoured but it has to contend with the fact that some countries are insisting that their own nationals should be used wherever possible.

It is also interesting to note the findings of research conducted by Scullion (1991) who found that although 50 per cent of the companies surveyed had formal policies favouring host country nationals, in practice two thirds of them used expatriates to manage their overseas operations.

## Management development strategy

The management development strategy has to consider the extent to which a truly international perspective can be furthered throughout the global organization by means of processes of identifying talent and potential, job rotation, special assignments, distance learning programmes, regional or central management training, attendance on management programmes run by international business schools and the provision of career guidance and monitoring processes from the centre

## Recruitment across international boundaries

International personnel management may mean recruiting local or third country nationals to work for parent country subsidiaries, plants or agencies in a foreign country or overseas territory.

### *Definition of requirements*

The starting point, as in all recruitment exercises, is a job description (what the job entails) and a person specification (what sort of people are most likely to be suitable).

The job description should set out any special features of the job. Reference can be made to career prospects locally and internationally and to any mobility requirements, ie the likelihood of future moves within the country or elsewhere. An indication of what the executive will be expected to achieve should be included. This would define objectives, targets and deadlines and would be particularly appropriate in a start-up situation.

The following is an example of a somewhat demanding person profile for a 'euro-executive' produced by a consultant:

> Fluent in at least one other Community language, of greater importance is exposure to a diversity of cultures stemming both from family background — he or she is likely to have a mixed education, multi-cultural marriage and parents of different nationalities — and working experience ... graduating from an internationally-orientated business school ... line management experience in a foreign culture company ... experience through various career moves of different skills, roles and environments.

Job descriptions and person specifications should be reasonably consistent with the format used by the parent company to assist in making international comparisons. Clearly they will emphasise the international features of the role and will spell out the cultural factors to be taken into account during the selection process.

## Help with recruitment

When setting up an overseas company or plant it is generally advisable to use international or local executive search or selection consultants to help find people for the more senior posts. The consultants should be familiar with the market for the executive or senior professional and technical staff they are looking for, will know the best recruitment media (or have good local contacts) and should be aware of the special legal requirements concerning employment. If a personnel director or personnel manager is appointed he or she can deal later with at least some of the selections.

## Interviewing

Candidates for key appointments should still, however, be interviewed by a parent company executive who will want to establish not only if the individual is capable of doing the job but also if she or he is mobile and is potentially capable of making an international career with the organization.

The recruitment of local nationals to an established overseas company or plant is best left to local management, possibly operating within broad policy guidelines provided by the parent company. One of the objectives set to the local company may be to create a reputation for good employment practices which will enable it to recruit good quality people. As Akinnusi (1991) comments:

> In spite of what may be said about the multinational companies in terms of their economic impact, the fact remains that the personnel policies and practices of the large ones tend, by and large, to command respect and, therefore, are able to attract and retain more qualified employees.

## International employee development

International employee development is concerned with enabling home, parent and third country nationals to become more effective in their present job in an overseas location. It also aims to develop the competences required to progress either within the local organization or internationally and, overall, to ensure that the organization has the number and quality of executives it is likely to need to manage multi-country or global operations in the future.

The basic approaches and techniques used to formulate and implement international employment development strategies and programmes will broadly be along the lines described in Part VI of this book. But there are a number of significantly different factors to be taken into consideration which are mainly related to the complexity of international operations. These are:

- cultural diversity factors and the impact of different legal, political, social and value systems
- the extent to which training should be left to local initiatives or centrally controlled
- the specific competences required by international executives.

## Cultural factors

The factors which will affect how training is delivered in different countries or internationally are:

- *legal* — local legal requirements relating to the provision of training opportunities without discriminating on the basis of race, sex or religion
- *political* — the national training and education framework including support for youth and vocational training and further education facilities
- *social* — national approaches to learning and training, including the relative importance attached to on-the-job and off-the-job training, the significance of further education, graduate and post-graduate qualifications
- *value systems* — the cultural factors which influence how people learn.

An illustration of what happens when international training programmes are being run is illustrated by Stanton (1992) based on the experience of Coopers & Lybrand:

> The practicalities of training presents some Euro-hazards too. Recently when training together managers from the German, French, Spanish, Belgian and British subsidiaries of a large manufacturer, we found the different expectations of teaching styles and levels to be a greater barrier than expected. The German preference for formal teaching, with much documentation and high specificity and accuracy, together with the French similar preference for a formal approach, but oral rather than written, and the British penchant for group work and open-ended sessions, meant that reduction to the lowest common denominator was not enough. We had first to teach learning.

## Local or central?

The usual approach is to devolve responsibility for the training of local country nationals in job skills to the subsidiary or overseas establishment. But central policy guidelines on training may be issued, a consultancy service may be provided, local managers may be trained in how to train (eg coaching skills) and the effectiveness of local training arrangements may be audited from the centre.

The development of international managers will be planned and coordinated centrally, although the aim may be to make the maximum use of local education and training facilities and business schools. Career development programmes may be devised centrally with provision for special courses or attendance on international business school programmes as appropriate. Some multinationals make special arrangements with business schools such as INSEAD.

## Competences for international managers

It will be necessary to decide on what particular competences international managers within a multinational may require (competences, as explained in chapter 11, are essentially the fundamental capabilities needed to do a job well). Many of these competences will be similar to those required of any effective manager in the organization, but specific competences which may be required by international managers include:

- building and leading multinational teams
- cultural sensitivity — capable of understanding the culture of the country in which they are located and adapting their behaviour to avoid conflicts with that culture and the values of the people with whom they work
- the capacity to manage ethical as well as cultural differences
- linguistic ability
- adaptability — capacity to adjust rapidly to new environments and working with people of different nationalities and cultures
- resilience — capacity to cope with pressure
- self-motivated — ability to motivate themselves and to take initiative in remote situations.

## Managing expatriates

The management of expatriates is probably one of the most difficult aspects of international personnel management. The research literature has suggested that the failure rate of expatriates is high, especially in the case of US nationals (Mendenhall and Oudall, 1985, report that the failure rate between 1965 and 1985 of the organizations they studied fluctuated between 25 and 40 per cent). This may be an overstatement of the incidence of failure and Scullion's (1991) study of 45 British and Irish multinationals found that 90 per cent of companies were generally satisfied with the overall performance of their expatriate managers. Under 10 per cent reported failure rates higher than 5 per cent and only two reported a failure rate of 20 per cent.

According to Scullion (1995) British multinationals experience lower expatriate failure rates than US companies. He suggests from the research evidence that this is the case because:

- they felt they had more effective personnel policies covering expatriates
- closer attention was paid to the selection of expatriates
- international experience was more highly valued
- it was believed that British managers were more international in their outlook than US managers.

To maximize success in the difficult job of managing expatriates it is necessary to pay close attention to the following considerations: selection, preparation, management and development overseas, re-entry and remuneration. The latter aspect is examined in Chapter 37, the others are considered below.

## Selection

The selection of managers for international assignments must be based on a well-researched competence profile which details not only the managerial, professional or technical knowledge and skills required but also the preferred behavioural characteristics in such areas as cultural sensitivity.

The additional points to look for in selecting people for international assignments are:

- previous experience overseas
- the ability of the person to adopt to new cultures
- any evidence that the values of the person are in accord with those of the culture in which he or she might work
- family circumstances — how well the person and his or her spouse/partner is likely to adjust to working overseas.

It is becoming harder to find people willing to take on international assignments. They are concerned about re-entry following the assignment, the possibility that the value of overseas experience will not be recognised, and disruption to family life and the education of their children. Spouses may not be willing to interrupt their careers by spending long periods overseas. These reactions have to be anticipated and steps taken to allay fears as far as this is possible, especially about re-entry problems.

## Preparation

The preparation for an overseas assignment should cover cultural familiarization — developing an understanding of the culture of the country in which the individual will work (sometimes called 'acculturisation') and of methods of ensuring that he or she will be able to lead and work in multi-national teams.

## Management development

The progress of expatriates abroad should be reviewed regularly using performance management processes as described in Chapter 13. Companies such as 3M and AT&T appoint career sponsors at headquarters to keep in touch with their expatriates and to act as mentors and helpers as necessary.

## Re-entry

Research conducted by Johnston (1991) found that the greatest problem met by international companies with their expatriates was re-integrating when they returned home. The main complaints made by the expatriates were lack of status, loss of autonomy, lack of career direction and lack of recognition of overseas experience.

# Part II
# Human Resource Management

*Human resource management (HRM) has been hyped as a fundamentally new approach to personnel management with a number of distinctive features; for example, strategic integration, an emphasis on mutuality, and treating people as a resource to be invested in rather than as a cost. The concept of HRM is based on the beliefs of various academics and management 'gurus' (mainly American). As a philosophy, if not a coherent set of policies and employment practices, it has been adopted by some managements which see it as a means of achieving commitment to their organisation's objectives, and, perhaps, marginalizing the trade unions.*

*Some commentators have dismissed HRM as rhetoric — and pernicious rhetoric at that. Others have suggested that the concept of HRM is riddled with contradictions. Yet others have denied that there is any real difference between HRM and 'best practice' personnel management.*

*Whether or not there are significant differences between HRM and personnel management the fact is that HRM has entered the vocabulary and, it can be claimed, has influenced the ways in which some managements and personnel practitioners approach the employment and development of people in organizations. It is therefore necessary in a book covering all aspects of personnel management to examine the concept of HRM — its origins, its characteristics as a philosophy, the reservations expressed about it and the differences, if any, between HRM and personnel management. This review of HRM is carried out in Chapter 9.*

*One of the fundamental characteristics claimed for HRM is that it is 'strategic', and the concept of strategic HRM is analysed in Chapter 10. Methods of translating this notion into realistic personnel strategies are considered in the next part of the book (Chapter 11).*

# 8

# The Concept of Human Resource Management

Conceptually, human resource management (HRM) can be regarded as a strategic and coherent approach to the management of an organization's most valued assets — the people working there who individually and collectively contribute to the achievement of the objectives of the business. HRM was described by Storey (1989) as a 'set of interrelated policies with an ideological and philosophical underpinning'. In 1995 Storey produced a more specific definition as follows:

> Human resource management is a distinctive approach to employment management which seeks to achieve competitive advantage through the strategic deployment of a highly committed and capable workforce, using an integrated array of cultural, structural and personal techniques.

The emphasis in HRM is on:

- the interests of management
- adopting a strategic approach — one in which HR strategies are integrated with business strategies
- treating people as assets to be invested in to further the interests of the organization
- obtaining added value from people by the processes of human resource development and performance management
- gaining their commitment to the objectives and values of the organization
- the need for a strong corporate culture expressed in mission and

value statements and reinforced by communications, training and performance management processes.

Human resource management is thus essentially a business-orientated philosophy concerning the management of people by line managers in order to achieve competitive advantage.

## Development of the HRM concept — the US models

HRM first emerged as a clearly defined concept in the mid-1980s when two models were produced by American academics. These were christened by Boxall (1992) as the 'matching model' and the 'Harvard framework'.

### The matching model of HRM

One of the first explicit statements of the HRM concept was made by Fombrun et al (1984). They asserted that HR systems and the organization structure should be managed in a way that is congruent with organizational strategy.

### The Harvard framework

The other founding fathers of HRM were Beer et al (1984). Their framework is based on the belief that the problems of historical personnel management can only be solved:

> ... when general managers develop a viewpoint of how they wish to see employees involved in and developed by the enterprise, and of what HRM policies and practices may achieve those goals. Without either a central philosophy or a strategic vision — which can be provided *only* by general managers — HRM is likely to remain a set of independent activities, each guided by its own practice tradition.

Beer and his colleagues were therefore the first to underline the HRM tenet that it belongs to line managers. They emphasized the need for coherence in HRM policies — perhaps one of the most difficult aspects of the concept to put into practice.

They also stated that:

> Human resource management involves all management decisions and action that affect the nature of the relationship between the organization and its employees — its human resources.

## The Concept of Human Resource Management

General managers are making strategic decisions all the time and these will have a profound impact on employees. For example, introducing new technology or deciding how the company should grow involve important HRM decisions. As can some financial decisions. None of these decisions and action resides in the personnel function.

They thought that: 'Today, many pressures are demanding a broader, more comprehensive and more strategic perspective with regard to the organization's human resources.' These pressures have created a need for:

> A longer-term perspective in managing people and consideration of people as potential assets rather than merely a variable cost.

Walton (1985b), also of Harvard, developed the concept of mutuality:

> The new HRM model is composed of policies that promote mutuality — mutual goals, mutual influence, mutual respect, mutual rewards, mutual responsibility. The theory is that policies of mutuality will elicit commitment which in turn will yield both better economic performance and greater human development.

The advantages of the Harvard model, according to Boxall (1992), are that it:

- incorporates recognition of a range of stakeholder interests
- recognizes the importance of 'trade-offs', either explicitly or implicitly, between the interests of owners and those of employees as well as between various interest groups
- widens the context of HRM to include 'employee influence', the organization of work and the associated question of supervisory style
- acknowledges a broad range of contextual influences on management's choice of strategy, suggesting a meshing of both product-market and socio-cultural logics
- emphasizes strategic choice — it is not driven by situational or environmental determinism.

The Harvard framework has exerted considerable influence over the theory and practice of HRM, particularly as a result of its contention that HRM is the concern of management in general rather than the personnel function in particular.

## UK versions of the HRM model

A number of British academics have made major contributions to the concept of HRM and their work is summarized below.

### David Guest

David Guest (1987, 1989a, 1989b, 1991) has taken the Harvard model and developed it further by defining four policy goals which he believes can be used as testable propositions:

1. *Strategic integration*: the ability of the organization to integrate HRM issues into its strategic plans, ensure that the various aspects of HRM cohere and provide for line managers to incorporate an HRM perspective into their decision-making.
2. *High commitment*: a behavioural commitment to pursue agreed goals, and attitudinal commitment reflected in a strong identification with the enterprise.
3. *High quality*: this refers to all aspects of managerial behaviour which bear directly on the quality of goods and services provided, including the management of employees and investment in high-quality employees.
4. *Flexibility*: functional flexibility and the existence of an adaptable organization structure with the capacity to manage innovation.

Guest (1989a) believes that the driving force behind HRM is 'the pursuit of competitive advantage in the market-place through provision of high-quality goods and services, through competitive pricing linked to high productivity and through the capacity swiftly to innovate and manage change in response to changes in the market-place or to breakthroughs in research and development.'

He considers that HRM values are:

- *unitarist* to the extent that they assume no underlying and inevitable differences of interest between management and workers
- *individualistic* in that they emphasize the individual–organization linkage in preference to operating through group and representative systems.

Guest has asserted (1989b) that HRM has been 'talked up' and its impact has been on attitudes rather than behaviour. He stated (1989a) that the term 'runs the risk of becoming a catch-all phrase, reflecting general intentions but devoid of specific meaning'.

# The Concept of Human Resource Management

## Karen Legge

Karen Legge (1989) considers that the common themes of typical definitions of HRM are that:

Human resource policies should be integrated with strategic business planning and used to reinforce an appropriate (or change an inappropriate) organizational culture, that human resources are valuable and a source of competitive advantage, that they may be tapped most effectively by mutually consistent policies that promote commitment and which, as a consequence, foster a willingness in employees to act flexibly in the interests of the 'adaptive organization's' pursuit of excellence.

Like other writers, Legge (1995) comments on the *rhetoric* of HRM. She refers to HRM rhetoric as being consistent with the enterprise culture and states that:

Without doubt, the language of HRM — and its close cousin, the language of excellence — is that of managerial triumphalism. Managers create missions for their organizations; they change their cultures, they act as transformational leaders that gain the commitment of employees to the values of quality, service, customer sovereignty, that is translated into bottom-line success. In the interests of achieving these values, employees must take responsibility, become empowered — as also are the supreme arbiters, the customers.

## Chris Hendry and Andrew Pettigrew

Hendry and Pettigrew (1990) play down the prescriptive element of the Harvard model and extend the analytical elements. As pointed out by Boxall (1992), such an approach rightly avoids labelling HRM as a single form and advances more slowly by proceeding more analytically. It is argued by Hendry and Pettigrew that 'better descriptions of structures and strategy-making in complex organizations, and of frameworks for understanding them, are an essential underpinning for HRM'.

Hendry and Pettigrew believe that, as a movement, HRM expressed a mission to achieve a turnaround in industry: 'HRM was thus in a real sense heavily normative from the outset: it provided a diagnosis and proposed solutions'. They also suggested that: 'What HRM did at this point was to provide a label to wrap around some of the observable changes, while providing a focus for challenging deficiencies — in attitudes, scope, coherence, and direction — of existing personnel management'.

## John Purcell

John Purcell (1993) thinks that 'the adoption of HRM is both a product of and a cause of a significant concentration of power in the hands of management', while the widespread use 'of the language of HRM, if not its practice, is a combination of its intuitive appeal to managers and, more importantly, a response to the turbulence of product and financial markets'.

He considers that HRM policies and practices, when applied within a firm as a break from the past, are often associated with words such as commitment, competence, empowerment, flexibility, culture, performance, assessment, reward, teamwork, involvement, cooperation, harmonization, quality and learning. But 'the danger of descriptions of HRM as modern best-management practice is that they stereotype the past and idealize the future'.

## Keith Sisson

Keith Sisson (1990) suggests that there are four main features increasingly associated with HRM:

1. A stress on the integration of personnel policies both with one another and with business planning more generally.
2. The locus of responsibility for personnel management no longer resides with (or is 'relegated to') specialist managers.
3. The focus shifts from manager–trade union relations to management–employee relations, from collectivism to individualism.
4. There is a stress on commitment and the exercise of initiative, with managers now donning the role of 'enabler', 'empowerer' and 'facilitator'.

## John Storey

John Storey (1993) suggests four aspects which constitute the *meaningful* version of HRM:

- a particular constellation of beliefs and assumptions
- a strategic thrust informing decisions about people management
- the central involvement of line managers
- reliance upon a set of 'levers' to shape the employment relationship — these are different from those used under proceduralist

and joint regulative regimes typical of classical industrial relations systems.

The concept locates HRM policy formulation firmly at the strategic level and insists that a characteristic of HRM is its internally coherent approach.

He has written (1989) that: 'In stereotyped form it (HRM) appears capable of making good each of the main shortcomings of personnel management'. The HR function becomes recognized as a central business concern and training and development assumes a higher profile: 'Its performance and delivery are integrated into line management: the aim shifts from merely securing compliance to the more ambitious one of winning commitment'.

In 1995 he commented that thre is often a certain evangelism about HRM and associated managerial movement and suggested that:

> HRM is an amalgam of description, prescription, and logical deduction. It describes the beliefs and assumptions of certain leading-edge practitioners. It prescribes certain priorities. And it deduces certain consequent actions which seem to follow from the series of propositions.

He makes a distinction (1989) between the 'hard' and 'soft' versions of HRM:

- *hard HRM* emphasizes the quantitative, calculative and business-strategic aspects of managing the headcount resource in as 'rational' a way as for any other economic factor
- *soft HRM* traces its roots to the human-relations school, it emphasizes communication, motivation and leadership.

## Characteristics of HRM

The combined contributions of the writers mentioned above and others suggest that the characteristic features of HRM as a new paradigm for managing people are that:

- it is a top management driven and management-orientated activity
- the performance and delivery of HRM is a line management responsibility
- it emphasizes the need for strategic fit — the integration of business and HR strategies
- it stresses the importance of gaining commitment to the organization's mission and values — it is 'commitment-orientated'
- it can take either a 'hard' or 'soft' form as defined by Storey (1989)

- it involves the adoption of a comprehensive and coherent approach to the provision of mutually supporting employment policies and practices
- importance is attached to strong cultures and values
- it is performance-orientated, emphasizing the need for ever higher levels of achievement to meet new challenges
- employee relations are unitarist rather than pluralist, individual rather than collective, high trust rather than low trust
- organizing principles are organic and decentralized with flexible roles and more emphasis on teamwork — flexibility and team-building are important policy goals
- there is strong emphasis on the delivery of quality to customers and the achievement of high levels of customer satisfaction
- rewards are differentiated according to performance, competence or skill.

## Reservations about HRM

On the face of it, HRM has much to offer, at least to management. But strong reservations have been expressed about it by a number of academics and by one practitioner, Alan Fowler (1987) in a typically trenchant comment in *Personnel Management*.

These reservations can be summed up as follows:

- HRM does not pass muster either as a reputable theory or as an alternative and better form of personnel management
- HRM is, in David Guest's (1991) words, an 'optimistic but ambiguous concept', it is all rhetoric, hype and hope
- even if HRM does exist as a distinct process, which many doubt, it is full of contradictions, manipulative, and, according to the Cardiff school (Blyton and Turnbull, 1992), downright pernicious.

### HRM as a theory

Noon (1992) has commented that HRM has serious deficiencies as a theory:

> It is built with concepts and propositions, but the associated variables and hypotheses are not made explicit. It is too comprehensive. . . . If HRM is labelled a 'theory' it raises expectations about its ability to describe and predict.

## HRM is simplistic

As Alan Fowler (1987) has written:

> The HRM message to top management tends to be beguilingly simple. Don't bother too much about the content or techniques of personnel management, it says. Just manage the context. Get out from behind your desk, bypass the hierarchy, and go and talk to people. That way you will unlock an enormous potential for improved performance.

There are two aspects of HRM which worry many people. The first is the HRM rhetoric which presents it as an all or nothing process which is ideal for any organization, despite the evidence that different business environments require different approaches.

The second concerns industrial relations. As Fowler (1987) also stated:

> At the heart of the concept is the complete identification of employees with the aims and values of the business — employee involvement but on the company's terms. Power, in the HRM system, remains very firmly in the hands of the employer. Is it really possible to claim full mutuality when at the end of the day the employer can decide unilaterally to close the company or sell it to someone else?

## Contradictions in HRM

Karen Legge (1989) believes that the concept of HRM contains the following internal contradictions:

- the complementarity and consistency of 'mutuality' policies designed to generate commitment, flexibility, quality etc.
- problems over commitment — as Guest (1987) asked, 'commitment to what?'
- HRM appears torn between preaching the virtues of individualism (concentration on the individual) and collectivism (team work etc)
- there is a potential tension between the development of a strong corporate culture and employees' ability to respond flexibly and adaptively.

## A flawed approach to people management

The Director-General of the Institute of Personnel and Development,

Geoff Armstrong (*People Management*, February 1995, p 57) believes that the HRM concept is fundamentally flawed:

> What I cannot accept is that there is a coherent and comprehensive approach to people management under the HRM umbrella, sufficiently distinctive to form the model or benchmark against which managerial performance is judged. It is part of the answer, not the whole picture ... The HRM rhetoric doesn't survive the business realists. Managers see their overriding priorities as being to cut costs, focus on core activities, outsource everything else, and satisfy the expectations of investing institutions above other stakeholders. And the drive for continuous improvement usually means fewer jobs. So the HRM ideals — empowerment, involvement, personal growth — are bound to be frustrated.

## The morality of HRM

As far back as 1987, Alan Fowler, in one of the first and most perceptive comments about HRM from a practitioner, asked whether HRM enthusiasts are over-simplifying some of the issues and solutions:

> Are they all genuinely concerned with creating a new, equal partnership between employer and employed, or are they really offering a covert form of employee manipulation dressed up as mutuality?

In spite of all their protestations to the contrary, the advocates of HRM could be seen to be introducing alternative and more insidious forms of 'control by compliance' when they emphasize the need for employees to be committed to doing what the organization wants them to do. As Legge (1989) pointed out:

> In its emphasis on 'strong culture', in theory HRM is able to achieve a cohesive workforce, but without the attendant dilemma of creating potentially dysfunctional solidarity. For a 'strong culture' is aimed at uniting employees through a shared set of managerially sanctioned values ('quality', 'service', 'innovation' etc) that assume an identification of employee and employer interests. Such co-optation — through cultural management of course — reinforces the intention that autonomy will be exercised 'responsibly', ie in management's interests.

In other words, say the accusers, HRM is manipulative. The forces of internal persuasion and propaganda may have to be deployed to get people to accept values with which they may not be in accord and which in any case may be against their interests.

Some commentators seem to regard HRM as totally evil. Keenoy and Anthony (1992), for example, observe that HRM is 'A wide and contradictory variety of regenerative initiatives have been introduced under the name of HRM and force-fed to a battered, bewildered and defensive workforce and a newly confident management.'

The morality of HRM has also been questioned by Peter Herriot (1996). He states that : 'Human resources implies that employees are human capital. Like plant and investment, they are assets to be used. And their sole use is to achieve business success.' He went on to say:

> Many top managements have indeed acted as though they own their employees. Faced with constant pressures to demonstrate a healthy bottom line, they have divested themselves of their human assets in the same way as their corporate ones. And this is where they have destroyed trust and respect more than by any other single act, including even their own remuneration excesses. For employees do not like being discarded as though they were now just another liability.

## The practicality of HRM

To put the concept of HRM into practice would involve strategic integration, developing a coherent and consistent set of employment policies, and gaining commitment. This requires high levels of determination and competence at all levels of management and a strong and effective HR function staffed by business-orientated people. It is difficult to meet all these criteria, especially when the proposed HRM culture conflicts with traditional managerial attitudes and behaviour.

It is contended by some opponents of the HRM concept that the development of integrated HR strategies, a central feature of HRM, is difficult if not impossible in companies which lack any real sense of strategic direction. Business strategies, they say, where they *are* formulated, tend to be dominated by product-market imperatives, leading to product and systems developments. To support these, priority is given, understandably enough, to obtaining financial resources and maintaining a sound financial base. Human resource considerations often come off a poor second.

Furthermore, a coherent and strategic approach may be difficult in the increasing number of decentralized organizations. As Kirkpatrick *et al* (1992) assert: 'Can the long-term aspects of HRM, so central to its whole philosophy, survive in a decentralized line environment dominated by short-term pressures? Our analysis suggests not.'

## HRM and personnel management

In the words of David Guest (1989b), 'HRM and personnel management: can you tell the difference'?

An earlier answer to this question was provided by Armstrong (1987):

> HRM is regarded by some personnel managers as just a set of initials or old wine in new bottles. It could indeed be no more and no less than another name for personnel management, but as usually perceived, at least it has the virtue of emphasizing the virtue of treating people as a key resource, the management of which is the direct concern of top management as part of the strategic planning processes of the enterprise. Although there is nothing new in the idea, insufficient attention has been paid to it in many organizations. The new bottle or label can help to overcome that deficiency.

Derek Torrington (1989) argued that:

> Personnel management has grown through assimilating a number of additional emphases to produce an ever-richer combination of expertise. . . . HRM is no revolution but a further dimension to a multi-faceted role.

HRM could, however, be regarded as high-concept personnel management and it is believed by suporters of the HRM philosophy that awareness among personnel directors and managers of the need to be more strategically and business-orientated might not have developed to its present state without the influence of HRM.

### Similarities

It can be argued that the similarities between personnel management and HRM are as follows:

- Personnel management strategies, like HRM strategies, flow from the business strategy.
- Personnel management, like HRM, recognizes that line managers are responsible for managing people. The personnel function provides the necessary advice and support services to enable managers to carry out their responsibilities.
- The values of personnel management and at least the 'soft' version of HRM are identical with regard to 'respect for the individual', balancing organizational and individual needs, and developing

people to achieve their maximum level of competence both for their own satisfaction and to facilitate the achievement of organizational objectives.

- Both personnel management and HRM recognize that one of their most essential functions is that of matching people to ever-changing business requirements.
- The same range of selection, competence analysis, performance management, training, management development and reward management techniques are used in HRM and personnel management.
- Personnel management, like the 'soft' version of HRM, attaches importance to the processes of involvement, participation and communication within an employee relations system.

## *Differences*

The differences between personnel management and HRM can be seen as a matter of emphasis and approach rather than one of substance. Or, as Hendry and Pettigrew (1990) put it, HRM can be perceived as a 'perspective on personnel management and not personnel management itself'.

From her review of the literature, Legge (1989) has identified three features which seem to distinguish HRM and personnel management:

1. Personnel management is an activity aimed primarily at non-managers whereas HRM is less clearly focused but is certainly more concerned with managerial staff.
2. HRM is much more of an integrated line management activity whereas personnel management seeks to influence line management.
3. HRM emphasizes the importance of senior management being involved in the management of culture whereas personnel management has always been rather suspicious of organization development and related unitarist, social psychologically orientated ideas.

The strategic nature of HRM is another difference commented on by a number of people who, in effect, dismiss the idea that traditional personnel management was ever really involved in the strategic areas of business. Hendry and Pettigrew (1990), for example, believe that the strategic character of HRM is distinctive.

Perhaps the most significant difference is that the concept of HRM is based on a management and business-orientated philosophy. It is claimed to be a central, senior management-driven strategic activity which is developed, owned and delivered by management as a whole to promote the interests of the organization which they serve. As Beardwell and Holden (1994) comment:

> The 'liberal' conception of personnel management as standing between employer and employee — moderating and soothing the interaction between them — is viewed as untenable. HRM is about shaping and delivering corporate strategies with commitment and results.

HRM purports to be a holistic approach concerned with the total interests of the organization — the interests of the members of the organization are recognized but subordinated to those of the enterprise. Hence the importance attached to strategic integration and strong cultures, which flow from top management's vision and leadership, and which require people who will be committed to the strategy, who will be adaptable to change, and who will fit the culture. By implication, as Guest (1991) says: 'HRM is too important to be left to personnel managers.'

## The take-up of HRM

The acronyms HRM and HR seem to have been generally accepted as part of the current management vocabulary, in spite of all the doubts about the concept of HRM itself or the extent to which it is different from personnel management. But how much of the HRM concept is simply rhetoric? To what extent has HRM in a distinctive form been taken up?

Research conducted by Storey (1992) in 15 mainstream UK organizations showed that there was an extensive adoption of many HRM-style approaches. Notably, many of these initiatives had been devised, as well as driven and delivered, by line management.

Further research in Leicestershire (Storey, 1995) covering 560 organizations with more than 15 employees, found that employers had taken up a number of new employment initiatives to a remarkable extent. The initiatives included culture change programmes, teamworking, team briefing, harmonized terms and conditions and increased flexibility between jobs. Teamworking had been introduced by 76 per cent of employers and 87 per cent of those employers had sustained it. Increased flexibility had taken place in 75 per cent of the organizations and had been sustained by 89 per cent of those who had introduced it.

In general, employee relations is the area in which the HRM philosophy has been most frequently put into practice. The HRM approach to employee relations is discussed in Chapter 40 and its application has included the extension of direct links between management and individual employees through involvement programmes which have by-passed the trade unions.

## Conclusions

It is probably true that there is no such thing as a universal model of HRM. It is certainly true that when comparing the concepts of HRM and personnel management all that usually happens is the production of distinctions without differences. As David Guest (1989a) has written: 'The HRM model is just one among a variety of forms of personnel management, and for some companies it may not be the most viable.'

Perhaps it is best to regard HRM as simply a notion of how people can best be managed *in the interests of the organization*. This echoes Torrington and Hall's (1991) argument that personnel management is *workforce centred* and therefore directs itself to employees, while HRM is *resource centred* and concerns itself with the overall human resource needs of the organization.

If this distinction is allowed, then concepts such as strategic integration, culture management, commitment and total quality management, and a unitary philosophy (the interests of management and employees coincide) all fit in well with the HRM model. Certainly, these notions have entered into the vocabulary of managers and support the idea that something which could be broadly described as HRM (although they may not use this phrase) will help them to improve organizational performance in the longer term.

There can be no doubt that there is something, whether you like it or not, which can be described as an HRM philosophy. But as research conducted by Armstrong and Long (1994) established, it can be put into practice by people who are described as personnel directors just as well or even better than those who have been retitled human resource directors. HRM can be seen as an approach to personnel management which is shared between line managers and personnel specialists and which, among other things, emphasizes the importance of human resources as assets rather than costs and the strategic nature of personnel management as a process which exists to enable the organization to achieve its objectives and, importantly, provide for the needs of its stakeholders. Strategic HRM, as discussed in the next chapter, is a convenient label to attach to the strategic aspects of this approach, and seems to have gained a measure of general acceptability as such, but it could equally well be called strategic personnel management.

# 9

# Strategic Human Resource Management

## Strategic HRM defined

Strategic HRM is an approach to making decisions on the intentions of the organization concerning people — essential components of the organization's business strategy. It is about the relationship between HRM and strategic management in the organization. Strategic HRM refers to the overall direction the organization wishes to pursue in achieving its objectives through people. It is argued that, because in the last analysis it is people who implement the strategic plan, top management must take this key factor fully into account in developing its corporate strategies. Strategic HRM, in this perspective, is an integral part of those strategies. It is also argued that the strategic capability of a firm — the achievement of sustained competitive advantage — is dependent on its resource capability, and people clearly constitute a major resource.

Strategic HRM can be regarded as an approach to dealing with longer-term people issues as part of the strategic management thrust of the business. It covers macro-organizational concerns relating to structure and culture, organizational effectiveness and performance, matching resources to future business requirements, and the management of change.

Overall, it will address any major people issues which affect or are affected by the strategic plans of the organization and it will provide agendas for change which set out intentions on how these issues will be handled.

Wright and Snell (1989) have suggested that in a business, strategic HRM deals with 'those HR activities used to support the firm's competitive strategy'. Another business-orientated definition was provided by Miller (1989) as follows:

> Strategic human resource management encompasses those decisions and actions which concern the management of employees *at all levels* in the business and which are directed towards creating and sustaining *competitive advantage.*

Walker (1992) defined strategic HRM as 'the means of aligning the management of human resources with the strategic content of the business' and Boxall (1994) expressed the view that 'the critical concerns of human resource management are integral to strategic management in any business'.

## The aims of strategic HRM

Strategic HRM aims to provide a sense of direction in an often turbulent environment so that organizational and business needs can be translated into coherent and practical policies and programmes. Strategic HRM should provide guidelines for successful action, and the ultimate test of the reality of strategic HRM is the extent to which it has stimulated such action.

Strategic HRM is based on the concepts of HRM as discussed in the last chapter and strategic management as considered below.

## Strategic management

### Strategic management defined

Strategic management can be regarded as a continuing process consisting of a sequence of activities — ie strategy formulation, strategic planning, implementation, review and updating. It has been defined as follows:

> Strategic management is the set of decisions and actions resulting in the formulation and implementation of strategies designed to achieve the objectives of an organization.
> Pearce and Robinson (1988)

> Strategic management is concerned with policy decisions affecting the entire organization; the overall objective being to position the organization to deal effectively with its environment.
> Gunnigle and Moore (1994)

Strategic management means that managers are looking ahead at what they need to achieve in the middle or relatively distant future. Although, as Fombrun et al (1984) put it, they are aware of the fact that businesses, like managers, must perform well in the present to succeed in the future, they are concerned with the broader issues they are facing and the general directions in which they must go in order to deal with these issues and achieve longer-term objectives. They do not take a narrow or restricted view.

Strategic management deals with both ends and means. As an end it describes a vision of what something will look like in a few years time. As a means, it shows how it is expected that the vision will be realized. Strategic management is therefore visionary management, concerned with creating and conceptualizing ideas of where the organization should be going. But it is also empirical management which decides how in practice it is going to get there.

Strategy is the means to create value and the starting point is top management's vision of how that will be achieved. The focus is then on identifying the organization's mission and strategies, but attention is also given to the resource base required to make it succeed. Managers who think strategically will have a broad and long-term view of where they are going. But they will also be aware that they are responsible first for planning how to allocate resources to opportunities which contribute to the implementation of strategy and, secondly, for managing these opportunities in ways which will significantly add value to the results achieved by the firm.

The purpose of strategic management has been expressed by Kanter (1984) who believes that strategic plans 'elicit the present actions for the future' and become 'action vehicles — integrating and institutionalizing mechanisms for change'. She goes on to say:

> Strong leaders articulate direction and save the organization from change by drift. ... They see a vision of the future that allows them to see more clearly what steps to take, building on present capacities and strengths.

## Key concepts of strategic management

The key concepts of strategic management are:

- *Competitive advantage* — as described by Porter (1985) this arises out of a firm creating value for its customers. To achieve it, firms select markets in which they can excel and present a moving target to their competitors by continually improving their position.

159

- *Resource capability* — as Hamel and Prahalad (1989) expressed it, strategy is about maintaining strategic fit between resources and opportunities. Successful firms have 'distinctive competences' which define they are good at and the extent to which they are unique in terms of the resources or capabilities available.
- *Critical success factors* — those areas of corporate performance — the 'drivers' — which are vital for the achievement of the organization's goals.
- *Synergy* — this happens when the combined performance of a company's resources is greater than the sum of its parts.

## Formulating strategies

Strategic management is primarily about the formulation of business strategy. This has been defined by Miller (1991) as:

> A market-led concept affected by product-market considerations and directed at the achievement of competitive advantage.

Business strategy is a statement of what the organization wants to become, where it wants to go and, broadly, how it means to get there. In its crudest form, strategy answers the questions: 'What business are we in?' and 'How are we going to make money out of it?' Strategy determines the direction in which the enterprise is going in relation to its environment in order to achieve sustainable competitive advantage. It is a declaration of intent which defines means to achieve ends, and is concerned with the long-term allocation of significant company resources. Strategy is a perspective on the way in which critical issues or success factors can be addressed. Strategic decisions aim to make a major and long-term impact on the behaviour and success of the organization.

The formulation of corporate strategy can be defined as a process for developing a sense of direction. It has often been described as a logical, step-by-step affair, the outcome of which is a formal written statement which provides a definitive guide to the organization's long-term intentions. Many people still believe and act as if this were the case, but it is a misrepresentation of reality. This is not to dismiss completely the ideal of adopting a systematic approach — it has its uses as a means of providing an analytical framework for strategic decision-making and a reference point for monitoring the implementation of strategy. But in practice the formulation of strategy can never be as rational and linear a process as some writers describe it or as some managers attempt to make it.

It has been said (Bower, 1982) that 'strategy is everything not well defined or understood'. This may be going too far but, in reality, strategy formulation can best be described as 'problem solving in unstructured situations' (Digman, 1990), and strategies will always be formed under conditions of partial ignorance. The difficulty is that strategies are often based on the questionable assumption that the future will resemble the past.

Strategy formulation is not necessarily a rational and continuous process, as was pointed out by Mintzberg (1978, 1987). He believes that, rather than being consciously and systematically developed, in practice 'a realized strategy can emerge in response to an evolving situation', and the strategic planner is often 'a pattern organizer, a learner if you like, who manages a process in which strategies and visions can emerge as well as be deliberately conceived.' Strategy develops as a pattern in a stream of activities. Mintzberg thinks that strategy formulation is about 'preferences, choices, and matches' rather than an exercise 'in applied logic'. As he sees them, all strategies exist in the minds of those people they make an impact upon. What is important is that people in the organization share the same perspective 'through their intentions and/or by their actions'. This is what Mintzberg calls the collective mind, and reading that mind is essential if we are 'to understand how intentions ... become shared, and how action comes to be exercised on a collective yet consistent basis'.

The dangers of adopting an unduly rationalistic model of strategy were underlined by Whittington (1993), but Kay (1993) warns against the 'nihilist' conclusion that 'firms do what they do because they are what they are', and the notion that strategy can be described but not prescribed. He accepts that it may be incremental and adaptive but believes it can be 'analysed, managed and controlled'.

## Origins of the concept of strategic HRM

The concept of strategic HRM was first formulated by Fombrun et al (1984), who wrote that three core elements are necessary for firms to function effectively:

- mission and strategy
- organization structure
- human resource management.

They defined strategy as a process through which the basic mission and objectives of the organization are set, and a process through which the organization uses its resources to achieve its objectives. They also made a distinction between the three levels of managerial work:

- *strategic level* — policy formulation and overall goal setting
- *managerial level* — concerned with the availability and allocation of resources to carry out the strategic plan
- *operational level* — day-to-day management.

But their most important conclusion was that:

> HR systems and organizational structures should be managed in a way which is congruent with organizational strategy.

## The rationale for strategic HRM

The rationale for strategic HRM rests on the perceived advantage of having an agreed and understood basis for developing approaches to managing people in the longer term. The rationale also contains the belief that declarations of intent in human resource management should be integrated with the needs of both the organization and the people in it.

It has also been suggested by Lengnick-Hall and Lengnick-Hall (1990) that underlying this rationale in a business is the concept of achieving competitive advantage through HRM:

> Competitive advantage is the essence of competitive strategy. It encompasses those capabilities, resources, relationships and decisions which permit an organization to capitalize on opportunities in the market-place and to avoid threats to its desired position.

Increasingly, they claim, it is being acknowledged that the management of people is one of the key links to generating a competitive edge.

## The meaning of strategic HRM

According to Hendry and Pettigrew (1986), strategic HRM has four meanings:

- the use of planning
- a coherent approach to the design and management of personnel systems based on an employment policy and manpower strategy and often underpinned by a 'philosophy'

- matching HRM activities and policies to some explicit business strategy
- seeing the people of the organization as a 'strategic resource' for the achievement of 'competitive advantage'.

## Strategic integration: integrating business and HR strategies

The whole concept of strategic HRM is predicated on the belief that HR strategies should be integrated with corporate or business strategies. Miller (1989) believes that for this state of affairs to exist it is necessary to ensure that management initiatives in the field of HRM are consistent with those decisions taken in other functional areas of the business, and consistent with an analysis of the product–market situation.

The key is to make operational the concept of 'fit' — the fit of human resource management with the strategic thrust of the organization. It could be said that the development of operational linkages is what strategic HRM is all about.

Tyson and Witcher (1994) consider that 'human resource strategies can only be studied in the context of corporate and business strategies'.

Strategic integration is necessary to provide congruence between business and human resource strategy so that the latter supports the accomplishment of the former and, indeed, helps to define it. The aim is to provide strategic fit and consistency between the policy goals of human resource management and the business.

This point was originally made by Fombrun et al (1984) who stated that:

> Just as firms will be faced with inefficiencies when they try to implement new strategies with outmoded structures, so they will also face problems of implementation when they attempt to effect new strategies with inappropriate HR systems. The critical management task is to align the formal structure and the HR systems so that they drive the strategic objectives of the organization.

Guest (1989b) has suggested that strategic human resource management is largely about integration. He sees this as one of the key policy goals for HRM, as listed in Chapter 3 — to ensure that HRM 'is fully integrated into strategic planning so that HRM policies cohere both across policy areas and across hierarchies, and HRM practices are used by line managers as part of their everyday work'.

Walker (1992) has pointed out that HR strategies are functional strategies like financial, marketing, production or IT strategies. In many organizations long-range functional planning is a mandated element of the long-range business planning process.

HR strategies are different, however, in the sense that they are intertwined with all other strategies. The management of people is not a distinct function but the means by which all business strategies are implemented. HR planning should be an integral part of all other strategy formulations. Where it is separate, it needs to be closely aligned.

## The difficulties

Achieving this alignment is easier said than done for the following reasons:

### Diversity of strategic processes, levels and styles

The different levels at which strategy is formulated, as described above, and the different styles adopted by organizations, may make it difficult to develop a coherent view of what sort of HR strategies will fit the overall strategies and what type of HR contributions are required during the process of formulation.

It has been argued by Miller (1987) that to achieve competitive advantage, each business unit in a diversified corporation should tailor its HRM policy to its own product-market conditions, irrespective of the HRM policies being pursued elsewhere in the corporation. If this is the case, there may be coherence within a unit but not across the whole organization and it may be difficult to focus HR strategies on corporate needs.

### The complexity of the strategy formulation process

As Hendry and Pettigrew (1986) maintain, strategy formulation and implementation is a complex, interactive process heavily influenced by a variety of contextual and historical factors. In these circumstances, as David Guest (1991) has asked, how can there be a straightforward flow from the business strategy to the HR strategy?

### The evolutionary nature of business strategy

This phenomenon, and the incremental nature of strategy-making, may make it difficult to pin down the HR issues which are likely to be relevant. Hendry and Pettigrew (1990) suggest that there are limits to the extent to which rational HR strategies can be drawn up if the process of business strategic planning is itself irrational. Even if Mintzberg's (1978) description of strategy as the *pattern* in a stream of decisions over time is accepted, it may be difficult to 'fit' HR strategy into the process in any well-defined way. HR strategies would therefore have to be equally evolutionary and just as difficult to pin down to a set of definitive statements. If this is the case, why bother to seek the holy grail of strategic fit, which implies a certain rigidity which is not in keeping with the realities of organizational life and the chaotic conditions in which organizations have to exist?

*The absence of articulated business strategies*
If, because of their evolutionary nature, business strategies have not been clearly articulated, this would add to the problems of clarifying the business strategic issues which human resource strategies should address. But it should be noted that 'articulation' in this context means that the business strategies are fully understood by those concerned. It does *not* mean that they have to be written down, although this may help to create understanding.

*The qualitative nature of HR issues*
Business strategies tend, or at least aim, to be expressed in the common currency of figures and hard data on portfolio management, growth, competitive position, market share, profitability etc. HR strategies may deal with quantifiable issues such as resourcing and skill acquisition but are equally likely to refer to qualitative factors such as commitment, motivation, good employee relations and high employment standards. The relationship between the pursuit of policies in these areas and individual and organizational performance may be difficult to establish.

*Integration with what?*
The concept of strategic HRM implies that HR strategies must be totally integrated with corporate/business strategies in the sense that they both flow from and contribute to such strategies. But as Brewster (1993) argues, HR strategies will be subjected to considerable environmental pressure — for example, in Europe, legislation about employee involvement. These may mean that HR strategies cannot be entirely governed by corporate/business strategies.

The question also needs to be asked: 'to what extent should HR strategy take into account the interests of all the stakeholders in the organization — employees in general as well as owners and management?'

In Storey's (1989) terms, 'soft strategic HRM' will place greater emphasis on the human relations aspect of personnel management, stressing security of employment, continuous development, communication, involvement and the quality of working life. 'Hard strategic HRM' on the other hand will emphasize the yield to be obtained by investing in human resources in the interests of the business. As Lengnick-Hall and Lengnick-Hall (1990) put it:

> There is now a growing realization that the overriding concern should be the yield from employees. Yield concentrates on the intricate web of costs and benefits that result from investing in and focusing human resource activities toward a certain set of activities and away from other behaviours and attitudes. Yield recognizes both trade-offs and choices. Yield depends on shared responsibilities and collaboration across functional units and hierarchical levels.

Ideally, strategic integration should attempt to achieve a proper balance between the hard and soft elements. The emphasis may be on achieving corporate or business objectives but this should be a process, in Quinn-Mills' (1983) phrase, of 'planning with people in mind', taking into account the needs and aspirations of all the members of the organization.

## The concept of 'strategic fit'

The concept of strategic integration or 'strategic fit' may be beguiling, but it is a difficult one. David Guest (1991) wondered if the fit should be to business strategy, a set of values about the quality of working life or the stock of human resources, or what? He also asked:

- Are there inevitable conflicts between the different types of fit?
- How do we identify or measure fit?
- How do we integrate the various HRM policies?

Neither he nor anyone else has been able to supply definitive answers to these questions, although Walker (1992) has put forward a useful analytical model for assessing the degree of fit or integration. He suggests that the following three types of processes are used in developing and implementing HR strategy:

*The integrated process*
In this approach, HR strategy is an integral part of the business

strategy, along with all the other functional strategies. In strategy review discussions, HR issues are addressed as well as financial, product-market and operational ones. However, the focus is not on 'downstream' matters such as staffing, individual performance or development but rather on people-related business issues, resource allocation, the implications of internal and external change and the associated goals, strategies and action plans.

### The aligned process

In this approach, HR strategy is developed together with the business strategy. They may be presented and discussed together but they are distinct outcomes of parallel processes. By developing and considering them together 'there is some likelihood that they will influence each other and be adopted as a cohesive or at least an adhesive whole!'

### The separate process

In this, the most common approach, a distinct HR plan is developed. It is both prepared and considered separately from the overall business plan. It may be formulated concurrently with strategic planning, before (and an input to) or following (to examine its implications). The environmental assessment is wholly independent. It focuses on human resource issues and, so far as possible, looks for the 'business-relativeness' of the information obtained. Since the assessment is outside the strategic planning process, consideration of HR strategy depends on a review of the current and past business strategies. The value of the HR strategy is therefore governed by the sufficiency (or insufficiency) of the business-related data. This approach perpetuates the notion of HR as a staff-driven, functionally specialist concern.

## The concept of coherence

Another aspect of strategic HRM is the concept of coherence. This could be described as the development of a mutually reinforcing and inter-related set of personnel and employment policies and programmes which jointly contribute to the achievement of the organization's strategies for matching resources to organizational needs, improving performance and quality and, in commercial enterprises, achieving competitive advantage.

In one sense, strategic HRM is holistic; it is concerned with the organization as a total entity and addresses what needs to be done across the organization as a whole in order to enable it to achieve its corporate strategic objectives. It is not interested in isolated programmes and techniques, or in the *ad hoc* development of personnel policies and programmes.

## The requirements for strategic HRM

Strategic HRM is most likely to be practised in organizations with the following characteristics:

- strong, visionary and often charismatic leadership from the top
- well-articulated missions and values, the latter often including a strong emphasis on quality and customer service (Tyson and Witcher, 1994, noted the importance their respondents attached to corporate values)
- a clearly expressed business strategy which had been implemented successfully
- a positive focus on well-understood critical success factors
- the organization offers a closely related range of products or services to customers
- a cohesive top management team
- a personnel/HR director who plays an active part in discussing corporate/business issues as well as making an effective and corporate/business-orientated contribution on HR matters.

## Conclusions

The fundamental concept of strategic HRM is based on the assumption that human resource strategy can contribute to the business strategy but is also justified by it. The validity of this concept depends on the extent to which it is believed that people create added value and should therefore be treated as a strategic resource. If this assumption is accepted, and it is difficult to challenge, then the validity of the concept of strategic HRM does depend on the extent to which it can be applied in practice and the outcomes of such applications.

As Armstrong and Long (1994) stated on the basis of their research:

> The reality of strategic HRM is that it does not and cannot exist except as a concept: a notion of how longer-term HR issues should be managed, an attitude of mind, an approach, a 'pattern in a stream of activities', a perspective.

Strategic HRM is only real when it is translated into specific personnel strategies which are then implemented. The formulation of such strategies is discussed in the first part of Chapter 10.

# Part III
# Personnel Processes and Activities

*This part is concerned with those processes and activities which, in one way or another, underpin all personnel and development activities, namely: the formulation and implementation of personnel strategies, policies and procedures, competence-based personnel management, job and competence analysis and performance management. These processes can play a major part in ensuring that an integrated and coherent approach to personnel management is achieved.*

# 10

# Personnel Strategies, Policies and Procedures

Personnel strategies, policies and procedures can be distinguished from one another as follows:

- *Personnel strategies* define the intentions of the organization concerning the direction it wants to go in developing and implementing personnel and development policies and practices.
- *Personnel policies* provide guidelines for implementing strategies and for carrying out personnel practices.
- *Personnel procedures* define the steps to be taken to meet specified requirements or deal with particular issues concerning people.

## Personnel strategies — nature and content

Personnel strategies define the intentions of the organization on what needs to be done and what needs to be changed in all aspects of personnel and development management in order to facilitate the attainment of corporate goals.

The key areas in which personnel strategies may be developed and the parts of this book in which they are considered are:

- employee resourcing (Part V)
- employee development (Part VI)
- employee reward (Part VII)
- employee relations (Part VIII).

### Strategic HRM and personnel strategies

The terms strategic HRM, as discussed in Chapter 9 and HR or personnel strategy are often used interchangeably, but a distinction can be made between them.

Strategic HRM can be regarded as a general approach to the strategic management of human resources in accordance with the intentions of the organization on the future direction it wants to take. By this definition, strategic HRM is integrated with the process of strategic management used by the organization. What emerges from this process is a stream of decisions over time which form the pattern adopted by the organization for managing its human resources and define the areas in which specific personnel strategies need to be developed. As described by Tyson and Witcher (1994), these strategies indicate 'the intentions and plans for utilizing human resources to achieve business objectives'.

According to the above analysis, strategic HRM decisions are built into the strategic plan while personnel strategy decisions are derived from it. But the formulation of personnel strategies should not be seen as a reactive or passive process. The strategic HRM concept requires that their thrust and purpose should be determined while developing the overall strategy. This is likely to require some iterations.

To sum up, it could be said that the relationship between strategic HRM and personnel or HR strategies is comparable with the relationship between strategic management and corporate or business strategies. Both strategic HRM and strategic management are terms which describe an approach that may be adopted by top management when focusing on longer-term issues and setting the overall direction. Personnel and corporate/business strategies can be outcomes of this approach which specify in more detail the intentions of the organization concerning key issues and particular functions or activities.

## Developing personnel strategies — general considerations

It is necessary to underline the interactive (not unilinear) relationship between business and personnel strategy, as have Hendry and Pettigrew (1990). They emphasize the limits of excessively rationalistic models of strategic and HR planning. It is also necessary to stress that coherent and integrated HR strategies are only likely to be developed if the top team understand and act upon the strategic imperatives associated with the employment, development and motivation of people, and this will be achieved more effectively if there is a personnel director who is playing an active and respected role as a business partner.

## Personnel Strategies, Policies and Procedures

Many different approaches may be adopted to the formulation of personnel strategies — as the research conducted by Armstrong and Long (1994) confirmed, there is no one right way. A similar point was also made by Tyson and Witcher (1994) on the basis of their research at 30 well-known companies: 'The different approaches to strategy formation reflect different ways to manage change and different ways to bring the people part of the business into line with business goals'.

When formulating strategies, process may be as important as content. Tyson and Witcher (1994) noted from their research that:

> The process of formulating HR strategy was often as important as the content of the strategy ultimately agreed. It was argued that by working through strategic issues and highlighting points of tension, new ideas emerged and a consensus over goals was found.

A distinction is made by Purcell (1989) between:

- *'upstream' first-order decisions* which are concerned with the long-term direction of the enterprise or the scope of its activities
- *'downstream' second-order decisions* which are concerned with internal operating procedures and how the firm is organized to achieve its goals — cf Chandler's (1962) dictum that 'structure follows strategy' which may be an over-simplified view of how structures develop, but does present a fundamental truth, that organization structure must be contingent on business strategy and how this relates to the environment in which the business is operating
- *'downstream' third-order decisions* which are concerned with choices on human resource structures and approaches and are strategic in the sense that they establish the basic parameters of employee relations management in the firm.

It can indeed be argued that personnel strategies, like all other functional strategies such as marketing, manufacturing and the introduction of new technology, will always be developed within the context of the overall enterprise or corporate strategy, but this need not imply that personnel strategies come third in the pecking order. Armstrong and Long (1994) noted from their research that there were only two clearly distinguishable levels of strategy formulation in the organizations they studied:

1.  The corporate strategy relating to the vision, mission and objectives of the organization and the business it is in or aspires to be in.
2.  The specific strategies within the corporate strategy concerning

product-market development, acquisitions and divestments, human resources, finance, new technology, organization and such overall aspects of management as quality, flexibility, productivity, innovation and cost reduction.

There was no question of personnel considerations being relegated to some sort of third division.

Boxall (1993) has drawn up the following propositions about the formulation of HR strategy from the literature:

- there is typically no single HR strategy in a firm
- business strategy may be an important influence on HR strategy but it is only one of several factors and the relationship is not unilinear
- implicit (if not explicit) in the mix of factors that influence the shape of HR strategies is a set of historical compromises and trade-offs from stakeholders
- management may seek to shift the historical pattern of HR strategy significantly in response to major contextual change, but not all managements will respond in the same way or equally effectively
- the strategy formation process is complex, and excessively rationalistic models that advocate formalistic linkages between strategic planning and HR planning are not particularly helpful to our understanding of it
- descriptions of the dimensions that underpin HR strategies are critical to the development of useful typologies but remain controversial, as no one set of constructs has established an intellectual superiority over the others.

## Approaches to the formulation of personnel strategies

The formulation of personnel strategies requires answers to just three fundamental questions:

- Where are we now?
- Where do we want to be in one, two, three or even five years time?
- How are we going to get there?

The process of answering these questions can be modelled as shown in Figure 10.1.

There is much to be said for adopting a systematic approach to formulating personnel strategies which considers all the relevant organizational, business and environmental issues, and a methodology for this purpose was developed by Dyer and Holder (1988) as follows:

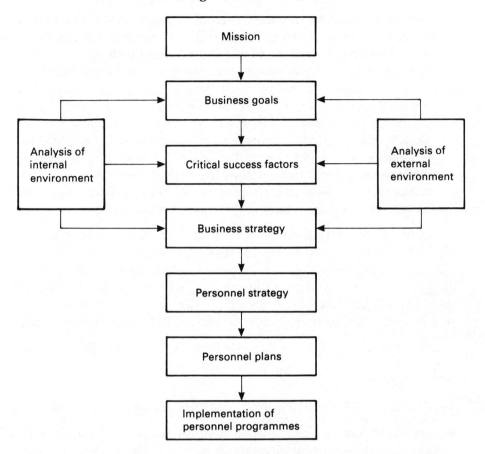

**Figure 10.1** Personnel strategy model

1. *Assess feasibility* — from an HR point of view, feasibility depends on whether the numbers and types of key people required to make the proposal succeed can be obtained on a timely basis and at a reasonable cost and whether the behavioural expectations assumed by the strategy are realistic (eg retention rates and productivity levels).

2. *Determine desirability* — examine the implications of strategy in terms of sacrosanct HR policies (eg a strategy of rapid retrenchment would have to be called into question by a company with a full employment policy).

3. *Determine goals* — these indicate the main issues to be worked on and they derive primarily from the content of the corporate/business strategy. For example, a strategy to become a lower-cost

producer would require the reduction of labour costs. This in turn translates into two types of HR goal: higher performance standards (contribution) and reduced head counts (composition).

4.  *Decide means of achieving goals* — the general rule is that the closer the external and internal fit, the better the strategy, consistent with the need to adapt flexibly to change. External fit refers to the degree of consistency between HR goals on the one hand and the exigencies of the underlying corporate/business strategy and relevant environmental conditions on the other. Internal fit indicates the extent to which HR means follow from HR ends or goals and other relevant environmental conditions, as well as the degree of coherency or synergy among the various HR means.

In addition, the HR or personnel strategist should take pains to understand the levels at which corporate/business strategies are formed, the critical success factors of the organization and the style adopted by the organization in creating strategies and monitoring their implementation. It will then be easier to focus on those corporate or business unit issues which are likely to have personnel implications.

## Key issues

The key issues which may impact on personnel strategies include:

- intentions concerning growth or retrenchment, acquisitions, mergers, divestments, diversification, product/market development
- proposals on increasing competitive advantage or organizational effectiveness through higher levels of productivity, improved quality/customer service, cost reduction (downsizing)
- the felt need to develop a more positive, performance-orientated culture
- any other culture management imperatives associated with changes in the philosophies of the organization in such areas as gaining commitment, mutuality, communications, involvement, empowerment, devolution, teamworking and developing a 'climate of success'
- any external environmental factors (opportunities and threats) which may impinge on the organization, such as government interventions, European legislation, competition or economic pressures (recession).

Corporate strategies in these areas may be influenced by personnel factors but not excessively so. Personnel strategies are, after all, about making corporate/business strategies work. But the corporate strategy must take into account the key opportunities and constraints to do with people.

Corporate strategy sets the agenda for personnel strategy in the following areas:

- mission
- values, culture and style
- organizational philosophy and approach to the management of people
- top management as a corporate resource
- resourcing
- skills acquisition and development
- commitment
- productivity
- performance management
- rewards
- employee relations.

## Questions to be answered

The specific questions to which answers are required when formulating personnel strategies include:

- What kind of skills and competences do we need in the future?
- Are performance levels high enough to meet demands for increased profitability, higher productivity, better quality and improved customer service?
- Will the organization's structure, processes and systems in their present form be able to cope with future challenges?
- Are we making the best use of the skills and capacities of our employees?
- Are we investing enough in developing those skills and capacities?

The answers to these and similar questions define the areas in which personnel strategies should be developed. The important thing is to give an overall sense of purpose to personnel activities by linking them explicitly to the needs of the organization and its employees. A strategic approach along these lines should address the requirement to achieve coherence in its development of new personnel practices and can, in fact, provide an important means of achieving such coherence.

Perhaps the two primary considerations to be borne in mind when developing personnel strategies are the fundamental concepts of strategic HRM as described in Chapter 9, namely:

- the need to achieve strategic integration or strategic fit (vertical integration)
- the need to adopt a coherent approach (horizontal integration).

## Personnel policies

### What are personnel policies?

Personnel policies are continuing guidelines on the approach the organization intends to adopt in managing its people. They define the philosophies and values of the organization on how people should be treated, and from these are derived the principles upon which managers are expected to act when dealing with personnel matters. Personnel policies therefore serve as reference points when personnel management practices are being developed and when decisions are being made about people. They help to define 'the way things are done around here'.

Personnel policies support the achievement of personnel strategies in each of the major areas of personnel management. They are particularly concerned with the employment relationship, prescribing how people should be treated equitably, fairly and consistently. They play an important part in defining the psychological contract which defines what employees and employers want and expect from one another.

### Why have personnel policies?

Personnel or employment policies help to ensure that when dealing with matters concerning people a consistent approach in line with corporate values is adopted throughout the organization. Personnel or employment policies provide frameworks within which consistent decisions are made. They promote equity in the way in which people are treated. Because they provide guidance on what managers should do in particular circumstances they facilitate decentralization and delegation. And, while they should fit the corporate culture, they can also help to shape it.

## *Do policies need to be formalized?*

All organizations have personnel policies. Sometimes, however, the policies exist implicitly as a philosophy of management and an attitude to employees that is expressed in the way in which personnel issues are handled; for example, the introduction of new technology. The advantage of explicit policies in terms of consistency and understanding may appear to be obvious, but there are disadvantages: written policies can be inflexible, constrictive, platitudinous, or all three. To a degree, policies have often to be expressed in abstract terms and managers do not care for abstractions. But they do prefer to know where they stand — people like structure — and formalized personnel policies can provide the guidelines they need.

Formalized personnel policies can be used in induction and in team leader and management training to help participants understand the philosophies and values of the business and how they are expected to behave within that context.

## *Personnel policy areas*

Personnel policies can be expressed as overall statements of the philosophy of the organization and of its values. Examples of the specific policy areas, which may be contained in the overall statement or issued as separate documents, are:

- employment
- equal opportunity
- managing diversity
- reward
- development and training
- employee involvement
- employee relations
- new technology
- health and safety
- harassment
- smoking.

The main points that could be covered in each of these policies are summarized below.

## *Overall policy*

The overall policy defines how the organization fulfils its social responsibilities for its employees and sets out its attitudes towards them. It is an expression of its values or beliefs about how people should be treated. Peters and Waterman (1982) wrote that if they were asked for one all-purpose bit of advice for management, one truth that they could distil from all their research on what makes a company excellent, it would be: 'Figure out your value system. Decide what the company stands for.' Selznick (1957) emphasized the key role of values in organizations when he wrote: 'The formation of an institution is marked by the making of value commitments, that is, choices which fix the assumptions of policy makers as to the nature of the enterprise, its distinctive aims, methods and roles.'

The values expressed in an overall statement of personnel policies may explicitly or implicitly refer to the following concepts:

● *Equity* — treating employees fairly and justly by adopting an 'even-handed' approach. This includes protecting individuals from any unfair decisions made by their managers, providing equal opportunities for employment and promotion and operating an equitable payment system.
● *Consideration* — taking account of individual circumstances when making decisions which affect the prospects, security or self-respect of employees.
● *Quality of working life* — consciously and continually aiming to improve the quality of working life as a means of increasing motivation and improving results. This involves increasing the sense of satisfaction people obtain from their work by, so far as possible, reducing monotony, increasing variety and responsibility and avoiding placing people under too much stress.
● *Working conditions* — providing healthy, safe and, so far as practicable, pleasant working conditions.

These values are espoused by many organizations in one form or another. But to what extent are they practised when making 'business-led' decisions, which can of course be highly detrimental to employees if, for example, they lead to redundancy? The principle of mutuality ('what's good for the business is good for the people in the business') sounds suspiciously like the president of General Motors saying 'what's good for General Motors is good for America'.

One of the dilemmas facing all those who formulate personnel policies is: 'How can we pursue business-led policies focusing on business success *and* fulfil our obligations to employees in such terms as equity, consideration, quality of working life and working conditions?' To argue, as some do, that HR or personnel strategies should be entirely business-led seems to imply that human considerations are unimportant. Organizations have obligations to all their stakeholders, not just their owners.

It may only be difficult to express these policies in generalized terms, but employers are increasingly having to recognize that they are subject to external as well as internal pressures which act as constraints on the extent to which they can disregard the higher standards of behaviour towards their employees that are expected of them.

## Employment policies

Employment policies cover the following areas:

- *Human resource planning* — a commitment by the company to planning ahead in order to maximize the opportunities for employees to develop their careers within the organization and to minimize the possibility of compulsory redundancy.
- *Quality of employees* — an organization may deliberately set out in its policy statement that, as a company which is dedicated to the pursuit of excellence and professionalism in all it does, it believes in recruiting people who have the ability or potential to meet the high standards of performance that will be expected of them.
- *Promotion* — the policy would state the company's wish to promote from within wherever this is appropriate as a means of satisfying its requirements for high-quality staff. The policy would, however, recognize that there will be occasions when the organization's present and future needs can only be met by recruitment from outside. The point could be made that a vigorous organization needs infusions of fresh blood from time to time if it is not to stagnate. In addition, the policy might state that employees will be encouraged to apply for internally advertised jobs and will not be held back from promotion by their managers, however reluctant the latter may be to lose them.
- *Equal opportunity* — a reference should be made in the general employment policy statement to the fact that the firm is an equal opportunity company.
- *Managing diversity* — how the organization manages the diverse people it employs.
- *Ethnic monitoring* — how the company deals with monitoring the employment of ethnic minorities.

- *Age and employment* — the policy would define the approach the company adopts to engaging, training and promoting older employees.
- *Redundancy* — the redundancy policy could state that it is the organization's intention to use its best endeavours to avoid involuntary redundancy through its redeployment and retraining procedures. However, if redundancy is unavoidable those affected will be given fair and equitable treatment, the maximum amount of warning, and every help that can be provided by the company to obtain suitable alternative work.
- *Discipline* — the disciplinary policy should state that employees have the right to know what is expected of them and what could happen if they infringe the company's rules. It would also make the point that, in handling disciplinary cases, the company will treat employees in accordance with the principles of natural justice.
- *Grievances* — the policy should state that employees have the right to raise their grievances with their manager, to be accompanied by a representative if they so wish, and to appeal to a higher level if they feel that their grievance has not been resolved satisfactorily.
- *Sexual harassment* — the policy would express the company's strong disapproval of sexual harassment and the measures taken to eliminate it.
- *Smoking* — the policy would define no-smoking rules.
- *Substance abuse* — how the company treats employees with drink or drug problems.
- *AIDS* — how the company approaches the employment of people who are HIV positive or actually suffering from AIDS.

## Equal opportunity policy

The equal opportunity policy should spell out the company's determination to give equal opportunities to all, irrespective of sex, race, creed or marital status. It could also state that the company will use its best endeavours to provide equal opportunities to disabled people. The policy should also deal with the extent to which the organization wants to take 'affirmative action' to redress imbalances between the numbers employed according to sex or race or to differences in the levels of qualifications and skills they have achieved.

The following is an example of an equal opportunity policy statement :

The Council of the London Borough of Richmond on Thames is an equal opportunity employer.

The Council's objective is to ensure that no job applicant or employee receives less favourable treatment, directly or indirectly, on the grounds of sex, sexual orientation, age, disability, marital status, creed/religion, colour, ethnic or national origin.

Where appropriate and where permissible under the relevant legislation and codes of practice, employees of under-represented groups will be given positive training and encouragement to achieve equal opportunity within the Council's organization.

The Council will implement a positive and continuing programme of action to make this policy fully effective. For example, selection criteria and all other personnel procedures will be reviewed initially and regularly thereafter to ensure that individuals are appointed, promoted and treated on the basis of their relevant merits and abilities.

## Managing diversity policy

A policy on managing diversity recognizes that there are differences among employees and that these differences, if properly managed, will enable work to be done more efficiently and effectively. It does not focus exclusively on issues of discrimination but instead concentrates on recognizing the differences between people. As Kandola and Fullerton (1994) express it, the concept of managing diversity 'is founded on the premise that harnessing these differences will create a productive environment in which everyone will feel valued, where their talents are fully utilized, and in which organizational goals are met'.

Managing diversity is a concept which recognizes the benefits to be gained from differences. It differs from equal opportunity, which aims to legislate against discrimination, assumes that people should be assimilated into the organization and, often, relies on affirmative action. Managing diversity policy will:

- acknowledge cultural and individual differences in the workplace
- state that the organization values the different qualities which people bring to their jobs
- emphasize the need to eliminate bias in such areas as selection, promotion, performance assessment, pay and learning opportunities
- focus attention on individual differences rather than group differences.

## Pay policy

A pay policy could cover such matters as:

- paying market rates
- paying for performance
- gainsharing — sharing in the gains (added value) or profits of the company
- providing an equitable pay system
- equal pay for work of equal value, subject to overriding market considerations.

## Employee development policy

The employee development policy should express the company's commitment to the continuous development of the skills and abilities of employees in order to maximize their contribution and to give them the opportunity to enhance their skills, realize their potential and advance their careers.

## Involvement and participation policy

The involvement and participation policy should spell out the company's belief in involvement and participation as a means of generating the commitment of all employees to the success of the enterprise. This policy could also refer to the basis upon which the company intends to communicate information to employees.

## Employee relations policy

The employee relations policy will set out the company's approach to the rights of employees to represent their interests to management through trade unions, staff associations or some other form of representative system. It will also cover the basis upon which the company works with trade unions — eg emphasizing that this should be regarded as a partnership.

## New technology policy

A new technology policy could be incorporated in the employment policy, but in most organizations these days the introduction of new technology is so significant that it justifies a separate policy statement. Such a statement would refer to consultation about the introduction of new technology and to the steps that would be taken by the company to minimize the risk of compulsory redundancy.

## Health and safety policy

Health and safety policies cover how the company intends to provide healthy and safe places and systems of work.

## Sexual harassment policy

Sexual harassment policies can:

- define harassment
- state unequivocally that sexual harassment at work is not tolerated and is regarded as a matter of gross misconduct
- define the role of managers in preventing harassment and dealing with complaints
- provide for a counselling service for those concerned about harassment
- set out the procedure for dealing with harassment.

## Smoking policy

Smoking policies will spell out whether or not there is a complete ban on smoking and, if not, the arrangements for restricting smoking to designated smoking areas.

## Formulating personnel policies

Personnel policies should both reflect and underpin the values of the organization concerning how people should be treated. They must be formulated in a way which will facilitate consistency, fairness and equity in dealing with employment and reward matters. Their content may simply codify existing practices but they can be developed in the light of best practice in order to achieve change.

It will, however, be necessary to achieve a balance between best practice and best fit. It may be highly desirable to go for the best but it could be an unrewarding exercise if 'best practice' as advocated by the pundits or implemented in other organizations will not fit the culture, organization and technology of the business. It will be difficult to introduce a 'best practice' policy if this is out of line with the existing values and norms of management. When framing policies, it is necessary to remember the role of the dominant coalition. In accordance with the behavioural theory of the firm as expressed by Cyert and March (1963), an organization can be viewed as a coalition of individuals who are, in turn, members of sub-coalitions. Various coalitions within the firm are likely to have different ideas as to how personnel policies should be formulated and the views of these coalitions, which, of course include employees generally and their representatives, should be taken into account through processes of consultation and involvement when developing policies. But there will be a dominant coalition (usually the top management team, but sometimes a combination of top managers and powerful senior managers), which will exert a considerable influence on personnel and development philosophy and practice, and progress can usually only be made if this coalition agrees with the direction new policies are taking. Thus, while it may be highly desirable to give more emphasis to achieving 'best practice' than to pursue a 'best fit' approach which simply reflects current but improvable policies, it will have to be recognized that the dominant coalition will need to be convinced of the need for change.

The following steps should be taken when formulating or revising personnel policies:

1. Gain an understanding of the corporate culture and its shared values.
2. Analyse existing policies — written and unwritten. Personnel policies will exist in any organization, even if they are implicit rather than expressed formally.
3. Analyse external influences. Personnel policies are subject to the influence of UK and EU employment legislation and the official codes of practice issued by bodies in the UK, such as ACAS (the Advisory, Conciliation and Arbitration Service), EOC (Equal Opportunities Commission), CRR (Commission on Racial Relations) or the Health and Safety Executive. The codes of practice issued by the professional institutions, especially the Institute of Personnel and Development, should also be consulted.
4. Assess any areas where new policies are needed or existing policies are inadequate.
5. Check with managers, preferably starting at the top, on their

views about personnel policies and where they think they could be improved.

6.  Seek the views of employees about personnel policies, especially the extent to which they are inherently fair and equitable and are implemented fairly and consistently. Consider doing this through an attitude survey.
7.  Seek the views of union representatives.
8.  Analyse the information obtained in the first seven steps and prepare draft policies.
9.  Consult, discuss and agree policies with management and union representatives.
10. Communicate the policies with guidance notes on their implementation as required (although policies should be as self-explanatory as possible). Supplement these communications with training.

## Personnel procedures

It is desirable to have the key personnel procedures written down so that everyone knows precisely what steps need to be taken, bearing in mind that procedures spell out exactly what should be done without normally leaving much room for manoeuvre. But don't overdo it. The danger of creating a bureaucratic system which hampers people in making decisions and taking action in accordance with the requirements of their situations should be avoided. Personnel management is about empowering managers and team leaders to handle their own personnel problems. It is not about engulfing them with rules and regulations.

There are, however, some areas of personnel practice where legal and ethical considerations demand that procedures are defined and steps taken to ensure that they are enforced. These include disciplinary, grievance and redundancy procedures, as described in Chapter 45 where approaches to dealing with equal opportunity, managing diversity, ethnic monitoring, promotion, age discrimination, sexual harassment, smoking, substance abuse and AIDS are also considered.

# 11

# Competence-related Personnel Management

Competence-related personnel management is about enabling the organization to obtain, manage, develop and reward people who have the capabilities required to maximize their contributions to achieving its goals.

The language of competence has dominated much of personnel thinking and practice in recent years. Competence has become a unifying concept which influences and integrates personnel processes in the key areas of resourcing, development and reward.

The concept of competence has achieved this degree of prominence because it is essentially about performance. It is directly concerned with the factors contributing to high levels of individual contribution and, therefore, organizational effectiveness. As Prahalad and Hamel (1990) have stated: 'An obsession with competence building will characterize the global winners of the 1990s'.

In this chapter the concept of competence and how it is defined is explained in depth, one of the problems being that there seem to be as many definitions of competence, competency, competences and competencies as there are people who write about the subject — and there are a lot of those. The whole competence scene is riddled with jargon and esoteric distinctions between, for example, competence and competency. The chapter aims to explain the jargon and develop a useable concept of competence. Applications of competence are summarized in the last part of the chapter and methods of analysing competence are described in Chapter 12.

## The concept of competence

The concept of competence was first popularized by Boyatzis (1982) who defined it as:

> A capacity that exists in a person that leads to behaviour that meets the job demands within the parameters of the organizational environment and that, in turn, brings about desired results.

He suggested the following 'clusters' of competences:

- goal and action management
- directing subordinates
- human resources management
- leadership.

Since the contribution of Boyatzis to the subject, however, there have been many alternative definitions of competence and a number of different views have been expressed about just what the concept means and how it can be applied. Lists of competences have also proliferated.

## *Definitions of competence*

The following is a selection of definitions of competence:

- Competence is a wide concept which embodies the ability to transfer skills and knowledge to new situations within the occupational area. It encompasses organization and planning of work, innovation and coping with non-routine activities. It includes those qualities of personal effectiveness that are required in the workplace to deal with co-workers, managers and customers. (Training Agency, 1988)
- The ability and willingness to perform a task. (Burgoyne, 1988a)
- The behavioural dimensions that affect job performance. (Woodruffe, 1990)
- Any individual characteristic that can be measured or counted reliably and that can be shown to differentiate significantly between effective and ineffective performance. (Spencer *et al*, 1990)
- The fundamental abilities and capabilities needed to do the job well. (Furnham, 1990)
- Any personal trait, characteristic or skill which can be shown to be directly linked to effective or outstanding job performance. (Murphy, 1993)

What these definitions have in common is that they all refer to those characteristics of individuals which affect their performance in work roles. There are, however, some complications to the concept of competence arising from the different types of competences that have been identified and the varying views which have been expressed on the meaning of competence and its constituents.

## Types of competences

Competences can be behavioural (personal) or work-based, generic or specific, threshold or performance, or differentiating, as described below.

### Behavioural/personal or work-based/occupational

*Behavioural or personal competences* are the underlying personal characteristics of individuals which they bring to their work roles. They are sometimes referred to as being concerned with 'soft skills'. Behavioural competences include such characteristics as interpersonal skills, leadership, analytical skills and achievement orientation. This type of competence is typically used in performance management processes, selection and development. Such competences are 'criterion validated', ie they are derived from the analysis of the behaviour of performers in an occupational role.

*Work-based or occupational competences* refer to expectations of workplace performance and the standards and outputs that people carrying out specified roles are expected to attain. They are derived from explicit behavioural or outcome-based statements and are sometimes described as 'hard' competences. Their concern is with effect rather than effort; with impact rather than input. These types of competences are used in NVQ (National Vocational Qualifications) systems. They are referred to as being 'criterion-referenced standards of occupational performance' and are developed by 'functional analysis' of what people in particular roles are expected to do and the standards they are required to reach.

These two aspects of competences have one thing in common: they relate to real-life requirements of performance. This means that they both concentrate on the outcomes of behaviour, not the levels of knowledge and skills required.

*Generic, core and specific competences* — competences can be universally generic, applying to all people in an occupation such as management irrespective of the organization they belong to, or their particular role. The list of competences drawn up by the Management Charter Initiative (MCI) comes into this category.

They can be organizationally generic, either general and applied to all staff (core competences), or focused on a job family or category of employees such as managers, scientists, professional staff or office/administrative staff. They may be defined for a job family hierarchy or, in some instances, all jobs, level by level. Competences may also be defined which are specific to individual roles.

## Threshold and performance competences

A distinction was made by Boyatzis (1982) between threshold and performance competences. Threshold competences are basic competences required to do the job but do not differentiate between high and low performers. Performance competences do make this distinction.

However, as Woodruffe (1991) comments, a problem with the distinction between threshold and performance competences is that a good proportion of the competences for a job are both threshold and performance. People need a certain level even to start a job, but any extra is welcome.

## Differentiating competences

Differentiating competences define the behavioural characteristics which high performers display as distinct from those characterizing less effective people — the performance dimensions for their job. The definitions of the level of competence expected of high performers in certain areas can be used as behavioural models for discussion at the performance agreement and performance review stages of performance management.

One way of setting out the difference between high and less effective performers is to derive positive and negative indicators for each competence heading as in the following example for leadership.

### Definition
Guiding, encouraging and motivating individuals and teams to achieve a desired result.

### Positive indicators

- Achieves high level of performance from team.

- Defines objectives, plans and expectations clearly.
- Continually monitors performance and provides good feedback.
- Maintains effective relationships with individuals and the team as a whole.
- Develops a sense of common purpose in the team.
- Builds team morale and effectively motivates individual members of the team by recognizing their contribution while taking appropriate action to deal with poor performers.

*Negative indicators*

- Does not achieve high levels of performance from team.
- Fails to clarify objectives or standards of performance.
- Pays insufficient attention to the needs of individuals and the team.
- Neither monitors nor provides effective feedback on performance.
- Inconsistent in rewarding good performance or taking action to deal with poor performers.

# The meaning of competence

One of the problems about the meaning of competence is the word itself. This, as we have seen, can be described in all sorts of ways and there are differences of opinion, discussed below, as to what the constituents of competence are.

The problem is accentuated by the fact that in common parlance 'competence' has a slightly grudging implication — someone who is described as 'competent' may be thought to be just getting by. The word has to be qualified as incompetent, barely competent or highly competent. In this sense the word is all about how well someone does in a job.

The use of competence in the NVQ systems adds to the confusion. An element of competence in NVQ language is a description of something which people in given work areas should be able to do. They are assessed on being competent or not yet competent. No attempt is made to assess the degree of competence, and the accent is more on what people should be able to do than on how they should behave in doing it.

*John Burgoyne* (1988a) points out that being competent is different from having competences. Simply having competences begs the question of how they are used, who uses them and how the user develops. He also questions the use of generic managerial competences in management development.

*Adrian Furnham* (1990) questions two aspects of the competence concept:

- Are competences an all-or-nothing phenomenon, under which people can and should be categorized into types, or are they dimensional, with a continuum from high to low competence? Most organizations talk in terms of types but measure along dimensions. The very concept of a competence certainly implies the former, with an implicit idea that someone is competent or not.
- Is the opposite of competency no competency or incompetency? What tasks can be done effectively if a particular competency does not exist or is insufficient? There is quite a difference between knowing how to do a job and doing it badly, which is incompetence, and not knowing how to do it, which is no competence.

*Charles Woodruffe* (1991) believes that the word competency is being used both to refer to the ability to perform a job or part of a job competently and to the sets of behaviour the person must display in order to perform the tasks and functions of a job with competence.

He therefore thinks that to avoid a potential minefield of misunderstanding and complications, the two senses of the word should be kept quite separate:

- First, it can be used to refer to areas of work at which the person is competent — *areas of competence.*
- Second, it is used to refer to the dimensions of behaviour lying behind competent performance. This is the person-related sense for which Woodruffe reserves the word *competency.*

Woodruffe points out that some of the competence lists produced by organizations mix up the two variables of aspects of the job and aspects of the person as if they were directly comparable. He suggests that 'such a list cannot be used satisfactorily to assess people, for example, because any particular behaviour will be both evidence of the competency and of the area of competency. Those making the assessment become confused and double mark any given behaviour.'

Finally, Woodruffe states that areas of competence are quite specific because they are based on functional analysis which proceeds by breaking down jobs into such areas. On the other hand, 'analysis of person-related competences proceeds in the other direction. It starts from specific types of behaviour and groups these types under the competencies.'

*Len Holmes* (1992) makes the point that competence should be regarded not as a thing but as a concept which can indicate a perceived relationship between expected performance and required performance based on information about previous or current performance. A statement that someone is competent therefore means: 'This person has been observed to perform in ways that lead us to believe that they would perform as required in the future'. In the NVQ approach the occupational standards are descriptions of required performance and assessment involves the comparison of current or past evidence relating to performance with the standards of performance set. But Holmes believes that this approach fails to provide adequate guidance on how competence can be inferred from observations of past performance. A 'model' of competence is therefore required; a conceptual approach to identifying the key components of performance, ie what makes a difference between 'good' and 'poor' performance'.

## The constituents of competence

The different definitions of competence referred to above are confusing enough but the situation is made even worse by the different views on the constituents of competence. Some hold that the concept of competence embodies the behaviour of individuals in carrying out their functions *and* the knowledge and skills which affect or underpin that behaviour. Many people believe that competence is only about *behaviour*. Personal attributes such as knowledge, skills and 'expertise' should be considered separately as the input job holders bring to their work which are transformed by their behaviour into outputs.

Shirley Fletcher (1991) stresses that 'it is application of knowledge and not knowledge itself that is important to competent performance'. One of the issues faced when developing the NVQ system, which is founded on 'competence-based standards', was the role of knowledge and understanding within these standards. Concern was expressed on how those who have been able to demonstrate effective performance 'would be able to do but not understand what they do'. Eventually the view emerged that 'underpinning knowledge and understanding' could be *inferred* from performance and the NVQ definition of an element of competence is therefore:

> A description of something which a person who works in a given occupational area should be able to do. It reflects action, behaviour or

outcomes which have real meaning in the occupational sector to which it relates.

Coombe (1996) has suggested that competences can be described as inputs, outputs or processes:

- As an *input*, competence is the capacity or potential existing within a person to perform a task well. Capacity includes knowledge, skills and attitudes. Input competences may take two forms: either those that can be acquired through study, training or experience, or those innate to the individual which are harder to influence. The problem with treating competence as an input is that of measurement, either to establish the extent to which learning results in performance improvements or to indicate how successful someone has been in applying the inputs.
- The *output model* is therefore based on the proposition that the concept of competence is only meaningful when it can be demon-strated that competences have been used effectively.
- The *process* model describes competences as the processes that link inputs and outputs. The inputs are knowledge and skills, the out-puts are the achievement of expected results, and the process of using knowledge and skills to achieve objectives is competence. Competence outputs are measured by assessing the degree to which competences have been used effectively.

## Using the concept

To cut through all this jargon it is best to define competence simply as the behaviour needed to attain the required levels of performance. This is the process aspect of competence and it will be affected by the level of inputs (knowledge and skills) and measured by an analysis of out-puts (actual behaviours and results). For recruitment and training purposes competence can be treated as an input. Performance man-agement systems may refer to all three elements and competence-related pay focuses more on outputs.

## Describing competences

Descriptions of competences may be called competence frameworks, competence maps or competence profiles.

- *Competence frameworks* are definitions of competence requirements which cover all the key jobs in an organization or all the jobs in a job family. A job family is a related set of jobs, often in a hierarchy, in a discrete area of activity, for example retail assistants, store managers and area managers in a retailing organization. The frameworks may therefore consist of 'generic competences'.
- *Competence maps* which describe the different aspects or categories of competent behaviour in an occupation against competence dimensions such as strategic capability, resource management and quality. An example of a competence map for personnel specialists is given in Chapter 4, page 101).
- *Competence profiles* which set out the competences required for effective performance in a specified role. These may be set out in the form of 'differentiating competences' as in the example given on pages 199 to 200.
- *Competence clusters and lists* — these, as described below, simply describe the main competence dimensions for individuals in frameworks, maps or profiles.

## Competence lists

Competence lists may be prepared generically or specifically as the basis for competence frameworks, maps or profiles (methods of competence analysis are described in Chapter 12). The lists may be prepared as 'clusters' of behaviours associated with core competences as in this example for senior managers at Manchester Airport:

- *Understanding what needs to be done* — critical reasoning, strategic visioning, business know-how.
- *Getting the job done* — achievement drive, a proactive approach, confidence, control, flexibility, concern for effectiveness, direction.
- *Taking people with you* — motivation, interpersonal skills, concern for output, persuasion, influence.

In this case differentiating competence definitions were used as in the following example:

### Getting the job done — direction

*Definition* — being able to tell others what they must do and confront performance problems; to plan, organize, schedule, delegate and follow up.

- *Low* — unable to confront others about performance problems to enforce rules, or to insist that subordinates comply with directives.
- *Outstanding* — confronts staff when they fail to meet standards. Has contingency plans for all objectives. Sets demanding objectives for staff. Demonstrates the ability to organize large numbers of people.

The following are some examples of competence lists:

## Management generic competences (Dulewicz, 1989)

| | |
|---|---|
| *Intellectual* | <ul><li>strategic perspective</li><li>analysis and judgement</li><li>planning and organizing</li></ul> |
| *Interpersonal* | <ul><li>managing staff</li><li>persuasiveness</li><li>assertiveness and decisiveness</li><li>interpersonal sensitivity</li><li>oral communication</li></ul> |
| *Adaptability* | <ul><li>adaptability and resilience</li></ul> |
| *Results* | <ul><li>energy and initiative</li><li>achievement motivation</li><li>business sense.</li></ul> |

## BP — competence clusters

- Achievement orientation
  - personal drive
  - organizational drive
  - impact
  - communication
- *People orientation*
  - awareness of others
  - team management
  - persuasiveness
- *Judgement*
  - analytical power
  - strategic thinking
  - commercial judgement

● *Situational flexibility*

— adaptive orientation

## Cadbury Schweppes

- Strategy
- Drive
- Leadership
- Persuasion
- Analysis
- Relationships
- Implementation
- Followership
- Personal factors

## Civil Service — graduates, grades 1–3

- Leadership
- Intellect and creativity
- Communication skills
- Management of people
- Delivery of results
- Personal effectiveness
- Strategic thinking and planning
- Expertise
- Management of financial and other resources

## WH Smith

- Planning and organizing skills
- Leadership
- Analytical and reasoning skills
- Written communication
- Oral communication
- Personal strength
- Team membership
- Decision making

The following is an example of a competence definition and scale:

*Personal drive* — self-confident and assertive drive to win with decisiveness and resilience:

1. Decisive even under pressure, assertive and tough-minded in arguing his/her case, very self-confident, shrugs off set-backs.
2. Will commit him/herself to definite opinions, determined to be heard, can come back strongly if attacked.
3. May reserve judgement where uncertain, but stands firm on important points, aims for compromise, fairly resilient.
4. Avoids making rapid decisions, takes an impartial coordinator role rather than pushing own ideas.
5. Doesn't pursue his/her own points, goes along with the group, allows criticisms setbacks to deter him/her.

## Differentiating competences

Differentiating competences can be defined by listing positive and contra-indicators as in the following examples:

### *Strategic perspective*

*Definition*
Taking a long-term and imaginative view of the direction to be followed in the future.

*Positive indicators*

- Rises above the detail to see the broader issues and implications.
- Takes account of wide-ranging influences and situations before creating and conceptualizing ideas about the future.
- Has a very clear sense of the longer-term goals to be achieved.

*Negative indicators*

- Takes a limited and short-term view of future developments.
- Is preoccupied with immediate issues and has no sense of the wider future implications of current trends.
- Loses sight of the goals to be achieved.

### *Analytical ability*

*Definition*
Identifying and relating different pieces of information and interpreting the data to obtain an overview of the situation or issue.

*Positive indicators*

- Seeks all relevant information.
- Quickly dissects complex situations and identifies the key elements in them.
- Relates and synthesizes relevant elements in the situation to develop a logical and internally consistent overview.
- Goes to the root of problems — establishing causes and likely effects.

*Negative indicators*

- Adopts an unsystematic and superficial approach to sizing up situations.
- Jumps to conclusions without having properly sifted the evidence.
- Concentrates on symptoms rather than causes.
- Produces woolly and unsubstantiated opinions.

## *Judgement*

*Definition*
Reaching appropriate conclusions and making sensible decisions on the basis of analysis and experience.

*Positive indicators*

- Alternative courses of actions are carefully explored before reaching a decision.
- Decisions founded on logical assumptions based on factual information.
- Quickly identifies what needs to be achieved in a given situation.
- Reaches sound decisions which indicate clearly the most appropriate course of action and the objectives to be achieved.
- Decisions or recommendations can be and are implemented effectively.

*Negative indicators*

- Fails to take account of some of the key factors in situations.
- Fails to think through the implications of the decision.
- Frequently comes to the incorrect conclusion because of flawed assumptions, inadequate analysis or inability to make good use of experience.

## Applications of Competence

The concept of competence lies at the very heart of personnel management. It is directly linked to a fundamental aim of strategic HRM — to obtain and develop highly competent people who will readily achieve their objectives and thus maximize their contribution to the attainment of the goals of the enterprise.

## Integrated personnel management

The language of competence and the existence of a competence framework can provide an invaluable basis for integrating key personnel activities and achieving a coherent approach to the management of people. The integrated elements of personnel management around the competence framework are illustrated in Figure 11.1.

Applications in each of these areas — all linked together by the common language of competence — are summarized below.

## Recruitment and selection

A competence approach to recruitment and selection focuses on *performance* rather than job *content*. This means defining performance criteria in terms of the competence profile for the jobs.

Human resource planning processes can be related to forecasts of future competence requirements and an analysis of the gaps to be filled between the likely demand for particular types of competences and the anticipated supply of people with those competences.

Competence-related recruitment processes are based on the identification of competences that meet the following criteria:

- candidates have demonstrated their competence in their working or academic life — eg initiative

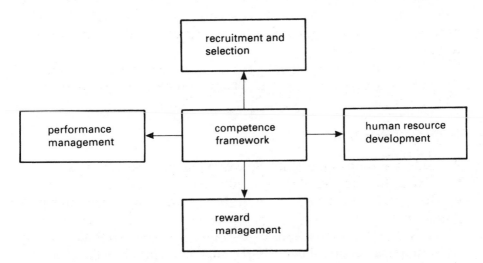

**Figure 11.1** Competence-based integrated personnel management

- they are likely to predict successful job performance, eg achievement motivation
- they can be assessed in a targeted behavioural event interview in which, for example, if team management is a key competence-area, candidates can be asked to give examples of how they have successfully built a team and got it into action
- they can be used as criteria in an assessment centre (see below).

Assessment centres use a range of assessment techniques to determine whether or not candidates are suitable for a particular job or for promotion. The focus of an assessment centre is always on behaviour, which is defined in terms of the competence dimensions that distinguish high performance. Various exercises are used to capture and stimulate the key behavioural aspects of the job and assessors rate candidates, using a scoring system for each dimension.

## Performance management

Performance management is a process for assessing and improving performance based on the agreement of objectives and development needs, the measurement of achievements and performance in relation to those needs and the agreement of new objectives and development plans on the basis of that measurement.

A full performance management process is concerned not only with outputs in the form of results but also with the behavioural aspects of how the role is being carried out which determine the outcome — the level of performance achieved. Assessing these indicates what may need to be done to modify that behaviour in order to improve performance.

The assessment of behaviour is best done by reference to agreed competence dimensions, either generic competences applying to a whole occupation, or individual job competences.

## Employee development

An understanding of the competences required in particular jobs is the best basis for creating learning situations: self-managed learning, coaching and counselling, or more formal training events and programmes.

The NVQ system is a means of assessing whether or not individuals have achieved defined standards of competence, NVQs are *not* training modules but they can be used as a basis for defining learning needs.

## Competence-related Personnel Management

A competence framework, competence maps and competence profiles will indicate learning needs — the specific competence dimensions which need to be addressed through the provision of learning opportunities and the stimulation of self-development.

Development centres using assessment centre methodology based on competences can help in the identification of development needs (see Chapter 29).

### Employee reward

One of the most recent developments in reward management practices has been the use of competence-related pay — relating grades and amounts of pay to the achievement of defined levels of competence. This approach is being used in job evaluation, pay structures and pay-for-performance schemes (see Part VII).

# 12

# Job and Competence Analysis

The analysis of jobs and roles (which incorporates skills and competence analysis) is one of the most important techniques in personnel management. It provides the information required to produce job descriptions and person and learning/training specifications. It is of fundamental importance in organization and job design, recruitment and selection, performance management, training, management development, career management, job evaluation and the design of pay structures. These constitute most of the key processes of personnel management.

This chapter deals with the subject under the following headings:

- definitions
- job analysis
- role analysis
- skills analysis
- competence analysis
- job descriptions
- role definitions.

## Definitions

### Job analysis

Job analysis is the process of collecting, analysing and setting out information about the content of jobs in order to provide the basis for a job description and data for recruitment, training, job evaluation and performance management. Job analysis concentrates on what job holders are expected to do.

## Role analysis

Role analysis also collects information relating to jobs but essentially, it looks at the part that people play in carrying out their jobs rather than the tasks they carry out. In other words, it is concerned not so much with job content as with the broader aspects of behaviour expected of job holders in achieving the overall purpose of the job, for example, working with others, working flexibly, and the styles of management they use. In practise, the determination of the content of jobs and the roles job holders play is carried out by similar analytical processes although the objective of the analysis will be somewhat different.

Some people use the term role analysis to cover both the job content and behavioural aspects of jobs. Others seem to use the terms interchangeably. But the distinction between what someone has to do and the part they play in doing it (the behavioural requirements) is worth making.

## Attributes analysis

Attributes analysis examines what people need to know and be able to do to perform their jobs effectively. The analysis is therefore concerned with knowledge, skill and expertise requirements. Attribute analysis may use various forms of skills analysis techniques as described later in this chapter.

## Competence analysis

Competence analysis is concerned with functional analysis to determine work-based competences and behavioural analysis to establish the behavioural dimensions that affect job performance. *Work-based or occupational competences* refer to expectations of workplace performance — what people should be capable of doing — and the standards and outputs that people carrying out specified roles are expected to attain. *Behavioural or personal competences* are the personal characteristics of individuals which they bring to their work roles.

## Job description

A job description sets out the purpose of a job, where it fits in the organization structure, the context within which the job holder functions and the principal accountabilities of job holders, or the main tasks they have to carry out.

## Role definition

A role definition describes the part to be played by individuals in fulfilling their job requirements. It may expand on the information contained in a job description by setting out the behavioural competences that characterize the role.

## Person specification

A person specification , also known as a job or personnel specification, sets out the education, qualifications, training, experience, personal attributes and competences a job holder requires to perform her or his job satisfactorily. Person specifications are used in recruitment and selection as described in Chapter 24.

## Learning or training specification

A learning or training specification defines the knowledge and skills needed to achieve an acceptable level of performance. It is used as the basis for devising learning and development programmes (see Chapter 27). Learning specifications may be drawn up on the basis of attribute, skills and competence analyses.

# Job analysis

Job analysis produces the following information about a job:

- *Overall purpose* — why the job exists and, in essence, what the job holder is expected to contribute.
- *Content* — the nature and scope of the job in terms of the tasks and operations to be performed and duties to be carried out — ie the processes of converting inputs (knowledge, skills and abilities) into outputs (results).
- *Accountabilities* — the results or outputs for which the job holder is accountable.
- *Performance criteria* — the criteria, measures or indicators which enable an assessment to be carried out to ascertain the degree to which the job is being performed satisfactorily.

- *Responsibilities* — the level of responsibility the job holder has to exercise by reference to the scope and input of the job; the amount of discretion allowed to make decisions; the difficulty, scale, variety and complexity of the problems to be solved; the quantity and value of the resources controlled; and the type and importance of interpersonal relations.
- *Organizational factors* — the reporting relationships of the job holder, ie to whom he or she reports either directly (the line manager) or functionally (on matters concerning specialist areas, such as finance or personnel management); the people reporting directly or indirectly to the job holder; and the extent to which the job holder is involved in teamwork.
- *Motivating factors* — the particular features of the job that are likely to motivate or demotivate job holders if, in the latter case, nothing is done about them.
- *Developmental factors* — promotion and career prospects and the opportunity to acquire new skills or expertise.
- *Environmental factors* — working conditions, health and safety considerations, unsocial hours, mobility, and ergonomic factors relating to the design and use of equipment or work stations.

## Approach to job analysis

The essence of job analysis is the application of systematic methods to the collection of information about jobs. Job analysis obtains information about the content of jobs (what employees do) and subjects this to analysis.

Job analysis is essentially about data collection and the basic steps are described below.

## Data collection — basic steps

The basic steps required to collect information about jobs are as follows:

- obtain documents such as existing organization, procedure or training manuals which give information about the job
- ask managers for fundamental information concerning the job, the overall purpose, the main activities carried out, the responsibilities involved and the relationships with others
- ask the job holders similar questions about their jobs — it is

sometimes helpful to get them to keep a diary or a detailed record of work activities over a week or two

- for certain jobs, especially those involving manual or office/administrative skills, observe job holders at work — even with managers or professional staff it is helpful, if time permits, to spend time with them.

There are a number of job analysis techniques used for data collection; these are described below.

## Interviews

### Information required

To obtain the full flavour of a job, it is necessary to interview job holders and check the findings with their managers or team leaders. The aim of the interview should be to obtain all the relevant facts about the job which comprises:

- the job title of the job holder
- the job title of the job holder's manager or team leader
- the job titles and numbers of people reporting to the job holder (best recorded by means of an organization chart)
- a brief description (one or two sentences) of the overall role or purpose of the job
- a list of the main tasks or duties that the job holder has to carry out; as appropriate, these should specify the results or output expected, the resources controlled, the equipment used, the contacts made and the frequency with which the tasks are carried out.

These basic details can be supplemented by questions designed to elicit from the job holders some information about the level of their responsibilities and the demands made upon them by the job. Such questions can be difficult to phrase and answer in a meaningful way. The replies may be too vague or misleading and usually have to be checked with the job holders' managers and in subsequent interviews. But they at least give job holders an opportunity to express their feelings about the job and they can provide useful leads for development in discussion. These questions can cover such aspects of the job as:

- the amount of supervision received and the degree of discretion allowed in making decisions
- the typical problems to be solved and the amount of guidance available when solving the problems

- the relative difficulty of the tasks to be performed
- the qualifications and skills required to carry out the work.

*Conducting the interview*
Job analysis interviews should be conducted as follows:

- work to a logical sequence of questions which help interviewees to order their thoughts about the job
- probe as necessary to establish what people really do — answers to questions are often vague and information may be given by means of untypical instances
- ensure that job holders are not allowed to get away with vague or inflated descriptions of their work — if, for example, the interview is part of a job evaluation exercise, they would not be human if they did not present the job in the best possible light
- sort out the wheat from the chaff: answers to questions may produce a lot of irrelevant data which must be sifted before preparing the job description
- obtain a clear statement from job holders about their authority to make decisions and the amount of guidance they receive from their manager or team leader — this is not easy, if asked what decisions they are authorized to make, most people look blank because they think about their job in terms of duties and tasks rather than abstract decisions
- avoid asking leading questions which make the expected answer obvious
- allow the job holder ample opportunity to talk by creating an atmosphere of trust.

*Job analysis interview checklists*
It is helpful to use a checklist when conducting the interview. Elaborate checklists are not necessary, they only confuse people. The essence of the art of job analysis is 'keep it simple'. The points to be covered are:

- What is your job title?
- To whom are you responsible?
- Who is responsible to you? (an organization chart is helpful)
- What is the main purpose of your job? (ie in overall terms, what are you expected to do?)
- To achieve that purpose, what are your main areas of responsibility (eg principal accountabilities, key result areas or main tasks)?

Describe *what* you have to do, not, in any detail, *how* you do it. Also indicate *why* you have to do it, ie the results you are expected to achieve by carrying out the task.

- What are the dimensions of your job in such terms of output or sales targets, numbers of items processed, numbers of people managed, number of customers?
- Is there any other information you can provide about your job to amplify the above facts such as:

    — how your job fits in with other jobs in your department or elsewhere in the company
    — flexibility requirements in terms of having to carry out a range of different tasks
    — how work is allocated to you and how your work is reviewed and   approved
    — your decision-making authority
    — the contacts you make with others, inside and outside the company
    — the equipment, plant and tools you use
    — other features of your job such as travelling or unsocial hours or effort or stamina demands or hazards
    — the major problems you meet in carrying out your work
    — the knowledge and skills you need to do your work.

The aim is to structure the job analysis interview in line with these headings.

### Checking the information
It is always advisable to check the information provided by job holders with their managers or team leaders. Different views can be held about the job and these should be reconciled. Job analysis often reveals such problems as well as various forms of organizational problems. This information can provide a useful spin-off from the job analysis process.

### Advantages and disadvantages
The advantages of the interviewing method are that it is very flexible, can provide in-depth information and is easy to organize and prepare. But interviewing can be time-consuming and the results are not always easy to analyse. That is why in large analysis exercises, questionnaires are used to provide advance information about the job, thus speeding up the interviewing process or even replacing the interview altogether, although this means that much of the 'flavour' of the job — ie what it is

*really* like — may be lost, and this flavour is needed if an understanding of the full role of the individual is to be obtained.

## Questionnaires

Questionnaires covering the points included in the checklist given above can be completed by job holders and approved by the job holder's manager or team leader. They are helpful when a large number of jobs are to be covered. They can also save interviewing time by recording purely factual information and by enabling the analyst to structure questions in advance in cover areas which need to be explored in greater depth.

The advantage of questionnaires is that they can produce information quickly and cheaply for a large number of jobs. But a substantial sample is needed and the construction of a questionnaire is a skilled job which should only be carried out on the basis of some preliminary fieldwork. It is highly advisable to pilot-test questionnaires before launching into a full-scale exercise. The accuracy of the results also depends on the willingness and ability of job holders to complete questionnaires. Many people find it difficult to express themselves in writing about their work, however well they know and do it.

## Checklists and inventories

A checklist for completion by job holders is similar to a questionnaire, but response requires fewer subjective judgements and tends to be of the YES or NO variety. Checklists can cover as many as 100 activities; job holders tick those tasks that are included in their jobs.

Like questionnaires, checklists need to be thoroughly prepared and a field trial is essential to ensure that the instructions for completion are adequate and that the responses make sense. Checklists can be used only where a large number of job holders exist. If the sample is below 30, the results can be erratic.

Rating scales or inventories are an improvement on the relatively crude checklist. Like the checklist, they present job holders with a list of activities. But instead of simply asking them to mark those they carry out, scales are provided for them to give a rating, typically from one to seven, according to the amount of time spent and, sometimes, the importance of the task. These scales could look like those given in Table 12.1.

There are a number of general purpose inventories available, the

**Table 12.1** Example of a job analysis rating scale

| | *Job analysis rating scale* | |
|---|---|---|
| *Activity description* | *Time spent — the activity occupies:* | *Importance of activity* |
| Dealing with requests for information by telephone | 1. Hardly any time (less than 10%) | 1. Extremely unimportant |
| | 2. A small proportion of the job (10%–24%) | 2. Very unimportant |
| | 3. Rather less than half the job (25%–44%) | 3. Not very important |
| | 4. About half the job (45%–54%) | 4. Fairly important |
| | 5. A fairly large proportion of the job (55%–74%) | 5. Important |
| | 6. A very large proportion of the job (75%–89%) | 6. Very important |
| | 7. Almost the whole of the job (90% or more) | 7. Extremely important |

most widely used of which is the *Position Analysis Questionnaire* developed by McCormick *et al* (1972). This was based on studies of over 3700 jobs, from which six major work factors were identified.

1. The input of information
2. Mental processes; for example, decision making
3. Work input; for example, the use of machine controls
4. Relationships with people
5. Work environment
6. Other characteristics.

Scales were devised under each heading to measure specific requirements for almost 200 job elements. Each scale describes the activity and has benchmark descriptions for each rating point, as in the example given in Table 12.2.

*The Position Analysis Questionnaire* has the advantage of being generally applicable and comprehensive and having benchmarks. However, it is time-consuming to administer and requires some specialist knowledge.

## Observation

Observation means studying job holders at work, noting what they do, how they do it, and how much time it takes. It is appropriate for situations where a relatively small number of key jobs need to be analysed in depth, but it is time-consuming and difficult to apply in jobs which involve a high proportion of unobservable mental activities, or in highly skilled manual jobs where the actions are too speedy to observe accurately.

## Self-description

Job holders can be asked to analyse their own jobs and prepare job descriptions. This saves the considerable time a job analyst can spend in interviewing or observing a job holder. But people do not always find this easy, perhaps because what they do is so much part of themselves that they find it difficult to be detached and dissect the information into its various elements. Some guidance is therefore required in most cases. If a number of job holders are involved, for

**Table 12.2** Position Analysis Questionnaire — example of benchmark scale for an element (McCormick)

---

*Near visual discrimination (visual discrimination of objects within arm's reach)*

---

| | |
|---|---|
| 7 | Inspects precision watch parts for defect |
| 6 | Proofreads newspaper articles before publishing |
| 5 | Reads electric house meters |
| 4 | Makes entries on sales tickets |
| 3 | Observes position of knife when carving beef |
| 2 | Paints house walls |
| 1 | Sweeps street with push broom |
| 0 | Makes no near visual discrimination |

---

example, in a job evaluation exercise, it is advisable to run special training sessions in which they practise analysing their own and other people's jobs. This method can be taken even further by getting the job holders together and, under the guidance of a job analyst, preparing their analyses and job descriptions on the spot. It is always helpful to produce a model job description to illustrate the format required.

## Diaries and logs

This approach to job analysis requires job holders to analyse their own jobs by keeping diaries or logs of their activities. These can be used by the job analyst as the basic material for a job description. Job holders need guidance on how to prepare their diaries or logs. They can be asked to describe a typical day on an hour-by-hour basis, or they can record their activities in narrative form at the end of a period, usually a day. Diaries and logs are best used for managerial jobs which are fairly complex and where the job holders have the analytical skills required, as well as the ability to express themselves on paper.

## Hierarchical task analysis

Hierarchical task analysis, as developed by Annet and Duncan (1971), breaks down jobs or areas of work into a hierarchical set of tasks, sub-tasks and plans. Tasks are defined in terms of objectives or end-products and the plan needed to achieve the objective is also analysed. The process starts with an analysis of the overall task. This is then subjected to further analysis in order to develop a hierarchy of sub-tasks, together with their outputs and produce definitions of the sub-plans needed to achieve them.

The method involves:

- using action verbs which describe, in clear and concrete terms, what has to be done
- defining performance standards, ie the level of performance which has to be achieved in carrying out a task or operation satisfactorily
- listing the conditions associated with task performance, which might include environmental factors such as working in areas of high noise.

This approach is mostly used for process or manufacturing jobs, but the principles of defining outputs and performance standards and analysing sub-tasks are relevant when analysing any type of job.

## Choice of method

In the selection of a method of job analysis, the criteria for choice are the purpose for which it will be used, its effectiveness in obtaining the data required, the degree of expertise required to conduct the analysis and the resources and amount of time available for the analysis programme. The following is a summary of the advantages or disadvantages of each method:

- *Interviewing* — this is the basic method of analysis and, as such, is the one most commonly used. It requires skill on the part of the analyst and is time-consuming. Analysts need to be trained, and their effectiveness is increased by the use of a checklist.
- *Questionnaires, checklists, and inventories* — these can be a useful aid in helping individuals to describe their jobs and they save interviewing time. But it may still be necessary to invest a lot of time in constructing and evaluating questionnaires, which, ideally, should be related to the particular job. They may fail to reveal the full flavour of the job. If they are over generalized it will be too easy for job holders to provide vague or incoherent answers.
- *Observation* — the most accurate technique for analysing job content (what people actually do). But it is so time-consuming that it is seldom used except when preparing training specifications for manual or clerical jobs.
- *Self-description* — this is the quickest and most economical form of job analysis. But it relies on the often limited ability of people to describe their own jobs. It is therefore necessary to provide them with guidance in the form of questionnaires and checklists.
- *Diaries and logs* — most useful for managerial jobs but they make great demands on job holders and can be difficult to analyse.
- *Hierarchical task analysis* — this provides a helpful structure for job analysis in terms of outputs — a particularly useful feature of this approach — plans (inputs) and relationships. It can be used when analysing the data obtained by interviews or other methods.

Perhaps the most commonly used method is the interview, often supplemented with questionnaires. In a large scale job evaluation exercise the key 'benchmark' jobs upon which the evaluation will be based may be analysed by interview, while questionnaires would be used for the other jobs.

## Role analysis

Role analysis is an extension of job analysis and is generally conducted by means of interviews, possibly supplemented by one of the more advanced competence analysis techniques. It will concentrate on the competences job holders require and the part they play in carrying out their work, with particular reference to how they work with other people (their relationships with their managers or team leaders, colleagues, customers, suppliers and any other people they deal with outside the organization), how they fit into the organization structure, the amount of independent action they are expected to take and how they establish their objectives and priorities.

## Skills analysis

Skills analysis determines the skills required to achieve an acceptable standard of performance. It is mainly used for technical, craft, manual and office jobs to provide the basis for devising learning and training programmes, as discussed in Chapters 27 and 28. Skills analysis starts from a broad job analysis but goes into detail of not only what job holders have to do but also the particular abilities and skills they need to do it. The skills analysis techniques described below are mainly developed for use in manual or clerical jobs:

- job breakdown
- manual skills analysis
- task analysis
- faults analysis
- job learning analysis.

### *Job breakdown*

The job breakdown technique analyses a job into separate operations, processes, or tasks which can be broken down into manageable parts for instructional purposes.

A job breakdown analysis is recorded in a standard format of three columns:

- *The stage column* in which the different steps in the job are described — most semi-skilled jobs can easily be broken down into their constituent parts.

- *The instruction column* in which a note is made against each step of how the task should be done. This, in effect, describes what has to be learned by the trainee.
- *The key points column* in which any special points such as quality standards or safety instructions are noted against each step so that they can be emphasized to a trainee learning the job.

## Manual skills analysis

Manual skills analysis is a technique developed from work study. It isolates for instructional purposes the skills and knowledge employed by experienced workers in performing tasks which require a high degree of manual dexterity. It is used to analyse short-cycle, repetitive operations such as assembly tasks and other similar factory work.

The hand, finger and other body movements of experienced operatives are observed and recorded in great detail as they carry out their work. The analysis concentrates on the tricky parts of the job which, while presenting no difficulty to the experienced operative, have to be analysed in depth before they can be taught to trainees. Not only are the hand movements recorded in great detail, but particulars are also noted of the cues (visual and other senses) which the operative absorbs when performing the tasks. Explanatory comments are added when necessary.

## Task analysis

Task analysis is a systematic analysis of the behaviour required to carry out a task with a view to identifying areas of difficulty and the appropriate training techniques and learning aids necessary for successful instruction. It can be used for all types of jobs but is specifically relevant to clerical tasks.

The analytical approach used in task analysis is similar to those adopted in the job breakdown and manual skills analysis techniques. The results of the analysis are usually recorded in a standard format of four columns as follows:

- *task* — a brief description of each element
- *level of importance* — the relative significance of each task to the successful performance of the whole job
- *degree of difficulty* — the level of skill or knowledge required to perform each task

- *training method* — the instructional techniques, practice and experience required.

## Faults analysis

Faults analysis is the process of analysing the typical faults which occur when performing a task, especially the more costly faults. It is carried out when the incidence of faults is high.

A study is made of the job and, by questioning workers and team leaders, the most commonly occurring faults are identified. A faults specification is then produced which provides trainees with information on what faults can be made, how they can be recognized, what causes them, what effect they have, who is responsible for them, what action the trainees should take when a particular fault occurs, and how a fault can be prevented from recurring.

## Job learning analysis

Job learning analysis, as described by Pearn and Kandola (1993), concentrates on the inputs and process rather than the content of the job. It analyses nine learning skills which contribute to satisfactory performance. A learning skill is one used to increase other skills or knowledge and represents broad categories of job behaviour which need to be learnt. The learning skills are the following:

- *physical skills* requiring practice and repetition to get right
- *complex procedures* or sequences of activity which are memorized or followed with the aid of written material such as manuals
- *non-verbal information* such as sight, sound, smell, taste and touch which is used to check, assess or discriminate, and which usually takes practice to get right
- *memorizing* facts or information
- *ordering, prioritizing and planning,* which refer to the degree to which a job holder has any responsibility for and flexibility in, determining the way a particular job activity is performed
- *looking ahead* and anticipating
- *diagnosing, analysing and problem solving,* with or without help
- *interpreting or using written manuals* and other sources of information such as diagrams or charts
- *adapting* to new ideas and systems.

In conducting a job learning analysis interview, the interviewer obtains information on the main aims and principal activities of the job, and then, using question cards for each of the nine learning skills, analyses each activity in more depth, recording responses and obtaining as many examples as possible under each heading.

## Competence analysis

### Definition

Competence analysis is concerned with functional analysis to determine work-based competences and behavioural analysis to establish the behavioural dimensions that affect job performance.

### Approaches to competence analysis

There are seven approaches to competence analysis. Starting with the simplest, these are:

- expert opinion
- structured interview
- workshops
- functional analysis
- critical-incident technique
- repertory grid analysis
- job competency assessment.

### Expert opinion

The basic, crudest and least satisfactory method is for an 'expert' member of the personnel department, possibly in discussion with other 'experts' from the same department to draw up a list from their own understanding of 'what counts' coupled with an analysis of other published lists such as those given in Chapter 11.

This is unsatisfactory because the likelihood of the competences being appropriate to the organization, realistic and measurable in the absence of detailed analysis, is fairly remote. The list tends to be bland and, because line managers and job holders have not been involved, unacceptable.

### Structured interview

The structured interview method begins with a list of competences drawn up by 'experts' and proceeds by subjecting a number of job holders to a structured interview. This starts by identifying the key result areas or principal accountabilities of the role and goes on to analyse the behavioural characteristics which distinguish performers at different levels of competence.

The basic question is: 'What are the positive or negative indicators of behaviour which are conducive or non-conducive to achieving high levels of performance?' These may be analysed under such headings as:

- personal drive (achievement motivation)
- impact on results
- analytical power
- strategic thinking
- creative thinking (ability to innovate)
- decisiveness
- commercial judgement
- team management and leadership
- interpersonal relationships
- ability to communicate
- ability to adapt and cope with change and pressure
- ability to plan and control projects.

In each area instances will be sought which illustrate effective behaviour.

One of the problems with this approach is that it relies too much on the ability of the expert to draw out information from interviewees. It is also undesirable to use a deductive approach which pre-empts the analysis with a prepared list of competence headings. It is far better to do this by means of an inductive approach which starts from specific types of behaviour and then groups them under competence headings. This can be done in a workshop by analysing positive and negative indicators to gain an understanding of the competence dimensions of an occupation or job as described below.

## Workshops

Workshops bring a group of people together who have 'expert' knowledge or experience of the job — managers and job holders as appropriate — with a facilitator, usually but not necessarily, a member of the personnel department or an outside consultant.

The workshop begins with an analysis of the 'core' competences of the organization — what it has to be good at doing in order to achieve success. Definitions are then agreed on the job-related competence areas — the key activities carried out by the people in the roles under consideration. These are defined in output terms, ie what has to be achieved in that particular aspect of the role. Existing role definitions can be used for this purpose.

Using the competence areas as a framework, the members of the group develop examples of effective behaviour, ie behaviour which is likely to produce the desired results. The basic question is: 'What sort of things do they do and how do they behave when they perform their role effectively?' The answers to this question are expressed in the form: 'Someone in this role will be doing it well when he/she...'. Actual examples of the type of behaviour referred to are given wherever possible. The answers are then recorded on flip charts. The group, with the aid of the facilitator, next analyses its answers and distils them into a number of competence headings which are defined in terms of the actual behaviours noted earlier. The group's words are used as far as possible so that they can 'own' the outcome. These headings form the basis for the generic competence framework or specific competence profile.

For example, one of the competence areas in a divisional personnel director's role might be human resource planning, defined as:

> Prepare forecasts of human resource requirements and plans for the acquisition, retention and effective utilization of employees which ensure that the company's needs for human resources are met.

The competence dimensions for this area could be expressed as: 'Someone in this role will be doing it well when he/she:

- seeks involvement in business strategy formulation
- contributes to business planning by taking a strategic view of longer-term human resource issues which are likely to affect business strategy
- networks with senior management colleagues to understand and respond to the human resource planning issues they raise
- suggests practical ways to improve the use of human resources.

The facilitator's role in the workshop is to prompt, help the group to analyse its findings and assist generally in the production of a set of competence dimensions which can be illustrated by behaviour-based examples.

## Functional analysis

Functional analysis is the method used to define competence-based standards for National Vocational Standards. This starts by describing the key purpose of the occupation and then identifies the key *functions* undertaken.

A distinction is made between *tasks*, which are the activities undertaken at work and *functions* which are the purposes of activities at work. The distinction is important because, as explained in more detail in Chapter 28, the analysis must focus on the outcomes of activities in order to establish expectations of workplace performance as the information required to define standards of competence.

When the units and elements of competence, as defined in Chapter 28, have been established, the next question asked is 'what are the qualities of the outcomes' in terms of the performance criteria which an NVQ assessor can use to judge whether or not an individual's performance meets the required standards.

Functional analysis is directed towards the definition of NVQ standards, it will not result directly in the development of definitions of the behavioural dimensions of competence, especially when generic definitions are required for a whole occupational area, for example, managers or team leaders.

## Critical-incident technique

The critical-incident technique is a means of eliciting data about effective or less effective behaviour which is related to examples of actual events — critical incidents. The technique is used with groups of job holders and/or their managers or other 'experts' (sometimes, less effectively, with individuals) as follows:

- Explain what the technique is and what it is used for, ie — 'to assess what constitutes good or poor performance by analysing events which have been observed to have a noticeably successful or unsuccessful outcome, thus providing more factual and 'real' information than by simply listing tasks and guessing performance requirements.'
- Agree and list the key areas of responsibility — the principal accountabilities — in the job to be analyzed. To save time, the analyst can establish these prior to the meeting but it is necessary to ensure that they are agreed provisionally by the group, which can

be told that the list may well be amended in the light of the forth-coming analysis.

- Each area of the job is taken in turn and the group is asked for examples of critical incidents. If, for example, one of the job responsibilities is dealing with customers, the following request could be made:

    I want you to tell me about a particular occasion at work which involved you — or that you observed — in dealing with a customer. Think about what the circumstances were, eg who took part, what the customer asked for, what you or the other member of the staff did and what the outcome was.

- Collect information about the critical incident under the following headings:

    — what the circumstances were
    — what the individual did
    — the outcome of what the individual did.

    This information should be recorded on a flip chart.

- Continue this process for each area of responsibility.
- Refer to the flip chart and analyse each incident by obtaining ratings of the recorded behaviour on a scale such as 1 for least effective to 5 for most effective.
- Discuss these ratings to get initial definitions of effective and ineffective performance for each of the key aspects of the job.
- Refine these definitions as necessary after the meeting — it can be difficult to get a group to produce finished definitions.
- Produce the final analysis which can list the competences required and include performance indicators or standards of performance for each principal accountability or main task.

## Repertory grid

Like the critical incident technique, the repertory grid can be used to identify the dimensions which distinguish good from poor standards of performance. The technique is based on Kelly's (1955) personal construct theory. Personal constructs are the ways in which we view the world. They are personal because they are highly individual and they influence the way we behave or view other people's behaviour.

223

The aspects of the job to which these 'constructs' or judgements apply are called 'elements'.

To elicit judgements, a group of people are asked to concentrate on certain elements, which are the tasks carried out by job holders, and develop constructs about these elements. This enables them to define the qualities which indicate the essential requirements for successful performance.

The procedure followed by the analyst is know as the 'triadic method of elicitation' (a sort of three card trick) and involves the following steps:

1. Identify the tasks or elements of the job to be subjected to repertory grid analysis. This is done by one of the other forms of job analysis, eg interviewing.
2. List the tasks on cards.
3. Draw three cards at random from the pack and ask the members of the group to nominate which of the these tasks is the odd one out from the point of view of the qualities and characteristics needed to perform it.
4. Probe to obtain more specific definitions of these qualities or characteristics in the form of expected behaviour. If, for example, a characteristic has been described as the 'ability to plan and organize', ask questions such as: 'What sort of behaviour or actions indicate that someone is planning effectively?', or 'How can we tell if someone is not organizing his or her work particularly well?'.
5. Draw three more cards from the pack and repeat steps 3 and 4.
6. Repeat this process until all the cards have been analysed and there do not appear to be any more constructs to be identified.
7. List the constructs and ask the group members to rate each task on every quality, using a six or seven point scale.
8. Collect and analyze the scores in order to assess their relative importance. This can be done statistically as described by Markham (1987).

Like the critical-incident technique, repertory grid analysis helps people to articulate their views by reference to specific examples. An additional advantage is that the repertory grid makes it easier for them to identify the behavioural characteristics or competences required in a job by limiting the area of comparison through the triadic technique.

Although a full statistical analysis of the outcome of a repertory grid exercise is helpful, the most important results which can be obtained are the descriptions of what constitute good or poor performance in each element of the job.

Both the repertory grid and the critical incident techniques require a skilled analyst who can probe and draw out the descriptions of job characteristics. They are quite detailed and time consuming but even if the full process is not followed, much of the methodology is of use in a less elaborate approach to competence analysis.

## Which approach?

Techniques such as critical-incident technique and repertory grid analysis can be used effectively but they are time-consuming and need experience to apply them effectively.

For those who have not got the time to use either of these approaches, the workshop approach as described above is probably the best. But if you have not carried out this type of analysis it is advisable to enlist the support of an external consultant who has the relevant experience. Functional analysis is used when the main objective is to develop NVQ standards.

## Job descriptions

Job descriptions are derived from the job analysis. They provide basic information about the job under the headings of the job title, reporting relationships, overall purpose and principal accountabilities or main tasks or duties.

The basic data may be supplemented by other information giving more details about the nature and scope of the job, the factors or criteria which indicate its level for job evaluation purposes, or the competences required as an aid to the preparation of training programmes and for use in assessment centres. This can convert the basic job description into a full role definition if it concentrates on the behavioural aspects of the role played by job holders.

### Use of job descriptions for organizational, recruitment and performance management purposes

The basic job description can be used to:

- define the place of the job in the organization and to clarify for job holders and others the contribution the job makes to achieving organizational or departmental objectives

225

- provide the information required to produce person specifications for recruitment and to inform applicants about the job
- be the basis for the contract of employment
- provide the framework for setting objectives
- be the basis for job evaluation and grading jobs.

Job descriptions should not go into too much detail. What needs to be clarified is the contribution job holders are expected to make, expressed as the results to be achieved (expressed as principal accountabilities, key result areas or main tasks, activities or duties) and their positions in the organization (reporting relationships).

There are two factors to take into account when preparing this type of job description:

- *Flexibility* — operational flexibility and multiskilling are becoming increasingly significant. It is therefore necessary to build flexibility into the job descriptions. This is achieved by concentrating on results rather than spelling out what has to be done — job descriptions should not become straitjackets by spelling out in detail the tasks to be carried out. The emphasis should be on the role job holders have to play in using their skills and competences in specified broad areas of responsibility to achieve results. The aim is to ensure that job holders who are expected to work flexibly cannot say 'No, it's not in my job description.'
- *Teamwork* — flatter organizations rely more on good teamwork and this requirement needs to be stressed.

*Format*

The format of a job description for organizational, recruitment or contractual purposes comprises simply:

- the job title
- a definition of the overall purpose or objectives of the job
- a list of principal accountabilities, key result areas, tasks, activities or duties (what these are called does not matter too much, although the terms 'principal accountabilities' and 'key result areas' do emphasize the end results the job holder is expected to achieve).

Examples of job descriptions are given in Appendix A.

## Job descriptions for job evaluation purposes

For job evaluation purposes, the job description should contain the information included in an organizational description as well as a 'factor analysis' of the job by reference to the job evaluation factors or criteria used to assess relative job values (see Chapter 32). In addition, it is often helpful to include a narrative describing the nature and scope of the job, as used in the Hay job evaluation system. This narrative gives general information on the environment in which the job operates. The nature of the job is described in broad terms to give evaluators an overall view of what sort of job it is. This puts flesh on the bones of a list of principal accountabilities. The scope of the job is defined wherever possible by quantifying the various aspects of the job, such as the resources controlled, the results to be achieved, budgets, the proportion of time spent on different aspects of the job, and the number of occasions over a certain period of time when decisions have to be made or actions taken.

The factor analysis attached to the job description describes the incidence of each job evaluation factor such as knowledge and skills, responsibility, decisions, complexity and contacts.

## Job descriptions for training purposes

For training purposes, job descriptions should be based on the format for an organizational job description, although the details on the nature and scope of the job and the factor analysis contained in job descriptions for job evaluations contain useful additional information. The training job description and specification include an analysis of the attributes (knowledge and skills) and competences used in the job. This means that a more detailed description of the tasks the job holder has to carry out may be necessary as well as spelling out attribute and competence requirements.

## Writing a job description

Job descriptions should be based on a detailed job analysis and should be as brief and factual as possible. The headings under which the job description should be written and notes for guidance on completing each section are set out below.

*Job title* — the existing or proposed job title should indicate as clearly as possible the function in which the job is carried out and the level of the job within that function. The use of terms such as 'manager', 'assistant manager' or 'senior' to describe job levels should be reasonably consistent between functions with regard to gradings of the jobs.

*Reporting to* — the job title of the manager or supervisor to whom the job holder is directly responsible should be given under this heading. No attempt should be made to indicate here any functional relationships the job holder might have to other managers.

*Reporting to job holder* — the job titles of all the posts directly reporting to the job holder should be given under this heading. Again, no attempt should be made here to indicate any functional relationships that might exist between the job holder and other employees.

*Overall purpose* — this section should describe as concisely as possible the overall purpose of the job. The aim should be to convey in one sentence a broad picture of the job which will clearly distinguish it from other jobs and establish the role of the job holders and the contribution they should make towards achieving the objectives of the company and their own function or unit. No attempt should be made to describe the activities carried out under this heading, but the overall summary should lead naturally to the analysis of activities in the next section. When preparing the job description, it is often best to defer writing down the definition of overall responsibilities until the activities have been analysed and described.

*Principal accountabilities or main tasks* — the steps required to define principal accountabilities or main tasks are:

- identify and produce an initial list of the main activities or tasks carried out by the job holder
- analyse the initial list of tasks and group them together so that no more than about ten main activity areas remain — most jobs can be analysed into seven or eight areas and if the number is extended much beyond that, the job description will become over-complex and it will be difficult to be specific about accountabilities or tasks
- define each activity as in effect a statement of accountability (although it need not be called that) — an accountability statement expresses what the job holder is expected to achieve (outputs) and will therefore be held responsible (accountable) for
- define the accountability in one sentence which should:

  — start with a verb in the active voice which provides a positive indication of what has to be done and eliminates unnecessary wording; for example: plans, prepares, produces, implements,

processes, provides, schedules, completes, dispatches, maintains, liaises with, collaborates with
— describe the object of the verb (what is done) as succinctly as possible; for example: tests new systems, posts cash to the nominal and sales ledgers, dispatches to the warehouse packed output, schedules production, ensures that management accounts are produced, prepares marketing plans
— state briefly the purpose of the activity in terms of outputs or standards to be achieved for example: tests new systems to ensure they meet agreed systems specifications, posts cash to the nominal and sales ledgers in order to provide up-to-date and accurate financial information, dispatches the warehouse planned output so that all items are removed by carriers on the same day they are packed, schedules production in order to meet laid-down output and delivery targets, ensures that management accounts are produced which provide the required level of information to management and individual managers on financial performance against budget and on any variances, prepares marketing plans which support the achievement of the marketing strategies of the enterprise, are realistic, and provide clear guidance on the actions to be taken by the development, production, marketing and sales departments.

Statements of accountability which emphasize the outputs required in terms of the results expected, provide essential data for use in agreeing standing and short-term objectives in performance management processes as described in Chapter 13, and in defining work-based competences.

*Nature and scope* — the nature and scope section of a job description (sometimes called the 'context' section) provides an opportunity to describe the job and the job holder's role in more general terms within the context of the organization. It may contain examples of what is done and an indication of the relative significance of its different aspects. It is often easier to get job holders to write a narrative of their jobs, from which can be distilled the principal accountabilities or main tasks. Nature and scope descriptions add 'flavour' to the job in order that job evaluators and trainers in particular, can obtain a better picture of what the job entails than from a mere list of duties. There are no rules for writing nature and scope descriptions except that they should not be too long or repetitive.

An example of a nature and scope description is given in Appendix A.

*Factor analysis* — when preparing job descriptions for job evaluation purposes, factor analysis techniques are used. Factor analysis is the process of taking each of the job evaluation factors such as knowledge and skills and responsibility and assessing the level at which they are present in the job. When writing factor analyses, reference should be made to the factor and level definitions in the job evaluation factor plan (see Chapter 32). The analysis should be backed up as far as possible with facts and examples. An example of a factor analysis is given in Appendix A.

## Role definitions

Is job analysis concerned with jobs or roles or both? The terms 'job' and 'role' are often used interchangeably, but there is an important difference:

- a *job* consists of a group of finite tasks to be performed (pieces of work) and duties to be fulfilled in order to achieve an end-result)
- a *role* describes the part played by people in meeting their objectives by working competently and flexibly within the context of the organization's objectives, structure and processes.

When describing a job the traditional approach has been to concentrate on why it exists (its overall purpose) and the activities to be carried out. The implication is that these are fixed and are performed by job holders as prescribed. On the face of it, there is no room for flexibility or interpretation of how best to do the work. Jobs are the same, in fact should be the same, whoever carries them out.

The concept of a role is much wider because it is people and behaviour-orientated — it is concerned with what people do and how they do it rather than concentrating narrowly on job content. When faced with any situation, eg carrying out a job, individuals have to enact a role in order to perform effectively within that situation. People at work are, in a sense, often acting a part; they are not simply reciting the lines but are interpreting them in terms of their own perceptions of how they should behave within their work context.

Role definitions cover the behavioural aspects of work — the competences required to achieve acceptable levels of performance and contribution — as well as the tasks to be carried out or the results to be achieved. They can stress the need for flexibility and multiskilling, and for adapting to the different demands that are made on people in project and team-based organizations where the emphasis is on process rather than hierarchical structure.

## *Preparation of role definitions*

Role definitions are prepared on the basis of the job, skills and competence analysis process described above. The 'nature and scope' or 'context' section of a job description may broadly describe the role of the job holder. It may be difficult to describe a role in precise terms and it is often better to clarify roles on a face-to-face basis rather than trying to get people to express them in writing. The concept of a role is essentially one that describes relationships and types of behaviours rather than precise facts. There is no standard format for a role definition but examples of typical definitions are given in Appendix B.

## *Generic role definitions*

Role definitions are often 'generic' that is, they cover groups of roles which are essentially similar. Their advantage is that they can be used to define broad recruitment and learning specifications for people who carry out those roles. They provide a basis for performance management agreements and reviews where these are concerned with typical competence requirements. They can also be used in job evaluation as the point of reference for grading a role, especially in a broad-banded or job family structure (these terms are defined in chapter 33).

Generic role definitions are prepared by means of normal job and competence analysis techniques as described earlier in this chapter. These aim to identify the common characteristics of such roles and distil them into a generalised definition. Examples are given in Appendix B.

# 13

# Performance Management

Performance management processes have come to the fore in recent years as a means of providing a more integrated and continuous approach to the management of performance than was provided by previous more isolated, and often inadequate, merit rating or performance appraisal schemes. Performance management is based on the principle of management by agreement or contract rather than management by command. It emphasizes development and the initiation of self-managed learning plans as well as the integration of individual and corporate objectives. It can, in fact, play a major role in providing for an integrated and coherent range of personnel processes which are mutually supportive and contribute as a whole to improving organizational effectiveness.

Performance management is considered in this chapter under the following headings:

- purpose
- background
- the process of performance management
- documentation
- introduction
- evaluation.

## Purpose

Performance management is a means of getting better results from the organization, teams and individuals by understanding and managing performance within an agreed framework of planned goals, standards and competence requirements. It is a process for establishing shared understanding about what *is* to be achieved, and an approach to managing and developing people in a way which increases the probability that it *will* be achieved in the short and long term. It is owned and driven by line management.

The key words in this definition are:

- *An agreed framework of planned goals, standards and competence requirements* — the basis of performance management is an agreement between the manager and the individual on expectations in relation to each of these headings. Performance management is largely about managing such expectations.
- *A process* — performance management is not just a system of forms and procedures. It is about the actions which people take to achieve the day-to-day delivery of results and manage performance improvements in themselves and others.
- *Shared understanding* — to improve performance, individuals need to have a shared understanding about what high levels of performance and competence look like and what they are working towards.
- *An approach to managing and developing people* — performance management is focused on three things. First, how managers and team leaders work effectively with those around them. Second, how individuals work with their managers and with their teams and third, how individuals can be developed to improve their knowledge, skills and expertise (their attributes) and their levels of competence and performance.
- *Achievement* — ultimately, performance management is about the achievement of job-related success for individuals so that they can make the best use of their abilities, realize their potential and maximize their contribution to the success of the organization.
- *Owned and driven by line managers* — performance management is a natural process of management, not a procedure forced onto line managers by top management and the personnel department.

Performance management is concerned with the interrelated processes of work, management, development and reward. It can become a powerful integrating force, ensuring that these processes are linked together properly as a fundamental part of the human resource management approach which should be practised by every manager in the organization. This concept is illustrated in Figure 13.1.

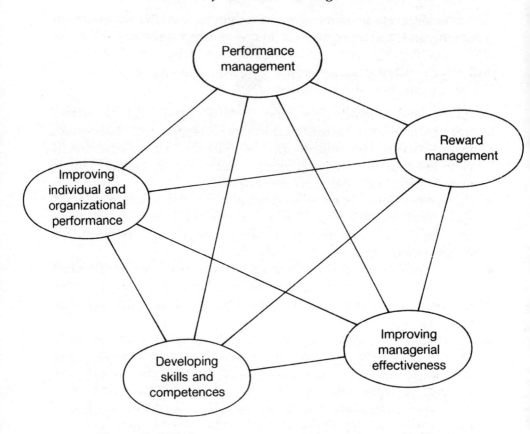

**Figure 13.1** Performance management as an integrating force

## Background to performance management

The concept of performance management has been one of the most important developments in the sphere of management in recent years. It began to take shape in the later 1980s, growing out of the realization that a more continuous and integrated approach was needed to manage and reward performance. All too often, crudely developed and hastily implemented performance-related pay and appraisal systems were not delivering the results that, somewhat naively, people were expecting from them.

Performance management has risen like a phoenix from the old-established but somewhat discredited systems of merit rating and management by objectives. Many of the more recent developments in performance appraisal have also been absorbed into the concept of performance management, which aims to be a much wider, more comprehensive and more natural process of management.

## Principles of performance management

Following their in-depth, case-study research into what they termed performance management systems (PMS) on behalf of the Institute of Personnel Management (1992a), Fletcher and Williams (1992) came to the conclusion that 'the real concept of performance management is associated with an approach to creating a shared vision of the purpose and aims of the organization, helping each individual employee understand and recognize their part in contributing to them, and in so doing manage and enhance the performance of both individuals and the organization.'

They suggested four underlying principles of effective performance management:

1. That it is owned and driven by line management and not by the HR department.
2. That there is an emphasis on shared corporate goals and values.
3. That performance management is not a package solution, it is something that has to be developed specifically and individually for the particular organization.
4. That it should apply to all staff, not just part of the managerial group.

## The process of performance management

Performance management is a continuous and flexible process which involves managers and those whom they manage acting as partners within a framework which sets out how they can best work together to achieve the required results. It focuses on future performance planning and improvement rather than on retrospective performance appraisal. It provides the basis for regular and frequent dialogues between managers and individuals or teams about performance and development needs. Performance management is mainly concerned with individual performance and development but, increasingly, the approaches described below are being used for or by teams.

Performance management reviews provide the inputs required to create personal or team development plans, and to many people performance management is essentially a developmental process.

Performance reviews can, however, produce the data in the form of individual ratings which are needed for performance-related pay decisions.

To a larger extent, performance management is a process for measuring outputs in the shape of delivered performance compared with expectations expressed as objectives. That is why it focuses on targets, standards and performance measures or indicators. But it is also concerned with inputs and processes — the knowledge, skills and behaviour required to produce the required results. It is by defining these input requirements and assessing the extent to which the expected levels of performance have been achieved by using skills and competences effectively that developmental needs are identified.

## Performance management activities

Performance management can be described as a continuous self-renewing cycle, as illustrated in Figure 13.2. There is a clear link to business plans so that objectives agreed with individuals and teams are integrated with and support the achievement of business objectives. The key activities are:

- *The performance agreement or contract.* This defines expectations — what the individual or team has to achieve in the form of objectives — how performance will be measured and the competences needed to deliver the required results.
- *The performance and development plan.* This sets out an agreement on performance and personal development needs, the latter may be expressed as a personal development plan (see chapter 27).
- *Managing performance throughout the year.* This is the continuous process of providing feedback on performance, conducting informal progress reviews and, where necessary, dealing with performance problems.
- *Performance review.* This is the formal review of performance over a period covering achievements and problems as the basis for agreeing as necessary revisions to the performance agreement and performance plan. It can also lead to performance ratings.

These activities are described in the next four sections of this chapter.

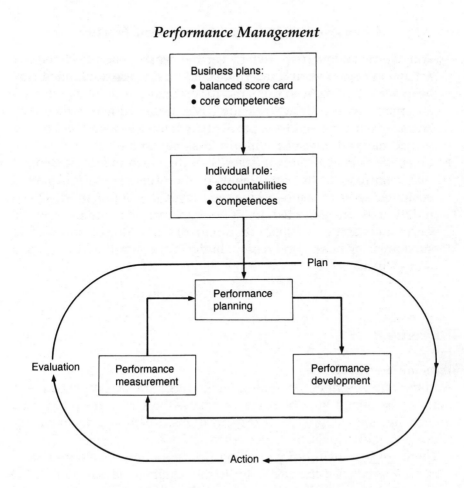

**Figure 13.2** The performance management cycle

## Performance agreements

### *Contents*

Performance agreements, also known as performance contracts, define expectations — the results to be achieved and the competences required to attain these results. Agreements cover the following points:

- *Objectives and standards of performance*
- *Performance measures and indicators* to assess the extent to which objectives and standards of performance have been achieved.
- *Competences* — definitions of the knowledge and skills necessary

and the behaviour required to get the work done effectively by achieving objectives and meeting standards. These definitions may be generic, having been prepared for occupations or job families on an organization or function-wide basis. Less frequently, they may be job-specific, agreed for a particular job by the job holder and his or her manager, possibly with professional advice.

● *Corporate core values or requirements* — the performance agreement may also refer to the core values of the organization for quality, customer service, teamworking, employee development etc which individuals are expected to uphold in carrying out their work. Certain general operational requirements may also be specified in such areas as health and safety, budgetary control, cost reduction and security.

These components of a performance agreement are discussed below.

## Objectives

*What are objectives?*
An objective describes something which has to be accomplished — a point to be aimed at. Objectives or goals (the terms are often used interchangeably) define what organizations, functions, departments, teams and individuals are expected to achieve.

There are two main types of objectives: work and developmental.

*Work or operational objectives* refer to the results to be achieved or the contribution to be made to the accomplishment of team, departmental and corporate objectives. At corporate level they are related to the organization's mission, core values and strategic plans.

At departmental or functional level they are related to corporate objectives, spelling out the specific mission, targets and purposes to be achieved by a function or department.

At team level they will again be related specifically to the purpose of the team and the contribution it is expected to make to achieving departmental and corporate goals.

At individual level they are job-related, referring to the main activity areas or key tasks which constitute the individual's job. They focus on the results individuals are expected to achieve and how they contribute to the attainment of team, departmental and corporate goals and to upholding the organization's core values. They will also clarify the basis upon which performance in attaining these results can be measured.

Ideally, performance management sets out not only to define objectives at each of these levels but also to integrate them so that a shared vision of performance requirements is created throughout the organization, all contributing to the ultimate goal of organizational effectiveness and success.

*How are individual work objectives expressed?*
Individual objectives can take the form of:

- *Quantified output or improvement targets* (open 24 new accounts by 31 December, reduce cost per unit of output by 2.5 per cent by 30 June) or in terms of projects to be completed (open distribution depot in Northampton by 31 October). Targets may be reset regularly, say once a year or every six months, or be subject to frequent amendments to meet new requirements or changed circumstances.
- *Standing objectives* which are concerned with the permanent or continuing features of a job. They incorporate or lead to defined standards of performance which may be expressed in quantified terms such as the requirement to ensure that all deliveries are made within three days of receiving an order. Alternatively, they may have to be defined as qualitative standards such as:

    Performance will be up to standard if requests for information are dealt with promptly and helpfully on a can do/will do basis and are delivered in the form required by the user.

Qualitative standing objectives may also be defined for behaviour which will contribute to upholding the core values of the organization.

A good work or operational objective will be:

S = stretching
M = measurable
A = agreed
R = realistic/relevant
T = time related.

The process of agreeing objectives need not be unduly complicated. It should start from an agreed list of main tasks or what are sometimes referred to as principal accountabilities or key result areas. It is then a matter of jointly examining each area and agreeing targets and standards of performance as appropriate. Agreement can also be reached on any projects to be undertaken which might be linked to a specific accountability, or the agreement may refer to more general projects which fall broadly within the remit of the job holder.

If the main tasks have been defined in output terms (as they should have been), ie if they indicate that the job holder has to do something *in order to* achieve a specified result, this may in itself define a standing objective. However, the definition may need to be expanded and short-term targets could be attached to it. It would, of course, also need to be amended regularly as output requirements change. One of the purposes of the review meeting and the performance agreement that arises from it is to examine job descriptions so that these requirements and the standing objectives that arise from them are updated accurately to reflect revised expectations.

*Developmental objectives*, ie personal or learning objectives, are concerned with what individuals should do and learn to improve their performance (performance improvement plans) and/or their knowledge and skills and competences (personal development plans).

Personal objectives emerge from the analysis and discussions which take place about the individual's performance compared with agreed work or operational objectives and the requirements for certain attributes (skill and knowledge) and levels of competence. The latter may be generic for all individuals in similar jobs or job families, or specific to the job holders.

The discussions will consider the factors which have contributed to achieving, meeting or failing to achieve objectives. These may be personal factors referring to the behaviour of the individual and the levels of skill or competence displayed, or external factors which may be outside the direct control of the individual but which he or she could reasonably be expected to manage.

In so far as the results obtained by individuals are attributable to the way in which they have carried out their work, learning needs and areas of strength or weakness for development or improvement are established.

## Performance measures

Measurement is a key aspect of performance management on the grounds that 'if you can't measure it you can't improve it'. It is pointless to define objectives or performance standards unless there is agreement and understanding on how performance in achieving these objectives or standards will be measured.

Performance measures should provide evidence of whether or not the intended result has been achieved and the extent to which the job holder has produced that result. This will be the basis for generating feedback information for use not only by managers but also by individuals to monitor their own performance.

Performance measures will only work if they are derived from clear main task definitions which focus on end results and suggest measurement. The definitions can indicate the measure to be used. For example, if one of the principal accountabilities of a sales manager is to develop new accounts, a target may be set to obtain 20 new customers within the next three months each of which generate sales of at least £15,000 a year. The performance measures of the number and the quality of the accounts are indicated in this target quite clearly.

However, the same sales manager may have a principal accountability which is to achieve and maintain a high degree of customer satisfaction. In this case measures of customer satisfaction would have to be agreed such as repeat or expanding business, absence of justifiable complaints, or response to a customer satisfaction survey. These measures may be quantified as targets or standards.

Performance measures may refer to such matters as income generation, sales, output, units processed, productivity, costs, delivery-to-time, 'take up' of a service, speed of reaction or turnround, achievement of quality standards or customer/client reactions.

It is important to agree performance measures at the same time as objectives are defined. This is the only way in which a fair assessment of progress and achievements can be made and the successful definition of performance measures will provide the best basis for feedback.

The following are guidelines for defining performance measures:

- measures should relate to results not efforts
- the results must be within the job holder's control
- measures should be objective and observable
- data must be available for measurement
- existing measures should be used or adapted wherever possible.

## Competences

The agreement of objectives and measures enables performance to be assessed by reference to outputs and contribution. But performance management is also concerned with the level of competence needed to achieve satisfactory results. Generic competence requirements can be analysed and defined as described in Chapter 12 and competence frameworks or maps may be used as the basis for agreeing expectations and reviewing actual behaviour.

If generic competence frameworks have not been prepared it is still desirable for managers and individuals to discuss and agree what competences are required. This should focus on the following questions which could be discussed in relation to each major aspect of the job:

- What do we think needs to be done to ensure that this part of the job is performed well?
- Can we think of any ways in which this task might be approached which would result in it not being done so well?
- Can we now agree on the sort of behaviour in carrying out this task which is likely to produce good or poor results?

The aim would be to produce an agreement which would ensure that individuals understand the sort of behaviours expected of them and appreciate that if they fulfil these expectations they will be regarded as having performed well.

## Values

Increasingly, organizations are setting out the core values that they think should govern the behaviour of their employees.

Typical values which organizations incorporate into their performance management schemes include:

- customer service (internal as well as external)
- quality
- equal opportunity
- team work
- (for managers) developing the performance of staff
- maintaining health and safety standards.

Definitions of the behaviour expected in upholding these values can be prepared for the organization as a whole and managers would be required to discuss with individuals the extent to which the latter's behaviour has supported the core value. This is an effective method of ensuring that espoused values are put into practice.

## Performance plans

Performance plans record the actions agreed to improve performance and to develop knowledge, skills and competences. The performance plan is likely to concentrate on development in the current job — to improve the ability to perform it well and also, importantly, to enable individuals to take on wider responsibilities, extending their capacity to undertake a broader role. This plan therefore contributes to the achievement of a policy of continuous development which is predicated on the belief that everyone is capable of learning more and doing better in their jobs. But the plan will also contribute to enhancing the potential of individuals to carry out higher level jobs.

Performance plans provide answers to the following questions which can be discussed with job holders:

- What areas of your performance do you feel in need of development?
- What do you think you need to do to develop your performance in any particular areas?
- Do you think you need further training in any aspect of your work?
- How can I (ie the manager) help to improve your performance?
- What development and training actions should we agree? (on the basis of the answers to the earlier questions).

The results of this agreement could be set out in a personal development plan as described in Chapter 27.

## Managing performance throughout the year

Perhaps one of the most important concepts of performance management is that it is a continuous process which reflects normal good management practices of setting direction, monitoring and measuring performance and taking action accordingly. Performance management should not be imposed on managers as something 'special' they have to do. It should be treated as a natural process which all good managers follow. The sequence of performance management activities as described in this book does no more than provide a framework within which managers, individuals and teams work together in whatever ways best suit them to gain better understanding of what is to be done, how it is to be done and what has been achieved. This framework and the philosophy that supports it can form the basis for training newly appointed or would-be managers in this key area of their responsibilities. It can also help in improving the performance of managers who are not up to standard in this respect.

Conventional performance appraisal systems are usually built around an annual event, the formal review, which tended to dwell on the past. This was carried out at the behest of the personnel department, often perfunctorily, and then forgotten. Managers proceeded to manage without any further reference to the outcome of the review and the appraisal form was buried in the personnel record system.

A formal, often annual review, is still an important part of a performance management framework but it is not the most important part. Equal — indeed more — prominence is given to the performance agreement and the continuous process of performance management, as illustrated in Figure 13.3.

## *The continuing process of performance management*

Performance management should be regarded as an integral part of the continuing process of management. This is based on a philosophy which emphasizes:

- the achievement of sustained improvements in performance
- continuous development of skills and overall competence
- that the organization is a 'learning organization'.

Managers and individuals should therefore be ready, willing and able to define and meet development and improvement needs as they arise. As far as practicable, learning and work should be integrated. This

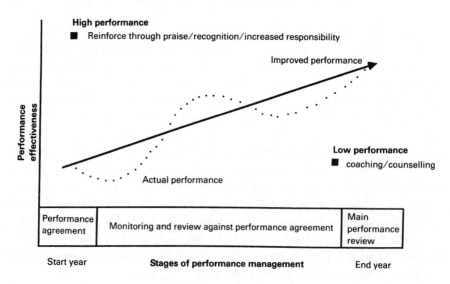

**Figure 13.3** Managing performance throughout the year

means that encouragement should be given to all managers and members of staff to learn from the successes, challenges and problems inherent in their day-to-day work.

The process of continuing assessment should be carried out by reference to agreed objectives and to work, development and improvement plans. Progress reviews can take place informally or through an existing system of team meetings. But there should be more formal interim reviews at predetermined points in the year, eg quarterly. For some teams or individual jobs these points could be related to 'milestones' contained in project and work plans. Deciding when such meetings should take place would be up to individual managers in consultation with their staff and would not be a laid-down part of a 'system'.

Managers would be encouraged to consider how to accommodate the need for regular dialogue within the established pattern of briefings, team or group meetings or project review meetings.

In addition to the collective meetings, managers may have regular one-to-one meetings with their staff. If performance management is to be effective, there needs to be a continuing agenda through these regular meetings to ensure that good progress is being made towards achieving the objectives agreed for each key result area.

During these interim meetings, progress in achieving agreed operational and personal objectives and associated work, development and improvement plans, can be reviewed. As necessary, objectives and plans are revised.

Interim review meetings should be conducted along the lines of the main review meetings as described below. Any specific outcomes of the meeting should be recorded as amendments to the original agreement and objectives and plans.

The issues which may arise in the course of managing performance throughout the year are:

- updating objectives and work plans
- continuous learning
- dealing with performance problems.

## Updating objectives and work plans

Performance agreements and plans are working documents. New demands, new situations arise, and provision therefore needs to be made for updating or amending objectives and work plans.

This involves:

- discussing what the job holder has done and achieved
- identifying any shortfalls in achieving objectives or meeting standards
- establishing the reasons for any shortfalls, in particular examining changes in the circumstances in which the job is carried out, identifying new demands and pressures and considering aspects of the behaviour of the individual *or* the manager which have contributed to the problem
- agreeing any changes required to objectives and work plans in response to changed circumstances
- agreeing any actions required by the individual or the manager to improve performance.

Any changes in duties and responsibilities should also be incorporated in the job description as they arise. Job descriptions are part of the performance management process and should also be regarded as working documents.

## Managing continuous learning

Performance management aims to enhance what Alan Mumford (1994) calls 'deliberate learning from experience', which means learning from the problems, challenges and successes inherent in people's day-to-day activities.

The premise is that every task individuals undertake presents them with a learning opportunity, as long as they reflect or are helped to reflect on what they have done and how they have done it and draw conclusions as to their future behaviour if they have to carry out a similar task. This principle can be extended to any situation when managers issue instructions to individuals or agree with them what needs to be achieved, followed by a review, which may be quite informal, of how well the task was accomplished. Such day-to-day contacts provide training as well as learning opportunities, and performance management emphasizes that these should be deliberate acts. In other words, that managers, with their complete teams and with the individual members of their teams, should consciously agree on the lessons learnt from experience and how this experience could be put to good use in the future.

## Dealing with performance problems

The approach to dealing with performance problems (managing underperformers) should be based on reinforcement theory. It is a positive process which is based on feedback throughout the year and looks forward to what can be done by individuals to overcome performance problems and, importantly, how managers can help.

The five basic steps required to handle performance problems are:

1. *Identify and agree the problem.* Analyse the feedback and, as far as possible, obtain agreement from the individual on what the shortfall has been. Feedback may be provided by managers but it should be built into the job. This takes place when individuals are aware of their targets and standards, know what performance measures will be used and either receive feedback/control information automatically or have easy access to it. They will then be in a position to measure and assess their own performance and, if they are well-motivated and well-trained, take their own corrective actions. In other words, a self-regulating feedback mechanism exists. This is a situation which managers should endeavour to create on the grounds that prevention is better than cure.

2. *Establish the reason(s) for the shortfall.* When seeking the reasons for any shortfalls the manager should not crudely be trying to attach blame. This is management by agreement, not management by blame. The aim should be for the manager and the individual jointly to identify the facts that have contributed to the problem. It is on the basis of this factual analysis that decisions can be made on what to do about it by the individual, the manager or the two of them working together.

    It is necessary first to identify any causes which are external to the job and outside the control of either the manager or the individual. Any factors which *are* within the control of the individual and/or the manager can then be considered. What needs to be determined is the extent to which the reason for the problem is because the individual:

    - did not receive adequate support or guidance from his/her manager
    - did not fully understand what he/she was expected to do
    - could not do it — ability
    - did not know how to do it — skill
    - would not do it — attitude.

3. *Decide and agree on the action required.* Action may be taken by the individual, the manager or both parties. This could include:

   - taking steps to improve skills or change behaviour — the individual
   - changing attitudes — this is up to individuals as long as they accept that their attitudes need to be changed. The challenge for managers is that people will not change their attitudes simply because they are told to do so. They can only be helped to understand that certain changes to their behaviour could be beneficial not only to the organization but also to themselves. A counselling approach is desirable
   - providing more support or guidance
   - clarifying expectations — job requirements, objectives and standards
   - developing abilities and skills — joint, in the sense that individuals may be expected to take steps to develop themselves but managers may provide help in the form of coaching, additional experience or training.

   Whatever action is agreed both parties must understand how they will know that it has succeeded. Performance measures and feedback arrangements should be agreed.

4. *Resource the action.* Provide the coaching, training, guidance, experience or facilities required to enable agreed actions to happen.

5. *Monitor and provide feedback.* Steps are taken to monitor performance, ensure that feedback is provided or obtained and analysed, and agree on any further actions that may be necessary. Individuals should be encouraged to monitor their own performance and take further action as required. This can be described as a 'self-managed learning process'.

## Performance reviews

Performance review discussions enable a perspective to be obtained on past performance as a basis for making plans for the future. An overall view is taken of the progress made. Examples are used to illustrate that overview, and the analysis of performance concentrates not only on what has happened but also on *why* it has happened so that data is obtained for planning purposes. Obtaining historical perspective through analysis is a necessary part of a performance review. But reaching agreement about what should be done in the future is what the discussion is really all about.

## The basis of the performance review

The performance review discussion provides the means through which the five key elements of performance management can be achieved. These are:

1.  *Measurement* — assessing results against agreed targets and standards.
2.  *Feedback* — giving the individual information on how he or she has been doing.
3.  *Positive reinforcement* — emphasizing what has been done well so that it will be done even better in the future; only making constructive criticisms, ie those that point the way to improvement.
4.  *Exchange of views* — ensuring that the discussion involves a full, free and frank exchange of views about what has been achieved, what needs to be done to achieve more and what individuals think about their work, the way they are guided and managed and their aspirations.
5.  *Agreement* — jointly coming to an understanding about what has to be done by both parties to improve performance and overcome any work problems raised during the discussion.

## Key aspects of the discussion

When a manager and an individual get together they are there to engage in a dialogue about the latter's performance and development. This is not an interview in which one person asks the questions and the other provides the answers. It is more like a meeting in which views are exchanged so that an agreed conclusion can be reached.

Describing the formal review meeting as a discussion implies that it is a free-flowing affair in which both parties are fully involved. This impression is correct, but it should not be assumed that the discussion can be allowed to meander to some inconclusive end. This is a conversation with a purpose; that purpose being to reach firm and agreed conclusions about the future development of the appraisee, any areas for improvement and how that improvement will be achieved. As such, the discussion has to be initiated with care and a variety of approaches and interpersonal skills are used to bring it to a successful conclusion.

## On what should the performance review meeting focus?

There are two focus issues in performance review meetings: first, on the emphasis which should be placed on performance improvement as distinct from broader developmental needs; second, on the degree to which the meeting should be forward rather than backward looking.

A single-minded focus on performance improvement at the expense of broader issues is unlikely to produce much motivation. The focus should also be on the individual's development, bearing in mind that no one is simply being prepared for vertical movement up the hierarchy. This means helping people to widen their range of abilities (multiskilling in shop floor terms) to enable them to meet the demands of future change and the additional activities they may be required to carry out. This particularly applies to the core of middle-of-the-road performers.

Performance review meetings which are used or are perceived as being used simply to generate ratings for performance-related pay purposes will almost inevitably fail to achieve what should be regarded as their most important objectives — to motivate and develop people.

The slogan which should be imprinted on the minds of all reviewers is that 'Yesterday is only useful if it teaches us about today and tomorrow.' The analysis of past performance is a necessary precursor to the preparation of performance and development plans for the future. But the tendency to dwell on the past rather than looking to the future must be avoided if the review is going to make any positive motivational impact.

## Conducting the discussion

There is no one right way of conducting a discussion — the approaches used will be strongly influenced by the circumstances, including the personalities and attitudes of the people involved. But the following guidelines should be taken into account by those conducting review meetings:

*Preliminary phases*

- Prepare carefully.
- Work to a clear but flexible structure.
- Create a supportive atmosphere.

*General guidelines*

- Let the appraisee do most of the talking.
- Encourage self-appraisal.
- Keep the whole year under review.
- No surprises — do not suddenly launch criticisms about past behaviour which should have been discussed at the time.
- Be positive, criticize constructively.

*Using interpersonal skills*

- Seek information by asking the right questions.
- Listen carefully.
- Be sensitive to the other person's concerns.
- Observe and respond to non-verbal signals.
- Maintain open, friendly body language.
- Be open to criticism.
- Test understanding.
- Reach agreement.

*Completing the discussion*

- Check understanding.
- Plan ahead.
- Rate performance, if that is part of the process.
- Complete documentation.
- End the meeting on a positive note.

## 360-degree feedback

Another approach to performance reviews is 360-degree feedback in a form marketed by *Pilat UK Limited*, (also known as 360-degree appraisal multi-rater assessment and multi-source assessment) is designed to give a complete, multi-dimensional picture of an individual's performance — from his or her manager, temporary project leaders in a matrix organization, direct and indirect reports, peers, and internal and external customers.

360-degree feedback is a means of establishing how successful individuals are in all their work relationships — the manager is unlikely to know the full story. Individuals are also asked to assess themselves. The emphasis is on skills, competences and behaviour. The feedback should be directed at describing behaviour rather than judging it. The usual approach is to use structured questionnaires which are completed anonymously and are confidential to the individual. However, it is desirable to provide some form of counselling which enables individuals to interpret the feedback and prepare action plans for self-development.

# Performance rating

Performance assessments are sometimes summarized following a review meeting by means of overall ratings which, if a performance-related pay scheme exists, provide a basis for deciding on increases. A rating scale format can either be behavioural, with examples of good, average and inadequate performance, or graphic which simply present a number of scale points along a continuum. The scale points or anchors in the latter may be defined alphabetically (a,b,c etc), numerically (1,2,3 etc) or by means of initials (ex for excellent etc) which purport to disguise the hierarchical nature of the scale. The scale points may be further described adjectivally, for example: excellent (A), highly acceptable (B), acceptable (C), not entirely acceptable (D) and unacceptable (E).

The ratings might be made against a series of standard headings, which in traditional schemes were generalized performance characteristics or personality traits such as effective output, knowledge of work, judgement, initiative, cooperation and reliability.

In results-orientated schemes (ie those reviewing performance against objectives) a rating or indication of the level of achievement might be made of the level of achievement for each objective, for example: achieved, partly achieved, not achieved. Alternatively, or additionally, an overall rating of performance may be made using an alphabetical behaviourally defined scale.

## Arguments for and against rating

The arguments for ratings are that:

- they are a convenient way of summing up judgements which might otherwise be submerged in verbiage
- it is not possible to have performance-related pay without them (assuming that performance-related pay is wanted or needed)
- they provide a means of identifying the exceptional performers or under-performers and those who are the reliable core performers so

that action can be taken (developmental or some form of non-financial reward)

- they can provide a basis for predicting potential on the assumption that people who perform well in the present are likely to go on doing so in the future — however, past performance is only a predictor of future performance when there is a connecting link, ie there are elements of the present job which are also important in a higher level job.

The arguments against ratings are that:

- they are largely subjective and it is difficult to achieve consistency between different rates
- to sum up the total performance of a person with a single rating is a gross over-simplification of what may be a complex set of factors influencing that performance
- to make judgements about potential on the basis of an overall rating which masks dissimilarities between these elements is dangerous, although, obviously, poor overall performance should not be followed or rewarded by promotion
- to label people as 'average' or 'below average', or whatever equivalent terms are used, is both demeaning and demotivating.

Some organizations which do not have performance-related pay reject ratings altogether because of the objections listed above.

## Achieving consistency

Perhaps the greatest of the problems mentioned above is that it is very difficult, if not impossible without very careful management, to ensure that a consistent approach is adopted by managers responsible for rating. It is almost inevitable that some people will be more generous than others, while others will be harder on their staff. Ratings can, of course, be monitored and questioned if their distribution is significantly out of line, and computer-based systems have been introduced for this purpose in some organizations. But many managers want to do the best for their staff, either because they genuinely believe that they are better or because they are trying to curry favour. It can be difficult in these circumstances to challenge them, and it could be argued that if responsibility for human resource management is being genuinely devolved to line management, it is up to them to decide how they are going to distribute their ratings.

If consistency is required, however, there are four approaches that can be adopted, as described below.

*Forced distribution* — the forced distribution of ratings requires managers to conform to a pattern which quite often corresponds with the normal curve of distribution on the assumption that performance levels are distributed normally. A typical distribution would be:

| Rating | % |
|--------|----|
| A | 5 |
| B | 15 |
| C | 60 |
| D | 15 |
| E | 5 |

However, the assumption that performance and consequential reward is distributed normally is questionable. It tends to produce win-lose situations. In the many evaluations of performance management and performance-related pay that have been conducted over the last few years, forced choice distributions and quotas have come in for particular criticism. There is no rule which states that performance or ability should be normally distributed within an organization. There are many examples of high-performance organizations where key departments such as marketing are well staffed with above average people who are delivering a new business strategy, and others where to fill departments such as finance with super-achieving accountants would be quite inappropriate and in any case would result in them withering away from boredom. There is also the view that the level of fully acceptable performance needs to be ratcheted up every year — so what was defined as a good contribution in one year is less than acceptable in the next. This is one of the arguments that can be used to contain rating drift.

The clinching argument against forced distribution, however, is that it totally removes from line management any feeling of ownership of the rating system, and this is the surest way possible to destroy a performance management scheme.

*Ranking systems* — an alternative approach is to rank staff in order of merit and then distribute performance ratings through the rank order. Shell UK, for example, gets managers together to rank groups of up to 100 employees and allocate them according to a forced distribution into four performance bands.

A typical forced distribution in a ranking system would be to give the top 10 per cent an A rating, the next 15 per cent a B rating, the next 60 per cent a C rating and the remaining 15 per cent a D rating. Such forced distribution systems do ensure a consistent distribution of ratings but still depend on the relative objectivity and accuracy of the rankings. They are also just as mechanistic as a normal forced distribution system and take away line management's responsibility for the ratings.

*Behaviourally anchored rating scales (BARS)* — these are designed to reduce the rating errors which it was assumed are typical of conventional scales. They include a number of performance dimensions such as teamwork, and managers rate each dimension on a scale as in the following example:

A   Continually contributes new ideas and suggestions. Takes a leading role in group meetings but is tolerant and supportive of colleagues and respects other people's points of view. Keeps everyone informed about own activities and is well aware of what other team members are doing in support of team objectives.

B   Takes a full part in group meetings and contributes useful ideas frequently. Listens to colleagues and keeps them reasonably well informed about own activities while keeping abreast of what they are doing.

C   Delivers opinions and suggestions at group meetings from time to time but is not a major contributor to new thinking or planning activities. Generally receptive to other people's ideas and willing to change own plans to fit in. Does not always keep others properly informed or take sufficient pains to know what they are doing.

D   Tendency to comply passively with other people's suggestions. May withdraw at group meetings but sometimes shows personal antagonism to others. Not very interested in what others are doing or in keeping them informed.

E   Tendency to go own way without taking much account of the need to make a contribution to team activities. Sometimes uncooperative and unwilling to share information.

F   Generally uncooperative. Goes own way, completely ignoring the wishes of other team members and taking no interest in the achievement of team objectives.

It is believed that the behavioural descriptions in such scales discourage the tendency to rate on the basis of generalized assumptions about personality traits (which are probably highly subjective) by focusing attention on specific work behaviours. But they do take a considerable amount of effort to develop properly and there is still room for making subjective judgements based on different interpretations of the definitions of levels of behaviour.

*Training and review* — the best way to deal with this issue is as part of the developmental process associated with performance management. This involves running regular consistency workshops with managers from across departments to discuss how ratings are perceived, explore differences, test out fair rating on 'case study' performance reviews and, over time, build up a better common understanding and level of comfort with the rating process.

This can be extended to bringing managers together after their performance ratings have been made and getting them to exchange information and, where necessary justify their distribution of assessments.

Another, and effective, support to the development of improved consistency is to provide for a 'grandparent' or boss's boss to check on both the quality of formal performance reviews and the consistency of performance ratings. Again this needs to be supported by training workshops, but it can and does prove a useful integrating influence on the ownership of performance management in a part of the organization.

The personnel department can play a useful part in helping to achieve fairly distributed and consistent ratings. Not by taking on a 'policing' role and compelling managers to accept a forced distribution, but by providing guidance and by encouraging managers to reconsider their ratings if they seem to be misjudged.

## Rating and performance-related pay

If the organization does have a performance-related pay system this will require some form of rating as the basis for determining the level of pay increases. But if these ratings are incorporated in a performance management review, there is a distinct possibility that the review will be dominated by pay considerations leading to the neglect of the key developmental aspects of the process.

This danger is avoided by some organizations by conducting a separate pay review in which managers are given a budget and simply asked to indicate whether they want to award an exceptionally high increase, an above average increase, a below average increase or no increase at all. Of course such judgements are related to assessments of performance and there is therefore a 'read across' from the performance review. But decisions about pay increases can be based on a number of factors besides performance in the current job, including the market worth of individuals and their potential.

## Documentation

It is the processes of performance management as practised jointly by managers and individuals which are important, not the content of the system; and the content often seems to consist largely of documents. Performance management is about managing and improving performance. It is not about completing forms.

A case could be made for having no forms at all. The parties involved could be encouraged to record the conclusions of their discussion and their agreements on blank sheets of paper to be used as working documents during the continuing process of managing performance throughout the year.

There is much to be said for having a format which can help in the orderly presentation of plans and comments. The mere existence of a form or a set of forms does demonstrate that this is a process which everyone is expected to take seriously.

### *Performance management forms as working documents*

The main function of performance management forms is to act as working documents. They should be completed jointly by managers and individuals. The manager should not deliver a completed form to an individual and say 'What do you think?'. In the past merit ratings were sometimes not shown to the individuals concerned at all, which was a remarkable denial of the whole reason for reviewing performance.

Forms should be in continual use as reference documents on objectives and plans when reviewing progress. They should also record agreements on performance achievements and actions to be taken to improve performance or develop competence and skills. They should be dog-eared from much use — they should not be condemned to moulder away in a file.

It can be argued that for this reason the forms should be owned by the manager and the individual (both parties should have a copy). Any information the personnel department needs on ratings (for performance related pay or career planning purposes), or requests for training, would be incorporated in a separate form for their use.

Individuals can be protected against unfair assessments and ratings by providing for their manager's manager (the so-called 'grandparent') to see and comment on the completed report. These comments could be shown to individuals who should have the right to appeal through a grievance procedure if they are still unhappy about the report.

There is, however, a good case for the personnel department having sight of completed review forms for quality assurance purposes, especially in the earlier days of operating performance management.

A typical set of forms which include an overall performance rating section is illustrated in Appendix C.

## Introducing performance management

Performance management processes need to be introduced with great care. Too many ambitious schemes fail because the seemingly obvious requirement has been neglected.

When planning the programme of introduction the following points need to be covered:

- where and how should performance management be introduced?
- who should be covered?
- what use should be made of pilot tests?
- what briefing arrangements should be made?
- how to monitor and evaluate?

### *Where and how should performance management be introduced?*

Performance management is usually introduced on an organization-wide basis, starting at the top. In many cases the philosophy, principles and key procedures and processes are developed centrally.

In a highly decentralized organization, separate business units may be allowed to decide for themselves whether or not they want performance management and if they do, develop it on their own.

An intermediate approach adopted by some decentralized organizations is for the centre (top management) to require all divisions and business units to introduce performance management in accordance with certain general principles which the centre lays down. The business units proceed to develop their own processes, but the centre provides help as required and may monitor the introduction of performance management on each division to ensure that it is happening according to plan and in line with corporate principles and values.

The most common and best method of introduction is to set up a project team or working group for this purpose with management and staff representatives. This provides for different opinions and experiences to be considered, serves as a base for wider consultation and communications to take place and generally helps to achieve understanding and acceptance of the process.

## Who should be covered?

Another important decision to be made at the outset is who should be covered by performance management. At one time most schemes were restricted to managers, but performance management is now more generally being extended to all professional, administrative, technical and support staff. Some organizations also include shop floor workers, especially high-tech firms, those that rely on production by high performance work teams, companies with integrated pay structures and terms and conditions of employment (often high-tech and/or international firms) and companies with performance-related pay for manual workers. There is much to be said for having a universal scheme as part of a completely integrated terms and conditions of employment policy and as a means of increasing commitment by demonstrating that all employees are regarded as important.

While some organizations believe that it would be invidious to distinguish between levels so far as the essence of the approach is concerned, they might accept that different performance measures may be used.

Some organizations do distinguish between roles where quantified and regularly updated short-term objectives will be set and those where continuing performance standards are more usual. In the former case they may refer to the key result areas of the job as 'principal accountabilities'; in the latter they may use terms such as 'main tasks' or 'key activities'.

It may also be recognized that the objective setting and review process in more routine jobs may not need to be as exhaustive as for those in managerial or professional roles.

## Pilot tests

Pilot testing of performance management is highly desirable — bearing in mind that the usual cycle lasts 12 months and it may therefore be difficult to pilot test the whole process.

Examples of aspects of performance management which can be tested are drawing up performance agreements, objective setting and document completion.

## *Prepare briefing papers*

It is advisable to issue an overall description of performance management to all employees which sets out its objectives and method of operation and the benefits it is expected to provide for the organization and its managers and employees. Some organizations have prepared elaborate and lengthy briefing documents but fairly succinct documents often suffice as long as they are written in simple language and are well produced.

It is also advisable to supplement written with oral briefings through a briefing group system, if there is one, or a special briefing programme. In a large or dispersed organization this briefing will have to be carried out by line managers and they should be issued with special briefing packs and, possibly, a list of typical questions and their answers.

## Monitoring and evaluating performance management

It is important to monitor the introduction of performance management very carefully but it is equally vital to continue to monitor and evaluate it regularly, especially after its first year of operation.

The best method of monitoring and evaluation is to ask those involved — managers, individuals and teams — how it worked. As many as possible should be seen, individually and in groups, to discuss the points set out in the last section of this chapter. It is also desirable to scrutinize a sample of completed forms to check on how well and thoroughly they have been completed. The evaluation can be carried out by members of the project team and/or by the personnel function. An independent consultant or adviser can be used to conduct a special review.

Individual and group discussions can be supplemented by a special survey of reactions to performance management which could be completed anonymously by all managers and staff. The results should be fed back to all concerned and analyzed to assess the need for any amendments to the process or further training requirements.

The ultimate test, of course, is analysing organizational performance to establish the extent to which improvements can be attributed to performance management. It may be difficult to establish a direct connection but more detailed assessments with managers and staff on the impact of the process may reveal specific areas in which performance has been improved which could be linked to an overall performance measure.

# Part IV
# Organizational Behaviour

*People perform their roles within complex systems
called organizations. The study of organizational
behaviour is concerned with how these people act
within their organizations, individually or in groups,
and how organizations function, in terms of their
structure and processes. All managers and personnel
specialists are in the business of influencing behaviour
in directions which will meet the need of the enterprise.
An understanding of organizational processes and
skills in the analysis and diagnosis of patterns of
organizational behaviour are therefore important. As
Nadler and Tushman (1980) have said:*

> *The manager needs to be able to understand the
> patterns of behaviour that are observed to predict
> in what direction behaviour will move (particu-
> larly in the light of managerial action), and to use
> this knowledge to control behaviour over the
> course of time. Effective managerial action
> requires that the manager be able to diagnose the
> system he or she is working in.*

*The purpose of this part of the book is to outline a basic
set of concepts and to provide analytical tools which
will enable personnel specialists to diagnose organizational behaviour and to take appropriate actions.*

*This purpose is achieved by initially (Chapter 14)
providing a general analysis of individuals at work —
individual differences, the nature of skill and*

*competence, what happens to people over time, the sources of social influence, how we make judgements about people and the factors affecting behaviour, including orientation to work and roles.*

*The next chapter (15) examines the nature of work, the employment relationship and the psychological contract — all aspects of managing people which need to be understood when developing and applying personnel policies and practices.*

*The concepts of individual motivation and commitment are then explored in Chapters 16 and 17 before reviewing generally in Chapter 18 the ways in which organizations function — formal and informal structures and how people work together in groups. The cultural factors which affect organizational behaviour are then examined in Chapter 19.*

# 14

# The Individual at Work

To manage people effectively, it is necessary to understand the factors that affect how people behave at work and influence their motivation and commitment, as discussed in Chapters 16 and 17. In this chapter these factors are examined under the following headings:

- Individual differences.
- The nature of skilled performance and competence.
- What happens to people over time.
- The sources of social influence on individuals.
- Attribution theory — how we make judgements about people at work.
- Behaviour at work — the factors that affect behaviour and its manifestation in attitudes, frustration and aggression, stress, and resistance to change.
- The approaches or orientation adopted by people towards work.
- The roles people play at work.
- The psychological contract.

## Individual differences

Personnel management would be much easier if everyone were the same, but they are, of course, hugely different because of their background (the environment in which they were brought up), their needs and wants, as described in Chapter 15, and their attributes — ability, intelligence and personality, as discussed below.

### Ability

Ability is the quality that makes an action possible. Abilities have been analysed by UK psychologists such as Burt (1954) and Vernon (1961). They classified abilities into two major groups:

V:ed — standing for verbal, numerical, memory and reasoning abilities.
K:m — standing for spatial and mechanical abilities, as well as perceptual (memory) and motor skills relating to physical operations such as eye/hand co-ordination and mental dexterity.

It has been suggested that overriding these abilities there is a 'g' or general intelligence factor which accounts for most variations in performance.

An alternative classification was produced by a US psychologist, Thurstone (1940), as follows:

S — spatial ability
P — perceptual speed
N — numerical ability
V — verbal meaning
M — memory
F — verbal fluency
I/R — inductive reasoning

An additional three ability headings were identified by Argyle (1989):

● *Judgement* — the capacity to make realistic assessments of practical solutions to particular problems.
● *Creativity* — the ability to see situations from a new point of view and to propose original solutions.
● *Social skills* — the capacity to persuade, to carry out various kinds of conversation effectively and to sustain good relationships with others.

## Intelligence

Intelligence has been defined as:

● 'The capacity to solve problems, apply principles, make inferences and perceive relationships.' (Argyle, 1989)
● 'The capacity for abstract thinking and reasoning with a range of different contents and media.' (Toplis, Dulewicz and Fletcher, 1991)
● 'What is measured by intelligence tests.' (Wright and Taylor, 1970)

The last, tautological definition is not facetious. It expresses the difficulty many writers have had in producing a universal definition. An operational definition of this kind can at least be related to the specific aspects of reasoning, inference, cognition (ie knowing, conceiving) and perception (ie understanding, recognition) which intelligence tests attempt to measure.

General intelligence, as noted above, consists of a number of mental abilities which enable a person to succeed at a wide variety of intellectual tasks which use the faculties of knowing and reasoning. The mathematical technique of factor analysis has been used to identify the constituents of intelligence, such as Thurstone's (1940) multiple factors listed above. But there is no general agreement among psychologists as to what these factors are or, indeed, whether there is such a thing as general intelligence.

An alternative approach to the analysis of intelligence was put forward by Guilford (1967), who distinguished five types of mental operation:

- thinking
- remembering
- divergent production (problem solving which leads to unexpected and original solutions)
- convergent production (problem solving which leads to the one, correct solution)
- evaluating.

He then suggested that there are six types of products of these operations (units, classes, relations, systems, transformations and implications), and he finally defined four types of content upon which operations are performed (figural, symbolic, semantic and behavioural). These classifications generate 120 distinguishable abilities, a number which suggests a much more complex (and probably realistic) concept of intelligence.

### Implications for personnel specialists

Personnel specialists need not bother too much about the subtleties of the definitions listed above of ability and intelligence. It is, however, useful to understand the broad concept and the definitions in order to use psychometric tests properly (see Chapter 24) and to analyse performance and competences.

## Personality

Personality can be defined as the relatively stable and enduring aspects of individuals which distinguish them from other people. This is the 'trait' concept of personality, traits being predispositions to behave in certain ways in a variety of different situations. The assumption that people are consistent in the ways they express these traits is the basis for making predictions about their future behaviour. We all attribute traits to people in an attempt to understand why they behave the way they do. As Chell (1987) says:

> This cognitive process gives a sense of order to what might otherwise appear to be senseless uncoordinated behaviours. Traits may therefore be thought of as classification systems, used by individuals to understand other people's and their own behaviour.

Perhaps the best known classification of traits is that produced by Cattell (1963). It forms the basis for the Sixteen Personality Factor Questionnaire (the 16PF personality test). Cattell's extensive empirical work used factor analysis to produce the following 16 dimensions or factors:

| Factor | High-score description | Low-score description |
| --- | --- | --- |
| A | Outgoing | Reserved |
| B | More intelligent | Less intelligent |
| C | Emotionally stable | Affected by feelings |
| E | Assertive | Humble |
| F | Happy-go-lucky | Sober |
| G | Conscientious | Expedient |
| H | Venturesome | Shy |
| I | Tender minded | Tough-minded |
| L | Suspicious | Trusting |
| M | Imaginative | Practical |
| N | Shrewd | Forthright |
| O | Apprehensive | Placid |
| Q1 | Experimenting | Conservative |
| Q2 | Self-sufficient | Group-dependent |
| Q3 | Controlled | Casual |
| Q4 | Tense | Relaxed |

Other classifications of traits form the basis for the following personality tests:

- *Myers-Briggs Type Indicator* — which contains four scales: introversion-extroversion; sensing-intuition; thinking-feeling; judging-perspective

- *Saville and Holdsworth's Occupational Personality Questionnaire (OPQ)* — which covers three domains of personality: relationships with people; thinking style; feelings and emotions.
- *Gordon Personal Profile and Inventory* — in which the profile measures ascendancy, responsibility, emotional stability and sociability; and the inventory measures cautiousness, original thinking, personal relations and vigour.

The use of personality tests as selection aids is discussed in Chapter 24.

Another factor analysis study by Eysenck (1953) identified three structural dimensions of personality: extroversion/introversion, neuroticism and psychoticism. He developed a hierarchical model of personality structure in which, for example, under the type level of introversion, trait levels were placed consisting of persistence, rigidity, subjectivity, shyness and irritability. These are expressed first in an habitual response level and finally in a specific response level.

However, the trait theory of personality has been attacked by people such as Mischel (1981), Chell (1985), and Harre (1979). The main criticisms have been:

- People do not necessarily express the same trait across different situations or even the same trait in the same situation. Different people may exhibit consistency in some traits and considerable variability in others.
- Classical trait theory, as typified by Eysenck (1953) and Cattell (1963), assumes that the manifestation of trait behaviour is independent of the situations and the persons with whom the individual is interacting — this assumption is questionable, given that trait behaviour usually manifests itself in response to specific situations.
- Trait attributions are a product of language — they are devices for speaking about people and are not described as objective features of action.

It is also noticeable that, as Chell (1987) points out:

> When people account for their own behaviour they point to some feature of the situation; when they account for other people's behaviour, they tend to make reference to traits. This is especially true when behaviour might be thought to be reprehensible in some way. This suggests that trait ascriptions are part of a moral commentary upon oneself and others; in general, they lead to the disapproval of others and credit for oneself.

These criticisms suggest that, while it is inevitable that we attribute certain dispositions (eg extroversion/introversion) to people, we should be careful to avoid assuming that they are fixed traits and that they will be displayed consistently in all situations. This is an argument against using traits as the basis for judgements when interviewing, testing and assessing performance. For this purpose, it may be best to adopt the following definition of personality produced by Toplis, Dulewicz and Fletcher (1991), which incorporates interaction with the environment and avoids the assertion that there are stable and enduring traits that can be used to predict future behaviour.

> The term personality is all-embracing in terms of the individual's behaviour and the way it is organised and co-ordinated when he or she interacts with the environment.

## The nature of skilled performance and competence

### Skilled performance

Skilled performance is achieved when a person reaches defined standards in the accomplishment of specified tasks. For manual jobs, it is sometimes described as an experienced worker's standard' (EWS). Skilled performance is always measured in terms of what the individual can actually do. The achievement of skilled performance levels is recorded by profiling, which assesses performance in specified skills, such as using a micrometer or word processing, or by reference to predetermined standards or criteria (sometimes called 'criterion-referenced' assessment).

### Competence

Competence can be defined in a number of ways as set out in Chapter 11. Essentially, however, the concept of competence refers to those characteristics of the behaviour of individuals which determine the extent to which they are effective in work roles. It is a term which has become increasingly fashionable in recent years, extending into many aspects of personnel management, especially those concerned with employee development, performance management, job evaluation and reward management. It is also used as the basis for the National Vocational Qualification (NVQ).

## What happens to people over time

Personnel management is continually concerned not only with what people are doing now but also with how they develop over time. These considerations affect employment policies and practices for older workers and the way in which career management programmes are structured (see Chapter 30). The three processes which need to be considered are maturation, development and ageing.

## Maturation

Maturation can be defined as progress towards the achievement of maturity, which means possessing fully developed powers of body and mind. The implication of this definition is that maturation ceases when the optimal development level of a characteristic or trait is reached. Maturation is both physiological and behavioural and occurs through growth and ageing. It is sometimes distinguished from learning, which can be defined as changes due to environment (nurture rather than nature). But the processes of maturing and learning are not independent — the development of behaviour should be regarded as a single, continuous process.

There is, in fact, considerable overlap between the concepts of maturity and development. Maturity can be regarded as a state which people reach because of what they are — their innate and endogenous (ie growing from within) characteristics — and because of what happens to them (their environment). A mature person could therefore be regarded as someone who has reached this state. Development, however, could be described as a continuous process which does not stop when a condition of physical or emotional maturity is reached. Development relies more on experience (or learning) and is concerned with abilities and aptitudes as well as personality.

Maturation can also be described as the achievement of full potential through a process of self-actualization. As Argyris (1957) describes it, from the individuals point of view, self-actualization is achieved when the person is attempting to:

- develop from a state of passivity to one of increased activity as an adult
- develop from a state of dependence to one of independence
- increase his or her skills, abilities and repertoire of behaviours
- develop from having merely short-term perspectives to much longer-term perspectives
- develop from being in a subordinate position to aspiring to be in an equal or superordinate position

- develop from a lack of awareness of self to an awareness and control over oneself as an adult.

This assumes a concept of personality which can mature and develop throughout life — people do not reach a certain level of maturity and then stop. They continue to grow, given the right environment.

## *Development*

Development is a continuous process of change in behaviour and personality which can take place as people get older. It involves maturation, but other changes may occur which could not be regarded as an increase in maturity. Sheehy (1976) has suggested the following stages or 'passages' of adult development:

1. *Pulling up roots* — which occurs in the later teens when the adolescent is striving for independence and freedom. This stage is often characterized by a brash show of confidence and the hiding of fears. It often involves an identity crisis.
2. *The trying 20s* — this is a period of exploration of one's identity. It is characterized by two strong urges: first, to build up a safe and secure base; and second, to experiment and take advantage of opportunities.
3. *Catch-30* — this is a period of reassessment in the early 30s and is characterized by an urge to burst out of the routine which had been established in the 20s. It is a time for reassessing ones career and moving into a more down-to-earth, realistic stage.
4. *The deadline decade* — this starts at about the age of 35 and involves a re-evaluation of the self. It might be described as an authenticity crisis. The earlier sense of independence gives way to a sense of isolation and awful responsibility for ones actions and ones destiny. There is a feeling that 'last chances must be taken now' and the individual may become more self-assertive.
5. *Renewal or resignation* — in the mid-40s stability may eventually be gained either by a process of renewal arising from the previous stage, or by one of resignation because the renewal has not been achieved.

Another model of adult development was conceived by Levinson (1978), who suggested that the 'individual life structure' is shaped by three types of external event:

1. The socio-cultural environment.

2. The roles one plays and the relationships one has.
3. The constraints and opportunities that enable or inhibit people in expressing and developing their personality.

## *Ageing*

It is commonly believed that, as people age, apart from any physical deteriorations, there is a tendency for them to become less flexible, less willing to take on extra responsibilities and slower in learning. But it would be wrong to assume that these changes are inevitable during a person's working life or that every worker will deteriorate (if there is any deterioration at all) at the same rate. Even if, for example, the speed of learning *has* declined, it is quite conceivable that older people will be just as conscientious and determined to learn as their younger colleagues, if not more so. Again, it would be rash to assume that maturity in judgement always increases with age, but there is no reason to suppose that it will inevitably decline.

It is usually found that older people are more satisfied with their jobs — as established by research conducted by Kalleberg and Loscocco (1983) and others. This could be because older people tend to have more rewarding and higher-status jobs. But it is more likely to happen because they become more adjusted to their work and more ready to accept the level they have reached. In other words, their attainments and aspirations have come closer together.

A study of job satisfaction as reported by Robertson and Smith (1985) showed that satisfaction with work tended to increase with age, but that there is a dip in satisfaction in the 40–50 years age group, suggesting that this group is the most difficult to motivate. In particular, satisfaction with promotion prospects falls to very low levels during the ages of 40–50 before rising again, possibly because people over the age of 50 become resigned to the status quo. As Robertson and Smith comment: 'The age distribution within an organization forms an implicit career timetable and people use this timetable to decide whether their own careers are on or off schedule. In one study, managers who saw themselves as "behind time" had more negative attitudes to work than other managers.'

## Sources of social influences on individuals

The sources of influence on individuals are the family, social contacts outside work and the work group. The work group is likely to make the most immediate impact. Socially, people have a strong need to conform to the norms of the group to which they belong. Norms are shared ways of behaving, shared attitudes and beliefs, and shared ways of feeling and perceiving, particularly in relation to the central tasks or activities of the group.

Acceptance of group norms commonly goes through two stages — compliance and internalization. Initially, a group member complies in order not to be rejected by the group, although he or she may behave differently when away from the group. Progressively, however, the individual accepts the norm whether with the group or not — the group norm has been internalized. As noted by Chell (1987), pressure on members to conform can cause problems when:

- there is incompatibility between a member's personal goals and those of the group
- there is no sense of pride from being a member of the group
- the member is not fully integrated with the group
- the price of conformity is too high.

## Attribution theory — how we make judgements about people

The ways in which we perceive and make judgements about people at work are explained by attribution theory, which concerns the assignment of causes to events. We make an attribution when we perceive and describe other people's actions and try to discover why they behaved in the way they did. We can also make attributions about our own behaviour. Heider (1958) has pointed out that: 'In everyday life we form ideas about other people and about social situations. We interpret other peoples' actions and we predict what they will do under certain circumstances.'

In attributing causes to peoples actions we distinguish between what is in the person's power to achieve and the effect of environmental influence. A personal cause, whether someone does well or badly, may, for example, be the amount of effort displayed, while a situational cause may be the extreme difficulty of the task. Kelley (1967) has suggested that there are four criteria which we apply to decide whether behaviour is attributable to personal rather than external (situational) causes:

1. *Distinctiveness* — the behaviour can be distinguished from the behaviour of other people in similar situations.

2. *Consensus* — if other people agree that the behaviour is governed by some personal characteristic.
3. *Consistency over time* — whether the behaviour is repeated.
4. *Consistency over modality* (ie the manner in which things are done) — whether or not the behaviour is repeated in different situations.

Attribution theory is also concerned with the way in which people attribute success or failure to themselves. Research by Weiner (1974) and others has indicated that when people with high achievement needs have been successful they ascribe this to internal factors such as ability and effort. High achievers tend to attribute failure to lack of effort and not lack of ability. Low achievers tend not to link success with effort but to ascribe their failures to lack of ability.

## Behaviour at work

### Factors affecting behaviour

Behaviour at work is dependent on both the personal characteristics of individuals and the situation in which they are working. These factors interact, and this theory of behaviour is sometimes called inter-actionism. It is because of this process of interaction and because there are so many variables in personal characteristics and situations that behaviour is difficult to analyse and predict.

The headings under which personal characteristics can vary have been classified by Mischel (1968) as follows:

- *Competences* — abilities and skills (current definitions of competence as set out in Chapter 11 differ from this one)
- *Constructs* — the conceptual framework which governs how people perceive their environment.
- *Expectations* — what people have learned to expect about their own and others' behaviour.
- *Values* — what people believe to be important.
- *Self-regulatory plans* — the goals people set themselves and the plans they make to achieve them.

Environmental or situational variables include the type of work individuals carry out; the culture, climate and management style in the organization (these cultural organizational features are discussed in Chapter 19); the social group within which individuals work; and the 'reference groups' which individuals use for comparative purposes (eg comparing conditions of work between one category of employee and another).

The behaviour of individuals at work also manifests itself and is affected by the following factors: attitudes, frustration and aggression, stress and resistance to change.

## Attitudes

An attitude can broadly be defined as a settled mode of thinking. Thus, attitudes are developed through experience and then influence behaviour. But they can change as new experiences are gained. Attitude surveys can be used to measure attitudes but, because attitudes vary as a result of situational changes, such measurements cannot be used accurately to predict behaviour. They can indicate, however, where changes to personnel policies and practices may be necessary and can also suggest areas where measures need to be taken by the organization in order to attempt to change attitudes (attitude surveys are discussed in more detail in Chapter 42).

## Frustration and aggression

Frustration occurs when individuals find that they are prevented from achieving their goals which means that their wants and needs are unlikely to be satisfied. Frustration can produce three types of reaction:

1. *Aggression* (fight) as discussed below.
2. *Regression* (flight) — a return to earlier habits.
3. *Fixation* — continuing mechanically and unthinkingly to do the same thing.

According to Lorenz (1966), aggression is a natural instinct. But it is generally held by psychologists that even if there is some instinctive tendency to be aggressive, it is usual for aggression to be either stimulated or learned as an appropriate mode of behaviour.

Aggressive responses to frustrating situations are, in the first place, directed towards whoever causes the frustration. But the aggression may be displaced. Instead of attacking the boss, an individual may take it out on a member of his or her family. Aggression, however, is often whipped up by the individual as it occurs rather than being discharged elsewhere. Aggressive behaviour can be learned. If individuals find that aggression succeeds, they will use it to gain their ends on later occasions.

## Stress

Unfortunately, stress is a feature of organizational life associated with getting work done, relating to other people, and being subjected to change, supervision and the exercise of power.

The main causes of stress are:

- the work itself — over-pressurized; actual or perceived failure
- role in the organization — ambiguity in what is expected of the individual or conflict between what he or she wants to do and can do (role ambiguity)
- poor relationships within the organization — lack of information, little effective consultation, restrictions on behaviour, office politics
- feelings about job or career — lack of job security, over-promotion, or under-promotion
- external pressures — clash between demands made by the organization and those made by the family or other external interests. Home interface problems of excessive hours (why should people be expected by means of cultural pressures to start early and stay late?), lots of travelling, company moves, etc can be extremely stressful and organizations tend to ignore these problems.

### Coping with stress

How people deal with stress depends on their personality, tolerance for ambiguity and ability to live with change. Some people revel in highly pressurized jobs. Others cannot cope. Motivation is also an influence and can act as a form of pressure. People can be too highly motivated and pressure becomes stress when they cannot achieve what they set out or are expected to do.

Stress can be coped with through adaptive behaviour. An overworked manager may adapt successfully by delegating some work, but someone else may accept the overload with the result that his performance deteriorates. As Torrington and Cooper (1977) point out, managers who adapt successfully to role ambiguity will seek clarification with their superior or colleagues, but managers who cannot adapt will withdraw from some aspect of their work role.

Approaches to managing stress in organizations are discussed in Chapter 43.

## Resistance to change

People resist change because it is seen as a threat to familiar patterns of behaviour as well as to status and financial rewards. Joan Woodward (1968), made this point clearly:

> When we talk about resistance to change we tend to imply that management is always rational in changing its direction, and that employees are stupid, emotional or irrational in not responding in the way they should. But if an individual is going to be worse off, explicitly or implicitly, when the proposed changes have been made, any resistance is entirely rational in terms of his own best interest. The interests of the organization and the individual do not always coincide.

Specifically, the main reasons for resisting change are as follows:

- *The shock of the new* — people are suspicious of anything which they perceive will upset their established routines, methods of working or conditions of employment. They do not want to lose the security of what is familiar to them. They may not believe statements by management that the change is for their benefit as well as that of the organization; sometimes with good reason. They may feel that management has ulterior motives and sometimes, the louder the protestations of managements, the less they will be believed. Economic fears — loss of money, threats to job security.
- *Inconvenience* — the change will make life more difficult.
- *Uncertainty* — change can be worrying because of uncertainty about its likely impact.
- *Symbolic fears* — a small change which may affect some treasured symbol, such as a separate office or a reserved parking space, may symbolize big changes, especially when employees are uncertain about how extensive the programme of change will be.
- *Threat to interpersonal relationships* — anything that disrupts the customary social relationships and standards of the group will be resisted.
- *Threat to status or skill* — the change is perceived as reducing the status of individuals or as deskilling them.
- *Competence fears* — concern about the ability to cope with new demands or to acquire new skills.

Techniques of managing change are discussed in Chapter 22.

## Orientation to work

Orientation theory examines the factors which are instrumental, ie serve as a means, in directing peoples choices about work. An orientation is a central organizing principle which underlies peoples attempts to make sense of their lives. In relation to work, as defined by Guest (1984) : 'An orientation is a persisting tendency to seek certain goals and rewards from work which exists independently of the nature of the work and the work content.' The orientation approach stresses the role of the social environment factor as a key factor affecting motivation.

Orientation theory is primarily developed from fieldwork carried out by sociologists rather than from laboratory work conducted by psychologists. Goldthorpe *et al* (1968) studied skilled and semi-skilled workers in Luton, and, in their findings they stressed the importance of instrumental orientation, that is, a view of work as a means to an end, a context in which to earn money to purchase goods and leisure. According to Goldthorpe, the 'affluent' worker interviewed by the research team valued work largely for extrinsic reasons:

> Considerations of pay and security appear most powerful in binding men to their present job. Workers in all groups within our sample tend to be particularly motivated to increase their power as consumers and their domestic standard of living, rather than their satisfaction as producers and the degree of their self-fulfilment in work.

He went on to emphasize the economic returns as the key factor:

> The workers have in effect chosen in favour of work which enables them to achieve a higher level of economic return ... a decision has been made to give more weight to the *instrumental* at the expense of the expressive aspects of work.

However, it was recognized that while pay may be the dominant factor in the choice of employer, or a decision to remain with that employer, there is no evidence that the level of pay determined the degree of satisfaction with the work itself.

In their research carried out with blue-collar workers in Peterborough, Blackburn and Mann (1979) found a wider range of orientations. They suggested that different ones could come into play with varying degrees of force in different situations. The fact that workers, in practice, had little choice about what they did contributed to this diversity — their orientations were affected by the choice or lack of choice presented to them and this meant that they might be forced to accept alternative orientations.

But Blackburn and Mann confirmed that pay was a key preference area, the top preferences being:

279

1. Pay
2. Security
3. Workmates
4. Intrinsic job satisfaction
5. Autonomy.

They commented that: 'An obsession with wages clearly emerged.... A concern to minimise unpleasant work was also widespread.' Surprisingly, perhaps, they also revealed that the most persistent preference of all was for outside work, 'a fairly clear desire for a combination of fresh air and freedom'.

## Roles

When faced with any situation, eg carrying out a job, people have to enact a role in order to manage that situation. This is sometimes called the 'situation-act model'. As described by Chell (1985), the model indicates that: 'The person must act within situations: situations are rule-governed and how a person behaves is often prescribed by these socially acquired rules. The person thus adopts a suitable role in order to perform effectively within the situation.'

At work, the term *role* describes the part to be played by individuals in fulfilling their job requirements. Roles therefore indicate the specific forms of behaviour required to carry out a particular task or the group of tasks contained in a *position* or job. Work role definitions primarily define the requirements in terms of the ways tasks are carried out rather than the tasks themselves. They may refer to broad aspects of behaviour, especially with regard to working with others and styles of management. The concept of a role emphasizes the fact that people at work are, in a sense, always acting a part, they are not simply reciting the lines but are interpreting them in terms of their own perceptions of how they should behave in relation to the context in which they work, especially with regard to their interactions with other people.

The role individuals occupy at work — and elsewhere — therefore exists in relation to other people — their *role set*. These people have expectations about the individuals' role, and if they live up to these expectations they will have successfully performed the role. Performance in a role is a product of the situation individuals are in (the organizational context and the direction or influence exercised from above or elsewhere in the organization) and their own skills, competences, attitudes and personality. Situational factors are important, but the role individuals perform can both shape and reflect their personalities. Stress and inadequate performance result when roles are ambiguous, incompatible, or in conflict with one another.

## Role ambiguity

When individuals are unclear about what their role is, what is expected of them, or how they are getting on, they may become insecure or lose confidence in themselves.

## Role incompatibility

Stress and poor performance may be caused by roles having incompatible elements, for example, when there is a clash between what other people expect from the role and what individuals believe is expected of them.

## Role conflict

Role conflict results when, even if roles are clearly defined and there is no incompatibility between expectations, individuals have to carry out two antagonistic roles. For example, conflict can exist between the roles of individuals at work and their roles at home.

## Implications for personnel specialists

The main implications for personnel specialists of the factors which affect individuals at work are as follows:

- *Individual differences* — when designing jobs, preparing training programmes, assessing and counselling staff, developing reward systems and dealing with grievances and disciplinary problems, it is necessary to remember that all people are different. What fulfils one person may not fulfil another. Abilities, aptitudes and intelligence differ widely and it is necessary to take particular care in fitting the right people in the right jobs and giving them the right training. The definitions contained in the section on individual differences in this chapter provide useful points of reference when preparing person specifications (see also Chapter 24). Personalities should not be judged simplistically in terms of stereotyped traits. People are complex and they change, and account has to be taken of this. The problem for personnel specialists and managers in general is that, while they have to accept and understand these differences and take full account of them, they have ultimately to proceed on the basis of fitting them to the requirements of the situation, which are essentially what the organization needs to achieve. There is always a limit to the extent to which an organization which relies on collective effort to achieve its goals can adjust itself to the specific needs of individuals. However, the organization has to appreciate that the pressures it makes on people can result in stress and therefore can become counter-productive.

- *Skilled performance and competence* — the need is for personnel specialists to be capable, first, of defining and measuring standards of performance and competence and then, of preparing recruitment, employment, training and development programmes which take account of these definitions and measures.

- *What happens to people over time* — in structuring employment policies and career development programmes, it is necessary to bear in mind the impacts of the processes of maturation, development and ageing. It should not be assumed that performance at work inevitably declines with age.

- *Social influences* — it is always necessary to remember that at work, as elsewhere, people are constantly subject to the influence of others. Whatever plans we make to motivate or influence individuals, they are always under pressure to conform to the norms of the group to which they belong. And the more cohesive the group, the more powerful the pressure. This can sometimes be a good thing from the viewpoint of the organization if the pressure is not unreasonably high and is directed at achieving desirable work standards. But groups can work against the interests of the organization in defending their own cohesion and they can exert undesirable pressure on individuals to conform. The extent to which individuals resist group pressures will vary considerably so that, as ever, it is not possible to generalize about the motives or behavioural influences on people.

- *Judgements about people* (attribution theory) — we all ascribe motives to other people and attempt to establish the causes of their behaviour. We must be careful, however, not to make simplistic judgements about causality (ie what has motivated someone's behaviour — for ourselves as well as in respect of others — especially when we are assessing performance).

- *Behaviour at work* — it is helpful to analyse attitudes by the use of some form of attitude survey. We must be aware, however, that we cannot predict what the attitudes are likely to be in the future and we should bear in mind that, although it is possible to change attitudes, this can be a difficult and long haul, especially when they are deep-seated, as they often are. An understanding of the causes of aggression and the effects of frustration should help us to deal with conflict and misbehaviour at work. Resistance to change as a natural phenomenon should be recognized and anticipated in change management programmes.

- *Orientation theory* - the significance of orientation theory is that it stresses the importance of the effect of environmental factors on the motivation to work.
- *Role theory* — role theory helps us to understand the need to clarify with individuals what is expected of them in behavioural terms and to ensure when designing jobs that they do not contain any incompatible elements. We must also be aware of the potential for role conflict so that steps can be taken to minimize stress.

# 15

# The Nature of Work, the Employment Relationship and the Psychological Contract

## The nature of work

Work is the exertion of effort and the application of knowledge and skills to achieve a purpose. Most people work to earn a living — to make money. But they also work because of the other satisfactions it brings, such as doing something worthwhile, a sense of achievement, prestige, recognition, the opportunity to use and develop abilities, the scope to exercise power, and companionship. Within organizations, the nature of the work carried out by individuals and what they feel about it is governed by the employment relationship and the psychological contract as discussed later in this chapter.

### The future of work

Charles Handy suggested some time ago (1984) that future developments in the nature of work would include:

- many more people than at present not working in an organization — an increase in outworkers and subcontracting facilitated by information technology in the shape of computer networks and electronic mail; shorter working hours
- fewer mammoth bureaucracies, more federal organizations and more small businesses
- more requirements for specialists and professionals in organizations

- more importance given to the informal, uncounted economy of the home and the community
- a manufacturing sector that is smaller in terms of people but larger in terms of output
- a smaller working population and a larger dependent population
- a greatly increased demand for education, often provided by distance learning
- new forms of social organization to complement the employment organization.

Certainly, Handy's forecasts have become actualities in such areas as a vast increase in the use of part-timers, a marked propensity for organizations to sub-contract work and to outsource services, and a greater requirement for specialists (knowledge workers) and professionals in organizations. Projections made by Business Strategies (BSL) in 1995 as reported by Coyle (1996) indicated that in ten years' time nearly half the work force would be covered by 'flexible' arrangements such as temporary contracts, self employment and part-time jobs. This will include 2.5 million people in short-term employment by 2005, a million more than in 1995. The BSL research confirmed that most part-timers and temporary workers are women, but most of those in self-employment are men. Men also account for the bulk of the new growth in temporary jobs.

Under the pressures to be competitive and to achieve 'cost leadership', organizations are not only 'downsizing' but are also engaging people on short-term contracts and make no pretence that they are there to provide careers. They want specific contributions to achieving organizational goals now and, so far as people are concerned, they may let the future take care of itself, believing that they can purchase the talent required as and when necessary. This may be short-sighted, but it is the way many businesses now operate.

When preparing and implementing human resource plans, personnel practitioners need to be aware of these factors and trends within the context of their internal and external environments. A further factor which affects the way in which the labour market operates and therefore human resource planning decisions is unemployment.

## Unemployment

As Hutton (1995) commented: 'For two decades unemployment has been a grim fact of British life, bearing particularly hard on men ...

One in four of the country's males of working age is now either officially unemployed or idle, with incalculable consequences for our well-being and social cohesion'. High levels of unemployment are not a British phenomenon. They exist throughout Europe — France, for example has a higher rate of youth unemployment than Britain — and indeed the world. But that is no consolation.

Economists seem unable to agree on the causes of or cures for unemployment (or anything else it seems). The essence of the Keynsian explanation is that firms demand too little labour because individuals demand too few goods. The classical view was that unemployment was voluntary and could be cleared by natural market forces. The neoclassical theory is that there is a natural rate of unemployment which reflects a given rate of technology, individual preferences and endowments. With flexible wages in a competitive labour market, wages adjust to clear the market and any unemployment that remains is voluntary. The latter view was that held by Milton Friedman and strongly influenced Conservative policy in the early 1980s. There is, of course, no simple explanation of unemployment and no simple solution. All that appears to be certain is that unemployment will continue at a high level, especially if the main thrust of economic policy is to keep down the rates of inflation.

## Career expectations

It is often said that the days of the life-long career are over, especially for white collared workers and that the job security which they previously enjoyed no longer exists. Although downsizing and delayering may have increased the risk to executives and administrative staff of being made redundant, data from the Department of Education and Employment as quoted by Elliott (1996) shows that in the decade between 1985 and 1995 there was very little change in the average length of job tenure. For men, it was down a fraction, for women, it was actually up a little. Burgess and Rees (1996) established that between 1975 and 1992 there was a fall of around 10 per cent in the length of time spent on a job. But they commented that: 'The data emphatically do not support the view that the dramatic changes in the labour market, technology and competition, have spelt the end of "jobs for life".'

## The nature of the employment relationship

The starting point of the employment relationship is an undertaking by an employee to provide skill and effort to the employer in return for which the employer provides the employee with a salary or a wage. Initially the relationship is founded on a legal contract. This may be a written contract but the absence of such a contract does not mean that no contractual relationship exists. Employers and employees still have certain implied legal rights and obligations. The employer's obligations include the duty to pay salary or wages, provide a safe workplace, to act in good faith towards the employee and not to act in such a way as to undermine the trust and confidence of the employment relationship. The employee has corresponding obligations, which include obedience, competence, honesty and loyalty.

An important factor to remember about the employment relationship is that generally, it is the employer who has the power to dictate the contractual terms unless they have been fixed by collective bargaining. Individuals, except when they are much in demand, have little scope to vary the terms of the contract imposed upon them by employers.

Two types of contracts defining the employment relationship have been distinguished by MacNeil (1985) and Rousseau and Wade-Benzoni (1994):

- *Transactional contracts,* which have well-described terms of exchange which are usually expressed financially. They are of limited duration with specified performance requirements.
- *Relational contracts,* which are less well-defined with more abstract terms and refer to an open-ended membership of the organisation. Performance requirements attached to this continuing membership are incomplete or ambiguous.

However, the employment relationships can also be expressed in terms of a *psychological contract* which, according to Guzzo and Noonan (1994), has both transactional and relational qualities. The concept of a psychological contract expresses the view that at its most basic level the employment relationship consists of a unique combination of beliefs held by an individual and his or her employer about what they expect of one another. In this chapter the concept of a psychological contract is defined and its nature and development are described. This is followed by a discussion of the significance of the employment relationship. The chapter concludes with an examination of the factors affecting the management of the employment relationship and the influence that can be exerted by the personnel function on the psychological contract.

## The psychological contract defined

The psychological contract is the set of reciprocal but unwritten expectations which exist between individual employees and their employers. As defined by Schein (1965):

> The notion of a psychological contract implies that there is an unwritten set of expectations operating at all times between every member of an organisation and the various managers and others in that organization.

This definition was amplified by Rousseau and Wade-Benzoni (1994) who stated that:

> Psychological contracts refer to beliefs that individuals hold regarding promises made, accepted and relied upon between themselves and another. (In the case of organizations, these parties include an employee, client, manager, and/or organization as a whole.) Because psychological contracts represent how people *interpret* promises and commitments, both parties in the same employment relationship (employer and employee) can have different views regarding specific terms.

Within organizations, as Katz and Kahn (1964) pointed out, every role is basically a set of behavioural expectations. These expectations are often implicit — they are not defined in the employment contract. Basic models of motivation — expectancy theory (Vroom, 1964) and operant conditioning (Skinner, 1974) — maintain that employees behave in ways they expect will produce positive outcomes. But they do not necessarily know what to expect. As Rousseau and Greller (1994) comment:

> The ideal contract in employment would detail expectations of both employee and employer. Typical contracts, however, are incomplete due to bounded rationality which limits individual information seeking, and to a changing organisational environment that makes it impossible to specify all conditions up front. Both employee and employer are left to fill up the blanks.

Employees may expect to be treated fairly as human beings, to be provided with work which uses their abilities, to be rewarded equitably in accordance with their contribution, to be able to display competence, to have opportunities for further growth, to know what is expected of them and to be given feedback (preferably positive) on how they are doing. Employers may expect employees to do their best on behalf of the organization — 'to put themselves out for the company' — to be fully committed to its values, to be compliant and loyal, and to enhance the image of the organisation with its customers and suppliers. Sometimes these assumptions are justified — often they are not. Mutual misunderstandings can cause friction and stress and lead to recriminations and poor performance, or to a termination of the employment relationship.

## The basic nature of the psychological contract

A psychological contract is a system of beliefs which encompasses, on the one hand, the actions employees believe are expected of them and what response they expect in return from their employer and, on the other, the behaviour employers expect from their employees. It creates attitudes and emotions which form and govern behaviour. A psychological contract is implicit. It is also dynamic — it develops over time.

The psychological contract may provide some indication of the answers to the two fundamental employment relationship questions which individuals pose: 'What can I reasonably expect from the organization?' and ' What should I reasonably be expected to contribute in return?' But it is unlikely that the psychological contract and therefore the employment relationship will ever be fully understood by either party.

The aspects of the employment relationship covered by the psychological contact will include from the employee's point of view:

- how they are treated in terms of fairness, equity and consistency
- security of employment
- scope to demonstrate competence
- career expectations and the opportunity to develop skills
- involvement and influence
- trust in the organization to keep its promises.

From the employer's point of view, the psychological contact covers such aspects of the employment relationship as:

- competence
- effort
- compliance
- commitment
- loyalty.

Some interesting insights into the nature of the psychological contract were provided by the IPD/Templeton College research conducted in 1995. This revealed that:

- 65 per cent of respondents felt that they had a lot of direct involvement in deciding how to do their jobs and organize their work
- 40 per cent had a lot of loyalty to their company
- 26 per cent trusted their company a good deal to keep its promises to employees.

## The changing nature of the psychological contract

The nature of the psychological contract is changing in many organizations in response to changes in their external and internal environments — the impact of global competition and the effect this has had on how businesses operate and are organized to become, for example, 'lean and mean'.

As Baillie (1995) has suggested:

> For the last 50 years the psychological contract was not an issue. People knew what to expect — you turned up to work, did what was required, and the organization provided security and development. It was not a complicated relationship, and for most organizations it worked well, providing them with a loyal, committed and dependable workforce.

But the psychological contract has not been an issue because it usually did not change much. This is no longer the case. Research commissioned by the IPD and conducted by the Harris Research Centre (IPD and Templeton College, 1995) established through 1006 telephone interviews that the proportion of employees affected by various changes were as follows:

- redundancy/layoffs — 57%
- introduction of new technology — 85%
- introduction of new working practices — 79%
- takeover/merger — 30%
- restructuring — 75%

Kissler (1994) summed up the differences between old and new employment contracts as follows:

### The Nature of Work

| Old | New |
|---|---|
| • Relationship is pre-determined and imposed | Relationship is mutual and negotiated |
| • You are who you work for and what you do | You are defined by multiple roles, many external to the organisation |
| • Loyalty is defined by performance | Loyalty is defined by output and quality |
| • Leaving is treason | People and skills only needed when required |
| • Employees who do what they are told will work until retirement | Long-term employment is unlikely, expect and prepare for multiple relationships. |

Perhaps one of the most important changes which has been taking place to the employment relationship as expressed by the psychological contract is that employees are now being required to bear risks which were previously carried by the organisation. As Elliott (1996) notes: 'The most profound change in the labour market over the past two decades has been the massive shift in power from employee to employer. This has not only meant that workers have had their rights eroded, but also that much of the risk involved in a business has been shifted from capital to labour.'

## How psychological contracts develop

Psychological contracts are not developed by means of a single transaction. There are many contract makers who exert influence over the whole duration of an employee's involvement with an organization. As Spindler (1994) comments:

> Every day we create relationships by means other than formal contracts ... As individuals form relationships they necessarily bring their accumulated experience and developed personalities with them. In ways unknown to them what they expect from the relationship reflects the sum total of their conscious and unconscious learning to date.

The problem with psychological contracts is that employees are often unclear about what they want from the organisation or what they can contribute to it. Some employees are equally unclear about what they expect from their employees.

Because of these factors, and because a psychological contract is essentially implicit, it is likely to develop in an unplanned way with unforeseen consequences. Anything that management does or is perceived as doing which affects the interests of employees will modify the psychological contract. Similarly the actual or perceived behaviour of employees, individually or collectively, will affect an employer's concept of the contract.

## The significance of the psychological contract

As suggested by Spindler (1994): 'A psychological contract creates emotions and attitudes which form and control behaviour'. The significance of the psychological contract was further explained by Sims (1994) as follows:

> A balanced psychological contract is necessary for a continuing, harmonious relationship between the employee and the organisation. However, the violation of the psychological contract can signal to the participants that the parties no longer shared (or never shared) a common set of values or goals.

The concept highlights the fact that employee/employer expectations take the form of unarticulated assumptions. Disappointments on the part of management as well as employees may therefore be inevitable. These disappointments can, however, be alleviated if managements appreciate that one of their key roles is to manage expectations, which means clarifying what they believe employees should achieve, the competences they should possess and the values they should uphold. And this is a matter not just of articulating these requirements but of discussing and agreeing them with individuals and teams.

The psychological contract governs the continuing development of the employment relationship, which is constantly evolving over time. But how the contract is developing and the impact it makes may not be fully understood by any of the parties involved. As Spindler (1994) comments:

> In a psychological contract the rights and obligations of the parties have not been articulated much less agreed to. The parties do not express their expectations and, in fact, may be quite incapable of doing so.

People who have no clear idea about what they expect may, if such unexpressed expectations have not been fulfilled, have no clear idea why they have been disappointed. But they will be aware that something does not feel right.

## Managing the employment relationship

The dynamic and often nebulous nature of a psychological contract increases the difficulty of managing the employment relationship. The problem is compounded because of the multiplicity of the factors which influence the contract — the culture of the organisation, the prevailing management style, the values, espoused and practised, of top management, day-to-day interactions between employees and line managers, and the personnel policies and practices of the business.

The latter are particularly important. The nature of the employment relationship is formed by personnel actions. These cover all aspects of personnel and development management. But the way in which people are treated in such areas as recruitment, performance reviews, promotion, career development, reward, involvement and participation, grievance handling, disciplinary procedures and redundancy will be particularly important. How people are required to carry out their work (including flexibility and multiskilling), how performance expectations are expressed and communicated, how work is organised and how people are managed will also make a significant impact on the employment relationship.

By definition, a psychological contract is implied and inferred rather than stated and agreed. It also evolves over time. Managing the employment relationship cannot therefore simply be a matter of spelling out the psychological contract. However, the personnel function can make a major contribution to shaping the psychological contract and developing a more productive employment relationship in the following ways:

- during *recruitment interviews* — presenting the unfavourable as well as the favourable aspects of a job in a 'realistic job preview'
- in *induction programmes* — communicating to new starters the organisation's personnel policies and procedures and its core values, indicating to them the standards of performance expected in such areas as quality and customer service, and spelling out requirements for flexibility
- by issuing and updating *employee handbooks* which reinforce the messages delivered in induction programmes

- by developing *performance management* processes which ensure that performance expectations are agreed and reviewed regularly
- by encouraging the use of *personal development plans* which spell out how continuous improvement of performance can be achieved, mainly by self-managed learning
- by using *training and management development programmes* to under-pin core values and define performance expectations
- by ensuring through *manager and team leader training* that managers and team leaders understand their role in managing the employment relationship through such processes as performance management and team leadership
- by encouraging the maximum amount of *contact* between managers and team leaders and their team members to achieve mutual understanding of expectations and to provide a means of two-way communications
- by adopting a general policy of *transparency* — ensuring that on all matters which affect them, employees know what is happening, why it is happening and the impact it will make on their employment, development and prospects
- by developing *personnel procedures* covering grievance handling, discipline, equal opportunities, promotion and redundancy and ensuring that they are implemented fairly and consistently
- by developing and communicating *personnel policies* covering the major areas of employment, development, reward and employee relations
- by ensuring that the *reward system* is developed and managed to achieve equity, fairness and consistency in all aspects of pay and benefits.

These approaches to managing the employment relationship cover all aspects of people management. It is important to remember, however, that this is a continuous process. The effective management of the relationship means ensuring that values are upheld and that a transparent, consistent and fair approach is adopted in dealing with all aspects of employment.

# 16

# Motivation

All organizations are concerned with what should be done to achieve sustained high levels of performance through people. This means giving close attention to how individuals can best be motivated through such means as incentives, rewards, leadership and, importantly, the work they do and the organization context within which they carry out that work. The aim, of course, is to develop motivation processes and a work environment which will help to ensure that individuals deliver results in accordance with the expectations of management.

Motivation theory examines the process of motivation. It explains why people at work behave in the way they do in terms of their efforts and the directions they are taking. It also describes what organizations can do to encourage people to apply their efforts and abilities in ways which will further the achievement of the organization's goals as well as satisfying their own needs.

Unfortunately, approaches to motivation are too often underpinned by simplistic assumptions about how it works. The process of motivation is much more complex than many people believe and motivational practices are most likely to function effectively if they are based on proper understanding of what is involved. This chapter therefore:

- defines motivation
- offers a somewhat simplified explanation of the basic process of motivation
- describes the two basic types of motivation; intrinsic and extrinsic
- explores in greater depth the various theories of motivation which explain and amplify the basic process
- examines the practical implications of the motivation theories.

## Definition of motivation

Motivation is inferred from or defined by goal-directed behaviour. It is concerned with the strength and direction of that behaviour.

Motivation takes place when people expect that a course of action is likely to lead to the attainment of a goal and a valued reward — one which satisfies their particular needs

Well-motivated people are those with clearly defined goals who take action which they expect will achieve those goals. They make effective contributions at work because of strongly developed feelings of behavioural commitment — they acknowledge that their efforts are required to further both the needs of the organization and their own interests.

## The process of motivation

The process of motivation can be modelled as shown in Figure 16.1. This is a needs-related model and it suggests that motivation is initiated by the conscious or unconscious recognition of unsatisfied needs. These needs create wants, which are desires to achieve or obtain something. Goals are then established which it is believed will satisfy these needs and wants and a behaviour pathway is selected which it is expected will achieve the goal. If the goal is achieved the need will be satisfied and the behaviour is likely to be repeated the next time a similar need emerges. If the goal is not achieved the same action is less likely to be repeated.

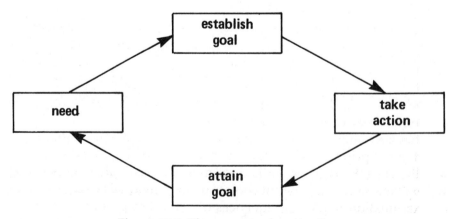

**Figure 16.1** The process of motivation

This model describes in a somewhat over-simplified form how individual motivation takes place. It is based on the motivational theories related to needs, goals and expectancy, as described later in this chapter. It is also influenced by three concepts relating to motivation and behaviour: reinforcement, homeostasis and open-systems theory.

From an organizational point of view, the model can be used to illustrate a process of motivation which involves setting goals that are likely to meet individual needs and wants, and encouraging the behaviour required to achieve those goals.

## Reinforcement

As experience is gained in taking action to satisfy needs, people perceive that certain actions help to achieve their goals while others are less successful. Some actions bring rewards; others result in failure or even punishment. Reinforcement theory as developed by Hull (1951) suggests that successes in achieving goals and rewards act as positive incentives and reinforce the successful behaviour which is repeated the next time a similar need emerges. The more powerful, obvious and frequent the reinforcement, the more likely it is that the behaviour will be repeated until, eventually, it can become a more or less unconscious reaction to an event. Conversely, failures or punishments provide negative reinforcement, suggesting that it is necessary to seek alternative means of achieving goals. This process has been called the law of effect.

The degree to which experience shapes future behaviour does, of course, depend, first, on the extent to which individuals correctly perceive the connection between the behaviour and its outcome and, second, on the extent to which they are able to recognize the resemblance between the previous situation and the one that now confronts them. Perceptive ability varies between people as does the ability to identify correlations between events. For these reasons, some people are better at learning from experience than others, just as some people are more easily motivated than others.

It has been suggested that behavioural theories based on the law of effect or the principle of reinforcement are limited because they imply, in Allport's (1954) phrase, a 'hedonism of the past'. They assume that the explanation of the present choices of an individual is to be found in an examination of the consequences of his or her past choices. Insufficient attention is paid in the theories to the influence of expectations, and no indication is given of any means of distinguishing in advance the class of outcomes which would strengthen responses and those which would weaken them.

## Homeostasis

The human organism, like all other living organisms, is constantly in a state of disequilibrium. It expends energy to stay alive and must replenish this energy. Automatic mechanisms exist to maintain a normal body temperature. This is called the homeostatic principle and it underlies all behaviour and motivation. The drive to satisfy unsatisfied needs is actuated by the constant move towards equilibrium.

Another concept which has some affinity with the principle of homeostasis is the desire to master one's immediate environment. Individuals subjectively organize their environment by reference to past experience, present needs and future expectations. This develops into a pattern which is taken for granted until some external influence affects it. The individual then engages in interpretative or problem-solving activity in an attempt to absorb or resist the change.

## Open-system theory

Open-system theory was originally formulated by Von Bertalanffy (1952), who wrote:

A living organism is an open-system which continually gives up matter to the outer world and takes in matter from it, but which maintains itself in the continuous exchange in a steady state.

Allport (1960) further developed this definition by setting out the following features of an open system:

- intake and output of both matter and energy
- achievement and maintenance of steady (homeostatic) states so that the intrusion of outer energy will not seriously disrupt internal form and order
- increase in order over time owing to an increase in complexity and differentiation of parts
- extensive transactional commerce with the environment.

The concept was developed by Lawrence and Lorsch (1969), who suggested that an individual can usefully be conceived as a system of biological needs, psychological motives, values and perceptions. The individual's system operates so as to maintain its internal balance in the face of the demands placed upon it by external forces and it develops in response to his or her basic needs to solve the problems presented by the external environment. But each individual system will have unique characteristics because, as Lawrence and Lorsch say:

1. Different individual systems develop with different patterns of needs, values and perceptions.
2. Individual systems are not static, but continue to develop as they encounter new problems and experiences.

## Intrinsic and extrinsic motivation

Motivation at work can take place in two ways. First, people can motivate themselves by seeking, finding and carrying out work (or being given work) which satisfies their needs or at least leads them to expect that their goals will be achieved. Secondly, people can be motivated by management through such methods as pay, promotion, praise, etc.

These two types of motivation can be described as:

- *Intrinsic motivation* — the self-generated factors which influence people to behave in a particular way or to move in a particular direction..These factors include responsibility (feeling that the work is important and having control over one's own resources), freedom to act, scope to use and develop skills and abilities, interesting and challenging work and opportunities for advancement.
- *Extrinsic motivation* — what is done to or for people to motivate them. This includes rewards, such as increased pay, praise, or promotion, and punishments, such as disciplinary action, withholding pay, or criticism.

Extrinsic motivators can have an immediate and powerful effect, but it will not necessarily last long. The intrinsic motivators, which are concerned with the 'quality of working life' (a phrase and movement which emerged from this concept), are likely to have a deeper and longer-term effect because they are inherent in individuals and not imposed from outside.

## Motivation theories

The process of motivation as described above is broadly based on a number of motivation theories which attempt to explain in more detail what it is all about. These theories have proliferated over the years. Some of them, like the crude 'instrumentality' theory which was the first to be developed, have largely been discredited, at least in psychological circles, although they still underpin the beliefs of some managers about motivation and pay systems (instrumentality theory is described below).

Immensely popular and influential motivation theories which were produced by Maslow (1954), and Herzberg (1957), have been severely criticized, although they are still regarded by many people as *the* motivation theories. A number of other significant and more convincing theories have been developed over the years and in their different ways they help us to appreciate the complexity of the process of motivation and the futility of believing that there are any easy or quick answers to motivating anybody.

The following leading motivation theories are summarized in the next sections of this chapter:

- *instrumentality theory* — based largely on the writings of Taylor (1911)
- *needs or content theory* — as developed by Maslow (1954), Alderfer (1972) and McClelland (1975)
- *process or cognitive theory* — which is concerned with the psychological processes or forces which influence motivation as affected by people's perceptions of their working environment and the ways in which they interpret and understand it — this embraces expectancy theory, goal theory, reactance theory and equity theory
- *Herzberg's (1957)* — two factor (motivation-hygiene) theory
- *behavioural theory*
- *social-learning theory* — as developed by Bandura (1977)
- *attribution theory*
- *role-modelling theory*

## Instrumentality theory

'Instrumentality' is the belief that if we do one thing it will lead to another. In its crudest form, instrumentality theory states that people only work for money.

The theory emerged in the second half of the nineteenth century with its emphasis on the need to rationalize work and on economic outcomes. It assumes that a person will be motivated to work if rewards and penalties are tied directly to his or her performance; thus the awards are contingent upon effective performance. Instrumentality theory has its roots in the scientific management methods of Taylor (1911), who wrote: 'It is impossible, through any long period of time, to get workmen to work much harder than the average men around them unless they are assured a large and permanent increase in their pay.'

This theory is based on the principle of reinforcement and the so-called law of effect as described earlier in this chapter (page 297). Motivation using this approach has been, and still is, widely adopted and can be successful in some circumstances. But it is based exclusively on a system of external controls and fails to recognize a number of other human needs. It also fails to appreciate the fact that the formal control system can be seriously affected by the informal relationship existing between workers.

## Needs (content) theory

The basis of this theory is the belief that an unsatisfied need creates tension and a state of disequilibrium. To restore the balance a goal is identified which will satisfy the need, and a behaviour pathway is selected which will lead to the achievement of the goal. All behaviour is therefore motivated by unsatisfied needs.

Not all needs are equally important for a person at any one time — some may provide a much more powerful drive towards a goal than others, depending on the individual's background and present situation. Complexity is further increased because there is no simple relationship between needs and goals. The same need can be satisfied by a number of different goals and the stronger the need and the longer its duration, the broader the range of possible goals. At the same time, one goal may satisfy a number of needs — a new car provides transport as well as an opportunity to impress the neighbours.

Needs theory has been developed by:

- *Maslow* (1954), who developed the concept of a hierarchy of needs which he believed were fundamental to the personality.
- *Alderfer* (1972), who produced a simpler and more flexible model of three basic needs (ERG theory).
- *McClelland* (1975), who identified three needs which motivate managers, and who, while agreeing with Maslow that needs motives are part of the personality, believed they are triggered off by environmental factors.

These theories are described below. In addition, Herzberg (1957) postulated a two-factor model of needs in order to identify those aspects of
the work environment which motivate people. His approach is
described on pages 304 to 306 of this chapter.

## Maslow's hierarchy of needs

The most famous classification of needs is the one formulated by
Maslow (1954). He suggested that there are five major need categories
which apply to people in general, starting from the fundamental
physiological needs and leading through a hierarchy of safety, social
and esteem needs to the need for self-fulfilment, the highest need of all.
Maslow's hierarchy is as follows:

1. *Physiological* — the need for oxygen, food, water and sex.
2. *Safety* — the need for protection against danger and the depriva-
   tion of physiological needs.
3. *Social* — the need for love, affection and acceptance as belonging to
   a group.
4. *Esteem* — the need to have a stable, firmly based, high evaluation of
   oneself (self-esteem) and to have the respect of others (prestige).
   These needs may be classified into two subsidiary sets: first, the
   desire for achievement, for adequacy, for confidence in the face of
   the world, and for independence and freedom, and, second, the
   desire for reputation or status defined as respect or esteem from
   other people, and manifested by recognition, attention, importance, or appreciation.
5. *Self-fulfilment (self-actualization)* — the need to develop potentiali-
   ties and skills, to become what one believes one is capable of
   becoming.

Maslow's theory of motivation states that when a lower need is satisfied the next highest becomes dominant and the individual's attention
is turned to satisfying this higher need. The need for self-fulfilment,
however, can never be satisfied. He said that 'man is a wanting animal';
only an unsatisfied need can motivate behaviour and the dominant
need is the prime motivator of behaviour. Psychological development
takes place as people move up the hierarchy of needs, but this is not
necessarily a straightforward progression. The lower needs still exist,
even if temporarily dormant as motivators, and individuals constantly
return to previously satisfied needs.

One of the implications of Maslow's theory is that the higher order needs for esteem and self-fulfilment provide the greatest impetus to motivation — they grow in strength when they are satisfied, while the lower needs decline in strength on satisfaction. But the jobs people do will not necessarily satisfy their needs, especially when they are routine or deskilled.

Maslow's needs hierarchy has an intuitive appeal and has been very influential. But it has not been verified by empirical research and it has been criticized for its apparent rigidity — different people may have different priorities and it is difficult to accept that people's needs progress steadily up the hierarchy. In fact, Maslow himself expressed doubts about the validity of a strictly ordered hierarchy.

## Alderfer's ERG theory

ERG theory (the needs for existence, relatedness and growth), as formulated by Alderfer (1972), is about the subjective states of satisfaction and desire. Satisfaction concerns the outcome of events between people and their environment. It is a subjective reaction which refers to the internal state of people who have obtained what they are seeking and is synonymous with getting and fulfilling. Desire is even more subjective because it refers exclusively to the internal state of a person related to needs, wants, preferences and motives. ERG theory adopts an 'open system' approach as described on pages 298–9 to understanding the human personality.

From this basis, Alderfer devised a theory of human needs which postulated three primary categories:

1.  *Existence needs,* which reflect the requirement people have for material and energy exchange and the need to reach and maintain a homeo-static equilibrium with regard to the provision of certain material substances. Hunger and thirst represent deficiencies and are existence needs. Pay, fringe benefits and working conditions are other types of existence needs.
2.  *Relatedness needs,* which acknowledge that people are not self-contained units but must engage in transactions with their human environment. The basic characteristic of relatedness needs is that their satisfaction depends on a process of sharing or mutuality. Acceptance, understanding, confirmation and influence are elements of the relatedness process.
3.  *Growth needs* emerge from the tendency of open systems to increase in internal order and differentiation over time as a con-

sequence of going beyond the environment. Growth needs impel people to make creative or productive efforts for themselves. The satisfaction of growth needs depends on a person 'finding the opportunities to be what he is most fully and to become what he can.'

## McClelland's achievement — affiliation — power needs

An alternative way of classifying needs was developed by McClelland (1975), who based it mainly on studies of managers. He identified three needs as being most important:

1.  The need for *achievement*, defined as the need for competitive success measured against a personal standard of excellence.
2.  The need for *affiliation*, defined as the need for warm, friendly, compassionate relationships with others.
3.  The need for *power*, defined as the need to control or influence others.

Different individuals have different levels of these needs. Some have a greater need for achievement, others a stronger need for affiliation, and still others a stronger need for power. While one need may be dominant, however, this does not mean that the others are non-existent.

The three needs may be given different priorities at different levels of management. High need for achievement is particularly important for success in many junior- and middle-management jobs where it is possible to feel direct responsibility for task accomplishment. But in senior-management positions a concern for institutionalized as opposed to personal power becomes more important. A strong need for affiliation is not so significant at any level.

### Herzberg's two-factor model

The two-factor model of satisfiers and dissatisfiers was developed by Herzberg *et al* (1957) following an investigation into the sources of job satisfaction and dissatisfaction of accountants and engineers. It was assumed that people have the capacity to report accurately the conditions which made them satisfied and dissatisfied with their jobs. Accordingly, the subjects were asked to tell their interviewers about the times during which they felt exceptionally good and exceptionally bad about their jobs and how long their feelings persisted. It was found that the accounts of 'good' periods most frequently concerned the content of the job, particularly achievement, recognition, advancement, responsibility, and the work itself. On the other hand, accounts of 'bad' periods most frequently concerned the context of the job. Company policy and administration, supervision, salary and working conditions more frequently appeared in these accounts than in those told about 'good' periods. The main implications of this research, according to Herzberg, are that:

> The wants of employees divide into two groups. One group revolves around the need to develop in one's occupation as a source of personal growth. The second group operates as an essential base to the first and is associated with fair treatment in compensation, supervision, working conditions and administrative practices. The fulfilment of the needs of the second group does not motivate the individual to high levels of job satisfaction and to extra performance on the job. All we can expect from satisfying this second group of needs is the prevention of dissatisfaction and poor job performance.

These groups form the two factors in Herzberg's model: one consists of the satisfiers or motivators, because they are seen to be effective in motivating the individual to superior performance and effort. The other consists of the dissatisfiers, which essentially describe the environment and serve primarily to prevent job dissatisfaction, while having little effect on positive job attitudes. The latter were named the hygiene factors in the medical use of the term, meaning preventive and environmental.

## Reservations about Herzberg's theory

Herzberg's two-factor has been strongly attacked. The research method has been criticized because no attempt was made to measure the relationship between satisfaction and performance. It has been suggested that the two-factor nature of the theory is an inevitable result of the questioning method used by the interviewers. It has also been suggested that wide and unwarranted inferences have been drawn from small and specialized samples and that there is no evidence to suggest that the satisfiers do improve productivity.

In spite of these criticisms (or perhaps because of them, as they are all from academics), the Herzberg theory continues to thrive; partly because for the layman it is easy to understand and seems to be based on 'real-life' rather than academic abstractions, and partly because it fits in well with the highly respected ideas of Maslow and McGregor in its emphasis on the positive value of the intrinsic motivating factors. It is also in accord with a fundamental belief in the dignity of labour and the Protestant ethic — that work is good in itself. As a result, Herzberg had immense influence on the job enrichment movement, which sought to design jobs in a way which will maximize the opportunities to obtain intrinsic satisfaction from work and thus improve the quality of working life. His emphasis on the distinction between intrinsic and extrinsic motivation is also important.

## Process theory

In process theory, the emphasis is on the psychological processes or forces which affect motivation, as well as on basic needs. It is also known as cognitive theory because it is concerned with people's perceptions of their working environment and the ways in which they interpret and understand it. According to Guest (1992b), the process theory provides a much more relevant approach to motivation that replaces the theories of Maslow and Herzberg which, he suggests, have been shown by extensive research to be wrong.

Process or cognitive theory can certainly be more useful to managers than needs theory because it provides more realistic guidance on motivation techniques. The processes are:

- expectations (expectancy theory)
- goal achievement (goal theory)
- behavioural choice (reactance theory)
- feelings about equity (equity theory).

### Expectancy theory

The concept of expectancy was originally contained in the valency-instrumentality-expectancy (VIE) theory which was formulated by Vroom (1964). Valency stands for value, instrumentality is the belief that if we do one thing it will lead to another, and expectancy is the probability that action or effort will lead to an outcome. This concept of expectancy was defined in more detail by Vroom as follows:

Whenever an individual chooses between alternatives which involve uncertain outcomes, it seems clear that his behaviour is affected not only by his preferences among these outcomes but also by the degree to which he believes these outcomes to be possible. An expectancy is defined as a momentary belief concerning the likelihood that a particular act will be followed by a particular outcome. Expectancies may be described in terms of their strength. Maximal strength is indicated by subjective certainty that the act will be followed by the outcome, while minimal (or zero) strength is indicated by subjective certainty that the act will not be followed by the outcome.

The strength of expectations may be based on past experiences (reinforcement), but individuals are frequently presented with new situations — a change in job, payment system, or working conditions imposed by management — where past experience is an inadequate guide to the implications of the change. In these circumstances, motivation may be reduced.

Motivation is only likely when a clearly perceived and usable relationship exists between performance and outcome, and the outcome is seen as a means of satisfying needs. This explains why extrinsic financial motivation — for example, an incentive or bonus scheme — works only if the link between effort and reward is clear and the value of the reward is worth the effort. It also explains why intrinsic motivation arising from the work itself can be more powerful than extrinsic motivation; intrinsic motivation outcomes are more under the control of individuals, who can place greater reliance on their past experiences to indicate the extent to which positive and advantageous results are likely to be obtained by their behaviour.

This theory was developed by Porter and Lawler (1968) into a model which follows Vroom's ideas by suggesting that there are two factors determining the effort people put into their jobs:

1. The value of the rewards to individuals in so far as they satisfy their needs for security, social esteem, autonomy, and self-actualization.
2. The probability that rewards depend on effort, as perceived by individuals — in other words, their expectations about the relationships between effort and reward.

Thus, the greater the value of a set of awards and the higher the probability that receiving each of these rewards depends upon effort, the greater the effort that will be put forth in a given situation.

But, as Porter and Lawler emphasize, mere effort is not enough. It has to be effective effort if it is to produce the desired performance. The two variables additional to effort which affect task achievement are:

- *ability* — individual characteristics such as intelligence, manual skills, know-how

307

- *role perceptions* — what the individual wants to do or thinks he or she is required to do. These are good from the viewpoint of the organization if they correspond with what it thinks the individual ought to be doing. They are poor if the views of the individual and the organization do not coincide.

## Goal theory

Goal theory as developed by Latham and Locke (1979) states that motivation and performance are higher when individuals are set specific goals, when goals are difficult but accepted, and when there is feedback on performance. Participation in goal setting is important as a means of getting agreement to the setting of higher goals. Difficult goals must be agreed and their achievement reinforced by guidance and advice. Finally, feedback is vital in maintaining motivation, particularly towards the achievement of even higher goals.

Erez and Zidon (1984) emphasized the need for acceptance of and commitment to goals. They found that, as long as they are agreed, demanding goals lead to better performance than easy ones. Erez (1977) also emphasized the importance of feedback. As Robertson *et al* (1992) point out:

> Goals inform individuals to achieve particular levels of performance, in order for them to direct and evaluate their actions; while performance feedback allows the individual to track how well he or she has been doing in relation to the goal, so that, if necessary, adjustments in effort, direction or possibly task strategies can be made.

Goal theory is in line with the 1960s concept of management by objectives. The latter approach, however, often failed because it was tackled bureaucratically without gaining the real support of those involved and, importantly, without ensuring that managers were aware of the significance of the processes of agreement, reinforcement and feedback, and were skilled in practising them.

Goal theory, however, plays a key part in the performance management processes which was evolved from the largely discredited management-by-objectives approach. Performance management is dealt with in Chapter 13.

## Reactance theory

Reactance theory as formulated by Brehm (1966) starts from the premise that, to the extent that people are aware of their needs and the behaviour necessary to satisfy these needs, and providing they have the appropriate freedom, they can choose behaviour so as to maximize need satisfaction. If, however, this freedom to act is threatened, people will react, that is, they will, in accordance with the principle of homeostasis, be motivationally aroused to the avoidance of any further loss of freedom. In essence, as Brehm says:

> Given that a person has a set of free behaviours, he (sic) will experience reactance whenever any of these behaviours is eliminated or threatened with elimination, and when a free behaviour of an individual is eliminated (or threatened) his desire for that behaviour or for the object of it will increase.

In other words, individuals are not passive receivers and responders. Instead, they actively strive to make sense of their environment and to reduce uncertainty by seeking to control factors influencing rewards. Management may have all sorts of wonderful ideas about motivating employees, but they will not necessarily work unless they make sense to the people concerned in terms of their own values and orientations.

## Equity theory

Equity theory is concerned with the perceptions people have about how they are being treated as compared with others. To be dealt with equitably is to be treated fairly in comparison with another group of people (a reference group) or a relevant other person. Equity involves feelings and perceptions and it is always a comparative process. It is not synonymous with equality, which means treating everyone the same, since this would be inequitable if they deserve to be treated differently.

Equity theory states, in effect, that people will be better motivated if they are treated equitably and demotivated if they are treated inequitably. It explains only one aspect of the processes of motivation and job satisfaction, although it may be significant in terms of morale.

As suggested by Adams (1965), there are two forms of equity: distributive equity, which is concerned with the fairness with which people feel they are rewarded in accordance with their contribution and in comparison with others; and procedural equity, which is concerned with the perceptions employees have about the fairness with which company procedures in such areas as performance appraisal, promotion and discipline are being operated.

Interpersonal factors are closely linked to feelings about procedural fairness. Five factors that contribute to perceptions of procedural fairness have been identified by Tyler and Bies (1990). These are:

1. Adequate considerations of an employee's viewpoint.
2. Suppression of personal bias towards the employee.
3. Applying criteria consistently across employees.
4. Providing early feedback to employees concerning the outcome of decisions.
5. Providing employees with an adequate explanation of the decision made.

## Self-efficacy theory

This theory was developed by Bandura (1982) who defined self-efficacy as 'how well one can execute courses of action required to deal with prospective situations'. It is concerned with an individual's self-belief that he or she will be able to accomplish certain tasks, achieve certain goals or learn certain things.

Locke (1984) has established that self-efficacy is positively related to goal level and goal commitment for self-set goals and performance.

## Behavioural theory

Behavioural psychologists such as Skinner (1974) emphasize that behaviour is learnt from experience. They play down, even dismiss, the significance of internal psychological factors and instinct and are only interested in the external factors that directly influence behaviour. They believe that learning takes place mainly through the process of reinforcement as described on page 297 of this chapter.

## Social learning theory

Social learning theory as developed by Bandura (1977) combines aspects of both behavioural and expectancy theory. It recognizes the significance of the basic behavioural concept of reinforcement as a determinant of future behaviour but also emphasizes the importance of internal psychological factors, especially expectancies about the value of goals and the individual's ability to reach them. The term 'reciprocal determinism' is used to denote the concept that while the situation will affect individual behaviour individuals will simultaneously influence the situation.

Robertson and Cooper (1983) have pointed out that 'there are many similarities between social learning theory and expectancy theory in their joint emphasis on expectancies, individual goals and values and the influence of both person and situational factors'.

## Attribution theory

Attribution theory is concerned with how we explain our performance after we have invested considerable effort and motivation in a particular task. Four types of explanation may be used to account for either success or failure — these are ability, effort, task difficulty and luck. For example, if success or failure is explained in terms of effort, then high motivation may follow. If, on the other hand, failure to achieve is explained in terms of task difficulty or bad luck, the result may be a loss of motivation. Incorrect attributions may be the result of inadequate feedback, and managers can do much to influence attributions and therefore motivation by feedback, communication, appraisal and guidance. This will affect subsequent motivation.

As Guest (1992b) explains:

> The activity of the manager in this context can be described as *social information processing*. Essentially this entails communicating information to influence social perception of aspects of the work setting. It works best in highly ambiguous situations. For example, where there is little clear feedback from the job on performance, if someone tells you are doing well, if the source is credible and there is an absence of other information, you will be inclined to believe you are doing well and therefore to persist in your behaviour.

## Role modelling

People can be motivated by modelling their behaviour on a 'role model', that is, someone whose approach to work and ability to get things done produces a measure of inspiration and a desire to follow the example provided by the model who could be a manager or a colleague. Role modelling can take place when inspirational leadership is provided and it is also one of the forces which can operate within groups. There is, of course a negative side to role modelling. The behaviour of a manager or of fellow team members can produce de-motivation.

## The key messages of motivation theory

The key messages provided by motivation theory are summarized below.

## Extrinsic and intrinsic motivating factors

Extrinsic rewards provided by the employer, including pay, will be important in attracting and retaining employees and, for limited periods, increasing effort and minimizing dissatisfaction. Intrinsic rewards related to responsibility, achievement and the work itself may have a longer-term and deeper impact on motivation.

## The significance of needs and wants

People will be better motivated if their work experience satisfies their social and psychological needs and wants as well as their economic needs.

## The influence of goals

Individuals at work are motivated by having specific goals, and they perform better when they are aiming for difficult goals which they have accepted and when they receive feedback on performance.

## The importance of expectations

The degree to which people are motivated will depend not only upon the perceived value of the outcome of their actions — the goal or reward — but also upon their perceptions of the likelihood of obtaining a worthwhile reward — ie their expectations. They will be highly motivated if they can control the means to attain their goals.

## Self-efficacy

Some people have to be helped to believe that they can do more or better.

## Behavioural theory

This claims that learning takes place mainly through the process of reinforcement but this may be an over-simplification.

## Social learning theory

Expectancies, individual goals and values and the influence of both person and situational factors are all key factors in motivating people.

## Attribution theory

This tells us that if someone tells you are doing well, if the source is credible and there is an absence of other information, you will be inclined to believe you are doing well and therefore to persist in your behaviour.

## Role modelling

This phenomenon draws attention to the importance of positive leadership and team building.

## The influence of orientations and reactance

Organizations may have expectations about how their motivating strategies will improve performance as well as helping to attract and retain employees. But the situation may not be under as much control as they would wish because of the influence of *orientations* (people's preferences for what they want to get out of work) and *reactance* (people attempt to control their own environment irrespective of what the organization wants them to do).

# The relationship between motivation and performance

The basic requirements for job satisfaction may include comparatively higher pay, an equitable payment system, real opportunities for promotion, considerate and participative management, a reasonable degree of social interaction at work, interesting and varied tasks and a high degree of control over work pace and work methods. The degree of satisfaction obtained by individuals, however, depends largely upon their own needs and expectations and the environment in which they work.

But research has not established any strongly positive connection between satisfaction and performance. A satisfied worker is not necessarily a high producer, and a high producer is not necessarily a satisfied worker. Some people claim that good performance produces satisfaction rather than the other way round, but their case has not been proved.

## Motivation and money

Money, in the form of pay or some other sort of remuneration, is the most obvious extrinsic reward. Money provides the carrot which most people want.

Doubts have been cast by Herzberg *et al* (1957) on the effectiveness of money because, they claimed, while the lack of it can cause dissatisfaction, its provision does not result in lasting satisfaction. There is something in this, especially for people on fixed salaries or rates of pay who do not benefit directly from an incentive scheme. They may feel good when they get an increase; apart from the extra money, it is a highly tangible form of recognition and an effective means of helping people to feel that they are valued. But this feeling of euphoria can rapidly die away. Other dissatisfactions from Herzberg's list of hygiene factors, such as working conditions or the quality of management, can loom larger in some people's minds when they fail to get the satisfaction they need from the work itself. However, it must be re-emphasized that different people have different needs and wants and Herzberg's two factor theory has not been validated. Some will be much more motivated by money than others. What cannot be assumed is that money motivates everyone in the same way and to the same extent. Thus it is naive to think that the introduction of a performance-related (PRP) scheme will miraculously transform everyone overnight into well-motivated, high-performing individuals.

Nevertheless, money provides the means to achieve a number of different ends. It is a powerful force because it is linked directly or indirectly to the satisfaction of many needs. It clearly satisfies basic needs for survival and security, if it is coming in regularly. It can also satisfy the need for self-esteem (as noted above, it is a visible mark of appreciation) and status — money can set you in a grade apart from your fellows and can buy you things they cannot to build up your prestige. Money satisfies the less desirable but still prevalent drives of acquisitiveness and cupidity.

Money may in itself have no intrinsic meaning, but it acquires significant motivating power because it comes to symbolize so many intangible goals. It acts as a symbol in different ways for different people, and for the same person at different times. As noted by Goldthorpe *et al* (1968) from their research into the 'affluent worker', pay is the dominant factor in the choice of employer and considerations of pay seem most powerful in binding people to their present job.

Do financial incentives motivate people? The answer is yes, for those people who are strongly motivated by money and whose expectations that they will receive a financial reward are high. But less confident employees may not respond to incentives which they do not expect to achieve. It can also be argued that extrinsic rewards may erode intrinsic interest — people who work just for money could find their tasks less pleasurable and may not, therefore, do them so well. What we do know is that a multiplicity of factors is involved in performance improvements and many of those factors are interdependent.

Money can therefore provide positive motivation in the right circumstances not only because people need and want money but also because it serves as a highly tangible means of recognition. But badly designed and managed pay systems can demotivate. Another researcher in this area was Jaques (1961), who emphasized the need for such systems to be perceived as being fair and equitable. In other words, the reward should be clearly related to effort or level of responsibility and people should not receive less money than they deserve compared with their fellow workers. Jaques called this the 'felt-fair' principle.

## Motivation strategies

Motivation strategies aim to create a working environment and to develop policies and practices which will provide for higher levels of performance from employees. They will be concerned with:

- measuring motivation to provide an indication of areas where motivational practices need to be improved
- ensuring, so far as possible, that employees feel they are valued
- developing behavioural commitment
- developing an organization climate which will foster motivation
- improving leadership skills
- job design
- performance management
- reward management
- the use of behavioural modification approaches.

### *Measuring motivation*

There are, of course, no direct means by which motivation can be measured. But indications of the level of motivation can be obtained through attitude surveys (see Chapter 42), measures of productivity, employee turnover and absenteeism, analysis of the results of performance reviews, analysis of issues raised through a grievance procedure and the enthusiasm with which employees participate in suggestion schemes, quality circles and the like.

## Valuing employees

Motivation *and* commitment are likely to be enhanced if employees feel that they are valued. This means investing in their success, trusting and empowering them, giving them the opportunity to be involved in matters with which they are concerned, keeping them fully in the picture, treating them fairly and like human beings, rather than 'resources' to be exploited in the interests of management, and providing them with rewards (financial and non-financial) which demonstrate the extent to which they are valued.

## Behavioural commitment

Behavioural commitment means that individuals will direct their efforts to achieving organizational and job objectives. It can be engendered by getting people involved in setting objectives, giving people more responsibility to manage their own jobs as individuals or as teams (empowerment) and providing for rewards to be clearly related to success in achieving agreed goals.

## Organizational climate

The organizational climate and core values should emphasize the importance of high performance. Managers and team leaders should be encouraged to act as role models of the sort of behaviour expected from employees.

## Leadership skills

Managers and team leaders should be helped to learn about the process of motivation and how they can use their knowledge to improve the motivation of their team members.

## Job design

Job design should involve the application of motivation theory, especially those aspects of the theory which relate to needs and motivation through the work itself (intrinsic motivation). Job design methods are discussed in Chapter 21.

## Performance management

Performance management processes, as described in Chapter 13, can provide for goal setting, feedback and reinforcement.

## Reward management

Reward management processes as covered in Part VII can provide direct motivation through various forms of performance pay as long as close attention is given to the significance of expectancy and equity theory.

## Employee or human resource development

Employee development is about personal development, and motivation theory indicates clearly that progress through self-development — self-managed learning — is the best form of development.

Learning theory as discussed in Chapter 27 emphasizes the importance of motivating people to learn. This will be carried out most effectively if the factors affecting motivation, including self-efficacy and social learning are taken into account.

## Behavioural modification

Behavioural modification or organizational behaviour (OB) modification uses the behavioural principle 'operant conditioning' (ie influencing behaviour by its consequences). Five steps for behavioural modification have been defined by Luthans and Kreitner (1975):

1. *Identify the critical behaviour* — what people do or do not do which needs to be changed.
2. *Measure the frequency* — obtain hard evidence that a real problem exists.
3. *Carry out a functional analysis* — identify the stimuli that precede the behaviour and the consequences in the shape of reward or punishment which influence the behaviour.
4. *Develop and implement an intervention strategy* — this may involve

the use of positive or negative reinforcement to influence behaviour (ie providing or withholding financial or non-financial rewards).

5. *Evaluate the effects of the intervention* — what improvements, if any, happened and if the interventions were unsuccessful, what needs to be done next?

## Conclusions

Motivation strategy will incorporate all the elements referred to in the last section. David Guest (1994) has summed up neatly (Figure 16.2) some of the ways in which the process of motivation can further a number of desirable aims in the management of people.

| | | |
|---|---|---|
| autonomy | ←——————→ | job design |
| achievement | ←——————→ | goal setting |
| responsibility | ←——————→ | behavioural commitment |
| confidence | ←——————→ | self-efficacy |
| incentives | ←——————→ | expectancy theory |
| progress | ←——————→ | personal development |

**Figure 16.2** Approaches to motivation

# 17

# Commitment

The concept of commitment plays an important part in HRM philosophy. As Guest (1987) has indicated, HRM policies are designed to 'maximise organizational integration, employee commitment, flexibility and quality of work'. The chapter explores the measuring and significance of organizational commitment, considers certain problems about the concept and discusses how it can be developed.

## The meaning of organizational commitment

Commitment refers to attachment and loyalty. As defined by Mowdray *et al* (1982) commitment consists of three components: an identification with the goals and values of the organization; a desire to belong to the organization and a willingness to display effort on behalf of the organization.

An alternative, although closely related, definition of commitment emphasizes the importance of behaviour in creating commitment. As Salancik (1977) put it: 'Commitment is a state of being in which an individual becomes bound by his actions to beliefs that sustain his activities and his own involvement'. Three features of behaviour are important in binding individuals to their acts: the visibility of the acts, the extent to which the outcomes are irrevocable, and the degree to which the person undertakes the action voluntarily. Commitment, according to Salancik can be increased and harnessed 'to obtain support for organizational ends and interests' through such ploys as participation in decisions about actions.

## The significance of commitment

There have been two schools of thought about commitment. One, the 'from control to commitment' school, was led by Walton (1985a and b), who saw commitment strategy as a more rewarding approach to human resource management, in contrast to the traditional control strategy. The other, 'Japanese/excellence' school, is represented by writers such as Pascale and Athos (1981) and Peters and Waterman (1982) who looked at the Japanese model and related the achievement of excellence to getting the wholehearted commitment of the workforce to the organization.

## From control to commitment

The importance of commitment was highlighted by Walton (1985a and b). His theme was that improved performance would result if the organization moved away from the traditional control-orientated approach to workforce management, which relies upon establishing order, exercising control and 'achieving efficiency in the application of the workforce'. He argued that this approach should be replaced by a commitment strategy. He suggested that workers respond best — and most creatively — not when they are tightly controlled by management, placed in narrowly defined jobs, and treated like an unwelcome necessity, but, instead, when they are given broader responsibilities, encouraged to contribute and helped to achieve satisfaction in their work.

Walton (1985a) suggested that in the new commitment-based approach:

> Jobs are designed to be broader than before, to combine planning and implementation, and to include efforts to upgrade operations, not just to maintain them. Individual responsibilities are expected to change as conditions change, and teams, not individuals, often are the organizational units accountable for performance. With management hierarchies relatively flat and differences in status minimized, control and lateral coordination depend on shared goals. And expertise rather than formal position determines influence.

Put like this, a commitment strategy does not sound like a crude attempt to manipulate people to accept management's values and goals as some have suggested. In fact, Walton does not describe it as being instrumental in this manner. His prescription is for a broad HRM approach to the ways in which people are treated, jobs are designed and organizations are managed. And he quotes a number of examples in America where unions have cooperated with management; talking about common interests and agreeing to sponsor quality-of-working-life programmes and employee involvement activities.

## The Japanese/excellence school

Attempts made to explain the secret of Japanese business success by such writers as Ouchi (1981) and Pascale and Athos (1981) led to the theory that the best way to motivate people is to get their full commitment to the values of the organization by leadership and involvement. This might be called the 'hearts and minds' approach to motivation and, among other things, it popularized such devices as quality circles.

The baton was taken up by Peters and Waterman (1982) and their imitators later in the 1980s. This approach to excellence was summed up by Peters and Austin (1985) when they wrote:

> Trust people and treat them like adults, enthuse them by lively and imaginative leadership, develop and demonstrate an obsession for quality, make them feel they own the business, and your workforce will respond with total commitment.

# Problems with the concept of commitment

A number of commentators have raised questions about the concept of commitment. These relate to three main problem areas: (1) its unitary frame of reference, (2) commitment as an inhibitor of flexibility, and (3) whether high commitment does in practice result in improved organizational performance.

## Unitary frame of reference

A comment frequently made about the concept of commitment is that it is too simplistic in adopting a unitary frame of reference; in other words, it assumes unrealistically that an organization consists of people with shared interests. It has been suggested by people like Cyert and March (1963), Mangham (1979) and Mintzberg (1983a) that an organization is really a coalition of interest groups where political processes are an inevitable part of everyday life. The pluralist perspective recognizes the legitimacy of different interests and values and therefore asks the question 'commitment to what?' Thus, as Coopey and Hartley (1991) put it 'commitment is not an all-or-nothing affair (though many managers might like it to be) but a question of multiple or competing commitments for the individual'.

Legge (1989) also raises this question in her discussion of strong culture as a key requirement of HRM through 'a shared set of managerially sanctioned values'.

However, managerial values for quality, service, equal opportunity and innovation are not necessarily wrong *because* they are managerial values. But it is reasonable to believe that pursuing a value such as innovation could work against the interests of employees by, for example, resulting in redundancies. And it would be quite reasonable for any employee encouraged to behave in accordance with a value supported by management to ask 'what's in it for me?'. It can also be argued that the imposition of management's values on employees without their having any part to play in discussing and agreeing them is a form of coercion.

## Commitment and flexibility

It was pointed out by Coopey and Hartley (1991) that: 'The problem for a unitarist notion of organizational commitment is that it fosters a conformist approach which not only fails to reflect organizational reality, but can be narrowing and limiting for the organization.' They argue that if employees are expected and encouraged to commit themselves tightly to a single set of values and goals they will not be able to cope with the ambiguities and uncertainties which are endemic in organizational life in times of change. Conformity to 'imposed' values will inhibit creative problem solving, and high commitment to present courses of action will increase both resistance to change and the stress which invariably occurs when change takes place.

If commitment is related to tightly defined plans then this will become a real problem. To avoid it, the emphasis should be on overall strategic directions. These would be communicated to employees with the proviso that changing circumstances will require their amendment. In the meantime, however, everyone can at least be informed in general terms where the organization is heading and, more specifically, the part they are expected to play in helping the organization to get there. If they can be involved in the decision-making processes on matters that affect them (which includes management's values for performance, quality and customer service), so much the better.

Values need not necessarily be restrictive. They can be defined in ways which allow for freedom of choice within broad guidelines. In fact, the values themselves can refer to such processes as flexibility, innovation and responsiveness to change. Thus, far from inhibiting creative problem solving, they can encourage it.

## The impact of high commitment

A belief in the positive value of commitment has been confidently expressed by Walton (1985a):

> Underlying all these (human resource) policies is a management philo-sophy, often embedded in a published statement, that acknowledges the legitimate claims of a company's multiple stakeholders — owners, employees, customers and the public. At the centre of this philosophy is a belief that eliciting employee commitment will lead to enhanced per-formance. The evidence shows this belief to be well founded.

However, a review by Guest (1991) of the mainly North American literature, reinforced by the limited UK research available, led him to the conclusion that: 'High organizational commitment is associated with lower labour turnover and absence, but there is no clear link to performance'.

It is probably wise not to expect too much from commitment as a means of making a direct and immediate impact on performance. It is not the same as motivation. Commitment is a wider concept and tends to be more stable over a period of time and less responsive to transitory aspects of an employee's job. It is possible to be dissatisfied with a particular feature of a job while retaining a reasonably high level of commitment to the organization as a whole.

In relating commitment to motivation it is useful to distinguish, as do Buchanan and Huczynski (1985), three perspectives.

1. The goals towards which people aim. From this perspective, goals such as the good of the company, or effective performance at work, may provide a degree of motivation for some employees, who could be regarded as committed in so far as they feel they own the goals.
2. The process by which goals and objectives at work are selected, which is quite distinct from the way in which commitment arises within individuals.
3. The social process of motivating others to perform effectively. From this viewpoint, strategies aimed at increasing motivation also affect commitment. It may be true to say that, where commitment is present, motivation is likely to be strong, particularly if a long-term view is taken of effective performance.

It is reasonable to believe that strong commitment to work is likely to result in conscientious and self-directed application to do the job, regular attendance, nominal supervision and a high level of effort. Commitment to the organization will certainly be related to the intention to stay — in other words, loyalty to the company.

## Creating a commitment strategy

In spite of these reservations, it is difficult to deny that it is desirable for management to have defined strategic goals and values. And it is equally desirable from management's point of view for employees to behave in ways which support these strategies and values.

However, in enlisting this support by means of a commitment strategy, account should be taken of the reservations discussed above. First, it has to be accepted that the interests of the organization and of its members do not necessarily coincide. It can be asserted by management that everyone will benefit from organizational success in terms of security, pay, opportunities for advancement etc. But employees and their trade unions may be difficult to convince that this is the case if they believe that the success is to be achieved by such actions as disinvestments, downsizing, cost reductions affecting pay and employment, tougher performance standards or tighter management controls. When defining values, it is important not to impose them on employees. They should be involved in their formulation and in discussing with management how they are to be upheld. This avoids what Legge (1989) refers to as a process of 'co-optation' in which management forces its own set of values down the throats of its employees. Involving employees makes sense in that they are thus much more likely to own and practice the values.

Secondly, management must not define and communicate values in such a way as to inhibit flexibility, creativity and the ability to adapt to change. Strategies have to be defined in broad terms with caveats that they will be amended if circumstances change. Values have to emphasize the need for flexibility, innovation and teamworking as well as the need for performance and quality.

Thirdly, too much should not be expected from campaigns to increase commitment. Management may reduce employee turnover, increase identification with the organization and develop feelings of loyalty among its employees. They may increase job satisfaction, but there is no evidence that higher levels of job satisfaction necessarily improve performance. They may provide a context within which motivation and therefore performance will increase. But there is no guarantee that this will take place, although the chances of gaining improvements will be increased if the campaign is focused upon a specific value such as quality.

It may be naive to believe that 'hearts and minds' campaigns to win commitment will transform organizational behaviour overnight. But it is surely useful for organizations to do what they can along the lines described below to influence behaviour, to support the achievement of objectives and to uphold values that are inherently worthwhile. It is good management practice to define its expectations in terms of objectives and standards of performance. It is even better management practice to discuss and agree these objectives and standards with employees.

Steps to create commitment will be concerned with both strategic goals and values. They may include communication, education and training programmes, initiatives to increase involvement and 'ownership', and the development of performance and reward management systems.

## Communication programmes

It seems to be strikingly obvious that commitment will only be gained if people understand what they are expected to commit to. But managements too often fail to pay sufficient attention to delivering the message in terms which recognize that the frame of reference for those who receive it is likely to be quite different from their own. Management's expectations will not necessarily coincide with those of employees: pluralism prevails. In delivering the message, the use of different and complementary channels of communication such as newsletters, briefing groups, videos, notice board, etc is often neglected.

## Education

Education is another form of communication. An educational programme is designed to increase both knowledge and understanding of, for example, total quality management. The aim will be to influence behaviour and thereby progressively change attitudes.

## Training

Training is designed to develop specific competences. For example, if one of the values to be supported is flexibility, it will be necessary to extend the range of skills possessed by members of work teams through multiskilling programmes.

Commitment is enhanced if managers can gain the confidence and respect of their teams, and training to improve the quality of management should form an important part of any programme for increasing commitment. Management training can also be focused on increasing the competence of managers in specific areas of their responsibility for gaining commitment, eg performance management.

## Developing ownership

A sense of belonging is enhanced if there is a feeling of 'ownership' among employees. Not just in the literal sense of owning shares (although this can help) but in the sense of believing they are genuinely accepted by management as a key part of the organization. This concept of 'ownership' extends to participating in decisions on new developments and changes in working practices which affect the individuals concerned. They should be involved in making those decisions and feel that their ideas have been listened to and that they have contributed to the outcome. They will then be more likely to accept the decision or change because it is owned by them rather than being imposed by management.

## Developing a sense of excitement in the job

A sense of excitement in the job can be created by concentrating on the intrinsic motivating factors such as responsibility, achievement and recognition, and using these principles to govern the way in which jobs are designed. Excitement in the job is also created by the quality of leadership and the willingness of managers and team leaders to recognize that they will obtain increased motivation and commitment if they pay continuous attention to the ways in which they delegate responsibility and give their staff the scope to use their skills and abilities.

## Performance management

Performance management as described in Chapter 13 can help to cascade corporate objectives and values throughout the organization so that consistency is achieved at all levels. Expectations of individuals are defined in terms of their own job, which they can more readily grasp and act upon than if they were asked to support some remote and, to them, irrelevant overall objectives. But individual objectives can be described in ways which support the achievement of those defined for higher levels in the organization.

## Reward management

Reward management processes can make it clear that individuals will be rewarded in accordance with the extent to which they achieve objectives *and* uphold corporate values. This can reinforce the messages delivered through other channels of communication.

## Commitment and mutuality

The notion of mutuality is closely associated with the concept of commitment. Mutuality in organizations is said to exist when it is perceived generally that the interests of management and employees coincide. Management and employees are interdependent and both parties benefit from this interdependence. Mutuality means that management is concerned in the well-being of employees as well as the success of the organization, and employees are just as concerned in the success of the organization as in their own well-being. The principle of mutuality is linked to the stakeholder concept — that both management and employees as well as owners, customers and suppliers have a stake in the organization and full consideration should therefore be given to their mutual interests. Mutuality could be regarded as a unitarist concept in that it assumes that there are no underlying and inevitable differences of interest between management and workers.

The ideal of mutuality is part of the rhetoric of human resource management and Walton (1985b) emphasized the importance of mutual goals and mutual responsibility. Kochan and Dyer (1995) have suggested that the principles guiding mutual commitment firms are as follows:

1.  *Strategic level*:

    - supportive business strategies
    - top management value commitment
    - effective voice for HR in strategy making and governance

2.  *Functional (human resource policy) level*:

    - staffing based on employment stabilization

- investment in training and development
- contingent compensation that reinforces co-operation, participation and contribution.

3. *Workplace level:*

- selection based on high standards
- broad task design and teamwork
- employee involvement in problem solving
- climate of co-operation and trust.

## Mutual commitment strategy

A mutual commitment strategy will be based on the principle of high
commitment management, which was defined by Wood (1996) as
being:

> ... a form of management which is aimed at eliciting a commitment so
> that behaviour is primarily self-regulated rather than controlled by
> sanctions and pressures external to the individual and relations within
> the organization are based on high levels of trust.

A mutual commitment strategy to achieve this end will incorporate the
various approaches described in pages 324 to 327 of this chapter. But its
foundation should be a philosophy that recognises employees as
valued stakeholders in the organization. In the words of Kochan and
Dyer (1995):

> Staffing policies must be designed and managed in such a way that they
> reinforce the principle of employment security and thus promote the
> commitment, flexibility and loyalty of employees. This does not guar-
> antee lifetime employment, but it does imply that the first instinct in
> good times and bad should be to build and protect the firm's investment
> in human resources, rather than to indiscriminately add and cut people
> in knee-jerk responses to short-term fluctuations in business conditions.

# 18

# How Organizations Function

### Basic considerations

Organizations can be regarded as systems (Miller and Rice, 1967) which exist within an ever-changing and often turbulent environment, in order to transform inputs (human, financial and physical resources) into outputs (goods or services). The transformation is affected by the socio-technical system (Trist *et al*, 1963) in which social processes (interactions between people) are interrelated with the technologies and operational processes of the organization.

The two factors which determine how an organization functions in relation to its internal and external environment are its structure and the processes that operate within it. Organizations are also affected by the culture they develop, that is, the values and norms which affect behaviour. This subject is dealt with separately in Chapter 14.

Much has been written to explain how organizations function and the first part of this chapter summarizes the various theories of organization, namely:

- the *classical school* whose members believed in system, predictability and order
- the *human relations school* whose members emphasized the significance of group behaviour and the distinction between the formal and informal organization
- the *behavioural scientists* who applied their concepts of how people behave to the way in which organizations function
- the *bureaucratic model* in which the emphasis was on logic and rationality
- the *system school* whose members saw the organization as a socio-technical system

- the *contingency school* the members of which emphasized the influence of the environment on the design and functioning of organizations
- the *modernists* who include those who analyse the new flexible organization operating in a world of competition, change, chaos and information technology.

These theories provide the background to the last three sections of the chapter which describe how organizations function in terms of organization structure, organizational processes and types of organizations.

## The classical school

The classical or scientific management school, as represented by Fayol (1916), Taylor (1911) and Urwick (1947) believed in control, order and formality. Organizations need to minimize the opportunity for unfortunate and uncontrollable informal relations, leaving room only for the formal ones. From these overriding principles the following concepts are derived:

- *Structure.* Formal structures are required to provide orderly relationships between functions. The basic structure contains the line organization, which exercises delegated authority in performing the functions of the enterprise, and the staff organization which offers advice and provides services required by the line organization. Structural considerations include the span of control, which relates to the number of subordinates an executive can manage and the number of levels in the hierarchy.
- *Specialization.* As the human organization grows, work must be broken down along lines as naturally as possible to provide well-defined areas of specialization. This is the classical economic theory of the division of labour and all other scientific-management principles are derived from it.
- *Co-ordination.* The need for specialization creates the need for co-ordination. The many different functions performed by the members of an organization must be coordinated or linked together in order that they contribute jointly to the end result. To achieve this, members have to carry out their work as and when required so that each contribution fits the contribution of others.
- *Authority.* Organizations achieve order and regularity by the use of authority implemented through a defined hierarchy or chain of command.

- *Continuity.* Organizations should be designed to achieve continuity, stability and predictability. This must be done by minimizing disruptions caused by personality and individual idiosyncrasy. The organization consists of replaceable members, and its design should not be affected by the people who happen to be employed in it.

The classical or scientific management model has been attacked vigorously because it is too rigid and because it makes no allowance for situational factors such as the environment or technology. Neither does it take account of change or human factors, including the informal organization. But the formal approach, with its emphasis on organization charts and manuals, job descriptions, clear definitions of responsibility and authority and limited spans of control, still thrives. As Lupton (1975) pointed out: 'The attraction of the classical design from the point of view of top management is that it seems to offer them control.' Managers like to think they are rational and this has all the appearance of a rational approach. Many line managers when asked to describe their organizations will draw hierarchical charts, produce job descriptions and use such expressions as chain of command, levels of authority, line and staff and span of control. This is the language of classical theory and it is not inherently wrong — most people prefer some structure and find it difficult to tolerate ambiguity. But it must not be applied too rigidly, there are other considerations.

## The human relations school

The classical school reigned supreme until the late 1930s and still holds sway in the 1990s, as mentioned above. But Barnard (1938) emphasized the importance of the informal organization — the network of informal roles and relationships which, for better or worse, strongly influences the way the formal structure operates. He wrote: 'Formal organizations come out of and are necessary to informal organization: but when formal organizations come into operation, they create and require informal organizations.' More recently, Child (1977) has pointed out that it is misleading to talk about a clear distinction between the formal and the informal organization. Formality and informality can be designed into structure. Unofficial policies do exist in organizations but they are not to be confused with informality. Organization designers recognize the relevance of informal relationships but do not implement unofficial structures.

Roethlisberger and Dickson (1939) reported on the Hawthorne

Studies — the first large-scale investigation of productivity and industrial relations, which took place at the Hawthorne plant at Western Electric. This highlighted the importance of informal groups, work restriction norms and decent, humane leadership.

It is widely, if unfairly, believed that supporters of the human relations school approach only wanted organizations to be nice to people. But by appearing to ignore business needs, that is the impression they often made.

## The behavioural science school

In the 1960s a number of behavioural scientists emerged who would not like to be described as part of the human relations school. They did, however, subscribe to some of the fundamental beliefs of that school, although these beliefs were refined and re-presented on the basis of further study and research. The most notable contributors to this postwar development were McGregor, Likert and Argyris.

### Douglas McGregor

The central principle of organizations that McGregor (1960) derived from his Theory Y is that of integration — the process of recognizing the needs of both the organization and the individual and creating conditions which will reconcile these needs so that members of the organization can work together for its success and share in its rewards: 'Man will exercise self-direction and self-control in the service of objectives to which he is committed'.

### Rensis Likert

Likert (1961) derived his concept of organizations based on supportive relationships from his research at the University of Michigan. The initial studies distinguished between job-centred and employee-centred supervisors, and established that employee-centred supervisors were higher producers than the job-centred ones. The studies also distinguished between general and close supervision and showed that general rather than close supervision is more often associated with a high rather than a low level of productivity.

From his analysis of high-producing managers, Likert found that their operations were characterized by attitudes of identification with the organization and its objectives and a high sense of involvement in achieving them. This situation was created by 'harnessing effectively all the major motivational forces which can exercise significant influence in an organizational setting and which, potentially, can be accompanied by co-operative and favourable attitudes.'

The integrating principle of supportive relationships was derived from this analysis and states that:

> The leadership and other processes of the organization must be such as to ensure a maximum probability that in all interactions and all relationships with the organization each member will, in the light of his background, values and expectations, view the experience as supportive and one which builds and maintains his sense of personal worth and importance.

## Chrys Argyris

The research carried out by Argyris (1957) into personality development in organizations suggested to him that 'the formal organization creates in a healthy individual feelings of failure and frustration, short time perspective and conflict'. He further concluded that the formal work organization requires many members to act in immature rather than adult ways: 'At all levels there is behaviour that is not productive in the sense of helping the organization achieve its objectives. For example, at the lower levels we found apathy, indifference and non-involvement. At the upper levels we found conformity, mistrust, inability to accept new ideas, and fear of risk-taking.'

To overcome this problem, Argyris wants individuals to feel that they have a high degree of control over setting their own goals and over defining the paths to these goals. The strategy should be:

> To develop a climate in which the difficulties can be openly discussed, the employee's hostility understood and accepted, and a programme defined in which everyone can participate in attempting to develop new designs. Wherever this is impossible, the attempt will be made to design new work worlds that can be integrated with the old and that help the employee obtain more opportunity for psychological success.

Lest this seem too idealistic (a tendency shared by all members of the human relations school), Argyris stresses the need for some structure to provide the 'firm ground on which to anchor one's security'. Organization design has therefore to plan for integration and involvement, although these processes will probably have to take place within the traditional pyramidal structure.

## Other contributions to the behavioural science movement

The behavioural science movement, pioneered by the writers mentioned above, but furthered by people such as Herzberg (1957) and Blake and Mouton (1964), continued to emphasize that in organizations the proper study of mankind is man. The research conducted by Herzberg *et al* (1957) suggests that improvements in organization design must centre on the individual job as the positive source of motivation. If individuals feel that the job is stretching them, they will be moved to perform it well.

Blake and Mouton (1964) concentrated on management style — the way in which managers manage, based on their beliefs and values. They suggest that there are two factors: 'concern for people and concern for production'. This is in line with the distinction made by the Ohio State University researchers Halpin and Winer (1957) between leadership styles based on 'consideration' or 'initiating structure'.

The concepts of these and other behavioural scientists provided the impetus for the organization development movement as described in Chapter 22.

## Views on the behavioural science school

No one can quarrel with the values expressed by the members of the behavioural science school — we are all in favour of virtue. But there are a number of grounds on which the more extreme beliefs of the school can be criticized:

- It claims that its concepts are universally applicable, yet organizations come in all shapes and sizes with different activities and operating in different contexts.
- It ignores the real commercial and technological constraints of industrial life. Instead, it reflects more of an ideological concern for personal development and the rights of the individual rather than a scientific curiosity about the factors affecting organizational efficiency.
- It over-reacts against the excessive formality of the classical or scientific management school by largely ignoring the formal organization.
- Its emphasis on the need to minimize conflict overlooks the point that conflict is not necessarily undesirable, and may rather be an essential concomitant of change and development.

To be fair, not all behavioural scientists were so naive. Although McGregor's Theory Y was somewhat idealistic, he at least recognized that 'industrial health does not flow automatically from the elimination of dissatisfaction, disagreement, or even open conflict. Peace is not synonymous with organizational health; socially responsible management is not co-extensive with permissive management.'

## The bureaucratic model

Meanwhile, as Perrow (1980) expressed it:

> In another part of the management forest, the mechanistic school was gathering its forces and preparing to outflank the forces of light. First came the numbers men — the linear programmers, the budget experts, the financial analysts. Armed with emerging systems concepts, they carried the 'mechanistic' analogy to its fullest — and it was very productive. Their work still goes on, largely untroubled by organizational theory; the theory, it seems clear, will have to adjust to them, rather than the other way around.... Then the works of Max Weber, not translated until the 1940s ... began to find their way into social science thought.

Max Weber (1964) coined the term 'bureaucracy' as a label for a type of formal organization in which impersonality and rationality are developed to the highest degree. Bureaucracy, as he conceived it, was the most efficient form of organization because it is coldly logical and because personalized relationships and non-rational, emotional considerations do not get in its way. The ideal bureaucracy, according to Weber, has the following features:

- maximum specialization
- close job definition as to duties, privileges and boundaries
- vertical authority patterns
- decisions based on expert judgement, resting on technical knowledge and on disciplined compliance with the directives of superiors
- policy and administration are separate
- maximum use of rules
- impersonal administration of staff.

At first, with his celebrations of the efficiency of bureaucracy, Weber was received with only reluctant respect, even hostility. Many commentators were against bureaucracy. But it turned out that managers are not. They tend to prefer clear lines of communication, clear specifications of authority and responsibility and clear knowledge of whom they are responsible to. Admittedly, in some situations, as Burns and Stalker (1961) point out, managers might want absolute clarity but they can't get it. On the other hand there are circumstances when the type of work carried out in an organization requires a bureaucratic approach in the Weberian, not the pejorative 'red tape', sense. The problem with both the human relations and bureaucratic schools of thought were that they were insufficiently related to context. It is necessary to look at how organizations worked as systems within their environment — this was the approach adopted by the systems school. It is also necessary to look at how organizations have to adapt to that environment. This was done by the contingency school.

## The systems school

The systems approach to organizations as formulated by Miller and Rice (1967) states that organizations should be treated as open systems which are continually dependent upon and influenced by their environments. The basic characteristic of the enterprise as an open system is that it transforms inputs into outputs within its environment.

As Katz and Kahn (1964) wrote: 'Systems theory is basically concerned with problems of relationship, of structure and of interdependence.' As a result there is a considerable emphasis on the concept of transactions across boundaries — between the system and its environment and between the different parts of the system. This open and dynamic approach avoided the error of the classical and human relations theorists, who thought of organizations as closed systems and analysed their problems with reference to their internal structures and processes of interaction, without taking account either of external influences and the changes they impose or of the technology in the organization.

### The socio-technical model

The concept of the organization as a system was extended by the Tavistock Institute researchers into the socio-technical model of organizations. The basic principle of this model is that in any system of organization, technical or task aspects are inter-related with the human or social aspects. The emphasis is on inter-relationships between, on the one hand, the technical processes of transformation carried out within the organization, and, on the other hand, the organization of work groups and the management structures of the enterprise.

## The contingency school

The contingency school consists of writers, such as Burns and Stalker (1961), Woodward (1965), Lawrence and Lorsch (1967), and Perrow (1970) who have analysed a variety of organizations and concluded that their structures and methods of operation are a function of the circumstances in which they exist. They do not subscribe to the view that there is one best way of designing an organization or that simplistic classifications of organizations as formal or informal, bureaucratic or non-bureaucratic are helpful. They are against those who see organizations as mutually opposed social systems (what Burns and Stalker refer to as the 'Manichean world of the Hawthorne studies') which set up formal against informal organizations. They are also against those who impose rigid principles of organization irrespective of the technology or environmental conditions.

### Burns and Stalker

Burns and Stalker (1961) based their concept of mechanistic and organic organizations on research into a number of Scottish firms in the electronics industry. They emphasized the rate of change in the environment of the organization as being the key factor in determining how it could operate.

In stable conditions a highly structured or 'mechanistic' organization emerges with specialized functions, clearly defined roles, strict administrative routines and a hierarchical system of exercising authoritarian control. In effect, this is the bureaucratic system. However, when the environment is volatile, a rigid system of ranks and routines inhibits the organization's speed and sensitivity of response. In these circumstances the structure is, or should be, 'organic' in the sense that it is a function of the situation in which the enterprise finds itself rather than conforming to any predetermined and rigid view of how it should operate. Individual responsibilities are less clear cut and members of the organization must constantly relate what they are doing to its general situation and specific problems.

Perhaps the most important contribution made by Burns and Stalker was the stress they placed on the suitability of each system to its own specific set of conditions. They concluded their analysis by writing:

We desire to avoid the suggestion that either system is superior under all circumstances to the other. In particular, nothing in our experience justifies the assumption that mechanistic systems should be superseded by organic in conditions of stability. The beginning of administrative wisdom is the awareness that there is no one optimum type of management system.

## Woodward

Woodward's (1965) ideas about organization derived from a research project carried out in Essex designed to discover whether the principles of organization laid down by the classical theorists correlate with business success when put into practice. She found considerable variations in patterns of organization which could not be related to size of firm, type of industry or business success. She also found that there was no significant correlation between adherence to the classical principles relating to matters such as span of control or number of levels in the hierarchy, and business success. After further analysis, she concluded: that different technologies demand different structures and procedures and create different types of relationships.

## Lawrence and Lorsch

Lawrence and Lorsch (1967) developed their contingency model on the basis of a study of six firms in the plastics industry. Organization, as they define it, is the process of coordinating different activities to carry out planned transactions with the environment. The three aspects of environment upon which the design of the organization is contingent are the market, the technology (ie the tasks carried out) and research and development. These may be differentiated along such dimensions as rate of change and uncertainty. The process of reacting to complexity and change by differentiation creates a demand for effective integration if the organization as a whole is to adapt efficiently to the environment. The concept of differentiation and integration is, in fact, the greatest contribution of Lawrence and Lorsch to organization theory. They suggested that:

> As organizations deal with their external environments, they become segmented into units, each of which has as its major task the problem of dealing with a part of the conditions outside the firm.... These parts of the system need to be linked together towards the accomplishment of the organization's overall purpose.

Their research showed that the two organizations with the most successful records had, in fact, achieved the highest degree of integration, and were also among the most highly differentiated. The differentiation of the various units was more in line with the demands of the environment for those two organizations than for the others.

One of the most important implications of the Lawrence and Lorsch model for organization designers is that, although differentiation demands effective integration, this must not be achieved by minimizing differences and producing a common bland outlook. Instead, integration should be achieved by allowing each department to be as different in its outlook and its structure as its tasks demand — that is, to be highly distinctive — but to use mediating devices such as committees, ad hoc project groups and assigned 'integrators' who stand midway between the functions with which they are concerned and are not dominated by any of them. Integration can therefore be achieved by structural means as well as by organizational development interventions designed to increase trust and understanding between groups and to confront conflict.

## Perrow

The model developed by Perrow (1970) recognizes the importance of structure and the inevitable tendency towards routinization, standardization and bureaucracy in organizations. In accordance with the views of other members of the contingency school, he suggests that different structures can exist within the same firm and that a bureaucratic structure is as appropriate for some tasks as a non-bureaucratic structure is for other tasks.

# The modernists

The modernists include Mintzberg, Drucker (still capable after all these years of coming up with original and stimulating ideas) and the management 'gurus' such as Richard Pascale who emerged in the 1980s and who based their ideas on an analysis of contemporary events, the Japanese approach to organization and, in Charles Handy's case, an apocalyptical view of the future.

## Mintzberg

Mintzberg (1983b) developed the following hypotheses from his research into the structure of organizations:

- the older the organization, the more formalized its behaviour
- structure reflects the age of founding of the industry
- the larger the organization, the more elaborate its structure — that is, the more specialised its tasks, the more differentiated its units and the more developed its administrative component
- the larger the organization, the more formalized its behaviour.

Mintzberg analysed organizations into five broad types or configurations:

1. *Simple structures* which are dominated by the top of the organization with centralized decision-making.
2. *Machine bureaucracy* which is characterized by the standardization of work processes and the extensive reliance on systems.
3. *Professional bureaucracy* where the standardization of skills provide the prime coordinating mechanism.
4. *Divisionalised structures* in which authority is drawn down from the top and activities are grouped together into units which are then managed according to their standardized outputs.
5. *Adhocracies* where power is decentralized selectively to constellations of work that are free to coordinate within and between themselves by mutual adjustments.

## Drucker

In *The coming of the new organization* (1988) Drucker has drawn attention to the impact of new technology.

> The typical large business 20 years hence will have fewer than half the levels of management of its counterpart today, and no more than a third the managers.... Businesses, especially large ones, have little choice but to become information-based. Demographics, for one, demands the shift. The centre of gravity in employment is moving fast from manual and clerical workers to knowledge workers who resist the command-and-control model that business took from the military 100 years ago.

Drucker also points out that organizations have established, through the development of new technology and the extended use of knowledge workers, 'that whole layers of management neither make decisions nor lead. Instead, their main, if not their only, function, is to serve as relays — human boosters for the faint, unfocused signals that pass for communications in the traditional pre-information organization.'

## Pascale

Pascale (1990) believes that the new organizational paradigm functions as follows:

- *From* the image of organizations as machines, with the emphasis on concrete strategy, structure and systems, *to* the idea of organizations as organisms, with the emphasis on the 'soft' dimensions — style, staff, and shared values.
- *From* a hierarchical model, with step-by-step problem solving, *to* a network model, with parallel nodes of intelligence which surround problems until they are eliminated.
- *From* the status-driven view that managers think and workers do as they are told, *to* a view of managers as 'facilitators', with workers empowered to initiate improvements and change.
- *From* an emphasis on 'vertical tasks' within functional units *to* an emphasis on 'horizontal tasks' and collaboration across units.
- *From* a focus on 'content' and the prescribed use of specific tools and techniques *to* a focus on 'process' and a holistic synthesis of techniques.
- *From* the military model *to* a commitment model.

## Charles Handy

Handy (1989) describes two types of organization; the 'shamrock' and the federal.

The *shamrock* organization consists of three elements:

- the core workers (the central leaf of the shamrock) — professionals, technicians and managers
- the contractual fringe — contract workers
- the flexible labour force consisting of temporary staff.

The *federal* organization takes the process of decentralization one stage further by establishing every key operational, manufacturing or service provision activity as a distinct, federated unit. Each federal entity runs its own affairs although they are linked together by the overall strategy of the organization and, if it is a public company, are expected to make an appropriate contribution to corporate profitability in order to provide the required return on their shareholders' investments and to keep external predators at bay.

The centre in a federal organization maintains a low profile. The federated activities are expected to provide the required initiative, drive and energy. The centre is at the middle of things, not at the top. It is not just a banker but it does provide resources. Its main role is to coordinate, advise, influence, suggest and help to develop integrated corporate strategies.

## Organizational structure

Each of the members of the various schools were, in effect, commenting on the factors affecting organization structure. The next section of this chapter takes an overall view of structure.

All organizations have some form of more or less formalized structure which has been defined by Child (1977) as comprising 'all the tangible and regularly occurring features which help to shape their members' behaviour'. Structures incorporate a network of roles and relationships and are there to help in the process of ensuring that collective effort is explicitly organized to achieve specified ends.

Organizations vary in their complexity, but it is always necessary to divide the overall management task into a variety of activities, to allocate these activities to the different parts of the organization and to establish means of controlling, coordinating and integrating them.

The structure of an organization can be regarded as a framework for getting things done. It consists of units, functions, divisions, departments and formally constituted work teams into which activities related to particular processes, projects, products, markets, customers, geographical areas or professional disciplines are grouped together. The structure indicates who is accountable for directing, coordinating and carrying out these activities and defines management hierarchies — the 'chain of command' — thus spelling out, broadly, who is responsible to whom for what at each level in the organization.

### Organization charts

Structures are usually defined in the form of an organization chart. This places individuals in boxes which denote their job and their position in the hierarchy and traces the direct lines of authority (command and control) through the management hierarchies.

Organization charts are vertical in their nature and therefore misrepresent reality. They do not give any indication of the horizontal and diagonal relationships that exist within the framework between people in different units or departments, and do not recognize the fact that within any one hierarchy, commands and control information do not travel all the way down and up the structure as the chart implies. In practice information jumps (especially computer-generated information) and managers or team leaders will interact with people at levels below those immediately beneath them.

Organization charts have their uses as means of defining — simplistically — who does what and hierarchical lines of authority. But even if backed up by organization manuals (which no one reads and which are, in any case, out of date as soon as they are produced) they cannot convey how the organization really works. They may, for example, lead to definitions of jobs — what people are expected to do — but they cannot convey the roles these people carry out in the organization; the parts they play in interacting with others and the ways in which, like actors, they interpret the part they are given.

## Organizational processes

The structure of an organization as described in an organization chart does not give any real indication of how it functions. To understand this, it is necessary to consider the various processes that take place within the structural framework; those of change, flexibility, interaction and networking, communication, group behaviour, teamwork, leadership, command and control, power, politics and conflict.

### Change

Everything is in a perpetual state of change. As Heraclitus of Ephesus said in c 500 BC:

> Everything flows and nothing abides. Everything gives way and nothing stays fixed.

And this phenomenon applies particularly to organizations and the life that goes on within them. To survive and thrive, businesses have to grow. They must innovate, develop new products, expand into new markets, reorganize, introduce new technology, and change working methods and practices. Even if this does not happen voluntarily, change may be forced upon them by competition and changes in the business, political and social environment. Managers have to be able to introduce and to manage change and gain the commitment of their teams to it. Members of the personnel function have a key role as facilitators or 'change agents' in ensuring that change can be managed effectively in the organization.

Change can create instability and ambiguity and replace order and predictability with disharmony and surprise. The organization's culture, as discussed in Chapter 19, can create solidarity and meaning and can inspire commitment and productivity. But the culture can actively and forcefully work against an organization when change becomes necessary. If not properly managed, change can decrease morale, motivation and commitment and create conditions of conflict within an organization.

Change, as Rosabeth Moss Kanter (1984) suggested, can be regarded as the process of analyzing 'the past to elicit the present actions required for the future'. It involves moving from a present state, through a transition state to a future desired state.

Conceptually, the change process starts with an awareness of the need for change. An analysis of this situation and the factors that have created it leads to a diagnosis of their distinctive characteristics and an indication of the direction in which action needs to be taken. Possible courses of action can then be identified and evaluated and a choice made of the preferred action.

It is then necessary to decide how to get from here to there. Managing change during this transition state is a critical phase in the change process. It is here that the problems of introducing change emerge and have to be managed. These problems can include resistance to change, low stability, high levels of stress, misdirected energy, conflict and loss of momentum. Hence the need to do everything possible to anticipate reactions and likely impediments to the introduction of change.

The installation stage can also be painful. When planning change there is a tendency for people to think that it will be an entirely logical and linear process of going from A to B. It is not like that at all. As described by Pettigrew and Whipp (1991), the implementation of change is an 'iterative, cumulative and reformulation-in-use process'.

To manage change, it is first necessary to understand the types of change and why people resist change. It is important to bear in mind that while those wanting change need to be constant about ends, they have to be flexible about means. This requires them to come to an understanding of the various models of change that have been developed. In the light of an understanding of these models they will be better equipped to make use of the guidelines for change which are set out at the end of this chapter.

There are two main types of change: strategic and operational.

*Strategic change* is concerned with broad, long-term and organization-wide issues. It is about moving to a future state which has been defined generally in terms of strategic vision and scope.

*Operational change* relates to new systems, procedures, structures or technology which will have an immediate effect on working arrangements within a part of the organization. But their impact on people can be more significant than broader strategic change and they have to be handled just as carefully.

## Flexibility

It was suggested by Atkinson (1984) that there are three kinds of flexibility:

1. *Functional flexibility* which is sought so that employees can be redeployed quickly and smoothly between activities and tasks. Functional flexibility may require multiskilling — craft workers who possess and can apply a number of skills covering, for example, both mechanical and electrical engineering, or manufacturing and maintenance activities.
2. *Numerical flexibility* which is sought so that the number of employees can be quickly and easily increased or decreased in line with even short-term changes in the level of demand for labour.
3. *Financial flexibility* which provides for pay levels to reflect the state of supply and demand in the external labour market and also means the use of flexible pay systems which facilitate either functional or numerical flexibility.

It was also claimed by Atkinson that there is a growing trend for firms to seek all three kinds of flexibility by developing an entirely new organization structure. This results in the development of what he termed the 'flexible firm'.

The new structure in the flexible firm involves the break-up of the labour force into increasingly peripheral, and therefore numerically flexible, groups of workers clustered around a numerically stable core group which will conduct the organization's key, firm-specific activities. At the core, the emphasis is on functional flexibility. Shifting to the periphery, numerical flexibility becomes more important. As the market grows, the periphery expands to take up slack; as growth slows, the periphery contracts. At the core, only tasks and responsibilities change; the workers here are insulated from medium-term fluctuations in the market and can therefore enjoy job security, whereas those in the periphery are exposed to them.

## Interaction and networking

Interactions between people criss-cross the organization creating networks for getting things done and exchanging information which are not catered for in the formal structure. 'Networking' is an increasingly important process in flexible and delayered organizations where more fluid interactions across the structure are required between individuals and teams. Individuals can often get much more done by networking than by going through formal channels. At least this means that they can canvass opinion and enlist support to promote their projects or ideas.

People also get things done in organizations by creating alliances — getting agreement on a course of action with other people and joining forces to get things done.

## Communications

The communications processes used in organizations have a marked effect on how it functions, especially if they take place through the network, which can then turn into the 'grapevine'. Electronic means of communication through computers (E-Mail) encourage the instant flow of information but may inhibit the face-to-face interactions which are often the best ways of getting things done.

## Group behaviour

Organizations consist of groups of people working together. Interactions take place within and between groups and the degree to which these processes are formalized varies according to the organizational context. To understand and influence organizational behaviour, one must understand how groups behave. In particular, this means considering the nature of:

- formal groups
- informal groups
- the processes that take place within groups
- group cohesion

- the factors that make for group effectiveness
- approaches to improving teamwork.

*Formal groups*
Formal groups are set up by organizations to achieve a defined purpose. People are brought together with the necessary skills to carry out the tasks and a system exists for directing, co-ordinating and controlling the groups activities. The structure, composition and size of the group will depend largely on the nature of the task; although tradition, organizational culture and management style may exert considerable influence. The more routine or clearly defined the task is the more structured the group will be. In a highly structured group the leader will have a positive role and may well adopt an authoritarian style. The role of each member of the group will be precise and a hierarchy of authority is likely to exist. The more ambiguous the task the more difficult it will be to structure the group. The leader's role is more likely to be supportive — she or he will tend to concentrate on encouragement and co-ordination rather than on issuing orders. The group will operate in a more democratic way and individual roles will be fluid and less clearly defined.

*Informal groups*
Informal groups are set up by people in organizations who have some affinity for one another. It could be said that formal groups satisfy the needs of the organization while informal groups satisfy the needs of their members. One of the main aims of organization design and development should be to ensure, so far as possible, that the basis upon which activities are grouped together and the way in which groups are allowed or encouraged to behave satisfy both these needs. The values and norms established by informal groups can work against the organization. This was first clearly established in the Hawthorne studies which revealed that groups could regulate their own behaviour and output levels irrespective of what management wanted. An understanding of the processes that take place within groups can, however, help to make them work *for*, rather than against, what the organization needs.

*Group processes*
As mentioned above, the way in which groups function is affected by the task and by the norms in the organization. An additional factor is size. There is a greater diversity of talent, skills and knowledge in a

347

large group, but individuals find it more difficult to make their presence felt. According to Handy (1981), for best participation and for highest all-round involvement, the optimum size is between five and seven. But to achieve the requisite breadth of knowledge the group may have to be considerably larger, and this makes greater demands on the skills of the leader in getting participation. The main processes that take place in groups as described below are interaction, task and maintenance functions, group ideology, group cohesion, group development and identification.

## Interaction

Three basic channels of communication within groups were identified by Leavitt (1951) and are illustrated in Figure 18.1. The characteristics of these different groups are as follows:

- *Wheel groups*, where the task is straightforward, work faster, need fewer messages to solve problems and make fewer errors than circle groups, but they are inflexible if the task changes.
- *Circle groups* are faster in solving complex problems than wheel groups.
- *All-channel groups* are the most flexible and function well in complex, open-ended situations.

The level of satisfaction for individuals is lowest in the circle group, fairly high in the all-channel group and mixed in the wheel group, where the leader is more satisfied than the outlying members.

## Task and maintenance functions

The following functions need to be carried out in groups:

- *task* — initiating, information seeking, diagnosing, opinion-seeking, evaluating, decision-managing
- *maintenance* — encouraging, compromising, peace-keeping, clarifying, summarizing, standard-setting.

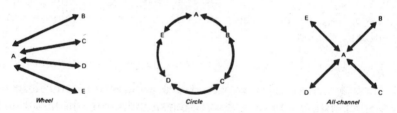

Figure 18.1 Channels of communication within groups (after Leavitt)

It is the job of the group leader or leaders to ensure that these functions operate effectively. Leaderless groups can work, but only in special circumstances. A leader is almost essential — whether official or self-appointed. The style adopted by a leader affects the way the group operates. If the leader is respected, this will increase group cohesiveness and its ability to get things done. An inappropriately authoritarian style creates tension and resentment. An over-permissive style means that respect for the leader diminishes and the group does not function so effectively.

### Group ideology

In the course of interacting and carrying out its task and maintenance functions, the group develops an ideology which affects the attitudes and actions of its members and the degree of satisfaction which they feel.

### Group cohesion

If the group ideology is strong and individual members identify closely with the group, it will become increasingly cohesive. Group norms or implicit rules will be evolved which define what is acceptable behaviour and what is not. The impact of group cohesion can, however, result in negative as well as positive results. Janis's (1972) study of the decision making processes of US foreign policy groups established that a cohesive group of individuals, sharing a common fate, exerts a strong pressure towards conformity. He coined the term 'group think' to describe the exaggeration of irrational tendencies which appears to occur in groups and argued that a group setting can magnify weakness of judgement.

To be 'one of us' is not always a good thing in management circles. A sturdy spirit of independence, even a maverick tendency, may be more conducive to correct decision making. Team working is a good thing but so is flexibility and independent judgement. These need not be incompatible with team membership, but could be if there is too much emphasis on cohesion and conformity within the group.

### Group development

Tuckman (1965) has identified four stages of group development:

1. *Forming* when there is anxiety, dependence on the leader and testing to find out the nature of the situation and the task, and what behaviour is acceptable.

2. *Storming* where there is conflict, emotional resistance to the demands of the task, resistance to control and even rebellion against the leader.
3. *Norming* when group cohesion is developed, norms emerge, views are exchanged openly, mutual support and cooperation increase and the group acquires a sense of identity.
4. *Performing* when interpersonal problems are resolved, roles are flexible and functional, there are constructive attempts to complete tasks and energy is available for effective work.

### Identification

Individuals will identify with their groups if they like the other members, approve of the purpose and work of the group and wish to be associated with the standing of the group in the organization. Identification will be more complex if the standing of the group is good.

## Teamworking

As defined by Katzenbach and Smith (1993):

> A team is a small number of people with complementary skills who are committed to a common purpose, performance goals and approach for which they hold themselves mutually accountable.

They suggested that some of the main characteristics of teams are as listed below:

- Teams are the basic units of performance for most organizations. They meld together the skills, experiences and insights of several people.
- Team work applies to the whole organization as well as specific teams. It represents 'a set of values that encourage behaviours such as listening and responding cooperatively to points of view expressed by others, giving others the benefit of the doubt, providing support to those who need it and recognizing the interests and achievements of others.'
- Teams are created and energized by significant and demanding performance challenges.
- Teams outperform individuals acting alone or in large organizational groupings, especially when performance requires multiple skills, judgements and experiences.

- Teams are flexible and responsive to changing events and demands. They can adjust their approach to new information and challenges with greater speed, accuracy and effectiveness than can individuals caught in the web of larger organizational connections.
- High-performance teams invest much time and effort exploring, shaping and agreeing on a purpose that belongs to them, both collectively and individually. They are characterized by a deep sense of commitment to their growth and success.

## Reservations about the significance of teamwork

The popular expectation is that group decisions will be superior to those made by individuals working alone. However, West and Slater (1995) found that research evidence (eg Diehl and Stroebe, 1987) is consistent in suggesting that the quality of decision-making by groups generally equals but does not exceed the quality of decisions made by individual members. The quality of decision-making of the most able members is generally not matched.

As noted by West and Slater, 'It is commonly assumed that cohesive teams, ie those characterised by a strong sense of mutual support and sharing, will be more effective than less cohesive teams'. West and Slater quote research by Mullen and Cooper (1994) and Tannenbaum *et al* (1992). The former indicated that effective team performance created cohesiveness rather than the other way round. Tannenbaum *et al*'s review of research on teambuilding interventions suggests that they have a relatively positive impact on member attitudes and perceptions but have no reliable impact on team performance. West and Slater comment that 'in studies conducted in organizational settings, there is no reliable impact of team building interventions upon task effectiveness or team performance. In particular, interventions designed to change the interpersonal processes in groups are least likely to effect any change in performance'.

## Team effectiveness

To summarize, an effective team is one in which the structure, leadership and methods of operation are relevant to the requirements of the task. The Tavistock Institute studies (Trist *et al*, 1963) emphasized the importance of commitment to the whole group task and the need to group people in a way which ensures that they are related to each other by way of the requirements of task performance and task interdependence.

In an effective team, its purpose is clear and its members feel that the task is important both to them and the organization (the concept of saliency). It was established by Bales (1950) that effective teams need people who help to get things done. They also need people who are concerned with the social side of working in a group. Task-orientated team members are most influential but socially inclined members are most liked. There are a number of roles that team members can play and an understanding of them helps in the teambuilding process. Two of the best known classifications are described below.

*Belbin's team roles*
Belbin (1981) identified eight different roles played by management team members.

1. *Chairmen* — control the way in which a team moves towards the group objectives by making the best use of team resources; recognizing where the team's strengths and weaknesses lie and ensuring that the best use is made of each team member's role.
2. *Shapers* — specify the ways in which team effort is applied, directing attention generally to the setting of objectives and priorities and seeking to impose some shape or pattern on group discussion and on the outcome of group activities.
3. *Company workers* — turn concepts and plans into practical working procedures and carry out agreed plans systematically and efficiently.
4. *Plants* — specify new ideas and strategies, with special attention to major issues. They look for possible breaks in approaches to the problems with which the team is confronted.
5. *Resource investigators* — explore and report on ideas, developments and resources outside the team, creating external contacts that might be useful to the team and conducting any subsequent negotiations.
6. *Monitor-evaluators* — analyse problems and evaluate ideas and suggestions so that the team is better placed to take better decisions.
7. *Team workers* — support members in their strengths (ie building on their suggestions), underpin members on their shortcomings, improve communications between members and foster team spirit generously.
8. *Completer-finishers* — ensure that the team is protected from mistakes, actively search for work which needs more than a usual degree of attention, and maintain a sense of urgency in the team.

Belbin suggests that although the main roles of team members can be slotted into one or other of these categories, most people have an alternative, back-up role which they use as necessary.

*Team Management Systems*

Team Management Systems (UK) markets another approach to the construction of balanced teams and the improvement of team performance. This includes an alternative classification of roles and was developed by Margerison and McCann (1986). The eight roles are:

- *Reporter-adviser*: gathers information and expresses it in an easily understandable form.
- *Creator-innovator*: enjoys thinking up new ideas and ways of doing things.
- *Explorer-promoter*: takes ideas and promotes them to others.
- *Assessor-developer*: takes ideas and makes them work in practice.
- *Thruster-organizer*: gets things done, emphasizing targets, deadlines and budgets.
- *Concluder-producer*: sets up plans and standard systems to ensure outputs are achieved.
- *Controller-inspector*: concerned with the details and adhering to rules and regulations.
- *Upholder-maintainer*: provides guidance and help in meeting standards.

According to Margerison and McCann a balanced team needs members with preferences for each of these eight roles. Teams that are balanced in terms of these preferences will consist of very different types of people whose contributions may be difficult to link together but the alternative, homogeneous team is likely to suffer from 'group think' and thus have a blinkered approach. Conflict in a team is seen as a healthy sign but means that special efforts have to be made to link the team into a coherent and effective unit.

## Leadership

The function of leaders is to achieve the task set for them with the help of the group. Leaders and their groups are therefore inter-dependent.

Leaders have two main roles. First they must achieve the task. Secondly, they have to maintain effective relationships between themselves and the group and the individuals in it — effective in the sense that they are conducive to achieving the task. These two roles were first identified by the Ohio State University researchers (Halpin and Winer, 1957), who identified the two dimensions of leadership behaviour:

- *Initiating structure* — specifying ways and means of accomplishing the goals of the group and co-ordinating the activities of its members.
- *Consideration* — motivating the members of the group to accept the group goals and to work at the group task while at the same time maintaining internal harmony and satisfaction.

In fulfilling their roles, leaders have to satisfy the following needs:

1. *Task needs.* The group exists to achieve a common purpose or task. The leaders' role is to ensure that this purpose is fulfilled. If it is not, they will lose the confidence of the group and the result will be frustration, disenchantment, criticism and, possibly, the ultimate disintegration of the group.
2. *Group maintenance needs.* To achieve its objectives, the group needs to be held together. The leaders' job is to build up and maintain team spirit and morale.
3. *Individual needs.* Individuals have their own needs which they expect to be satisfied at work. The leaders' task is to be aware of these needs so that where necessary they can take steps to harmonize them with the needs of the task and the group.

As Adair (1973) pointed out, these three needs are interdependent. The leaders' actions in one area affect both the others; thus successful achievement of the task is essential if the group is to be held together and its members motivated to give their best effort to the job. Action directed at meeting group or individual needs must be related to the needs of the task. It is impossible to consider individuals in isolation from the group or to consider the group without referring to the individuals within it. If any need is neglected, one of the others will suffer and the leader will be less successful.

The kind of leadership exercised will be related to the nature of the task and the people being led. It will also depend on the environment and, of course, on the actual leader. Analysing the qualities of leadership in terms of intelligence, initiative, self-assurance and so on has only limited value. The qualities required may be different in different situations. It is more useful to adopt a contingency approach and take account of the variables leaders have to deal with;

especially the task, the group and their own position relative to the group.

Fiedler (1967), in particular, concentrated upon the relationship between the leader and the group and the structure of the task as determinants in the choice of the most effective style of leadership. His research indicated that the leaders of the most effective groups tended to maintain greater distance between themselves and their subordinates than the leaders of less effective groups. He found that an 'initiating structure' approach was most effective when the situation was either very favourable or unfavourable to the leader, while 'consideration' was more appropriate when the situation was only moderately favourable. Fiedler also emphasized the 'situational' aspects of leadership.

Leadership performance depends as much on the organization as on the leaders' own attributes. Except perhaps for the unusual case, it is simply not meaningful to speak of an effective leader and an ineffective leader; we can only speak of a leader who tends to be effective in one situation and ineffective in another.

The most effective leaders fit their style to the situation, which includes their own preferred style of operating and personal characteristics as well as the nature of the task and the group.

## Command and control

The 'command and control' approach to organizing is regarded with distaste by some people. Handy (1989) advocates the development of a 'culture of consent,' and the emphasis of most contemporary organization theorists is on the virtues of decentralization, empowerment and self-managed teams.

However, the culture of many organizations — their prevailing management style — is still authoritarian, and the ways in which this authority is exercised in order to obtain compliance is of interest to the organization analyst. The analysis must go beyond the espoused values to what really happens. It can be argued, as does Guest (1991), that the pursuit of increased commitment is really a means of gaining compliance — employees are expected to be committed to what the organization wants them to do.

## Power

Organizations exist to get things done and in the process of doing this people or groups exercise power. Directly or indirectly, the use of power in influencing behaviour is a pervading feature of organizations, whether it is exerted by managers, specialists, informal groups or trade union officials.

Power is clearly linked to position and rank: but to a certain degree it has to be earned. Managers give orders to their subordinates but they will get more out of them if they obtain their willing cooperation rather than their grudging submission. Power is bestowed upon managers, but they also have to justify their use of it. There are, however, other sources of power, namely:

- *Access to people with power*. Proximity or a direct line obviously gives people more scope to exert influence, actual or perceived. That is why personal assistants or secretaries are important.
- *Control over information*. 'Knowledge is power' or, alternatively, 'authority goes to the one who knows'. If people are in the know, they are in a better position to control events or, if they want to play politics, to put a spoke in other people's wheels.
- *Control over results*. Power goes to those who can control what the organization achieves. When trade unions strike, they are exercising this sort of power.
- *Control over resources*. Power goes to those who exercise control over resources that everyone else needs, such as money, people, information, equipment or services that anyone else needs, the person in that position will have power.
- *Control over rewards and punishments*. People have power if they can give rewards or punishments or influence others who control them.
- *Expertise*. People gain and keep power if they can convince others that they are the experts.
- *Identification*. Power can be achieved over others if they identify with what is being done or with the individual concerned. This is what charismatic visionary leaders do by enthusiasm, dedication, getting people involved and sheer force of personality.

## Politics

Power and politics are inextricably mixed, and in any organization there will inevitably be people who want to achieve their satisfaction by acquiring power, legitimately or illegitimately.

Organizations consist of individuals who, while they are ostensibly there to achieve a common purpose, are, at the same time, driven by their own needs to achieve their own goals. Effective management is the process of harmonizing individual endeavour and ambition to the common good. Some individuals genuinely believe that using political means to achieve their goals will benefit the organization as well as themselves. Others rationalize this belief. Yet others unashamedly pursue their own ends.

It can be argued that a political approach to management is inevitable and even desirable in any organization where the clarity of goals is not absolute, where the decision-making process is not clear cut and where the authority to make decisions is not evenly or appropriately distributed. And there can be few organizations where one or more of these conditions do not apply. Kakabadse (1983) recognizes this point when he says: 'Politics is a process, that of influencing individuals and groups of people to your point of view, where you cannot rely on authority.' In this sense, a political approach can be legitimate as long as the ends are justifiable from the viewpoint of the organization.

## Conflict

Conflict is inevitable in organizations because they function by means of adjustments and compromises among competitive elements in their structure and membership. These elements produce conflict of two kinds: horizontal conflict between functions, departments and groups, and vertical conflict between different levels in the hierarchy.

Conflict also arises when there is change, because it may be seen as a threat to be challenged or resisted, or when there is frustration — this may produce an aggressive reaction; fight rather than flight. Conflict is not to be deplored. It is an inevitable result of progress and change and it can and should be used constructively.

Conflict between individuals raises fewer problems than conflict between groups. Individuals can act independently and resolve their differences. Members of groups may have to accept the norms, goals, and values of their group. The individual's loyalty will usually be to his or her own group if it is in conflict with others.

## Types of organization

The basic types of organization are:

- the 'line and staff' organization
- the divisionalized organization
- matrix organization

- the flexible organization
- the process-based organization.

## Line and staff

The line and staff organization was the type favoured by the classical theorists. Although the term is not so much used today, except when referring to line managers, it still describes many structures. The line hierarchy in the structure consists of functions and managers who are directly concerned in achieving the primary purposes of the organization, for example, manufacturing and selling or directing the organization as a whole. 'Staff' in functions such as finance, personnel and engineering provide services to the line to enable them to get on with their job.

## Divisionalized organizations

The process of divisionalization, as first described by Sloan (1963) on the basis of his experience in running General Motors, involves structuring the organization into separate divisions each concerned with discrete manufacturing, sales, distribution or service functions, or with serving a particular market. At group headquarters functional departments may exist in such areas as finance, planning, personnel, legal and engineering to provide services to the divisions and importantly, to exercise a degree of functional control over their activities. The amount of control exercised will depend on the extent to which the organization has decided to decentralize authority to strategic business units which are positioned close to the markets they serve.

## Decentralized organizations

Some organizations, especially conglomerates, decentralize most of their activities and retain only a skeleton headquarters staff to deal with financial control matters, strategic planning, legal issues and sometimes, but not always, personnel issues, especially those concerned with senior management on an across the group basis (recruitment, development and remuneration).

As Goold and Campbell (1986) established through their research in a number of major UK conglomerates and divisionalized organizations, there are three ways in which the centre of the organization may relate to its component businesses:

- *strategic planning* — the centre develops strategy with the business units and sets broad, strategic performance targets
- *financial control* — the centre exercises control through financial budgeting processes and by measuring performance in relation to profit targets; planning influence is low
- *strategic control* — the centre leaves the units to develop their strategic plans but exercises tight control against strategic targets.

## Matrix organizations

Matrix organizations are project-based. Development, design or construction projects will be controlled by project directors or managers or, in the case of a consultancy, assignments will be conducted by project leaders. Project managers will have no permanent staff except, possibly, some administrative/secretarial support. They will draw the members of their project teams from discipline groups, each of which will be headed up by a director or manager who is responsible on a continuing basis for resourcing the group, developing and managing its members and ensuring that they are assigned as fully as possible to project teams. When these individuals are assigned to a project team they will be responsible to the team leader for delivering the required results, but they will continue to be accountable generally to the head of their discipline for their overall performance and contribution.

Matrix organizations are a logical way of organizing when the business is mainly concerned with project management, but they produce obvious stresses and strains on individuals who, in effect, are working for two bosses.

## Flexible organizations

Flexible organizations may conform broadly to the Mintzberg (1983b) category of an adhocracy in the sense that they are capable of quickly adapting to new demands and operate fluidly. They may organize themselves along the lines of Handy's (1989) 'shamrock' organization with core workers carrying out the fundamental and continuing activities of the organization and contract and temporary staff being employed as peripheral workers when needed, ie numerical flexibility.

## The process-based organization

Classical structure doctrine focuses attention on vertical relationships and authority-based management — the 'command and control structure'. Horizontal processes that cut across organizational boundaries received little attention except by the systems school which had relatively little influence on practising managers. But times have changed, as Ghoshal and Bartlett (1995) have stated:

> In recent years, however, managers have begun to notice that horizontal processes matter. Total quality management was such a process. It was not top down. It cut across the boundaries separating organizational units to invest quality in the company's products and services. Likewise, re-engineering showed companies how to integrate functionally separated tasks into unified horizontal work processes. Through such experimentation, managers are beginning to deal with their organizations in some fundamentally different ways. Rather than seeing them as a hierarchy of static roles, they think of them as a portfolio of dynamic processes.... They see core organizational processes that overlay and often dominate the vertical, authority-based processes of the hierarchical structure.... They see another process that builds competence across the organization's internal boundaries.

# 19

# Organizational Culture

## Definition

Organizational or corporate culture is the pattern of shared beliefs, attitudes, assumptions, norms and values in an organization which may not have been articulated but in the absence of direct instructions, shape the way people act and interact and strongly influence the ways in which things get done.

This definition emphasizes that organizational culture refers to a number of abstractions (beliefs, norms, attitudes, etc) which pervade the organization although they may not have been defined in specific terms. Nevertheless, they can significantly influence people's behaviour.

A more comprehensive psychologist's definition was provided by Schein (1984):

> Organizational culture is the pattern of basic assumptions that a given group has invented, discovered or developed in learning to cope with its problems of external adaptation and internal integration, and that have worked well enough to be considered valid, and, therefore, to be taught to new members as the correct way to perceive, think and feel in relation to those problems.

## The importance of culture to organizations

Culture is a key component in the achievement of an organization's mission and strategies, the improvement of organizational effectiveness and the management of change.

The significance of culture arises because it is rooted in deeply held beliefs. It reflects what has worked in the past, being composed of responses which have been accepted because they have met with success.

Culture can work for an organization by creating an environment which is conducive to performance improvement and the management of change. It can work against an organization by erecting barriers which prevent the attainment of corporate strategies. These barriers include resistance to change and lack of commitment.

The impact of culture can include:

- conveying a sense of identity and unity of purpose to members of the organization
- facilitating the generating of commitment and 'mutuality'
- shaping behaviour by providing guidance on what is expected.

## Components of organizational culture

Organizational culture can be described in terms of *values, norms and artifacts*. It will be perceived by members of the company as *organizational climate*, and it will influence, and be influenced by, the organization's strategy, structure and systems.

### Values

Values refer to what is regarded as important. They are expressed in beliefs in what is best or good for the organization and what sort of behaviour is desirable. The 'value set' of an organization may only be recognized at top level, or it may be shared throughout the firm so that the enterprise could be described as being 'value driven'.

Clearly, the more strongly based the values the more they will affect behaviour. This does not depend upon their having been articulated. Implicit values which are deeply embedded in the culture of an organization and are reinforced by the behaviour of management can be highly influential, while espoused values which are idealistic and are not reflected in managerial behaviour may have little or no effect. Areas in which values can be expressed might be:

- care and consideration for people
- care for customers
- competitiveness
- enterprise
- equal opportunity
- equity in the treatment of employees

- excellence
- growth
- innovation
- managing diversity
- market/customer orientation
- priorities between people and organizational needs
- performance orientation
- productivity
- quality
- social responsibility
- teamwork.

Values are translated into reality through *norms* and *artifacts* as described below. They may also be expressed through the media of language (organizational jargon), rituals, stories and myths.

## *Norms*

Norms are the unwritten rules of behaviour, the 'rules of the game' which provide informal guidelines on how to behave. Norms tell people what they are supposed to be doing, saying, believing, even wearing. They are never expressed in writing — if they were, they would be policies or procedures. They are passed on by word of mouth or behaviour and can be enforced by the reactions of people if they are violated. They can exert very powerful pressure on behaviour because of these reactions — we control others by the way we react to them.

Norms refer to such aspects of behaviour as

- how managers treat the members of their teams and how the latter relate to their managers
- the prevailing work ethic, eg 'work hard, play hard', 'come in early, stay late', 'if you cannot finish your work during business hours you are obviously inefficient', 'look busy at all times', 'look relaxed at all times'
- status — how much importance is attached to it; the existence or lack of obvious status symbols
- ambition — naked ambition is expected and approved of, or a more subtle approach is the norm
- performance — exacting performance standards are general; the highest praise that can be given in the organization is to be referred to as very professional
- power — recognized as a way of life; executed by political means,

dependent on expertise and ability rather than position; concentrated at the top; shared at different levels in different parts of the organization

- politics — rife throughout the organization and treated as normal behaviour; not accepted as overt behaviour
- loyalty — expected, a cradle to grave approach to careers; discounted, the emphasis is on results and contribution in the short term
- anger — openly expressed; hidden, but expressed through other, possibly political, means
- approachability — managers are expected to be approachable and visible; everything happens behind closed doors
- formality — a cool, formal approach is the norm; forenames are/are not used at all levels; there are unwritten but clearly understood rules about dress.

## Artifacts

Artifacts are the visible and tangible aspects of an organization which people hear, see or feel. Artifacts can include such things as the working environment, the tone and language used in letters or memoranda, the manner in which people address each other at meetings or over the telephone, the welcome (or lack of welcome) given to visitors and the way in which telephonists deal with outside calls. Artifacts can be very revealing.

## Organizational climate

Organizational climate is less encompassing than the concept of organizational culture and is more readily measured.

Organizational climate is how people perceive (see and feel about) the culture that has been created in their company or unit. It has been defined by French *et al* (1985) as 'the relatively persistent set of perceptions held by organization members concerning the characteristics and quality of organizational culture'.

Perceptions about climate can be measured by questionnaires such as that developed by Litwin and Stringer (1968) which cover nine categories:

1. *Structure* — feelings about constraints and freedom to act and the degree of formality or informality in the working atmosphere.

2.  *Responsibility* — the feeling of being trusted to carry out important work.
3.  *Risk* — the sense of riskiness and challenge in the job and in the organization; the relative emphasis on taking calculated risks or playing it safe.
4.  *Warmth* — the existence of friendly and informal social groups.
5.  *Support* — the perceived helpfulness of managers and co-workers; the emphasis (or lack of emphasis) on mutual support.
6.  *Standards* — the perceived importance of implicit and explicit goals and performance standards; the emphasis on doing a good job; the challenge represented in personal and team goals.
7.  *Conflict* — the feeling that managers and other workers want to hear different opinions; the emphasis on getting problems out into the open rather than smoothing them over or ignoring them.
8.  *Identity* — the feeling that you belong to a company; that you are a valuable member of a working team.

## Management style

Management style describes the way in which managers set about achieving results through people. It is how managers behave as team leaders and how they exercise authority. Managers can be autocratic or democratic, tough or soft, demanding or easy-going, directive or laissez-faire, distant or accessible, destructive or supportive, task orientated or people orientated, rigid or flexible, considerate or unfeeling, friendly or cold, keyed up or relaxed. How they behave will depend partly on themselves — their natural inclinations, partly on the example given to them by their managers and partly on organizational values and norms.

## Culture and strategy

To paraphrase Chandler (1962), it seems possible that culture follows strategy; in other words, strategic choices on such matters as growth, innovation, product-market development and human resource development will shape behaviour and, progressively, change values and norms. But the culture of the organization could equally help to shape its strategy. For example, a company with an open, enterprising and flexible culture is more likely to adopt this approach when developing its business strategies. Culture and strategy are inter-dependent.

## Culture and process

Process describes how things get done, not what gets done. It embraces such aspects of organizational behaviour as leading, motivating, gaining commitment, managing change, communicating, networking, working in teams and planning and coordinating activities. Policies, procedures, structures and systems are means of making process work.

Culture management will involve influencing behaviour, attitudes and beliefs through process. For example, total quality as a concept can be developed through various quality control mechanisms but will only be fully achieved if processes in the organization fully support its achievement.

## Culture and structures or systems

Culture will affect the ways in which the organization is structured and its operational systems. These will include the amount of rigidity or flexibility allowed in the structure, the extent to which informal processes of interaction and communication override or replace formal channels, the amount of authority which is devolved from the top or the centre, and the degree to which jobs are compartmentalized and rigidly defined. It may affect the number of layers of management, the spans of control of managers and the extent to which decisions are made by teams rather than by individuals.

The development and use of systems will also be affected by the corporate culture and will in turn help to shape it. A bureaucratic or mechanistic organization will attempt to govern everything through systems or manuals. An organic approach will only allow systems which are functions of the situation in which the enterprise finds itself rather than conforming to any pre-determined and rigid view of how it should operate. In some organizations, people follow systems to the letter, in others, people take pride in 'bucking the system' and cutting corners to get things done. Systems can be used as control mechanisms to enforce conformity or they can be flexed to allow scope for adapting and responding to new situations as they arise.

# Development of culture

The norms and values which are the basis of culture will be developed over time as a result of the influence of the organization's external environment and its internal processes, systems and technology.

## Organizational Culture

The external environment covers economic, market, competitive and social trends, technological innovations, and government interventions. Internally, culture is shaped by the purpose, strategy and technology of the organization and by particularly significant events, such as a major crisis or the impact of a dynamic, visionary and inspirational chief executive. In fact, the philosophy and values of top management over the years will have played a dominant role.

## Varieties of culture

The strength of a culture will clearly influence its impact on corporate behaviour. Strong cultures will have more widely shared and more clearly expressed beliefs and values. These values will probably have been developed over a considerable period of time and they will be perceived as functional in the sense that they help the organization to achieve its purpose.

There may be one culture pervading the organization but there will almost certainly be a number of sub-cultures in different departments, functions or divisions. This can complicate culture management because of possible inconsistencies or conflicts between cultures.

In fact, an important question to answer when considering cultural change is the extent to which a common culture should be developed (or imposed) throughout the organization, or the degree to which strategic business units should continue to maintain their own distinctive cultures.

The answer to this question will depend on the philosophy of top management, which in turn will affect and be affected by the nature of the organization and its operation. In each of Goold and Campbell's (1986) categories of strategic planning, financial control and strategic control companies, different approaches will be used.

Culture may also be strongly influenced by different product-market conditions or different technologies.

The more operational responsibility is devolved the less pressure there will be from the centre to adopt a common culture on the basis of what matters is 'what you achieve rather than how you achieve it'.

The companies with the strongest and most pervasive cultures such as Hewlett-Packard, Marks and Spencer or IBM are likely to be those which are well established and operationally homogeneous. In Peters and Waterman's (1982) phrase, they 'stick to their knitting'.

## Implications

Culture is developed and manifests itself in different ways in different organizations. It is not possible to say that one culture is better than another, only that it is dissimilar in certain ways. There is no such thing as an ideal culture, only an appropriate culture. This means that there can be no universal prescription for managing culture, although there are certain approaches which can be helpful, as described in the next section.

## Culture management

Culture management is the process of developing or reinforcing an appropriate culture — that is, one which helps the organization to fulfil its purpose.

Culture management is concerned with:

- *Culture change* — the development of attitudes, beliefs and values which will be congruent with the organization's mission, strategies, environment and technologies. The aim is to achieve significant changes in organizational climate, management style and behaviour which positively support the achievement of the organization's objectives.
- *Culture reinforcement* — which aims to preserve and reinforce what is good or functional about the present culture.
- *Change management* — which is concerned with enabling the culture to adapt successfully to change and gaining acceptance to changes in organization, systems, procedures and methods of work (see Chapter 22).
- *Commitment gain* — which is concerned with the commitment of members of the organization to its mission, strategies and values (see Chapter 17).

## Aims of culture management

The aims of culture management are to:

- develop an ideology which guides management on the formulation and implementation of coherent HRM strategies and policies
- create and maintain a positive climate within an organization which indicates the behaviour which is expected of members of that organization in the course of their work

- promote understanding and commitment to the values of the organization.

Culture management does not, however, aim to impose a uniform and bland culture on an organization. It recognizes that different cultures may be appropriate in different parts of the firm. And although there will be certain values which management believe are important, the process of disseminating these values will recognize that members of the organization will have their own sets of values which they will only modify if they are convinced that it is in their own interests as well as those of the organization.

The management of the organization's culture is a central activity for senior management with the advice and help of personnel or HR specialists in their increasingly important role as internal consultants (this role was discussed in Chapter 4).

Managements, according to Legge (1989), use strong culture to unite employees through a set of managerially sanctioned values. They set the direction and establish a culture which helps them to maintain it. Legge also points out that:

> The relationship between 'strong' cultures, employee commitment and adaptability contains a series of paradoxes. Strong cultures allow for a rapid response to familiar conditions, but inhibit immediate flexibility in response to the unfamiliar because of the commitment generated to a (now) inappropriate ideology.

Weak cultures are potentially more adaptable but will not be so effective in generating commitment to action.

The implication is that the pursuit of new strategic goals in response to environmental changes may require action to change the culture. However, changing strong cultures can be a prolonged affair, except in crisis conditions.

## Approaches to culture management

Culture management is about reinforcing or embedding an existing functional culture or changing a dysfunctional culture. The approach will be affected by certain overall considerations as discussed below. With these in mind, culture management is a matter of analysis and diagnosis followed by the application of appropriate reinforcement or change levers.

Schein (1987), has suggested that the most powerful primary mechanisms for culture embedding and reinforcement are:

- what leaders pay attention to, measure and control
- leaders' reactions to critical incidents and crises
- deliberate role modelling, teaching and coaching by leaders
- criteria for allocation of rewards and status
- criteria for recruitment, selection, promotion and commitment.

Because cultures have evolved over the years and are usually deeply rooted, they are difficult to change. It is very hard to get people to alter long held attitudes and beliefs, and attempts to do so often fail. All you can do is to get them to alter their behaviour in ways which will reduce dysfunctional elements in the culture and support the introduction of functional elements.

But changing behaviour is not always easy, although it will happen in traumatic circumstances such as a crisis, a change in ownership or the arrival of a powerful, autocratic, charismatic and visionary leader.

## Culture analysis

The analysis of culture and the diagnosis of what management action needs to be taken can be carried out on a continuous basis by observation and noting behaviours which indicate the values and norms prevalent in the organization.

A more searching analysis would use instruments such as interviews, questionnaires, focus groups (representative groups of employees whose views are sought on organizational or work issues), attitude surveys and workshops.

## Culture management strategies

One or more of the following approaches can be used to help in managing culture:

- Creating mission and value statements which explicitly state where the organization is going and the values it adopts in getting there — but these statements must represent reality and must be followed up by workshops, training and discussions which translate the words into deeds. They will make far more impact on culture if they are drawn up by a process of involvement and discussion possibly by means of workshops held at all levels in the organization.
- Organizational development interventions designed to improve the effectiveness with which the organization functions and to enable it to respond to or manage change.

- Employee development interventions which aim to increase acceptance and understanding of the organization's core values and to influence behaviour so that it upholds those values.
- Performance management processes which ensure through the mechanisms of objective setting and performance appraisal that the values, norms and behaviours which the cultural change programme is developing are absorbed and acted upon as part of the normal process of management.
- Reward management processes which reward people for behaviour which is in accord with the values built into the culture change programme.
- Behavioural modification techniques as described in Chapter 16, bearing in mind that it is often easier to influence behaviour than to change attitudes.

Such programmes can be used not only to change but also to reinforce a culture. Ideally, they should be conducted on an organization-wide basis but it may have to be recognized that different parts of the organization may legitimately have different cultures and that it could be counter-productive to impose an alien culture upon them.

Individual managers can make a vital contribution by first understanding their culture, secondly getting involved as far as possible in the definition of the aims and constituents of a culture management programme and, finally, playing their part by practising the required behaviour themselves, developing it in their staff, and instilling or reinforcing the value system of the organization.

# 20

# Organization Design

The management of people in organizations constantly raises questions such as 'Who does what?', 'How should activities be grouped together?', 'What lines and means of communication need to be established?', 'How should people be helped to understand their roles in relation to the objectives of the organization and the roles of their colleagues?' 'Are we doing everything that we ought to be doing and nothing that we ought not to be doing?' and 'Have we got too many unnecessary layers of management in the organizations?'

These are questions involving people which must concern personnel practitioners in their capacity of helping the business to make the best use of its people. Personnel specialists should be able to contribute to the processes of organization design or re-design as described below because of their understanding of the factors affecting organizational behaviour and because they are in a position to take an overall view of how the business is organized which it is difficult for the heads of other functional departments to obtain.

## The process of organizing

The process of organizing can be described as the design, development and maintenance of a system of coordinated activities in which individuals and groups of people work co-operatively under leadership towards commonly understood and accepted goals. The key word in that definition is 'system'. Organizations are systems which, as affected by their environment, have a structure which has both formal and informal elements.

The process of organizing may involve the grand design or redesign of the total structure, but most frequently it is concerned with the organization of particular functions and activities and the basis upon which the relationships between them are managed.

Organizations are not static things. Changes are constantly taking place in the business itself, in the environment in which the business operates, and in the people who work in the business. There is no such thing as an 'ideal' organization. The most that can be done is to optimize the processes involved, remembering that whatever structure evolves it will be contingent on the environmental circumstances of the organization, and one of the aims of organization is to achieve the 'best fit' between the structure and these circumstances.

An important point to bear in mind is that organizations consist of people working more or less cooperatively together. Inevitably, and especially at managerial levels, the organization may have to be adjusted to fit the particular strengths and attributes of the people available. The result may not conform to the ideal, but it is more likely to work than a structure which ignores the human element. It is always desirable to have an ideal structure in mind, but it is equally desirable to modify it to meet particular circumstances, as long as there is awareness of the potential problems that may arise. This may seem an obvious point, but it is frequently ignored by management consultants and others who adopt a doctrinaire approach to organization, often with disastrous results.

## Aim

Bearing in mind the need to take an empirical and contingent approach to organizing, as suggested above, the aim of organization design could be defined as being to *optimize* the arrangements for conducting the affairs of the business. To do this it is necessary, as far as circumstances allow, to:

- clarify the overall purposes of the organization — the strategic thrusts which govern what it does and how it functions
- define as precisely as possible the key activities required to achieve that purpose
- group these activities logically together to avoid unnecessary overlap or duplication
- provide for the integration of activities and the achievement of cooperative effort and teamwork in pursuit of a common purpose
- build flexibility into the system so that organizational arrangements can adapt quickly to new situations and challenges

- provide for the rapid communication of information throughout the organization
- define the role and function of each organizational unit so that all concerned know how it plays its part in achieving the overall purpose
- clarify individual roles, accountabilities and authorities
- design jobs to make the best use of the skills and capacities of the job holders and to provide them with high levels of intrinsic motivation (job design is considered in Chapter 21)
- plan and implement organization development activities to ensure that the various processes within the organization operate in a manner which contributes to organizational effectiveness
- set up teams and project groups as required to be responsible for specific processing, development, professional or administrative activities or for the conduct of projects (teambuilding and team management processes are considered in Chapter 18).

## Conducting organization reviews

Organization reviews are conducted in the following stages:

1. An *analysis*, as described below, of the existing arrangements and the factors which may affect the organization now and in the future.
2. A *diagnosis* of what needs to be done to improve the way in which the organization is structured and functions.
3. A *plan* to implement any revisions to the structure emerging from the diagnosis, possibly in phases. The plan may include longer term considerations about the structure and the type of managers and employees who will be required to operate within it.
4. *Implementation* of the plan.

## Organization analysis

The starting point for an organization review is an analysis of the existing circumstances, structure and processes of the organization and an assessment of the strategic issues that might affect it in the future. This covers:

- *The external environment.* The economic, market and competitive factors that may affect the organization. Plans for product-market development will be significant.
- *The internal environment.* The mission, values, organization climate,

management style, technology and processes of the organization as they affect the way it functions and should be structured to carry out those functions. Technological developments in such areas as cellular manufacturing may be particularly important as well as the introduction of new processes such as just-in-time or the development of an entirely new computer system.

- *Strategic issues and objectives.* As a background to the study it is necessary to identify the strategic issues facing the organization and its objectives. These may be considered under such headings as growth, competition and market position and standing. Issues concerning the availability of the required human, financial and physical resources would also have to be considered.

- *Activities.* Activity analysis establishes what work is done and what needs to be done in the organization to achieve its objectives within its environment. The analysis should cover what is and is not being done, who is doing it and where, and how much is being done. An answer is necessary to the key questions: 'Are all the activities required properly catered for?' 'Are there any unnecessary activities being carried out, ie those which do not need to be done at all or those which could be conducted more economically and efficiently by external contractors or providers?'

- *Structure.* The analysis of structure covers how activities are grouped together, the number of levels in the hierarchy, the extent to which authority is decentralized to divisions and strategic business units (SBUs), where functions such as finance, personnel and research and development are placed in the structure (eg as central functions or integrated into divisions or SBUs) and the relationships that exist between different units and functions (with particular attention being given to the way in which they communicate and cooperate with one another). Attention would be paid to such issues as the logic of the way in which activities are grouped and decentralized, the span of control of managers (the number of separate functions or people they are directly responsible for), any overlap between functions or gaps leading to the neglect of certain activities, and the existence of unnecessary departments, units, functions or layers of management.

## Organization diagnosis

The diagnosis should be based on the analysis and an agreement by those concerned with what the aims of the organization should be. The present arrangements can be considered against these aims and future requirements to assess the extent to which they meet them or fall short.

It is worth repeating that there are no absolute standards against which an organization structure can be judged. There is never one right way of organizing anything and there are no absolute principles which govern organizational choice. The current fashion for de-layering organizations has much to commend it but it can go too far, leaving units and individuals adrift without any clear guidance on where they fit into the structure and how they should work with one another, and making the management task of coordinating activities more difficult.

## Organization guidelines

There are no 'rules' or 'principles' of organization but there are certain guidelines which are worth bearing in mind in an organization study. These are:

- *Allocation of work.* The work that has to be done should be defined and allocated to functions, units, departments, work teams, project groups and individual positions. Related activities should be grouped together, but the emphasis should be on process rather than hierarchy latching on to account the need to manage processes which involve a number of different work units or teams.
- *Differentiation and integration.* It is necessary to differentiate between the different activities that have to be carried out, but it is equally necessary to ensure that these activities are integrated so that everyone in the organization is working towards the same goals.
- *Teamwork.* Jobs should be defined and roles described in ways which facilitate and underline the importance of teamwork. Areas where cooperation is required should be emphasized. The organization should be designed and operated in such a way as to facilitate horizontal processes and cooperation across departmental or functional boundaries. Wherever possible, self-managing teams should be set up and given the maximum amount of responsibility to run their own affairs, including planning, budgeting and exercising quality control. Networking should be encouraged in the sense of people communicating openly and informally with one another as the need arises. It is recognized that these informal processes can be more productive than rigidly 'working through channels' as set out in the organization chart.
- *Flexibility.* The organization structure should be flexible enough to

respond quickly to change, challenge and uncertainty. Flexibility should be enhanced by the creation of core groups and by using part-time, temporary and contract workers to handle extra demands. At top management level and elsewhere, a collegiate approach to team operation should be considered in which people share responsibility and are expected to work with their colleagues in areas outside their primary function or skill.

- *Role clarification.* People should be clear about their roles as individuals and as members of a team. They should know what they will be held accountable for and be given every opportunity to use their abilities in achieving objectives which they have agreed and are committed to. Job/role descriptions should define key result areas but should not act as straitjackets, restricting initiative and unduly limiting responsibility.
- *Decentralization.* Authority to make decisions should be delegated as close to the scene of action as possible. Profit centres should be set up as strategic business units which operate close to their markets and with a considerable degree of autonomy. A multiproduct or market business should develop a federal organization with each federated entity running its own affairs, although they will be linked together by the overall business strategy.
- *Delayering.* Organizations should be 'flattened' by stripping out superfluous layers of management and supervision in order to promote flexibility, facilitate swifter communication, increase responsiveness, enable people to be given more responsibility as individuals or teams and reduce costs.

Organization design leads into organization planning — assessing implications of structural changes on future manpower requirements and taking steps to meet those requirements.

## Organization planning

Organization planning is the process of converting the analysis into the design. It determines structure, relationships, roles, human resource requirements and the lines along which changes should be implemented. There is no one best design. There is always a choice between alternatives. Logical analysis will help in the evaluation of the alternatives but the law of the situation will have to prevail. The final choice will be contingent upon the present and future circumstances of the organization. It will be strongly influenced by personal and human considerations — the inclinations of top management, the strengths and weaknesses of management generally, the availability of people to man the new organization and the need to take account of the feelings of those who will be exposed to change. Cold logic may sometimes have to override these considerations. If it does, then it must be deliberate and the consequences must be appreciated and allowed for when planning the implementation of the new organization.

It may have to be accepted that a logical regrouping of activities cannot be introduced in the short term because no one with the experience is available to manage the new activities, or because capable individuals are so firmly entrenched in one area that to uproot them would cause serious damage to their morale and would reduce the overall effectiveness of the new organization.

The worst sin that organization designers can commit is that of imposing their own ideology on the organization. Their job is to be eclectic in their knowledge, sensitive in their analysis of the situation and deliberate in their approach to the evaluation of alternatives.

Having planned the organization and defined structures, relationships and roles, it is necessary to consider how the new organization should be implemented. It may be advisable to stage an implementation over a number of phases, especially if new people have to be found and trained.

## Who does the work?

Organization design may be carried out by line management with or without the help of members of the personnel function acting as internal consultants, or it may be done by outside consultants. Personnel management should always be involved because organization design is essentially about people and the work they do. The advantage of using outside consultants is that an entirely independent and dispassionate view is obtained. They can cut through internal organizational pressures, politics and constraints and bring experience of other organizational problems they have dealt with. Sometimes, regrettably, major changes can be obtained only by outside intervention. But there is a danger of consultants suggesting theoretically ideal organizations which do not take sufficient account of the problems of making them work with existing people. They do not have to live with their solutions as do line and personnel managers. If outside consultants are used, it is essential to involve people from within the organization so they can ensure that they are able to implement the proposals smoothly.

# 21

# Job Design

## What is job design?

Job design has been defined by Davis (1966) as 'The specification of the contents, methods, and relationships of jobs in order to satisfy technological and organizational requirements as well as the social and personal requirements of the job holder.'

Job design has two aims: first, to satisfy the requirements of the organization for productivity, operational efficiency and quality of product or service, and second, to satisfy the needs of the individual for interest, challenge and accomplishment. Clearly, these aims are interrelated and the overall objective of job design is to integrate the needs of the individual with those of the organization.

The process of job design must start from an analysis of what work needs to be done — the tasks that have to be carried out if the purpose of the organization or an organizational unit is to be achieved. This is where the techniques of process planning, systems analysis and work study are used to achieve improvement in organizational performance — the first aim of job design. They concentrate on the work to be done, not the worker. They may lead to a high degree of task specialization and assembly line processing; of paper work as well as physical products. It can also lead to the maximization of individual responsibility and the opportunity to use personal skills.

It is necessary, however, to distinguish between efficiency and effectiveness. The most efficient method may maximize outputs in relation to inputs in the short run, but it may not be effective in the longer term in that it fails to achieve the overall objectives of the activity. The pursuit of short-term efficiency by imposing the maximum degree of task specialization may reduce longer-term effectiveness by demotivating job holders and increasing employee turnover and absenteeism.

Job design has to start from work requirements because that is why the job exists — too many writers on job design seem to imply that job design is only concerned with human needs. When the results to be achieved have been determined it should then be the function of the job designer to consider how the jobs can be set up to provide the maximum degree of intrinsic motivation for those who have to carry them out with a view to improving performance and productivity. Consideration has also to be given to another important aim of job design: to fulfil the social responsibilities of the organization to the people who work in it by improving the quality of working life, an aim which, as stated in Wilson's (1973) report on this subject, 'depends upon both efficiency of performance and satisfaction of the worker'.

## Factors affecting job design

Job design is fundamentally affected by the technology of the organization, the changes that are taking place in that technology and the environment in which the organization operates. Job design has therefore to be considered within the context of organizational design, as described in Chapter 13, but it must also take into account the following factors:

- the process of intrinsic motivation
- the characteristics of task structure
- the motivating characteristics of jobs
- the implications of group activities.

## The process of intrinsic motivation

The case for using job design techniques is based on the premise that effective performance and genuine satisfaction in work follow mainly from the intrinsic content of the job. This is related to the fundamental concept that people are motivated when they are provided with the means to achieve their goals. Work provides the means to earn money, which as an extrinsic reward satisfies basic needs and is instrumental in providing ways of satisfying higher-level needs. But work also provides intrinsic rewards which are under the direct control of the worker.

## Characteristics of task structure

Job design requires the assembly of a number of tasks into a job or a group of jobs. An individual may carry out one main task which consists of a number of interrelated elements or functions. Or task functions may be allocated to a team working closely together in a manufacturing 'cell' or customer service unit, or strung along an assembly line. In more complex jobs, individuals may carry out a variety of connected tasks, each with a number of functions, or these tasks may be allocated to a team of workers or divided between them. In the latter case, the tasks may require a variety of skills which have to be possessed by all members of the team (multiskilling) in order to work flexibly.

Complexity in a job may be a reflection of the number and variety of tasks to be carried out, the different skills or competences to be used, the range and scope of the decisions that have to be made, or the difficulty of predicting the outcome of decisions.

The internal structure of each task consists of three elements: planning (deciding on the course of action, its timing and the resources required), executing (carrying out the plan), and controlling (monitoring performance and progress and taking corrective action when required). A completely integrated job includes all these elements for each of the tasks involved. The worker, or group of workers, having been given objectives in terms of output, quality and cost targets, decides on how the work is to be done, assembles the resources, performs the work, and monitors output, quality and cost standards. Responsibility in a job is measured by the amount of authority someone has to do all these things.

## Motivating characteristics of jobs

The ideal arrangement from the point of view of intrinsic motivation is to provide for fully integrated jobs containing all three task elements. In practice, management and team leaders are often entirely responsible for planning and control, leaving the worker responsible for execution. To a degree, this is inevitable, but one of the aims of job design is often to extend the responsibility of workers into the functions of planning and control. This can involve empowerment — giving individuals and teams more responsibility for decision-making and ensuring that they have the training, support and guidance to exercise that responsibility properly.

## The job characteristics model

A useful perspective on the factors affecting job design and motivation is provided by Hackman and Oldham's (1974) job characteristics model. They suggest that the 'critical psychological states' of 'experienced meaningfulness of work, experienced responsibility for outcomes of work and knowledge of the actual outcomes of work' strongly influence motivation, job satisfaction and performance.

As Robertson *et al* (1992) point out, 'This element of the model is based on the notion of personal reward and reinforcement.... Reinforcement is obtained when a person becomes aware (knowledge of results) that he or she has been responsible for (experienced responsibility) and good performance on a task that he or she cares about (experienced meaningfulness).'

## Providing intrinsic motivation

Three characteristics have been distinguished by Lawler (1969) as being required in jobs if they are to be intrinsically motivating:

1. *Feedback* — individuals must receive meaningful feedback about their performance, preferably by evaluating their own performance and defining the feedback. This implies that they should ideally work on a complete product, or a significant part of it which can be seen as a whole.
2. *Use of abilities* — the job must be perceived by individuals as requiring them to use abilities they value in order to perform the job effectively.
3. *Self-control* — individuals must feel that they have a high degree of self-control over setting their own goals and over defining the paths to these goals.

## Approaches to job design

Job design should start with an analysis of task requirements, using the job analysis techniques described in Chapter 12. These requirements will be a function of the purpose of the organization, its technology and its structure. The analysis has also to take into account the decision-making process — where and how it is exercised and the extent to which responsibility is devolved to individuals and work teams.

Robertson and Smith (1985) suggest the following five approaches to job design.

## Job Design

1. To influence skill variety:

   — provide opportunities for people to do several tasks
   — combine tasks.

2. To influence task identity:

   — combine tasks
   — form natural work units.

3. To influence task significance:

   — form natural work units
   — inform people of the importance of their work.

4. To influence autonomy: give people responsibility for determining their own working systems.

5. To influence feedback:

   — establish good relationships
   — open feedback channels.

Turner and Lawrence (1965) identified six important characteristics which they called 'requisite task characteristics', namely: variety, autonomy, required interactions, optional interactions, knowledge and skill and responsibility'. And Cooper (1973) outlined four conceptually distinct job dimensions: variety, discretion, contribution and goal characteristics.

An integrated view suggests that the following motivating characteristics are of prime importance in job design:

- autonomy, discretion, self-control and responsibility
- variety
- use of abilities
- feedback
- belief that the task is significant.

These are the bases of the approach which are used in job enrichment, as described later in this chapter.

The main approaches to job design are:

- *Job rotation*, which comprises the movement of employees from one task to another to reduce monotony by increasing variety.
- *Job enlargement*, which means combining previously fragmented tasks into one job, again to increase the variety and meaning of repetitive work.

- *Job enrichment*, which goes beyond job enlargement to add greater responsibility to a job and is based on the job characteristics approach.
- *Empowerment*, which gives people more autonomy in their work.
- *Self-managing teams (autonomous work groups)* — these are self-regulating teams who work largely without direct supervision. The philosophy on which this technique is based is a logical extension of job enrichment but is strongly influenced by socio-technical systems theory (see Chapter 18).

Of these five techniques, it is generally recognized that, although job rotation and job enlargement have their uses in developing skills and relieving monotony, they do not go to the root of the requirements for intrinsic motivation and for meeting the various motivating characteristics of jobs as described above. These are best satisfied by using, as appropriate, job enrichment, empowerment or autonomous work groups within a quality of working life strategy as described at the end of this chapter.

## Job enrichment

Job enrichment aims to maximize the interest and challenge of work by providing the employee with a job that has the following characteristics:

- it is a complete piece of work in the sense that the worker can identify a series of tasks or activities that end in a recognizable and definable product
- it affords the employee as much variety, decision-making responsibility and control as possible in carrying out the work
- it provides direct feedback through the work itself on how well the employee is doing his or her job.

Job enrichment as proposed by Herzberg (1968) is not just increasing the number or variety of tasks; nor is it the provision of opportunities for job rotation. It is claimed by supporters of job enrichment that these approaches may relieve boredom, but they do not result in positive increases in motivation.

### Impact of job enrichment

The advocates of job enrichment have been so dedicated to their cause that one cannot help feeling sometimes that their enthusiasm for the philosophy of their movement has clouded their judgement of its real benefits to the organization, let alone to the individuals who are supposed to have been enriched.

There have been a number of case studies which have indicated success, although this has often been measured in subjective terms. However, a study by Hulin and Blood (1968), of all relevant research on job enrichment concluded that the effects of job enrichment on job satisfaction or worker motivation are generally overstated and in some cases unfounded. They argue convincingly that many shop-floor workers are not alienated from the work environment but are alienated from the work norms and values of the middle class, especially its belief in the work-related elements of the Protestant ethic and in the virtue of striving for the attainment of responsible positions.

Fein's (1970) study of worker motivation reached essentially the same conclusion. He states:

> Workers do not look upon their work as fulfilling their existence. Their reaction to their work is the opposite of what the behaviouralists predict. It is only because workers choose not to find fulfilment in their work that they are able to function as healthy human beings. By rejecting involvement in their work which simply cannot be fulfilling, workers save their sanity.... The concepts of McGregor and Herzberg regarding workers' needs to find fulfilment through their work are sound only for those workers who choose to find fulfilment through their work.... Contrary to their postulates, the majority of workers seek fulfilment outside their work.

## Empowerment

### *What is empowerment?*

Empowerment is the process of giving people more scope or 'power' to exercise control over, and take responsibility for, their work. It provides greater 'space' for individuals to use their abilities by enabling and encouraging them to take decisions close to the point of impact.

The concept of empowerment has been termed 'the elixir of the 1990s' (Burdett, 1991). Of course the term is not new. It has been around in its current usage since the early 1980s and can often appear to be indistinguishable from job enrichment. There is nothing original in a philosophy which says: 'Enrich people's jobs, push decisions downwards to the point of impact, trust people rather than assume that they will cheat you, avoid unnecessary layers of management etc.'

These ideas were inherent in Herzberg's (1968) concept of job enrichment and McGregor's (1960) Theory Y, and the need to eliminate unnecessary layers of management was one of the principles advocated by the scientific management school in the 1930s.

Perhaps the reason for empowerment emerging as a concept for our times is that, although organizations are now driven by realists under profit generating, cost reduction and 'time to market' pressures, some of these realists have perceived the need to generate energy release in their people by providing visionary leadership and a supporting environment, and by treating them as a precious asset to be invested in rather than as a cost.

However, as Cave (1994) points out, it is difficult to get to grips with the notoriously elusive quality of the empowerment vocabulary: 'Even by the standards of management jargon it is a notoriously slippery concept, apparently used by different people to convey many quite different meanings'.

## Reasons for empowerment

The reasons usually advocated for empowerment are that it:

- can speed up decision-making processes and reaction times
- releases the creative and innovative capacities of employees
- provides for greater job satisfaction, motivation and commitment
- gives people more responsibility
- enables employees to gain a greater sense of achievement from their work
- reduces operational costs by eliminating unnecessary layers of management, staff functions and quality control and checking operations.

## The process of empowerment

Empowerment can be achieved through:

- structural means — organizational and work grouping
- the behaviour or style of individual managers
- enlisting the support of employees in tackling immediate organizational issues
- job enrichment as described earlier in this chapter.

*Structural empowerment — organizational*
An empowered organization is likely to have a flat structure with the

minimum number of management layers. A multi-layered structure filters the two-way flow of information and hinders decision-making from penetrating as far down the organization as it should.

*Structural empowerment — work group*
As suggested by Christian Schumacher (1976/77) of *Small is beautiful* fame, empowerment can be achieved at the work group level by applying the following principles:

1.  Work should be organized around basic operations to form 'whole tasks'.
2.  The basic organizational unit should be the primary workgroup (ie 4–20 people).
3.  Each workgroup should include a designated leader.
4.  Each workgroup and its leader should, as far as possible, plan and organize its own work.
5.  Each workgroup should be able fully to evaluate its performance against agreed standards of excellence.
6.  Jobs should be structured so that workgroup members can personally plan, execute and evaluate at least one operation in the process.
7.  All workgroup members should have the opportunity to participate in the group's processes of planning, problem solving and evaluation.

*Management style*
Managers empower the members of their teams not by giving up control but by changing the way control is exercised. They have to learn to delegate more and to allow individuals and teams more scope to plan, act and monitor their own performance.

However, they still have the responsibility to provide guidance and support to their staff as required. They must also help them to develop the skills and competences they need to function effectively in an empowered organization.

*Involvement in issues*
Empowerment can be achieved by involving people in developing their own solutions to specific issues. This can be done by expecting teams, not simply to propose ways forward or to hope that someone else will do something, but actually to solve the problem in their part of the organization, in accordance with the resources they have and the constraints within which they work.

## Self-managing teams

A self-managing team or autonomous work group (also known as a self-directed work group) is allocated an overall task and given discretion over how the work is done. This provides for intrinsic motivation by giving people autonomy and the means to control their work, which will include feedback information. The basis of the autonomous work group approach to job design is socio-technical systems theory, which suggests that the best results are obtained if grouping is such that workers are primarily related to each other by way of task performance and task interdependence. As Emery (1980) has stated:

> In designing a social system to efficiently operate a modern capital-intensive plant the key problem is that of creating self-managing groups to man the interface with the technical system.

A self-managing team:

- enlarges individual jobs to include a wider range of operative skills (multiskilling)
- decides on methods of work and the planning, scheduling and control of work
- distributes tasks itself among its members.

The advocates of self-managing teams or autonomous work groups claim that this approach offers a more comprehensive view of organizations than the rather simplistic individual motivation theories which underpin job rotation, enlargement and enrichment. Be that as it may, the strength of this system is that it does take account of the social or group factors and the technology as well as the individual motivators. Fully self-managing teams are, however, fairly rare.

## A quality of working life strategy

The phrase 'quality of working life' first came to the fore in the 1970s. Wilson's (1975) report on the subject emphasized that efficiency of performance depended on job satisfaction and the concept of quality of working life (QWL) referred primarily to how jobs can be designed to increase satisfaction and therefore performance. Much of the thrust for QWL was provided by Herzberg (1968) who advocated job enrichment.

In the more pragmatic and entrepreneurial 1980s the QWL approach fell into some disrepute as a seemingly 'soft' approach to management.

Earlier studies by people like Brayfield and Crockett (1955) and Vroom (1964) which concluded that there was little evidence of any marked correlation between satisfaction and performance were recalled, as were the output of a number of American researchers such as Hulin and Blood (1968) who questioned the whole job enrichment process as a method of improving job satisfaction or motivation.

However, QWL has made something of a comeback in the post-entrepreneurial 1990s as was exemplified by an ACAS (1991) publication which suggested that improvement in organizational effectiveness and competitive edge is best achieved by changing the ways of managing people from a 'control' to a 'quality of working life strategy' aimed at bringing together the goals of the organization and the development of people in it. ACAS say that the main contributions a QWL strategy can make are that:

- people will be better motivated if their work experience satisfies their social and psychological needs in addition to economic needs
- people work more effectively if they are managed in a participative way
- factors which satisfy people at work are essentially different from those factors which cause dissatisfaction (this is Herzberg's (1957) two-factor model)
- individual motivation and therefore greater efficiency can be enhanced by attention to the design of jobs and work organization
- there is a need to see an organization as a balance between its technical systems (the way goods and services are produced) and its social systems (the way that people are organized, managed, trained and consulted) ie socio-technical theory.

# 22

# Organizational Development

## What is organizational development?

Organizational development is concerned with the planning and implementation of programmes designed to improve the effectiveness with which an organization functions and responds to change. The aim of organization development is to provide a coherent approach which changes for the better the ways in which people carry out their work and interact with others.

Organizational development, as described above, should be distinguished from management development, although the two often overlap. Management development (discussed in Chapter 29) is mainly aimed at the improvement of the performance and potential of individuals, while organizational development is more concerned with improving the overall effectiveness of the organization — in particular, the way its various processes function and its people work together.

## Basis of organizational development

Organizational development approaches are traditionally based on the concepts of the behavioural scientists. The philosophy of organizational development was defined by Bennis (1960) as follows:

1. A new concept of man based on increased knowledge of his complex and shifting needs, which replaces an oversimplified, push-button notion of man.
2. A new concept of power, based on collaboration and reason, which replaces a model of power based on coercion and threat.
3. A new concept of organization values, based on humanistic-

democratic ideals, which replaces the mechanistic value system of bureaucracy.

Essentially, the philosophy of organizational development is humanistic. The central belief is that each of us has within ourselves the capacity to develop in a healthy and creative way. This is very much in line with McGregor's (1960) *Theory Y* which expressed his view that 'the capacity to exercise a relatively high degree of imagination, ingenuity and creativity in the solution of organizational problems is widely, not narrowly, distributed in the population'. As a humanistic approach, organizational development in the 1970s tended to have an idealistic flavour about it, but at least the better practitioners saw the organization as a whole and based their proposals on a coherent view of how the various processes taking place there should be managed.

## Methods of organizational development

Organizational development programmes in their original form were usually characterized by three main features:

1.  They were managed, or at least strongly supported, from the top but often made use of third parties or 'change agents' to diagnose problems and to manage change by various kinds of planned activity or 'intervention'.
2.  The plans for organization development were based upon a systematic analysis and diagnosis of the circumstances of the organization and the changes and problems affecting it.
3.  They used behavioural science knowledge and aimed to improve the way the organization copes in times of change through such processes as interaction, communications, participation, planning and conflict.

Typical organizational development activities include:

* introducing new structures or processes
* working with teams on team development
* working on inter-group relationships either in defining roles or resolving inter-group conflict
* various educational activities for improving personal and interpersonal skills.

Organizational development programmes have consisted of any one or a mix of these activities, and this is why it is difficult to describe 'OD', as it is familiarly known, in a satisfactorily comprehensive way. In some companies an OD programme is no more than a glorified management development package, using a few team-building exercises and informal training courses and, perhaps, dabbling in some interactive skills training such as transactional analysis. In others the programme embraces a number of different but related activities, all designed to achieve a measurable improvement in the performance of the organization.

Organizational development may be based on some form of process consulting which is used for analytical and diagnostic purposes prior to designing and implementing a programme.

## Process consulting

Process consultancy, as described by Schein (1969), is a technique used in OD assignments but it is equally valid in culture management and other approaches for improving organizational effectiveness. Process consulting involves helping clients to generate information which they can understand about their projects and problems and creating conditions for clients to own the solutions to the problems by gaining internal commitment to their choice.

As Schein describes it, process consultation:

> Involves the manager and the consultant in a period of *joint* diagnosis. The process consultant is willing to come into an organization without a clear mission or a clear need, because of an underlying assumption that most organizations could probably be more effective than they are if they could identify what processes (work flow, interpersonal relations, communications, intergroup relations, etc) need improvement. A closely related assumption is that no organization is perfect, that every organizational form has strengths and weaknesses. The process consultant would urge any manager with whom he (sic) is working not to leap into an action program, particularly if it involves any kind of changes in organizational structure, until the organization itself has done a thorough diagnosis and assessment of the strengths and weaknesses of the present structure.

The process consultant is usually someone from outside the organization but it is possible for people from within the company to operate in this capacity as internal consultants as long as they can preserve their objectivity and a measure of independence. Suitably qualified and experienced members of the personnel function can do this, but it is not an easy task to fulfil the following ten roles that a process consultant plays as a facilitator of change:

1. Sharer
2. Challenger
3. Interventionist
4. Catalyst
5. Provider of insight
6. Process analyst
7. Listener/observer
8. Provider of structure
9. Developer of ownership
10. Action stimulator.

## Analysis and diagnosis

The analysis concentrates on the internal processes of the organization as affected by change imposed externally or from within. This leads to a diagnosis and when making it, most OD practitioners take a normative view, in other words, they establish in their minds values or norms of behaviour which they think should be adopted by the organization. The following is a list of typical OD values as set out by Beckhard (1969) who defined a 'healthy' organization from the point of view of a behavioural scientist as having the following characteristics:

1. The total organization, the significant subparts, and individuals manage their work against goals and plans for the achievement of these goals.
2. Form follows function (the problem, or task or project, determines how the human resources are organized).
3. Decisions are made by and near the source of information, regardless of where these sources are located on the organization chart.
4. The reward system is such that managers and supervisors are rewarded (and punished) comparably for:

   — short-term profit or production performance
   — growth and development of their subordinates
   — creating a viable working group.

5. Communication laterally and vertically is relatively undistorted. People are generally open and confronting. They share all the relevant facts, and their feelings.
6. There is a minimum amount of inappropriate win/lose activity between individuals and groups. Constant effort exists at all

levels to treat conflict and conflict situations as problems subject to problem-solving methods.

7. There is a high conflict (clash of ideas) about tasks and projects, and relatively little energy spent in clashing over interpersonal difficulties because they have been generally worked through.

8. The organization and its parts see themselves as interacting with each other and with a larger environment. The organization is an open system.

9. There is a shared value, and management strategy to support it, of trying to help each person (or unit) in the organization to maintain his or her (or its) integrity and uniqueness in an interdependent environment.

10. The organization and its members operate in an 'action research' way. General practice is to build in feedback mechanisms so that individuals and groups can learn from their own experience.

'Action research', as mentioned by Beckhard, is an approach developed by Lewin (1947) which takes the form of collecting data from people about process issues and feeding them back in order to identify the likely causes of problems so that possible actions can be tested. This is the basis of *group-dynamics* as a method of training used in OD programmes (see Appendix D).

Another analytical approach used by OD practitioners in its heyday (ie the 1970s), was Bales analysis (Bales, 1950) which is a method of studying the ways in which groups solve problems which can be used to reveal certain patterns of behaviour which are quite predictable.

## Planning organizational development programmes

The steps required after the diagnosis are to define what the programme is intended to achieve, establish criteria for measuring the success of the programme and prepare an action plan.

There will be a number of alternative courses of action, depending on the situation. At one end of the scale it may simply be a matter of introducing new structures or processes. At the other end the requirement might be for fundamental changes in values and attitudes. It is in the latter area that what have in the past been called 'OD' programmes have been transmogrified into 'culture management' programmes as described in Chapter 19. The name has changed but not the substance. In between these two extremes are the situations where there is a specific problem, for example, inter-departmental conflict, which needs to be resolved.

The programme may include the implementation of changed structures or processes and the approaches used would be based on change management processes. It may incorporate various 'interventions' into group processes which could include team development or building activities (see Chapter 28) or conflict resolution techniques for use in developing inter-group relations as described below. It may include, or in some cases be entirely based on, an educational programme. These activities are described below.

## Change management

### Change models

The best known change models are those developed by Lewin (1951) and Beckhard (1969). But other important contributions to an understanding of the mechanisms for change have been made by Thurley (1979), Bandura (1986) and Bêer *et al* (1990).

### Lewin

The basic mechanisms for managing change, according to Lewin (1951), are as follows:

- *Unfreezing*— altering the present stable equilibrium which supports existing behaviours and attitudes. This process must take account of the inherent threats change presents to people and the need to motivate those affected to attain the natural state of equilibrium by accepting change.
- *Changing* — developing new responses based on new information.
- *Refreezing* — stabilizing the change by introducing the new responses into the personalities of those concerned.

Lewin also suggested a methodology for analysing change which he called 'field force analysis'. This involves:

- Analysing the restraining or driving forces which will affect the transition to the future state. These restraining forces will include the reactions of those who see change as unnecessary or as constituting a threat.
- Assessing which of the driving or restraining forces are critical.
- Taking steps both to increase the critical driving forces and to decrease the critical restraining forces.

## Beckhard

According to Beckhard (1969), a change programme should incorporate the following processes:

- setting goals and defining the future state or organizational conditions desired after the change
- diagnosing the present condition in relation to these goals
- defining the transition state activities and commitments required to meet the future state
- developing strategies and action plans for managing this transition in the light of an analysis of the factors likely to affect the introduction of change.

## Thurley

Thurley (1979) described the following five approaches to managing change:

1. *Directive* — the imposition of change in crisis situations or when other methods have failed. This is done by the exercise of managerial power without consultation.
2. *Bargained* — this approach recognizes that power is shared between the employer and the employed and change requires negotiation, compromise and agreement before being implemented.
3. *'Hearts and minds'* — an all-embracing thrust to change the attitudes, values and beliefs of the whole workforce. This 'normative' approach (ie one which starts from a definition of what management thinks is right or 'normal') seeks 'commitment' and 'shared vision' but does not necessarily include involvement or participation.
4. *Analytical* — a theoretical approach to the change process using models of change such as those described above. It proceeds sequentially from the analysis and diagnosis of the situation, through the setting of objectives, the design of the change process, the evaluation of the results and, finally, the determination of the objectives for the next stage in the change process. This is the rational and logical approach much favoured by consultants — external and internal. But change seldom proceeds as smoothly as this model would suggest. Emotions, power politics and external pressures mean that the rational approach, although it might be the right way to start, is difficult to sustain.

5. *Action-based* — this recognizes that the way managers behave in practice bears little resemblance to the analytical, theoretical model. The distinction between managerial thought and managerial action blurs in practice to the point of invisibility. What managers think is what they do. Real life therefore often results in a 'ready, aim, fire' approach to change management. This typical approach to change starts with a broad belief that some sort of problem exists, although it may not be well defined. The identification of possible solutions, often on a trial or error basis, leads to a clarification of the nature of the problem and a shared understanding of a possible optimal solution, or at least a framework within which solutions can be discovered.

When analysing the potential impact of change in one part of the organization, it is necessary not only to consider how it directly affects the people in that area but also to take a view of how the proposed changes will affect the organization as a whole. In making this analysis, the individual introducing the change, who is often called the 'change agent' should recognize that new ideas are likely to be misunderstood and should make ample provision for the discussion of reactions to proposals to ensure complete understanding of them. It is also necessary to try to gain an understanding of the feelings and fears of those affected so that unnecessary worries can be relieved and, as far as possible, ambiguities can be resolved.

## *Bandura*

The ways in which people change was described by Bandura (1986) as follows:

1. People make conscious choices about their behaviours.
2. The information people use to make their choices comes from their environment.
3. Their choices are based upon:

   - the things that are important to them
   - the views they have about their own abilities to behave in certain ways
   - the consequences they think will accrue to whatever behaviour they decide to engage in.

For those concerned in change management, the implications of this theory are that:

- the tighter the link between a particular behaviour and a particular outcome, the more likely it is that we will engage in that behaviour
- the more desirable the outcome, the more likely it is that we will engage in behaviour that we believe will lead to it
- the more confident we are that we can actually assume a new behaviour, the more likely we are to try it.

To change people's behaviour, therefore, we have first to change the environment within which they work, secondly, convince them that the new behaviour is something they can accomplish (training is important) and, thirdly, persuade them that it will lead to an outcome that they will value. None of these steps is easy.

## *Beer* et al

Beer *et al* (1990) believe that most change management programmes are guided by a theory of change which is fundamentally flawed. This theory states that changes in attitudes lead to changes in behaviour. 'According to this model, change is like a conversion experience. Once people "get religion", changes in their behaviour will surely follow.'

They believe that this theory gets the change process exactly backwards:

> In fact, individual behaviour is powerfully shaped by the organizational roles people play. The most effective way to change behaviour, therefore, is to put people into a new organizational context, which imposes new roles, responsibilities and relationships on them. This creates a situation that in a sense 'forces' new attitudes and behaviour on people.

They prescribe six overlapping steps to effective change which concentrate on what they call 'task alignment' — reorganizing employee's roles, responsibilities and relationships to solve specific business problems in small units where goals and tasks can be clearly defined. The aim of following the steps is to build a self-reinforcing cycle of commitment, coordination and competence. The steps are:

1. Mobilize commitment to change through the joint analysis of problems.
2. Develop a shared vision of how to organize and manage to achieve goals such as competitiveness.
3. Foster consensus for the new vision, competence to enact it, and cohesion to move it along.

4. Spread revitalization to all departments without pushing it from the top — don't force the issue, let each department find its own way to the new organization.
5. Institutionalize revitalization through formal policies, systems and structures.
6. Monitor and adjust strategies in response to problems in the revitalization process.

This approach is fundamental to the effective management of changes but there are no easy solutions to achieving the acceptance of change. There are, however, the following guidelines.

## Guidelines for change management

- The achievement of sustainable change requires strong commitment and visionary leadership from the top.
- Understanding is necessary of the culture of the organization and the levers for change which are most likely to be effective in that culture.
- Those concerned with managing change at all levels should have the temperament and leadership skills appropriate to the circumstances of the organization and its change strategies.
- It is important to build a working environment which is conducive to change. This means developing the firm as a 'learning organization'.
- Although there may be an overall strategy for change, it is best tackled incrementally (except in crisis conditions). The change programme should be broken down into actionable segments for which people can be held accountable.
- People support what they help to create. Commitment to change is improved if those affected by change are allowed to participate as fully as possible in planning and implementing it. The aim should be to get them to 'own' the change as something they want and will be glad to live with.
- The reward system should encourage innovation and recognize success in achieving change.
- Change implies streams of activity across time and 'may require the enduring of abortive efforts or the build up of slow incremental phases of adjustment which then allow short bursts of incremental action to take place' — Pettigrew and Whipp (1991).
- Change will always involve failure as well as success. The failures must be expected and learned from.

- Hard evidence and data on the need for change are the most powerful tools for its achievement, but establishing the need for change is easier than deciding how to satisfy it.
- It is easier to change behaviour by changing processes, structure and systems than to change attitudes or the corporate culture.
- There are always people in organizations who can act as champions of change. They will welcome the challenges and opportunities that change can provide. They are the ones to be chosen as change agents.
- Resistance to change is inevitable if the individuals concerned feel that they are going to be worse off — implicitly or explicitly. The inept management of change will produce that reaction.
- In an age of global competition, technological innovation, turbulence, discontinuity, even chaos, change is inevitable and necessary. The organization must do all it can to explain why change is essential and how it will affect everyone. Moreover, every effort must be made to protect the interests of those affected by change.

## Conflict resolution

The basic assumptions about conflict made by Blake, Shepart and Mouton (1964) are that:

- Conflict is inevitable; agreement is impossible.
- Conflict is not inevitable, yet agreement is not possible.
- Although there is conflict, agreement is possible.

The third assumption is clearly the most hopeful. Three approaches can be adopted if this belief is held:

1. *Peaceful co-existence*. People are encouraged to work happily with one another. There is the maximum amount of information, contact and exchange of views, and people move freely between groups. This is a pleasant ideal but it may lead to smoothing over real differences and is not practicable in all circumstances.
2. *Compromise*. Splitting the difference by negotiation or bargaining. This approach assumes that there is no right or best answer and is essentially pessimistic, although it may be inevitable if the other two approaches are tried and do not work.
3. *Problem solving*. The joint development of solutions to the problem and the sharing of responsibility to see that the solutions work. This is clearly the best approach. It emphasizes the need to find a

genuine solution to the problem, rather than simply accommodating different points of view.

The problem-solving approach may involve some form of confrontation. According to Walton (1969), the confrontation is most likely to be successful if:

- Both parties have incentives to resolve the dispute.
- Equal power is established between the two parties.
- Adequate time is allowed for the 'differentiation' phase before moving into the 'integration' phase when the aim is to identify common ground.
- Conditions are created which favour openness.
- Mutual understanding is increased through effective communication.
- Stress and tension in the situation is, as far as possible, kept at a moderate level.

## Educational activities in organizational development

Educational activities have traditionally played a major role in OD programmes. Some of the most commonly used approaches are:

- group dynamics
- sensitivity or 'T-group' (ie training group) training
- interactive skills training.

These methods are described in Appendix D.

## The role of the OD practitioner

OD programmes have generally been 'facilitated' by consultants on the assumption that external 'interventions' are likely to be more effective than internal ones. Argyris (1970) summarized the primary tasks of the OD practitioner or interventionist as being to:

- generate and help clients to generate valid information which they can understand about their problems
- create opportunities for the clients to search effectively for solutions to their problems and to make free choices
- create conditions for internal commitment to these choices and apparatus for the continual monitoring of the action taken.

## Where has OD got to?

The original OD programmes, as mentioned earlier, were based on a set of values. But the approaches used by OD practitioners lost a great deal of credibility in the 1970s because, as McClean (1981) commented:

> The theory of change and change management which is the foundation of most OD programmes is based on over-simplistic generalizations which offer little specific guidance to practitioners faced with the confusing complexity of a real change situation... Writers are facing up to the naivety of early beliefs and theories in what may be described as a climate of sobriety and new realism. There is an increasing recognition of the existence of human traits other than those of trust, openness and sharing. Such traits as competitiveness, political ambition, distrust and dislike are coming to be seen as endemic and enduring features of organizational life. The signs are that more recent theories and concepts are beginning to incorporate these new perspectives.

Another reason for the decline of traditional 'OD' is that its practitioners surrounded it with awful jargon which put off many people.

Since then, the 'new realism' has recognized the complexity of organizational processes and the fact that simplistic solutions as advocated in some OD educational programmes are unlikely to work. The emphasis has shifted to a more contingent approach which recognizes all the forces that impinge on organizational effectiveness and does not seek to solve them by a few 'interventions', however well directed. Hence the increased attention being paid to culture management which recognizes the impossibility of instant solutions. The focus on, empowerment, teambuilding, change management, flexibility and total quality management as specific approaches to improving organizational effectiveness has in a sense replaced OD. But it could be argued that these all fit into the traditional organizational development framework and the term is still a useful way of describing any approach which concentrates on process within organizations.

# Part V
# Employee Resourcing

*Employee resourcing means ensuring that the organization knows and gets what it wants in the way of the people it needs in terms of both numbers and skills and competence levels. It starts from an initial analysis of the strategic objectives of the company and continues with an analysis of the human resources required to achieve them.*

*Human resource planning uses demand and supply forecasting techniques to set out needs in both quantitative (how many people) and qualitative (what sort of people) terms. It provides the basis for resourcing programmes which use recruitment procedures and selection techniques to ensure that requirements are met in accordance with quality, quantity and time specifications.*

# 23

# Human Resource Planning

## Definition

Human resource planning has been defined by the Institute of Personnel and Development as:

> The systematic and continuing process of analysing an organization's human resource needs under changing conditions and developing personnel policies appropriate to the longer-term effectiveness of the organization. It is an integral part of corporate planning and budgeting procedures since human resource costs and forecasts both affect and are affected by longer-term corporate plans.

Human resource planning is generally concerned with matching resources to business needs in the longer term (more than one year ahead) although it will sometimes address shorter-term requirements and it will constantly be looking at approaches to improving employee utilization now as well as in the future.

## The labour market

Human resource planning processes take place within the context of the labour market. As defined by Elliott (1991): 'The market for labour is an abstraction; it is an analytical construction used to describe the context within which the buyers and sellers of labour come together to determine the pricing and allocation of labour services.' A distinction can be made between the external labour market and the internal labour market.

*The external labour market* comprises the local, regional, national and international labour markets. When formulating human resource plans and making decisions on where to find the people required it is necessary to analyse which of these labour markets is likely to provide the best source. Distinct skills and occupations also constitute labour markets. There is, for example, a market for IT specialists and this will indicate availability and price (the market rates for different types of computer skills).

*The internal labour market* is the market for labour within firms. It refers to the stocks available and the flows of people within the firm from entry through various stages of their career (if any) until they leave. The internal labour market can be the main source of future labour requirements through policies of development, training, 'promotion from within', career planning and management succession. Human resource planning is concerned with the future supply of labour and will assess the extent to which requirements can be satisfied from within the firm (the internal labour market) or outside (the external labour market). Both sources are generally used, but to different extents, depending on the size of the firm, its rate of growth or decline, and its employee resourcing policies. The latter may consist of explicit or implicit policies to the effect that the company prefers to rely on the internal market and wants to develop its own skills base, for example through apprenticeship or youth training schemes, and to provide long-term careers for its staff. Alternatively, implicit policies may exist of relying mainly on the external market, recruiting on an *ad hoc* basis, leaving other firms to do the training and, perhaps, seeking to 'inject fresh blood' into the organization.

## Aims

The aims of human resource planning are to ensure that the organization:

- obtains and retains the number of people it needs with the skills, expertise and competences required
- makes the best use of its human resources
- is able to anticipate the problems of potential surpluses or deficits of people
- can develop a well-trained and flexible workforce, thus contributing to the organization's ability to adapt to an uncertain and changing environment
- reduces its dependence on external recruitment when key skills are in short supply — this means formulating retention, as well as employee development strategies.

## Achieving the aims

Human resource planning is usually assumed to consist of four clear steps:

- forecasting future needs
- analysing the availability and supply of people
- drawing up plans to match supply to demand
- monitoring the implementation of the plan.

As Casson (1978) pointed out, this conventional wisdom represents human resource planning as an 'all-embracing, policy-making activity producing, on a rolling basis, precise forecasts using technically sophisticated and highly integrated planning systems'. But he suggests that it is better regarded as:

- a regular *monitoring* activity, through which human resource stocks and flows and their relationship to business needs can be better understood, assessed and controlled, problems highlighted and a base established from which to respond to unforeseen events
- an *investigatory* activity by which the human resource implications of particular problems and change situations can be explored and the effects of alternative policies and actions investigated.

It is not the function of human resource planning to take over the decision-making role. It simply supplies the context in which sensible policies can be formulated. And, as Casson points out, it is not about producing *the* manpower plan: 'Such spurious precision has little value when reconciled with the complex and frequently changing nature of manpower, the business and the external environment'. The typical concept of human resource planning as a matter of forecasting the long-term demand and supply of people fails because the ability to make these estimates must be severely limited by the difficulty of predicting the influence of external events. Human resource planning today is likely to concentrate on deciding what skills and competences will be required in the future and simply providing a broad indication of the numbers required in the longer term (more than one year ahead).

There is however a strong case for giving systematic attention to likely human resource requirements, if only to provide the context and guidelines for decisions designed to ensure that as far as possible people are available to meet the needs of the business. Human resource planning is therefore a key element in the strategic human resource management process. It aims to produce personnel policies and plans for the acquisition, training, development, retention and utilization of human resources which are integrated with the requirements of the business plan. It also provides an important input into the process of achieving coherence in the development of personnel policies and programming so that recruitment, training and steps to improve commitment and performance are integrated with a particular end in view — seeing that the organization has the people it wants.

Human resource planning as described later in this chapter can attempt to be highly analytical, making use of computer models for forecasting purposes. These systematic approaches are not made irrelevant by the problems of forecasting future demand and supply figures mentioned above, as long as it is remembered that the projections can only be used as guides to decision-making and that they will have to be continuously updated.

However, the process of human resource planning can be, and usually is, conducted without the use of elaborate models, concentrating as it does on answering the following questions by the exercise of informed judgement:

- How many people will be needed?
- What skills, knowledge and competences will be required in the future?
- Will existing human resources meet the identified need?
- Is further training or development needed?
- Is recruitment necessary?
- When will the new people be needed?
- When should training or recruitment start?
- If numbers are to be reduced to cut costs or because of lower activity levels, what will be the best way to tackle it?
- What other 'people' implications are there in such areas as productivity and commitment?
- How do we achieve the necessary degree of flexibility on the use of people?

Achieving the aims is discussed in this chapter under the headings of:

- resourcing strategy
- turning broad strategies into action plans
- demand forecasting
- supply forecasting — analysing existing resources, employee turnover and wastage, analysing the effect of promotions and

transfers, analysing changes in conditions of work and absenteeism, analysing sources of supply
- forecasting requirements
- flexibility
- productivity and cost analysis
- action planning — overall, human resource development, recruitment, retention, flexibility, productivity, downsizing
- control.

## Employee resourcing strategy

Employee resourcing strategy contributes both to the formulation and the implementation of business strategies.

### Formulation of business strategies

Resourcing strategy contributes to the formulation of business strategy by identifying opportunities to make the best use of existing human resources and by pointing out how human resource constraints may affect the implementation of the proposed business plans unless action is taken. Those constraints might include skill shortages, high recruitment, training and employment costs, or insufficient flexibility.

### Implementation strategies

These consist of:

- *acquisition strategies*, which define how the resources required to meet forecast needs will be obtained
- *retention strategies*, which indicate how the organization intends to keep the people it wants
- *development strategies*, which describe what needs to be done to extend and increase skills (multiskilling) to fit people for greater responsibility, and also define the outputs required from training programmes
- *utilization strategies*, which indicate intentions to improve productivity and cost-effectiveness
- *flexibility strategies*, which show how the organization can develop more flexible work arrangements
- *downsizing strategies*, which define what needs to be done to reduce the numbers employed.

## The basis of employee resourcing strategies

The basis for employee resourcing strategies is provided by longer-term business plans and shorter-term budgets and programmes. These indicate future activity levels, new demands for skills and competences and intentions 'to take cost out of the business' by reducing the size of the workforce, delayering, sub-contracting work or relying more on outworkers or part-timers.

The business strategies, plans and budgets define demand requirements. But the strategy must also deal with the supply side, from within and outside the organization. Internal supply-side planning means forecasting the output of training schemes and losses through employee turnover. The impact of absenteeism also has to be considered.

External supply-side planning means looking at demographics — the likely supply of school-leavers, professionally qualified staff and university graduates entering the local and national labour market. The 'demographic time bomb' which was identified in the 1980s consisted of a projected accelerated decline in the number of young people entering the labour market in the early 1990s while noting that the numbers will slowly increase in the second half of the decade. The time bomb was defused by the early 1990s recession but the problem may recur and no organization can be complacent about getting the people it needs, especially in the professional and highly skilled categories.

A further key factor is the increasing demand from employers for 'knowledge workers' coupled with their requirement for workers with a wider range of skills in the core of the new, flexible firm.

## Turning broad strategies into action plans

Resourcing strategies show the way forward through the analysis of business strategies and demographic trends. They are converted into action plans based on the outcome of the following interrelated planning activities:

- *Demand forecasting* — estimating future needs for people and competences by reference to corporate and functional plans and forecasts of future activity levels.
- *Supply forecasting* — estimating the supply of manpower by reference to analyses of current resources and future availability, after allowing for wastage.

- *Forecasting requirements* — analysing the demand and supply forecasts to identify future deficits or surpluses with the help of models, where appropriate.
- *Productivity and cost analysis* — analysing productivity, capacity, utilization and costs in order to identify the need for improvements in productivity or reductions in cost.
- *Action planning* — preparing plans to deal with forecast deficits or surpluses of people, to improve utilization, flexibility and productivity or to reduce costs.
- *Budgeting and control* — setting human resource budgets and standards and monitoring the implementation of the plan against them.

Although these are described as separate areas, and are analysed as such in later sections of this chapter, they are, in fact, closely interrelated and often overlap. For example, demand forecasts are estimates of future requirements, and these can be prepared only on the basis of assumptions about the productivity of employees. But the supply forecast will also have to consider productivity trends and how they might affect the supply of people.

A flow chart of the process of human resource planning is shown in Figure 23.1.

## Demand forecasting

Demand forecasting is the process of estimating the future numbers of people required and the likely skills and competences they will need. The basis of the forecast is the annual budget and longer-term business plan, translated into activity levels for each function and department or decisions on 'downsizing'. In a manufacturing company the sales budget would be translated into a manufacturing plan giving the numbers and types of products to be made in each period. From this information the number of hours to be worked by each skill category to make the quota for each period would be computed.

Details are required of any organization plans which would result in increased or decreased demands for employees. For example, setting up a new regional organization, creating a new sales department, decentralizing a head office function to the regions. Plans and budgets for reducing employment costs and their implications on the future numbers of people to be employed would also have to be considered.

The planning data would refer to expected changes in productivity or employee levels arising from changes in working methods or

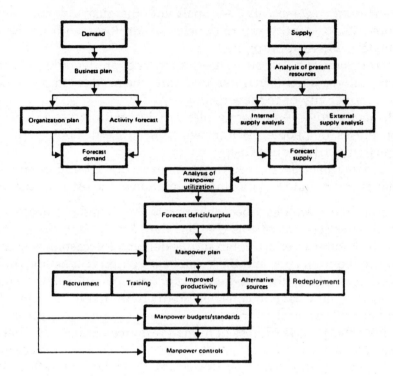

**Figure 23.1** The process of human resource planning

procedures, the introduction of new technology, or computerization. These could be set out as a crude percentage increase in productivity which could be used to adjust the required hours for a given level of output. Or they might give specific instances of cases where the numbers employed in, for example, a machine tool section or cell, a production line, a distribution centre, an office section or a sales office is to be increased or decreased.

## Demand forecasting methods

There are four basic demand forecasting methods for estimating the numbers of people required:

1. Managerial judgement
2. Ratio-trend analysis
3. Work study techniques
4. Modelling.

These are described separately below, although in many cases a combination of, say, managerial judgement and statistical techniques would be used.

*Managerial judgement*

The most typical method of forecasting used is managerial judgement. This simply requires managers to sit down, think about their future workloads, and decide how many people they need. It might be done on a 'bottom-up' basis with line managers submitting proposals for agreement by senior management.

Alternatively, a 'top-down' approach can be used, in which company and departmental forecasts are prepared by top management, possibly acting on advice from the personnel departments. These forecasts are reviewed and agreed with departmental managers. A less directive approach is for top management to prepare planning guidelines for departmental managers setting out the planning assumptions and the targets they should try to meet.

Perhaps the best way of using managerial judgement is to adopt both the 'bottom-up' and 'top-down' approach. Guidelines for departmental managers should be prepared which indicate broad company assumptions about future activity levels which will affect their departments. Targets are also set where necessary. Armed with these guidelines, departmental managers prepare their forecasts to a laid-down format. They are encouraged to seek help at this stage from the personnel departments. Meanwhile, the personnel department prepares a company human resource forecast. The two sets of forecasts can then be reviewed by a human resource planning committee consisting of functional heads. This committee reconciles with departmental managers any discrepancies between the two forecasts and submits the final amended forecast to top management for approval. This is sometimes called the 'right-angle method'.

An example of a forecast form using managerial judgement is shown in Figure 23.2.

*Ratio-trend analysis*

Ratio-trend analysis is carried out by studying past ratios between, say, the number of direct (production) workers and indirect (support) workers in a manufacturing plant, and forecasting future ratios, having made some allowances for changes in organization or methods. Activity level forecasts are then used to determine, in this

413

| Category of staff .................................................................. Year ............................ | | |
|---|---|---|
| *Staff members and movements* | *No. of staff to be provided* | *Remarks* |
| 1. Number of staff at 1.1 ..... (excluding known resignations) 75 | — | Age groups: <br> Under 25       30 <br> 25–34       20 <br> 35–44       15 <br> 45 and over   10 |
| 2.(a) Expected retirements, transfers out, and promotions during year   8 <br> (b) Less expected transfers in, promotions, and new appointments already made   3 | 5 | (dates to be specified) <br><br> Increase in number to be substantiated by O&M report |
| 3.(a) Number of staff required at 1 January, next year   80 <br> (b) Less present staff   75 | 5 | |
| 4. Expected staff losses due to normal wastage of existing staff   15 | 15 | Estimated by age groups: <br> Under 25       12 <br> 25–34       2 <br> 35–44       1 <br> 45 and over   — |
| 5. Expected losses of staff to be recruited in the period   5 | 5 | Short service staff turnover at 20% of 25 (events 2. + 3. + 4. above) |
| 6. Total staff to be provided during period | 30 | 5 to be recruited by 1 February — others to be programmed later |

**Figure 23.2** Forecast form

example, direct labour requirements, and the forecast ratio of indirects to directs would be used to calculate the number of indirect workers needed.

## Work study techniques

Work study techniques can be used when it is possible to apply work measurement to calculate how long operations should take and the number of people required. The starting point in a manufacturing company is the production budget prepared in terms of volumes of saleable products for the company as a whole, or volumes of output for individual departments. The budgets of productive hours are then compiled by the use of standard hours for direct labour, if standard labour times have been established by work measurement. The standard hours per unit of output are then multiplied by the planned volume of units to be produced to give the total planned hours for the period. This is divided by the number of actual working hours for an individual operator to show the number of operators required. Allowance may have to be made for absenteeism and forecast levels of idle time. The following is a highly simplified example of this procedure:

- Planned output for year = 20,000 units
- Standard hours per unit = 5 hours
- Planned hours for year = 100,000 hours
- Productive hours per person year (allowing normal overtime, absenteeism and down time) = 2000 hours
- Number of direct workers required (planned hours divided by productive hours per person year = 50 hours).

Work study techniques for direct workers can be combined with ratio-trend analysis to calculate the number of indirect workers needed.

*Modelling*
Mathematical modelling techniques using computers can help in the preparation of demand and supply forecasts. They are described on pages 424 to 427.

## Forecasting skill and competence requirements

Forecasting skill and competence requirements is largely a matter of managerial judgement. This judgement should, however be exercised on the basis of a careful analysis of the impact of projected product-market developments and the introduction of new technology, either information technology, computerized production methods such as manufacturing requirements planning (MRP2) or computer integrated manufacturing (CIM), or some form of automation or robotics.

## Supply forecasting

Human resources comprise the total effective effort that can be put to work as shown by the number of people and hours of work available, the capacity of employees to do the work and their productivity. Supply forecasting measures the number of people likely to be available from within and outside the organization (ie the internal and external labour markets), having allowed for absenteeism, internal movements and promotions, wastage and changes in hours and other conditions of work. The supply analysis covers:

● existing human resources
● potential losses to existing resources through employee wastage
● potential changes to existing resources through internal promotions
● effect of changing conditions of work and absenteeism
● sources of supply from within the organization
● sources of supply from outside the organization in the national and local labour markets.

The information required and the methods of analysis that can be used are considered below. As in the case of demand forecasting, the process of supply forecasting can be greatly facilitated by the use of human resource modelling techniques.

## Analysing existing human resources

The basic analysis should classify employees by function or department, occupation, level of skill and status.

The aim should be to identify from this analysis 'resource centres' consisting of broadly homogenous groups for which forecasts of supply need to be made. There is endless scope for cross analysis in preparing human resource inventories, but beware of collecting useless data; it is necessary to subject the analytical scheme to rigorous analysis, and for each category to ask the questions: 'Why do we need this information?' and 'What are we going to do with it when we get it?'

Some detailed analysis may be essential. For example, the review of current resources may need to cut across organizational and occupational boundaries to provide inventories of skills and potential. It may be important to know how many people the organization has with special skills or abilities; for example, engineers, chemists, physicists, mathematicians, economists or linguists. From the point of view of management succession planning and the preparation of management development programmes, it may be equally important to know how many people with potential for promotion exist and where they can be found.

An analysis of employees by age helps to identify problems arising from a sudden rush of retirements, a block in promotion prospects, or a preponderance of older employees. Age distribution can be illustrated graphically, as in Figure 23.3, which shows that a large number of employees will retire shortly and that the proportion of employees in the older age brackets is unduly high.

Length of service analysis may be even more important because it will provide evidence of survival rates, which, as discussed later, are a necessary tool for use by planners in predicting future resources.

The analysis of current resources should look at the existing ratios between different categories of employees: for example, managers and team leaders to employees, skilled to semi-skilled, direct to indirect, or office staff to production. Recent movements in these ratios should be studied to provide guidance on trends and to highlight areas where rapid changes may result in supply problems.

## Employee turnover or wastage

Employee turnover should be analysed in order to forecast future losses and to identify the reasons for people leaving the organization.

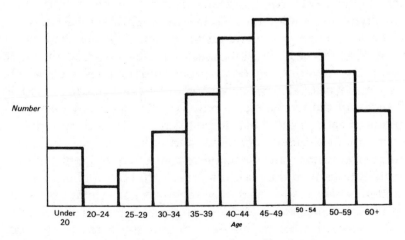

**Figure 23.3** Analysis of age distribution

Plans can then be made to attack the problems causing unnecessary wastage and to replace uncontrollable losses. The human resource planner therefore has to know how to measure wastage and how to analyse its causes. This can be done in various ways as described below.

## Turnover index

The turnover index (often referred to as the employee or labour wastage rate) is the traditional formula for measuring wastage:

$$\frac{\text{Number of leavers in a specified period (usually 1 year)}}{\text{Average number of employees during the same period}} \times 100$$

This method is in common use because it is easy to calculate and to understand. It is a simple matter to work out that if last year 30 out of an average force of 150 employees left (20 per cent turnover), and this trend continues, then the company will have to recruit 108 employees during the following year, in order to increase and to hold the work-force at 200 in that year (50 extra employees, plus 40 to replace the 20 per cent wastage of the average 200 employees employed, plus 18 to replace wastage of the 90 recruits).

This wastage formula is simple to use, but it can be positively misleading. The main objection to the measurement of turnover in terms of the proportion of those who leave in a given period is that the figure may be inflated by the high turnover of a relatively small proportion of the workforce, especially in times of heavy recruitment. Thus, a company employing 1000 people might have had an annual wastage rate of 20 per cent, meaning that 200 jobs had become vacant during the year. But this could have been spread throughout the company, covering all occupations and long as well as short service employees. Alternatively, it could have been restricted to a small sector of the workforce — only 20 jobs might have been affected although each of these had to be filled ten times during the year. These are totally different situations, and unless they are understood, inaccurate forecasts would be made of future requirements and inappropriate actions would be taken to deal with the problem. The turnover index is also suspect if the average number of employees upon which the percentage is based is unrepresentative of recent trends because of considerable increases or decreases during the period in the numbers employed.

## Stability index

The stability index is considered by many to be an improvement on the turnover index. The formula is:

$$\frac{\text{Number with 1 year's service or more}}{\text{Number employed 1 year ago}} \times 100$$

This index provides an indication of the tendency for longer-service employees to remain with the company, and therefore shows the degree to which there is a continuity of employment. But this too can be misleading because the index will not reveal the vastly different situations that exist in a company or department with a high proportion of long-serving employees in comparison with one where the majority of employees are short service.

## Length of service analysis

This disadvantage of the stability index may be partly overcome if an analysis is also made of the average length of service of people who leave, as in the example shown in Table 23.1 on page 420.

This analysis is still fairly crude, because it deals only with those who leave. A more refined analysis would compare for each service category the numbers leaving with the numbers employed. If, in the example shown, the total numbers employed with fewer than three months' service were 80 and the total with more than five years were 80, the proportion of leavers in each category would be, respectively, 50 per cent and 10 per cent — much more revealing figures, especially if previous periods could be analysed to reveal adverse trends.

## Survival rate

Another method of analysing turnover which is particularly useful for human resource planners is the survival rate: the proportion of employees who are engaged within a certain period who remain with the organization after so many months or years of service. Thus, an analysis of trainees who have completed their training might show that after two years, ten of the original cohort of 20 trainees were still with the company, a survival rate of 50 per cent.

The distribution of losses for each entry group, or cohort, can be plotted in the form of a 'survival curve' as shown in Figure 23.4 on page 421.

Table 23.1 Analysis of leavers by length of service

| Occupation | Leavers by Length of Service 19...... | | | | | | Total no. leaving | Average no. employed | Index of labour turnover |
| | less than 3 months | 3-6 months | 6 months- 1 year | 1-2 years | 3-5 years | 5 or more years | | | % |
| --- | --- | --- | --- | --- | --- | --- | --- | --- | --- |
| Skilled | 5 | 4 | 3 | 3 | 2 | 3 | 20 | 200 | 10 |
| Semi-skilled | 15 | 12 | 10 | 6 | 3 | 4 | 50 | 250 | 20 |
| Unskilled | 20 | 10 | 5 | 3 | 1 | 1 | 40 | 100 | 40 |
| **Totals** | **40** | **26** | **18** | **12** | **6** | **8** | **100** | **550** | **20** |

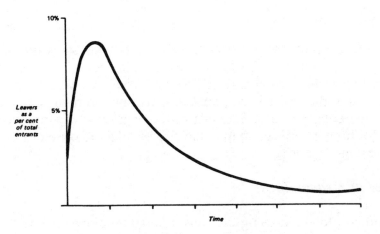

**Figure 23.4** A survival curve

The basic shape of this curve has been found to be similar in many situations, although it has been observed that the peak of the curve may occur further along the time scale and/or may be lower when it relates to more highly skilled or trained entry cohorts. Table 23.2 would tell human resource planners that they have to allow for half the number of recruits in any one year to be lost over the next five years, unless something can be done about the factors causing wastage. Thus, to achieve a requirement of 50 trained staff in five years' time, 100 people would have to be engaged this year.

**Table 23.2** Survival rates analysis

| Entry cohort | Original strength | No. surviving to end of year after engagement | | | | |
| | | Year 1 | Year 2 | Year 3 | Year 4 | Year 5 |
| --- | --- | --- | --- | --- | --- | --- |
| A | 40 | 35 | 28 | 26 | 22 | 20 |
| B | 32 | 25 | 24 | 19 | 18 | 17 |
| C | 48 | 39 | 33 | 30 | 25 | 23 |
| D | 38 | 32 | 27 | 24 | 22 | 19 |
| E | 42 | 36 | 30 | 26 | 23 | 21 |
| Average survival rate | 100% | 83% | 71% | 62% | 55% | 50% |

## *Half-Life Index*

A simpler concept derived from survival rate analysis is that of the half-life index, which is defined as the time taken for a group or cohort of starters to reduce to half its original size through the wastage process (five years in the above example). Comparisons can then be made for successive entry years or between different groups of employees in order to show where action may have to be taken to counter undesirable wastage trends.

## *Choice of measurement*

It is difficult to avoid using the conventional employee (labour) turnover index as the easiest and most familiar of all methods of measurement. But it needs to be supplemented with some measure of stability — an analysis of turnover or wastage as part of a human resource planning exercise requires detailed information on the length of service of leavers to identify problem areas and to provide a foundation for supply forecasts.

## Analysing the effect of promotions and transfers

The supply forecast should indicate the number of vacancies that will have to be filled to meet the demand forecast. Vacancies arise because people leave, but the exit of a senior manager may produce a chain reaction of replacements. Transfers between departments and divisions may also have to be allowed for.

In a large organization, persistent patterns of promotion or transfer may develop and it may be possible to predict the proportions of employees in particular categories who are likely to be promoted or moved in the future by starting with a forecast of the chain reaction factor, to give a broad indication of the number of displacements that may occur. For example, where there are three levels of management:

| | | | | |
|---|---|---|---|---|
| 3rd line management | : | 41 promotions | = | 3 moves |
| 2nd line management | : | 5 promotions | = | 10 moves |
| 1st line management | : | 25 promotions | = | 25 moves |
| **Total promotions/moves** | | **31** | | **38** |

But this is pretty crude, and in most companies, management succession planning has to be worked out specifically by reference to known retirements and transfers.

## Assessing changes in conditions of work and absenteeism

This assessment should cover factors operating within the firm such as changes in all of the following: normal weekly hours of work, overtime policies, the length and timing of holidays, retirement policy, the policy for employing part-timers, and shift systems.

The effect of absenteeism on the future supply of employees should also be allowed for, and trends in absenteeism should be analysed to trace causes and identify possible remedial actions.

## Analysing sources of supply

Internal labour market sources include the output from established training schemes or management development programmes and the reservoirs of skill and potential that exist within the organization. But the availability of people from the local and national labour markets is also a vital factor when preparing development plans. Too often, corporate or functional plans make assumptions about the availability of people locally or nationally which could easily be proved wrong after a brief investigation. It is particularly necessary to identify at an early stage any categories of employees where there might be difficulties in recruiting the numbers required so that action can be taken in good time to prepare a recruiting campaign, to tap alternative sources, or to develop training or retraining programmes to convert available staff to meet the company's needs. The factors which can have an important bearing on the supply of manpower are listed below.

### Local labour market

- population densities within reach of the company
- current and future competition for employees from other employers
- local unemployment levels
- the traditional pattern of employment locally, and the availability of people with the required qualifications and skills
- the output from the local educational system and training establishments
- the pattern of immigration and emigration within the area
- the attractiveness of the area as a place to live
- the attractiveness of the company as a place to work
- the availability of part-time employees
- local housing, shopping and transport facilities.

## National labour market

- demographic trends in the number of school leavers and the size of the working population
- national demands for special categories of employees — graduates, professional staff, technologists, technicians, skilled workers
- the output of the universities, professional institutions and other education and training establishments
- the effect of changing educational patterns
- the impact of national training initiatives
- the impact of government employment regulations.

## Forecasting human resource requirements

Human resource requirements are forecast by relating the supply to the demand forecasts and establishing any deficits or surpluses of employees that will exist in the future. Models can be used for this purpose as described below.

## Demand and supply forecasting models

A model is a representation of a real situation. It depicts interrelationships between the relevant factors in that situation and, by structuring and formalizing any information about these factors, presents reality in a simplified form.

Models can help to:

- increase the decision makers understanding of the situation in which a decision has to be made and the possible outcomes of that decision
- stimulate new thinking about problems by, among other things, providing answers to 'what if?' questions (sensitivity analysis)
- evaluate alternative courses of action.

Human resource modelling techniques can be used to prepare general human resource forecasts; to understand, predict and measure wastage, and to assist in career evaluation. If a computerized personnel information system exists, as described in Chapter 46, the information contained on the database can be exploited swiftly to provide detailed analyses of quantities of data which can be turned into projections of future demand and supply flows, and forecasts of employee requirements.

## Human Resource Planning

The 'what if?' questions that can be answered by a model include the impact on human resource requirements of alternative activity level forecasts or variations in assumptions about wastage rates, promotions and transfers, or changing patterns in the use of skills and competences arising from the introduction of new technology or changes in marketing strategy.

The data required for setting up and operating human resource models are essentially the same as those used for demand and supply forecasting. But they may have to be organized on a more systematic basis to fit the modelling process.

The main headings under which data need to be assembled are:

- *The human resource system* which describes how people move into and out of the organization or any of its units and how they progress between the various organizational levels or grades. A highly simplified representation of the system is illustrated in Figure 23.5.
- *Stocks* — the number of people employed in each grade, which are analysed in age or length of service bands.
- *Flows* — leavers, recruits and promotion flows are also analysed by grade and age or length of service.
- *Assumptions* — alternative assumptions can be made about the future behaviour of the system so that the implication of the different outcomes can be evaluated. These assumptions might include a 'push' analysis of flows where the organization 'pushes' people

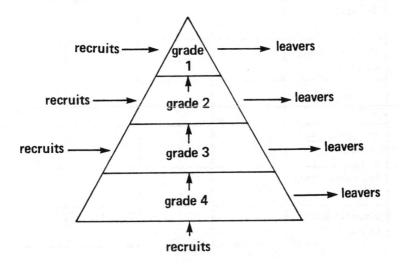

**Figure 23.5** A human resource system

through the system as their career progresses without having fixed grade sizes (this type of system uses pay curves rather than pay ranges, as discussed in Chapter 33). In a graded system the assumptions will be concerned with targets for grade sizes expressed as a growth or shrinkage percentage rate per grade, or target numbers from the operational plan.

- *Careers analysis* — a 'careers prospectus' can be built up by analysing data on promotions between grade and career progression curves, and by projecting trends. The model can link this data to information on the database about the potential of current employees in order that future stocks for promotion can be estimated.

The data on stocks and flows can be recorded on a form such as the one illustrated in Figure 23.6.

Models such as those developed by the Institute of Employment Studies can be obtained to use on a computerized personnel information system, as described in Chapter 46. The advice given by the

| Grade | Age ranges | | | |
|---|---|---|---|---|
| Grade 4 | 16–24 | 25–34 | 35–44 | 45–65 |
| Stocks at beginning of year | | | | |
| Recruits during year | | | | |
| Recruits leaving during year | | | | |
| Leavers during year | | | | |
| Promotions to grade 3 | | | | |
| Promotions from grade 5 | | | | |
| Stocks at end of year | | | | |

Figure 23.6 Stocks and flows data schedule

Institute of Employment Studies in operating its models includes the following points:

- understand why a model is being used, what outputs are required and what assumptions have to be included
- in making assumptions about the manpower system, flows and targets, start by asking what happens if current practices continue to be operated and then consider possible changes in market conditions, the use of new technologies, etc.
- use time series data, ie trend analysis, wherever possible to provide the basis for extrapolations
- although disaggregation, ie splitting mass data into subdivisions, can apparently lead to greater accuracy, this could be spurious if it involves manipulating very small numbers
- do not push the data further than they will go — when dealing with small or doubtful numbers, smooth or aggregate where necessary or sensible
- cross-check assumptions about wastage rates with other companies to ensure they are reasonable
- carry out sensitivity analysis, ie the study of alternative assumptions in order to predict alternative outcomes, depending on the assumption
- look first for significant results in the model's output, especially changes in workforce composition and unusually large or small flows.

### Flexibility arrangements

Flexibility arrangements which aim to achieve increased organizational effectiveness can take the following forms:

- *contract-based* — new forms of employment contracts
- *time-based* — shift working and flexible hours
- *job-based* — job-related flexibilities
- *skills-based* — multiskilling
- *organization-based* — the use of contract workers and part-timers
- *pay-based* — more flexible reward systems.

### *Contract-based flexibility*

Contract-based flexibility refers to employee contracts which specify flexibility as a key aspect of terms and conditions. Job descriptions are written in terms which emphasize the overall purpose of the job and its principal accountabilities. These are defined by reference to the results to be achieved. The job description does not specify the tasks to be carried out by the job holder. It may be replaced by a role definition which sets out competence and behavioural requirements, not duties. Contract-based flexibility can be achieved by employing contract workers to work on any task or in any area appropriate to their range of skills. It can also involve the use of fixed-term contracts to avoid long-term commitments.

## Time-based flexibility

Time-based flexibility can be achieved by the use of flexible hours. The most familiar method is flexitime in which employees can vary their daily hours of work on either side of the core-time when they have to be present, providing the longer-term required hours are completed. Time flexibility can be achieved in companies with marked seasonal fluctuations in labour requirements, such as photo-processing, by negotiating annual hours agreements. These specify the annual hours to be worked and paid for, but within that total they incorporate provisions for longer hours at peak periods and shorter hours during troughs.

## Job-based flexibility (functional flexibility)

Job-based flexibility means that workers can be moved from task to task and may be expected to use a wider range of skills within their capability. Firms may want to introduce this type of flexibility because they need to make the fullest use of their workforce, especially when they are using increasingly sophisticated equipment and systems which must be properly maintained if they are to produce at their optimum level. Functional flexibility also means that where work loads in different parts of a factory fluctuate widely, people can be moved in quickly to handle the extra demands.

In the United Kingdom, the 1970s and the 1980s saw the end of many of the old demarcation rules which had bedeviled flexibility in British industry. A typical union agreement (Nissan Motor) stipulated that:

1. To ensure the fullest use of facilities and manpower, there will be complete flexibility and mobility of employees.
2. It is agreed that changes in technology, processes and practices will

be introduced and that such changes will affect both productivity and manning levels.

3. To ensure such flexibility and change, employees will undertake training for all work as required by the company. All employees will train other employees as required.

These arrangements are fairly typical, especially in international firms setting up in green-field sites. Full functional flexibility is often associated with integrated pay schemes and the harmonization of terms and conditions of employment so that all staff, both office and factory workers, are covered by the same pay structure and are treated alike as far as benefits are concerned.

## Skill-based flexibility (multiskilling)

Functional flexibility is only possible when employees have the range of skills required to perform different tasks, for example machine operators having the necessary skills not only to operate their machinery but also to carry out basic maintenance and deal with minor faults and breakdowns.

At Hardy Spicer a form of 'just-in-time' manufacture was introduced which included an integrated flexible flow line of dedicated CNC (computer numerical control) machine cells, linked by a robotized pallet convey or system and programmable controls. This type of manufacturing system pointed to the need for multiskilling in which 'system technicians' on the production line had to have a range of skills including machine set up and basic maintenance, as well as taking responsibility for loading, quality and output. These technicians had to have a wide understanding of tool gauging, hydraulics, electrics and basic electronics. A 20 week training programme was required.

Multiskilling is about developing the capacities of people to undertake a wider range of tasks and to exercise greater responsibility. It is therefore consistent with human resource management philosophy which emphasizes the importance of investing in people and, therefore, of human resource development. Multiskilling, however, makes considerable demands on the organization to provide the training required and to motivate people to learn.

Multiskilling is based on two principles as defined by Michael Cross (1991). The first is competency within the workplace, ie the ability of a single individual to assess and rectify problems as they occur day by day, regardless of the nature of the problem. The second is the full utilization of capabilities, ie the only limitations on who does what, how and when, are the skills that an individual has or can acquire, the time available to perform any new or additional tasks, and the requirements of safety.

It is necessary to set clear objectives for the levels of benefit expected from multiskilling, including better use of resources, focusing attention on critical success factors and increased productivity. It is also essential to decide how the success of multiskilling can be measured and to introduce methods of monitoring progress.

### Organization-based

Organization-based approaches to flexibility include making more use of part-time and temporary staff or contract workers (peripheral workers).

## Productivity and costs

Human resource planning is just as concerned with making the best use of people as with forecasting and getting the numbers and skills required. An increase in activity levels can be catered for by improving productivity as well as by recruiting more employees and one of the main concerns of many organizations is how they can reduce and/or control costs. This means looking at productivity and employment costs as well as the possibility of treating human resources as assets rather than liabilities, to be invested in, maintained and allocated on the same rational basis that is used for all other assets.

### Productivity

Fundamentally, productivity represents the output of goods and services which can be obtained from a given input of employees. Within the firm, productivity should be monitored by using such measures as employment costs per unit of output, employment costs at a ratio of sales value, added value per employee, added value per £ of employment costs, sales value per employee, tons of product handled per person hour, or labour costs as a percentage of added value (the difference being production costs and sales value). Internal and external comparisons through a process of 'benchmarking' may then reveal areas where improvement is required by introducing new technology, improved management, a more flexible approach to resourcing or other means.

## *Employment costs*

Employment costs can be grouped under these headings:

- remuneration costs — pay, employee benefits, national insurance contributions
- recruitment costs
- training costs
- relocation costs
- leaving costs, including loss of production, redundancy payments, replacement and training
- the cost of health and safety and other employee services and policies, eg restaurants, welfare facilities, long service awards, suggestion schemes.
- personnel administration costs — personnel department costs, other than those allocated under other headings.

It may be difficult to collect and allocate expenses under all these headings, but the more detailed the analysis the better the control that can be exercised over employment costs.

# Action planning

Action plans are derived from the broad resourcing strategies and the more detailed analysis of demand and supply factors. However, the plans often have to be short-term and flexible because of the difficulty of making firm predictions about human resource requirements in times of rapid change.

Action plans should be made in the following areas:

- an overall plan as required to deal with shortages arising if there are demographic pressures
- a human resource development plan
- a recruitment plan
- a retention plan
- a plan to achieve greater flexibility
- a productivity plan
- a downsizing plan, if required.

# Overall plan

Demographic pressures may not make much impact during recessions, and many organizations, even in times of recovery, still pursue downsizing policies in order to reduce costs. But there are still areas where skill shortages exist and these may multiply in the future. It is therefore advisable to be prepared to take a selection of the following steps as part of an overall human resource plan:

- improving methods of identifying the sort of young people the organization wants to recruit
- establishing links with schools and colleges to gain their interest in the organization
- developing career programmes and training packages to attract young people
- widening the recruitment net to include, for example, more women re-entering the labour market
- finding ways of tapping alternative pools of suitable workers, eg part-time employees
- adapting working hours and arrangements to the needs of new employees and those with domestic responsibilities
- providing more attractive benefit packages; for example, child-care facilities
- developing the talents and making better use of existing employees
- providing retraining for existing and new employees to develop different skills
- making every effort to retain new recruits and existing staff.

## The human resource development plan

The human resource development plan will show:

- the number of trainees required and the programme for recruiting and training them
- the number of existing staff who need training or retraining and the training programmes required
- the new learning programmes to be developed or the changes to be made to existing programmes and courses
- how the required flow of promotable managers can be maintained.

## The recruitment plan

The recruitment plan will take account of the flow of trainees or retrained staff and set out:

- the numbers and types of employees required to make up any deficits and when they are needed

- the likely sources of recruits
- methods of attracting good candidates; these may include training and development programmes, attractive pay and benefit packages, 'golden hellos' (sums of money paid up front to recruits), flexible working arrangements, generous relocation payments, child-care facilities and, generally, improving the image of the company as an employer
- how any special problems in the supply of recruits will be dealt with by the recruitment programme.

## The retention plan

The retention plan should be based on an analysis of why people leave. Exit interviews may provide some information but they can be unreliable — people rarely give the full reasons why they are going. A better method is to conduct attitude surveys at regular intervals. The retention plan should address each of the areas in which lack of commitment and dissatisfaction can arise. The actions to be considered under each heading are listed below.

- *Pay* — problems arise because of uncompetitive, inequitable or unfair pay systems. Possible actions include:

  — reviewing pay levels on the basis of market surveys
  — introducing job evaluation or improving an existing scheme to provide for equitable grading decisions
  — ensuring that employees understand the link between performance and reward
  — reviewing performance-related pay schemes to ensure that they operate fairly (criteria for such schemes are set out in Chapter 34)
  — adapting payment-by-results systems to ensure that employees are not penalized when they are engaged only on short runs
  — tailoring benefits to individual requirements and preferences
  — involving employees in developing and operating job evaluation and performance-related pay systems.

- *Jobs* — dissatisfaction results if jobs are unrewarding in themselves. Jobs should be designed to maximize skill variety, task significance, autonomy and feedback, and they should provide opportunities for learning and growth.
- *Performance* — employees can be demotivated if they are unclear about their responsibilities or performance standards, are unin-

formed about how well they are doing, or feel that their performance assessments are unfair. The following actions can be taken:

— express performance requirements in terms of hard but attainable goals

— get employees and managers to agree on those goals and the steps required to achieve them

— encourage managers to praise employees for good performance but also get them to provide regular, informative and easily interpreted feedback — performance problems should be discussed as they happen in order that immediate corrective action can be taken

— train managers in performance review techniques such as counselling; brief employees on how the performance management system works and obtain feedback from them on how it has been applied.

● *Training* — resignations and turnover can increase if people are not trained properly, or feel that demands are being made upon them which they cannot reasonably be expected to fulfil without proper training. New employees can go through an 'induction crisis' if they are not given adequate training when they join the organization. Learning programmes and training schemes should be developed and introduced which:

— give employees the competence and confidence to achieve expected performance standards

— enhance existing skills and competences

— help people to acquire new skills and competences so that they can make better use of their abilities, take on greater responsibilities, undertake a greater variety of tasks and earn more under skill and competence-based pay schemes

— ensure that new employees quickly acquire and learn the basic skills and knowledge needed to make a good start in their jobs.

● *Career development* — dissatisfaction with career prospects is a major cause of turnover. To a certain extent, this has to be accepted. More and more people recognize that to develop their careers they need to move on, and there is little their employers can do about it, especially in today's flatter organizations where promotion prospects are more limited. These are the individuals who acquire a 'portfolio' of skills and may consciously change direction several times during their careers. To a certain degree, employers should welcome this tendency. The idea of providing 'cradle to grave' careers is no longer as relevant in the more changeable job markets of today, and this self-planned, multiskilling process provides for the availability of a greater number of qualified people. But there is still everything to be said in most organizations for maintaining a stable workforce and in this situation employers should still plan to provide career opportunities by:

— providing employees with wider experience
— introducing more systematic procedures for identifying potential such as assessment or development centres
— encouraging promotion from within
— developing more equitable promotion procedures
— providing advice and guidance on career paths.

● *Commitment* — this can be increased by:

— explaining the organizations mission, values and strategies and encouraging employees to discuss and comment on them
— communicating with employees in a timely and candid way, with the emphasis on face-to-face communications through such means as briefing groups
— constantly seeking and taking into account the views of people at work
— providing opportunities for employees to contribute their ideas on improving work systems
— introducing organization and job changes only after consultation and discussion.

● *Lack of group cohesion* — employees can feel isolated and unhappy if they are not part of a cohesive team or if they are bedeviled by disruptive power politics. Steps can be taken to tackle this problem through:

— teamwork, setting up self-managing or autonomous work groups or project teams
— team building, emphasizing the importance of teamwork as a key value, rewarding people for working effectively as members of teams and developing teamwork skills.

● *Dissatisfaction and conflict with managers and supervision* — a common reason for resignations is the feeling that management in general, or individual managers and team leaders in particular, are not providing the leadership they should, or are treating people unfairly or are bullying their staff (not an uncommon situation). This problem should be remedied by:

— selecting managers and team leaders with well-developed leadership qualities
— training them in leadership skills and in methods of resolving conflict and dealing with grievances
— introducing better procedures for handling grievances and disciplinary problems, and training everyone in how to use them.

- *Recruitment, selection, and promotion* — rapid turnover can result simply from poor selection or promotion decisions. It is essential to ensure that selection and promotion procedures match the capacities of individuals to the demands of the work they have to do.
- *Over-marketing* — creating expectations about career development opportunities, tailored training programmes and varied and interesting work can, if not matched with reality, lead directly to dissatisfaction and early resignation. Care should be taken not to oversell the firm's employee development policies.

## The flexibility plan

The aims of the flexibility plan should be to:

- provide for greater operational flexibility
- improve the utilization of employees skills and capacities
- reduce employment costs
- help to achieve downsizing smoothly and in a way which avoids the need for compulsory redundancies
- increase productivity.

In preparing the plan, the possibility of introducing more flexible patterns of work, as described on pages 437–9, should be explored.

The steps to be considered when formulating a flexibility plan are as follows:

- take a radical look at traditional employment patterns to find alternatives to full-time, permanent staff — this may take the form of segregating the workforce into a 'core group' and one or more peripheral groups
- new arrangements for flexible hours

- new overtime arrangements
- new shift-working arrangements.

## Alternatives to full-time permanent staff

The first step in reducing the number of full-time, permanent staff is to identify the 'core' of permanent, full-time employees who are essential to the direction, coordination and development of the firm's activities. The core may include:

- managers, but in reduced numbers because of flattened hierarchies and more decentralization
- team leaders, ie those needed to lead teams of core workers or peripherals
- professional staff in fields such as finance, legal and personnel who are involved continually and at high level in providing professional advice and services; bearing in mind, however, that many of these services could be purchased outside, possibly at less cost than maintaining professional staff permanently on the pay roll
- knowledge workers who are involved in the development and management of new technology, including information technology
- technicians and highly skilled workers in laboratories, design offices, and manufacturing departments etc, who need to be continuously available as the core element in project or work teams.

Employees in the core group need to be highly flexible and adaptable.

Having identified the core group, the next step is to consider how, where, and to what extent peripheral workers can be used. The choice lies between:

- temporary workers
- part-time workers
- job sharing
- new technology — homeworking and teleworking
- sub-contracting.

*Temporary workers* — can be used as part of a flexibility plan to reduce the company's commitment to the cost of employing people on a permanent basis. Their numbers can easily be increased or reduced to match fluctuations in the level of business activity. Temporary workers are also employed for the traditional reasons of providing cover for staff shortages, sickness or holidays.

The two main new trends in temporary working are:

- to establish permanent staffing levels to meet minimum or normal levels of demand and rely on temporary staff to cover peaks
- to develop a 'two-tier' workforce in order to provide greater job security for the core workers by employing a certain percentage of temporary staff at the periphery.

*Part-time workers*, where the advantages of using them include:

- more scope for flexing hours worked
- better utilization of plant and equipment by, for example, the introduction of a 'twilight shift'
- lower unit labour costs because overtime levels for full-time workers are reduced
- higher productivity on repetitive work because part-time workers can give more attention to their work during their shorter working day.

The disadvantages are:

- part-timers are generally less willing to undertake afternoon or evening work, may find it more difficult to vary their hours of work, and may be less mobile
- rates of employee turnover may be higher among part-timers
- part-timers may be less committed than full-time employees.

*Job-sharing* is an arrangement whereby two employees share the work of one full-time position, dividing pay and benefits between them according to the time each works. Job-sharing can involve splitting days or weeks or, less frequently, working alternate weeks. The advantages of job-sharing include reduced employee turnover and absenteeism because it suits the needs of individuals. Greater continuity results because if one-half of the job-sharing team is ill or leaves, the sharer will continue working for at least half the time. Job-sharing also means that a wider employment pool can be tapped for those who cannot work full-time but want permanent employment. The disadvantages are the administrative costs involved and the risk of responsibility being divided.

*New technology (homeworking and teleworking)* home-based employees, can be employed in such jobs as consultants, analysts, designers, programmers or various kinds of administrative work. The advantages of these arrangements are:

- flexibility to respond rapidly to fluctuations in demand
- reduced overheads

- lower employment costs if the homeworkers are self-employed (care, however, has to be taken to ensure that they are regarded as self-employed for income tax and national insurance purposes).

Teleworking involves people working at home with a terminal which is linked to the main company or networked with other outworkers. Its aim is to achieve greater flexibility, rapid access to skills and the retention of skilled employees who would otherwise be lost to the company. Teleworkers can be used in a number of functions such as marketing, finance, personnel and management services. The arrangement does, however, depend for its success on the involvement and education of all employees (full-time and teleworkers), the careful selection and training of teleworkers, allocating adequate resources to them and monitoring the operation of the system.

*Subcontracting* enables:

- resources to be concentrated on core business activities
- employment costs to be reduced
- flexibility and productivity to be increased
- job security for core employees to be enhanced.

The potential drawbacks include:

- the legal status of subcontractors — this has to be clarified for income tax, national insurance and employment legislation purposes
- the degree to which subcontractors will be able to meet delivery and quality requirements — it may be more difficult to control their work
- negative reactions from employees and trade unions who prefer work to be kept within the company.

The decision on how much work can be subcontracted is mainly an operational one, but the flexibility plan should cover the implications of subcontracting on employment levels and employee relations.

## Flexible hour arrangements

Flexible hour arrangements can be included in the flexibility plan in one or more of the following ways:

- flexible daily hours — these may follow an agreed pattern day by day according to typical or expected work loads (eg flexitime systems)

- flexible weekly hours — providing for longer weekly hours to be worked at certain peak periods during the year
- flexible daily and weekly hours — varying daily or weekly hours or a combination of both to match the input of hours to achieve the required output. Such working times, unlike daily or weekly arrangements, may fluctuate between a minimum and a maximum
- compressed working weeks in which employees work fewer than the five standard days
- annual hours — scheduling employee hours on the basis of the number of hours to be worked, with provisions for the increase or reduction of hours in any given period, according to the demand for goods or services.

## Overtime arrangements

A flexibility plan can contain proposals to reduce overtime costs by the use of flexible hours, new shift arrangements (eg twilight shifts), time off in lieu and overtime limitation agreements. The reduction of overtime is often catered for in formal productivity deals which include a *quid pro quo* in the form of increased pay for the elimination of overtime payments and the introduction of flexible work patterns.

## Shift-working arrangements

These can be introduced or modified to meet demand requirements, reduce overtime or provide for better plant or equipment utilization.

## The productivity plan

The productivity plan sets out programmes for improving productivity or reducing employment costs in such areas as:

- improving or streamlining methods, procedures and systems mechanization, automation or computerization
- the use of financial and non-financial incentives.

These will be additional to any proposals contained in the flexibility plan.

The productivity plan should also set productivity or efficiency targets such as those mentioned earlier in this chapter.

## The downsizing plan

If all else fails, it may be necessary to deal with unacceptable employment costs or surplus numbers of employees by what has euphemistically come to be known as 'downsizing'. The downsizing plan should be based on the timing of reductions and forecasts of the extent to which these can be achieved by natural wastage or voluntary redundancy. The plan should set out:

- the total number of people who have to go and when and where this needs to take place
- arrangements for informing and consulting with employees and their trade unions
- a forecast of the number of losses which can be taken up by natural wastage
- any financial or other inducements to encourage voluntary redundancy
- a forecast of the likely numbers who will volunteer to leave
- a forecast of the balance of employees, if any, who will have to be made redundant (the plan should, of course, aim to avoid this through natural wastage and voluntary redundancy)
- the redundancy terms
- any financial inducements to be offered to key employees whom the company wishes to retain
- any arrangements for retraining employees and finding them work elsewhere in the organization
- the steps to be taken to help redundant employees find new jobs by counselling, contacting other employers or offering the services of outplacement consultants
- the arrangements for telling individual employees about the redundancies and how they are affected, and for keeping the trade unions informed.

## Control

The human resource plan should include budgets, targets, and standards. It should also clarify responsibilities for implementation and control, and establish reporting procedures which will enable achievements to be monitored against the plan. These may simply report on the numbers employed against establishment (identifying both those who are in post and those who are in the pipeline), and on the numbers recruited against the recruitment targets. But they should also report employment costs against budget and trends in wastage and employment ratios.

# 24

# Recruitment and Selection

## The recruitment and selection process

The overall aim of the recruitment and selection process should be to obtain at minimum cost the number and quality of employees required to satisfy the human resource needs of the company. The three stages of recruitment and selection are:

1. *Defining requirements* — preparing job descriptions and specifications; deciding terms and conditions of employment.
2. *Attracting candidates* — reviewing and evaluating alternative sources of applicants, inside and outside the company, advertising, using agencies and consultants.
3. *Selecting candidates* — sifting applications, interviewing, testing, assessing candidates, assessment centres, offering employment, obtaining references; preparing contracts of employment.

The flow of work and main decisions required in a recruitment and selection procedure are shown in Figures 24.1 and 24.2.

This chapter starts with a description of approaches to defining requirements and then discusses the following main features of the recruitment and selection process in the areas of obtaining and selecting candidates under the following headings:

- defining requirements
- attracting candidates
- advertising
- using agencies
- using recruitment consultants
- using executive search consultants

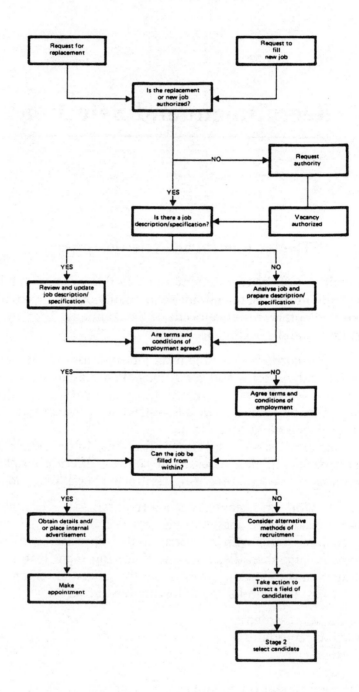

**Figure 24.1** Recruitment flow chart — part 1: preliminary stages

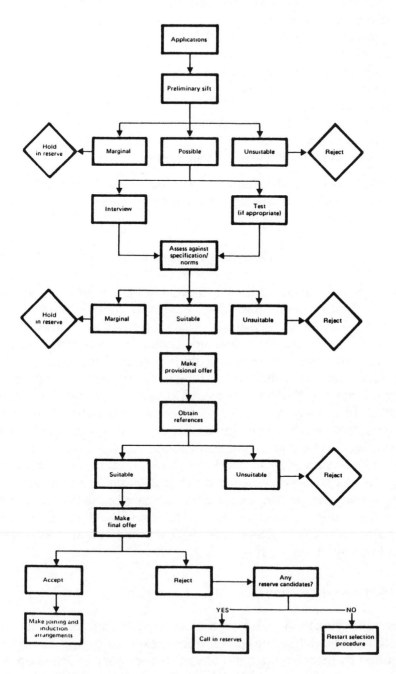

**Figure 24.2** Recruitment flow chart — part 2:
interviewing and selection stages

- recruiting from educational and training establishments
- sifting applications
- types of interview
- assessment centres
- interviewing arrangements
- interviewing techniques
- selection testing
- improving selection procedures
- references and offers
- induction and follow-up arrangements.

At the end of the chapter consideration is given to evaluating the selection process and the legal and ethical frameworks for recruitment and selection.

## Defining requirements

The number and categories of people required should be specified in the recruitment programme, which is derived from the human resource plan. In addition, there will be demands for replacements or for new jobs to be filled, and these demands should be checked to ensure that they are justified. It may be particularly necessary to check on the need for a replacement or the level or type of employee that is specified.

In a large organization it is useful to have a form for requisitioning staff, as illustrated in Figure 24.3. However, even when a requisition form is completed, it may still be necessary to supplement the brief information contained in the form about the job, and it will almost certainly be necessary to check on the specification. If a requisition form is not available, then the job has to be analysed and a job description and person specification prepared. Existing descriptions and specifications should be checked to ensure that they are up to date. It is also necessary to establish or check on the terms and conditions of employment at this stage.

### Person specifications

Person specifications, also known as recruitment, personnel or job specifications, define the qualifications, experience and competences required by the job holder and any other necessary information on the special demands made by the job, such as physical conditions, unusual hours, or travel away from home. They also set out or refer to terms

| STAFF REQUISITION | | | |
|---|---|---|---|
| To<br>Personnel Department | From | Department | Date |

| REQUIREMENTS | |
|---|---|
| Job title | Permanent ☐          Temporary ☐ |
| Salary grade | Date needed |
| | If temporary, specify the period<br>from                    to |
| Brief outline of main duties | Education and qualifications required |
| | Experience required |
| | Special skills, mental or personality<br>requirements |
| | Age limits (if any) |
| | Who will supervise<br>the employee? |
| | Whom will the<br>employee supervise? |

**IF A REPLACEMENT, COMPLETE THE FOLLOWING**

| Employee replaced | Job title | Salary | Date terminated |
|---|---|---|---|
| Reason for termination | | | |
| Performance<br>☐ Above average   ☐ Satisfactory   ☐ Unsatisfactory | | Would you re-engage?<br>☐ Yes  ☐ No | |

**IF INCREASE IN ESTABLISHMENT, COMPLETE THE FOLLOWING**

| What has created the need for an increase? | | |
|---|---|---|
| Explain why it is not possible to avoid this increase by organizational or other<br>re-arrangements | | |
| Increase in establishment approved | Signed | Date |

**Figure 24.3** Staff requisition form

and conditions of employment such as pay, employee benefits, hours and holidays.

The information on the qualifications and work-based and behavioural competences required should be derived from job and competence analysis as described in Chapter 12. These should be specified; for example, the skills a machine operator requires to operate a machine or group of machines, the knowledge of word processing needed by a secretary, the persuasive ability needed by a sales representative, or the competence in delivering training required by a personnel manager. The list should be as precise as possible in order that at the interviewing stage interviewers can structure their interviews by focusing their questions on what the candidate knows and can do.

Lists can be developed of the competences relevant for particular jobs. These can be used as criteria in the selection procedure as part of an interviewing or assessment centre process. At the individual job level, competence analysis identifies:

- *inputs* — what the job holder needs to know and be able to do; this identifies job-based or work-related competences
- *process* — how the job holder applies knowledge and skill to do the work; this identifies the behavioural requirements
- *outputs* — the value added to the organization as a result of the job holder's contribution; this sets out what job holders are expected to achieve as a basis for objective setting.

The biggest danger to be avoided at this stage is that of overstating the qualifications and competences required. Perhaps it is natural to go for the best, but setting an unrealistically high level for candidates increases the problems of attracting applicants, and results in dissatisfaction among recruits when they find their talents are not being used. Understating requirements can, of course, be equally dangerous, but it happens much less frequently. The best approach is to distinguish between those requirements that are essential and those that are desirable.

When the requirements have been agreed, they should be analysed under suitable headings. The ways of doing this were traditionally the seven-point plan developed by Rodger (1952) and the five-fold grading system produced by Munro-Fraser (1954).

## The seven-point plan

The seven-point plan covers:

1. *Physical make-up* — health, physique, appearance, bearing and speech
2. *Attainments* — education, qualifications, experience
3. *General intelligence* — fundamental intellectual capacity
4. *Special aptitudes* — mechanical, manual dexterity, facility in the use of words or figures
5. *Interests* — intellectual, practical, constructional, physically active, social, artistic
6. *Disposition* — acceptability, influence over others, steadiness, dependability, self-reliance
7. *Circumstances* — domestic circumstances, occupations of family.

## The five-fold grading system

The five-fold grading system covers:

1. *Impact on others* — physical make-up, appearance, speech and manner
2. *Acquired qualifications* — education, vocational training, work experience
3. *Innate abilities* — natural quickness of comprehension and aptitude for learning
4. *Motivation* — the kinds of goals set by the individual, his or her consistency and determination in following them up, and success in achieving them
5. *Adjustment* — emotional stability, ability to stand up to stress and ability to get on with people.

## Choice of method

Of these two systems the seven-point plan has the longer pedigree. The five-fold grading scheme is simpler, in some ways, and places more emphasis on the dynamic aspects of the applicant's career. Both can provide a good framework for interviewing. However, more and more recruiters are now using the language of competences as a basis for the person specification and for a structured interview. These competences will be defined in terms of:

● *work-based competences* — which refer to expectations of what people have to be able to do if they are going to achieve the results required in the job — these are the areas of competence, which will be expressed in terms of outputs and the standards of performance they must reach in all the job's main elements

*449*

| Part 1: JOB SPECIFICATION | |
|---|---|
| Department | Section |
| Job title | Job grade |
| Reporting to (job title) | |
| Reporting to job holder (job titles) | |
| Overall purpose of job | |
| Main activities/tasks | |
| Special requirements (tools and equipment used, external contacts, etc) | |
| Other features of job: shift or night work, travel, working conditions, etc | |
| Location of job | |

**Figure 24.4(a)** Job and person specification form (part 1)

- *behavioural competences* — which refer to the personal characteristics and behaviour required for successful performance in such areas as interpersonal skills, leadership, personal drive, communication skills, team membership and analytical ability.

This information can be recorded on a person specification form, as shown in Figure 24.4 (a and b). An example of a person specification is given in Appendix A.

| Part 2: PERSON SPECIFICATION | |
| --- | --- |
| **Education, qualifications and special training** | |
| **Experience** | |
| **Work-based competences** | |
| Essential | Desirable |
| **Behavioural competences** | |
| Essential | Desirable |

**Figure 24.4(b)** Job and person specification form (part 2)

## Attracting candidates

Attracting candidates is primarily a matter of identifying, evaluating and using the most appropriate sources of applicants. However, in cases where difficulties in attracting or retaining candidates are being met or anticipated, it may be necessary to carry out a preliminary study of the factors that are likely to attract or repel candidates — the strengths and weaknesses of the organization as an employer.

## Analysis of recruitment strengths and weaknesses

The analysis of strengths and weaknesses should cover such matters as the national or local reputation of the organization, pay, employee benefits and working conditions, the intrinsic interest of the job, security of employment, opportunities for education and training, career prospects, and the location of the office or plant. These need to be compared with the competition in order that a list of what are, in effect, selling-points, can be drawn up as in a marketing exercise, in which the preferences of potential customers are compared with the features of the product in order that those aspects which are likely to provide the most appeal to the customers can be emphasized. Candidates are, in a sense, selling themselves, but they are also buying what the organization has to offer. If, in the latter sense, the labour market is a buyer's market, then the company which is selling itself to candidates must study their needs in relation to what it can provide.

The aim of the study might be to prepare a better image of the organization for use in advertisements, brochures or interviews. Or it might have the more constructive aim of showing where the organization needs to improve as an employer if it is to attract more or better candidates *and* to retain those selected. The study could make use of an attitude survey to obtain the views of existing employees. One such survey mounted by the writer in an engineering company wishing to attract science graduates established that the main concern of the graduates was that they would be able to use and develop the knowledge they had gained at university. As a result, special brochures were written for each major discipline giving technical case histories of the sort of work graduates carried out. These avoided the purple passages used in some brochures (which the survey established were distinctly off-putting to most students) and proved to be a most useful recruitment aid. Strong measures were also taken to ensure that research managers made proper use of the graduates they recruited.

## Sources of candidates

First consideration should be given to internal candidates, although some organizations with powerful equal opportunity policies (often local authorities) insist that all internal candidates should apply for vacancies on the same footing as external candidates. If there are no people available within the organization, or if the policy is to advertise all vacancies externally as well as internally the main sources of candidates as described in the next five sections are:

- advertising
- agencies
- recruitment consultants
- executive search consultants
- educational establishments.

# Advertising

Advertising is the most obvious method of attracting candidates. Nevertheless, the first question to ask is whether an advertisement is really justified. This means looking at the alternative sources mentioned above and confirming, preferably on the basis of experience, that they will not do. Consideration should be given as to whether it might be better to use an agency or a selection consultant. When making the choice, refer to the three criteria of cost, speed and the likelihood of providing good candidates. The objectives of an advertisement should be to:

- *attract attention* — it must compete for the interest of potential candidates against other employees
- *create and maintain interest* — it has to communicate in an attractive and interesting way information about the job, the company, the terms and conditions of employment and the qualifications required
- *stimulate action* — the message needs to be conveyed in a manner which will not only focus peoples eyes on the advertisement but also encourage them to read to the end, as well as prompt a sufficient number of replies from good candidates.

To achieve these aims, it is necessary to:

- analyse the requirement
- decide who does what
- write the copy
- design the advertisement
- plan the media
- evaluate the response.

## Analyse the requirement

First it is necessary to establish how many jobs have to be filled and by when. Then turn to the job description and person specification to obtain information on responsibilities, qualifications and experience required and any other data needed to draft the advertisement.

The next step is to consider where suitable candidates are likely to come from; the companies, jobs or education establishments they are in; and the parts of the country where they can be found.

Finally, think about what is likely to attract them about the job or the company so the most can be made of these factors in the advertisement. Consider also what might put them off, for example, the location of the job, in order that objections can be anticipated. Analyse previous successes or failures to establish what does or does not work.

## Using an advertising agency

When planning a campaign or recruiting key people, there is much to be said for using an advertising agency. An agency can provide expertise in producing eye-catching headlines and writing good copy. It can devise an attractive house style and prepare layouts which make the most of the text, the logo and any 'white space' round the advertisement. Moreover, it can advise on ways of achieving visual impact by the use of illustrations and special typographical features. Finally, an agency can advise on media, help in response analysis and take up the burden of preparing blocks and placing advertisements.

The following steps should be taken when choosing an advertising agency:

- check its experience in handling recruitment advertising
- see examples of its work
- check with clients on the level of service provided
- meet the staff who will work on the advertisements
- check the fee structure
- discuss methods of working.

## Write the copy

A recruitment advertisement should start with a compelling headline and then contain information on:

- the organization
- the job
- the person required — qualifications, experience etc
- the pay and benefits offered

- the location
- the action to be taken.

The headline is all important. The simplest and most obvious approach is to set out the job title in bold type. To gain attention, it is advisable to quote the salary (if it is worth quoting) and to put 'plus car' if a company car is provided. Salaries and cars are major attractions and should be stated clearly. Applicants are rightly suspicious of clauses such as 'salary will be commensurate with age and experience' or 'salary negotiable'. This usually means either that the salary is so low that the company is afraid to reveal it, or that salary policies are so incoherent that the company has no idea what to offer until someone tells them what he or she wants.

The name of the company should be given. Do not use box numbers — if you want to be anonymous, use a consultant. Add any selling-points, such as growth or diversification, and any other areas of interest to potential candidates, such as career prospects. The essential features of the job should be conveyed by giving a brief description of what the job holder will do and, as far as space permits, the scope and scale of activities. Create interest in the job but do not oversell it.

The qualifications and experience required should be stated as factually as possible. There is no point in overstating requirements and seldom any point in specifying exactly how much experience is wanted. This will vary from candidate to candidate and the other details about the job and the rate of pay should provide them with enough information about the sort of experience required. Be careful about including a string of personal qualities such as drive, determination, and initiative. These have no real meaning to candidates. Phrases such as 'proven track record' and 'successful experience' are equally meaningless. No one will admit to not having either of them.

The advertisement should end with information on how the candidate should apply. 'Brief but comprehensive details' is a good phrase. Candidates can be asked to write, but useful alternatives are to ask them to telephone or to come along for an informal chat at a suitable venue.

Remember that the Sex Discrimination Act 1975 makes it unlawful to discriminate in an advertisement by favouring either sex, the only exceptions being a few jobs which can be done only by one sex. Advertisements must therefore avoid sexist job titles such as 'salesman' or 'stewardess'. They must refer to a neutral title such as 'sales representative', or amplify the description to cover both sexes by stating 'steward or stewardess'. It is accepted, however, that certain job titles are unisex and therefore non-discriminatory. These include director, manager, executive and officer. It is best to avoid any reference to the sex of the candidate by using neutral or unisex titles and referring only to the 'candidate' or the 'applicant'. Otherwise you must specify 'man or woman' or 'he or she'.

The Race Relations Act 1976 has similar provisions, making unlawful an advertisement which discriminates against any particular race. As long as race is never mentioned or even implied in an advertisement, you should have no problem in keeping within the law.

## Design the advertisement

The main types of advertisement are the following:

- Classified/run-on, in which copy is run-on, with no white space in or around the advertisement and no paragraph spacing or indentation. They are cheap but suitable only for junior or routine jobs.
- Classified/semi-display, in which the headings can be set in capitals, paragraphs can be indented and white space is allowed round the advertisement. They are fairly cheap and semi-display can be much more effective than run-on advertisements.
- Full display, which are bordered and in which any typeface and illustrations can be used. They can be expensive but obviously make the most impact for managerial, technical and professional jobs.

## Plan the media

An advertising agency can advise on the choice of media (press, radio, television) and its cost. British Rates and Data (BRAD) can be consulted to give the costs of advertising in particular media.

The so-called 'quality papers' are best for managerial, professional and technical jobs. The popular press, especially evening papers, can be used to reach staff such as sales representatives and technicians. Local papers are obviously best for recruiting office staff and manual workers. Professional and trade journals can reach your audience directly, but results can be erratic and it may be advisable to use them to supplement a national campaign.

Avoid Saturdays and be cautious about repeating advertisements in the same medium. Diminishing returns can set in rapidly.

## *Evaluate the response*

Measure response to provide guidance on the relative cost-effectiveness of different media. Cost per reply is the best ratio.

# Using recruitment agencies

Most private agencies deal with secretarial and office staff. They are usually quick and effective but quite expensive. London agencies charge a fee of 15 per cent or so of the first year's salary for finding someone. It can be cheaper to advertise, especially when the company is in a buyer's market. Shop around to find the agency which suits the organization's needs at a reasonable cost.

Agencies should be briefed carefully on what is wanted. They produce unsuitable candidates from time to time but the risk is reduced if they are clear about your requirements.

# Using recruitment consultants

Recruitment consultants generally advertise, interview and produce a short list. They provide expertise and reduce workload. The organization can be anonymous if it wishes. Most recruitment consultants charge a fee based on a percentage of the basic salary for the job, usually ranging from 15 to 20 per cent.

The following steps should be taken when choosing a recruitment consultant:

- check reputation with other users
- look at the advertisements of the various firms in order to obtain an idea of the quality of a consultancy and the type and level of jobs with which it deals
- check on special expertise — the large accountancy firms, for example, are obviously skilled in recruiting accountants
- meet the consultant who will work on the assignment to assess his or her quality
- compare fees, although the differences are likely to be small, and the other considerations are usually more important.

When using recruitment consultants it is necessary to:

- agree terms of reference
- brief them on the organization, where the job fits in, why the appointment is to be made and any special requirements

457

- give them every assistance in defining the job and the person specification, including any special demands that will be made on the successful candidate in the shape of what he or she will be expected to achieve — they will do much better if they have comprehensive knowledge of what is required and what type of person is most likely to fit well into the organization
- check carefully the proposed programme and the draft text of the advertisement
- clarify the basis upon which fees and expenses will be charged
- ensure that arrangements are made to deal directly with the consultant who will handle the assignment.

## Using executive search consultants

Use an executive search consultant, or 'head hunter', for senior jobs where there are only a limited number of suitable people and a direct lead to them is wanted. They are not cheap. Head hunters charge a fee of 30 to 50 per cent or so of the first year's salary, but they can be quite cost-effective.

Executive search consultants first approach their own contacts in the industry or profession concerned. The good ones have an extensive range of contacts and their own data bank. They will also have researchers who will identify suitable people who may fit the specification or can provide a lead to someone else who may be suitable. The more numerous the contacts, the better the executive search consultant.

When a number of potentially suitable and interested people have been assembled, a fairly relaxed and informal meeting takes place and the consultant forwards the names of suitable candidates to the client.

There are some good and some not-so-good executive search consultants. Do not use one unless a reliable recommendation is obtained.

## Educational and training establishments

Many jobs can, of course, be filled by school leavers. For some organizations the major source of recruits for training schemes will be universities and training establishments as well as schools. Graduate recruitment is a major annual exercise for some companies which go to great efforts to produce glossy brochures, visit campuses on the 'milk run' and use elaborate sifting and selection procedures to vet candidates, including 'biodata' and assessment centres as described later in this chapter.

## Sifting applications

When the vacancy or vacancies have been advertised and a fair number of replies received, the typical sequence of steps required to process and sift applications is as follows:

- List the applications on a standard control sheet such as the one illustrated in Figure 24.5.
- Send a standard acknowledgement letter to each applicant unless an instant decision can be made to interview or reject.
- The applicant may be asked to complete and return an application form. This ensures that all applicants are considered on the same basis — it can be very difficult to plough through a pile of letters, often ill-written and badly organized, although the quality of CVs (curriculum vitae which set out the applicant's qualification and experience) is likely to be higher if the applicant has been receiving advice from an 'outplacement' consultant, ie one who specializes in finding people jobs. However, to save time, trouble, expense and irritation, many recruiters prefer to make a decision on the initial letter where it is quite clear that an applicant meets or does not meet the specification rather than ask for a form.
- Compare the applications with the key criteria in the job specification: qualifications, competences, training, experience, achievements and location, and sort them initially into three categories: possible, marginal and unsuitable.
- Scrutinize the possibles again to draw up a short list for interview. This scrutiny could be carried out by the personnel or employment specialist, and, preferably, the manager. The numbers on the short list should ideally be between four and eight or so. Fewer than four leaves relatively little choice (although such a limitation may be forced on you if an insufficient number of good applications have been received). More than eight will mean that too much time is spent on interviewing and there is a danger of diminishing returns setting in.
- Draw up an interviewing programme. The time you should allow for the interview will vary according to the complexity of the job. For a fairly routine job, 30 minutes or so should suffice. For a more senior job, 60 minutes or more is required. It is best not to schedule too many interviews in a day — if you try and carry out more than five or six exacting interviews you will quickly run out of steam and do neither the interviewee or your company any justice. It is

advisable to leave about 15 minutes between interviews to write up notes and prepare for the next one.

- Invite the candidates to interview, using a standard letter where large numbers are involved. At this stage, candidates should be asked to complete an application form, if they have not already done so. There is much to be said at this stage for sending candidates some details of the organization and the job so that you do not have to spend too much time going through this information at the interview.

- Review the remaining possibles and marginals and decide if any are to be held in reserve. Send reserves a standard 'holding' letter and send the others a standard rejection letter. The latter should thank candidates for the interest shown and inform them briefly, but not too brusquely, that they have not been successful. A typical reject letter might read as follows:

> Since writing to you on ... we have given careful consideration to your application for the above position. I regret to inform you, however, that we have decided not to ask you to attend for an interview. We should like to thank you for the interest you have shown.

| Ref | Vacancy | | | | | | |
|---|---|---|---|---|---|---|---|
| **Media** | | | | | | | |
| No. | Media Ref | Name | Address | Grading | Acknow-ledge | Inter-view | Final letter |
| 1 | | | | | | | |
| 2 | | | | | | | |
| 3 | | | | | | | |
| 4 | | | | | | | |
| 5 | | | | | | | |
| 6 | | | | | | | |
| 7 | | | | | | | |
| 8 | | | | | | | |
| 9 | | | | | | | |
| 10 | | | | | | | |

**Figure 24.5** Recruitment control sheet

## Application forms

Application forms are required as a means of setting out the information on a candidate in a standardized format. They provide a structured basis for drawing up short lists, the interview itself and for the subsequent actions in offering an appointment and in setting up personnel records. An example of a form is given in Appendix C.

## Electronic CVs

Computers can read CVs by means of high-grade, high-speed scanners using optical character recognition (OCR) software. CVs are scanned and converted into basic text format. The system's artificial intelligence reads the texts and extracts key data such as personal details, skills, educational qualifications, previous employers and jobs, and relevant dates. Search criteria are created listing mandatory and preferred requirements such as qualifications, companies in which applicants have worked and jobs held. The system carries out an analysis of the CVs against these criteria, lists the candidates that satisfy all the mandatory requirements and ranks them by the number of these requirements each one meets. The recruiter can then use this ranking as a shortlist or can tighten the search criteria to produce a shorter list. Essentially, the computer is looking for the same key words as human recruiters but it can carry out this task more systematically and quicker, cross-referencing skills. Any recruiter knows the problem of dealing with a large number of applications and trying, often against the odds, to extract a sensible shortlist.

## Biodata

A highly structured method of sifting applications is provided by the use of biodata. These are items of biographical data which are criterion based (ie they relate to established criteria in such terms as qualifications and experience which indicate that individuals are likely to be suitable). These are objectively scored and, by measurements of past achievements, predict future behaviour.

The items of biodata consist of demographic details (sex, age, family circumstances), education and professional qualifications, previous employment history and work experience, positions of responsibility outside work, leisure interests and career/job motivation. These items are weighted according to their relative importance as predictors, and a range of scores is allocated to each one. The biodata questionnaire (essentially a detailed application form) obtains information on each item, which is then scored.

Biodata are most useful when a large number of applicants are received for a limited number of posts. Cut-off scores can then be determined, based on previous experience. These scores would indicate who should be accepted for the next stage of the selection process and who should be rejected, but they would allow for some possible candidates to be held until the final cut-off score can be fixed after the first batch of applicants have been screened.

Biodata criteria and predictors are selected by job and functional analysis, which produces a list of competences. The validity of these items as predictors and the weighting to be given to them are established by analyzing the biodata of existing employees who are grouped into high or low performers. Weights are allocated to items according to the discriminating power of the response. Biodata questionnaires and scoring keys are usually developed for specific jobs in an organization. Their validity compares reasonably well with other selection instruments but they need to be developed and validated with great care and they are only applicable when large groups of applicants have to be screened.

# Types of interview

## Individual interviews

The individual interview is the most familiar method of selection. It involves face-to-face discussion and provides the best opportunity for the establishment of close contact — rapport — between the interviewer and the candidate. If only one interviewer is used, there is more scope for a biased or superficial decision, and this is one reason for using a second interviewer or an interviewing panel.

## Interviewing panels

Two or more people gathered together to interview one candidate may be described as an interviewing panel. The most typical situation is that in which a personnel manager and line managers see the candidate at the same time. This has the advantage of enabling information to be shared and reducing overlaps. The interviewers can discuss their joint impressions of the candidate's behaviour at the interview and modify or enlarge any superficial judgements.

## *Selection boards*

Selection boards are more formal and, usually, larger interviewing panels convened by an official body because there are a number of parties interested in the selection decision. Their only advantage is that they enable a number of different people to have a look at the applicants and compare notes on the spot. The disadvantages are that the questions tend to be unplanned and delivered at random, the prejudices of a dominating member of the board can overwhelm the judgements of the other members, and the candidates are unable to do justice to themselves because they are seldom allowed to expand. Selection boards tend to favour the confident and articulate candidate, but in doing so they may miss the underlying weaknesses of a superficially impressive individual. They can also underestimate the qualities of those who happen to be less effective in front of a formidable board, although they would be fully competent in the less formal or less artificial situations that would face them in the job.

## Assessment centres

A more comprehensive approach to selection is provided by the use of assessment centres. These incorporate a range of assessment techniques and typically have the following features:

- The focus of the centre is on behaviour.
- Exercises are used to capture and simulate the key dimensions of the job. These include one-to-one role-plays, 'in-tray' exercises and group exercises. It is assumed that performance in these simulations predicts behaviour on the job.
- Interviews and tests will be used in addition to group exercises.
- Performance is measured in several dimensions in terms of the competences required to achieve the target level of performance in a particular job or at a particular level in the organization.
- Several candidates or participants are assessed together to allow interaction and to make the experience more open and participative.
- Several assessors or observers are used in order to increase the objectivity of assessments. Involving senior managers is desirable to ensure that they 'own' the process. Assessors must be carefully trained.

Assessment centres provide good opportunities for indicating the extent to which candidates match the culture of the organization. This will be established by observations of their behaviour in different but typical situations, and the range of the tests and structured interviews which are part of the proceedings. Assessment centres also give candidates a better feel for the organization and its values so that they can decide for themselves whether or not they are likely to fit. They are most appropriate for candidates who are being considered for jobs with complex competence profiles.

A well-conducted assessment centre can achieve a better forecast of future performance and progress than judgements made by line or even personnel managers in the normal, unskilled way.

## Interviewing arrangements

The interviewing arrangements will depend partly on the procedure being used, which may consist of individual interviews, an interviewing panel, a selection board or some form of assessment centre, sometimes referred to as a group selection procedure. The main features of these alternative procedures were described above but, in most cases, the arrangements for the interviews should conform broadly to the following pattern:

● The candidate who has applied in writing or by telephone should be told where and when to come and whom to ask for. The interview time should be arranged to fit in with the time it will take to get to the company. It may be necessary to adjust times for those who cannot get away during working hours. If the company is difficult to find, a map should be sent with details of public transport. The receptionist or security guard should be told who is coming. Candidates are impressed to find that they are expected.

● Applicants should have somewhere quiet and comfortable in which to wait for the interview, with reading material available and access to cloakroom facilities.

● The interviewers or interviewing panel should have been well briefed on the programme. Interviewing rooms should have been booked and arrangements made, as necessary, for welcoming candidates, for escorting them to interviews, for meals and for a conducted tour round the company.

● Comfortable private rooms should be provided for interviews with little, if any, distractions around them. Interviewers should preferably not sit behind their desks, as this creates a psychological barrier. During the interview or interviews, time should be allowed to tell candidates about the company and the job and to discuss with them conditions of employment. Negotiations about pay and other benefits may take place after a provisional offer has been made, but it is as well to prepare the ground during the interviewing stage.

- Candidates should be told what the next step will be at the end of the interview. They may be asked at this stage if they have any objections to references being taken up.
- Follow-up studies should be carried out of the performance of successful candidates in their jobs compared with the prediction made at the selection stage. These studies should be used to validate the selection procedure and to check on the capabilities of inter-viewers.

When making arrangements for an interview it is essential that the people who are going to conduct the interview are properly briefed on the job and the procedures they should use. There is everything to be said for including training in interviewing techniques as an automatic part of the training programmes for manager and team leaders.

It is particularly important that everyone is fully aware of the pro-visions of the Sex and Race Discrimination Acts. It is essential that any form of prejudiced behaviour or any prejudiced judgements are eliminated completely from the interview and the ensuing discussion. Even the faintest hint of a sexist or racist remark must be totally avoided. When recording a decision following an interview it is also essential to spell out the reasons why someone was rejected, making it clear that this was absolutely on the grounds of their qualifications for the job and had nothing to do with their race or sex.

Another important consideration in planning and executing a recruitment programme is to behave ethically towards candidates. They have the right to be treated with consideration and this includes acknowledging replies and informing them of the outcome of their application without undue delay.

## Interviewing

The purpose of the interview is to obtain and assess information about a candidate which will enable a valid prediction to be made of his or her future performance in the job in comparison with the predictions made for any other candidates. Interviewing therefore involves pro-cessing and evaluating evidence about the capabilities of a candidate in relation to the job specification. Some of the evidence will be on the application form, but this must be supplemented by the more detailed or specific information about experience and personal characteristics that can be obtained in a face-to-face meeting. Further evidence may be obtained from selection tests or from references, but the interview is generally regarded as the most useful source of information although its accuracy has often been questioned.

## The aim of an interview

Selection interviews aim to provide answers to three fundamental questions:

1. *Can* the individual do the job? Is he or she competent?
2. *Will* the individual do the job? Is she or he motivated?
3. *How* is the individual likely to fit into the organization?

## The nature of an interview

An interview can be described as a conversation with a purpose. It is a conversation because candidates should be induced to talk freely with their interviewers about themselves and their careers. But the conversation has to be planned, directed and controlled to achieve the main purpose of the interview, which is to make an accurate prediction of the candidate's future performance in the job for which he or she is being considered.

Interviews, however, have other aims. One is to provide the candidate with information about the job and the company. An interview is basically an exchange of information which will enable both parties to make a decision: to offer or not to offer a job; to accept or not to accept the offer. It may be better for the candidates to 'de-select' themselves at this stage if they do not like what they hear about the job or the company rather than take on a disagreeable job. A further aim is to give the candidate a favourable impression of the organization to encourage the good candidate to join.

But it is unwise to paint too rosy a picture of the company or the job. This might only create dissatisfaction when the employee finds out what it is really like. The aim should be to provide what has been termed a 'realistic job preview'. This presents the unfavourable as well as the favourable aspects of the job and spells out the expectations of the business about what employees have to achieve. It can provide the basis for a mutually agreed psychological contract.

Good interviewers know what they are looking for and how to set about finding it. They have a method for recording their analyses of candidates against a set of assessment criteria which will be spelt out in a person specification using a format such as one of those described earlier in this chapter. The main elements of a good interview are:

- preparation
- sequence and timing
- starting and finishing
- structuring
- interviewing techniques
- analysing the result.

## Preparation

Careful preparation is essential and this means a careful study of the person specification and the candidate's application form and/or CV. It is necessary at this stage to identify those features of the applicant which do not fully match the specification so that these can be probed more deeply during the interview. It can be assumed that the candidate has only been short-listed because there is a reasonable match, but it is most unlikely that this match will be perfect. It is also necessary to establish if there are any gaps in the job history or items which require further explanation.

As Fowler (1991b) suggests, there are two fundamental questions that need to be answered at this stage:

- What more do I need to find out at the interview to ensure that the candidate meets the essential selection criteria?
- What further information do I need to obtain at the interview to ensure that I have an accurate picture of how well the candidate meets the desirable and useful, though not wholly essential criteria?

The preparation should include making notes of the specific questions the interviewer needs to ask to establish the relevance of the candidate's experience and the extent to which he or she has the skills, knowledge and levels of competence required. It is essential to probe during an interview to establish what the candidate really can do and has achieved. Applicants will generally aim to make the most of themselves and this can lead to exaggerated, even false, claims about their experience and capabilities.

## Sequence and timing

There is no one best sequence to follow. As Fowler points out: 'Some interviewers prefer to go through the candidate's history chronologically, some work backwards from the current job, others may chose to examine various aspects in turn, but not necessarily in date order'. What is important is to decide in advance what sequence to follow. It is also important to get the balance right. You should concentrate most on recent experience and not dwell too much on the distant past. You should allow time not only for the candidate to talk about his or her career but also to ask probing questions as necessary. You should certainly not spend too much time at the beginning of the interview talking about the company and the job. It is highly desirable to issue that information in advance to save interview time and simply encourage the candidate to ask questions at the end of the interview (the quality of the questions can indicate something about the quality of the candidate).

## Starting and finishing

You should start interviews by putting candidates at their ease. You want them to provide you with information and they are not going to talk freely and openly if they are given a cool reception.

In the closing stages of the interview candidates should be asked if they have anything they wish to add in support of their application. They should also be given the opportunity to ask questions. At the end of the interview the candidate should be thanked and told what the next step will be. If some time is likely to elapse before a decision is made the candidate should be informed accordingly so as not to be left on tenterhooks. It is normally better not to announce the final decision during the interview. It may be advisable to obtain references and, in any case, time is required to reflect on the information received.

## Structured and behaviourally-based interviews

The problem with interviews are that they are often inadequate as predictors of performance — an hour's interview may not cover the essential points unless it is carefully planned and, sadly, the general standard of interviewing is low. This is not simply a result of many people using poor interviewing techniques (eg they talk rather than listen). More importantly it is a result of not carrying out a proper analysis of the competences required with the result that they do not know the information they need to obtain from the candidate as a basis for structuring the interview.

The aim of a structured interview, also known as a targeted or behaviourally-based interview, is to assess the degree to which candidates have the competences which have been identified by the organization as being necessary to attain the required standard of performance in a job. Such interviews are behaviourally based in the sense that they are founded on the assumption that past performance is the best predictor of future performance. Predetermined questions are put to candidates which are designed to elicit from them behavioural evidence as proof that they are competent in specific areas. Typical questions could be:

- describe a situation in which you persuaded others to take an unusual course of action
- describe an occasion when you completed a task in the face of great difficulties
- describe any contribution you have made as a member of a team in achieving a successful result
- describe any situation in which you took the lead in getting something worthwhile done.

'Behavioural event' questions can also be put to candidates on how they would behave in situations which have been identified as critical to effective job performance. A typical interview may include about ten pre-prepared questions and the answers provided by candidates are assessed by means of specially developed scales. Behaviourally-based structured interviews are particularly useful when large numbers of candidates have to be assessed, for example when interviewing graduates. It was noted by Latham *et al* (1980) that interviewers using this technique produced reasonably consistent and reliable assessments.

## Interviewing techniques

As mentioned earlier, an interview is a conversation with a purpose. The interviewee should be encouraged to do most of the talking — one of the besetting sins of poor interviewers is that they talk too much. The interviewer's job is to draw the candidate out at the same time ensuring that the information required is obtained. To this end it is desirable to ask a number of open-ended questions — questions which cannot be answered by yes or no and which promote a full response. But a good interviewer will have an armoury of other types of questions to be asked as appropriate, such as:

- *probing questions* which ask for more detailed and specific explanations of a candidate's work experience, knowledge, skills and competences
- *play-back questions* which test the interviewer's understanding of what a candidate has said by playing back what a candidate appears to have told him or her
- *closed questions* to clarify a point of fact
- *hypothetical questions* which involve putting a situation to candidates and asking how they would respond.

The questions to avoid are leading questions, which supply their own answer and do not tell you anything, and multiple questions, which only serve to confuse the candidate, and you.

To enable a valid prediction to be made about likely success in a job it is useful to take the job description and help the candidate to identify areas of past experience which positively relate to it. It is also necessary to establish any aspects of the job in which the candidate has little or no experience. In these areas the interviewer has to make a judgement on the importance of such gaps and how readily they can be filled by training and experience. If a competence analysis has been carried out (and this is highly desirable) the interviewer can similarly go through the key competence areas and discuss with the candidate how she or he feels they match the competence profile. This approach provides the basis for a structured interview as described on pages 468 to 469.

Interviewers should always bear in mind that the quality of the answers provided by candidates depends on the quality of the questions. That is why it is a good idea to have prepared in advance some basic questions although these should be used with discretion — it is no good firing a string of questions at candidates. They should be introduced naturally and at appropriate times, and interviewers should be prepared to ask follow-up questions. The sort of general questions which can be put to candidates to get them talking about themselves and thus to reveal the information required include:

- Now you know more about the job, which parts of your experience do you believe are most relevant?
- Is there any aspect of the job that you are not sure you are qualified to do at present?

- What steps have you taken recently to extend your knowledge or develop your skills?
- What are the most significant things you have achieved over the last year or two?
- What has been the most difficult aspect of your present job and why?
- Is there anything else you would like to tell me about your qualifications, experience and achievements that we have not covered?

The dos and don'ts of interviewing are summarized in Table 24.1.

## *Analysing the result*

The analysis of the result of the interview should concentrate on establishing the extent to which the candidate has met the specification. Reference should be made to each of the essential and desirable requirements set out on the person specification and an indication given of how the candidate measures up to them. Candidates who fail to demonstrate that they have the essential qualities required can be eliminated. The final choice will be made on the basis of the candidate who rates highest on both the essential and desirable characteristics.

It is essential not to be beguiled by a pleasant, articulate and confident interviewee who is all surface without any substance in the shape of a good track record and the potential to succeed in the job for

**Table 24.1** Dos and don'ts of interviewing

| Do | Don't |
|---|---|
| ☐ plan the interview | ☐ start the interview unprepared |
| ☐ establish an easy and informal relationship | ☐ plunge too quickly into demanding questions |
| ☐ encourage the candidate to talk | ☐ ask leading questions |
| ☐ cover the ground as planned | ☐ jump to conclusions on inadequate evidence |
| ☐ probe where necessary | |
| ☐ analyse career and interests to reveal strengths, weaknesses, patterns of behaviour | ☐ pay too much attention to isolated strengths or weaknesses |
| | ☐ allow the candidate to gloss over important facts |
| ☐ maintain control over the direction and time taken by the interview | ☐ talk too much |

which he or she is being considered. Beware of the 'halo' effect which occurs when one or two good points are seized upon leading to the neglect of negative indicators. The opposite 'horns' effect should also be avoided.

## Advantages and disadvantages of interviews

The advantages of interviews as a method of selection are that they:

- enable a face-to-face encounter to take place so that the interviewer can make an assessment of how the candidate might fit in the organization and what they would be like to work with
- allow the interviewer to describe the job and the organization in more detail
- provide opportunities for interviewers to ask probing questions about the candidate's experience
- provide opportunities to candidates to ask questions about the job and clarify issues
- enable a number of interviewers to assess candidates, where appropriate.

The disadvantages of interviews are that they:

- generally lack validity as a means of predicting performance and reliability in the sense of measuring the same thing for different candidates (but a structured and behaviourally based approach and the use of tests or an assessment centre can help to overcome this problem)
- rely on the skill of the interviewer, but many people are in fact very poor at interviewing (this problem can and should be alleviated by training)
- do not necessarily assess directly competence in carrying out the various tasks which the job involves (again this problem can be alleviated by structured interviews, tests and, where appropriate, assessment centres)
- can lead to biased and subjective judgements by interviewers (again, training helps and it is generally desirable to get a second or even third opinion and compare notes).

### Selection tests

The purpose of a psychometric selection test is to provide an objective means of measuring individual abilities or characteristics. These involve the application of standard procedures to subjects which enable their responses to be quantified. The differences in the numerical scores represent differences in abilities or behaviour.

A good test has the following four characteristics:

1. It is a *sensitive* measuring instrument which discriminates well between subjects.
2. It has been *standardized* on a representative and sizeable sample of the population for which it is intended so that any individuals score can be interpreted in relation to that of others.
3. It is *reliable* in the sense that it always measures the same thing. A test aimed at measuring a particular characteristic, such as intelligence, should measure the same characteristic when applied to different people at the same or a different time, or to the same person at different times.
4. It is *valid* in the sense that it measures the characteristic which the test is intended to measure. Thus, an intelligence test should measure intelligence (however defined) and not simply verbal facility. A test meant to predict success in a job or in passing examinations should produce reasonably convincing (statistically significant) predictions.

The main types of psychometric tests used for selection are intelligence tests, aptitude and attainment tests, and personality tests.

## Intelligence tests

Intelligence tests are the oldest and most frequently used psychological tests. Test scores may be expressed in the form of intelligence quotients, or IQs. The IQ is the ratio of the mental age, as measured by a Binet-type test, to the actual (chronological) age. When the mental and chronological age correspond, the IQ is expressed as 100. It is assumed that intelligence is distributed normally throughout the population; that is, the frequency distribution of intelligence corresponds to the normal curve shown in Figure 24.6.

The most important characteristic of the normal curve is that it is symmetrical — there are an equal number of cases on either side of the mean, the central axis. Thus, the distribution of intelligence in the population as a whole consists of an equal number of people with IQs above and below 100.

The difficulty with intelligence tests is that they have to be based on a theory of what constitutes intelligence and then have to derive a series

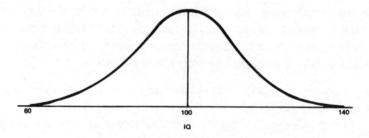

**Figure 24.6** A normal curve

of verbal and non-verbal instruments for measuring the different factors or constituents of intelligence. But intelligence is a highly complex concept. There is no agreed definition of it among psychologists and the variety of theories about intelligence and the consequent variations in the test instrument or battery available make the choice of an intelligence test a difficult one. For general selection purposes, a test which can be administered to a group of candidates is the best, especially if it has been properly validated, and it is possible to relate test scores to 'norms' in such a way as to indicate how the individual taking the test compares with the rest of the population, in general or in a specific area. Such tests do not usually attempt to measure IQs.

## Aptitude and attainment tests

Aptitude tests are designed to predict the potential an individual has to perform a job or specific tasks within a job. They can cover such areas as clerical aptitude, numerical aptitude, mechanical aptitude and dexterity.

All aptitude tests should be properly validated. The usual procedure is to determine the qualities required for the job by means of a job analysis. A standard test or a test battery is then obtained from a test agency. Alternatively, a special test is devised by or for the organization. The test is then given to employees already working on the job and the results compared with a criterion, usually managers' or team leaders' ratings. If the correlation between test and criterion is sufficiently high, the test is then given to applicants. To validate the test further, a follow-up study of the job performance of the applicants selected by the test is usually carried out. This is a lengthy procedure, but without it no real confidence can be attached to the results of any aptitude test. Many do-it-yourself tests are worse than useless because they have not been properly validated.

Attainment tests measure abilities or skills that have already been acquired by training or experience. A typing test is the most typical example. It is easy to find out how many words a minute a typist can type and compare that with the standard required for the job.

## Personality tests

'Personality' is an all-embracing and imprecise term which refers to the behaviour of individuals and the way it is organized and coordinated when they interact with the environment. There are many different theories of personality and, consequently, many different types of personality tests. These include self-report personality questionnaires and other questionnaires which measure interests, values or work behaviour.

Self-report personality questionnaires are the ones most commonly used. They usually adopt a 'trait' approach, defining a trait as a fairly independent but enduring characteristic of behaviour which all people display but to differing degrees. Trait theorists identify examples of common behaviour, devise scales to measure these, and then obtain ratings on these behaviours by people who know each other well. These observations are analysed statistically, using the factor analysis technique to identify distinct traits and to indicate how associated groups of traits might be grouped loosely into 'personality types'.

'Interest' questionnaires are sometimes used to supplement personality tests. They assess the preferences of respondents for particular types of occupation and are therefore most applicable to vocational guidance but can be helpful when selecting apprentices and trainees.

'Value' questionnaires attempt to assess beliefs about what is 'desirable or good' or what is 'undesirable or bad'. The questionnaires measure the relative prominence of such values as conformity, independence, achievement, decisiveness, orderliness and goal-orientation.

Specific work behaviour questionnaires cover behaviours such as leadership or selling.

Personality questionnaires were shown to have the low validity coefficient of 0.15 on the basis of research conducted by Schmitt et al (1984). But as Saville and Sik (1992) point out, this was based on a rag-bag of tests, many developed for clinical use and some using 'projective' techniques such as the Rorschach inkblots test, the interpretation of which relies on a clinician's judgement and is therefore quite out of place in a modern selection procedure. Smith's (1988) studies based on modern self-report questionnaires revealed an average validity coefficient of 0.39.

The following rule of thumb guide was produced by Smith (1984) on whether a validity coefficient is big enough:

over 0.5          excellent
0.40–0.49      good
0.30–0.39      acceptable
less than 0.30  poor

On this basis, only ability tests, biodata and (according to Smith's figures) personality questionnaires reach acceptable levels of validity.

A vigorous attack was launched on personality tests by Steve Blinkorn and Charles Johnson of Psychometric Research and Development (as reported in *Personnel Management Plus,* January 1991, p. 3). As they commented: 'We see precious little evidence of personality tests predicting job performance.' But as Clive Fletcher, Professor of Psychology at Goldsmith's College, wrote in the same issue:

> Like any other selection procedure they (psychometric tests) can be used well or badly. But it would be foolish to dismiss all the evidence of the value of personality assessment in selection on the basis of some misuse. Certainly the majority of applied psychologists feel the balance of the evidence supports the use of personality inventories.

Personality tests can provide interesting supplementary information about candidates which is free from the biased reactions that frequently occur in face-to-face interviews. But they have to be used with great care. The tests should have been developed by a reputable psychologist or test agency on the basis of extensive research and field testing and they must meet the specific needs of the user. Advice should be sought from a member of the British Psychological Society on what tests are likely to be appropriate.

## Choosing tests

It is essential to choose tests which meet the four criteria of sensitivity, standardization, reliability and validity. It is very difficult to achieve the standards required if an organization tries to develop its own test batteries unless it employs a qualified psychologist or obtains professional advice from a member of the British Psychological Society. This organization, with the full support and understanding of the reputable test suppliers, exercises rigorous control over who can use what tests and the standard of training required and given. Particular care should be taken when selecting personality tests — there are a lot of charlatans about.

Do-it-yourself tests are always suspect unless they have been properly validated and realistic norms have been established. Generally speaking, it is best to avoid using them.

## The use of tests in a selection procedure

Tests are most likely to be helpful when they are used as part of a selection procedure for occupations where a large number of recruits are required, and where it is not possible to rely entirely on examination results or information about previous experience as the basis for predicting future performance. In these circumstances it is economical to develop and administer the tests, and a sufficient number of cases can be built up for the essential validation exercise.

Intelligence tests are particularly helpful in situations where intelligence is a key factor, but there is no other reliable method of measuring it. It may, incidentally, be as important to use an intelligence test to keep out applicants who are too intelligent for the job as to use one to guarantee a minimal level of intelligence.

Aptitude and attainment tests are most useful for jobs where specific and measurable skills are required, such as typing or computer programming. Personality tests are potentially of greatest value in jobs such as selling where 'personality' is important, and where it is not too difficult to obtain quantifiable criteria for validation purposes.

Tests should be administered only by staff who have been thoroughly trained in what the tests are measuring, how they should be used, and how they should be interpreted.

It is essential to evaluate all tests by comparing the results at the interview stage with later achievements. To be statistically significant, these evaluations should be carried out over a reasonable period of time and cover as large a number of candidates as possible.

In some situations a battery of tests may be used, including various types of intelligence, aptitude and personality tests. These may be a standard battery supplied by a test agency, or a custom-built battery may be developed. The biggest pitfall to avoid is adding extra tests just for the sake of it, without ensuring that they make a proper contribution to the success of the predictions for which the battery is being used.

## Graphology

Graphology can be defined as the study of the social structure of a human being through his or her writing. Its use in selection is to draw conclusions from a candidate's handwriting about his or her personality as a basis for making predictions about future performance in a role. The use of graphology as a selection aid is extensive on the Continent but relatively uncommon here — Fowler (1991a) quotes research findings which indicate that only between 0.5 and 1.0 per cent of employers use it in this country. This very small proportion may be attributed to the suspicion the great majority of recruiters have that graphology is in some way spurious and using it as a predictor will be a waste of time and money. In an extensive review of the research literature, Fowler (1991a) established that some studies had indicated a predictive validity coefficient in the range of 0.1 to 0.3 although zero results have also been obtained. By reference to the guidelines quoted on page 476, these are low figures which achieve only a poor level of validity. Fowler's conclusion was that: 'Clues about personality characteristics can be deduced by skilled graphologists. But the use of graphology as a single or standard predictor cannot be recommended'. He also suspects that for some people, the real attraction of graphology is that it can be used without the subject's knowledge.

## Improving the effectiveness of recruitment and selection

An HRM approach can be adopted to recruitment which involves taking much more care in matching people to the requirements of the organization as a whole as well as to the particular needs of the job. These requirements will include commitment and ability to work effectively as a member of a team.

Examples of this approach in Japanese companies in the UK include the establishment of the Nissan plant in Washington and Kumatsu in Newcastle. As described by Townley (1989), both followed a conscious recruitment policy with rigorous selection procedures. Aptitude tests, personality questionnaires and group exercises were used and the initial pre-screening device was a detailed 'biodata' type questionnaire which enabled the qualifications and work history of candidates to be assessed and rated systematically. Subsequent testing of those who successfully completed the first stage was designed to assess individual attitudes as well as aptitude and ability. As Wickens (1987) said of the steps taken at Nissan to achieve commitment and teamworking: 'It is something which develops because management genuinely believes in it and acts accordingly — and recruits or promotes people who have the same belief.'

The need for a more sophisticated approach to recruitment along these lines is characteristic of HRM. The first requirement, as discussed below, is to take great care in specifying the competences, attitudes and behavioural characteristics required of employees. The second is to use a wider range of methods to identify candidates who match the specifications.

As a device for predicting success in a job, the traditional unstructured interview is inadequate. Other methods such as ability tests and biodata have greater validity. A study was made by Hunter and Hunter (1984), of the validity of alternative methods as predictors of performance for people moving into their first job. If total validity is achieved (ie 100 per cent accuracy in prediction) the score (the correlation coefficient) would be 1.00. The mean validity (a statistical method for comparing and averaging results over a large number of studies) actually achieved by these methods was:

- ability tests                .53
- biodata                      .37
- interview                    .14
- academic achievements        .11
- education                    .10
- age                          −.01

It is generally accepted that higher levels of validity can be attained if the selection process uses a wider range of methods than just an interview. These may be brought together in an assessment centre.

## Evaluating the recruitment process

The efficiency and effectiveness of the recruitment process should be monitored and evaluated under the following headings:

- ability to identify human resource requirements in terms of numbers and skills from business plans and developments and to take appropriate action
- speed of response to requests for help from line managers
- quality of advice on sources of recruits and on people specifications
- selection of appropriate media for recruitment
- the effectiveness of advertising in such terms as cost per reply

- the efficiency with which recruitment and selection projects are managed and administered
- the length of time taken to recruit people from the initial request to joining the firm
- the quality of recruits
- the retention rate of recruits.

# The legal framework

The legal framework to recruitment is provided by:

- *The Employment Protection (Consolidation) Act 1978 as amended by the Employment Act (1982) and the Trade Union Reform and Employment Rights Act (1993)* provide for written particulars of the main terms and conditions of employment to be given to all employees working eight or more hours a week within two months of starting work.
- *The Sex Discrimination Acts 1975 and 1986* make it unlawful to discriminate on the grounds of sex or marital status in relation to who is offered employment and the terms on which employment is offered. When advertising, it is unlawful to use a 'sexist' job title such as waiter or stewardess unless that the job is open to both men and women. Particular care has therefore to be taken in briefing all interviewers on the need to avoid discrimination and to record the reason, which must be non-discriminatory, for making decisions about candidates. These requirements should be enforced by disciplinary action against anyone who has been guilty of discrimination. Equal care must be taken in wording advertisements.
- *The Race Relations Act 1976* prohibits discrimination on racial grounds and between racial groups against candidates in the arrangements for deciding who should be employed (eg racially biased advertisements), in the terms on which employment is offered or by refusing or deliberately omitting to offer employment. Similar precautions to those required to prevent sexual discrimination should be enforced.

# The ethical framework

The ethical framework for recruitment and selection should cover the following points:

- Candidates should be treated fairly and not discriminated against on the grounds of sex, race or religion.

- Candidates should be treated courteously. Their letters of application should be acknowledged promptly and they should be informed as quickly as possible of the results of their application or interview. They should be treated with consideration at interviews, not being kept waiting too long and not being harassed or browbeaten by the interviewer. Interviews are stressful enough without undue pressure being exerted in a 'stress interview', which is likely to be counterproductive. But this does not mean that probing questions to elicit the full facts should not be used.
- Candidates should be treated honestly — they should be given all the information they need about the company and the job so that they can make a rational decision as to whether or not to accept an offer (dishonest information at an interview will inevitably rebound to the discredit of the firm and the interviewer and will prejudice the achievement of a satisfactory employment relationship).
- Good professional practice should be followed in selecting and using tests. The results of tests should be carefully and considerately fed back to those candidates who want to know how they performed in lay terms.

## References and offers

After the interviewing and testing procedure has been completed, a provisional decision to make an offer by telephone or in writing can be made. This is normally 'subject to satisfactory references' and the candidate should, of course, be told that these will be taken up. If there is more than one eligible candidate for a job it may be advisable to hold one or two people in reserve. Applicants often withdraw, especially those whose only purpose in applying for the job was to carry out a 'test marketing' operation, or to obtain a lever with which to persuade their present employers to value them more highly.

### References

The purpose of a reference is to obtain in confidence factual information about a prospective employee and opinions about his character and suitability for a job.

The factual information is straightforward and essential. It is simply necessary to confirm the nature of the previous job, the period of time in employment, the reason for leaving (if relevant), the salary or rate of pay and, possibly, the attendance record.

Opinions about character and suitability are less reliable and should be treated with caution. The reason is obvious. Previous or present employers who give references tend to avoid highly detrimental remarks either out of charity or because they think anything they say or write may be construed as slanderous or libellous (references are, in fact, privileged as long as they are given without malice and are factually correct).

Personal referees are, of course, entirely useless. All they prove is that the applicant has at least one or two friends.

Written references save time, especially if they are standardized. They may take the form of an invitation to write a letter confirming the employment record and commenting on the applicant's character in general. If brief details about the job are included (these may be an extract from the advertisement — they should certainly not be an over-elaborate job description), previous employers can be asked to express their views about the suitability of the individual for the job. But this is asking a lot. Unless the job and companies are identical, how well can existing or ex-employers judge the suitability of someone they may not know particularly well for another job in a different environment?

More precise answers may be obtained if a standard form is provided for the employer to complete. The questions asked on this form should be limited to the following:

- What was the period of employment?
- What was the job title?
- What work was carried out?
- What was the rate of pay or salary?
- How many days' absence over the last 12 months?
- Would you re-employ (if not, why not)?

The last question is the key one, if it is answered honestly.

Telephone references may be used as an alternative or an addition to written references. The great advantage of a telephone conversation is that people are more likely to give an honest opinion orally than if they have to commit themselves in writing. It may also save time to use the telephone.

Employer references are necessary but they are unreliable. A satisfactory reference has to be treated at its face value — all one can be reasonably certain about is that the factual details are correct. A very glowing reference may arouse suspicion, and it is worth comparing it with a reference from another employer (two employment references are desirable in any case). Poor or grudging references must create some alarm if only because they are so infrequent. But allowance should be made for prejudice and a check should be made, by telephone if possible.

## Confirming the offer

The final stage in the selection procedure is to confirm the offer of employment after satisfactory references have been obtained, and the applicant has passed the medical examination required for pension and life assurance purposes or because a certain standard of physical fitness is required for the work. The contract of employment should also be prepared at this stage.

## Contracts of employment

The basic information that should be included in a written contract of employment varies according to the level of job, contracts of employment are dealt with in Chapter 45.

## Induction and follow-up arrangements

Induction is the process of receiving and welcoming employees when they first join a company and giving them the basic information they need to settle down quickly and happily and start work. Induction has three aims:

- to smooth the preliminary stages when everything is likely to be strange and unfamiliar to the starter
- to establish quickly a favourable attitude to the company in the mind of the new employee so that he or she is more likely to stay
- to obtain effective output from the new employee in the shortest possible time.

## Company induction

The first stage in induction is when the employee arrives at the company. He or she should be welcomed by a responsible person (not simply a commissionaire or a junior wages clerk) who can provide basic information about the company and terms and conditions of employment. Some of the information will confirm what the employee has already been told, some will be new, but there is a limit to how much can be conveyed at this stage.

An employee handbook is useful for this purpose. It need not be too glossy, but it should convey clearly and simply what new staff need to know under the following headings:

- a brief description of the company — its history, products, organization and management
- basic conditions of employment — hours of work, holidays, pension scheme, insurance
- pay — pay scales, when paid and how, deductions, queries
- sickness — notification of absence, certificates, pay
- leave of absence
- company rules
- disciplinary procedure
- grievance procedure
- promotion procedure
- union and joint consultation arrangements
- education and training facilities
- health and safety arrangements
- medical and first-aid facilities
- restaurant and canteen facilities
- social and welfare arrangements
- telephone calls and correspondence
- travelling and subsistence expenses.

If the organization is not large enough to justify a printed handbook, the least that can be done is to prepare a typed summary of this information.

Company induction procedures, however, should not rely on the printed word. The member of the personnel department or other individual who is looking after new employees should run through the main points with each individual or, when larger numbers are being taken on, with groups of people. In this way, a more personal touch is provided and queries can be answered.

When the initial briefing has been completed, new employees should be taken to their place of work and introduced to their manager or team leader for the departmental induction programme. Alternatively, they may go straight to a training school and join the department later.

### Departmental induction

The departmental induction programme should, wherever possible, start with the departmental manager, not the immediate team leader.

The manager may give only a general welcome and a brief description of the work of the department before handing new employees over to their team leaders for the more detailed induction. But it is important for the manager to be involved at this stage so that he or she is not seen as a remote figure by the new employee. At least this means that the starter will not be simply a name or a number to the manager.

The detailed induction is probably best carried out by the immediate team leader, who should have five main aims:

- to put the new employee at ease
- to interest the employee in the job and the organization
- to provide basic information about working arrangements
- to indicate the standards of performance and behaviour expected from the employee
- to tell the employee about training arrangements and how he or she can get on with the company.

## Follow-up

It is essential to follow up newly engaged employees to ensure that they have settled in and to check on how well they are doing. If there are any problems it is much better to identify them at an early stage rather than allowing them to fester.

Following up is also important as a means of checking on the selection procedure. If by any chance a mistake has been made, it is useful to find out how it happened so that the selection procedure can be improved. Misfits can be attributed to a number of causes — for example, inadequate job description or specification, poor sourcing of candidates, weak advertising, poor interviewing techniques, inappropriate or invalidated tests, or prejudice on the part of the selector. If any of these are identified, steps can be taken to prevent their recurrence.

# 25

# Release from the Organization

## General considerations

The employment relationship may be ended voluntarily by someone moving elsewhere. Or it may finish at the end of a career by retirement. Increasingly, however, people are having to go involuntarily. Organizations are becoming mean as well as lean. They are terminating the relationship through redundancy and they are tightening up disciplinary procedures to handle not only cases of misconduct but also those of incapability — as judged by the employer. Resourcing policies and practices concerning release from the organization have also to cover voluntary turnover and retirement

### Causes of redundancy

Redundancy, like the poor which it helps to create, has always been with us. At one time, however, it was mainly a result of adverse trading conditions, especially during times of recession. This is, of course, still a major cause of redundancy, exacerbated by the pressures of global competition and international recession. But the drive for competitive advantage has forced organizations to 'take cost out of the business' — a euphemism for getting rid of people, employment costs being the ones on which companies focus, as they are usually the largest element in their cost structures. The result has been delayering (eliminating what are deemed to be unnecessary layers of management and supervision) and 'downsizing' (another euphemism) or even 'right-sizing' (a yet more egregious euphemism).

The introduction of new technology has contributed hugely to the reduction in the number of semi-skilled or unskilled people in offices and on the shop floor. But the thrust for productivity (more from less) and added value (increasing the income derived from the expenditure on people) has led to more use of such indices as added value per £ of employment costs to measure business performance with regard to the utilization of its 'human resources', (the use of human resources in this connection implies a measure of exploitation). Business process re-engineering techniques are deployed as instruments for downsizing. Benchmarking to establish which organizations *are* in fact doing more with less (and if so how they do it) is another popular way of preparing the case for 'downsizing'.

## Setting higher performance standards

The pressure for improved performance to meet more intense global competition explains why many organizations are setting higher standards for employees and are not retaining those who do not meet those standards. This may be done through disciplinary procedures but performance management processes as described in the previous chapter are being used to identify under-performers. Properly administered, such processes will emphasise positive improvement and development plans but they will inevitably highlight weaknesses and if these are not overcome disciplinary proceedings may be invoked.

## Voluntary release

Of course, people also leave organizations voluntarily to further their careers, get more money, move away from the district or because they are fed up with the way they feel they have been treated. They may also take early retirement (although this is sometimes involuntary) or volunteer for redundancy (under pressure or because they are being rewarded financially for doing so).

## Managing organizational release — the role of the personnel function

The personnel function is usually given the task of managing organizational release and, in its involuntary form, this is perhaps the most distasteful, onerous and stressful of all the activities with which personnel people get involved. In effect, the function is being asked to go into reverse. Having spent a lot of positive effort on employee resourcing and development it is now being placed in what appears to be an entirely negative position. Personnel people are indeed acting, however unwillingly, as the agents of the managements who make the 'downsizing' decisions or want to 'let someone go' (there are more euphemisms in this area of management than the rest of the areas put together). Being placed in this often invidious position means that there are ethical and professional considerations to be taken into account, as discussed below.

A more positive aspect of the function's involvement in organizational release is the part personnel people can play in easing retirement and analysing the reasons given by employees for leaving the organization so that action can be taken to correct organizational shortcomings.

## Ethical and professional considerations

Personnel professionals may have no choice about taking part in a 'downsizing' exercise — that is, if they wish to remain with the organization. But they can and should make an important contribution to managing the process in order to minimise the distress and trauma that badly handled redundancies can create, or the distress and bad-feeling that unfair or uncouth disciplinary practices can engender. They can press for policies and actions that will minimise, even if they cannot eliminate involuntary redundancy. They can emphasise the need to handle redundancies sensitively, advising line managers on the approach they adopt, helping them to communicate the decision to employees, advising generally on communication within and outside the organization and laying on counselling and outplacement services. Professionally, they should ensure that there are proper redundancy procedures (including those relating to consultation) which are in line with codes of practice and legal requirements, and they must see that these practices are followed.

Similarly, a professional approach to discipline means that personnel specialists should ensure that there are disciplinary procedures which conform to codes of practice and take into account legal implications. They have to communicate these procedures to line managers, provide training in how they are applied and advise on their use. Ethically, personnel professionals should do their best to see that people are treated fairly in accordance with the principles of natural justice.

## Career dynamics

Career dynamics is the term used to describe how careers progress within organizations or over a working life. As long ago as 1984 Charles Handy forecast that many more people would not be working in organizations. Instead there would be an increase in the number of outworkers and subcontractors facilitated by information technology. He also predicted that there would be more requirements for specialists and professionals (knowledge workers) within organizations. In later books (eg *The Empty Raincoat*, 1994) he developed his concept of a portfolio career — people changing their careers several times during their working lives, either because they have been forced to leave their jobs or because they have seized new opportunities.

The national culture has changed too. High levels of unemployment seem set to continue, more people are working for themselves (often because they have to) and short-term contracts are becoming more common, especially in the public sector. Some commentators believe that organizations are no longer in the business of providing 'life-long careers' as they slim down, delayer and rely on a small core of workers. Clearly, this *is* taking place in some companies but employees do not all necessarily see it this way. The IPD/Templeton College 1995 survey established that 46 per cent of their respondents viewed their current job as a long-term one which they intended to stay in. However, 16 per cent saw their present job as part of a career or profession that would probably take them to different companies and 15 per cent saw their job as one they would leave as not part of their career.

## *Organizational release activities*

Against this background, organizational release activities as described in this chapter deal with redundancy, outplacement, dismissal, voluntary turnover and retirement.

## Redundancy

'Downsizing' is one of the most demanding areas of people management with which personnel professionals can become involved. Their responsibilities, as discussed below, are to:

- plan ahead to achieve downsizing without involuntary redundancy
- advise on and implement other methods of reducing numbers or avoiding redundancy
- encourage voluntary redundancy if other methods fail
- develop and apply a proper redundancy procedure

- deal with payment arrangements for releasing employees.
- advise on methods of handling redundancies and take part as necessary to ensure that they are well-managed.

Personnel specialists should also be involved in organising out-placement services as described in the next section of this chapter.

## Plan ahead

Planning ahead means anticipating future reductions in people needs and allowing natural wastage to take effect. A forecast is needed of the amount by which the workforce has to be reduced and the likely losses through employee turnover. Recruitment can then be frozen at the right moment to allow the surplus to be absorbed by wastage.

The problem is that forecasts are often difficult to make, and in periods of high unemployment, natural wastage rates are likely to be reduced. It is possible therefore to overestimate the extent to which they will achieve the required reduction in numbers. It is best to be pessimistic about the time it will take to absorb future losses and apply the freeze earlier rather than later.

Ideally, steps should be taken to transfer people to other, more secure jobs and retrain them where possible.

## Use other methods to avoid redundancy

The other methods which can be used to avoid or at least minimize redundancy include, in order of severity:

- calling in outside work
- withdrawing all subcontracted labour
- reducing or preferably eliminating overtime
- developing work-sharing: two people doing one job on alternate days or splitting the day between them
- reducing the number of part-timers, remembering that they also have employment rights
- temporary lay-offs.

## Voluntary redundancy

Asking for volunteers — with a suitable pay-off — is one way of relieving the number of compulsory redundancies. The amount needed to persuade people to go is a matter of judgement. It clearly has to be more than the statutory minimum, although one inducement for employees to leave early may be the belief that they will get another job more easily than if they hang on until the last moment. Help can be provided to place them elsewhere.

One of the disadvantages of voluntary redundancy is that the wrong people might go, ie good workers who are best able to find other work. It is sometimes necessary to go into reverse and offer them a special loyalty bonus if they agree to stay on.

## Outplacement

Outplacement is the process of helping redundant employees to find other work or start new careers. It may involve counselling, which can be provided by firms who specialize in this area.

## Redundancy procedure

If you are forced to resort to redundancy, the problems will be reduced if there is an established procedure to follow. This procedure should have three aims:

- to treat employees as fairly as possible
- to reduce suffering as much as possible
- to protect management's ability to run the business effectively.

These aims are not always compatible. Management will want to retain its key and more effective workers. Trade unions, on the other hand, may want to adopt the principle of last in, first out, irrespective of the value of each employee to the company.

The following points should be included in any redundancy procedure:

- early warnings and consultation with unions and staff: in the UK, firms are required by law to inform the union and the Department of Employment if ten or more employees are to be made redundant, giving at least 30 days' notice
- means to be adopted to avoid or reduce redundancies
- the basis of selection for redundancy — the starting-point may be the principle of last in, first out, but the right has to be reserved to deviate from this principle where selection on the basis of service would prejudice operational efficiency

- the basis of compensating for redundancy, ie payments made by the company which are additional to the statutory minimum.
- the help the company will give to redundant employees to find other work.

An example of a redundancy procedure is given in Appendix E.

## Payment arrangements

Employers are required by law to make a lump sum redundancy payment to employees who have had at least two years' continuous service and are dismissed because of redundancy. There is a scale of payments for up to 20 complete years of service (eg one and a half week's pay for each complete year of employment in which the employee was not below the age of 41 up to the normal retiring age or to the age of 60, and one week's pay for each year of employment in which the employee was not below the age of 22 but was below the age of 41.

In addition to these minimum statutory payments it is now common for organizations to provide additional separation payments or compensation. This is to fulfil the employer's responsibility to provide some recognition and assistance to longer serving employees who, through no fault of their own, have been told that their job no longer exists. As stated in the Industrial Tribunal case of *Wynes v Southrepps Broiler Farm Ltd*:

> The purpose of redundancy pay is to compensate a worker for loss of a job, irrespective of whether that loss leads to unemployment. It is to compensate him (sic) for loss of security, possible loss of earnings and fringe benefits, and the uncertainty and anxiety of job change.

Organizations typically make higher extra redundancy payments to more senior staff and longer-serving or older employees. They may also be more generous to those who accept voluntary redundancy.

## Handling redundancy

The first step is to ensure that the redundancy selection policy has been applied fairly. It is also necessary to make certain that the legal requirements for consultation have been met. The information to be presented at any consultative meetings will need to cover the reasons for the redundancy, what steps the company has taken or will take to minimize the problem and the redundancy pay arrangements. An indication should also be given of the time scale. The basis for selecting people for redundancy as set out in the redundancy policy should be confirmed.

It will then be necessary to make a general announcement if it is a large scale redundancy or inform a unit or department if it is on a smaller scale. It is best if the announcement is made in person by an executive or manager who is known to the individuals concerned. It should let everyone know about the difficulties the organization has been facing and the steps that have been taken to overcome them. The announcement should also indicate in general how the redundancy will take place, including arrangements for individuals to be informed (as soon as possible after the general announcement), payment arrangements and, importantly, help to those affected in finding work through outplacement counselling or a 'job shop'.

If it is a fairly large redundancy the media will have to be informed, but only after the internal announcement. A press release will need to be prepared, again indicating why the redundancy is taking place and how the company intends to tackle it.

The next step is to inform those affected. It is very important to ensure that everything possible is done to ensure that the interviews with those who are to be made redundant are handled sensitively. Managers should be given guidance and, possibly, training on how to deal with what is sometimes called (another euphemism) a 'release interview'. It may well be advisable for a member of the personnel function to be present at all interviews, although it is best for the line manager to conduct them. Advance information should be obtained on the reasons why individuals were selected and how they may react. Their personal circumstances should also be checked in case there are any special circumstances with which the interviewer should be familiar.

The interview itself should explain as gently as possible why the individual has been selected for redundancy and how it will affect him or her (payment, timing etc). Time should be allowed to describe the help that the organization will provide to find another job and to get initial reactions from the individual which may provide guidance on the next steps.

## Outplacement

Outplacement is about helping redundant employees to find alternative work. It involves assisting individuals to cope with the trauma of redundancy through counselling, helping them to re-define their career and employment objectives and then providing them with knowledgeable but sensitive guidance on how to attain those objectives.

## Job shops

Help may be provided by the organization on an individual basis but in larger scale redundancies 'job shops' can be set up. The people who staff these scour the travel-to-work area seeking job opportunities for those who are being made redundant. This is often done by telephone. Further help may be given by matching people to suitable jobs, arranging interviews, training in CV preparation and interview techniques. Job shops are sometimes staffed by members of the personnel function (the writer successfully organized one in an aerospace firm some years ago). Alternatively, the organization may ask a firm of outplacement consultants to set up and run the job shop and provide any other counselling or training services which may be required.

## Outplacement consultancy services

As described by Eggert (1991), the outplacement process usually takes place along the following lines:

- initial counselling — gaining biographical data and discussing immediate issues of concern
- achievement list — clients write up all the achievements they can think of to do with their career
- skills inventory — clients develop from the achievement list a personal portfolio of saleable skills
- personal statement — clients develop a personal statement in 20 to 30 words about what is being presented to the job market
- personal success inventory — those recent or appropriate successes which can be quantified and which support the personal profile
- three jobs — identification of three possible types of jobs that can be searched for
- psychological assessment — development of a personality profile with a psychologist
- development and agreement of a CV (see below)
- identify job market opportunities
- practice interview
- plan job search campaign

## CVs

CVs provide the basic information for job searching and an out-placement consultant will guide individuals on how to write their CVs. The traditional CV uses what Eggert (1991) calls the 'tombstone' approach because it reads like an obituary. It sets out personal details and education and employment history in chronological order.

Outplacement consultants prefer what they call the 'achievement CV' which is structured on the principle of a sales brochure, providing information in simple, positive statements sequenced for the reader's convenience. The CV lists the most important areas of experience in reverse chronological order and sets out for each position a list of achievements beginning with such words as 'set up', 'developed', 'introduced', 'increased', 'reduced' and 'established'. This is designed to generate the thought in the reader's mind that 'if the individual can do it for them, he or she will be able to do it for us'. The career achievement history is followed by details of professional qualifications and education, and personal information.

## Selecting an outplacement consultant

There are some highly reputable outplacement consultants around; there are also some cowboys. It is advisable only to use firms which follow a code of practice such as that produced by the IPD or the Career Development and Outplacement Association.

# Dismissal

## The legal framework

The legal framework as described below is provided by employment statutory and case law relating to unfair dismissal. Under UK employment legislation, an employee who has been employed for two years or more has the right not to be unfairly dismissed. Complaints by an employee that he or she has been unfairly dismissed are heard by industrial tribunals.

### Definition of dismissal
Legally, dismissal takes place when:

- the employer terminates the employee's contract with or without

notice — a contract can be terminated as a result of a demotion or transfer as well as dismissal
- the employee terminates the contract (resigns) with or without notice by reason of the employer's behaviour in the sense that the employer's conduct was such that the employee could not be expected to carry on — this is termed 'constructive dismissal'
- the employee is employed under a fixed-term contract of one year or more which is not renewed by the employer when it expires
- an employee resigns while under notice following dismissal
- an employee is unreasonably refused work after pregnancy.

*Fundamental questions*
The legislation lays down that industrial tribunals should obtain answers to two fundamental questions when dealing with unfair dismissal cases:

1. Was there sufficient reason for the dismissal, ie was it fair or unfair?
2. Did the employer act reasonably in the circumstances?

*Fair dismissal*
Dismissals may be held by an industrial tribunal to be fair if the principal reason was one of the following:

- incapability, which covers the employee's skill, aptitude, health and physical or mental qualities
- misconduct
- failure to have qualifications relevant to the job
- a legal factor that prevents the employee from continuing work
- redundancy — where this has taken place in accordance with a customary or agreed redundancy procedure
- the employee broke or repudiated his or her contract by going on strike — as long as he or she was not singled out for this treatment, ie all striking employees were treated alike and no selective re-engagement took place
- the employee was taking part in an unofficial strike or some other form of industrial action
- some other substantial reason of a kind which would justify the dismissal of an employee holding the position which the employee held.

*Unfair dismissal*
Dismissals may be unfair if:

- the employer has failed to show that the principal reason was one of the admissible reasons as stated above, or if the dismissal was not reasonable in the circumstances (see below)
- a constructive dismissal has taken place
- they are in breach of a customary or agreed redundancy procedure, and there are no valid reasons for departing from that procedure.

The onus of proof is not on employers to show that they had acted reasonably in treating the reason for dismissal as sufficient. The industrial tribunal is required, in considering the circumstances, to take into account the size and administrative resources of the employer's undertaking.

*Reasonable in the circumstances*
Even if the employer can show to a tribunal that there was good reason to dismiss the employee (ie if it clearly fell into one of the categories listed above, and the degree of incapability or misconduct was sufficient to justify dismissal), the tribunal still has to decide whether or not the employer acted in a reasonable way at the time of dismissal. The principles defining 'reasonable' behaviour on the part of an employer are as follows:

- employees should be informed of the nature of the complaint against them
- the employee should be given the chance to explain
- the employee should be given the opportunity to improve, except in particularly gross cases of incapability or misconduct
- employees should be allowed to appeal
- the employee should be warned of the consequences in the shape of dismissal if specified improvements do not take place
- the employer's decision to dismiss should be based on sufficient evidence
- the employer should take any mitigating circumstances into account
- the employer should act in good faith
- the offence or misbehaviour should merit the penalty of dismissal rather than some lesser penalty.

A good disciplinary procedure as described in chapter 49 will include arrangements for informal and formal warnings and provisions to ensure that the other aspects of discipline are handled reasonably.

*Remedies*

Industrial tribunals which find that a dismissal was unfair can make an order for reinstatement or re-engagement and state the terms on which this should take place. The tribunal can consider the possibility of compensation for unfair dismissal, but only after the possibility of reinstatement or re-engagement has been examined.

## Incapability

Dismissal on the grounds of incapability has to be handled with particular care. Incompetence can be shown to exist by comparing actual against expected performance. But where measurement is difficult, as in managerial jobs, it can still be shown that a manager is incompetent if a responsible employer has come to that conclusion over an appropriate period of time. Employees should normally be given a reasonable period to improve. But, if there is clear evidence of inherent and irredeemable incapability such that an opportunity to improve is most unlikely to have any effect, the employer can fairly and lawfully dismiss the employee without going through the whole procedure, although the complaint should have been brought to the attention of the employee over a period of time.

It is often not possible to judge performance against clearly defined standards. A gradual decline in overall competence is particularly difficult to judge and, if someone has been allowed to get away with it in the past, it becomes progressively more difficult to do anything. That is why it is better for everyone's sake to take action at the time, if only to give a warning, rather than to let things slide. A soft approach now can lead to real problems in the future.

Those problems which are hardest to solve arise when the 'face doesn't fit' or attitudes to work are incompatible. Who is to blame if the boss cannot get on with his or her staff, or vice versa? How is it possible to substantiate accusations that someone is uncooperative or upsets colleagues? What is the point of warning people that things must improve or else, when the problem is one of an inherent personality characteristic which individuals may not accept as being a defect and, even if they did, could not do much about changing it? In any case, people who are vaguely accused of being uncooperative frequently respond with remarks to the effect that 'everyone is out of step but me'.

Criticisms of behaviour are difficult to make and even more difficult to substantiate. The only way to do it is to produce evidence of the effects of such behaviour or performance and make individuals recognize the fault and work out for themselves how to overcome it. And it is no good making blunt accusations. The best approach is to spot unsatisfactory behaviour when it starts and discuss it informally, using the non-directive counselling or interviewing techniques described in Chapter 45 (pages 835 to 836).

## Absenteeism and poor timekeeping

Absenteeism and poor timekeeping only lead to dismissal as a last resort after a full procedure of informal and formal warnings has been implemented. It is up to the employer to decide what level of absenteeism without proper explanation, or lateness is unacceptable. Employees should be made aware of this level and warned of the consequences if they do not meet the standards expected of them.

Warnings require a continuing commitment from the employee not to take days off without leave or satisfactory explanation, or to be late. They do not lapse simply because the employer retains the employee. But if the employer has agreed to ignore previous offences they cannot be taken into account if persistent absenteeism or lateness recurs.

Note that this raises the difficult question of time limits when an employer gives a final warning that absenteeism or timekeeping must improve by a certain date or else. If it does improve by that date, and the slate is wiped clean, it could be assumed that the disciplinary procedure starts again from scratch if absenteeism increases or timekeeping deteriorates again. But it is in the nature of things that some people cannot reduce absenteeism or sustain efforts to get to work on time for long, and deterioration often occurs. In these circumstances, does the employer have to keep on going through the warning cycles time after time? The answer ought to be no, and, although there are no conclusive rulings in case law on this point, the best approach seems to be to incorporate a fairly long warning period, say six months or more which means that employees have to maintain agreed standards of absence or timekeeping for some time and, it is hoped, having done so, are less likely to lapse (the same principle applies to warnings about poor performance). It may be advisable to avoid stating a finite end date to a final warning period (ie improve by a certain date) which implies a 'wipe the slate clean' approach. Instead, the final warning letter could simply say that timekeeping performance will be reviewed on a stated date. If it has not improved, disciplinary action can be taken. If it has, no action is taken, but the employee is warned that further deterioration will make him liable to disciplining which may well circumvent the normal procedure, perhaps by only using the final warning stage and by reducing the elapsed time between the warning and the review date.

In the face of persistent absenteeism, there comes a time, as the EAT said in *International Sports Co Ltd v Thomson* (1980), when the employer is entitled to say 'enough is enough' and dismiss. In *Gould v Weetabix Ltd* (1985) the EAT upheld an industrial tribunal's decision that it was fair for an employer who had reason to think that 'enough was enough' to dismiss an employee who had a very poor attendance record, even though the employer had failed to give the warnings required by their disciplinary procedure.

## Approach to handling disciplinary cases

The approach should be governed by the legal considerations described on pages 495 to 497 and the following three principles of natural justice:

1. Individuals should know the standards of performance they are expected to achieve and the rules to which they are expected to conform.
2. They should be given a clear indication of where they are failing or the rules are being broken.
3. Except in cases of gross misconduct, they should be given an opportunity to improve before disciplinary action is taken.

There should be a disciplinary procedure which is understood and applied by all managers and team leaders. The procedure should provide for the following three-stage approach before disciplinary action is taken:

- informal oral warnings
- formal oral warnings, which, in serious cases, may also be made in writing — these warnings should set out the nature of the offence and the likely consequences of further offences
- final written warnings which should contain a statement that any recurrence would lead to suspension, dismissal or some other penalty.

The procedure should provide for employees to be accompanied by a colleague or employee representative at any hearing. There should also be an appeal system and a list of offences which constitute gross misconduct and may therefore lead to instant dismissal. Managers and supervisors should be told what authority they have to take disciplinary action. It is advisable to have all final warnings and actions approved by a higher authority. In cases of gross misconduct, team leaders and junior managers should be given the right to suspend, if higher authority is not immediately available, but not to dismiss. The importance of obtaining and recording the facts should be emphasized. Managers should always have a colleague with them when issuing a formal warning and should make a note to file of what was said on the spot.

An example of a disciplinary procedure is given in Appendix E.

## Voluntary leavers

When people leave of their own volition three actions may be taken: conducting exit interviews, analysing reasons for turnover and providing references.

### *Exit interviews*

It is useful to interview employees when they leave to establish why they are going and identify problem areas on which action can be taken, although the information obtained is not always reliable. However, the purpose of exit interviews, which are usually carried out by members of the personnel department, is not to persuade people to stay. If it is felt that an attempt should be made to dissuade someone from leaving this should be done when the notice is first handed in (employees who do not give a proper notice are not worth bothering about). This may be more a matter for the line manager than a personnel specialist except that line managers should not be allowed to bribe people to stay and thus upset established relativities. If they do feel strongly that more money should be paid, this should be agreed with the personnel department and agreement should be given only if there is a cast iron case. It is dangerous to allow employees to believe they can get more money simply by presenting a pistol to their manager's head.

The aim of the exit interview should be to identify and classify the reasons employees give for leaving. These could be analysed under such headings as:

- more pay
- more security
- better prospects

- a career move (gaining experience, a significant increase in responsibility)
- moving away from the area (eg to follow a spouse)
- dissatisfaction with pay
- dissatisfaction with career progress and prospects
- dissatisfaction with working conditions
- poor relationships with management or supervision
- poor relationships with fellow workers
- feeling of insecurity
- bullying or harassment.

Some leavers will be forthcoming, others will not. It is up to the interviewer to encourage people to open up while at the same time controlling the string of abuse which is occasionally produced. The interviewer may have to probe skilfully and sensitively to establish reasons for dissatisfaction or unhappiness so that, where these feelings are justified, something can be done about them. Judgement, however, is required to sort out genuine complaints from unfounded or exaggerated ones.

## Analysing reasons for turnover

The results of exit interviews should be analysed under each heading to identify general (eg pay) or particular (eg harassment) problem areas. This can then be used as evidence when general actions are proposed or when an approach is made to feed back the information. It is necessary to be very careful about feeding back complaints. They could be quite unjustified. But if they have been made and the interviewer is reasonably confident that there may be some truth in them (possibly on the basis of other evidence) at least they should be brought to the manager's or team leader's attention but in a purely factual way: ... 'this has been raised, what comments would you like to make?' If a first time complaint is rejected as being inaccurate, malicious or frivolous, then nothing more is done. But if a pattern emerges from a number of exit interviews then a stronger line can be taken.

Statistical analyses from exit interviews should be examined to establish any trends so that action can be taken where necessary (approaches to dealing with high levels of employee turnover by retention planning were discussed in Chapter 23).

## References

Employers do not need to respond to requests for references. Neither do employees generally have the right to see a reference except when copies may be given to an employee as part of a settlement reached on termination of employment or when an appropriate legal claim requires the reference to be disclosed.

There is a clear legal liability for references. This does not mean that there is liability for every mis-statement or omission — only for those which due care would have avoided. Employers can be liable for negligence towards both employees and other employers. For liability in negligence to arise it must be foreseeable that damage or injury is likely to occur unless reasonable steps are taken to prevent it. Any opinions in a reference must be capable of being supported by the facts. Employers should therefore be careful only to give factual references. It is often advisable if a written reference is required to confine it simply to a statement of the dates in which the employee was with the company and the job(s) which he or she held. It is best not to hazard an opinion about whether the employee would be suitable for a job in another company. It is also preferable to restrict any views about the degree to which an employee is satisfactory to a subjective phrase such as 'satisfactory to us'. Employers are not obliged to answer the typical question 'would you re-employ yes/no?'.

## Retirement

Retirement is a major change and should be prepared for. Retirement policies need to specify:

- when people are due to retire
- the circumstances, if any, in which they can work on beyond their normal retirement date
- the provision of pre-retirement training
- the provision of advice to people about to retire.

Pre-retirement training can cover such matters as finance, insurance, State pension rights, health, working either for money or in a voluntary organization during retirement and sources of advice and help. The latter can be supplied by such charities as Help the Aged and Age Concern.

# Part VI
# Employee Development

*Employee development, often referred to as human resource development (HRD), is about the provision of learning, development and training opportunities in order to improve individual, team and organizational performance.*

*This part considers employee development under the following headings:*

- *The basis of employee development — definitions of the elements and processes of employee development and the factors to be considered when formulating human resource development strategies.*

- *Learning and development — a review of learning theory as the basis for developing training interventions, creating a learning organization and providing for continuous development, self-managed learning and other learning activities.*

- *Training — planning, conducting and evaluating training programmes to enable people to acquire the specific knowledge and skills required to carry out the jobs.*

- *Management development — improving the performance of managers, encouraging self-development and giving them opportunities for growth.*

- *Career management and management succession — ensuring that the organization has the people it*

*needs to provide for growth and management suc-*
*cession and that individual managers are given the*
*guidance and help they require to realize their*
*potential. This could be regarded as an aspect of*
*management development but is significant enough*
*in its own right to be dealt with separately.*

# 26

# The Basis of Employee Development

In this chapter employee development is considered in terms of its aims, activities, strategies, the context of employee development policies and practices and ways in which it can be marketed and evaluated within the organization.

## Definition of employee development

Employee development is concerned with providing learning and development opportunities, making training interventions and planning, conducting and evaluating training programmes.

## Aims

The overall aim of employee development is to see that the organization has the quality of people it needs to attain its goals for improved performance and growth. This aim is achieved by ensuring as far as possible that everyone in the organization has the knowledge and skills and reaches the level of competence required to carry out their work effectively, that the performance of individuals and teams is subject to continuous improvement, and that people are developed in a way which maximizes their potential for growth and promotion.

## Employee development activities

Employee development involves the following activities:

- *Learning* — defined by Bass and Vaughan (1967) as 'a relatively permanent change in behaviour that occurs as a result of practice or experience'.

- *Education* — the development of the knowledge, values and understanding required in all aspects of life rather than the knowledge and skills relating to particular areas of activity.
- *Development* — the growth or realization of a person's ability and potential through the provision of learning and educational experiences.
- *Training* — the planned and systematic modification of behaviour through learning events, programmes and instruction which enable individuals to achieve the levels of knowledge, skill and competence to carry out their work effectively.

## Employee development strategy

Employee development strategy is business-led in that it is initiated by the strategic plans of the enterprise which define where it is going, the resources it needs to get there and the levels of performance required to achieve business goals.

These business plans form the basis for human resource plans which define the numbers of people needed and the knowledge, skills and competences they will require. The human resource plans flow from the business plan but also contribute to it by spelling out how much more could be achieved by investing in people and by making better use of the organization's human resources.

Employee development strategy is a declaration of intent which states, in effect, that 'we believe a strategy for investing in people will pay off and this is what we are going to do about it'. The strategy sets out how employee development processes, policies and programmes will contribute to the achievement of the corporate goals contained in the business plan.

The employee development strategy should address the critical success factors of the business in the fields of product-market development, innovation, quality and cost leadership. It should demonstrate the real links between learning, development and training activities and business performance and indicate how these activities will add value and contribute to the achievement of competitive advantage. In a business enterprise their only justification will be the return that can be generated by investing in human resources, and how this will increase shareholder value. But the employee development strategy should be designed to benefit all the stakeholders in the enterprise: not only the shareholders but also employees, customers, suppliers and the community. This is why it should be prepared within the context of the employee development philosophy of the business which should be determined at top level and communicated throughout the organization.

The following is an example of a 'people development' strategy as formulated by ZENECA Pharmaceuticals.

1. The Pharmaceuticals business believes that its employees are its single most important asset and has therefore set the third strategic business objective as:

   > To ensure a well-motivated organization in which people are respected, enjoy their jobs and obtain fulfilment.

   This policy relates to all employees, not just to managers or people of high potential. It relates to the continuing development of ability and contribution in each person's current job and, if considered to have the potential to progress further, towards subsequent jobs.

2. People development strategies are vital to the well-being of the business but it is important that they support the key business strategies. The appropriate resources must be available to meet the key priorities for people development. Expenditure on education, training and development is regarded as a necessary and calculated investment yielding considerable pay-off in terms of enhanced business performance.

3. Managers have a clear responsibility to develop their subordinates. Performance management, which is a key management process that brings together the setting of personal work targets and development plans, is the preferred integrated approach by which employees' learning and development are managed continually in relation to all work activities.

4. All employees must have a personal development plan jointly agreed with their managers and this plan must be progressed and regularly reviewed and updated. It should be derived from the accountabilities of the job holder and the personal targets for the coming period, plus any anticipated future needs. The plan should cover on-job and off-the-job training and experience in the areas of business, individual and team skills, and professional and management skills.

5. All employees are to be encouraged continually to develop their skills and experience both for their own benefit and that of the business through the improved contribution which will result, thus maintaining and extending the business's competitive advantage.

6. Career planning will be a joint activity between the individual and the manager, with employees having a major responsibility for their own career management, including personal development.
7. The development of individuals must take into account that ZENECA Pharmaceuticals is a complex, globally managed business. Particular emphasis should be placed on the need for good business understanding and teamwork across the business worldwide. The nature of the business requires special attention in the areas of organization development activities, team building, project management and cross-cultural management skills.
8. People development activities will regularly be audited to ensure that appropriate, cost-effective investment is made in all parts of the organization to support current business priorities.

## The context of employee development

Employee development should be considered within the national and international contexts. Nationally it is influenced by government training initiatives such as the modern apprenticeship scheme. The approach to employee development within the firm will vary according to the technology, traditional policies and the values of management. The importance of achieving competitive advantage by raising the skills base is recognized by some companies but many ignore this possibility, treating training as a cost rather than an investment. Training provision in the UK lags seriously behind many of the country's international competitors. Multinational firms are more likely to invest in employee development programmes because they are aware of the need to develop talent on a worldwide basis. Global competition is a factor which is forcing some British companies to reconsider their *laissez faire* attitudes to training. Approaches to learning vary in different cultures. As Mayo and Lank (1994) comment:

> Not only do individuals learn in different ways, but they may be *conditioned* through their culture to be orientated towards certain styles. The West generally favours systematic rationality and programmed learning; the East, harmonious concepts and ideals and intuitive learning.

The culture of an organization will make a significant impact on employee development philosophies. The values of management and the norms governing the behaviour of line managers and team leaders will strongly influence their attitudes to training and their behaviour when dealing with the development needs of their staff. The concept of a 'learning organization' as discussed in Chapter 27 is mainly about developing an appropriate culture in which learning is seen as a continuous process that is fundamental to business success. It is not simply about introducing various employee development 'programmes'.

## Marketing employee development

As Moorby (1991) states:

> The internal employee development function needs to be seen as professional and competitive with outside suppliers. Its literature and standard of presentation as well as the quality of its products and professional staff should stand comparison with anyone — since they will be compared.

Marketing employee development can be carried out in the same way as marketing the personnel contribution as a whole (see Chapter 4). The difference is that employee development 'products' are more easily identifiable and there is stronger competition from external providers (although slimmed-down employee development functions are increasingly relying on external sources to deliver training). There is therefore a greater need to create a brand image (branding) which can be used to identify all information and communications about employee development initiatives. As suggested by Moorby, these may include a logo and distinctive course brochures.

The other approaches to marketing employee development which should be considered include:

- market research to identify customer needs and wants
- competitor analysis to establish what external providers are offering
- customer surveys to establish the degree to which internal customers are satisfied with the products on offer to them
- establishing target markets based on an analysis of the market segments in which the employee development function will concentrate and the marketing position it intends to adopt in each segment
- marketing planning to determine the actions required to develop new products or to reposition existing ones and what needs to be done to promote those products to customers (mainly internal, but some employee development departments market their products and services externally)
- sales promotion — the promotional and communication campaigns

required to assist product launches and to increase demand for the products on offer.

## Evaluating the employee development contribution

The employee development contribution should be evaluated overall against the aims as expressed in the strategy. Individual training interventions should be evaluated along the lines described in Chapter 28. The evaluation should be conducted by surveying the reactions of internal customers and, so far as possible, establishing the impact made on individual, team and organizational performance.

# 27

# Learning and Development

The employee development policies, strategies and practices of an organization must be driven by the business and human resource requirements of the enterprise. The starting point should be the approaches adopted to the provision of learning and development opportunities, bearing in mind the distinction between learning and development made by Pedler *et al* (1989) who see learning as being concerned with an increase in knowledge or a higher degree of an existing skill, whereas development is about moving towards a different state of being or functioning. Such approaches should be based on an understanding of how people learn — learning theory — and this will be considered in the first section of this chapter.

The remaining sections of this chapter deal with the application of learning theory in the following areas of learning and development policy and practice:

- the learning organization
- continuous development
- self-managed or self-directed learning.

This leads naturally into the next chapter in which consideration will be given to how learning and development can be facilitated through training interventions and programmes.

## How people learn

To understand how people learn it is necessary to consider

- the learning process
- the concept of the learning curve

- the key factors of learning psychology
- the main learning theories: reinforcement, stimulus-response, cognitive, self-efficacy
- Kolb's learning cycle and learning styles
- types of learning (Honey and Mumford)
- how this learning theory can be put to good use — conditions for effective learning.

## The learning process

There are three areas of learning:

- *knowledge* — what individuals need to know (cognitive learning)
- *skill* — what individuals need to be able to do
- *attitudes* — what people feel about their work.

As described by Reay (1994), learning is a continuous and natural phenomenon. And the best learning is closely related to practical experience — doing things.

## The learning curve

The concept of the learning curve refers to the time it takes an inexperienced person to reach the required level of performance in a job or a task. This is sometimes called the experienced worker's standard (ESW).

The standard learning curve is shown in Figure 27.1.

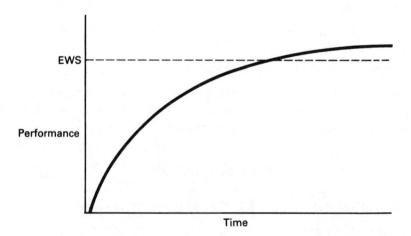

**Figure 27.1** A standard learning curve

But rates of learning vary, depending on the effectiveness of the training, the experience and natural aptitude of the learner, and the latter's interest in learning. Both the time taken to achieve the experienced worker's standard and the speed with which learning takes place at different times, which is likely to vary, affect the shape of the curve, as shown in Figure 27.2.

Learning is often stepped with one or more plateaux while further progress is halted. This may be because learners cannot continually increase their skills or speeds of work and need a pause to consolidate what they have already learnt. The existence of steps such as those shown in Figure 27.3 can be used when planning training to provide deliberate reinforcement periods when newly acquired skills are practised in order to achieve the expected standards.

When a training module is being prepared which describes what has to be learnt and the training required to achieve the required levels of skill and speed, it is often desirable to proceed step-by-step, taking one task or part of a task at a time, reinforcing it and then progressively adding other parts, consolidating at each stage. This is called the progressive parts method of training.

## Key factors of learning psychology

The key factors of learning psychology as listed by Reay (1994) are:

- *Motivation or a sense of purpose* — people learn best when they see a worthwhile end-product to the process.
- *Relevance to personal interest and choice* — learning will be motivated best if it is seen as relevant by the learner.

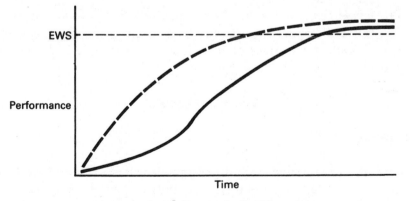

**Figure 27.2** Different rates of learning

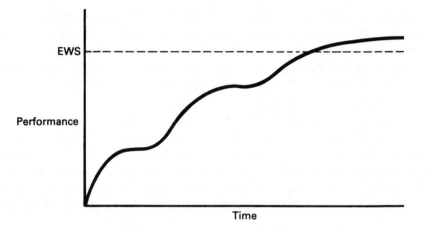

**Figure 27.3** A stepped learning curve

- *Learning by doing* — the old saying is: 'I hear and forget. I see and remember. I do and understand'. Understanding is essential to effective performance and only doing can promote real understanding.
- *Freedom to make mistakes in safety* — learning by doing means that people run the risk of failure. Learning events or experiences must therefore ensure that individuals know that it is safe and permitted to fail, but trainers have to help them learn from their mistakes. As Samuel Beckett expressed it 'Try. Fail. Try again. Fail again. Fail better.'
- *Feedback* — learners need feedback on how they are doing but this is best provided by giving learners the means to evaluate their own progress, ie self-checking.
- *Freedom for learners to learn in their own time and at their own pace* — learning will be more effective if trainees can manage it themselves in accordance with their own preferences as to how it should progress.

## Learning theory

### Reinforcement

Reinforcement involves commending learners when they have accomplished a task successfully, thus motivating them to extend their learning. Positive feedback and knowledge of results is an important way of ensuring that learning takes place. The concept of reinforcement has been strongly influenced by Skinner's (1974) conditioning and social engineering theories and, although they are sometimes criticized as being simplistic and manipulative, they continue to have a considerable effect on the design of training programmes.

## Cybernetic and information theories

Cybernetic and information theories suggest that feedback can control people's performance in the same way that a thermostat controls a heating system. Learners react to cues or stimuli which, if they are established by means of skills analysis, can be used as the basis for training programmes. If a task can be divided into a number of small parts, each with its own cue or stimulus, the learning of each part can be accelerated by ensuring that trainees concentrate on one easily assimilated piece of learning at a time.

## Cognitive theory

This describes the way in which people learn to recognize and define problems and experiment to provide solutions. If, according to this theory, people can discover things for themselves they are more likely to retain the skill or knowledge and use it when required to. Cognitive theory is the basis for discovery, self-managed learning or 'do-it-yourself' processes. It provides the rationale for workshop, participative, and case study training, which help people to 'own' the solution as one they have worked out for themselves rather than something they have been forced to accept by a trainer.

## Experiential learning

Experiential learning involves people reflecting on their experience in order to explain it and determine how it will be applied. Managers, team leaders and specialist trainers can help people to understand how best they can interpret and benefit from their experience.

## Stimulus-response theory

This theory, as developed by Gagne (1965), relates the learning process to a number of factors, including reinforcement, namely:

- *Drive* — there must be a basic need or drive to learn.
- *Stimulus* — people must be stimulated by the learning process.
- *Response* — people must be helped by the learning process to develop appropriate responses ie the knowledge, skills and attitudes which will lead to effective performance.
- *Reinforcement* — these responses need to be reinforced by feedback and experience until they are learnt.

## Self-efficacy

The concept of self-efficacy as developed by Bandura (1977), refers to the belief of people in their capability to learn and perform a task. As Guest (1992b) has noted, a strong feeling of self-efficacy has been shown to be positively related to improvements in learning performance.

## Kolb's learning cycle and learning styles

Kolb *et al* (1974) identified a learning cycle consisting of four stages as shown in Figure 27.4.

He defined these stages as follows:

1. *Concrete experience* — this can be planned or accidental.
2. *Reflective observation* — this involves actively thinking about the experience and its significance.
3. *Abstract conceptualization* (theorizing) — generalizing from experience in order to develop various concepts and ideas which can be applied when similar situations are encountered.
4. *Active experimentation* — testing the concepts or ideas in new situations. This gives rise to a new concrete experience and the cycle begins again.

The key to Kolb's model is that it is a simple description of how experience is translated into concepts which are then used to guide the choice of new experiences. To learn effectively, individuals must shift from being observers to participants, from direct involvement to a more objective analytical detachment. Every person has his or her own learning style and one of the most important arts that trainers have to develop is to adjust their approaches to the learning styles of trainees. Trainers must acknowledge these learning styles rather than their own preferred approach.

Kolb also defined the following learning styles of trainees:

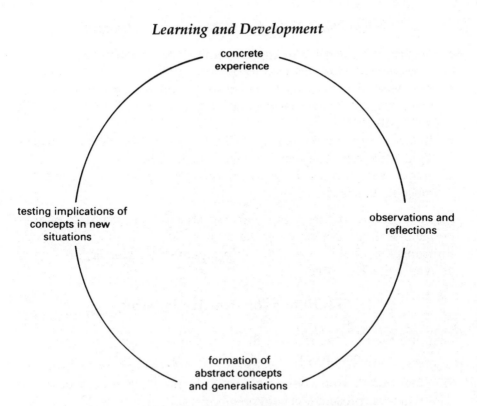

**Figure 27.4** The Kolb learning cycle

- *Accommodators* who learn by trial and error, combining the concrete experience and experimentation stages of the cycle.
- *Divergers* who prefer concrete to abstract learning situations and reflection to active involvement. Such individuals have great imaginative ability, and can view a complete situation from different viewpoints.
- *Convergers* who prefer to experiment with ideas, considering them for their practical usefulness. Their main concern is whether the theory works in action, thus combining the abstract and experimental dimensions.
- *Assimilators* who like to create their own theoretical models and assimilate a number of disparate observations into an overall integrated explanation. Thus they veer towards the reflective and abstract dimensions.

## Learning styles

Another analysis of learning styles was made by Honey and Mumford (1986). They identified four styles:

- *Activists* who involve themselves fully without bias in new experiences and revel in new challenges.
- *Reflectors* who stand back and observe new experiences from different angles. They collect data, reflect on it and then come to a conclusion.
- *Theorists* who adapt and apply their observations in the form of logical theories. They tend to be perfectionists.
- *Pragmatists* who are keen to try out new ideas, approaches and concepts to see if they work.

However, none of these four learning styles is exclusive. It is quite possible that one person could be both a reflector and a theorist and someone else could be an activist/pragmatist, a reflector/pragmatist or even a theorist/pragmatist.

## Conditions for effective learning

Learning theory suggests that there are ten main conditions required for learning to be effective:

1.  Individuals must be motivated to learn. They should be aware that their present level of knowledge, skill or competence, or their existing attitude or behaviour, needs to be improved if they are to perform their work to their own and to others' satisfaction. They must, therefore, have a clear picture of the behaviour they should adopt.
2.  Standards of performance should be set for learners. Learners must have clearly defined targets and standards which they find acceptable and can use to judge their own progress.
3.  Learners should have guidance. They need a sense of direction and feedback on how they are doing. Self-motivated individuals may provide much of this for themselves, but the trainer should still be available to encourage and help when necessary.
4.  Learners must gain satisfaction from learning. They are capable of learning under the most difficult circumstances if the learning is satisfying to one or more of their needs. Conversely, the best training schemes can fail if they are not seen as useful by the trainee.
5.  Learning is an active, not a passive process. Learners need to be actively involved with their trainer, their fellow trainees and the subject matter of the training programme.
6.  Appropriate techniques should be used. Trainers have a large

repertory of training tools and materials. But they must use these with discrimination in accordance with the needs of the job, the individual and the group.

7. Learning methods should be varied. The use of a variety of techniques, as long as they are equally appropriate, helps learning by maintaining the interest of trainees.

8. Time must be allowed to absorb the learning. Learning requires time to assimilate, test and accept. This time should be provided in the training programme. Too many trainers try to cram too much into their programmes and allow insufficient scope for practice and familiarization.

9. The learner must receive reinforcement of correct behaviour. Learners usually need to know quickly that they are doing well. In a prolonged training programme, intermediate steps are required in which learning can be reinforced.

10. It must be recognized that there are different levels of learning and that these need different methods and take different times. At the simplest level, learning requires direct physical responses, memorization and basic conditioning. At a higher level, learning involves adapting existing knowledge or skill to a new task or environment. At the next level, learning becomes a complex process when principles are identified in a range of practices or actions, when a series of isolated tasks have to be integrated or when the training deals with interpersonal skills. The most complex form of learning takes place when training is concerned with the values and attitudes of people and groups. This is not only the most complex area, but also the most difficult and dangerous.

## The learning organization

A 'learning organization' was defined by Wick and Leon (1995) as one that 'continually improves by rapidly creating and refining the capabilities required for future success'.

A learning organization has been described by Pedler et al (1989) as 'an organization which facilitates the learning of all its members and continually transforms itself'. As defined by Garvin (1993) it is one which is 'skilled at creating, acquiring, and transferring knowledge, and at modifying its behaviour to reflect new knowledge and insights'. He has suggested that learning organizations are skilled at five main activities:

1. *Systematic problem solving* which rests heavily on the philosophy and methods of the quality movement. Its underlying ideas include:

   ● relying on scientific method, rather than guesswork, for diagnosing problems — what Deming (1986) calls the 'plan-do-check-act' cycle and others refer to as 'hypothesis-generating, hypothesis-testing' techniques
   ● insisting on data rather than assumptions as the background to decision-making — what quality practitioners call 'fact-based management'
   ● using simple statistical tools such as histograms, Pareto charts and cause-and-effect diagrams to organize data and draw inferences.

   According to Garvin, this suggests that employees must be helped to become more disciplined in their thinking. They must be encouraged to ask, 'How do we know that's true?' and they must recognize 'that close enough is not good enough if real learning is to take place — they must push beyond obvious symptoms to ascertain underlying causes'.

2. *Experimentation* — this activity involves the systematic search for and testing of new knowledge. Continuous improvement programmes — 'kaizen' are an important feature in a learning organization.

3. *Learning from past experience* — learning organizations review their successes and failures, assess them systematically and record the lessons in a way that employees find open and accessible. This process has been called the 'Santayana principle' quoting the philosopher George Santayana who coined the phrase: 'Those who cannot remember the past are condemned to repeat it'.

4. *Learning from others* — sometimes the most powerful insights come from looking outside one's immediate environment to gain a new perspective. This process has been called SIS for 'steal ideas shamelessly'. Another word for it is benchmarking — a disciplined process of identifying best practice organizations and analysing the extent to which what they are doing can be transferred, with suitable modifications, to one's own environment.

5. *Transferring knowledge quickly and efficiently throughout the organization* by seconding people with new expertise, or by education and training programmes, as long as the latter are linked explicitly with implementation.

## Learning and Development

As Burgoyne (1994) has pointed out, learning organizations have to be able to adapt to their context and develop their people to match the context. Many individual jobs could be learned by processes of 'natural discovery' rather than formula learning. His definition (1988) of a learning organization is that it channels the career and life-planning activities of individual managers in a way that allows the organization to meet its strategic needs. This is done by encouraging the identification of individual needs, organic formulation of business strategy with inputs from training departments on current skills, and continual organizational review and learning from experience.

One approach, as advocated by Senge (1990), is to focus on collective problem-solving within an organization using team learning and a 'soft systems' approach whereby all the possible causes of a problem are considered in order to define more clearly those which can be dealt with and those which are insoluble.

Garratt (1990) believes that managers have to develop learning abilities as individuals, and work and learn as teams. He advocates the use of development activities such as job enlargement, job enrichment, monitoring, and various forms of team and project-based work.

Kandola and Fullerton (1994) have produced a six factor model of a learning organization as follows:

1.  *Shared vision* which enables the organization to identify, respond to and benefit from future opportunities.
2.  *Enabling structure* which facilitates learning.
3.  *Supportive culture* which encourages challenges to the *status quo* and the questioning of assumptions and established ways of doing things.
4.  *Empowering management* — managers genuinely believe that devolved decision-making and better team-working result in improved performance.
5.  *Motivated workforce* which wants to learn continuously.
6.  *Enhanced learning* — processes and policies exist to encourage learning amongst all employees.

The research conducted by Wick and Leon (1995) found that the characteristics of successful learning organizations were:

- a leader with a clearly defined vision
- the rapid sharing of information
- inventiveness

523

- a detailed, measurable action plan
- the ability to implement the action plan.

## Continuous development

A philosophy of continuous development states that for an organiza-tion simply to provide a measure of training to people at the start of their employment or at occasional points in their careers is insufficient. Learning should instead be regarded as a continuous process, with less emphasis on formal instruction and an increased requirement for people to be responsible for their own learning. Hence the develop-ment of such approaches as self-managed learning and learning con-tracts, action learning and computer-based training.

The Institute of Personnel and Development's code of practice on continuous development states:

> If learning activity in an organization is to be fully beneficial both to the organization and its employees, the following conditions must be met:
>
> - The organization must have some form of strategic business plan — it is desirable that the implications of the strategic plan, in terms of the skills and knowledge of the employees who will achieve it, should be spelled out.
> - Managers must be ready and willing (and able) to define and meet needs as they appear, all learning needs cannot be anticipated — organizations must foster a philosophy of continuous development.
> - As far as practicable, learning and work must be integrated. This means that encouragement must be given to all employees to learn from the problems, challenges and successes inherent in their day-to-day activities.
> - The impetus for continuous development must come from the chief executive and other members of the top management team (the board of directors, for example) — the top management team must regu-larly and formally review the way the competence of its management and workforce is being developed. It is important too that one senior executive is charged with responsibility for ensuring that continuous development activity is being effectively undertaken.
> - Investment in continuous development must be regarded by the top management team as being as important as investment in research, new product development or capital equipment — it is not a luxury which can be afforded only in the 'good times'. Indeed, the more severe the problems an organization faces the greater the need for learning on the part of its employees and the more pressing the need for investment in learning.

- Money spent within the organization on research and development into human resource development itself is money well spent. An evaluation of current human resource development procedures can confirm the effectiveness of current practice or point the way towards necessary change. Such research is as valuable as technical research.

## Self-managed learning

Self-managed or self-directed learning involves encouraging individuals to take responsibility for their own learning needs, either to improve performance in their present job or to satisfy their career aspirations. It can be based on a process of recording achievement and action planning which involves individuals reviewing what they have learnt, what they have achieved, what their goals are, how they are going to achieve those goals and what new learning they need to acquire.

Mumford (1994) suggests that self-managed learning can be carried out as follows:

- identify the individuals' learning style
- review how far their learning is encouraged or restricted by their learning style
- review their core learning skills of observation and reflection, analysis, creativity, decision-making and evaluation, and consider how to use them more effectively
- review the work and other experiences in which they are involved in terms of the kind of learning opportunity they offer
- look for potential helpers in the self-development process; managers, colleagues, trainers, or mentors (ie individuals other than the manager or a trainer who provide guidance and advice)
- draw up learning objectives and a plan of action — a personal development plan or learning agreement
- set aside some time each day to answer the question 'What did you learn today?'

Self-managed learning is based on the principle that people learn and retain more if they find things out for themselves. But they may still need to be given direction on what to look for and help in finding. Such direction can be provided through the performance management process as described in Chapter 13, in which the performance agreement can incorporate a personal learning/development plan but which also sets out the help the learner will receive from the manager and the organization.

The plan can be expressed in the form of a *learning agreement or contract*. This is an agreement, usually in writing, between individuals and their managers and, often, a trainer or mentor, to achieve a specified learning objective. The partners to the contract agree on how the objectives will be achieved and their respective roles.

Harrison (1992) emphasizes the need to create a climate of awareness about the opportunities for learning and development and to design training events to develop learning styles and skills.

In particular, the organization can encourage self-managed learning by ensuring that learners:

● define for themselves, with whatever guidance they may require, what they need to know to perform their job effectively
● are given guidance on where they can get the material or information which will help them to learn
● prepare a learning plan and programme as part of a learning contract
● prepare a personal development plan setting out what they need to learn, how they should develop and the actions they need to take to achieve learning and development goals.

## Personal development plans

### Defined

A personal development plan provides a clear developmental action plan for individuals which may include formal training but is also likely to incorporate a wider set of development activities such as self-managed learning, distance learning, coaching, project working, taking on new responsibilities (job enlargement), secondment, action learning, and developmental career moves, often lateral (ie to new roles at a broadly similar level which will extend the individual's skills and competences and provide the basis for further career development).

### Purpose

The purpose of a personal development plan may concentrate on the development required to improve performance in the current job. It may extend to the development required for future career moves and is thus part of a career development and planning process. Such plans are becoming more important in new flatter and process-based organizations where the emphasis is on continuous development, primarily through lateral career moves which, however, can still enhance people's skills and competences and provide additional challenge and reward.

Responsible employers also appreciate that, having cut back opportunities for promotion in their delayered organizations, they must do their best to provide lateral career development opportunities. Moreover, because of the more limited scope for advancement upwards and because job security has been reduced, they should be prepared to help employees to develop a portfolio of transferable skills which will make it easier to progress their careers if they have to move on.

## Preparing a personal development plan

The steps necessary to prepare a personal development plan as suggested by Gannon (1995) are to:

1. *Analyse current situation and development needs.* This means identifying skills, strengths and areas for development and improvement in the present role. As indicated by Gannon (1995) the starting point could be to categorize individuals' skills into those they:

- perform well and prefer using
- perform well but do not prefer using
- do not perform well but prefer using
- do not perform well and do not prefer using.

The primary aim is to get individuals to agree with their managers or team leaders the skills they use well and could be developed for the future in an extended role or possibly a new role — these might be termed their transferrable skills. Agreement has also to be reached on any areas where performance in using skills in the existing job need to be improved. However, another important aim is to consider how individuals can make even better use of their skills and competences. As Gannon states: 'Part of employee development planning is about assisting individuals to identify where their interests truly lie, and seeking to incorporate more of those interests into their roles to increase job satisfaction, thereby enhancing performance'.

2. *Set goals.* Goals can be set, as appropriate, under the headings of:

- improving performance
- working towards future changes in the current role
- enriching the current job
- moving across the organization
- moving upwards within the organization
- the improvement or acquisition of skills
- the extension of relevant knowledge
- the development of specified areas of competence.

3. *Prepare action plan.* This will be agreed by individuals with their managers and the organization to achieve developmental goals. It will include an appropriate mix of the activities listed above — for example, self-managed learning programmes for individuals, coaching by managers, projects, courses designed to meet specified training needs. The action plan could incorporate learning contracts — undertakings by individuals to learn or develop specified skills or to increase knowledge in defined areas.

# 28

# Training

## Definition

Training is the systematic modification of behaviour through learning which occurs as a result of education, instruction, development and planned experience. Training was defined in greater detail by the Manpower Services Commission (1981) as follows:

> A planned process to modify attitude, knowledge or skill behaviour through learning experience to achieve effective performance in an activity or range of activities. Its purpose, in the work situation, is to develop the abilities of the individual and to satisfy the current and future manpower needs of the organization.

## Aim

The fundamental aim of training is to help the organization achieve its purpose by adding value to its key resource — the people it employs. Training means investing in people to enable them to perform better and to empower them to make the best use of their natural abilities. The particular objectives of training are to:

- develop the competences of employees and improve their performance
- help people grow within the organization in order that, as far as possible, its future needs for human resources can be met from within
- reduce the learning time for employees starting in new jobs on appointment, transfer or promotion, and ensure that they become fully competent as quickly and economically as possible.

## Benefits

Effective training can:

- minimize learning costs
- improve individual, team and corporate performance in terms of output, quality, speed and overall productivity
- improve operational flexibility by extending the range of skills possessed by employees (multiskilling)
- attract high-quality employees by offering them learning and development opportunities, increasing their levels of competence and enhancing their skills, thus enabling them to obtain more job satisfaction, to gain higher rewards and to progress within the organization
- increase the commitment of employees by encouraging them to identify with the mission and objectives of the organization
- help to manage change by increasing understanding of the reasons for change and providing people with the knowledge and skills they need to adjust to new situations
- help to develop a positive culture in the organization, one, for example, which is orientated towards performance improvement
- provide higher levels of service to customers.

## Understanding training

To understand how training should be developed and operated within an organization, the first requirement is to appreciate learning theory and approaches to providing learning and development opportunities in organizations as discussed in Chapter 27. It is then necessary to understand the following approaches to training as described in this chapter:

- training philosophy — the basis upon which training philosophies and policies should be developed
- the process of training — how systematic training programmes and interventions can be planned, implemented and evaluated
- identifying training needs — establishing what type of training is required and ensuring that it is relevant to the requirements of individuals and the organization
- planning training — deciding how the longer- and shorter-term training needs of the organization and the teams and individuals

working in it can be satisfied and selecting and using training techniques
- conducting training — running training programmes for different categories of employees
- responsibility for training — determining who plans and executes training programmes
- evaluating training — establishing the extent to which training is achieving objectives by satisfying training needs.

## Training philosophy

The training philosophy of an organization expresses the degree of importance it attaches to training. Some firms adopt a *laissez-faire* approach, believing that employees will find out what to do for themselves or through, in the old phrase, 'sitting by Nellie'. If this sort of firm suffers a skill shortage, it is remedied by recruiting from firms who do invest in training.

Other companies pay lip service to training and indiscriminately allocate money to it in the good times. But in the bad times these firms are the first to cut their training budgets.

Organizations with a positive training philosophy understand that they live in a world where competitive advantage is achieved by having higher quality people than other firms employ, and that this need will not be satisfied unless they invest in developing the skills and competences of their people. They also recognize that actual or potential skills shortages can threaten their future prosperity and growth. In hard commercial terms, these firms persuade themselves that training is an investment that will pay off. They understand that it may be difficult to calculate the return on that investment but they believe that the tangible and intangible benefits of training, as described earlier in this chapter, will more than justify the cost.

It is not enough to believe in training as an act of faith. This belief must be supported by a positive and realistic philosophy of how training contributes to the bottom line. Underpinning this belief that is the need to set hard objectives for training in terms of a return on investment in the same way as other investments have to demonstrate a pay-back. The areas in which such a philosophy should be developed are described below.

### A strategic approach to training

Training strategy takes a long-term view of what skills, knowledge and levels of competence employees of the company need. Training philosophy emphasizes that training and development should be an integral part of the management process. Performance management requires managers to review regularly, with their teams and the individuals reporting to them, performance in relation to agreed objectives, the factors that have affected performance and the development and training needs that emerge from this analysis. The satisfaction of these needs is a joint process between managers, teams and individuals by means of coaching, counselling and relevant learning and training activities and interventions. Performance management leads to personal development plans and learning agreements or contracts.

## Relevant

While some organizations do not go in for training at all, others have tended to go in for 'training for training's sake'. Although in times of recession, this may be less likely, there is still the risk of organizations committing themselves to training in areas where the benefits in terms of improved performance in key activity areas have not been spelt out. Training must be relevant in that it satisfies identified and appropriate training needs.

## Problem-based

Training should be problem-based in the sense that it should be planned to fill the gaps between what people can do and what they need to do, now and in the future. The problem may be a negative one in the form of a weakness that needs to be remedied. Or it may be positive because it refers to how the need to develop new skills or enhance knowledge to meet future requirements will be satisfied.

## Action-orientated

Training philosophy should stress that training exists to make things happen, to get people into action, and to ensure that they can do things they are doing now better or will be able to do things that they could not do before. The objectives of any training event or programme should be defined in terms of 'deliverables' — this is what people will be able to do after training, and this is what they will achieve.

## *Performance-related training*

A performance-related training philosophy involves relating training specifically to performance and competence requirements — for example, those following the introduction of a new product, process or system.

## *Continuous development*

Training should not be regarded as simply the provision of short, isolated courses at various points in a person's career. Learning is a continuous process and a policy of continuous development as described in Chapter 27 should be pursued.

## *Training policies*

Training policies are expressions of the training philosophy of the organization. They provide guidelines on the amount of training that should be given (eg everyone in managerial, professional, technical or supervisory positions should undergo at least five days formal training every year), the proportion of turnover that should be allocated to training, the scope and aims of training schemes, and the responsibility for training.

# The process of training

## *Systematic training*

The concept of systematic training was originated by the Industrial Training Boards in the late 1960s. Systematic training is training which is specifically designed to meet defined needs. It is planned and provided by people who know how to train and the impact of training is carefully evaluated.

Systematic training is based on a simple four-stage model expressed as follows:

- define training needs
- decide what sort of training is required to satisfy these needs
- use experienced and trained trainers to plan and implement training
- follow up and evaluate training to ensure that it is effective.

The model provides a good basis for planning training programmes, but it is oversimplified — training is a more complex process than this. Another drawback to the concept of systematic training is that insufficient emphasis is placed on the responsibilities of managers and individuals for training. And under the influence of the training boards, a 'training industry' developed in the 1970s which imposed or tried to impose over-elaborate and bureaucratic routines on industry and commerce, an 'industry', which, understandably, was largely dismantled. But the essential validity of the concept of systematic training was not destroyed by the fact that it was badly implemented. What needed to be done was to develop a more realistic approach, which is described below as 'planned training'.

## Planned training

Planned training, as defined by Kenney and Reid (1994), is a 'deliberate intervention aimed at achieving the learning necessary for improved job performance'. The process of planned training, as shown in Figure 28.1, consists of the following steps:

- *Identify and define training needs* — this involves analysing corporate, team, occupational and individual needs to acquire new skills or knowledge or to improve existing competences. The analysis covers problems to be solved as well as future demands. Decisions are made at this stage on the extent to which training is the best and most cost-effective way to solve the problem.
- *Define the learning required* — it is necessary to specify as clearly as possible what skills and knowledge have to be learnt, what competences need to be developed and what attitudes need to be changed.
- *Define the objectives of training* — learning objectives are set which define not only what has to be learnt but also what learners must be able to do after their training programme.
- *Plan training programmes* — these must be developed to meet the needs and objectives by using the right combination of training techniques and locations.
- *Decide who provides the training* — the extent to which training is provided from within or outside the organization needs to be decided. At the same time, the division of responsibility between the training department, managers or team leaders and individuals has to be determined.

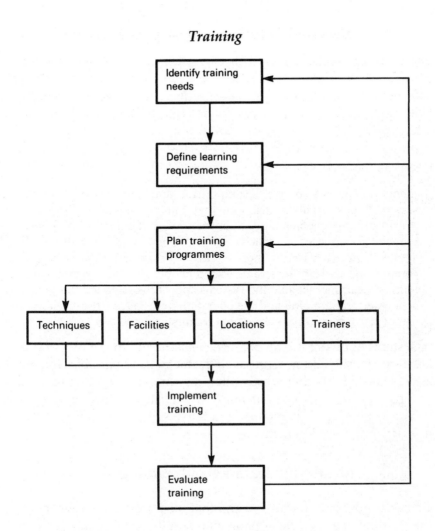

**Figure 28.1** The process of planned training

- *Implement the training* — ensure that the most appropriate methods are used to enable trainees to acquire the skills, knowledge, levels of competence and attitudes they need.
- *Evaluate training* — the effectiveness of training is monitored during programmes and, subsequently, the impact of training is assessed to determine the extent to which learning objectives have been achieved.
- *Amend and extend training as necessary* — decide, on the basis of evaluation, the extent to which the planned training programme needs to be improved and how any residual learning requirements should be satisfied.

## The systems approach to planned training

The training process just described will work effectively only if it is fully integrated with the systems of relationships, structures, inter-dependence and work in the organization. A systems approach to training has been defined by the Manpower Services Commission (1981) as the process of:

> Identifying inputs, outputs, components and sub-systems, and then seeking to identify the contribution that training can make to improving the operation by enhancing the contribution of the human components (people) as opposed to machinery and operational procedures. The systems approach is next applied to the training design, where the components are learning strategies and people, and the objectives are in terms of learning. Finally, the systems approach is applied to the inter-action between training and the operation to produce a feedback which can be used to improve subsequent training.

A systems approach requires those concerned with the preparation of training plans to take account of all the factors and variables that might affect learning. In other words, the programme of training for a job in one part of the organization might be affected by events elsewhere, within or outside the company, and the design of the course must take into account these interactions.

## Identifying learning and training needs

Training must have a purpose and that purpose can be defined only if the learning needs of the organization and the groups and individuals within it have been systematically identified and analysed.

### Training needs analysis — aims

Training needs analysis is partly concerned with defining the gap between what is happening and what should happen. This is what has to be filled by training (see Figure 28.2), ie the difference between what people know and can do and what they *should* know and be able to do.

However, it is necessary to avoid falling into the trap of adopting the 'deficiency model' approach which implies that training is only about putting things right that have gone wrong. Training is much more positive than that. It is, or should be, more concerned with identifying and satisfying development needs — multiskilling, fitting people to

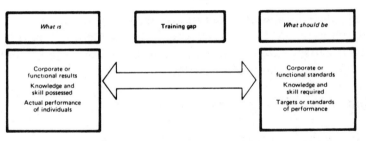

**Figure 28.2** The training gap

take on extra responsibilities, increasing all-round competence and preparing people to take on higher levels of responsibility in the future.

## *Training needs analysis — areas*

Training needs should be analysed, first, for the organization as a whole — corporate needs; second, for departments, teams, functions or occupations within the organization — group needs; and third, for individual employees — individual needs. These three areas are interconnected, as shown in Figure 28.3. The analysis of corporate needs will lead to the identification of training needs in different departments or occupations, while these in turn will indicate the training required for individual employees. The process also operates in reverse. As the needs of individual employees are analysed separately, common needs emerge which can be dealt with on a group basis. The sum of group and individual needs will help to define

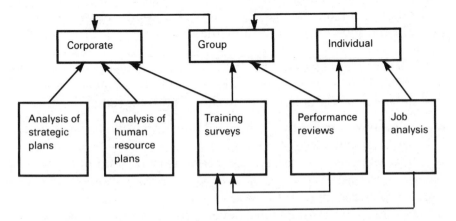

**Figure 28.3** Training needs analysis — areas and methods

corporate needs, although there may be some superordinate training requirements which can be related only to the company as a whole to meet its business development needs — the whole training plan may be greater than the sum of its parts.

## Methods of analysing training needs

The four methods of training needs analysis are:

- analysis of business and human resource plans
- job analysis
- analysis of performance reviews
- training surveys.

### Business and human resource plans
The training strategy of an organization should largely be determined by its business and personnel strategies and plans from which flow human resource plans. The plans should indicate in fairly general terms the types of skills and competences that may be required in the future and the numbers of people with those skills and competences who will be needed. These broad indicators have to be translated into more specific plans which cover, for example, the outputs from training programmes of people with particular skills or a combination of skills (multiskilling).

### Job analysis
Job analysis for training purposes means examining in detail the content of jobs, the performance standards required in terms of quality and output and the knowledge, skills and competences needed to perform the job competently and thus meet the performance standards.

The techniques of job, skills and competence analysis were described in Chapter 12. For training purposes, it would be necessary to ensure that the information obtained from this analysis specifies:

- any problems faced by job holders in learning the basic skills and applying them successfully
- any weaknesses in the performance of existing job holders arising from gaps in knowledge, lack of skill or poor motivation which need to be rectified by training
- any areas where competence levels are clearly not up to the standard required

- any areas where future changes in work processes, methods or job responsibilities indicate a learning need
- how training is carried out at present — and how effective it is.

The output of the job analysis should be a training specification, as described below.

### Training specification

A training specification is a product of job analysis. It breaks down the broad duties contained in the job description into the detailed tasks that must be carried out. It then sets out the characteristics or attributes that the individual should have in order to perform these tasks successfully. These characteristics are:

- *Knowledge* — what the individual needs to know. It may be professional, technical or commercial knowledge. Or it may be about the commercial, economic, or market environment; the machines to be operated; the materials or equipment to be used or the procedures to be followed; or the customers, clients, colleagues and subordinates he or she is in contact with and the factors that affect their behaviour. Or it may refer to the problems that occur and how they should be dealt with.
- *Skills* — what the individual needs to be able to do if results are to be achieved and knowledge is to be used effectively. Skills are built progressively by repeated training or other experience. They may be manual, intellectual or mental, perceptual or social.
- *Competences* — the work-based and behavioural competences required to achieve the levels of performance required.
- *Attitudes* — the disposition to behave or to perform in a way which is in accordance with the requirements of the work.
- *Performance standards* — what the fully competent individual has to be able to achieve.

### Performance reviews

Performance management processes, as described in Chapter 13, should be a prime source of information about individual learning and development needs. The performance management approach to learning concentrates on the preparation of performance improvement programmes and learning contracts or personal development plans which are related to jointly determined action plans. The emphasis is on continuous development. Every contact between managers and individuals throughout the year is regarded as a learning opportunity.

*Training surveys*

Training surveys assemble all the information obtained from the other methods of analysis in order to provide a comprehensive basis for the development of a training strategy and its implementation. It may be necessary to supplement that information by interviewing managers to establish their views about training needs and by discussing with people undergoing training or who have just completed a training course their opinions about its effectiveness.

A training survey pays particular attention to the extent to which existing training arrangements are meeting training needs. Further information should be derived from training evaluations, as described later in this chapter. It is also necessary to assess training programmes in terms of the quality of training provided, their output and the level of performance achieved by ex-trainees.

Attitude surveys can be used to obtain the opinions of employees about the present amount and level of training provision.

## Planning training programmes

Every training programme needs to be designed individually, and the design will continually evolve as new learning needs emerge, or when feedback indicates that changes are required. Before consideration is given to special aspects of training programmes for managers, team leaders, craft and technical trainees, and office staff, decisions are necessary in the areas discussed below.

## *Objectives*

It is essential to consider carefully the objectives of the training programme. Objectives can be defined as 'criterion behaviour', ie the standards or changes of behaviour on the job to be achieved if training is to be regarded as successful. This should be a definition of what the trainee will be able to do when he or she goes back to work on completing the course; in other words, terminal behaviour. Transfer of learning is what counts; behaviour on the job is what matters. Training objectives are best expressed as follows:

> On completing the training (or this part of the course) the trainee will be able to ... (read a balance sheet, program a microcomputer, operate a word processor, work to a high degree of accuracy, etc).

## Content

The content of the training programme should be determined entirely by the learning and training needs analysis and an assessment of what needs to be done to achieve the agreed training objectives.

## Length

The length of the training programme obviously depends on its content. But careful consideration should be given to how learning can be speeded up by the use of techniques such as computer-based training. Thought should also be given to where more time needs to be allowed for 'discovery learning' to take place, or for the amount of involvement required to ensure that those undergoing training have the opportunity fully to understand and 'own' the new ideas or techniques to which they have been exposed.

## Where should training take place?

There are three places where training can take place: in-company, on the job, off the job; and external, off the job. Each has its uses, and its advantages and disadvantages as discussed below.

### In-company, on-the-job

In-company, on-the-job training may consist of teaching or coaching by managers, team leaders or trainers at the desk or at the bench. It may also consist of individual or group assignments and projects and the use of mentors (see Appendix D). It is the only way to develop and practise the specific managerial, team leading, technical, selling, manual, and administrative skills needed by the organization. It has the advantage of actuality and immediacy. The individual works, learns and develops expertise at the same time. Theory is put into practice immediately and its relevance is obvious. Much of the learning can take place naturally as part of the performance management process and through day-to-day contacts although it will be most effective if specific learning objectives have been articulated.

The disadvantages are that the effectiveness of the learning is strongly influenced by the quality of the guidance and coaching provided on the job. Many managers and team leaders are unskilled at training and disinclined to carry it out or to encourage it. Relying on fellow employees — 'sit by me' training — had equally obvious disadvantages. The instruction may be inadequate and the training may perpetuate bad habits. Above all, the learner may be distracted by the environment and find it difficult to acquire the basic skills quickly. To overcome this problem, it is essential to provide training to managers and team leaders on how to train and even more important, to stress that this is expected of them as a key part of their jobs and will be one of the key areas in which there performance will be measured.

### In company, off the job

In-company, off-the-job training can take place on special courses or in training areas or centres which have been specially equipped and staffed for training. It is the best way to acquire advanced manual, office, customer service or selling skills and to learn about company procedures and products. It helps to increase the identification of the trainee with the company as a whole, and the use of systematic training techniques, special equipment and trained trainers means that the basic skills and knowledge can be acquired quickly and often economically.

The main disadvantage arises when trainees are transferred from the training course to a job to apply their knowledge and skills in practice. On a full-time manual skills course in a training centre, they will have been sheltered from the realities of the rough and tumble in most workshops, especially in batch production factories.

For managers and team leaders level, the problem of transferring from the 'training situation' to 'real life' may be even more difficult. This issue of transferring learning is important in all aspects of training but it is a particular problem with management and team leader training whether in-company or provided outside. This is partly because much management training tends to deal with relatively abstract concepts like motivation and leadership and the connection between what people learn in the class room (or out of doors) may not always be apparent. Strenuous efforts have to be made to ensure that learners perceive the reality of what they are learning and are expected to develop and implement action plans for putting it into practice. The concept of 'action learning', as developed by Revans (1989), is designed to mitigate this problem.

### External training

External training is useful for the development of managerial, team leaders, technical and social knowledge and skills, especially if the courses cover standard theory and practice which can easily be translated from the general to the particular. External training should be able to supply the quality of instruction which it might be uneconomic to provide from internal resources. It can be used to implant highly specialized knowledge or advanced skills and has the added advantage of broadening the horizons of those taking part, not least because they will be exposed to their peers from other organizations.

The main disadvantage is that of transferring learning into practice — even more acute with external courses. However effective the training, the knowledge and skills acquired may be quickly dissipated unless they are used immediately. It may also be difficult to select relevant courses from the bewildering variety available.

## Training programme design as an art

The art of designing training programmes is to select the right blend of on-the-job and off-the-job training. There are no rules for doing this. Each programme has to be considered individually. But the emphasis should always be towards putting learning into practice and, therefore, first consideration has to be given to what happens on the job — learning by doing with appropriate guidance from managers, colleagues or mentors.

Off-the-job courses, whether internal or external, should be regarded as complementary and supplementary activities which may stimulate learning or provide knowledge and skills that cannot be obtained internally. But they are always subsidiary to what individuals do and learn in their normal place of work.

## Training techniques

There is a wide variety of training techniques that can be used. These can be divided into:

- *On-the-job techniques*, which are practised on a day-to-day basis or as part of a specially tailored training programme. These include demonstration, coaching, job rotation, planned experience and mentoring.
- *Off-the-job techniques*, which are used in formal training courses away from the place of work. These include lectures, talks, discussions, the discovery method, case study, role-playing, simulation, group exercises, team building, distance learning, outdoor learning and workshops.
- On- or off-the-job techniques, which include instruction, question

and answer, action learning, assignments, projects, guided reading, computer-based training, inter-active video and video.

These techniques are described in Appendix D.

## Who provides the training?

On-the-job training can be provided by managers, team leaders, colleagues or 'mentors' (fellow employees who are given a particular responsibility to guide, advise and generally look after trainees — see Appendix D). As mentioned earlier, it is essential to train anyone involved in on-the-job training in techniques such as coaching, instructing and mentoring.

Off-the-job training may be provided by members of the training department, external education and training establishments, or training providers — training consultants or guest speakers. Increasingly, organizations are turning to external training providers rather than maintaining their own establishment of training staff.

Line managers should also be involved as much as possible to bring reality into the classroom, to ease the transfer of learning to work (always a difficult problem) and to underline their prime responsibility for training. Anyone who provides off-the-job training must be carefully selected, briefed and monitored to ensure that they make the right contribution. Natural trainers are fairly rare and even professionals need all the guidance you can give them to ensure that they are providing relevant training.

## Conducting training programmes

The only general rules for conducting training programmes are that first, the courses should continually be monitored to ensure that they are proceeding according to plan and within the agreed budget and second, all training should be evaluated after the event to check on the extent to which it is delivering the required results. This is the job of whoever has the responsibility for employee development, who should be required to report on progress against plan at regular intervals.

There are, however, a number of considerations which affect the conduct of training for specific occupations, and those concerning managers and team leaders (these are dealt with jointly because the basic principles are similar), sales staff, skilled workers and office staff are discussed briefly below. Special approaches may also be used for teambuilding training and particular groups of employees and these are also described below.

## Management and team leader training

As the old saying goes, managers learn to manage by managing under the guidance of a good manager. The emphasis should therefore always be towards on-the-job training, by planned experience, coaching or assignments. This can be supplemented — but never replaced — by off-the-job training to extend knowledge, fill in gaps, develop skills, or modify attitudes.

Management and team leader training courses can provide:

- concentrated knowledge
- an opportunity to acquire new skills or to develop and practise existing skills
- a framework for analysing past experience
- the chance to reflect on ways in which better use can be made of future experience
- a means of getting new ideas accepted and changing attitudes through group activities not available on the job.

However, management training courses do not always (some cynics would say 'often') achieve these objectives. Following extensive research, Mant (1970) noted that:

- the majority of managers do not benefit greatly from external management courses
- managers benefit more from well-designed and well-conducted internal courses, variously termed 'in-company', 'in-plant', or 'in-house', which are linked to the job and involve problem-orientated project work
- the organization, and not the individual, should be regarded as the main consumer of management training, the aim of which is to secure better results for the company.

Revans (1971) has taken the same standpoint in developing his concept of 'action learning' as described in Appendix D.

To get good results from external courses it is necessary to ensure that they will be relevant and well conducted and that managers are required to make practical use of what they have learnt.

Project training is one way of avoiding the problems of external courses. It provides managers and team leaders with new experiences and the opportunity to extend their knowledge over a wider range of problems and to exercise their analytical skills in solving them.

Management and team leader training should be seen as a continuous process. One of the greatest fallacies of the typical external management course is that this is sufficient. A management and team leader training programme should therefore be established as a continuing activity at all levels of management to avoid dissipation of the interest and enthusiasm that follows an isolated course, and to promote the progressive development of managerial and team leader skills as new experiences are encountered and as conditions change.

## Sales training

The aim of sales training should be to equip sales representatives with the knowledge, skills, attitudes and habits required to meet or exceed their sales targets.

The first requirement is knowledge of the company and its products, customers, competitors and sales administration procedures.

Secondly, they have to acquire and develop skills: prospecting, making the approach, making presentations, handling objections, closing the sale, and handling complaints. Perhaps the most important skill to be developed, however, is analytical ability. Sales representatives must be taught how to analyse their product into its technical characteristics and, most important, its selling points — those aspects of the product that are likely to appeal to particular customers. They must also be taught how to analyse their customers from the point of view of their buying habits and the features of the product that are most likely to appeal to them. In addition, they must be able to analyse themselves — their own strengths and weaknesses.

Thirdly, training should aim to develop attitudes: of loyalty to the company and belief in its products, and of understanding and tolerance with regard to potential and existing customers. The importance of customer service must be emphasized. Sales representatives have to believe in themselves; they must be given confidence and provided with the motivation to go out and sell — a task which requires courage, determination and persistence.

The fourth requirement is to develop sound work habits: organizing time, planning activities, following up leads, maintaining records and submitting reports.

Sales training, like any other form of training, should be based on an analysis of the job and the problems sales representatives are likely to meet. The training programme should be continuous; there can never be a time in any sales representative's career when he or she would not benefit from training. Use should be made of classroom training to provide basic knowledge and an opportunity to practise skills. But most training should be carried out on the job by sales managers or team leaders who can demonstrate sales techniques and observe and comment on the efforts of the sales representatives.

## Technical and skill or craft training

Technical and skill or craft training schemes can be divided into four main types:

- *Graduate* — postgraduate training leading to a professional qualification.
- *Student* — a course of education and practical training leading to a degree or some other qualification as an engineer, scientist or technologist or technician. In the UK the course may include 'block' release to college for periods of a number of months or the student may undergo a full degree course as the central part of the training while gaining experience before and after the course and during vacations.
- *Technician* — a course of education and training, which could last up to three or four years, leading to employment as a technician and an appropriate technician's qualification.
- *Skill or craft* — a course lasting a number of years, depending on the level of skill that has to be attained and often leading to a craft certificate or other record of achievement. At one time such training schemes were always called apprenticeships and the indenture agreement laid down a fixed period of training. But it did not specify what training should take place or indicate what standards had been achieved.

    The old apprenticeship agreement has generally been replaced by the training agreement. This stipulates the basic and general training, and the skill modules that have to be completed to satisfactory standards before the training is completed satisfactorily. A skill module is based on skills analysis and defines what training is required to achieve an 'experienced worker's standard' in a particular skill or task. It sets out the exercises to be carried out and how attainments should be tested. The training may be built round National Vocational Qualification (NVQ) specifications, although specific training modules will be built into the programme linked to the competence elements incorporated in the NVQ level which is to be attained. The training agreement may also specify the part-time period of further education that has to be completed.

*Phases of skill training*
In the major craft industries — engineering and construction — the skill training for craft trainees or apprentices consists of the following three phases.

*Basic training*
In the basic training period trainees receive training in basic skills in a basic training workshop. This training should consist of a series of modules. Clearly, the standard modules should be chosen on the basis of an analysis of the skills required, and additional modules should be specially developed if necessary. A basic course for engineering craft apprentices may last a full year, by which time the apprentices should be fully equipped with all the basic skills.

Each module should have defined objectives — criterion behaviour. There should be methods of measuring behaviour after the module has been completed. The training should be given by trained instructors in a space set aside for training.

*General training*
In the general training period trainees are given experience in a number of different departments, processes, or operations to consolidate training. If it is already decided that they are to become, say, computer numerically controlled machine tool operators in a flexible manufacturing system (FMS), they would be given an extended period of familiarization in the machine tool room. But they would also spend some time in related areas; for example, the design office, production planning and control and various fitting and assembly shops.

Technician, student and graduate trainees in engineering would also spend a general period of training 'round the shops' but would then move into the engineering, design or development departments, depending on their speciality. A production specialist, for example, would spend time in the planning, production control, work study and quality assurance departments.

During the period, graduate and student trainees should be given special projects which test their understanding of the design, development, engineering and manufacturing functions. Craft and technician trainees may return to the training school for advanced skill courses in machine operation, CADCAM (computer aided design and manufacturing) systems or any other speciality.

The biggest danger to avoid in this period of general training is that trainees aimlessly wander from shop to shop and find themselves relegated to a tedious job out of harms way because no one wants to know about them. To avoid this danger, it is essential to have a syllabus of training in every workshop which is based on an analysis of skill requirements. There should be one trained supervisor responsible for training in each workshop and in a large department, such as a machine shop, there may be more than one full-time training supervisor. The training department should also monitor the progress of trainees carefully to ensure that they are following the syllabus and are acquiring the knowledge and skill they need. In a large organization there may be one or more full-time supervisors who spend all their time in the shops chasing shop team leaders or supervisors and checking on the progress of trainees.

The trainees themselves should know what they are expected to learn at each stage in order that they can request a move if they feel they are wasting their time or are not covering the syllabus. They should also be required to keep logbooks to record what they have done. These should be seen regularly by their training officer as a check on their progress.

*Final training*

In the final training period trainees settle down in the department of their choice, or the department for which they are best fitted. During this period trainees will probably be doing the same work as experienced skilled operators, technicians or technologists. The aim is to ensure that they are equipped to apply their learning in normal working conditions and at the pace and level of quality expected from a fully experienced and competent individual.

Throughout these three stages the training department has to work closely with the educationists to ensure that, as far as possible, the theory is complementary to the practice.

The length of the period of training at each stage obviously depends on the level and complexity of the knowledge and skills that have to be acquired and on the type of apprenticeship. Traditional union agreements laid down the length of training in some cases but these have virtually disappeared. The experience of any company conducting training along the lines described above, however, has shown that if the basic training is sufficiently comprehensive and the period of experience is adequately planned and monitored, the length of time to reach a fully experienced worker's standard may be considerably less than the traditional period.

Training for other skilled crafts should follow the same pattern of basic training: familiarization with the application of different aspects of the craft, and final consolidation of knowledge and skills. The basic training period, however, may not be so elaborate and may well be carried out in a local training centre which is better equipped to provide the skilled instruction required.

## Training office staff

Office training is the most neglected form of training. Perhaps this is because both line and training managers often underestimate the skill content of most office work. This feeling has been intensified because of the tendency of systems analysts to deskill office jobs.

However, inefficiency in office work can be an important factor in reducing the efficiency of the organization as a whole. A company cannot afford to neglect training in office skills and departmental procedures.

Office training should be divided into three areas: basic training, further education, and continuation training. During the basic training stage, when the trainee is being taught how to carry out his or her first job, a foundation is being laid for the employees career. During this period, young trainees should obtain background knowledge of the company and acquire the basic knowledge and skills they need.

Office trainees should be encouraged to follow a further course of studies leading to a professional or commercial qualification or a NVQ. The course of studies should be decided by agreement between the employee, the departmental manager and the training department.

The third area is continuation training. Training and development should be a continuous process. When trainees have completed their basic training programme and, preferably, have obtained a qualification, their abilities should be developed by providing broader experience within the company and by short technical courses. The aim at this stage should be to ensure that staff with potential are not allowed to stagnate within a department and that they are prepared for greater responsibility.

## Team building training

Team building training can be defined as a structured attempt to improve and develop the effectiveness of a group of people who work (permanently or temporarily) together. This improvement may be defined in terms of outputs, for example the speed and quality of the decisions and actions produced by the team. It may also be defined in more nebulous terms, for example, the quality of relationships or greater cooperation.

The ways in which team building can influence attitudes and behaviour are illustrated in Figure 28.4.

Team building training aims to:

- increase awareness of the social processes which take place within teams
- develop the interactive or interpersonal skills which enable individuals to function effectively as team members
- increase the overall effectiveness with which teams operate in the organization.

To be effective, team building programmes should be directly relevant to the responsibilities of the participants and be seen as relevant by all participants. They need to support business objectives, fit in with practical working arrangements and reflect the values the organization wishes to promote. Team building training can be based on an appropriate mix of approaches described in Appendix D. These include action learning, group dynamics, group exercises, interactive skills training, interactive video, role-playing and simulation. Team building training is often based on either Belbin or Margerison and

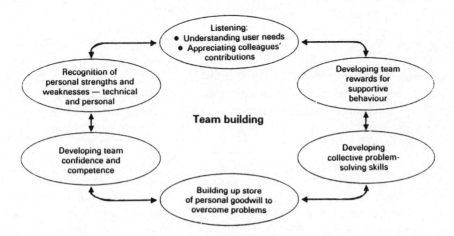

**Figure 28.4** Team building as an influence on attitudes and behaviour

McCann classifications of team roles as listed in Chapter 18 (pages 352 to 353).

Outdoor learning (outdoor-based development) as also described in Appendix D is a good method of providing team-building training. It can offer a closer approximation to reality than other forms of training. Participants tend to behave more normally and, paradoxically, it is precisely because the tasks are unrelated to work activities and are relatively simple that they highlight the processes involved in team work and provide a good basis for identifying how these processes can be improved.

## Meeting the training needs of special groups

Training needs analysis as described earlier in this chapter is often conducted entirely on an occupational basis but it is also necessary to consider the needs of special groups, especially the disabled and ethnic minorities. A separate needs analysis should be carried out which identifies the occupations they are likely to be in and any special training requirements arising from different types of disabilities or the particular ethnic group(s). Advice on approaches to training people with disabilities can be obtained from charities such as the Royal National Institute for the Blind, the Royal National Institute for the Deaf, the Royal Association for Disability and Rehabilitation and MENCAP. Ethnic groups may have to be given special training if there are any linguistic or cultural issues which need attention.

## Responsibility for training

As has been made clear throughout this chapter, most learning occurs on the job through coaching, planned experience and self-development. The onus is on managers and individuals to ensure that it takes place. Senior management must create a learning organization in which managers recognize that training and development are a key part of their role and one on which their performance will be assessed.

The role of a specialized training function is generally to provide advice and guidance to managers on their training responsibilities. In many organizations they are involved much less, if at all, in training delivery. Training functions are relying more and more on external providers to provide the actual training. This means that the huge training departments which used to exist in a lot of organizations have now been slimmed down considerably. Increasingly, the role of the company trainer is to act as an internal consultant.

The much smaller training function may still, however, be responsible for the following activities:

- developing training strategies which support the achievement of business strategies
- analyzing and identifying corporate and occupational training needs
- developing proposals on how these needs should be satisfied
- preparing plans and budgets for training activities
- identifying external training resources, selecting external training providers, specifying what is required from them and ensuring that their delivery of training meets the specification
- advising on external training courses for individuals or groups
- organizing internal courses and training programmes, but often relying on outside help for the whole or part of formal training courses
- training managers, supervisors and mentors in their training responsibilities
- providing help and guidance to individuals in the preparation and implementation of personal development plans
- monitoring and evaluating the effectiveness of training throughout the organization.

## Evaluation of training

It is at the planning stage that the basis upon which each category of training is to be evaluated should be determined. At the same time, it is necessary to consider how the information required to evaluate courses should be obtained and analysed.

The process of evaluating training has been defined by Hamblin (1974) as: 'Any attempt to obtain information (feedback) on the effects of a training programme, and to assess the value of the training in the light of that information.' Evaluation leads to control which means deciding whether or not the training was worthwhile (preferably in cost-benefit terms) and what improvements are required to make it even more cost-effective.

Evaluation is an integral feature of training. In its crudest form, it is the comparison of objectives (criterion behaviour) with effects (terminal behaviour) to answer the question of how far the training has achieved its purpose. The setting of objectives and the establishment of methods of measuring results are, or should be, an essential part of the planning stage of any training programme.

Evaluation can be difficult because it is often hard to set measurable objectives and even harder to collect the information on the results or to decide on the level at which the evaluation should be made.

## Evaluation levels

Hamblin has suggested that there are five levels at which evaluation can take place:

1.  *Reactions* of trainees to the training experience itself: how useful or even how enjoyable they feel the training is, what they think of individual sessions and speakers, what they would like put in or taken out, and so on.
2.  *Learning* evaluation requires the measurement of what trainees have learned as a result of their training — the new knowledge and skills they have acquired or the changes in attitude that have taken place.
3.  *Job behaviour* evaluation is concerned with measuring the extent to which trainees have applied their learning on the job. This constitutes an assessment of the amount of transfer of learning that has taken place from an off-the-job training course to the job itself. If the training is carried out on the job, there should be little difference between learning and job behaviour. This is the terminal behaviour that occurs after the training has finished.
4.  *Organizational unit* evaluation attempts to measure the effect of changes in the job behaviour of trainees on the functioning of the part of the organization in which they are employed. The measurement might be in such terms as improvements in output, productivity, quality, contribution, or sales turnover. In effect, the question answered by this type of evaluation is not simply what behavioural changes have taken place, but what good have those changes done for the unit or department in which the employee works.
5.  *Ultimate value* evaluation aims to measure how the organization as a whole has benefited from the training in terms of greater profitability, survival or growth. But it might also be defined in terms of the trainees personal goals rather than those of the sponsoring organization. Evaluation at this level is related to the

criteria by which the organization judges its efficiency and its success or failure. The difficulty is assessing how far training has contributed to the ultimate results.

As Hamblin points out, the five levels are links in a chain: training leads to reactions, which lead to learning, which leads to changes in job behaviour, which lead to changes in the organizational unit, which lead to changes in the achievement of ultimate goals. But the chain can be snapped at any link. Trainees can react favourably to a course — they can enjoy it — but learn nothing. They can learn something, but cannot, or will not, or are not allowed to, apply it. They apply it, but it does no good within their own area. It does some good in their function, but does not further the objectives of the organization.

Evaluation can start at any level. Ideally, some people might say, it starts and finishes at levels four and five; organizational and ultimate value. This is all that really matters, they assert. But it may be difficult, if not impossible, to measure the effect of training in these respects. In any case, it may be desirable to work backwards to find out what went wrong at earlier levels if the ultimate benefits arising from training are inadequate. Evaluation has to focus on the particular merits or otherwise of a training programme so that, if necessary, steps can be taken to revise the aims and content of the programme, to improve the delivery of training or to ensure that the transfer of learning does take place to good effect.

# 29

# Management Development

## What is management development?

Management development contributes to business success by helping the organization to grow the managers it requires to meet its present and future needs. It improves managers' performance, gives them development opportunities, and provides for management succession. As stated in the IPD's professional standards, development processes may be *anticipatory* (so that managers can contribute to long-term objectives), *reactive* (intended to resolve or pre-empt performance difficulties) or *motivational* (geared to individual career aspirations). The particular aims of management development are to:

- ensure that managers understand what is expected of them; agreeing with them objectives against which their performance will be measured and areas where competence levels need to be improved
- identify managers with potential, encouraging them to prepare and implement personal development plans and ensuring that they receive the required development, training and experience to equip them for more demanding responsibilities within their own locations and elsewhere in the organization
- provide for management succession, creating a system to keep this under review.

## Management development as a business-led process

The most important thing to remember about the process of management development is that it must be business-led even though it will be concerned with the development of individual performance and potential. The business has to decide what sort of managers it needs to achieve its strategic goals and the business must decide how it can best obtain and develop these managers. Even when the emphasis is on self-development, as it should be, the business must still indicate the directions in which self-development should go, possibly in the broadest of terms.

## The impact of management development

The capability of the organization to achieve its business strategies in the light of the critical success factors for the business (innovation, quality, cost leadership, etc) depends largely on the capability of its managers as developed within the organization to meet its particular demands and circumstances. The relationships involved are illustrated in Figure 29.1 (adapted from Fonda, 1989).

Fonda (1989) emphasizes the far-reaching nature of the management capabilities required as follows:

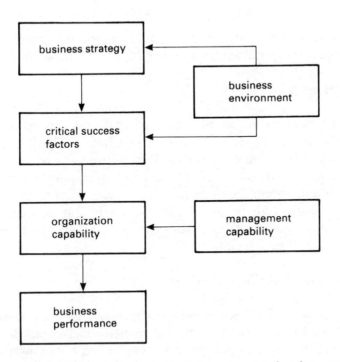

**Figure 29.1** The strategic impact of management development

- setting challenging ambitions
- developing product-market strategies which sustain the competitiveness of the business
- creating functional strategies which support strategic ambitions and product-market strategies
- developing and effectively using systems for managing the business
- shaping organizational culture for the future
- structuring and restructuring the parts and the whole of the business in line with emerging priorities
- optimizing profits by continually improving sales and service with today's customers and today's products.

## The processes of management development

As suggested by Harrison (1992) the three essential management development activities are the:

- analysis of present and future management needs
- assessment of existing and potential skills and effectiveness of managers against those needs
- production of policy, strategy and plans to meet those needs.

Management development also involves management succession planning and career management activities as described in this chapter.

### Analysis of needs

The analysis of the future needs for managers is carried out through human resource planning processes (see Chapter 23).

In today's changeable, if not chaotic, conditions it may not be feasible to make precise forecasts of the number of managers required. But what can and should be done is to assess the skills and competences managers will need to meet future demands and challenges arising from competitive pressures, new product-market strategies and the introduction of new technology.

### Assessment of skills and competences

The assessment of skills and competences against these needs can be carried out by performance management processes as described in Chapter 13. It will be important, however, to include in these processes a means of identifying specific development needs and the agreement of development plans to meet not only current needs but anticipated future requirements.

## Meeting the needs

To meet the needs it is necessary to:

- understand the nature of management development and the processes involved
- formulate management development strategies
- define the responsibilities for management development
- implement formal and informal approaches to management development
- make use of competence-based approaches to management development
- use development centres as a means of identifying potential and development needs.

These aspects of management development are discussed in the remaining sections of this chapter.

## The nature of management development

It has been suggested by Mumford (1993) that three elements have to be combined to produce an effective management development system:

- *self-development* — a recognition that individuals can learn but are unlikely to be taught, and that the initiative for development often rests with the individual
- *organization-derived development* — the development of the systems of formal development beloved of personnel and management development specialists
- *boss-derived development* — those actions undertaken by a senior manager with others, most frequently around real problems at work.

Mumford also makes the point that managers think in terms of activities, not learning opportunities and therefore: 'Our main concern must be to facilitate learning through our understanding of real work in the manager's world, rather than attempting to impose separate management development processes'. He suggests that formal management development processes do not always function as effectively as we would like because: 'We have put too much emphasis on planning ahead, and not enough on enabling managers to use, understand and then build on their past experiences'.

## Management development strategy

The management development strategy will be concerned overall with what the organization intends to do about providing for its future management needs in the light of its business plans. The strategy will be concerned with the roles of the parties involved and with the approaches the organization proposes to use to develop its managers.

An example of management development benchmark statements produced by the NHS Training Division is given in Table 29.1.

The prime aim of these benchmark statements is to identify the key facets that make up management development activities. They provide personnel and line managers with a means of conducting their own evaluation and analysis of the state of management development within their organization. Each facet or 'dimension' in the statements brings together such aspects as the links between management development and business strategy, the formulation of a management development plan, the assessment of skills and identification of skill gaps, and the delivery of appropriate and effective training and development.

The facets are broken down into four aspects of performance:

- commitment to management development
- reviewing the current position of management development
- making progress in management development
- excellence in management development.

The NHS Training Division emphasizes that the 'underpinning assumption in the framework is the importance of bringing together the elements of a management development strategy into a more integrated whole'. The various components do not have separate existences of their own.

## Responsibility for management development

Management development is not a separate activity to be handed over to a specialist and forgotten or ignored. The success of a management development programme depends upon the degree to which all levels of management are committed to it. The development of subordinates

**Table 29.1** Management development benchmark statements

| Management Development Strategy & Commitment | Identification of Need | Realizing Management Potential | Information Systems | Value for Money |
|---|---|---|---|---|
| A. There is a written, public, top level commitment to using Management Development, where appropriate, to develop individual managers, management teams and the organization. | A. There is a written, public, top level commitment to the consistent identification of development needs using a recognized system or process. | A. There is a written, public, top level commitment that all members of staff performing management tasks will have their contribution assessed and developed. | A. There is a written, public, top level commitment to make high quality information about Management Development activities available to all managers to make informed choices. | A. There is a written, public, top level commitment to achieving value for money in Management Development through the comon identification of costs and benefits. |
| B. Management Development activity is regularly reviewed to demonstrate its links to organizational objectives. | B. The organization regularly reviews, in terms of skills, knowledge, understanding and values, the development needs of its managers and management teams. | B. Management Development activity is regularly audited to demonstrate how it provides access and opportunity to staff to realize management potential. | B. The organization regularly reviews its information on Management Development provision and its usefulness to decision makers. | B. An accepted, common approach exists for the audit of the costs and benefits of Management Development. |
| C. All Management Development activity is driven by organizational objectives and is managed by line managers. | C. The organization bases its action on regular reviews, in terms of skills, knowledge, understanding and values, the development needs of its managers and management teams, both short and long-term. | C. The organization makes available resources to allow all managers, and others with management potential, to have their development needs identified and met. | C. Decisions on Management Development activity are based upon high quality information supplied to and received from line managers across the organization. | C. The organization bases its actions upon the accepted, common approach to the auditing of the costs and benefits of Management Development. |
| D. Management Development activity across the organization is integrated and coherent and meets declared organizational objectives. | D. The organization aligns and integrates its management skills, knowledge, understanding and values through a continuous process to meet declared organizational objectives. | D. Management Development activity realizes all available managerial potential and aligns and integrates it with declared organizational objectives. | D. Information is used to optimize the quality and cost effectiveness of Management Development provision to deliver the staff the organization needs in the short and long term. | D. The organization obtains optimal value for money in all Management Development activity taking account of costs, short-term benefits to individuals and the organization to meeting declared organizational objectives. |

*Source: NHS Training Division*

must be recognized as a natural and essential part of any manager's job. But the lead must come from the top.

The traditional view is that the organization need not concern itself with management development. The natural process of selection and the pressure of competition will ensure the survival of the fittest. Managers, in fact, are born not made. Cream rises to the top (but then so does scum).

The reaction to this was summed up in Humble's (1963) phrase, 'programmitis and crown princes'. Management development was seen in its infancy as a mechanical process using management inventories, multicoloured replacement charts, 'Cook's tours' for newly recruited graduates, detailed job rotation programmes, elaborate points schemes to appraise personal characteristics, and endless series of formal courses.

The true role of the organization in management development lies somewhere between these two extremes. On the one hand, it is not enough, in conditions of rapid growth (when they exist) and change, to leave everything to chance — to trial and error. On the other hand, elaborate management development programmes cannot successfully be imposed on the organization. As Peter Drucker wisely said many years ago (1955): 'Development is always self-development. Nothing could be more absurd than for the enterprise to assume responsibility for the development of a man. The responsibility rests with the individual, his abilities, his efforts.'

But he went on to say:

> Every manager in a business has the opportunity to encourage individual self-development or to stifle it, to direct it or to misdirect it. He (sic) should be specifically assigned the responsibility for helping all men working with him to focus, direct and apply their self-development efforts productively. And every company can provide systematic development challenges to its managers.

Executive ability is eventually something which individuals must develop for themselves while carrying out their normal duties. But they will do this much better if they are given encouragement, guidance and opportunities by their company and managers. In McGregor's (1960) phrase: managers are grown — they are neither born nor made. The role of the company is to provide conditions favourable to faster growth. And these conditions are very much part of the environment and organization climate of the company and the management style of the chief executive. The latter has the ultimate responsibility for management development. As McGregor wrote:

> The job environment of the individual is the most important variable affecting his development. Unless that environment is conducive to his (sic) growth, none of the other things we do to him or for him will be effective. This is why the 'agricultural' approach to management development is preferable to the 'manufacturing' approach. The latter leads, among other things, to the unrealistic expectation that we can create and develop managers in the classroom.

It is remarkable that today some people are still reciting these well-established principles as if they had just discovered them.

## Personal development plans

Managers must therefore take the main responsibility for their own development. The organization can help and the manager's boss must accept some responsibility for encouraging self-development and providing guidance as necessary. But individuals should be expected to draw up their own personal development plans (see also Chapter 27), the content of which would be based on answers to the following questions:

- What knowledge and/or skills do you intend to gain? and/or
- What levels of competence are you planning to achieve?
- What are your learning objectives? These should be set out in the form of definitions of the areas in which your performance will improve and/or what new things you will be able to do after the learning programme.
- How are you going to achieve your objectives? What tasks, projects, exercises or reading will you do? What educational or training courses would you like to attend? The development plan should be broken down into defined phases and specific learning events should be itemized. The duration of each phase and the total length of the programme should be set out together with the costs, if any.
- What resources will you need in the form of computer-based training material, books, videos, individual coaching, mentoring etc?
- What evidence will you show to demonstrate your learning? What criteria will be used to ensure that this evidence is satisfactory?

## *Role of the personnel/management development specialist*

Management development is not a separate activity to be handed over to a specialist and forgotten or ignored. The success of management development depends upon the degree to which it is recognized as an important aspect of the business strategy — a key organizational process aimed at delivering results. All levels of management must therefore be committed to it. The development of their staff must be recognized as a natural and essential part of any manager's job and one of the key criteria upon which their performance as managers will be judged. But the lead must come from the top.

However, personnel/management development specialists still have a number of important roles. They:

- interpret the needs of the business and advise on how management development strategies can play their part in meeting these needs
- act as advocates of the significance of management development as a business-led activity
- make proposals on formal and informal approaches to management development
- develop in conjunction with line management competence frameworks which can be used as the basis for management development
- provide guidance to managers on how to carry out their developmental activities
- provide help and encouragement to managers in preparing and pursuing their personal development plans — including advice on acquiring NVQ or academic qualifications
- provide the learning material managers need to achieve their learning objectives
- act as tutors or mentors to individual managers or groups of managers as required
- advise on the use and choice of external management education programmes
- facilitate action learning projects
- plan and conduct development centres as described at the end of this chapter
- plan and conduct other formal learning events with the help of external providers as required.

## The basis of management development

Management development should be regarded as a range of related activities rather than an all-embracing programme. The use of the word 'programme' to describe the process smacks too much of a mechanistic approach.

This does not imply that some systematization is not necessary; first, because many managers have to operate in more or less routine situations and have to be developed accordingly, and secondly, because organizations will not continue to thrive if they simply react to events. There must be an understanding of the approaches that can be used both to develop managers and also to assess existing managerial resources and how they meet the needs of the enterprise. And plans must be made for the development of those resources by selecting the best of the methods available. But this should not be seen as a 'programme' consisting of a comprehensive, highly integrated and rigidly applied range of management training and development techniques.

The management development activities required depend on the organization: its technology, its environment and its philosophy. A traditional bureaucratic/mechanistic type of organization may be inclined to adopt the programmed routine approach, complete with a wide range of courses, inventories, replacement charts, career plans and results-orientated review systems. An innovative and organic type of organization may rightly dispense with all these mechanisms. Its approach would be to provide its managers with the opportunities, challenge and guidance they require, seizing the chance to give people extra responsibilities, and ensuring that they receive the coaching and encouragement they need. There may be no replacement charts, inventories or formal appraisal schemes, but people know how they stand, where they can go and how to get there.

## Approaches to management development

It has often been said that managers learn to manage by managing — in other words, 'experience is the best teacher'. This is largely true, but some people learn much better than others. After all, a manager with ten years' experience may have had no more than one year's experience repeated ten times.

Differences in the ability to learn arise because some managers are naturally more capable or more highly motivated than others, while some will have had the benefit of the guidance and help of an effective boss who is fully aware of his or her responsibilities for developing managers. The saying quoted above could be expanded to read: 'Managers learn to manage by managing under the guidance of a good manager.' The operative word in this statement is 'good'. Some managers are better at developing people than others, and one of the aims of management development is to get all managers to recognize that developing their staff is an important part of their job. And for senior managers to say that people do not learn because they are not that way inclined, and to leave it at that, is to neglect one of their key responsibilities — to improve the performance of the organization by doing whatever is practical to improve the effectiveness and potential of the managers.

To argue that managers learn best 'on the job' should not lead to the conclusion that managers are best left entirely to their own devices or that management development should be a haphazard process. The organization should try to evolve a philosophy of management development which ensures that consistent and deliberate interventions are made to improve managerial learning. Revans (1989) wants to take management development back into the reality of management and out of the classroom, but even he believes that deliberate attempts to foster the learning process through 'action learning' (see Appendix D) are necessary.

It is possible to distinguish between formal and informal approaches to management development, as described below.

## Formal approaches to management development

The formal approaches to management development include:

- development on the job through coaching, counselling, monitoring and feedback by managers on a continuous basis associated with the use of performance management processes to identify and satisfy development needs, and with mentoring
- development through work experience, which includes job rotation, job enlargement, taking part in project teams or task groups, 'action learning', and secondment outside the organization
- formal training by means of internal or external courses
- structured self-development by following self-managed learning programmes agreed as a personal development plan or learning contract with the manager or a management development adviser — these may include guided reading or the deliberate extension of knowledge or acquisition of new skills on the job.

The formal approaches to management development are based on the identification of development needs through performance management or a development centre. The approach may be structured around a list of generic or core competences which have been defined as being appropriate for managers in the organization.

## *Informal approaches to management development*

Informal approaches to management development make use of the learning experiences which managers meet during the course of their everyday work. Managers are learning every time they are confronted with an unusual problem, an unfamiliar task or a move to a different job. They then have to evolve new ways of dealing with the situation. They will learn if they analyse what they did to determine how and why it contributed to its success or failure. This retrospective or reflective learning will be effective if managers can apply it successfully in the future.

This is potentially the most powerful form of learning. The question is: can anything be done to help managers make the best use of their experience? This type of 'experiential' learning comes naturally to some managers. They seem to absorb, unconsciously and by some process of osmosis, the lessons from their experience, although in fact they have probably developed a capacity for almost instantaneous analysis, which they store in their mental databank and which they can retrieve whenever necessary.

Ordinary mortals, however, either find it difficult to do this sort of analysis or do not recognize the need. This is where semi-formal approaches can be used to encourage and help managers to learn more effectively. These approaches include:

● emphasizing self-assessment and the identification of development needs by getting managers to assess their own performance against agreed objectives and analyse the factors that contributed to effective or less effective performance — this can be provided through performance management
● getting managers to produce their own personal development plans or self-managed learning programmes
● encouraging managers to discuss their own problems and opportunities with their bosses, colleagues or mentors in order to establish for themselves what they need to learn or be able to do.

## An integrated approach to management development

An integrated approach to management development will make

judicious use of both the formal and informal methods as described above. There are five governing principles:

- *The reality of management* — the approach to management develop-ment should avoid making simplistic assumptions on what man-agers need to know or do, based on the classical analysis of management as the processes of planning, organizing, directing and controlling. In reality managerial work is relatively disorganized and fragmented, and this is why many practising managers reject the facile solutions suggested by some formal management training programmes. As Kanter (1989) has said: 'Managerial work is undergoing such enormous and rapid change that many managers are reinventing their profession as they go.'

- *Relevance* — it is too easy to assume that all managers need to know about such nostrums as quantitative analysis, strategic planning, balance sheet analysis, zero-based budgeting, etc. These can be useful but they may not be what managers really need. Manage-ment development processes must be related to the needs of par-ticular managers in specific jobs and these processes may or may not include techniques such as those listed above. Those needs should include not only what managers should know now but also what they should know and be able to do in the future, if they have the potential. Thus, management development may include 'broadening programmes' aimed at giving managers an under-standing of the wider, strategic issues which will be relevant at higher levels in the organization.

- *Self-development* — managers need to be encouraged to develop themselves and helped to do so. Performance management will aim to provide this guidance.

- *Experiential learning* — if learning can be described as the modi-fication of behaviour through experience then the principal method by which managers can be equipped is by providing them with the right variety of experience, in good time, in the course of their careers, and by helping them to learn from that experience — action learning is a method of achieving this.

- *Formal training* — courses can supplement but can never replace experience and they must be carefully timed and selected or designed to meet particular needs.

## Competence-based management development

Competence-based management development uses competence

frameworks, maps or profiles (see Chapter 11) as a means of identifying and expressing development needs and pointing the way to self-managed learning programmes or the provision of learning opportunities by the organization.

Competence-based management development may concentrate on a limited number of core generic or competences which the organization has decided will be an essential part of the equipment of their managers if they are going to take the organization forward in line with its strategic plans. For example:

- *strategic capability* to understand the changing business environment, opportunities for product-market development, competitive challenges and the strengths and weaknesses of their own organization in order to identify optimum strategic responses
- *change management capability* to identify change needs, plan change programmes and persuade others to participate willingly in the implementation of change
- *team management capability* to get diverse groups of people from different disciplines to work well together
- *relationship management* to network effectively with others to share information and pool resources to achieve common objectives
- *international management* to be capable of managing across international frontiers working well with people of other nationalities.

## Development centres

The aim of development centres is to help participants build up an awareness of the competences their job requires and to construct their own personnel development plans to improve their performance in the present job and to enhance their careers.

Like assessment centres (see Chapter 24) development centres are built around definitions of competence requirements. Unlike assessment centres, however, development centres look ahead at the competences needed in the future. The other significant difference between a development centre and an assessment centre is that in the latter case the organization 'owns' the results for selection or promotion purposes, while in the former case the results are owned by the individual as the basis for self-managed learning.

Development centres are an event, not a physical location. The activities of the centre offer participants the opportunity to examine and understand the competences they require now and in the future.

Because 'behaviour predicts behaviour' the activities of the centre need to offer opportunities for competences to be observed in practice. Simulations of various kinds are therefore important features — these are a combination of case studies and role playing designed to obtain the maximum amount of realism. Participants are put into the position of practising behaviour in conditions very similar to those they will meet in the course of their every day work.

An important part of the centre's activities will be feedback reviews, counselling and coaching sessions conducted by the directing staff, which will consist of full-time tutors and line managers who have been given special training in the techniques required.

The stages of a typical development centre as described by Hall and Norris (1991) are:

*Prior to the centre* delegates assess themselves against defined competences

*Day 1*

- delegates test their pre-centre work with other delegates
- individual task
- structured self-insight
- business simulation

*Day 2*

- team roles questionnaire
- personal profiles questionnaire
- further counselling sessions and self-assessment procedures

*Day 3*

- numerical reasoning tests
- feedback on questionnaire
- counselling on personal development plans
- review of key points and findings.

# 30

# Career Management — Management Succession and Career Planning

## Definitions

Career management consists of the processes of career planning and management succession.

Career planning shapes the progression of individuals within an organization in accordance with assessments of organizational needs and the performance, potential and preferences of individual members of the enterprise.

Management succession planning takes place to ensure that, as far as possible, the organization has the managers it requires to meet future business needs.

## Overall aims

Career management has three overall aims:

1. To ensure that the organization's needs for management succession are satisfied.
2. To provide men and women of promise with a sequence of training and experience that will equip them for whatever level of responsibility they have the ability to reach.
3. To give individuals with potential the guidance and encouragement they need if they are to fulfil their potential and achieve a successful career with the organization in tune with their talents and aspirations.

## The process of career management

The process of career management is illustrated in Figure 30.1. The key aspects of this process are discussed below.

### Career dynamics and analysis

Career dynamics describes how career progression takes place — the ways in which people move through their careers either upwards through promotion or by enlarging or enriching their roles to take on greater responsibilities or make more use of their skills and capacities. Career analysis examines the characteristics of job ladders and families.

### Career dynamics

Figure 30.2 illustrates the ways in which career progression proceeds in the following stages:

- expanding at the start of a career, when new skills are being acquired, knowledge is growing rapidly, competences are developing quickly and aspirations and inclinations are being clarified
- establishing the career path, when skills and knowledge gained in the expanding stage are being applied, tested, modified and consolidated with experience, when full levels of competence have been achieved and when aspirations are confirmed or amended
- maturing when individuals are well established on their career path and proceed along it according to their motivation, abilities and opportunities.

Through each of these stages people develop and progress at different rates. This means that at the maturing stage they either continue to grow, 'plateau-out' (although still doing useful work), or stagnate and decline.

The study of career dynamics is a necessary prelude to the formulation of career management policies and the preparation of management succession plans. The study is carried out by analysing the progression of individuals within an organization — function by function — in relation to assessments of performance, as illustrated in Figure 30.3. This can be used to trace typical career progressions in relation to performance assessment and to compare actuals with the

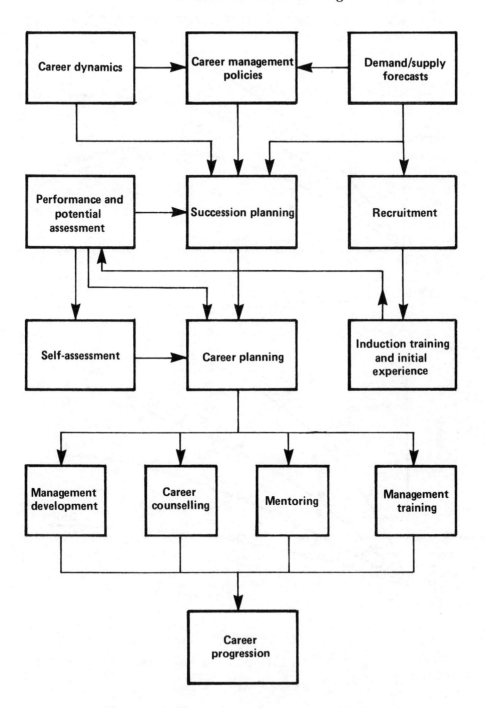

**Figure 30.1** The process of career management

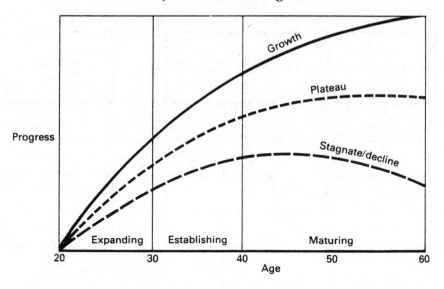

**Figure 30.2** Career progression curves

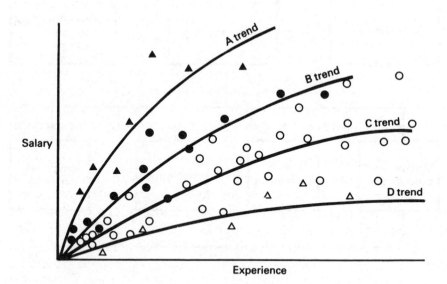

**Figure 30.3** Progress analysis

model that can be developed from the empirically determined trend lines. An analysis of career dynamics can also point the way towards any actions required to alter career path trends for promising individuals by means of specific career management actions. Finally, the analysis reveals anomalies such as over-promotions (victims of the Peter Principle who have been promoted to the level of their own incompetence) or problems of managers who are stagnating or have gone over the hill.

## Job ladders and families

A job ladder consists of the steps individuals can take as they progress through their career in a job family. A job family consists of jobs where the nature of the work is essentially the same although there may be significant differences in the level of work undertaken. Such occupations as scientists, engineers, accountants and personnel specialists could be grouped into job families.

Job family analysis starts by dividing the job population into job families of basically similar jobs. At the same time, the jobs which will need to be treated individually should be identified.

The next step is to analyze each family of jobs to establish the extent to which work is carried out at different levels. Where this is the case, the levels within each family are analysed and described in terms which differentiate them clearly and in the language of the family, thus creating a job ladder. These descriptions can usefully be made in competence terms.

Some job families are more diverse than others and it may be useful to divide the broad family of, say professional engineers, into homogeneous groups of, for example, design engineers, development engineers, and project engineers. A set of parallel ladders could then be developed. This broad family approach is more appropriate when career development is not simply up a series of parallel ladders but includes diagonal or even horizontal moves as people gain experience in a variety of roles. As Pritchard and Murlis (1992) put it: 'What is wanted is a wide staircase or scrambling net which can accommodate diversity of roles and career paths between them.'

The information gained from this analysis can be used for career planning purposes and to establish the attributes and competences required at each level. It can also be used to evaluate the jobs and develop pay structures.

## Career management policies

Career management policies cover the areas discussed below.

### Make or buy decisions

The organization needs to decide on the extent to which it:

- makes or grows its own managers (a promotion from within policy)
- recruits or buys-in deliberately from outside (bringing 'fresh blood' into the organization) which means adopting a policy that accepts a reasonable amount of wastage and even takes steps in good time to encourage people to develop their careers elsewhere if they are in danger of stagnating
- will have to buy-in talent from outside because of future shortfalls in the availability of managers, as revealed by demand and supply forecasts.

A make or buy policy may be expressed as follows: 'We plan to fill about 80 per cent of our management vacancies from within the organization. The remaining 20 per cent we expect to recruit from outside.'

### Short or long-term policies

Policies for determining the time scale for investing in careers fall into one or other of the following categories:

- *Short-term performance.* Employers who adopt, consciously or unconsciously, this policy, concentrate on the 'here and now'. They recruit and train high performers who will be good at their present job and are rewarded accordingly. If they are really good, they will be promoted — there are plenty of opportunities — and the enterprise will get what it wants. Deliberately to train managers for a future that may never happen is considered a waste of time. Top managers in this type of organization may well say: 'If we can get good people to do good work, the future will take care of itself. They'll prove and mature their abilities in their present job and be ready and indeed eager to take on extra responsibilities when the occasion arises. If there's no one around at the time, then we'll buy in someone from outside — no problem!'
- *Long-term plans.* Employers who believe in long-term career

planning develop highly structured approaches to career management. They go in for elaborate reviews of performance and potential, assessment centres to identify talent or confirm that it is there, 'high-flyer' schemes, and planned job moves in line with a predetermined programme.

- *Long-term flexibility.* Employers who follow this policy appreciate that they must concentrate on getting good performance now, and that in doing so they will, to a considerable extent, be preparing people for advancement. To this extent, they adopt the same attitude as short-term employers. However, they also recognize that potential should be assessed and developed by training which is not job-specific and by deliberately broadening experience through job rotation or the redirection of career paths. This approach avoids the possible short-sightedness of the here-and-now policy and the rigidity and, often, lack of realism, inherent in the structured system. In conditions of rapid development and change, how far is it actually possible to plan careers over the long term? The answer must be, to a very limited extent, except in a static organization which has implicitly recognized that it provides a 'cradle-to-grave' career for people who, in general, are willing to wait for 'Buggins' turn' — and there are fewer and fewer organizations setting out to provide 'jobs for life' nowadays.

As a generalization, the short-term system is likely to be more common in smallish, rapidly growing, 'organic' businesses where form follows function and the organization is fluid and flexible. The longer-term system is more prevalent in larger, bureaucratic, 'mechanistic' types of organization, where accurate forecasts of future needs can be made, significant changes in skill requirements are not likely to take place and there is a steady flow, according to easily assessed performance, up the promotion ladder. A longer-term flexibility approach is likely to be pursued by the majority of organizations who fall into neither of the other two categories, and this is probably the best approach in most circumstances.

## Specialists or generalists

Career management policies should cover the extent to which the organization is concerned about developing better and better specialists (broadly in line with the short-term approach) or whether it attaches equal, or even more, importance to developing the appropriate number of generalists who are capable of moving into general management. Obviously, all organizations have a mix of these two categories, but it may be a matter of policy to create a dual career structure with separate career ladders for pure specialists, who would be rewarded in accordance with their technical contribution and not in line with their place in a management grade hierarchy. There is no universal law that says a top-rate specialist who is not a manager and does not want to be one, must be paid less than someone who happens to have the skills and inclinations to take him or her along the management route.

Clearly, the policy depends on the type of organization, especially its technology and the extent to which it is either a hierarchy of managers and support staff with a few specialists on the side, or a hi-tech, research-based operation where the scientist and development engineers rule.

## Dealing with the 'plateaued' manager

Inevitably, the great majority of managers will eventually 'plateau-out' in their careers within an organization and this is more likely to happen in a flatter 'de-layered' organization where middle management jobs have been 'stripped out' as a result of a re-organization or business process re-engineering programme. Such activities may result in redundancies, which replace the problem of coming to a dead end in an organization with another problem. Some of those that remain may be reconciled to the end of the 'rat race' but continue to work effectively. Others will become bored and frustrated, especially rising stars on the wane. These may no longer be productive and can become positively disruptive. Steps must be taken either to reshape their careers so that they still have challenging work at the same level, even if this does not involve promotion up the hierarchy. Others may have to be encouraged to start new careers elsewhere. In either of these cases the organization should provide career advice, possibly through 'outplacement' consultants who provide a counselling service.

## Demand and supply forecasts

Demand and supply forecasts are provided by the use of human resource planning and modelling techniques (see Chapter 23). In larger organizations, modelling is a particularly fruitful method to use because it does allow for sensitivity analysis of the impact of different assumptions about the future (answering 'what if?' questions).

Expert systems, as described in Chapter 46, can also be used where this is an extensive database on flows, attribute requirements (person specifications), and performance and potential assessments. Such systems can establish relationships between the opportunities and the personal attributes they demand so that careers advisers can take a set of personal attributes and identify the most appropriate available opportunities. At the career planning stage, they can also identify people with the correct abilities and skills for particular jobs and provide information on the career management programmes required to ensure that attributes and jobs are matched and careers progress at an appropriate rate. Career management systems such as ExecuGROW (Control Data) have been specially developed for this purpose.

There is a limit, however, to sophistication. There are so many variables and unpredictable changes in both supply and demand factors that it may be possible to conduct only an annual check to see what the relationship is between the numbers of managers who will definitely retire over the next four or five years and the numbers at the next level who have the potential to succeed them. If this comparison reveals a serious unbalance, then steps can be taken to reduce or even eliminate the deficit or to consider other types of deployment for those who are unlikely to progress. This comparison is represented graphically in Figure 30.4, in which the two hypothetical examples illustrate a surplus situation (a) and a deficit situation (b).

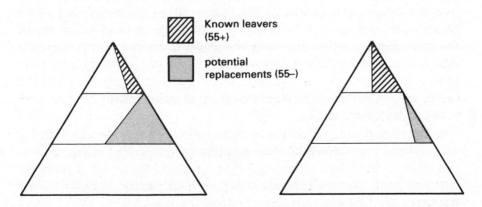

**Figure 30.4** Demand and supply models

## Succession planning

The aim of management succession planning is to ensure that, as far as possible, suitable managers are available to fill vacancies created by promotion, retirement, death, leaving, or transfer. It also aims to ensure that a cadre of managers is available to fill the new appointments that may be established in the future.

The information for management succession planning comes from organization reviews and demand-and-supply forecasts. The succession plans will be influenced by the career dynamics of the organization and also by the performance and potential assessments (see below), which provide information, often of limited validity, on who is ready now and in the future to fill projected vacancies. This information needs to be recorded so that decisions can be made on promotions and replacements, and training or additional experience arranged for those with potential or who are earmarked for promotion.

The records need not be elaborate. In practice, complex inventories and detailed succession charts replete with colour codes and other symbols are a waste of time, except in the largest and most bureaucratic organizations. All the information required can be recorded on a simple management succession schedule such as the one illustrated in Figure 30.5.

A computerized personnel information system, as described in Chapter 46, can, with the help of competence modelling techniques, store inventories of the skills, competences and experience of individual employees together with records of their performance and potential assessments. Lists of attributes for key jobs can also be stored, and this information can be linked to the other data mentioned above to provide guidance on who is available to fill present or future vacancies and on any career plans needed to ensure that potential is realized.

## Performance and potential assessment

The aim of performance and potential assessment is to identify training and development needs, provide guidance on possible directions in which an individual's career might go, and indicate who has potential for promotion. This information can be obtained from performance management processes, as described in Chapter 13.

The assessment of potential can be carried out formally by managers

| MANAGEMENT SUCCESSION SCHEDULE | | | | | | | Department | | | | Director/Manager | | |
|---|---|---|---|---|---|---|---|---|---|---|---|---|---|
| Present Managerial and Supervisory Staff | | | | | | | | | | | Possible successors | | |
| Name | Position | Age | Date due for replacement | Rating | | If promotable, indicate what position and when | | | | | Names (1st and 2nd choice) | Positions | When ready |
| | | | | Performance | Potential | | | | | | | | |
| | | | | | | | | | | | | | |
| | | | | | | | | | | | | | |
| | | | | | | | | | | | | | |
| | | | | | | | | | | | | | |
| | | | | | | | | | | | | | |
| | | | | | | | | | | | | | |

**Figure 30.5** Management succession schedule

following a performance review. They may be asked to identify managers who have very high potential, some potential or no potential at all. They may even be asked to indicate when their managers will be ready for promotion and how far they are likely to get. The problem with this sort of assessment is that the assessors find it difficult to forecast the future for the people they are reviewing — good performance in the current job does not guarantee that individuals will be able to cope with wider responsibilities, especially if this involves moving into general management. And managers may not necessarily be aware of the qualities required for longer-term promotion. But the organization does need information on those with potential and assessors should be encouraged in their comments section at least to indicate that this is someone who is not only performing well in the present job but may perform well in higher-level jobs. This information can identify those who may be exposed to assessment or development centres which can be used to establish potential and discuss career plans. (Assessment and development centres are described in Chapters 24 and 29 respectively).

## Recruitment

Career management means taking into account the fact that the organization will inevitably need to recruit new managers, who will then have to prove themselves while gaining their initial experience and undergoing induction training. As soon as they have been with the company long enough to show what they can do and where they might go, their performance and potential can be assessed and they can be fed into the career management system.

## Career planning

### *The process of career planning*

Career planning is the key process in career management. It uses all the information provided by the organization's assessments of requirements, the assessments of performance and potential and the management succession plans, and translates it into the form of individual career development programmes and general arrangements for management development, career counselling, mentoring and management training.

## *Career progression — the competence band approach*

It is possible to define career progression in terms of the competences required by individuals to carry out work at progressive levels of responsibility or contribution. These levels can be described as competence bands.

Competences would be defined as the attributes and behavioural characteristics needed to perform effectively at each discrete level in a job family as described earlier in this chapter. The number of levels would vary according to the range of competences required in a particular job family. For each band, the experience and training needed to achieve the competence level would be defined.

These definitions would provide a career map incorporating 'aiming points' for individuals, who would be made aware of the competence levels they must reach in order to achieve progress in their careers. This would help them to plan their own development, although support and guidance should be provided by their managers, personnel specialists and, if they exist, management development advisers or mentors (the use of mentors is discussed in Appendix D). The provision of additional experience and training could be arranged as appropriate, but it would be important to clarify what individual employees need to do for themselves if they want to progress within the organization.

The advantage of this approach is that people are provided with aiming points and an understanding of what they need to do to reach them. One of the major causes of frustration and job dissatisfaction is the absence of this information.

A competence band career development approach can be linked to a pay curve salary structure, as described in Chapter 33, thus providing a fully integrated approach to career and reward management which recognizes the need to join these together. The operation of a competence band career progression system is illustrated in Figure 30.6.

## *Career planning is for core managers as well as high-flyers*

The philosophy upon which career plans are based refers not only to advancing careers to meet organizational and individual requirements, but also to the need to maximize the potential of the people in the organization in terms of productivity and satisfaction under conditions of change, when development does not necessarily mean promotion. An obsession with high-flyers and 'fast-tracking' may

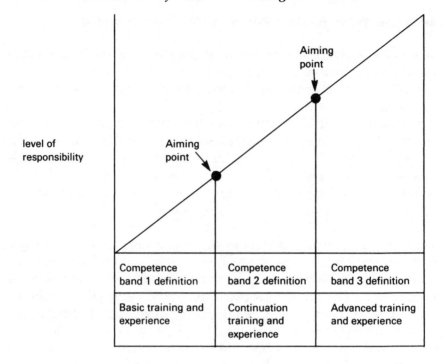

**Figure 30.6** Competence band career progression system

lead to a neglect of the majority of employees, who also need to be motivated, encouraged and given every opportunity to use their skills and abilities.

## *Career planning is for individuals as well as the organization*

Career planning procedures are always based on what the organization needs. But they have to recognize that organizational needs will not be satisfied if individual needs are neglected. Career planning has to be concerned with the management of diversity.

Career plans must therefore recognize that:

- members of the organization should receive recognition as individuals with unique needs, wants, and abilities
- individuals are more motivated by an organization which responds to their aspirations and needs
- individuals can grow, change and seek new directions if they are given the right opportunities, encouragement and guidance.

## Career planning techniques

Career planning uses all the information generated by the succession plans, performance, and potential assessments and self-assessments, to develop programmes and procedures which are designed to implement career management policies, achieve succession planning objectives and generally improve motivation, commitment and performance. The procedures used are those concerned with:

- training and management development, as described in Chapters 28 and 29
- mentoring as described in Appendix D
- career counselling as described in the following section.

In addition, career planning procedures may cater for the rising stars by 'fast-tracking' them, that is, deliberately accelerating promotion and giving them opportunities to display and enlarge their talents. But these procedures should pay just as much, if not more, attention to those managers who are following the middle route of steady, albeit unspectacular, progression.

## Career counselling

Performance management processes, as described in Chapter 13 should provide for counselling sessions between individuals and their managers. These sessions should give the former the opportunity to discuss their aspirations and the latter the chance to comment on them — helpfully — and, at a later stage, to put forward specific career development proposals to be fed into the overall career management programme.

Development centres as described in Chapter 29 can provide a valuable vehicle for career counselling and planning.

Career counselling is, however, a skilled job and the immediate boss is not always the best person to do it, although all managers should be trained in the techniques involved. Some large organizations have appointed specialists whose sole job is to provide a career counselling service to back up the efforts of line managers and to advise on what needs to be done for individuals or, more generally, by the organization as a whole. Mentoring can also be used for this purpose.

The individuals concerned may need an increased level of self-awareness, better access to information about career opportunities and improved decision-making skills.

## Career management in delayered organizations

The implications of 'delayering', ie removing layers of management and supervision, thus creating a flatter organization, is that opportunities for career progression upwards through the hierarchy may be significantly reduced. A study carried out by the Roffey Park Management Institute (Holbeche, 1994) into career development in flatter organizations estimated that about 95 per cent of UK based organizations have undertaken delayering exercises or are about to do so. This is making a major contribution to the demise of the 'job for life' notion, and employees are having to adjust their expectations about career development within their organization and recognize that they no longer have well defined career paths through promotion. Holbeche suggests that:

> Career management in flatter structures calls for an approach which explicitly takes into account both organizational needs and employee interests. It will encompass recruitment, personal development plans, international assignments, development positions, career bridges, lateral moves and support for employees who want to develop. It calls for creativity in identifying ways to provide development opportunities and enhance employee loyalty.

# Part VII
# Employee Reward

*Employee reward processes and practices are concerned with designing, implementing and maintaining reward systems which are geared to the improvement of organizational team and individual performance. This aspect of personnel management used to be called salary administration, but this is now regarded as a limited description of one aspect of the whole subject of remuneration. The alternative phrase 'compensation management' is used in the US and is gaining recognition in the UK. It is believed in some quarters that this term represents a more up-to-date approach to creating and managing pay systems, but the use of the word 'compensation' seems to imply that work is an unpleasant necessity which people have to be compensated for doing rather than spending their time more rewardingly elsewhere. The processes and systems described in this part are often referred to as 'reward management'.*

*This part describes employee reward systems in general and then considers the detailed components of such systems.*

# 31

# Employee Reward Systems

## Introduction

Employee reward is about how people are rewarded in accordance with their value to an organization. It is concerned with both financial and non-financial rewards and embraces the philosophies, strategies, policies, plans and processes used by organizations to develop and maintain reward systems. This chapter:

- describes the concept of a reward system in terms of its components, elements and aims
- discusses the economic and other factors that determine pay levels
- examines developments in thinking about employee reward as expressed by the 'new pay' philosophy
- discusses the foundations for employee reward systems provided by reward philosophies, strategies and policies
- reviews the current and future reward management scene.

## The employee reward system

An employee reward system consists of an organization's integrated policies, processes and practices for rewarding its employees in accordance with their contribution, skill and competence and their market worth. It is developed within the framework of the organization's reward philosophy, strategies and policies and contains arrangements in the form of processes, practices, structures, and procedures which will provide and maintain appropriate types and levels of pay, benefits and other forms of reward.

## Components of a reward system

A reward system consists of financial rewards (fixed and variable pay) and employee benefits, which together comprise total remuneration. The system also incorporates non-financial rewards (recognition, praise, achievement, responsibility and personal growth) and, in many cases, performance management processes.

# The elements of employee reward

The elements of an employee reward system are described below.

## Base pay

Base or basic pay is the fixed salary or wage which constitutes the rate for the job. For manual workers it may be referred to as time or day rate. It may provide the platform for determining additional payments related to performance, competence or skill. It may also govern pension entitlements and life insurance when they are related to pay. The basic levels of pay for jobs reflect both internal and external relativities. The internal relativities may be measured by some form of job evaluation which places jobs in a hierarchy (although the trend now is to play down the notion of hierarchy in the new process-based organizations). External relativities are assessed by tracking market rates. Alternatively, levels of pay may be agreed through negotiation (collective bargaining with trade unions) or by individual agreements. The base rate for a job is sometimes regarded as the rate for a competent or skilled person in a job. This rate may be varied in a skill-based or competence-based system according to the individual's skill or competence.

Levels of pay may be based on long-standing structures which were first created in the mists of time and have been updated since then in response to movements in market rates and inflation and through negotiations. In many organizations pay levels evolve — they are not planned or maintained systematically. Rates are fixed by managerial judgement of what is required to recruit and retain people. They may be adjusted in response to individual or collective pressures for increases or upgradings. This evolutionary and *ad hoc* process can result in a chaotic and illogical pay structure which is inequitable, which leads to inconsistent and unfair pay decisions and is difficult to understand, expensive to maintain and the cause of dissatisfaction and demotivation. Pay levels are affected by economic factors as discussed later in this chapter and by negotiations with trade unions which will influence levels of pay in accordance with whatever bargaining power they possess.

Base pay may be expressed as an annual, weekly or hourly rate and it may be adjusted to reflect increases in the cost of living or market rates by the organization unilaterally or by agreement with a trade union. Performance skill-based or competence-related pay increases may be added to or 'consolidated' into the basic rate. Similarly, consolidated increases may be given based on time in the grade. This is a fixed incremental pay system, which is often associated with a pay spine as described in Chapter 33. But some companies pay non-consolidated performance-related cash bonuses.

## Additions to base pay

Additional financial rewards may be provided which are related to performance, skill, competence or experience. Special allowances may also be paid. If such payments are not consolidated into base pay they can be described as 'variable pay'. Variable pay is sometimes defined as 'pay at risk,' as in the CBI/Wyatt survey (1993). For example, the pay of sales representatives on a 'commission only' basis is entirely at risk. The main types of additional pay are:

- *Individual performance-related pay* in which increases to base pay or cash bonuses are determined by performance assessment and ratings (also known as merit pay)
- *Bonuses* — rewards for successful performance which are paid as lump sums related to the results obtained by individuals, teams or the organization.
- *Incentives* — payments linked to the achievement of previously set targets which are designed to motivate people to achieve higher levels of performance. The targets are usually quantified in such terms as output or sales.
- *Commission* — a special form of incentive in which payments to sales representatives are made on the basis of a percentage of the sales value they generate.
- *Service-related pay* — pay which increases by fixed increments on a scale or pay spine depending on service in the job. There may sometimes be scope for varying the rate of progression through the scale according to performance.

- *Skill-based pay* (sometimes called knowledge-based pay) — pay which varies according to the level of skill achieved by the individual.
- *Competence-related pay* — pay which varies according to the level of competence achieved by the individual.
- *Allowances* — these are elements of pay which are provided as a separate sum of money for such aspects of employment as overtime, shift working, call-outs and living in London or other large cities. London or large city allowances are sometimes consolidated and organizations which are simplifying their pay structure may 'buy out' the allowance and increase base pay accordingly.

## Total earnings

Total earnings are usually calculated as the sum of base pay and any additional payments. They constitute the amount of money paid into the bank or placed in an employee's pay packet. When explaining to individual employees how their pay package is built up it is necessary to break the total pay down into the different components listed above and indicate how, in their case, they have combined to produce the final sum they are receiving.

## Employee benefits

Employee benefits, also known as indirect pay, include pensions, sick pay, insurance cover and company cars. They comprise elements of remuneration given in addition to the various forms of cash pay and also include provisions for employees which are not strictly remuneration such as annual holidays.

## Total remuneration

Total remuneration is the value of all cash payments (total earnings) and benefits received by employees.

## Non-financial rewards

These include any rewards which focus on the needs people have to varying degrees for achievement, recognition, responsibility, influence and personal growth.

## Pay levels

Pay levels are the rates of pay for jobs as determined by reference to market rates, formal or informal job evaluation processes and, sometimes, collective bargaining.

## Pay structures

The pay structure of an organization defines the pay levels for individual jobs. These may be grouped into grades, to each of which is attached a pay range which allows scope for pay progression related to performance, skill, competence or time. Alternatively they may be placed on a pay spine as described in Chapter 33.

The elements of a reward system and their interrelationships are illustrated in Figure 31.1.

# General factors determining pay levels

Pay levels for jobs and individuals are determined by a combination of the following factors:

- *the external value of the job (external relativities)* — the market rates for jobs as influenced by economic factors operating within external labour markets as described below, these rates are assessed by means of market rate surveys
- *the internal value of the job (internal relativities)* — the comparative value of jobs in the internal labour market as assessed by formal or informal job evaluation processes
- *the value of the person* — the value attached to individuals as measured by formal or informal appraisal or performance management processes
- *the contribution of the individual or team* — rewards to individuals or teams related to performance, skill or competence
- *collective bargaining* — pay negotiations with trade unions.

# Economic factors affecting pay levels

## Labour markets

Like all other markets, the labour market has buyers (employers) and sellers (employees). It is in the external market that the economic

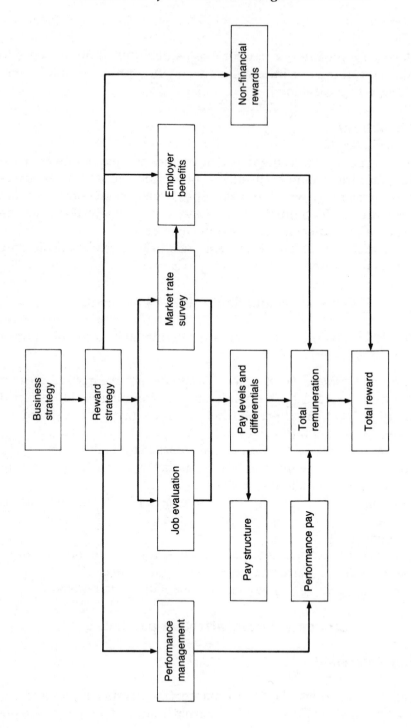

**Figure 31.1** The reward system

determinants of pay levels operate. In the internal labour market pay levels and relativities market may differ significantly between firms in spite of general external market pressures. These arise particularly when long-term relationships are usual, even though these are becoming less common. Pay progression related to length of service and an 'annuity' approach to pay increments (ie pay which goes up but does not come down, what economists call 'the sticky wage') may lead to higher internal rates. Pay in the internal market will also be affected by decisions on what individuals should be awarded for their particular contributions or specialised expertise, irrespective of the market rate for their job. But the relationship between internal and external rates will also depend on policy decisions within the firm on its levels of pay generally, or on the rates for specified occupations compared with 'the going rate', ie the market rate for comparable jobs. Within the external and internal labour markets the economic theories about pay are concerned with supply and demand, efficiency wage theory, human capital theory and agency theory.

## Supply and demand

Classical economic competitive theory states that pay levels in labour markets are determined by supply and demand considerations. Other things being equal, if the supply of labour exceeds the demand, pay levels go up; if the demand for labour exceeds the supply, pay goes down. Pay stabilises when demand equals supply at the 'market clearing' or 'market equilibrium wage'. This is sometimes known as the theory of equalizing differences. Classical theory, however, is based on the premises that 'other things are equal' and that a 'perfect market' for labour exists. In the real world, of course, other things are never equal and there is no such thing as a universally perfect market, that is, one in which everyone knows what the going rate is, there is free movement of labour within the market and there are no monopolistic or other forces interfering with the normal processes of supply and demand. The existence of internal markets means that individual firms exercise a good deal of discretion about how much they pay and how much attention they give to external market pressures.

## Efficiency wage theory

Efficiency wage theory proposes that firms will pay more than the market rate because they believe that high levels of pay will contribute to increases in productivity by motivating superior performance, attracting better candidates, reducing labour turnover and persuading workers that they are being treated fairly. This theory is also known as 'the economy of high wages'.

## Human capital theory

Human capital theory states that investment in people adds to their value to the firm. Individuals expect a return on their own investment and firms recognise that the increased value of their employees should be rewarded. Human capital theory encourages the use of skill-based or competence-related pay as a method of reward. It also underpins the concept of individual market worth which indicates that individuals have their own value in the marketplace which they acquire and increase through investments by their employer and themselves in gaining extra expertise and competence through training, development and experience. The market worth of individuals may be considerably higher than the market rate of their jobs, and if they are not rewarded accordingly they may market their talents elsewhere.

## Agency theory

Agency theory, or principal agent theory, in its purest form recognises that in most firms there is a separation between the owners (the principals) and the agents (the managers). However, the principals may not have complete control over their agents. The latter may therefore act in ways which are not fully revealed to their principals and which may not be in accordance with the wishes of those principals. This generates what economists call agency costs which arise from the difference between what might have been earned if the principals had been the managers, and the earnings achieved under the stewardship of the actual managers. To reduce these agency costs, the principals have to develop ways of monitoring and controlling the actions of their agents.

Agency theory as described above can be extended to the employment contract within firms. The employment relationship may be regarded as a contract between a principal (the employer) and an agent (the employee). The payment aspect of the contract is the method used by the principal to motivate the agent to perform work to the satisfaction of the employer. But according to this theory, the problem of ensuring that agents do what they are told remains. It is necessary to clear up ambiguities by setting objectives and monitoring performance to ensure that those objectives are achieved.

Agency theory also indicates that it is desirable to operate a system of incentives to motivate and reward acceptable behaviour. This process of 'incentive alignment' consists of paying for measurable results which are deemed to be in the best interests of the owners. Such incentive systems track outcomes in the shape of quantifiable indices of the firm's performance such as earnings per share rather than being concerned with the behaviour that led up to them. The theory is that if the incentives schemes for top managers are designed properly, those managers will out of self interest closely monitor performance throughout the organization.

## Aims of employee reward — the organization's requirements

A reward system expresses what the organization values and is prepared to pay for. It is governed by the need to reward the right things to get the right message across about what is important.

### *Overall aim*

The overall aim of employee reward is to support the attainment of the organization's strategic and shorter-term objectives by helping to ensure that it has the skilled, competent, committed and well-motivated workforce it needs.

### *Specific aims*

From the organization's point of view, the specific aims of employee reward are to:

- play a significant part in the communication of the organization's values, performance, standards and expectations
- encourage behaviour that will contribute to the achievement of the organization's objectives and reflect the 'balanced score card' of key performance drivers — two of the basic questions to be answered when developing reward systems are; 'What sort of behaviour do we want?' and 'How can reward processes promote that behaviour?'
- underpin organizational change programmes concerned with culture, process and structure

- support the realisation of the key values of the organization in such areas as quality, customer care, teamwork, innovation, flexibility and speed of response
- provide value for money — no reward initiative should be undertaken unless it has been established that it will add value, and no reward practice should be retained if it does not result in added value.

## Reward aims from the employee's point of view

From the employees' point of view the reward system should:

- treat them as stakeholders who have the right to be involved in the development of the reward policies that affect them
- meet their expectations that they will be treated equitably, fairly, and consistently in relation to the work they do and their contribution
- be transparent — they should know what the reward policies of the organization are and how they are affected by them.

## Achieving the aims

It is sometimes said that to achieve these aims an organization's pay practices should be 'internally equitable and externally competitive'. This is all right as far as it goes but it is not always easy to attain, and it presents a somewhat limited point of view. The first problem is that the goals of internal equity and external competitiveness are often hard to reconcile. The pressure of market forces may overcome internal equity considerations when people with scarce talents have to be recruited. On the other hand, a crude wish to be competitive may be inappropriate. As Schuster and Zingheim (1992) point out: 'The strategic view of competitive practices suggests that achieving competitive pay should be contingent upon providing a level of work quality, productivity, or performance which must justify pay levels that reflect expected reasonable goal performance'. In other words, competitive pay should be linked with competitive performance.

The aims of an employee reward system are best achieved if:

- reward strategies are developed as described later in this chapter which are aligned to the business strategies for financial performance, market share, product/market development, quality, customer focus and organizational development (cultural and structural change)

- reward policies are formulated as discussed later in this chapter which enable reward philosophies and strategies to be implemented consistently but are flexed in accordance with the changing needs of the business
- employees are valued according to their contribution, skill and competence
- the reward system is transparent and employees are treated as stakeholders who are entitled to make representations on any area of reward that affects their interests and who will be involved in the development of reward processes
- employee relations strategies are designed to build mutual trust and to develop a partnership approach which provides for increases in prosperity to be shared with all employees (not just the favoured few at the top)
- reward policies emphasise the need for equity and fairness while recognising that the ideal of internal equity may not be sustainable in full because of market pressures
- the maximum amount of responsibility is devolved to line managers to manage the reward system within their budgets and in accordance with broad policy guidelines
- there is a constant thrust to maximise the performance leverage of any money spent on pay
- reward initiatives are only taken if their interaction with other business and personnel policies is assessed, and an integrated approach is adopted to the development of mutually supportive processes.

## The new pay

When developing reward strategies and policies attention should be given to the philosophy of the 'new pay'. Lawler (1990) originated this phrase to reflect the need for an understanding of the organization's goals, values and culture and the challenges of a more competitive global economy when formulating reward policies. He advocated people-based as distinct from job-based pay — paying people according to their value in the market and in relation to their knowledge and skills. Lawler sees new pay as helping to achieve the individual and organizational behaviour that a company needs if its business goals are to be met. Pay systems must flow from the overall strategy and they can help to emphasise important objectives such as customer retention, customer satisfaction and product or service quality. Lawler's concept of the new pay was further developed by Schuster and Zingheim (1992) who stated that:

> The new pay view provides that organizations effectively use all elements of pay — direct pay (cash compensation) and indirect pay (benefits) — to help them form a partnership between the organization and its employees. By means of this partnership, employees can understand the goals of the organization, know where they fit in to those goals, become appropriately involved in decisions affecting them, and receive rewards to the extent the organization achieves those goals and to the extent they have assisted the organization to do so. New pay helps link the financial success of both the organization and its employees.

## Reward strategy

Reward strategy defines the intentions of the organization on how its reward policies and processes should be developed to meet business requirements. The fact that payroll costs can comprise 70 per cent or more of the total costs incurred by an organization explains the need to adopt a strategic approach to reward which ensures that added value is obtained from any investment in pay.

An effective reward strategy:

- is based on corporate values and beliefs
- flows from the business strategy but also contributes to it
- is driven by business needs and 'fits' the business strategy
- aligns organizational and individual competences
- is integrated with other personnel and development strategies
- is congruent with the internal and external environment of the organization — the content of the strategy will be contingent on those environments
- provides for the reward of results and behaviour that are consistent with key organizational goals, thus driving and supporting desired behaviour
- is linked to business performance, adopting a competitive strategy perspective
- is practical and implementable
- has been evolved in consultation with key stakeholders, taking full account of their views on what they believe is best for them — unless such account is taken, reward initiatives like performance pay can fail totally.

Reward strategy should be developed as an integrated part of the total personnel strategy of the organization. The aim should be to ensure that it will support initiatives in the fields of resourcing, development and the overall goals for improving organizational performance. The strategy should also take into account the employee relations climate and the processes for negotiating pay with trade unions.

## *Content of reward strategy*

The aspects of employee reward which may be regarded as key strategic issues include:

- competitive pay
- achieving a more equitable and definable pay system
- restructuring the pay system to take account of, indeed to underpin, organizational changes; for example, introducing broadbanding after a delayering exercise
- using pay as a lever for performance improvement and culture change
- devolution of pay decisions to line managers
- involvement of employees in reward matters
- developing teamwork
- increasing levels of competence and enlarging the skill base (support to multi-skilling)

## Reward policy

Reward policy provides guidelines for decision-making and action. It may include statements of guiding principles or common purposes. It addresses issues such as the following:

- *competitive pay* — the 'pay policy' or 'pay stance' of the organization indicates the extent to which it wants to be 'market-led', ie the relationship it wishes to maintain between its pay levels and market rates
- *internal equity* — the policy will indicate the degree to which internal equity is a prime consideration and the circumstances in which the need to be competitive may override the principle of internal equity
- *contingent pay* — the extent, if any, to which the firm believes that pay should vary according to performance, competence or skill
- *variable pay* — the extent to which it is believed that contingent pay should be at risk, ie, is not consolidated

- *individual or team reward* — the need for rewards to concentrate on individual or team performance
- *employee benefits* — the types and levels of employee benefits to be provided and the extent to which employees can choose the benefits they want
- *the total reward mix* — the mix of total rewards between base pay, variable pay and indirect pay (employee benefits) and the use of non-financial rewards, bearing in mind that there is always choice within a portfolio of reward practices
- *structure* — the extent to which the organization wants a hierarchical and relatively formal (narrow-banded structure) or one which is flexible and broad-banded
- *reward priorities* — the degree to which the organization wants to concentrate on 'piling the rewards high' for the relatively small number of key players, or recognises the need to provide rewards which will support the steady improvement of the many (in other words, who are the people likely to exert the most leverage on overall business performance who should be rewarded accordingly?)
- *differentials* — the levels of reward at the top of the organization compared with average and minimum reward levels
- *flexibility* — the amount of flexibility allowable in operating the reward system; the degree of consistency required in applying policies; the amount of control exercised from the centre
- *uniformity* — the extent to which pay structures and policies should apply to the whole organization or be flexed for different levels or categories of employees
- *devolution* — the amount of authority which will be devolved to line managers to make pay decisions
- *control* — how much control should be exercised from the centre over the implementation of reward policies
- *gender neutrality* — the approach which will be adopted towards eliminating gender bias in reward processes and structures so as to ensure that equal pay is provided for work of equal value
- *partnership* — the extent to which the organization believes in sharing success with employees
- *involvement* — how much employees will be involved in pay decisions which affect them, including the development of new approaches
- *transparency* — how much should be published about reward policies and practices.

## Developments in the reward management scene

A survey of pay systems practice in 480 British organizations conducted by the CBI and Hay Management Consultants (1996) found that: 'The most significant factors driving change in pay and benefit policy are the need to strengthen the link to business performance, cost control, support for organizational change and recruitment and retention pressures. The need to provide more flexibility in pay and benefits systems is expected to become more important.' The survey provided the following information on developments in the participating organizations:

- almost half had changed some area of their pay strategy or policy in the last two years, the main areas being in pay structure, pay progression practice and the introduction of profit-related pay
- 13 per cent plan to introduce team pay
- 30 per cent are making changes to their benefits packages, mainly to provide more flexibility
- around 17 per cent plan to introduce a broad banded pay structure
- 45 per cent have introduced or plan to introduce some form of competency or skill-based HR management, mainly for training and development purposes and as a basis for performance management.

This survey and other recent UK studies such as Armstrong and Baron (1995) have established that the main areas where changes are taking place or at least being contemplated in reward policies and practices are:

| From | To |
| --- | --- |
| Narrowly defined jobs and job standards. | Broader generic roles — emphasis on competence and continuous development. |
| Inflexible job evaluation systems sizing tasks, rewarding non-adaptive behaviour and empire building and encouraging point-grabbing. | Flexible job evaluation processes assessing the value added by people in their roles, often within job families. |
| Hierarchical and rigid pay structures in which the only way to get on is to move up. Focus is on the next promotion. | Broad-banded pay structures where the emphasis is on flexibility, career development pay and continuous improvement. Focus is on the next challenge. |
| Emphasis on individual PRP. | More focus on team performance through team-based pay. |
| Consolidation of rewards into base pay. | More emphasis on variable or 'at risk' pay. |

These movements include innovations such as competence-related pay, broadbanding and team pay, which are the most forward looking of the current developments taking place in the context of increased devolution of pay decisions to line management and more involvement of employees. They also reflect an increasing strategic concern about getting value for money from the reward system as evidenced by the increased interest in variable pay. The main areas of employee reward, including these innovations, are described in the rest of this part of the handbook.

# 32

# Evaluating and Pricing Jobs

Decisions on pay levels and structures provide the foundation for the reward system. These decisions are based on job evaluation and market pricing processes. In this chapter:

- job evaluation is defined
- its nature, main features and basic methodology are discussed
- the different types of job evaluation schemes are described
- the considerations to be taken into account when introducing and maintaining job evaluation are considered, including equal pay for work of equal value issues
- the techniques of conducting pay surveys to establish market rates (market pricing) are described.

## Job evaluation — definition and purpose

Job evaluation is a systematic process for establishing the relative worth of jobs within an organization. Its purpose is to:

- provide a rational basis for the design and maintenance of an equitable and defensible pay structure
- help in the management of the relativities existing between jobs within the organization
- enable consistent decisions to be made on grading and rates of pay
- establish the extent to which there is comparable worth between jobs so that equal pay can be provided for work of equal value.

Job evaluation enables a framework to be designed which underpins pay decisions. It can help with internal comparisons and, to a degree, external comparisons by providing a common language for use in discussing the relative worth of jobs and people.

Research conducted by Armstrong and Baron (1995) established that 55 per cent of the 316 organizations covered by the survey had a formal job evaluation scheme. It was confirmed that the primary reason given by organisations for introducing job evaluation is to ensure a more equitable pay structure. Organizations commonly introduce job evaluation because they want to replace chaos with order, inconsistency with consistency and political judgement with rational judgement.

However job evaluation is not a scientific and objective 'system' which, after it has been 'installed', will at a stroke remove all the problems they have experienced in managing internal relativities, fixing rates of pay and controlling the pay structure. This, of course, is asking far too much of job evaluation which should be regarded as a process rather than a system.This process may be systematic and it can reduce subjectivity, but it will always be more art than science; and, because it relies on human judgements, it can never be fully objective.

## The key features of job evaluation

Job evaluation can be regarded as:

- *A comparative process* — it deals with relationships not absolutes.
- *A judgemental process* — it requires the exercise of judgement in interpreting data on jobs and roles (job and role definitions or completed job analysis questionnaires), comparing one job with another, comparing jobs against factor level definitions and scales, and developing a grade structure from a rank order of jobs produced by job evaluation.
- *An analytical process* — job evaluation may be judgemental but it is based on *informed* judgements which in an analytical scheme are founded on a process of gathering facts about jobs, sorting these facts out systematically in order to break them down into various elements, and re-assembling them into whatever standard format is being used.
- *A structured process* — job evaluation is structured in the sense that a framework is provided which aims to help evaluators make consistent and reasoned judgements; this framework consists of language and criteria which are used by all evaluators, although, because the criteria are always subject to interpretation, they do not guarantee that judgements will be either consistent or rational.

## *Jobs and people*

Traditional job evaluation deliberately avoids considering the value of people. Human beings are treated as unnecessary intrusions in the pure world of job hierarchies with which job evaluation is concerned. Of course, the reason for the dogma that 'job evaluation measures the value of jobs not people' is to avoid contaminating the process of evaluation with considerations of the performance of individual job holders. And indeed it would be undesirable for job evaluators to get involved in performance assessment, which is a separate matter.

But the traditional view still implies that people have nothing to do with the value of the job they perform, and this is clearly ludicrous. It is equally misguided to make the universal assumption that people adapt to the fixed specification of their jobs rather than jobs being adapted to fit the characteristics of the people in them. In the new flexible organization roles are created and evolve according to the strengths and limitations of the people who design and fill them. To sum up, it is people who create value, not jobs.

## Basic methodology

The process of job evaluation begins by identifying which jobs are to be covered and the total number to be evaluated. A decision also has to be made on whether there should be one scheme for all employees or whether there should be separate schemes for different levels or categories of people. The next step is to chose one of the methods described later in this chapter. The final stages are to:

- select the representative 'benchmark' jobs which will be used as the basis for comparisons
- decide on the factors to be used in evaluating the jobs
- analyse the jobs and roles
- establish the relative value of jobs by applying a process of evaluation
- develop a pay structure — this usually means designing a grade structure and then deciding on the rates or ranges of pay in the structure through internal comparisons and 'market pricing'.

## Job evaluation schemes

Job evaluation schemes can be divided broadly into the following types: non-analytical, analytical, single factor, skill or competence based, market pricing, and the management consultants' schemes, the so-called proprietary brands.

*Non-analytical schemes* compare whole jobs with one another and make no attempt specifically to distinguish between the factors within the jobs which may differentiate them. Job ranking, paired comparison and job classification are usually regarded as the three main non-analytical schemes, although paired comparison is simply a statistical method of establishing rank order. Another non-analytical approach, which is not generally dignified with being called a scheme, is internal benchmarking. This may not be recognized as a proper form of job evaluation but it is, nevertheless, practised by a lot of organizations, even if they do not refer to it by that name. And once they have carried out their initial analytical job evaluation exercise, many organizations do in effect slot in jobs by internal benchmarking whenever they perceive a close affinity between the job in question and a representative benchmark job.

The *analytical schemes* are point-factor rating, as it is universally known in the United States (in the UK it is often called simply points rating or a points scheme), and factor comparison. Because of its complexity and a number of other fundamental flaws, the latter is little used in its traditional form and is therefore not dealt with in this chapter (a full description is given in Armstrong and Baron 1995). A modified form of what may be called graduated factor comparison is, however, sometimes adopted by the job evaluation 'experts' commissioned by industrial tribunals to report on equal value cases.

*Market pricing* is used in conjunction with other internally orientated evaluation schemes to price jobs by reference to market rates.

*Skill-based or competence-related schemes* value people rather than jobs in terms of their attributes and competences. These are described in Chapter 34.

*Management consultants' schemes* — a number of management consultants such as Hay Management Consultants, KPMG Management Consulting, PA Consulting, PE Consulting, Price Waterhouse, Saville and Holdsworth, Towers Perrin, and Watson Wyatt offer their own 'proprietary brands'. These are usually analytical and generally rely on some form of points scoring. Details of these and other consultants' schemes are provided in Neathey (1994).

The principal features of the job ranking, job classification, internal benchmarking, point-factor and market pricing approaches are summarized below.

## Job ranking

Job ranking is a non-analytical approach which compares whole jobs and does not attempt to assess separately different aspects of the jobs. It determines the position of jobs in a hierarchy by placing them in rank according to perceptions of their relative size.

If a graded pay structure is required (see Chapter 33), decisions are made on how the rank order should be divided into groups of jobs, the values of which are thought to be broadly comparable or at least within the same size range.

Ranking is the simplest and quickest form of job evaluation. It may be claimed that the process of assessing the value of the job as a whole to the organization is, in practice, what people do even when they go through the motions of assessing the different facets of a job in an analytical scheme. Ultimately, it can be argued, people will feel that their grading is fair by noting where their whole job is placed in relation to others.

The disadvantage of ranking, however, is that there is no rationale to defend the rank order — no defined standards for judging relative size. It is simply a matter of opinion, although it can be argued that analytical methods do no more than channel opinions into specified areas.

## Job classification

Job classification is also a non-analytical method which compares whole jobs to a scale, in this case a grade definition. It is based on an initial decision on the number and characteristics of the grades into which the jobs will be placed. The grade definitions attempt to take into account discernible differences in skill, competence or responsibility and may refer to specific criteria, such as level of decisions, knowledge, equipment used and education and training required to do the work. Jobs are allotted to grades by comparing the whole job description with the grade definition.

Job classification is a simple, quick and easily implemented method of slotting jobs into an established structure. It attempts to provide some standards for judgement in the form of grade definition. Its lack of complexity and the ease with which it can be learned and used means that it is suitable for large populations and for decentralized operations in which more complex systems might be difficult to operate consistently. But it cannot cope with complex jobs with features which will not fit neatly into one grade. Like other non-analytical systems it is not being accepted for use in equal value cases and there is a danger of the descriptions becoming so generalized that they provide little help in evaluating borderline cases, especially at higher levels. Job classification also tends to be inflexible in that it is not sensitive to changes in the nature and content of jobs.

## Internal benchmarking

Internal benchmarking is what people often do intuitively when they are deciding on the value of jobs. Evaluation by internal benchmarking simply means comparing the job under review with any internal benchmark job which is believed to be properly graded and paid, and slotting the job under consideration into the same grade as the benchmark job. The comparison is usually made on a whole job basis without analysing the jobs factor by factor. However, internal benchmarking is likely to be much more accurate and acceptable if it is founded on the comparison of role definitions which indicate key result areas and the knowledge, skills and competence levels required to achieve the specified results.

Internal benchmarking is simple and quick, and it is natural in the sense that it involves comparing one job with another which, essentially, is what job evaluation is all about. It can produce reasonable results as long as it is based on the comparison of accurate job or role descriptions. But it relies on judgements which may be entirely subjective and could be hard to justify. It is also dependent on the identification of suitable benchmarks which are properly graded and paid, and such comparisons may only perpetuate existing inequities. Importantly, it would not be acceptable in equal value cases.

## Point-factor rating

Point-factor rating is an analytical method of job evaluation using job-scale comparisons.

The method is based on the breaking down of jobs into factors or key elements. It is assumed that each of the factors will contribute to job size and are a part of all the jobs to be evaluated but to different degrees. Using numerical scales, points are allocated to a job under each factor heading according to the degree to which it is present in the job. The separate factor scores are then added together to give a total score which represents job size.

The point-factor method is built on a *factor plan* which consists of:

- the choice of factors to be used in the scheme
- the factor rating scales
- factor weighting.

## Choice of factors

A factor is a characteristic which occurs to a different degree in the jobs to be evaluated and can be used as a basis for assessing the relative value of the jobs. If, in common parlance, a job is said to be more responsible than another, and therefore worth more, responsibility is being used as a factor, however loosely responsibility is defined.

When we evaluate a job, even if there is no formal evaluation scheme, we always have some criterion in mind. It may be some generalized concept of 'responsibility', or may be more specifically related to the size of resources controlled or the contribution to end-results.

Point-factor schemes may have any number of factors, but to reduce complexity, there are normally between three and twelve. These can broadly be grouped under the three headings of:

- *Inputs* — the knowledge and skills and any other personal characteristics required to do the job. These may include such aspects as technical or professional knowledge, manual and mental skills, interpersonal skills and team-leading skills. The education, training and experience required to develop the knowledge and skills may also be regarded as a factor, as might the academic, technical or professional qualifications which indicate the level of knowledge acquired.
- *Process* — the characteristics of the work which determine the demands made by the job on job holders. These include such aspects as mental effort, problem solving, complexity, originality, creativity, judgement and initiative, teamworking, dealing with people (using interpersonal skills) and physical factors such as physical effort, working conditions and dangers or hazards associated with the work.
- *Outputs* — the contribution of impact the job holder can make on end-results taking into account such aspects of jobs as responsibility for output, quality, sales, profit etc, responsibility for resources such as people, assets and money, decision-making authority, and the effect of errors.

A typical list of factors would be:

- knowledge and skills (input)
- responsibility (output)
- decisions (process)
- complexity (process)
- interpersonal skills (process)

It is sometimes felt when drawing up a factor plan that a multiplicity of factors will guarantee more accurate judgements by evaluators. This is an illusion. The more factors there are, the greater the likelihood of overlap and duplication. Evaluators therefore find it difficult to make the fine distinctions required when making their judgements. And the extra work involved in using multi-factor schemes is considerable. It is seldom necessary to have more than six factors.

There are no absolute rules on what factors should be chosen although equal pay for work of equal value legislation and case law indicate that account should be taken of the demands made by a job on a worker under the headings of effort, skill and decisions. However, effort is usually only included in schemes for manual workers.

The choice of factors and the weighting given to them will be influenced by the values of the organization on what is considered to be important when valuing the contribution of people in their roles. The selection therefore conveys a message to employees about these values and this is a good reason for involving them in the design of a tailor-made scheme.

## Factor rating scales

Factor rating scales consist of definitions of the levels at which the factor can be present in any of the jobs to be evaluated. Jobs are analyzed in terms of these factors and the result of this analysis is compared with the factor level definitions to establish the factor level. The maximum points score for a factor is determined by factor weighting (see below), and when this has been established, each level can be allocated a points score or a range of scores. Points progression is usually arithmetic (eg 20, 40, 60, 80, 100).

The number of levels or degrees to each factor depends on the range of jobs to be covered and the amount of sensitivity the scheme is attempting to achieve. Most schemes seem to have up to six or seven levels but there is no rule that says all factors must have the same number of levels.

When defining factor levels the aim is to produce a graduated series of definitions which will produce clear guidance on how the factor should be scored. This is difficult to achieve and can become a semantic exercise in the use of comparative adjectives (big, bigger, biggest) to which no precise meaning can be attached. In some cases, however, it is possible to quantify levels in terms of outputs or the size of resources controlled. Successive levels can also be defined by reference to the use of specified skills or the need for particular qualifications, training or experience. In practice, level definitions become more meaningful to evaluators when they can relate them to benchmark jobs. What happens, in effect, is that the somewhat abstract level definition is brought to life by an example and the comparison is made from job to job as well as from job to scale.

An example of a definition of a factor and its levels is given in Figure 32.1.

## Factor weighting

A factor plan involves making decisions on the relative importance of the various factors — that is, their weighting for scoring purposes. It could be decided that all factors should be equally weighted but the great majority of points factor schemes do weight their factors differently.

Clearly, this is a critical decision. A factor which is overweighted in relation to its true significance as one of a number of factors could result in evaluations becoming badly skewed. For example, over-

### COMPLEXITY

*Factor definition*

The variety and diversity of tasks carried out by the job holder and the range of skills used.

*Level definitions*

1. Highly repetitive work where the same task or group of tasks is carried out without any significant variation.
2. A fairly narrow range of tasks are carried out which tend to be closely related to one another and involve the use of a limited range of skills.
3. There is some diversity in the activities carried out although they are broadly related to one another. A fairly wide variety of skills have to be used.
4. A diverse range of broadly related tasks are carried out. A wide variety of administrative, technical or supervisory skills are used.
5. A highly diverse range of tasks are carried out, many of which are unrelated to one another. A wide variety of professional and/or managerial skills are used.
6. The work is multi-disciplinary and involves fulfilling a broad range of highly diverse responsibilities.

**Figure 32.1** Example of a definition of a factor and its levels

weighting a factor which refers to the number of people controlled could unduly favour managers with large numbers of easily controlled staff rather than high-powered specialists. Weighting also has equal value implications. To overweight a factor such as physical effort which mainly applies to male job holders could be seen as discriminatory.

## The complete factor plan

A complete factor plan with weighted scores is illustrated in Table 32.1.

**Table 32.1** A factor plan

| Factor | Levels | | | | | |
|---|---|---|---|---|---|---|
| | *1* | *2* | *3* | *4* | *5* | *6* |
| Knowledge and skills | 20 | 40 | 60 | 80 | 100 | 120 |
| Responsibility | 20 | 40 | 60 | 80 | 100 | 120 |
| Decisions | 15 | 30 | 45 | 60 | 75 | 90 |
| Complexity | 10 | 20 | 30 | 40 | 50 | 60 |
| Contacts | 10 | 20 | 30 | 40 | 50 | 60 |

## Using the factor plan

The points-factor job evaluation process involves analysing a job in terms of the factors, comparing that analysis with the factor and level definition, allocating a level and score for each factor, and adding up the factor scores to produce a total job evaluation score for the job as shown in Table 32.2.

This can be compared with the scores for other jobs which produces a ranked order of jobs according to their score. If there is a graded pay structure, decisions are then made on how these jobs should be grouped into grades (this is often a matter of judgement). A separate decision is made on the pay ranges to be attached to the job grades which will be influenced by market rate considerations and what is considered to be an appropriate range of pay in a grade and the size of the pay differentials between grades.

## Advantages of point-factor schemes

The advantages of point-factor schemes are that:

**Table 32.2** Example of job evaluation score

| Factor | Evaluated level | Score |
|---|---|---|
| Knowledge and skills | 3 | 60 |
| Responsibility | 4 | 80 |
| Decisions | 4 | 60 |
| Complexity | 5 | 50 |
| Contacts | 3 | 30 |
| Total score | | 280 |

- Evaluators are forced to consider a range of factors which, as long as they are present in all the jobs and affect them in different ways, will avoid the over-simplified judgements made when using non-analytical schemes.
- Points schemes provide evaluators with defined yardsticks which should help them to achieve some degree of objectivity and consistency in making their judgements.
- They at least appear to be objective, even if they are not, and this quality makes people feel that they are fair.
- They provide a rationale which helps in the design of graded pay structures (see Chapter 33).
- They are acceptable in equal value cases.
- They adapt well to computerization.

## Disadvantages of point-factor schemes

Points schemes have these disadvantages:

- They are complex to develop, install and maintain.
- They give a somewhat spurious impression of scientific accuracy — it is still necessary to use judgement in selecting factors, defining levels within factors, deciding on weightings, and interpreting information about the jobs in relation to the definitions of factors and factor levels.
- They assume that it is possible to quantify different aspects of jobs on the same scale of values and then add them together. But skills cannot necessarily be added together in this way.
- They are based on the assumption that the factor weightings in the scheme apply equally to all jobs. But it is possible to argue that each job will have its own pattern of factor weights. In other words, not

only will the levels at which factors are present in jobs vary, but within a job the relative weight to be attached to that factor will be different from its weight in other jobs.

Apart from the complexity issue, however, this list of disadvantages simply confirms what we already know about any form of job evaluation. It is not a scientific process. It cannot guarantee total objectivity or absolute accuracy in sizing jobs. It can do no more than provide a broad indication of internal relativities where jobs should be placed in a pay structure. But the analytical nature of points-factor rating will at least give a more accurate indication than non-analytical methods. If the process of using this method is carefully managed the results are more likely to be acceptable (to be felt fair), and a sound basis for dealing with equal value issues will have been established. Additionally, and importantly, point-factor evaluation provides a good basis for designing a graded pay structure.

However, a powerful attack has been made by Lawler (1986) on point-factor evaluation for other reasons. He suggests that job evaluation was originally developed to support traditional bureaucratic management and the essential nature of point-factor schemes has not changed since they were first evolved in the early 1900s. He believes that job evaluation depersonalizes people by equating them with a set of duties rather than concentrating on what they are and what they can do. Job evaluation schemes strongly reinforce the concept of a management hierarchy and do not take account of organizations in which the emphasis is on knowledge and high technology work and where flexibility and multiskilling is important. He proposes that the emphasis should be on people rather than jobs and the key criteria for establishing the value of people to an organization should be the levels of skill and competence they need to make an effective contribution in their roles. There is much to be said for this argument, hence the importance of new skill or competence-based approaches to job evaluation as discussed below and the increased use of 'broad-banded' pay structures or pay curves as described in Chapter 33.

## Skill-based evaluation

Skill-based evaluation grades jobs according to the level of skills or expertise required to perform them. There may be a number of skill factors, each with a rating scale or the grades may be related to NVQ levels.

This method focuses on individuals and the inputs they are capable of providing. The assumption is made that the process demands made on job holders to deliver the expected outputs can be measured by the level of inputs required. It is therefore a person rather than a job-orientated approach to evaluation. Skill-based evaluation is flexible and can respond more quickly to demands for new skills, the acquisition or development of which need to be encouraged and rewarded. It is most commonly used for technical and operational jobs in manufacturing and process industries.

The problem with this approach is that the emphasis on inputs seems to imply that skills are rewarded even when they are not delivering results. This does not make sense. Skills should only be valued if they are used productively and the analysis and evaluation process should take account of this.

Skill-based evaluation is associated with skill-based pay (see Chapter 34). Skills analysis techniques were described in Chapter 12.

## Competence-based evaluation

Competence-based evaluation measures the size of jobs by reference to the level of competence required for their successful performance. The conceptual basis for this type of job measurement is that the level of competence demanded for the effective performance of different jobs is a measure of the relative value of those jobs.

Like skill-based evaluation, competence-based measurement focuses on people. It concentrates on inputs and processes and it can be argued that it fails to assess contribution. This drawback can be tackled by incorporating performance requirements in definitions of competency levels, bearing in mind that competence is essentially the ability to apply knowledge and skills successfully, not the knowledge and skills themselves.

## Market pricing

Many organizations reject the idea of formal job evaluation and base their decisions on job values on 'market pricing' which involves relating internal rates of pay to market rates on the assumption that 'a job is worth what the market says it is worth', and that therefore market rate relativities should dictate internal relativities.

The problem with this approach is that the concept of a market rate is much less precise than most people think. Market rates are also volatile and unpredictable. Relying on market rate comparisons alone will not necessarily result in the provision of a sufficiently reliable or stable basis for an equitable pay structure, although market rates will, of course, influence rates of pay within the structure.

A further problem with market pricing is that it may only be possible to get market rate data for some of the jobs in the organization. It can be difficult to obtain information for unique or highly specialized jobs. It could be equally hard to determine accurately the market worth of 'individual contributors' whose value to the organization depends more on their personal level of skill and competence than on their level of responsibility in a job hierarchy. Organizations which rely on market pricing still have to make decisions on how these jobs fit into the pay structure. If they have the most common type of structure, one which groups jobs into grades they will still have to make assumptions about the internal value of these jobs by slotting them into some form of rank order and placing them in grades. Even if they do not have a graded structure or a pay spine as described in Chapter 33, they will still need to determine internal relativities. The argument in favour of some form of systematic or analytical job evaluation process as described in this chapter is that this does at least produce a rationale for such decisions which provides for some degree of equity and consistency and, importantly, can be used to explain why decisions on job grades or values have been made.

## Pros and cons of formal job-centred evaluation

Although there are strong arguments in favour of a people rather than a job-focused approach and although market pricing recognizes the realities of the market place, many organizations prefer to adopt one of the more traditional approaches. Each of the job-centred schemes described above has its advantages and disadvantages, but before choosing between them it will be useful to summarize the arguments for and against a formal job-centred approach.

### Pros

The arguments in favour of formal job evaluation are that:

● a rational basis is required for making defensible decisions on job grades and rates of pay — such decisions are more likely to be accepted if the logic upon which they are based is clear

- a consistent approach is required to the management of relativities
- an equitable pay structure is unlikely to be achieved unless a logical method of measuring relative job size exists
- equal pay for work of equal value issues can ultimately only be resolved by the use of a formal and analytical method of job evaluation
- a reasonably formal approach to job evaluation provides a strategic framework within which rational decisions can be made in response to changing organization structures and roles and to market rate pressures
- a logical and consistent approach to measuring the relative size of jobs will not be achieved unless there is an agreed method and set of criteria for doing so which is used by all evaluators and represents the values of the organization as a whole.

## Cons

The arguments against formal, traditional approaches to job evaluation are that:

- no scheme has been proved to be valid in that it measures what it sets out to measure, or reliable in that it produces consistent results — an act of faith is required to believe in job evaluation
- 'whole-job' comparison schemes look wrong because they seem to oversimplify, but analytical systems are also suspect — apples and pears cannot be-added together; the quantification of subjective judgements does not make them any more objective
- job evaluation relies on human judgement; its methodology may be logical and it may provide guidelines on the exercise of judgement, but these are subject to different interpretations and varying standards among assessors, and their preconceived notions ensure that subjectivity creeps in.
- averaging a group of subjective judgements, as achieved when job evaluation panels reach a consensus view, does not make them any more objective
- all formal evaluation schemes deteriorate as the organization changes and as evaluators become more skilled at manipulating the system; grade drift — unjustified upgradings as a result of this manipulation — occurs and the pay structure is no longer equitable
- job evaluation schemes can be costly to install and maintain — installation costs include not only consultancy fees, if applicable, by

the inevitable increase in the pay bill after introducing job evaluation, usually at least three per cent

- is not the universal panacea that some businesses think it to be:
handling its introduction can be a very delicate matter; evaluations
can upset long-standing differentials and gradings and thus create
more problems than they solve; the installation of job evaluation
always creates expectations that everyone's pay will increase and
however carefully you explain that such increases will *not* happen, a
number of people, sometimes a lot of people, will inevitably be
disappointed.

And of course, there are the convincing arguments offered by Lawler
(1986) as mentioned on page 616.

To sum up, job evaluation attempts to impose objectivity on a process of subjective judgement. It can never fully succeed in the task. In
the last analysis, all job evaluation schemes boil down to organized
rationalization.

## Is job evaluation necessary?

The pros for job evaluation as given above appear to be self-evident,
but the cons are formidable and reading them prompts the question, 'Is
job evaluation really necessary?' The answer is, of course, yes. You
cannot avoid evaluating jobs. That is what you do every time you
decide on what one job should be paid in relation to another. Job
evaluation is therefore always necessary although it does not have to
take the form of one of the traditional methods.

## Introducing job evaluation

### Who should be covered?

Ideally, every job should be evaluated in order that comparisons can be
made throughout the organization, or at least between people in
comparable occupations at different levels. Some businesses, however,
exclude directors and possibly senior managers on the grounds that
their salary levels are largely determined on a personal basis. Senior
jobs are often built round the skills of particular individuals and they
can change, sometimes quite radically, when one manager leaves or is
promoted and is replaced by another. Where this happens, job evaluation would clearly mean evaluating the individual, not the job.

## How many schemes?

The tendency has been to have different systems for, say, managers, office staff and manual workers because of the perceived difficulty of designing a scheme which is equally applicable at all levels of responsibility or for completely different types of work.

Increasingly, however, organizations which have harmonized and integrated their pay structures, ie which place all employees in the same pay structure, are introducing single job evaluation schemes which cover every position except, possibly, board directors.

## Tailor-made scheme?

The main advantage of a specially designed scheme is clearly that it can take into account the particular values of the organization and any of the individual features of the organization, such as the need to cover different categories of employees or types of work. Special factors can be introduced at different levels and appropriate weightings can be applied. Tailor-made schemes are not necessarily less expensive to introduce than a job evaluation package because account has to be taken of the opportunity costs in the shape of the considerable amount of executive time that has to be spent in designing, developing and introducing a special scheme. This time can be reduced by getting help from management consultants, although that can be costly.

## Job evaluation package

The alternative to a tailor-made scheme is a job evaluation package — a 'proprietary brand'. This will have been carefully developed and tested over time, and, at a price, is readily installed by the consultants. Some schemes are used as the basis for comparing market rates, which can provide a valuable additional source of information. A ready-made scheme is simpler to install but may not fit the organization's needs so well as one that has been specially developed.

## What type of scheme?

When developing a tailor-made scheme, you have the choice between using a job-centred or people-centred approach. If you believe in the need to establish the position of jobs in a hierarchy and therefore do not want to take into account the individual characteristics of people in their different roles, a traditional job-centred approach will be appropriate. The choice is then between a job ranking or job classification system, or an analytical point-factor scheme. The natural way to evaluate jobs is to compare one whole job with another — people do this almost instinctively — but point-factor schemes are best in complex situations where it is felt that only a highly analytical approach provides an acceptable basis for evaluation, and they can provide a useful basis for designing a pay structure. Their objectivity may be suspect but their use may well be justified if it is considered that people are going to be favourably impressed both by the sheer amount of time and trouble involved in introducing the scheme, and by the apparent fairness of the process of analysis. In addition, an analytical scheme is required to avoid potential difficulties over equal pay for work of equal value claims where the leading case of *Bromley and Others v H & J Quick (1988)* established that a job evaluation scheme can only provide a defence if it is analytical in nature.

Point-factor schemes have been steadily increasing in popularity. Most organizations introducing job evaluation select this type of scheme because of their 'face validity'. People feel that they are scientific and therefore they must be all right.

People-focused skill- or competence-based schemes could be appropriate in relatively fluid organizations, especially those in the high-tech, scientific or research and development fields. Skills-based schemes may be relevant for highly skilled and multiskilled workers. Competence-based schemes may be right for professional, scientific and technical jobs and where career development tends to be progressive rather than by means of a series of steps in a job hierarchy. Such schemes can be designed to operate analytically by referring to a range of specifically defined skills and competences.

Market pricing can be adopted by those organizations which are very much exposed to market pressures and/or cannot be bothered with a formal scheme

## Developing a point-factor scheme

The majority of organizations which want to use a formal approach to job evaluation select a point-factor scheme. This section therefore describes the following steps which need to be taken when developing and introducing such a scheme.

- inform employees and agree on how they should be involved
- clarify trade union attitudes, where appropriate
- select benchmark jobs
- plan the job evaluation programme

## Informing and involving employees

Employees must obviously be informed about the exercise. It affects them deeply and their help is required in analysing jobs. The objectives and potential benefits should be discussed and it should be made absolutely clear that it is the jobs which are to be evaluated and not the performance of the people carrying out the jobs. The way in which employees are consulted will depend on the organization's normal policies for consultation and negotiation.

There is much to be said for involving people in the job evaluation programme. They can assist in selecting, analysing and evaluating benchmark jobs (ie the key jobs which can be used as reference points — see below). It is becoming increasingly common to set up job evaluation panels to establish and maintain the scheme and to hear appeals.

This approach is equally desirable if a skill or competence-based scheme is being introduced.

## Trade union attitudes

If the organization is unionized, the form in which consultation and participation takes place will be strongly influenced by union attitudes. Trade unions may insist on being involved in the job evaluation programme, although they might not be prepared to commit themselves in advance to accept its findings.

## Select benchmark jobs

In any exercise where there are more than 30 or 40 jobs to be evaluated, it is necessary to identify and select a sample of benchmark jobs which can be used for comparisons inside and outside the organization. The benchmark jobs should be selected to achieve a representative sample of each of the main levels of jobs in each of the principal occupations.

The size of the sample depends on the number of different jobs to be covered. It is usually difficult to produce a balanced sample unless at least 25 per cent of the distinct jobs at each level of the organization are included. The higher the proportion the better, bearing in mind the time required to analyse jobs (often as much as a day for each job).

## Draw up job evaluation programme

The steps to be taken in drawing up and implementing a job evaluation scheme are summarized in Figure 32.2.

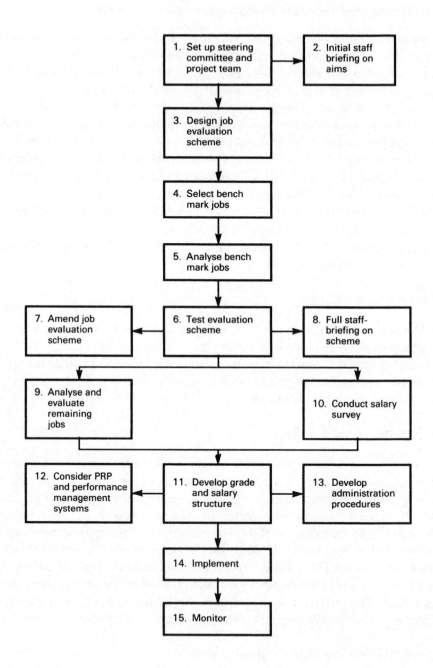

**Figure 32.2** Job evaluation programme

The particular points to be covered are the following:

1. *Roles*: who is responsible for analysis, evaluation, pay comparisons and the design of the salary structure.
2. *Briefing*: of management, employees and unions on the objectives of the exercise and how they are to be achieved.
3. *Procedures*: the terms of reference, membership and methods of working of any job evaluation panel, project team or committee.
4. *Training*: the training to be given to analysts and evaluators. This is a vital part of the programme. If training is carried out thoroughly, many of the limitations of job evaluation referred to earlier can be minimized.
5. *Pay comparisons*: methods of conducting market rate surveys and the timetable for completing them.
6. *Job evaluation*: methods and procedures, including appeals, and the timetable for completing the programme.
7. *Job analysis*: the methods to be used in job analysis, the jobs to be covered and the timetable for completing the programme.
8. *Pay structure design*: the type of structure (see Chapter 33), the design methods to be used and the timetable for completing the design.
9. *Communication and negotiation*: the approach to communicating the results of the exercise to employees and for negotiating the structure with unions. It is highly desirable to produce a booklet explaining the scheme.
10. *Implementation*: the procedures for implementing the scheme, including grading or re-grading jobs, deciding on how to deal with any increases, informing individual employees, drawing up maintenance procedures covering such points as evaluating or re-evaluating new or changed jobs and installing an appeal system.

When the programme has been drawn up, the detailed work of job analysis, pay comparisons and design of the structure can be carried out. The points to be covered when conducting a job evaluation exercise using a point-factor scheme are discussed below.

## Conducting the job evaluation exercise

### *How much time is involved?*

However much the organization may want to get the scheme fully implemented, it is unwise to rush job evaluation. Even the keenest evaluation panel can grade only a limited number of jobs in a day: eight is probably a realistic average maximum. After this, the quality of evaluation tends to drop, and more time has to be spent later in checking and assessing the validity of grading. The final review of all the grades allocated to check that no inconsistencies have occurred should be done meticulously and with enough time allowed for re-evaluation if necessary. Extra time devoted at this stage will help reduce appeals to the inevitable few. Careful preparation for the communication of job grades and of the handbooks or other documents describing the scheme and its operation will also assist acceptance.

## Responsibility for the exercise

Responsibility for the overall coordination of the introduction of job evaluation should be in the hands of a senior executive who can then report on progress to the board or management committee and advise it on ensuing salary policy developments.

Where there is a developed personnel function, the head of personnel will take control. In larger organizations with a department specializing in pay matters, the executive in charge of this function will normally take responsibility for the introduction and maintenance of the scheme. Provided adequate training is given at the outset, job analysis is an excellent way for new personnel or other trainees to familiarize themselves with the business and the work done in its different departments. Analysts must be taught the basic skills of interviewing and the elements of a concise descriptive style for writing job descriptions.

The use of analysts either to write job descriptions or check on those written by job holders and their managers often greatly improves the quality of job descriptions submitted for evaluation.

## Job evaluation panels

It is highly desirable to set up a job evaluation panel which can be involved in the design of a new scheme when a tailor-made one is to be introduced. The panel members may possibly carry out job analyses and will certainly evaluate the jobs using either their own scheme or, in conjunction with a management consultant acting in an advisory capacity, a 'proprietary brand'. The panel may continue to meet after the initial exercise to hear appeals and to conduct new evaluations or re-evaluations.

When deciding on the membership of the job evaluation panel, it is necessary to consider the extent to which different levels of employees will be included. The aim should be to set up a panel of no more than about eight members who between them have good first-hand knowledge of the jobs to be evaluated.

If trade unions are involved, they may wish to nominate an agreed number of representatives, balanced by management nominees and a mutually acceptable chairperson, preferably the head of personnel or the remuneration function who will more easily be able to act as a facilitator. When conducting evaluations the chairperson should play this role rather than acting as a decision-maker. Internal or external consultants may also be used as facilitators. Panel members will need to be trained in job analysis and evaluation techniques.

## Briefing for job evaluation

Thorough briefing of all employees who will be affected by job evaluation is essential. This can be done at a meeting or series of meetings at which the person responsible for the introduction of the scheme outlines its aims and emphasizes the long-term benefits in terms of a fair and equitable pay structure for all concerned. A simple question-and-answer sheet given out at the meeting and covering the common, if basic, questions employees normally ask will also help remove any misgivings that may arise. Some of the most common questions are the following:

- What is job evaluation?
- Why does this company need job evaluation?
- How will it work?
- Will my performance in my job be taken into account?
- How does it affect promotion policy?
- How will the system be kept up to date?
- Does job evaluation mean that everyone whose job is in the same grade gets the same rate of pay?
- How does the publication of job grades and pay bands affect confidentiality?
- How does the system cater for additions to or alterations in jobs?
- What impact is the exercise likely to have on pay?
- What happens if individuals disagree with their grading?
- How quickly will appeals on grading be dealt with?
- How will the company go about grading new jobs created as the result of change or expansion?

It is desirable to anticipate these questions and have answers ready for them. It is particularly important to emphasize that the scheme is evaluating jobs, not people. It is even more important to defuse any expectations that job evaluation will result in massive all-round pay increases. In fact, it is advisable to play down the pay aspect of the process and stress that job evaluation is about measuring the relative size of jobs so that they can be fairly graded. The scheme itself will not determine pay levels. It only helps in the development of a framework within which fair and consistent decisions on pay can be made.

## Briefing and training the job evaluation panel

Much of the success of a job evaluation panel depends on how well it is briefed and trained. The first meeting should discuss the collective responsibilities of the panel, go through the principles of job evaluation, and answer members' questions. Training should be given in job analysis and the principles of job evaluation.

If a tailor-made scheme is to be developed the panel, with the help of the internal specialist or external consultant will decide on the type of scheme and, if a points-factor scheme is to be used, the factor plan. If a proprietary brand is to be used the consultants will brief the panel.

The panel should try a few practice runs before the programme of analysis and evaluation begins.

## Conducting the panel meetings

The chairperson, the personnel adviser to the panel or the external consultant should act as a 'facilitator', helping the panel to understand the processes they are using and to reach consensus. Facilitators should not normally evaluate the jobs themselves — that is the function of the panel which must 'own' the final decision. But facilitators are there to provide advice on interpreting the scheme and how it is used, and they will try to achieve consensus. It is surprising how readily consensus is achieved with a well-conceived scheme, a balanced and well-trained panel and, importantly, an effective facilitator.

To begin with the panel will take some time to evaluate jobs. But as its members become familiar with how the scheme works, they will speed up. Bearing in mind that job evaluation is essentially a comparative process, consistency in judgements will more easily be achieved by comparing the evaluations for separate factors in different jobs (if a points scheme is used). Evaluating 'real' jobs will also help members to put flesh on the bones of the factor level descriptions in the scheme, which will necessarily be non-specific.

## Appeals procedure

Even the most committed and highly trained job evaluation committees make mistakes. Additionally, managers may expect the people they supervise to be more highly graded as a reflection of their own or their department's status, and individuals may feel that the importance of their job has been undervalued. An appeals procedure is therefore essential.

## Use of computers (computer-assisted job evaluation)

A job evaluation exercise can generate a lot of paper and take considerable time. The use of knowledge-based software systems, often referred to as expert systems, can organize the analytical processes in a way which makes the best use of the database, assists in making consistent judgements and records decisions to be added to the database. An expert system will do this by:

- defining the evaluation rules relating to the weighting of factors, the points, levels, or degrees attached to each factor, and the assessment standards which guide evaluators to the correct rating of jobs — these may take the form of benchmark jobs and/or level definitions
- programming the computer to ask appropriate questions concerning each factor in a job to enable it to apply the evaluation rules
- applying the rules consistently and determining the factor score for the job
- grading the job
- sorting the job into position in the rank order
- storing the job information entered in the form of a factor analysis into the computer's memory so that it can be called to the screen or printed at any time.

## Equal value

Under the equal value amendment to the UK Equal Pay Act, any person can claim equal pay with any other person if he or she believes that the work is equally demanding under such factors as effort, skill and decision-making. Equal value claims can be made whether or not job evaluation schemes exist, and they can cut across traditional boundaries, so that blue-collar workers can compare their jobs with those of white-collar workers and vice versa. Vulnerability to claims is highest where traditional, sex-based job segregation exists.

Claims are heard by industrial tribunals, who may ask independent 'experts' appointed by ACAS (the Advisory Conciliation and Arbitration Service) to assess equality of value between claimant and comparator. The experts carry out their evaluation by applying sets of factors to the job analysis such as knowledge, experience, judgement and decision-making, contacts, physical effort and consequence of errors.

Independent experts start with the job description to identify any areas where the content of the job is the cause of conflict. They attempt to get agreement on the facts and ask the employer to justify the differential. A precise point rating for each factor is usually considered neither necessary nor appropriate, but a general statement comparing the demands of each job under each factor heading is essential.

The existence of a job evaluation scheme which assigns values to the jobs under review can be used to prove that no discrimination is taking place only if the scheme itself is non-discriminatory. It is also desirable for it to be analytical in accordance with the ruling in *Bromley v Quick*. Job evaluation schemes can be discriminatory in the choice of factors and in the weightings attached to the factors as well as in the grading process — reflecting underlying discrimination.

The Equal Opportunities Commission has stated that job evaluation should not give a spurious objectivity to the status quo: 'a commitment to a fair job evaluation may require that some traditional assumptions are changed regarding the value attributed to work predominantly carried out by women.' It also advises that extremely high or low weightings should not be given to factors which are exclusively found in jobs performed predominantly by one sex.

## Establishing market rates

### *Purpose*

To ensure that pay levels are competitive, it is necessary to track market rates for the jobs within the business, especially those which are particularly vulnerable to market pressures because of scarcity factors.

Job evaluation schemes can be used to determine internal relativities, but, in themselves, they cannot price jobs. To a large extent, pay levels are subject to market forces which have to be taken into account in fixing the rates for particular jobs. Some specialized jobs may not be subject to the same external pressures as others, but it is still necessary to know what effect market rates are likely to have on the pay structure as a whole before deciding on internal pay differentials which properly reflect levels of skill and responsibility. It has also to be accepted that market pressures and negotiations affect differentials within the firm.

## The concept of the market rate

The concept of the market rate, even in the local labour market, is an imprecise one. There is no such thing as *the* market rate, unless this is represented by a universally applied national pay scale, and such cases are now rare. There is always a range of rates paid by different employers, even for identical jobs, because of different pay policies on how they want their rates to compare with the market rates. This is particularly so in managerial jobs and other occupations where duties can vary considerably, even if the job title is the same, and where actual pay is likely to be strongly influenced by the quality and value to the business of individuals. It is therefore possible to use pay surveys only to provide a broad indication of market rates. Judgement has to be used in interpreting the results of special enquiries or the data from published surveys. And there is often plenty of scope for selecting evidence which supports whatever case is being advanced.

## The information required

When making market comparisons, the aim should be to:

- obtain accurate and representative data covering base pay, bonuses and benefits
- compare like with like in terms of the type and size of the job and the type of organization — this is the process of 'job matching'
- obtain up-to-date information
- interpret data in the light of the organization's circumstances and needs
- present data in a way which indicates the action required.

## Job matching

The aim in conducting a pay survey is to compare like with like — the process of job matching. The various methods of job matching in ascending order of accuracy are:

- *job title* — often very misleading
- *brief (two or three lines) description of job and level of responsibility* — this provides better guidance for matching jobs but still leaves much scope for inaccuracy
- *capsule job descriptions* which define the job and its duties in two or three hundred words, some indication being given of the size of the job in such terms as resources controlled — these can provide a better basis for job matching but may still not produce the ideal degree of accuracy
- *full job descriptions* which provide more details about the job but demand a considerable amount of effort in making the comparisons
- *job evaluation* can be used in support of a job description to obtain reasonably accurate information on comparative job sizes, but it is very time consuming unless it is done through the UK surveys run on this basis by firms such as Hay and Wyatt.

## Presentation of data

Data can be presented in two ways:

1. *Measures of central tendency:*

   - arithmetic mean (average)
   - median — the middle item in a distribution of individual items, this is the most commonly used measure because it avoids the distortions to which arithmetic averages are prone.

2. *Measures of dispersion*

   - upper quartile — the value above which 25 per cent of the individual values fall
   - lower quartile — the value below which 25 per cent of the individual values fall
   - interquartile range — the difference between the upper and lower quartiles.

## Sources of information

The following sources of information are available on market rates:

- published surveys
- special surveys
- club surveys
- advertisements.

These are described below.

*Published surveys*
There is a wide range of published surveys which either collect general information about managerial salaries or cover the pay for specialist professional, technical or office jobs. The general surveys which are available 'over the counter' include those published by Reward, Monks Publications and Remuneration Economics. Incomes Data Services publishes a *Directory of Salary Surveys* which is a consumer's guide to all the major surveys.

When using a published survey it is necessary to check on:

- the information provided
- the size and composition of the participants
- the quality of the job matching information
- the extent to which it covers the jobs for which information is required
- the degree to which it is up to date
- how well data is presented.

Published surveys are a quick and not too expensive way of getting information. But there may be problems in job matching and the information may be somewhat out of date.

## Special surveys

Special surveys can be 'do it yourself' affairs or they can be conducted for you by management consultants. The latter method costs more but it saves a lot of time and trouble and some organizations may be more willing to respond to an enquiry from a reputable consultant.

Special surveys can be conducted as follows:

1. Decide what information is wanted.
2. Identify the 'benchmark' jobs for which comparative pay data is required. This could have been done as part of a job evaluation exercise.
3. Produce capsule job descriptions for those jobs.
4. Identify the organizations which are likely to have similar jobs.

5.  Contact those organizations and invite them to participate. It is usual to say that the survey findings will be distributed to participants (this is the *quid pro quo*) and that individual organizations will not be identified.

6.  Provide participants with a form to complete together with notes for guidance and capsule job descriptions.

7.  Analyse the returned forms and distribute a summary of the results to participants.

Special surveys can justify the time and trouble, or expense, by producing usefully comparable data. It may, however, be difficult to get a suitable number of participants to take part, either because organizations cannot be bothered or because they are already members of a survey club or take part in a published survey.

### Club surveys

Club surveys are conducted by a number of organizations who agree to exchange information on pay in accordance with a standard format and on a regular basis. They have all the advantages of special surveys plus the additional benefits of saving a considerable amount of time and providing regular information. It is well worth joining one if you can. If a suitable club does not exist you could always try to start one, but this takes considerable effort.

### Advertisements

Many organizations rely on the salary levels published in recruitment advertisements. But these can be very misleading as you will not necessarily achieve a good match and the quoted salary may not be the same as what is finally paid. However, although it is highly suspect, data from advertisements can be used to supplement other more reliable sources.

### Other market intelligence

Other market intelligence can be obtained from the publications of *Incomes Data Services* and *Industrial Relations Services*. This may include useful information on trends in the 'going rate' for general, across-the-board pay increases which can be used when deciding on what sort of uplift, if any, is required to pay scales.

## Using survey data

The use of market survey data as a guide on pay levels is a process based on judgement and compromise. Different sources may produce different indications of market rate levels. As a result you may have to produce what might be described as a 'derived' market rate based on an assessment of the relative reliability of the data. This would strike a reasonable balance between the competing merits of the different sources used. This is something of an intuitive process.

Once all the data available have been collected and presented in the most accessible manner possible (ie job by job for all the areas the structure is to cover), reference points can be determined for each pay range in a graded pay structure as described in Chapter 33. This process will take account of the place in the market the business wishes to occupy, ie its market 'stance' or 'posture'.

# 33

# Pay Structures

## Definition

A pay structure consists of an organization's pay ranges for jobs grouped into grades or for individual jobs, pay curves for job families, or pay scales for jobs slotted into a pay spine. However, a system of individual job rates (spot rates) could also be regarded as a pay structure.

In a typical graded structure, jobs will be allocated to job grades according to their relative size, which in a formal system will have been determined by some type of job evaluation. There will be a pay range for each grade which defines the minimum and maximum rates of pay for all the jobs in the grade. This pay range will take account of market rates for the jobs in the grade.

## Purpose

The purpose of a pay structure is to provide a fair and consistent basis for motivating and rewarding employees. The aim is to further the objectives of the organization by having a logically designed framework within which internally equitable and externally competitive reward policies can be implemented, although the difficulty of reconciling often conflicting requirements for equity and competitiveness has to be recognized.

The structure should help in the management of relativities and enable the organization to recognize and reward people appropriately according to their job/role size, performance, contribution, skill and competence. It should be possible to communicate with the aid of the structure the pay opportunities available to all employees.

*Pay Structures*

The pay structure should also help the organization to control the implementation of pay policies and budgets.

## Criteria for pay structures

Pay structures should:

- Be appropriate to the characteristics and needs of the organization: its culture, size, technology and complexity, the degree to which it is subjected to change, and the type and level of people employed.
- Be flexible in response to internal and external pressures, especially those related to market rates and skills shortages.
- Facilitate operational and role flexibility so that employees can be moved around the organization between jobs of slightly different sizes without the need to reflect that size variation by changing rates of pay.
- Give scope for rewarding high level performance and significant contributions while still providing appropriate rewards and recognition for the effective and reliable 'core' employees who form the majority in most organizations.
- Facilitate rewards for performance and achievement.
- Help to ensure that consistent decisions are made on pay in relation to job size, contribution, skill and competence.
- Clarify pay opportunities, developmental pathways and career ladders.
- Be constructed logically and clearly so that the basis upon which they operate can readily be communicated to employees.
- Enable the organization to exercise control over the implementation of pay policies and budgets.

## Number of pay structures

There may be different structures according to level or to the category of employee. For example, some organizations still have two structures: one for staff and one for manual workers. Other organizations even have three structures — for managerial and professional staff, for junior staff and for manual workers. Top management (directors) may be left out of the main structure altogether and their remuneration agreed individually. Fully integrated single structures covering all employees except, sometimes, directors, are becoming more common as organizations simplify their approaches and continue to reduce status differentials.

Organizations sometimes have separate parallel structures for different occupations. For example, there may be 'technical ladders' for scientists or research and development engineers, which recognize that progression can sometimes depend more on professional competence than the assumption of managerial responsibility for people and other resources. This principle may be extended to setting up separate structures for different job families or market groups.

## The basis of pay structures

Pay structures are based on decisions about internal relativities and external comparisons as established by job evaluation and market rate surveys.

### Internal relativities

Internal relativity decisions are usually formed through a process of job evaluation. This normally excludes personal factors, and the relative size of jobs is measured on the basis of what has to be done to achieve a standard and acceptable level of job performance. In an individual job range structure this provides the reference point for the rate within the range which should be paid to a fully competent person. In a conventional graded structure the same assumption is made for all the jobs grouped into the grade although in practice their relative size may differ.

### External comparisons

External comparisons are made through market rate surveys, and decisions on external relativities follow the organization's policy on how its pay levels should relate to market rates – its market or pay stance.

Market stance policy depends on the organization's views as to whether it should pay above the market, match the market or pay less than the market. These will be influenced by such factors as the level of people the organization wants to attract and retain, the degree to which it is thought that pay is a major factor affecting attraction and retention rates and, of course, what it can afford to pay.

Some organizations are 'market driven' in the sense that they pay a lot of attention to market rates when designing and maintaining their pay structures. Others take the view that they are not going to allow another company's business and reward strategies to drive their own structure. They pay people in accordance with their beliefs on what they are worth to them. They will not, because they cannot, ignore the market place and the need to be competitive but they do not allow these needs to dominate their thinking.

It is possible to design pay structures entirely on the basis of external relativities and allow these to determine internal differentials, ignoring internal equity considerations. But this extreme approach is rare except in small or rapidly growing organizations or within sectors such as some parts of the finance sector in the City where it is accepted as the norm. It is more usual to start by assessing the relative size of jobs by job evaluation and then price those jobs on the basis of external comparisons.

Thus the reference point in a pay range may be aligned at the average market rate for jobs in the grade or above or below that rate. This may result in tension between the need for both internal equity and external competitiveness.

This tension creates general problems of market rate differentials between distinct occupational categories and particular problems when the market rate for individual jobs or an individual's market worth are above the level suggested by internal equity considerations.

One approach to dealing with the problem of significant market rate differences between certain occupations is to set up separate 'market group' structures in a job family system as described later in this chapter.

When there is pressure for one job to be paid more because of its market rate a 'market premium' can be paid, although this should only be done when there is no alternative and the premium should be removed if market rate comparisons no longer justify it. This need not result in a decrease in pay for the individual concerned who might not, however, receive the same general or market-related increase as others, with the result that the premium could be progressively reduced and eventually consolidated into base pay.

Alternatively, in a structure with reasonably wide pay ranges, it may be possible to absorb market rate differentials within the range. But this approach can lead to problems with internal equity unless it is only embarked upon when absolutely necessary and is controlled carefully.

The types of pay structures described in this chapter are:

- graded pay structures
- broad-banded structures (a variant of graded structures)
- individual job ranges
- job family structures
- pay or progression/maturity curves
- spot rates
- pay spines
- pay structures for manual workers
- integrated pay structures
- rate for age.

## Graded pay structures

A graded pay structure consists of a sequence of job grades to each of which is attached a pay range. A typical graded structure with overlapping pay ranges is illustrated in Figure 33.1.

The main features of graded structures are described below.

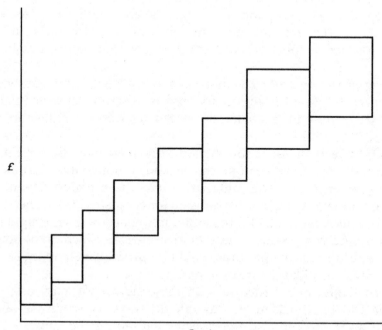

Grades

**Figure 33.1** A typical graded pay structure

## *Job grades*

Jobs are allocated to job grades on the basis of an assessment of their relative size and all jobs allocated to a grade are treated the same for pay purposes.

If a points-factor job evaluation process has been used, all jobs in a grade will be within the same job size range as defined by points scores. If some other method of job evaluation is adopted such as job classification, jobs in each grade are also assumed to be broadly within the same job size range, although this range would not be quantified in points terms.

## *Pay ranges and grades*

A pay range is attached to each grade. This defines the minimum and maximum rate payable to any job in the grade and indicates the scope provided for job holders to progress through the range. There is a reference point in the range (see below) which defines the rate of pay for a fully competent individual and which is related to market rates.

## *Defining a pay range*

A pay range may be defined in terms of the percentage increase between the lowest and highest points in the range, for example, a spread from £20,000 to £30,000 would be a 50 per cent range. Alternatively, a range may be defined in terms of a percentage of the midpoint, for example, a pay bracket of from £20,000 to £30,000 where the midpoint of £25,000 is designated as 100 per cent could be described as an 80 per cent to 120 per cent range.

## *Number of pay ranges*

The number of pay ranges will depend on the pay of the highest and lowest paid jobs in the structure, which gives the overall range of pay within which the pay ranges have to be fitted, the width of the pay ranges and the differentials between ranges.

## *Size of ranges*

The span of a range from the minimum to the maximum rate allows for pay flexibility where the policy is to have differential pay, ie pay levels for individuals will be differentiated according to their performance, skill or competence. The size of ranges can vary. In a narrow or fine-banded structure the span may be about 20 per cent above the minimum for each range. In a conventionally banded structure the span of the ranges might be around 30 to 50 per cent above the minimum. A span of 50 per cent above the minimum (ie 20 per cent on either side of the midpoint — a 80 to 120 per cent range) is fairly common for managerial grades, but the span tends to be less at more junior levels (20 to 30 per cent on the assumption that there is less scope for variations in performance).

## Reference point

In each range there will be a reference point, often the midpoint which defines what the organization is prepared to pay to job holders whose performance in a job of a particular size over a period of time is fully acceptable and who have reached the full level of competence required.

## Differentials

Differentials exist between adjacent ranges which provide adequate scope for recognizing differences in the value of jobs in the grades concerned. Differentials tend to be between 15 and 20 per cent, but 20 per cent is typical. Again, there are no fixed rules.

## Overlap

An overlap between adjacent pay ranges will exist whenever, in percentage terms, the span of the ranges exceeds the differential between them. Overlap is measured by the proportion of a range which is covered by the next lower range. Overlaps between ranges acknowledge that an experienced person doing a good job can be of more value to the organization than a newcomer to a position in the grade above. A large overlap of 40 to 50 per cent is typical in organizations with a wide variety of jobs where a reasonable degree of flexibility is required in grading them.

## Progression through ranges

Pay increases to individual job holders and progression within a range will typically vary according to assessments of performance, contribution, skill or competence and, to some degree, length of service or time in the grade.

## Advantages of graded structures

The advantages of this type of structure are that:

- Grades are easy to explain to employees and help in the communication of pay policies and practices. They clearly indicate the relativities between various job levels, especially when pay ranges are published. This is an important consideration — the management of relativities is perhaps the most onerous task facing those who are concerned with reward practices.
- Consistent methods of grading jobs and managing relativities can be maintained.
- The use of graded structures can be useful in communicating opportunities to progress through a range.
- Grades allow a degree of job flexibility and individuals can be moved round the organization to jobs of slightly different sizes without the need to change pay to reflect that size variation. The wider the grade, the greater the scope for flexibility but the greater is the need to pay close attention to the management of pay differentials.
- A well-defined and comprehensible framework exists for managing reward and career progression.
- Better control can be exercised over pay for new starters, individual performance-related pay increases and promotion increases.
- A grade structure with reasonably wide bands allows a degree of job flexibility and some scope to accommodate differences between the market rates of jobs in the grade.

## Disadvantages of graded pay structures

The disadvantages of this type of structure are that:

- The mechanics of designing and managing the grade structure and the processes of grading and regrading can create major problems. The fact that there are grade boundaries dividing groups of jobs into separate entities creates discontinuities. This in turn puts pressure on the evaluation process and the grade boundaries need to be selected with great care. This cannot be done scientifically. There is always room for judgement and the design of graded structures is often an empirical and iterative process.

- Inevitably there will be a tendency for grade drift to take place as jobs get pushed into the next grade above as a result of pressure from employees and, frequently, their managers.
- The grouping of jobs into grades means that there are different sizes of jobs within a single grade. As each grade is for pay management purposes a single unit, this inevitably means that smaller jobs in the grade will be over-paid while larger jobs will be under-paid.
- A graded pay structure can impose a degree of hierarchical rigidity which may be at odds with the fluidity with which some roles develop in an organization. For example, the careers of scientists or development engineers in high-tech organizations do not necessarily progress step by step up a promotion ladder. Some organizations are providing for even more flexibility by introducing broad-banded structures as described in the next section. Others adopt the pay curve approach as discussed later in this chapter.
- The existence of a known pay range generates expectations amongst employees that they will inevitably reach the top. However carefully the company spells out that progression depends on performance and may not go beyond a certain limit, people are still disappointed and aggrieved when their progression is halted. The result is that in many organizations managers tend to allow the pay of their staff to drift to the top of the range irrespective of their performance.
- Graded structures mean that some people will inevitably hit the ceiling of their range and, assuming the size of their jobs has not increased enough to justify regrading, they have nowhere to go unless they are promoted, which in today's flatter organizations may be less likely. Yet they may continue to make a real added value contribution and they are likely to be demotivated if they are not rewarded appropriately. This problem can be alleviated by providing for lump sum, re-earnable achievement or continuing superior level of performance bonuses (variable pay). These are typically not consolidated for pension purposes.

## Designing graded pay structures

The following basic steps are required when designing and implementing a graded pay structure:

1. Conduct a job evaluation and market rate survey exercise.
2. Decide on the pay policies of the organization — its pay or market stance and policies for differentials.
3. Develop a job grade structure and allocate jobs into the grades according to their evaluation. Jobs are allocated to grades by reference to points scores if a points-factor scheme has been used. But judgement will always be required in grading jobs so that all jobs placed in the same grade are perceived to be broadly within the same size range and it is possible to justify decisions on why jobs are placed in one grade rather than another. Overlapping pay ranges can reduce the critical nature of these judgements.
4. Define the pay ranges for each structure by reference to market rates and the differential policies of the organization.
5. Implement the structure. This may involve paying employees more than their job evaluated grade justifies, either because they have to be paid a market rate premium, or because they are over-graded and it has been decided not to reduce their pay. In these circumstances they are said to be 'red-circled' to indicate that they are anomalies.

## Conclusions

Historically, the advantage of graded structures was that they eased pay administration problems, especially when there were large numbers of jobs. However, with the advent of sophisticated reward management computer systems this becomes less necessary. Such systems enable organizations to manage and control individual job range, pay curve or spot rate structures more easily and avoid some of the difficulties mentioned above.

Conventional grading structures may be part of the culture and therefore difficult to change to some other form of structure or from a fine-graded structure to a broad-banded one. On the other hand, the introduction of a new type of structure may be a lever for assisting the process of culture change.

## Broad-banded pay structures

### Characteristics

The characteristics of a broad-banded structure are:

- a *limited number of ranges or bands* — there are four or five bands to cover all salaried employees (a structure with more than six or seven bands could better be described as a 'fat-graded' structure)

- *wider bands* — the range of salary in the band can be 100 per cent or more
- a *large overlap* between bands of 50 per cent or more — this provides room for individuals in a band to continue receiving 'career development' pay increases without having to be upgraded
- *no midpoints* — because of their spread, broad bands do not have midpoints as in a conventional graded pay structure to provide a basis for the traditional control systems of compa-ratios and mid-point management
- *target rates of pay* may be assigned to individual jobs or generic roles which are determined by reference to market values or job evaluation — but the range of pay around this target rate which can be earned by individuals may not be defined.

Alternatively, *pay zones* may be established for jobs within the band which are 'anchored' by market rates — these define the 'target' rate for a competent individual in the role and indicate that when someone is paid below market value, pay should be brought up to that rate as long as the individual achieves the required level of competence. People can be paid above the target rate within the zone if their competence and contribution is above that normally expected in their existing role. There is scope to move beyond the zone into the upper limits of the band, but pay progresses to this extent only when the role of individuals is enlarged or developed into new areas of responsibility and they demonstrate that they have the level of competence required to deliver the performance required in the extended role. The purpose of zones is to provide guidance for managers in making pay decisions and, unlike traditional salary ranges, it is possible for employees to be paid outside the zone without the need for special approvals or procedures. Although it is always emphasised that pay zones within a broadband are not the same as orthodox pay ranges, they can look remarkably similar.

## Defining bands

Bands can simply be defined in terms of the broad characteristics of the generic roles that may be allocated to them. To underline the message that a broadbanded structure is not the same as traditional graded structure hierarchies, most companies which introduce broadbanding do not designate bands by numbers or letters. Instead, they use general descriptive labels such as, in GE Plastics, 'professional, technical/ managerial, leadership, executive'.

Band boundaries are sometimes defined by means of job evaluation points so that all jobs with a score of between, say 750 and 1000 points are placed in one band. The minimum and maximum levels of pay in a band may be established by reference to market rate data for jobs in the band.

## Pay progression

In traditional graded structures it is usual to have rigid or prescribed methods of progressing pay through the relatively narrow grades. A much more flexible approach can be adopted in the wider and less structured ranges within broadbanded systems. Progression is based on managerial judgements about the individual's contribution, competence and ability to continue developing. It is recognized in today's flexible organizations that the set of responsibilities assumed to form a job is no longer stable. Roles become more dynamic as employees, especially the increasing proportion of knowledge workers, have greater scope to influence the content of their jobs. Progression is people rather than job-orientated.

The emphasis in broadbanding is on competence development, but competences are much more than a set of skills that may or may not be used. Progression within a band is based not on the *existence* of knowledge and skills but on their application in a series of career moves in which people are faced with new opportunities and challenges and rewarded accordingly.

## Advantages and disadvantages

The main advantages of broadbanding are that it:

- enhances organizational flexibility by reducing the number of vertical breakpoints
- speaks more directly to each employee's personal growth by paying for skills and competences
- encourages the development of multi-focus roles and a 'boundaryless' organization
- can help organizations to reward lateral career development and continuous learning.

The advantages of broadbanding may seem to be considerable but there are some important disadvantages. Broadbanding may mean that:

- the number of promotional opportunities appear to be restricted
- employees are concerned by the apparent lack of structure precision
- employees may expect more in the way of pay progression than they get
- payroll costs could escalate unless very careful control is exercised over the operation of the system, but this may be difficult.

Broad-banding is probably only an option for large, delayered organizations which are adopting a sophisticated approach to reward management.

## Individual job ranges

Where the content and size of jobs is widely different, for example at senior levels, an individual job grade structure may be preferable to a conventionally banded structure. An individual job grade structure avoids the problem of grouping a number of jobs with widely different job sizes into a grade, with the inevitable consequence that some jobs are underpaid while others are overpaid.

Individual job range structures simply define a separate pay range for each job. The relativities between jobs are usually determined by points-factor job evaluation which may in effect convert points to pounds by the application of a formula. There is a reference point in each range, often the midpoint, and the range is expressed as plus or minus a percentage of the reference point, typically 20 per cent. The reference point is aligned to market rates in accordance with the organization's pay stance. Where reliable market data is available this can be carried out job by job, which means that individual ranges can more readily be changed in response to market rate movements.

## Job family structures

The advantages of operating one pay structure for all jobs in terms of achieving consistency and facilitating control seem to be obvious. But it becomes progressively more difficult to do this in two situations. First, where market rate pressures operate differentially on particular occupations or categories of employees and second, when there are significant variations in the type of work carried out and the competences required by different occupational groups which cannot easily be catered for in a single pay structure.

Job family structures provide a method of dealing with these problems. A job family consists of jobs in a function or discipline such as research scientist, development engineer or personnel specialist. The jobs will be related in terms of the fundamental activities carried out and the basic skills required, but they will be differentiated by the level of responsibility, skill or competence involved. Job families may also be distinguished from one another in terms of the market rates for the occupations within the family. Significant differences in market rates may mean that a family will constitute a separate 'market group'.

A job family structure consists of separate graded pay structures for each of the job families which have been identified for this purpose. These structures are aligned individually to market rates and contain a number of pay ranges which reflect the particular levels of work within the job family.

Separate job families or market groups may only cover some occupations in the organization. The others would be catered for by a common graded pay structure.

Job family structures can be suitable where occupations need to be treated differently because of the nature of the work and/or their special market rate position. But they can be divisive and equity is more difficult to achieve, especially where they are strongly orientated towards market rates and individual competences. Unless great care is taken to justify differences in these terms, it can be difficult to ensure that the principle of equal pay for work of equal value is maintained and this important aspect has so far not been tested.

## Pay curves

Pay curves (sometimes referred to as maturity or progression curves) are related to job family structures. A pay curve system recognizes that different methods of handling pay determination and progression may have to be used in some job families, especially those containing knowledge workers. Pay curves are also concerned with the development of more integrated approaches to pay involving rewarding people according to a combination of their competence, performance and market worth.

Graded structures can work well when job evaluation is used to discriminate clearly between job responsibilities and progression is made in a series of steps representing a distinct hierarchy of increases in job size.

However, graded structures may not be so suitable for knowledge workers such as professional staff, engineers, scientists, technologists, technicians or IT specialists who may carry out innovative or at least highly variable work and whose skills may be readily transferable to a wide variety of projects or tasks. The basis upon which work is allocated to them and the level of work they carry out may depend entirely on their particular range of skills and expertise and not on their position in a defined hierarchy. It is often the case that the value of such people increases progressively as they mature in the sense of acquiring additional skills and competences and/or the ability to use an increasing range of skills more flexibly. These are the individuals whose experience over time will equip them to expand their role. They are likely to develop continuously as new opportunities and challenges arise. Their advancement will not be a matter of climbing distinct steps in a job hierarchy where job size can be determined by points-factor evaluation scores, although it may well be possible to define levels of competence to which they can aspire.

The basis of a pay curve system is therefore the value of individuals to the organization and their particular roles rather than the assumed comparative value of the jobs they carry out.

Pay curves as illustrated in Figure 33.2, provide different pay progression tracks along which people in a family of jobs can move according to their levels of competence and performance. Pay levels are determined by reference to market rates. The assumptions governing pay curves are that first, competence develops progressively through various levels or bands rather than between a number of fixed points, second, individuals will develop at different rates and will therefore deliver different levels of performance which should be rewarded accordingly and third, market rate considerations should be taken into account when determining levels of pay at each point in the curve.

The concept of pay curves is linked to that of competence-based evaluation (see Chapter 32), which, like skill-based evaluation, recognizes that roles may expand to the level of ability or competence of the job holder rather than being constrained within narrowly defined jobs in traditional hierarchies.

A job family pay curve contains a number of competence bands each of which constitutes a definable level of skill, competence and responsibility. Individuals move through these bands at a rate which is

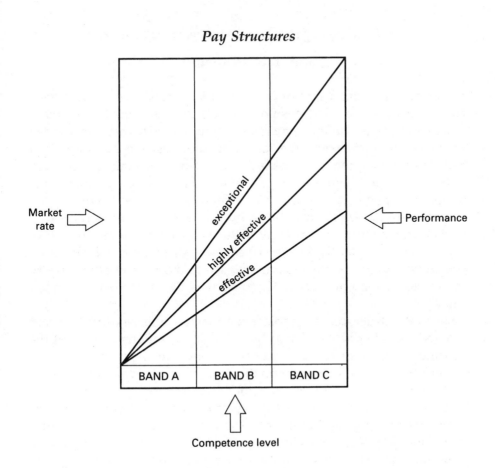

**Figure 33.2** A job family pay curve

related to their performance and their capacity to develop. They would not move into a new band until they have demonstrated that they have attained the level of competence required. Pay ranges in each band are related to market rates for the job family concerned in line with the organization's pay stance. Pay curves may be introduced for knowledge-workers alongside a more conventional structure for other employees.

Under this system there is usually no common level of movement for all employees. Instead, each set of job family pay curves will be amended as necessary to reflect market rate movements. Even within a job family there may not be a general increase in pay. Reviews take account of how the pay of individuals reflects their market worth (which is, of course, affected by their performance and competence) and their rate will be adjusted accordingly.

## Spot rate structures

In its simplest form, a spot or individual job rate structure allocates a specific rate for a job. There is no scope for the basic rate for the job to progress through a defined pay range, although individual rates of pay for job holders for whom the rates have not been negotiated with a trade union may change, possibly at the whim of management. Job holders may be eligible for performance pay through performance-related base pay progression, or an incentive or bonus scheme.

Spot rates can be fixed entirely by reference to market rates in a market driven structure and, unless this is done systematically, a spot rate system can hardly be described as a structure at all. In more structured systems, job evaluation is used to measure relative job size and establish a job hierarchy. The rates may be negotiated with trade unions.

Spot rate structures are typical for manual workers but they are adopted for other types of staff by some organizations who want the maximum degree of scope to pay what they like. Such organizations are very unlikely to use a systematic process of job evaluation.

Modifications can be made to spot rate structures so that they give some room for varying levels of pay other than by means of performance-related pay or incentives. These modifications can produce something akin to an individual job grade structure. There may be a provision for paying less than the spot rate for those on a learning curve where they are not fully qualified to do the job, or for paying more for specified skills, job responsibilities or conditions of work.

## Pay spines

Pay spines consist of a series of incremental points extending from the lowest to the highest paid jobs covered by the structure. Pay scales or ranges for different job grades may then be superimposed on the pay spine.

If performance-related pay is introduced, individuals can be given accelerated increments. The Civil Service has used this approach to add range points to the top of the normal scale which enable staff who achieve very high or consistently high performance ratings to advance above the maximum scale for the grade. The Civil Service is now, however, moving on to a diversity of approaches at different levels which involve more delegation of pay decisions to departments.

Pay spines are most often found in the public sector or in agencies and voluntary organizations which have adopted a public sector approach to reward management.

## Pay structures for manual workers

A pay structure for manual workers consists of the rates paid to employees who work on the shop floor, in distribution, transport, public services and anywhere else where the work primarily involves manual skills and tasks. The structure will be similar to any other pay structure in that it incorporates pay differentials between jobs which reflect real and assumed differences in skill and responsibility but are influenced by pressures from the local labour market, by custom and practice and by settlements reached between management and trade unions. These pay levels are underpinned by what can be described as the 'effort bargain'.

### The effort bargain

The task of management is to assess what level and type of inducements it has to offer in return for the contribution it requires from its workforce. The worker's aim is to strike a bargain about the relationship between what he or she regards as a reasonable contribution and what the employer is prepared to offer to elicit that contribution. This is termed the 'effort bargain' and is, in effect, an agreement which lays down the amount of work to be done for a rate of pay or wage rate, not just the hours to be worked. Explicitly or implicitly, all employees are in a bargaining situation with regard to pay. A system will not be accepted as effective and workable until it is recognized as fair and equitable by both parties.

### Rates of pay

The basic method of paying manual workers is the time rate for the job, which is paid according to the level of the job (eg skilled, semi-skilled or unskilled) and the hours worked as described below. There may also be an incentive element which is related to some measure of performance or skill. This arrangement is described in Chapter 34.

### Time rates

Time rates, also known as day rates or flat rates, are an arrangement under which workers are simply paid a predetermined rate per month, week, day or hour for the actual time worked. Pay is fixed in accordance with the level of the job or the skills regularly used and only varies with time, never with output, performance or any additional skills the worker acquires.

In some companies, what are termed high time or day rates are paid which are set at a level above the minimum rates. The high day rate may include a consolidated bonus element and is probably greater than the local labour market rate to attract and retain good quality workers. High day rates have been common in industries such as motor manufacturing where above average earnings are expected because of a history of payment-by-results, and where there is a high degree of machine control over output. They are appropriate in machine-paced assembly lines and in some high technology plants where multiskilling and flexibility are important — both these requirements may be inhibited by a traditional payment-by-results scheme.

Time rates are often used when it is believed that it is undesirable or impossible to operate an incentive scheme, for example, in maintenance work. But they are being increasingly introduced in situations where a payment-by-result scheme has proved to be unsatisfactory in the sense that it creates wage drift, is costly to run, creates conflict or is not providing value for money in the shape of increased productivity. Time rates may also be adopted where there is a focus on total quality.

From the point of view of many operators, time rates are better because earnings are predictable and steady and they do not have to engage in endless arguments with industrial engineers, rate fixers and supervisors about piecework rates or work measured time allowances.

The obvious argument against time rates is that they do not provide the motivation of a direct financial incentive which clearly relates pay to performance. The point is often made that people want money and will work harder to get it. The argument is a powerful one and is supported by the many successful incentive schemes that are still in operation, although the difficulty of maintaining an effective payment-by-result scheme should never be underestimated.

## Plus rates

Many structures incorporate various 'plus rates' for particular skills or demands made on employees. These may include shift rates, pay for 'unsocial working hours', overtime rates, and pay for difficult or unpleasant working conditions.

## Integrated pay structures

Integrated pay structures cover groups of employees who have traditionally been paid under separate arrangements. An integrated structure may have one grading system which includes all employees — managers, professional, technical and office staff *and* manual workers, although such structures frequently leave out senior management.

An integrated pay structure may be based on the same system of job evaluation which is applied to all employees. It will involve the harmonization to some extent of employee benefits and conditions of employment such as holidays, hours of work, sick pay and pensions, although the scale of such benefits may still be related to position in the grade hierarchy.

## Rate for age scales

Rate for age scales provide for a specific rate of pay or a pay bracket to be linked to age for staff in certain jobs. They are relatively uncommon nowadays because of changing patterns of work. The rationale for rate for age scales used to be the learning curve principle, but that can be catered for in a graded pay structure. They are, however, still in use for employees below the age of 21 on formal training schemes extending over two or three years.

## Choice of structure

Two factors determine the choice of structure: first, the type of people employed — the existence and proportions of managers, knowledge workers, sales staff, office workers and skilled or unskilled manual workers; and second, the type of organization — its size, technology, complexity, culture and traditions.

Larger enterprises and institutions with formal, hierarchical organization structures will trend to prefer conventional graded structures which provide for orderly administration and ease in managing internal relativities. High technology organizations who want to achieve rather more flexibility but within a defined framework may opt for a broad-banded structure or a pay curve system.

Individual job ranges may be favoured by organizations who want a degree of formality, for example in progressing people through a range, but do not wish to put 'one-off' jobs into what they may perceive as the straitjacket of a graded structure.

Organizations who are particularly concerned with maintaining competitive pay levels and have a number of different market groups among their employees may prefer a job family structure. They could also introduce such a structure if there were a number of distinctive job families. If they employ a large proportion of knowledge workers who are continually developing in their jobs, especially in their formative years, they may go further and introduce a pay curve system for certain categories of staff.

Smaller organizations, those whose environment induces a more flexible, less formalized approach to administration, companies which are market rate driven and fast-moving entrepreneurial companies who demand very high performance may prefer a spot rate structure, coupled, especially in the latter category, with a powerful pay-for-performance system.

# 34

# Paying for Individual Performance, Skill and Competence

## Paying for performance

### Defined

Paying for performance is the process of providing a financial reward to an individual which is linked directly to his or her performance. The principal types of performance pay are performance related pay (PRP), individual and team incentive and bonus schemes, and organization-wide profit or added value related plans.

### Advantages and disadvantages of paying for performance

Advocates of paying for performance claim that it improves individual, team and organizational performance by:

- focusing for employees the elements of their performance which deliver organizational success thus directing their attention and effort where it is most needed
- motivating employees
- increasing commitment and identification
- reinforcing or helping to change cultures and values — typically towards a more performance, quality and customer service orientated culture
- recognizing and rewarding contribution, not just effort
- differentiating consistently and equitably in the distribution of rewards in relation to contribution

- delivering positive messages about performance expectations
- improving the recruitment and retention of high quality employees
- flexing pay costs in line with organizational performance.

The potential disadvantages of paying for performance are that incentive and bonus schemes can:

- be inequitable and unfair if they do not clearly and properly relate reward to performance, which they often fail to do
- be divisive, prejudicing teamwork
- encourage 'short-termism' — for example, executives concentrating on short-term issues linked to annual targets rather than the achievement of longer-term plans
- encourage shop-floor workers to go for output at the expense of quality and sales staff to go for sales turnover rather than customer service
- are often all too easy to manipulate
- be demotivating if they are linked to corporate performance which is adversely affected by outside influences such as exchange rate fluctuations
- are often difficult to keep under control — earnings can increase to absurdly high limits (especially in some executive bonus schemes) without any commensurate improvement in performance
- add to remuneration costs without delivering real performance improvements.

These disadvantages can be formidable and should be weighed very carefully against the advantages set out earlier before introducing a new scheme or reviewing an existing one. Account should also be taken of the reservations expressed above about the effectiveness of performance pay. And Vicky Wright (1991) has emphasized that: 'Even the most ardent supporters of performance related pay recognize that it is extraordinarily difficult to manage well.'

However, the philosophical argument that it is equitable to relate pay to performance is overwhelming, and it does work well in many circumstances especially on the shop floor, in sales jobs, and in managerial or other jobs where there is a visible and direct relationship between focused effort and reward. It can also be argued strongly that performance pay schemes are an effective means of conveying the message that performance matters and channelling effort in the right direction.

## *Paying for performance — incentive or reward?*

When defining the objectives of their pay-for-performance schemes, many people treat the terms incentive and reward as being inter-changeable. But there are significant differences, and when defining objectives and evaluating results it is necessary to distinguish between them.

The essential distinction is that incentives are forward-looking while rewards are retrospective.

- *Financial incentives* are designed to motivate people to improve their performance — to make a greater contribution by increasing effort and output and by producing better results expressed in such terms as objectives and targets for profit, sales turnover, productivity, cost reduction, quality, customer service, turnaround and delivery on time.
- *Financial rewards* provide extra money for achievement in terms of contribution or output. The emphasis is on recognition and on equity, in the sense of paying people according to their just deserts ('the labourer is worthy of his hire'). Recognition is, of course, an important form of motivation and therefore may provide an incentive, but the relationship between pay and future performance is not always as clear as some people would like to believe.

This difference is important because it highlights the fact that schemes which are designed to provide motivation and incentives may in practice fail to do this directly, although they will be a useful means of recognizing contribution.

This distinction between incentives and rewards points the way to another aspect of reward processes about which there is often con-fusion — the difference between incentives and bonuses.

## *The difference between incentives and bonuses*

The terms incentive and bonus are often juxtaposed. In this book, the terms are used with special meaning. They resemble each other in that they are both payments which are linked in some defined way to performance. But there the similarity ends.

- *Incentives*: are payments linked to the achievement of previously set and agreed targets.
- *Bonuses*: are essentially rewards for success and are paid out as a lump sum.

## Criteria for success

As Lawler (1995) put it, pay-for performance systems 'must create a clear line of sight between an employee's behaviour and the receipt of important amounts of money'. In particular, the success criteria are:

- individuals need to be clear about the targets and standards of performance required, whatever they may be
- they must be in a position to influence their performance by changing their behaviour or decisions
- they should be clear about the rewards they will receive for achieving the required end-results
- the rewards should be meaningful enough to make the efforts required worthwhile — and the communication of the rewards should be positively handled
- the incentive or bonus formula should be easy to understand
- fair and consistent means are available for measuring performance — it can be said that 'you can't pay for performance unless you can measure performance'
- it is appropriate to the type of work carried out and the people employed on it and fits the culture of the organization
- the reward follows as closely as possible the accomplishment which generated it
- individuals should be able to track performance against targets and standards throughout the period over which performance is being assessed

These are demanding criteria, and it is no wonder that performance pay schemes often fail to meet expectations. But PRP (performance-related pay) schemes still flourish although payment-by-result schemes for manual workers are in decline.

## Types of pay-for-performance schemes

The main types of pay-for-performance schemes are:

- performance-related pay
- executive bonus schemes
- shop floor incentive schemes.

These are described below.

## Performance related pay

Performance related pay (PRP) bases additional financial rewards on ratings of performance and contribution. The ratings are derived from performance reviews and assessments of overall contribution, achievements against objectives, and competence as part of the performance management process described in Chapter 13.

The rewards may take the form of pay increases which progress individuals through a pay range at rates which will vary according to performance. But this can be described as 'a gift that goes on giving', and some businesses are using lump sum 'achievement bonuses' as an alternative. These are paid when an individual has done particularly well, 'beyond the normal line of duty', in delivering results or completing a project. They may also be paid to those who are at the top of their pay range but are still performing outstandingly well. This avoids the demotivating impact of coming to 'the end of the road' as far as financial rewards are concerned, if there are no promotion opportunities (and in today's flatter organizations, these may not be readily available).

PRP is generally applied to individuals. But the increasing attention being paid to developing good teamwork is encouraging some organizations to concentrate more on team pay, usually through some form of group bonus scheme. And individual PRP schemes are paying more attention to performance criteria related to teamwork.

### How PRP operates

Methods of operating PRP vary considerably but its typical main features are as follows.

- *Pay structure* — this is designed to provide scope for pay progression within pay brackets attached to job grades.
- *Pay progression and performance* — the rate and limits of progression through the pay brackets are determined by performance ratings.
- *Decelerated progression* — pay progression relating to performance is typically planned to decelerate through the grade because it is argued in line with learning curve theory that pay increases should be higher during the earlier period in a job when learning is at its highest rate.
- *Performance-related pay increases* may be added cumulatively to basic pay (ie consolidated) until either the maximum rate of pay for the

grade or a limit within the grade defined in terms of a level of performance is reached as was illustrated in Figure 34.1. PRP increases typically range from 3 per cent to 10 per cent with an average of about 5 per cent in times of low inflation. But this can vary considerably between organizations and between different categories of people within organizations. Alternatively, as mentioned below, they can be paid as non-consolidated lump sums although this is less common. The CBI/Wyatt 1994 survey on variable pay systems in the UK indicated that the average awards for individual bonus schemes were 10 per cent for senior management, 8 per cent for managerial and professional staff and 5 per cent for supervisory and clerical staff (note, however, that in this analysis 'individual bonus' included any type of bonus scheme as well as performance-related pay plans).

It has been suggested by Lawler (1990) that a pay change of 10 per cent to 15 per cent is probably required to increase motivation significantly and some commentators put the necessary change at an even higher level. Research indicates that a pay increase of 3 per cent to 5 per cent, while noticeable, is not sufficient to improve performance.

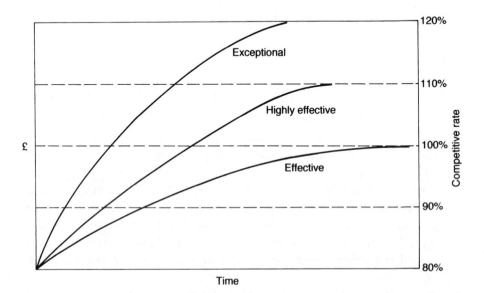

**Figure 34.1** Performance-related variable progression

## Methods of determining and controlling PRP increases

PRP increases are usually based on a performance rating as discussed in chapter 13 and the total amount spent on performance pay will be controlled by a payroll or a performance pay increase budget. The latter may be applied as a single figure, for example 5 per cent of pay roll throughout the organization, or flexed on the basis of assumptions about which departments or categories of employees should be given a larger or smaller budget than the norm. The main methods of determining PRP increases are described below, ranked in order of the amount of discretion allowed to line managers to make decisions.

### Line manager's discretion

Line managers can be given discretion to make PRP awards within their budgets, although they may be told the target rate of pay for a fully competent individual and the circumstances in which cash should be given rather than a pay increase. Devolving pay decisions to line managers can create a problem of ensuring that such decisions are equitable, fair and consistent. The responsibility of line managers for reward matters is discussed in Chapter 38.

### Guidelines

Guidelines to managers on PRP decisions can set out the minimum and maximum increases that can be given, for example, 3 per cent and 10 per cent. This, of course, must be within the PRP increase budget.

If a rating system is used, firmer guidelines can be produced suggesting that, within the budget, increases can be awarded as in the following example:

|   |   | % |
|---|---|---|
| A | = | 10 |
| B | = | 7.5 |
| C | = | 5 |
| D | = | 3 |
| E | = | 0 |

Even stronger guidelines can be provided which indicate the recommended distribution of awards between employees according to their ratings. These sometimes take the form of a normal distribution on the questionable assumption that competence and ability are distributed normally. Some companies skew the distribution to avoid this. Here are some examples of distribution patterns:

|   | % | % | % | % |
|---|---|---|---|---|
| A | 10 | 5 | 10 | 5 |
| B | 20 | 15 | 20 | 20 |
| C | 40 | 60 | 50 | 60 |
| D | 20 | 15 | 15 | 10 |
| E | 10 | 5 | 5 | 5 |

*PRP matrix*
A common approach to providing firm guidelines is to use a PRP matrix. This puts dimensions on the PRP curves illustrated in Figure 24.1 by indicating the percentage increase payable for different ratings according to the position of the individual's pay in the pay range. An example for an 80 to 120 per cent range is illustrated in Figure 34.2.

*Forced distribution*
Guidelines such as those mentioned above can be strengthened by requiring that managers must distribute their awards in accordance with a distribution pattern laid down centrally. This may achieve uniformity but it will certainly create resentment — no one likes being put in a straitjacket, and it can reasonably be argued that the distribution of ability and performance will vary between departments.

*Ranking*
Ranking is also an enforced approach to distributing awards and can cause just as much resentment. It means ranking employees according to the merit rating scores they have been given and then laying down the increases to be awarded to defined sections of the rank order, eg 10 per cent for the first 5 per cent, 8 per cent for the next 15 per cent and so

| | Position in pay range (compa-ratio) | | | |
|---|---|---|---|---|
| *Rating* | 80–90% | 91–100% | 101–110% | 111–120% |
| *Exceptional* | 12 | 10 | 8 | 6 |
| *Very effective* | 10 | 8 | 6 | 4 |
| *Effective* | 6 | 4 | 3 | 0 |
| *Developing* | 4 | 3 | 0 | 0 |
| *Ineligible* | 0 | 0 | 0 | 0 |

**Figure 34.2** A PRP matrix

on. Some flexibility could be introduced by varying the proportions between different departments, although this would be an arbitrary process.

## Arguments for PRP

The strongest argument in favour of PRP is that it is right and equitable to reward people according to their contribution. PRP provides a tangible means of recognizing achievement.

PRP is also a means of ensuring that everyone understands the performance imperatives of the organization.

It is also argued, of course, that PRP works as an incentive because money is the best motivator.

## Arguments against PRP

The arguments most frequently levelled against PRP are that:

- Its effectiveness as a motivator can be questioned — there is little firm evidence that people are motivated by their expectations on the rewards they will get from PRP, especially as these are often quite small.
- Financial incentives may work for some people because their expectations that they will be rewarded well are high. But such individuals will tend to be well-motivated anyway. Less confident employees will not respond so well to the possibility of rewards which they do not expect to receive.
- It can be difficult to measure individual performance objectively, especially in demand-led or process jobs — unfair assessments may be made in these circumstances because ratings tend to be both subjective and inconsistent.
- It can encourage people to focus narrowly on the tasks that will earn them 'brownie points' and to be less concerned about innovation, longer-term issues and quality.
- If there is undue emphasis on individual performance, teamwork will suffer.
- It can lead to pay rising faster than performance if proper control is not exercised — there is often a tendency for performance-related pay to drift upwards without any commensurate improvement in performance.

However, many organizations still feel that PRP is desirable, even when they recognize that it is seldom an effective motivator and in spite of the other arguments against it listed above. They favour PRP for three main reasons:

1. Rewards should be differentiated according to performance.
2. It can help to develop a more performance-orientated culture.
3. It can deliver messages about performance expectations.

Many employees also believe that their pay should be related to their performance — as long as this is done fairly.

But PRP schemes can easily fail — and often do — because they have been badly or hastily conceived. Many first generation schemes introduced in the heady days of the 1980s with much enthusiasm but little thought are now being replaced because they have been unpopular, ineffective, or both.

PRP will only work if:

● performance can be and is measured properly — a well-established and effective performance management process is in place which is accepted by managers and other employees alike
● individuals feel that PRP decisions are fair
● there is a climate of trust between management and employees
● the scheme is developed in consultation with the line managers who will make PRP decisions and with representatives of the employees who will be affected by it
● the aims of the scheme and how it will function are communicated thoroughly to employees
● the operation of the scheme is continually monitored and regular evaluations of its impact and costs are made
● the views of managers and employees about how PRP is working are obtained, listened to and acted upon whenever a real problem is revealed.

Everyone who has successfully introduced PRP stresses the needs to 'communicate, communicate, communicate' and 'involve, involve, involve'. This, of course, applies to any other reward or personnel and development innovation which affects the interests of employees — and when do they not affect their interests?

## Executive bonus and incentive schemes

Bonus and incentive schemes for directors and senior executives provide additional and often substantial sums in addition to base salary.

These payments generally reward the attainment of company growth and profitability targets although in some schemes they may be related to the achievement of individual objectives linked to specific accountabilities.

Executive bonuses and incentives incorporate an element of risk money into the remuneration package. Their use has extended rapidly because companies believe that this risk element is appropriate for their executives. It also allows for considerable rewards to be made for success. There is evidence, however, that excessively high payments can be made which are not justified by the individual contribution of the chief executive or director.

Another important reason for the spread of executive bonus and incentive schemes is that it is believed they are necessary to maintain competitive overall levels of remuneration for key people.

## Shop floor incentive schemes

Shop floor incentive schemes relate the pay or part of the pay received by employees to the number of items they produce or process, the time they take to do a certain amount of work and/or some other aspect of their performance. They usually provide for pay to fluctuate with performance in the short term, but they can, as in measured daywork, provide for a long-term relationship. They are often referred to as payment-by-result schemes.

Traditionally, the ratio of base rate to incentive has been 2:1, but the current trend is to reduce the target proportion of incentive pay to one-third or one-quarter to minimize fluctuations in earnings and to control wage or earnings drift (increases in incentive based earnings which are higher than the increases in output which generated the incentive payment — wage drift is an undesirable but common phenomenon associated with old and decaying payment-by-result schemes). Further reasons for reducing the incentive element is that many organizations find it more difficult to justify highly personalized differentiated pay because it can be counter-productive in terms of the achievement of quality and teamwork.

There might also be a guaranteed or 'fall-back' rate for workers in payment-by-results schemes which would be related to the con-solidated time rate for a worker at a similar level.

The main types of incentive or payment-by results schemes are individual piecework, work-measured schemes and measured day work.

## Individual piecework

In individual or straight piecework a uniform price is paid per unit of production. Operators are therefore rewarded according to the number of 'pieces' they produce or process, so pay is directly proportioned to results.

Most piecework schemes provide a fall-back rate or minimum earnings level. It is common for the minimum rate to be set at 70 to 80 per cent of average earnings, although some companies set it as low as 30 per cent and others set it equal to the minimum time rate. Companies may also provide guaranteed payments for downtime due to machine failure, maintenance work or waiting for materials.

The advantages to employers of piecework is that the system is easy to operate, simple to understand and can be left to run by itself, provided there is adequate supervision to ensure that quality does not suffer. Piecework can also enable employers to estimate and control manufacturing costs effectively. But employers can find that they lose control over the level of production, which depends largely on the self-motivation of the workforce. Quality can suffer if close supervision is not exercised and the negotiation of piece rates for new work can be time consuming and fractious.

The advantages to employees is that they can predict their earnings in the short term and regulate their pace of work in accordance with the level of pay they want to attain. But it may be difficult to predict longer-term earnings if work fluctuates from week to week. The intensity of work required in this system may lead to repetitive strain injury (RSI).

Piecework has become more inappropriate as an incentive method as new technology has changed work arrangements. In larger scale manufacturing it has largely been replaced by work-measured schemes or some other form of incentive or bonus payment.

## Work-measured schemes

In a work-measured scheme the job, or its component tasks, is timed and the incentive payment is related to performance above the standard time allowed for the job. The amount of incentive pay received depends on the difference between the actual time taken to perform the task and the standard time allowed. If a task is done in less than the standard time, then there is a time saving, which means that the operator's output will increase.

## Paying for Individual Performance, Skill and Competence

Work measurement involves working out standard values or times for a complete task, which can, however, be broken down into components to each of which standard minute values can be allocated. Work study or industrial engineers can measure the time taken for each component with the help of a stop-watch. A large number of timings will be made in each task to ensure that the variety of conditions under which an operator works are included so as to minimize distortions. Measurements may therefore be taken at different times of the day, and a number of operators may be timed on the same task to extend the range of timings and reduce the risk of errors.

The work study engineer who measures the job will be entirely objective about the stop-watch timing but a subjective assessment will also have to be made of the operator's speed, or effectiveness. This is known as the operator's effort rating. The performance of a qualified worker, if motivated, without over-exertion, is known as standard performance. Industrial engineers sometimes relate this to walking at a reasonably brisk pace, say four miles an hour. All operators who have been timed are given an effort rating relative to this standard and this is taken into account when deciding on standard times.

A refinement of individual work measurement is to adopt a predetermined motion time system such as methods time measurement (MTM). Such a system can be used when a mass of data has been assembled over a period of time which can lead to the production of 'synthetics' — standard times which can be applied to a particular task or operation. If these synthetics are based on reliable data they can eliminate the need for expensive and time-consuming work measurement and avoid disagreements about the accuracy of standards (especially when individual standards have involved the use of subjective effort rating).

When calculating standard values or times, allowances can be made to cover a reasonable amount of relaxation, personal needs, fatigue, and contingencies associated with the work, such as machine adjustments and maintenance.

When standard values have been calculated, a performance scale can be drawn up against which an operator's performance can be rated. Common scales include the British Standard Institution 100/133, on which 100 represents the performance of an average operator working conscientiously without financial motivation, and 133 represents the same worker's performance with financial motivation. Other scales are the BSI 75/100 or the 60/80 scale, which all work on the same principle, ie that the performance for a motivated worker will be set at one-third more than the performance of an operator working without an incentive.

Incentive payments are made when performance exceeds the standard. The relationship between pay and performance usually follows either the proportional or regressive pattern.

When proportional payments are made the incentive payment increases in direct proportion to performance. Thus on the BSI 100/133 scale the incentive may be one per cent of basic pay for every point above BSI 100. If, for example, the operator works at BSI 110, the incentive payment is ten per cent of base pay.

In a regressive or deaccelerated payment system the incentive payment increases proportionately less than output. For example, a performance of BSI 110 may produce a payment of eight per cent of basic pay, while one of BSI 120 may result in a payment of 14 per cent.

The proportionate payment method is the most equitable one, but a regressive system has the advantage for employers of making mistakes in rate-fixing less costly and lowering unit wage costs for output above standard performance. For obvious reasons, however, the latter approach is viewed with suspicion by trade unions and workers.

It is usual, and advisable, to establish a ceiling to the amount of incentive pay which can be earned to avoid excessive amounts being paid out because of loose rates or, some other form of degeneration (this is sometimes called 'capping'). Typically, the upper limit is set at 133 points in a BSI 100/133 scheme resulting in a maximum payment of 33 per cent of base pay in a proportional payment system or, less — for example, 20 per cent — in a regressive system.

## The problem of degeneration

Incentive schemes degenerate. The consultants and work study engineers who install them say they should not degenerate but they do. In an ideal world they would not. Managers and team leaders should be able to exercise the degree of control the consultants advise. But the latter do not always live in the real world where there are numerous opportunities for workers to gain more from an incentive scheme than they have earned. Both individual and group incentive schemes are prone to this type of degeneration, which is often called wage or earnings drift.

The main causes of degeneration are:

- *Special allowances.* All schemes have allowances for the payment of shop-average earnings or some other figure which includes a premium over the base rate in certain circumstances. The most common are for unmeasured work or waiting time. Clearly, the higher the proportion of the time when pay is unrelated to effort, the more the scheme degenerates.

- *Erosion of standards.* The type of work or the work mix can change almost imperceptibly over a period of time. It may not be possible to point to a change in method sufficient enough to justify a re-timing of the job under the rules of the scheme.

## Preventing degeneration

To avoid degeneration, it is advisable only to introduce a payment-by-result scheme when the following conditions apply:

- short-cycle, repetitive work
- changes in work mix, tasks or methods are infrequent
- shop-floor hold-ups are rare and not prolonged
- management and supervision are capable of controlling the scheme, not only technically, but also to prevent manipulation
- productivity is so low that the stimulus of a bonus scheme, even when it might cause problems later, is still worthwhile.

It is also necessary when introducing a scheme to use the best work study engineers available to ensure that accurate and even standards are obtained.

Recording systems and rules for booking time on non-bonus earning activities should be instituted which minimize the risk of allowance manipulation and cross-booking. Incentive earnings and performance rates should be monitored continuously and immediate action should be taken to crack down on drift. New jobs need to be timed properly and the implications of any changes in methods or work mix should be understood and reflected in altered standards — it is essential to agree initially with trade unions that changes can be made in these circumstances and when there has been an error in the original bonus calculation.

Importantly, managers, team leaders and industrial engineers should be trained in how to manage and control the scheme. It should be impressed upon them that they will be held accountable for productivity and ensuring that the scheme will not degenerate.

## Measured daywork

In measured daywork, the pay of employees is fixed on the understanding that they will maintain a specified level of performance, but pay does not fluctuate in the short term with their performance. The arrangement depends on work measurement to define the required level of performance and to monitor the actual level. The fundamental principles of measured daywork are that there is an incentive level of performance and that the incentive payment is guaranteed in advance, thereby putting employees under an obligation to perform at the effort level required. In contrast, a conventional work measured incentive scheme allows employees discretion on their effort level but relates their pay directly to the results they achieve. Between these two extremes there is a variety of alternatives, including banded incentives, stepped schemes and various forms of high day rate.

Measured daywork seeks to produce an effort–reward bargain in which enhanced and stable earnings are exchanged for an incentive level of performance. Its disadvantage is that the set performance target can become an easily attainable norm and may be difficult to change, even after extensive renegotiation.

The criteria for success in operating measured daywork are:

- total commitment of management, employees and trade unions, which can only be achieved by careful planning, joint consultation and a staged introduction of the scheme
- effective work measurement and efficient production planning and control and inventory control systems
- the establishment of a logical pay structure with appropriate differentials from the beginning of the scheme's operation — the structure should be developed by job evaluation and in consultation with employees
- the maintenance of good control systems so that swift action can be taken to correct any shortfalls on targets.

These are exacting requirements and this is one reason why measured daywork is relatively rare and has been abandoned by a number of organizations in favour of a high day rate system topped up with team or factory-wide bonuses.

## Skill-based pay

Skill-based pay is a payment method in which pay progression is linked to the number, kind and depth of skills which individuals develop and use. It involves paying for the horizontal acquisition of the skills required to undertake a wider range of tasks, and/or for the vertical development of the skills needed to operate at a higher level, or the development in depth of existing skills.

Skill-based pay systems are people rather than job orientated. Individuals are paid for the skills they are capable of using (as long as those skills are necessary) not for the job they happen to be doing at the time. There may be a basic job rate for individuals with the minimum level of skills, but above that level they will be paid for what they can do themselves and as members of teams. Skill-based pay, however, is not concerned with how well people use their skills. This is the role of performance-related pay, although it is possible to add a performance pay dimension to a skill-based pay system.

The creation of National Vocational Qualifications (NVQs) as a means of defining and assessing competence levels has arisen from the need to extend skills bases and has encouraged the growth of skill-based pay schemes.

## How skill-based pay operates

There are many varieties of skill-based pay, but a typical scheme for operatives is likely to have the following features:

- the scheme is based on defined skill blocks or modules — clusters or sets of skills which the organization is willing to reward with extra pay
- the type and number of skill blocks which individuals need to learn and can learn are defined
- the successful acquisition of the skills contained in a skills block or module results in an increment to base pay
- the incremental skills payments will be limited to a defined hierarchy or range of skills
- the order in which the skills must be acquired in a skills hierarchy may be defined or more freedom is allowed to build up a range of skills blocks (this freedom may however be restricted by defining the basic skills which have to be acquired first)
- training modules and programmes are defined for each skill block to provide the necessary 'cross-training'
- the achievement of levels of competence by experience and training can be accredited under the NVQ system through such organizations as BTEC or the City and Guilds Institute. Alternatively or additionally, the training may be certified by the company and/or an education and training institution.

673

Skill-based pay has a lot to offer organizations which are keen to extend their skillbase and increase multiskilling. It avoids many of the problems associated with performance pay but it can be expensive to introduce and operate.

## Competence-related pay

Competence-related pay links pay within a range or band to competence in the sense, not only of the acquisition of competence, but also its effective use.

The most typical approach is to use the headings and level definitions contained in a competence framework as assessment headings or levels. Individuals are rated or scored according to the level of competence they have demonstrated and these ratings are converted into a competence-related pay increase — a percentage increase to the existing rate of pay, an additional increment or, more rarely, a cash bonus. In practice, some of the schemes that have recently been introduced do not appear to differ much from traditional merit rating systems.

# 35

# Paying for Team and Organizational Performance

## Team rewards

Team-based rewards are payments or other forms of non-financial reward provided to members of a formally established team which are linked to the performance of that team. The rewards are shared amongst the members of teams in accordance with a published formula or on an *ad hoc* basis for exceptional achievements. Rewards for individuals may also be influenced by assessments of their contribution to team results.

The purpose of team rewards is to reinforce the behaviours that lead to and sustain effective team performance by:

- providing incentives and other means of recognising team achievements
- clarifying what teams are expected to achieve by relating rewards to the attainment of pre-determined and agreed targets and standards of performance or to the satisfactory completion of a project or a stage of a project
- delivering the message that one of the organisation's core values is effective team work.

Research conducted by Armstrong and Ryden (1996) established that the main reason organisations gave for developing team reward processes was the perceived need to encourage group endeavour and cooperation rather than to concentrate only on individual performance. It is argued that pay for individual performance systems prejudice team performance in two ways. First, they encourage individuals to focus on their own interests rather than those of their team. Second, they result in managers and team leaders treating their team members only as individuals rather than relating to them in terms of what the team is there to do and what they can do for the team.

## Types of teams

The choice of team rewards will be influenced by the type of team. There are four categories:

1. *Organizational teams* — these consist of individuals who are linked together organizationally as members of, for example, the 'top management team', departmental heads in an operational or research division, section heads or team leaders in a department, or even people carrying out distinct and often separate functions, as long as they are all contributing to the achievement of the objectives of their department or section.
2. *Work teams* — these are self-contained and permanent teams whose members work closely together to deliver results in terms of output, the development of products or processes, or the delivery of services to customers.
3. *Project teams* — these consist of people brought together from different functions to complete a task lasting several months to several years. After the project is completed the team disbands.
4. *Ad hoc teams* — these are functional or cross-functional teams set up to deal with an immediate problem. They are usually short-lived and operate as a task force. It is unusual to pay bonuses to such teams unless they deliver exceptional results.

## The basis of team rewards

In a sense, all of us do what we get rewarded for doing, whether acting as individuals or as members of a team. The emphasis in team reward systems is usually on team pay rather on than other forms of non-financial rewards. Pay is of course important, as a tangible means of recognition and reward and, in certain circumstances and within limits, as a motivator. But the ultimate reward for teams, especially project teams, is often the successful accomplishment of a task, as long as that is recognized. And cash is not the only means of recognition. The choice is not between financial and non-financial rewards but between financial team rewards enhanced by non-financial rewards and non-financial rewards alone.

## Team pay schemes

The most common method of providing team pay for managerial, professional, technical and office staff is to distribute a cash sum related to team performance amongst team members. Various formulae are used for calculating the bonus pool and there are a number of different ways in which bonus pools are divided between team members. There is no such thing as a typical team pay scheme for people in these categories. This is to be expected. The design of such schemes will be contingent on the requirements and circumstances of the organisation, and these will always differ.

In contrast, shop floor group incentive schemes tend to follow a similar pattern, bonuses being linked either to the physical output of teams or, in work-measured schemes, to the time saved on team tasks — the difference between allowed time and actual time.

## Requirements for team pay

Team pay works best if teams:

- stand alone as performing units for which clear targets and standards can be agreed
- have a considerable degree of autonomy — team pay is likely to be most effective in self-managed teams
- are composed of people whose work is interdependent — it is acknowledged by members that the team will only deliver the results expected of it if they work well together and share the responsibility for success
- are stable — members are used to working with one another, know what is expected of them by fellow team members and know where they stand in the regard of those members
- are mature — teams are well-established, used to working flexibly to meet targets and deadlines and capable of making good use of the complementary skills of their members
- are composed of individuals who are flexible, multi-skilled and good team players while still being capable of expressing a different point of view and carrying that point if it is for the good of the team.

## Introducing team pay

Team pay may be an unfamiliar device and it should therefore be introduced with care, especially if it is replacing an existing system of individual PRP. The process will be easier if employees have been involved in developing the scheme, but it is still essential to communicate in detail to all employees the reasons for introducing team pay, how it will work and how it will affect them.

It is better to introduce team pay into mature teams whose members are used to working together, trust one another and can recognise that team pay will work to their mutual advantage. Although it may seem an attractive proposition to use team pay as a means of welding new work teams together, there are dangers in forcing people who are already in a different situation to accept a radical change in their method of remuneration. It should be remembered that it may not be easy to get people in work teams to think of their performance in terms of how it impacts on others. It can take time for employees to adapt to a system in which a proportion of their pay is based on team achievement.

Clearly, this problem does not arise when teams are set up to tackle a special project. All the members of project or *ad hoc* teams know, or should know, that the project or task will only be completed successfully if they work well together.

## Relating rewards to organizational performance

Rewards can be related to organizational performance by means of profit-sharing, gainsharing, profit-related pay and share ownership schemes. Such rewards aim to:

- enable employees to share in the success of the organization
- increase the identification of employees with the organization
- focus employees' attention on what they can contribute to organizational success
- obtain tax advantages for employees through approved profit sharing or share schemes and profit-related pay — such 'tax-efficient' schemes enable the business to get better value for money from its expenditure on employee remuneration.

Schemes relating rewards to organizational performance, sometimes known as company-wide or factory-wide schemes, can be used to bring areas for improvement to the attention of employees. But they are not effective as individual motivators because the links between effort and reward are too remote.

### Profit sharing

Non-approved profit-sharing schemes are the traditional schemes which usually provide cash from a 'pool' to eligible employees on the basis of a formula, which may or may not be published. As reported by IDS (1995), in almost one-third of the schemes covered by their survey the size of the pool is decided at the discretion of the directors or the executive council. At General Accident, the directors are bound by one proviso; the size of the pool is subject to a minimum of 2–3 per cent of aggregate basic salaries. In some companies, the payout is triggered by the attainment of a set profit level. Others use a defined formula. In most non-approved schemes the profit-share is distributed to employees as a percentage of their pay.

The other form of profit sharing are the all-employee approved profit-sharing scheme which were originally introduced by the 1978 Finance Act. Such schemes, which must be company-wide, allow bonuses to be paid in free shares rather than in cash. Although they are known as profit-sharing schemes, there is no statutory requirement for share allocations to be directly related to company profits.

## Gainsharing schemes

Gainsharing is a formula-based company or factory-wide bonus plan which provides for employees to share in the financial gains made by a company as a result of its improved performance. The formula determines the share by reference to a performance indicator such as added value or another measure of productivity. In some schemes, the formula also incorporates performance measures relating to quality, customer service, delivery or cost reduction. Gainsharing aims to relate its payouts specifically to productivity and performance improvements within the control of employees.

## Profit-related pay

Profit-related pay schemes are arrangements approved by the Inland Revenue which have the following features:

- A portion of pay moves up and down with profit.
- Profit-related pay can be introduced or increased in amount in place of a conventional increase in pay, and this can be coupled with a conversion of some existing pay to profit-related pay. The latter is known as a salary sacrifice scheme and in such schemes employees have to accept that their pay may increase *or* decrease as profits rise or fall.

- Profit-related pay is free of income tax when it is the lower of 20 per cent of pay or £4,000 a year.
- All employees except controlling directors are eligible for tax relief under approved schemes. But employees with up to three years' service and part-timers working less than 20 hours a week may be excluded.

## Share ownership

Share ownership can be provided through approved profit sharing schemes but also by means of SAYE share option schemes or an employee share option plan (ESOP).

'Save-As-You-Earn' share option schemes provide for employees to be given options to buy shares in their company on a specified future date at the share price at the beginning of the contract or within an allowed discount to that price.

If share prices rise over the contract-period then the option price will be below the market price and a profit will be made. Whether employees opt for shares or cash there is no income tax to pay.

Employee share option schemes (ESOPs) are based on an employee benefit trust which borrows money and uses those funds to buy shares from the company to distribute to employees (including directors). The trust holds these shares on behalf of the employees to whom they have been distributed. These employees receive dividends on the shares which are taxed in the normal way. If the employees leave their shares in the employee benefit trust for at least five years, they pay no tax on them (unless the gain in value of these shares pushes an individual's tax gains over the capital gains tax threshold).

# 36

# Employee Benefits, Pensions and Allowances

## Employee benefits

### Definition

Employee benefits are elements of remuneration given in addition to the various forms of cash pay. They also include items which are not strictly remuneration such as annual holidays.

### Objectives

The objectives of the employee benefits policies and practices of an organization are to:

- provide an attractive and competitive total remuneration package which both attracts and retains high-quality employees
- provide for the personal needs of employees
- increase the commitment of employees to the organization
- provide for some people a tax-efficient method of remuneration.

Note that these objectives do not include 'to motivate employees'. This is because the normal benefits provided by a business seldom make a direct and immediate impact on performance. They can however create more favourable attitudes towards the business which can improve commitment and organizational performance in the longer term.

### Main types of employee benefits

Benefits can be divided into the following categories:

- *Pension schemes:* these are generally regarded as the most important employee benefit.
- *Personal security:* these are benefits which enhance the individual's personal and family security with regard to illness, health, accident or life insurance.
- *Financial assistance:* loans, house purchase schemes, relocation assistance and discounts on company goods or services.
- *Personal needs*: entitlements which recognize the interface between work and domestic needs or responsibilities, eg holidays and other forms of leave, child care, career breaks, retirement counselling, financial counselling and personal counselling in times of crisis, fitness and recreational facilities.
- *Company cars and petrol:* still a much appreciated benefit in spite of the fact that cars are now more heavily taxed.
- *Other benefits* which improve the standard of living of employees such as subsidized meals, clothing allowances, refund of telephone costs, mobile phones (as a 'perk' rather than a necessity) and credit card facilities.
- *Intangible benefits*: characteristics of the organization which contribute to the quality of working life and make it an attractive and worthwhile place in which to be employed.

## Taxation

It should be remembered that most benefits are taxable as 'benefits in kind', the notable exceptions being approved pension schemes, meals where these are generally available to employees, car parking spaces, professional subscriptions and accommodation where this is use solely for performing the duties of the job.

## Choice of benefits

It cannot always be assumed that the benefits a business is prepared to provide to its employees are those which are equally attractive to all employees. A 'cafeteria' or flexible remuneration system allows employees to exercise choice over a range of options within defined financial limits.

Cafeteria systems have not really been introduced to any great extent in the UK, probably because of the perceived problems of administering the system fairly and the amount of extra effort involved, although to a very limited extent some companies are allowing their executives to take a cash payment instead of their company car.

But such a system does enable businesses to:

- discover which benefits are popular and which are not, leading to the concentration of resources on those benefits welcomed by employees
- develop mechanisms to control benefit costs
- inform employees of the real costs of benefits which otherwise they take for granted.

## Total remuneration

The concept of total remuneration is based on the principle of treating all aspects of pay and benefits provision as a whole. The cost to the business and the value to the individual of each element can be assessed with the object of adjusting the package according to organizational and individual needs. Consideration can also be given to the overall competitiveness of the total package in the market place.

## Occupational pension schemes

The reasons for having a worthwhile pension scheme are that it:

- demonstrates that the organisation is a good employer
- attracts and retains high quality people by helping to maintain competitive levels of total remuneration
- indicates that the organization is concerned about the long-term interests of its employees.

## Definition

An occupational pension scheme is an arrangement under which an employer provides pensions for employees when they retire, income for the families of members who die, and deferred benefits to members who leave. A 'group scheme' is the typical scheme which provides for a number of employees.

## Operation

Occupational pension schemes are administered by trusts which are supposed to be outside the employer's control. The trustees are responsible for the pension fund from which pension benefits are paid. The pension fund is fed by contributions from employers and usually (but not always) employees. The size of the fund and its capacity to meet future commitments depends both on the size of contributions but also on the income the trustees can generate. They do this by investing fund money with the help of advisors in stocks, shares and other securities, or through an insurance company. In the latter case, insurance companies offer either a *managed fund* — a pool of money managed by the insurance company for a number of clients, or a *segregated fund* which is managed for a single client.

## Contributions

In a *contributory scheme* employees as well as employers make contributions to the pension fund. Pensionable earnings are total earnings from which may be excluded such payments as overtime or special bonuses. A sum equal to the State flat rate pension may also be excluded.

The level of contributions varies considerably, although in a typical contributory scheme, employees would be likely to contribute about 5 per cent of their earnings and employers would contribute approximately twice that amount.

## Approved scheme

Members of an occupational scheme which has been approved by the Inland Revenue (an *approved scheme)* obtain full tax relief on their contributions. The company also recovers tax on its contributions and the income tax deductible from gains realised on UK investments. This makes a pension fund the most tax-efficient form of saving available in the UK.

Employers can establish unapproved pension schemes which provide benefits in excess of approved schemes but at the expense of the generous tax allowances for the latter type of scheme.

## Retiring age and sex discrimination

Traditionally, the retiring age was 65 for men and 60 for women. However, under the Sex Discrimination Act (1986), it is unlawful for employers to require female employees to retire at an earlier age than male employees. In its judgement on the *Barber v Guardian Royal Exchange* case on 17 May 1990 the European Court ruled that pension was 'pay' under Article 119 of the Treaty of Rome (which provided for equal pay) and that it was unlawful to discriminate between men and women with regard to pension rights. It has since been agreed that pensions would not be considered as pay prior to 17 May 1990.

## Benefits statements

Every member of an occupational scheme is entitled to an annual statement setting out his or her prospective benefits.

## Contracting out

It is possible for a pension scheme to be contracted out of the State Earnings Related Scheme (SERPS) as long as it meets certain conditions.

## Types of occupational pension schemes

A defined benefit or *final salary* group pension scheme offers a guaranteed pension, part of which may be surrendered for a tax-free cash sum. In its final pay or salary form, the pension is a fraction of final pensionable earnings for each year of service (typically 1/60th). To achieve the maximum two-thirds pension in a 1/60th scheme would therefore take 40 years' service. Defined benefit schemes provide employers with a predictable level of pension. But for employers, they can be costly and unpredictable because they have to contribute whatever is necessary to buy the promised benefits.

In a defined contribution or *money purchase* scheme employers fix the contributions they want to pay for employees by undertaking to pay a defined percentage of earnings irrespective of the benefits available on retirement. The retirement pension is therefore whatever annual payment can be purchased with the money accumulated in the fund for a member.

A defined contribution scheme offers the employee unpredictable benefits because these depend on the total value of the contributions invested, the investment returns achieved and the rate at which the accumulated fund can be converted into pension on retirement. For the employer, however, it offers certainty of costs.

## Allowances and other payments to employees

The main areas in which allowances and other special payments may be made to employees are:

- *Location allowances* — London and large town allowances may be paid because of housing and other cost-of-living differentials. Allowances are paid as an addition to basic pay although many employers in effect consolidate them by paying the local market rates which takes into account explicit or implicit location allowances and costs.
- *Subsistence allowances* — the value of subsistence allowances for accommodation and meals vary greatly between organisations. Some have set rates depending on location or the grade of employee. Others allow 'reasonable' rates without any set scale but usually, and desirably, with guidelines on acceptable hotel and meal costs.
- *Overtime payments* — most manual workers are eligible for paid overtime as well as many staff employees up to management level. Higher paid staff may receive time off in lieu if they work longer hours. Typically, organisations which make overtime payments give time and a half as an overtime premium from Monday to Saturday, with double time paid on Sundays and statutory holidays. Some firms also pay double time from around noon on Saturday. Work on major statutory holidays such as Christmas Day and Good Friday often attracts higher overtime premia.
- *Shift payments* are made at rates which usually vary according to the shift arrangement. A premium of, say, one-third of basic pay may be given to people working nights while those on an early or late day shift may receive less, say, one-fifth of basic pay.
- *Stand-by and call-out allowances* may be made to those who have to be available to come in to work when required. The allowance may be made as a standard payment added to basic pay. Alternatively, special payments may be made for unforeseen call-outs.

# 37

# Rewarding Special Groups — Sales Staff, International Staff and Directors

There is considerable diversity in the ways in which employee reward systems function depending both on the type of organization and, within organizations the type of occupation. Special considerations apply to sales and international staff and to directors and these are summarized in this chapter.

## Sales staff

Salespeople operate at what they sometimes refer to as the 'sharp end' of the business, where, so they claim, they are primarily responsible for generating sales turnover and, therefore, profit. Because of the nature of their work, salespeople have traditionally been more results-orientated than other salaried employees. Their efforts can easily be measured in quantified terms such as sales volume, profit, gross margin or contribution to profit and the fixed expenses of the business (contribution is defined in accounting terms as sales revenue minus the variable costs of material, labour and other expenses). Increasingly, the customer service aspect of their work — creating and maintaining customer satisfaction and generating repeat business — is being measured through consumer reaction surveys and more sophisticated methods of quantifying continuing sales to satisfied customers.

These aspects of the role of sales representatives combine to create the belief in many organizations that salespeople are unique and should therefore be treated differently from all other employees. Whether this is true or not, reward packages for sales staff are often designed and operated quite separately from the reward system applied to other employees. Salespeople, for example, are much more likely to have a significant proportion of their earnings at risk, that is, dependent on their performance. Indeed they are sometimes entirely dependent on their performance for income when they are on commission only terms. Sales staff are often excluded from the job evaluation system and their base rates will be more influenced by market rates — job mobility is generally much higher than in other occupations because companies tend to adopt competitive pay policies to attract high performers from other firms.

This perceived difference means that in some businesses it is the sales management team which decides on the payment systems — the personnel function may not be consulted. But it can be disruptive if the sales force is treated as a special case without reference to reward strategies and policies elsewhere in the organization.

Depending on the type of sales operation and the views of sales management the elements which can be included in the sales reward mix as discussed below.

## Basic salary

Some organizations pay basic salary only. Although salary progression is likely to be performance-related, there are no specific commission or bonus schemes entirely related to sales volume or the achievement of sales targets.

This approach may be adopted when companies want to discourage 'quick sales at all costs' attitudes and actions. Their main concern is to encourage sales staff to build up long-term relationships with their customers, the emphasis being on customer service rather than on high-pressure selling.

Companies with a salary-only policy have to adopt competitive pay policies if they want to attract and retain high quality staff. They have to take account of the regular total earnings of sales staff in markets from which they recruit people or where their own staff move. If they cannot or do not want at least to match average earnings they may have to offer other inducements to join or stay with the company. These can include opportunities for promotion, learning new skills, more stable pay and greater security.

## Basic salary plus commission and/or bonus

While the advantages of basic salary only may be becoming more apparent in some businesses, many companies still believe that the special nature of selling activities and the type of person they need to attract to their sales force requires some form of additional bonus or commission to be paid. This is intended to act both as an incentive and as a reward and a means of recognizing achievement. The different types of commission or bonus schemes are considered below.

## Commission plans

Commission plans provide sales representatives with payments based on a percentage of the sales turnover they generate. The simplest form of plan is straight commission where the salesperson receives only a commission on sales and no basic salary is provided. More commonly, commission is paid in addition to a basic salary.

Commission only plans may be adopted when:

- the performance of sales staff depends primarily on their personal selling abilities and it can be measured by short-term results, ie immediate sales
- representatives are not required to perform any non-selling activities
- continuing relationships with customers are relatively unimportant.

Salary plus commission plans provide for a proportion of total earnings to be paid in commission, the rest is provided in the form of a fixed salary. The proportion of commission varies widely. As a general rule it is higher when results depend on the ability and effort of individual representatives and/or when there is less emphasis on non-selling activities.

The commission element of a salary plus commission plan may be designed to operate flexibly. Higher rates may be paid for new business. Differential rates may be attached to different products so that sales people will focus their efforts on more profitable areas.

The commission may be calculated as a fixed percentage of all sales, possibly with a 'cap' or upper limit on commission earnings. Alternatively an accelerating commission rate formula may be adopted which increases the rate at a series of sales value thresholds; for example, 5 per cent up to £250,000 of sales per quarter, 7.5 per cent on sales between £250,000 and £300,000 and so on. This is designed to encourage sales staff to strive for even higher levels of sales.

## Bonus schemes

Bonus schemes provide pay in addition to basic salary which is related to the achievement of defined and, preferably, agreed targets. These may refer simply to sales volume or profit, and such bonus arrangements are akin to commission schemes with one vital difference — they are based on the achievement of targets rather than on an essentially crude percentage of whatever sales have been attained. Such bonus plans, which are often called quota schemes, therefore clarify expectations of what is to be accomplished and have defined levels of achievement which will be rewarded.

## Choice of approach

The factors affecting choice between the main methods of payment are broadly as follows:

- *Basic salary only* when the aim is to build and maintain long-term relationships with customers through non-selling activities.
- *Salary plus commission* where a more flexible approach is required and non-selling activities are important.
- *Salary plus bonus* where flexibility in providing rewards for different aspects of the sales task is important and where attention needs to be focused on more profitable lines and the various selling and non-selling activities which contribute to effective sales performance.
- *Salary plus commission and bonus* where the company wants to get the best of both worlds — a clear link between sales revenue and reward and the scope to modify behaviour by rewarding particular aspects of the sales representative's performance. But this approach can be unduly complex.

## International pay and expatriate's rewards

When businesses carry out manufacturing, marketing or service activities internationally they may transfer staff to work abroad as 'expatriates' for periods of a few months to a number of years. This means that special expatriate's pay packages have to be devised and the two main approaches are described below.

## Home-based pay

The home-based pay approach aims to ensure that the value of the expatriate's salary is the same as in the home country. The home-base salary may be a notional one for long-term assignments (ie the assumed salary which would be paid to expatriates if they were employed in a job of an equivalent level in the parent company). For shorter-term assignments it may be the actual salary of the individual. The notional or actual home-base salary is used as the foundation upon which the total remuneration package is built. This is sometimes called the 'build-up' or 'balance sheet' approach.

The policy of most organizations which employ expatriates is to ensure that they are no worse off because they have been posted abroad. In practice, the various additional allowances or payments which are made to expatriates mean that they are usually better off financially than if they had stayed at home.

The salary 'build up' starts with the actual or notional home-base salary. To this is added a cost of living adjustment which is applied to 'spendable income' — the portion of salary which would be used at home for everyday living. It usually excludes income tax, social security, pensions and insurance and can exclude discretionary expenditure on major purchases or holidays on the grounds that these do not constitute day to day living expenses. The cost of housing in the home country (mortgage payments) is a special case. It is usually treated separately, consideration being given to factors such as the housing arrangements in the host country and any income earned from renting the home property.

Some or all of the following allowances as described later in this chapter may be added to this salary:

- incentive to work abroad premium
- hardship and location
- housing and utilities
- school fees
- 'rest and recuperation' leave.

The expatriate's total home-based remuneration package would consist of this sum plus, as appropriate, pension, insurance, company car and home leave. Total earnings expressed in the local currency may be paid entirely to the expatriates in their host country. Generally, however, the salary is split between the home and host countries. Expatriates can then pay for continuing domestic commitments such as mortgage and insurance payments and build up some capital (the opportunity to acquire capital is often a major inducement for people to work as expatriates).

A problem that can be caused by home-based pay is that it can create inequities between the remuneration of expatriates and that of their colleagues who are nationals of the host country. If a number of third country nationals from different parts of the world are employed, home-based pay can create an even more complicated situation.

## Host-based pay

The host-based pay approach provides salaries and benefits such as company cars and holidays to expatriates which are in line with those given to nationals of the host country in similar jobs.

The host-based method provides for equity between expatriates and host country nationals. It is adopted by companies using the so-called market rate system which ensures that the salaries of expatriates match the market levels of pay in the host country for similar jobs.

Companies using the host-based approach commonly pay traditional allowances such as school fees, accommodation and medical insurance. They may also fund long-term benefits like social security, life assurance and pensions from home.

The host-based method is certainly equitable from the viewpoint of local naturals, and it can be less expensive than home-based pay. But it may be much less attractive as an inducement for employees to work abroad, especially on unpleasant locations, and it can be difficult to collect market rate data locally to provide a basis for setting pay levels.

## Rewards for directors and senior executives

There is probably no aspect of remuneration which has attracted as much attention in recent years as that of the pay of directors and senior executives. The outcry over top executive reward levels led to the 1995 Greenbury Committee. Previously, the report of the Cadbury Committee in 1993 on the financial aspects of corporate governance made a number of important recommendations on the remuneration of directors.

## The Cadbury Report

The report of the Cadbury Committee in 1993 on the Financial Aspects of Corporate Governance increased the amount of disclosure and led to a large number of remuneration committees being set up. But this did not work. More information on pay resulted in a greater outcry and remuneration committees consisting of non-executive directors were criticised on the assumption (which is not necessarily true) that such committees would be filled by 'old pals' who were also executive directors in other companies and would support higher pay increases because that would advance their own interests.

## The Greenbury Report

The 1995 Greenbury report expressed the belief that 'UK companies mostly deal with directors' remuneration in a sensible and responsible way'. Although the report did state that:

> We fully understand the concerns which shareholders, employees and the public have expressed in recent times about executive remuneration and compensation payments. There have been, in our view, mistakes and misjudgments.

The key recommendation of the report was that remuneration committees should be set up consisting exclusively of non-executive directors. it was proposed that their role would be to make recommendations to the Board on the levels of remuneration package required to attract, retain and motivate directors but they should avoid paying more than is necessary. They should be sensitive to wider issues, eg pay and employment conditions elsewhere in the company and should take a robust line on the payment of compensation where performance has been unsatisfactory.

## Main elements of directors' and executives' remuneration

The main elements of directors' and executives' remuneration are basic pay, short and long term bonus or incentive schemes, share option and share ownership schemes, benefits and service contracts.

*Base salary*
Decisions on the base salary of directors and senior executives are usually founded on views about the market worth of the individuals concerned. At this level the positions may not be evaluated through a formal scheme and are frequently excluded from the pay structure, although most companies will pay some attention formally or informally to internal relativities. They might, for example, lay down that directors and senior managers should be paid respectively 70 per cent and 50 per cent of the chief executive's salary.

Remuneration on joining the company is usually settled by negotiation, often subject to the approval of a remuneration committee. Reviews to base salaries are then made by reference to market movements and success as measured by company performance. Decisions on base salary are important not only in themselves but also because the level agreed is likely to be the platform on which so much else rests. Bonuses are expressed as a percentage of base salary, share options may be allocated as a declared multiple of basic pay and, commonly, pension will be a proportion of final salary.

*Bonus schemes*

Bonus schemes provide directors and executives with cash sums on the basis of measures of company and, frequently, individual performance. Bonus schemes may be short or long-term and reward individual directors and executives on the basis of some measure of company and, often, individual performance. Cash payments are usually made annually, although shorter periods such as half-yearly are sometimes adopted in fast-moving businesses.

*Share options*

Executive share option schemes provide individual directors and executives with the right to buy a block of shares on some future date at the share price existing when the option was granted. They are a form of long term incentive on the assumption that executives will be motivated to perform more effectively if they can anticipate a substantial capital gain when they sell their shares at a price above that prevailing when the option was granted.

Share options have been severely criticised recently because of the enormous gains made by some executives in the privatised industries where the initial share price was set at an artificially low level. There is a strong feeling amongst the institutions and some companies that share options do not achieve community of interest between executives and shareholders and are in effect no more than a form of cash bonus in which the payout has little or nothing to do with the executive's performance.

Share option schemes may continue because they are well understood and have become an accepted feature of executive remuneration. But since the tax advantage has been reduced companies may be more interested in developing schemes which are medium to long-term and are designed to deal with pay for performance, accountability and shareholder alignment. Such schemes may require personal investment in shares.

*Share ownership schemes*

Share ownership schemes are relatively uncommon in the UK but more interest is now being expressed in them as an alternative to share options. Their aim is to align the interests of the executive with the shareholder which means that they take the same risks — they can lose as well as gain, which is not the case with share options.

## Benefits

Employee benefits for executives may amount to over 20 per cent of the total reward package. The most important element is the pension scheme, and directors may be provided with a much higher accrual rate in a final salary scheme. This means that, typically, the maximum two-thirds pension can be achieved after 20 years' service rather than the 40 years it takes in the usual 1/60ths scheme. Additional pensions through unapproved pension schemes (which do not attract income tax exemptions) may be provided to take the director's pension above the maximum amount permitted in an approved pension scheme (the 'cap').

Directors and executives may receive the same range of benefits as other staff but these could be on a larger scale (a bigger car) or in the form of more generous arrangements for such benefits as medical care.

## Service contracts

Three year service contracts for directors, which have been fairly typical, attracted much adverse publicity in the middle 1990s because of the high severance payments given to departing chief executives and directors, even when it is suspected or is actually the case that they have been voted off the board because of their inadequate performance. Following the outcry and the Greenbury report, rolling contracts for directors are likely to be restricted to one year in most cases.

# 38

# Managing Employee Reward

## Reward budgets and forecasts

Reward budgets and forecasts are concerned with overall payroll costs and the costs of general and individual pay increases.

### Payroll budgets

A payroll budget is a statement of the planned allocation and use of human resources required to meet the objectives of the organization. It is usually a major part of the master budget. The budget is based on forecast levels of activity which determine the number of people required. The annual payroll budget is a product of the number of people to be employed and the rates at which they will be paid during the budget year. It will incorporate the cost of benefits (eg pensions contributions) and the employer's National Insurance contributions. The budget will be adjusted to take account of forecasts covering increases or decreases to employee numbers, the likely costs of general and individual pay reviews, changes to the pay structure and increases to the cost of employee benefits.

Managers in charge of budget centres will have their own payroll budget which they have to account for. This budget will incorporate forecasts of pay increases as well as the manager's assessment of the numbers of employees needed in different categories. Managers will be required to ensure that individual pay increases are made within that budget, which may, however, be flexed upwards or downwards if activity levels or the assumptions on which forecast pay increases were based change.

## *Review budgets*

A general review budget simply incorporates the forecast costs of any across-the-board pay increases which may be granted or negotiated during the budget year. Individual performance review budgets may be expressed as the percentage increase to the payroll that can be allowed for performance, skill-based or competence-related increases. The size of the budget will be affected by the following considerations:

- the amount the organization believes it can afford to pay on the basis of budgeted revenue, profit, and payroll costs
- the organization's policies on pay progression — the size and range of increases
- any allowances that may need to be made for increasing individual rates of pay to remove anomalies, for example, after a job evaluation exercise.

The basic budget would be set for the organization as a whole but within that figure, departmental budgets could be flexed to reflect different needs and circumstances. Pay modelling techniques which cost alternative pay review proposals on distributions of awards can be used to prepare individual review budgets. Increasingly, organizations are replacing individual review budgets with a total payroll budgeting approach. This means that departmental heads have to fund individual increases from their payroll budget. In effect, they are expected to add value from performance pay or at least ensure that it is self-financing.

## Evaluating the reward system

The reward system should be audited regularly to assess its effectiveness, the extent to which it is adding value and its relevance to the present and future needs of the organisation. This audit should include an assessment of opinions about the reward system by its key users and those who are affected by it. This leads to a diagnosis of strengths and weaknesses and an assessment of what needs to be done and why.

The operation of the reward system should be monitored continually by the personnel department through such audits and by the use of compa-ratios and attrition analysis as discussed below. In particular it is necessary to analyse data on upgradings, the effectiveness with which performance management processes are functioning and the amount paid out on pay-for-performance schemes and the impact they are making on results.

Internal relativities should also be monitored by carrying out periodical studies of the differentials that exist vertically within departments or between categories of employees. The studies should examine the differentials built into the pay structure and also analyse the differences between the average rates of pay at different levels. If it is revealed that because of changes in roles or the impact of pay reviews differentials no longer properly reflect increases in job values and/or are no longer 'felt fair', then further investigations to establish the reasons for this situation can be conducted and, if necessary, corrective action taken.

External relativities should be monitored by tracking movements in market rates by studying published data and conducting pay surveys as described in Chapter 32.

No reward innovations should take place unless a cost-benefit analysis has forecast that they will add value. The audit and monitoring processes should establish that the extent to which the predicted benefits have been obtained and check on the costs against the forecast.

## Compa-ratio analysis

A compa-ratio (short for comparative ratio) measures the relationship in a graded pay structure between actual and policy rates of pay as a percentage. The policy value used is the midpoint or reference point in a pay range which represents the 'target rate' for a fully competent individual in any job in the grade. This point is aligned to market rates in accordance with the organization's market stance policy.

Compa-ratios are used to define where an individual is placed in a pay range. The analysis of compa-ratios indicates what action might have to be taken to slow down or accelerate increases if compa-ratios are too high or too low compared with the policy level. This process is sometimes called 'midpoint management'.

Compa-ratios are calculated as follows:

$$\frac{\text{actual rate of pay}}{\text{mid or reference point of range}} \times 100$$

A compa-ratio of 100 per cent means that actual and policy pay are the same. Compa-ratios which are higher or lower than 100 per cent mean that, respectively, pay is above or below the policy target rate. For example, if the target (policy) rate in a range were £20,000 and the average pay of all the individuals in the grade were £18,000, the compa-ratio would be 90 per cent.

Compa-ratios establish differences between policy and practice and the reasons for such differences need to be established.

## Analysing attrition

Attrition or slippage takes place when employees enter jobs at lower rates of pay than the previous incumbents. If this happens payroll costs will go down given an even flow of starters and leavers and a consistent approach to the determination of rates of pay. In theory attrition can help to finance pay increases within a range. It has been claimed that fixed incremental systems can be entirely self-financing because of attrition, but the conditions under which this can be attained are so exceptional that it probably never happens.

Attrition can be calculated by the formula: total percentage increase to payroll arising from general or individual pay increases minus total percentage increase in average rates of pay. If it can be proved that attrition is going to take place, the amount involved can be taken into account as a means of at least partly financing individual pay increases. Attrition in a pay system with regular progression through ranges and a fairly even flow of starters and leavers is typically between 2 and 3 per cent but this should not be regarded as a norm.

## Pay reviews

Pay reviews can be general or individual. General reviews give 'across-the-board-increases' in response to market trends, increases in the cost of living or negotiated pay settlements. Individual reviews decide on any performance, skill-based or competence related increases in pay for individual employees.

## General reviews

General reviews take place when an increase is given to employees in response to general market rate movements, increases in the cost of living or union negotiations. General reviews are often combined with individual reviews but employees are usually informed of the general and individual components of any increase they receive. Alternatively, the general review may be conducted separately to enable better control to be achieved over costs and to focus employees' attention on the performance-related aspect of their remuneration.

Many organizations, however, prefer not to link pay rises explicitly to the cost of living. Their policy is to respond to movements in market rates in order to maintain their competitive position, bearing in mind that increases in market rates are affected by the cost of living. They do not want to be committed to an 'index-linked' approach, even in times of low inflation.

## Individual reviews

Individual reviews determine performance, skill or competence-related pay increases, or special achievement or sustained good performance bonuses as additions or alternatives to base pay rate increases. They may be based on some form of performance and/or competence rating or the acquisition of additional skills.

Performance-related pay (PRP) reviews are conducted by reference to performance ratings as described in Chapter 34. Guidelines are provided to managers on the relationships between pay increases and performance rating and, frequently, the position of employees in their pay range (their compa-ratio). A PRP increase matrix may be used to indicate levels of increase, or guidelines may be given on the distribution of increases or the maximum and minimum increases that can be awarded. Line managers should work within a review or payroll budget.

Individual reviews usually take place on a fixed date, typically once a year, although fast-moving organisations may prefer more frequent reviews, say twice a year. The review date can be varied to suit the circumstances of the organization. Some organisations like to hold rolling reviews for individuals based on their birthday or starting/ promotion date in order to allow more attention to be given to the individual's review. But this system is more difficult to budget for and control.

## Control

Control over the implementation of pay policies generally and payroll costs in particular will be easier if it is based on:

- a clearly defined and understood pay structure
- specific pay review guidelines and budgets
- defined procedures for grading jobs and fixing rates of pay
- clear statements of the degree of authority managers have at each level to decide on rates of pay and increases

- a personnel (HR) function which is capable of monitoring the implementation of pay policies and providing the information and guidance managers require and has the authority and resources (including computer software) to do so
- a systematic process for monitoring the implementation of pay policies and costs against budgets.

## Reward procedures

Reward management procedures are required to achieve and monitor the implementation of reward management policies. They deal with methods of fixing pay on appointment or promotion and dealing with anomalies. They will also refer to methods of appealing against grading or pay decisions, usually through the organisation's normal appeals procedure.

### *Procedures for grading jobs*

The procedures for grading new jobs or re-grading existing ones should lay down that grading or re-grading can only take place after a proper job evaluation study. It is necessary to take action to control grade drift by insisting that this procedure is followed. Pressures to upgrade because of market forces or difficulties in recruitment or retention should be resisted. These problems should be addressed by such methods as market premiums or creating special market groups of jobs.

### *Fixing rates of pay on appointment*

Line managers should have a major say in pay offers and some free-dom to negotiate when necessary, but they should be required to take account of relevant pay policy guidelines which should set out the circumstances in which pay offers above the minimum of the range can be made. It is customary to allow a reasonable degree of freedom to make offers up to a certain point, eg the 90 per cent level in a 80 to 120 per cent pay range. Pay policies frequently allow offers to be made up to the midpoint or reference point depending on the extent to which the recruit has the necessary experience, skills and competences. Offers above the midpoint should be exceptional because they would leave relatively little room for expansion. Such offers will sometimes be made because of market pressures, but they need to be very carefully considered because of the inevitability of grade drift unless the individual is promoted fairly soon. If the current rates are too low to attract good candidates, it may be necessary to reconsider the scales or to agree on special market rate premiums. To keep the latter under control, it is advisable to require that they cannot be awarded unless they are authorized by the personnel department or a more senior manager. Many organizations require that all offers should be vetted and approved by a member of the personnel function and/or a higher authority.

## Promotion increases

Promotion increases should be meaningful, say 10 per cent or more. They should not normally take the promoted employee above the midpoint or reference point in the pay range for his or her new job so that there is adequate scope for performance-related increases. One good reason for having reasonably wide differentials is to provide space for promotions.

## Dealing with anomalies

Within any pay structure, however carefully monitored and maintained, anomalies will occur and they need to be addressed during a pay review. Correction of anomalies will require higher level increases for those who are under-paid relative to their performance and time in the job, and lower levels of increase for those who are correspondingly over-paid. It is worth noting that over-payment anomalies cannot be corrected in fixed incremental structures, and this is a major disadvantage of such systems. The cost of anomaly correction should not be huge in normal circumstances if at every review managers are encouraged to 'fine tune' their pay recommendations as suggested earlier.

In a severely anomalous situation, which may be found at the implementation stage of a new structure or at a major review, a longer-term correction programme may be necessary either to mitigate the demotivating effects of reducing relative rates of pay or to spread costs over a number of years.

As well as individual anomaly correction there may be a need to correct an historical tendency to over-pay or under-pay whole departments, divisions or functions by applying higher or lower levels of increases over a period of time. This would involve adjustments to pay review budgets and guidelines and, obviously, it would have to be handled with great care.

## Responsibility for reward

The trend is to devolve more responsibility for pay decisions to line managers, especially those concerned with individual pay reviews. But there are obvious dangers. These include inconsistency between managers' decisions, favouritism, prejudice (gender or racial) and illogical distributions of rewards. Research has shown that many managers tend not to differentiate between the performance of individual members of their staff. Ratings can be compressed, with most people clustered around the midpoint and very few staff rated as good or poor performers.

Devolving more authority to line managers may in principle be highly desirable but managers must be briefed thoroughly on their responsibilities, the organisation's pay policies (including methods of progressing pay), the principles to be followed in conducting reviews and how they should interpret and apply pay review guidelines. The need to achieve equity and a reasonable degree of consistency across the organization should be emphasized. Managers should be given whatever training, guidance and help they need to ensure that they are capable of exercising their discretionary powers wisely. This training should cover:

- how information on market rates supplied by the personnel department should be interpreted and used
- how data provided by the personnel department on the levels of pay and pay progression histories of individual members of staff and the distribution of pay by occupation throughout the department should be used as the basis for planning pay
- methods of assessing performance and contribution levels
- how to interpret any generic competence profiles to assess individual development needs and agree career pathways
- how to assess competence requirements for specific roles (as they exist now or as they may develop), and how to counsel employees on the preparation of personal development plans
- methods of reviewing progress in achieving these plans and in career development, and how to interpret information from these reviews when making pay decisions
- generally, how to distribute rewards within budgets, fairly, equit-

ably and consistently by reference to assessments of contribution, competence, progress or growth
- the guidance available from the personnel function on how to manage pay — it should be emphasised that guidance must always be sought if line managers have any doubts as to how they should exercise their discretion.

Full devolution implies that the decisions of managers on pay increases are not reviewed and questioned as long as they keep within their budgets. However, it is usual for senior managers, personnel or pay specialists to monitor pay proposals to spot inconsistencies or what appear to be illogical recommendations, especially when the scheme is initiated or with newly appointed managers. The use of computerised personnel information systems makes it easier for managers to communicate their proposals and for the personnel department to monitor them. If the personnel department is involved, it should aim to provide support and guidance, not to act as a police force. Monitoring can be relaxed as managers prove that they are capable of making good pay decisions.

## Communicating to employees

Employee reward systems communicate messages to employees about the beliefs of the organization on what is felt to be important when valuing people in their roles. They deliver two messages: this is how we value your contribution; this is what we are paying for. It is therefore important to communicate to employees collectively about the reward policies and practices of the organization and individually about how those policies affect them — now and in the future. Transparency is essential.

### What to communicate to employees generally

Employees generally should understand:
- the *reward policies* of the organization in setting pay levels, providing benefits and progressing pay
- the *pay structure* — grades and pay ranges and how the structure is managed
- the *benefits structure* — the range of benefits provided with details of each the pension scheme and other major benefits

- *methods of grading and regrading jobs* — the job evaluation scheme and how it operates
- *pay progression* — how pay progresses within the pay structure and how pay decisions affecting employees collectively and individually are made
- *pay-for-performance schemes* — how individual, team and organisation-wide schemes work and how employees can benefit from them
- *pay for skill or competence* — how any skill-based or competence-based schemes work, the aims of the organization in using such schemes, and how employees can benefit from them
- *performance management* — how performance management processes operate and the parts played by managers and employees
- *reward developments and initiatives* — details of any changes to the reward system, the reasons for such changes, and how employees will be affected by them — the importance of doing this thoroughly cannot be over-emphasized.

## What to communicate to individual employees

Individual employees should know and understand:

- their *job grade* and how it has been determined
- the basis upon which their *present rate* of pay has been determined
- the *pay opportunities* available to them — the scope in their grade for pay progression, the basis upon which their pay will be linked to their performance and the acquisition and effective use of skills and competences as their career develops, and what actions and behaviour are expected of them if their pay is to progress
- *performance management* — how their performance will be reviewed and the part they play in agreeing objectives and formulating personal development and performance improvement plans
- *the value of the employee benefits they receive* — the level of total remuneration provided for individuals by the organisation, including the values of such benefits as pension and sick pay schemes
- *appeals and grievances* — how they can appeal against grading and pay decisions or take up a grievance on any aspect of their remuneration.

# Part VIII
# Employee Relations

## *Employee relations defined*

*Employee relations consist of all those areas of personnel management which involve relationships with employees — directly and/or through collective agreements where trade unions are recognized. Employee relations are concerned with generally managing the employment relationship as considered elsewhere in this handbook, particularly in Chapter 15 and Part 10.*

*These relationships will be concerned with the agreement of terms and conditions of employment and with issues arising from employment. They will not necessarily be subject to collective agreements or joint regulation. Employee relations therefore cover a broader spectrum of the employment relationship than industrial relations, which are usually regarded as being essentially about dealings between managements and trade unions. This wider definition recognizes the move away from collectivism towards individualism in the ways in which employers relate to their employees. The move in this direction has been prompted by a growing insistence on management's prerogative supported by the philosophy of HRM (human resource management), the requirement to meet competition with slimmer and more efficient organizations, a massive restructuring of industry in the 1980s, the 1980s concept of the market economy and free enterprise and by trade union legislation.*

Employee relations practices include formal processes, procedures and channels of communication. It is important to remember, however, that employee relations are mainly conducted on a day-to-day informal basis by line managers and team leaders; within the framework of employment and employee relations policies but acting mainly on their own initiative.

## Role of the personnel function in employee relations

The personnel function provides guidance and training and will develop and help to introduce and maintain formal processes; but it does not do line managers' jobs for them. However, in their role as industrial relations specialists, personnel practitioners may deal directly with trade unions and their representatives. They are also likely to have a measure of responsibility for maintaining participation and involvement processes and for managing employee communications. They can and should play a major part in developing employee relations strategies and policies which aim to:

- achieve satisfactory employment relationships, taking particular account of the importance of psychological contracts

- build stable and cooperative relationships with employees which recognize that they are stakeholders in the organization and minimize conflict

- achieve commitment through employee involvement and communications processes

- develop mutuality — a common interest in achieving the organization's goals through the development of organizational cultures based on shared values between management and employees

- clarify industrial relations processes with trade unions and build harmonious relationships with them on a partnership basis.

In these capacities, personnel practitioners can make a

*major contribution to the creation and maintenance of a good employee relations climate.*

## Plan

*This part covers the broad subject of employee relations under the following headings:*

- *the context of employee relations — the conceptual framework to industrial relations, developments in industrial relations and the parties involved*

- *employee relations systems, processes and outcomes, including collective bargaining*

- *negotiating and bargaining skills*

- *processes for employee involvement, participation and communications.*

# 39

# The Employee Relations Framework

The purpose of this chapter is to provide a general introduction to the complex subject of employee relations. It starts with a summary of the content of employee relations and then deals with the following industrial relations concepts:

- the systems theory of industrial relations which sees the subject as a system of regulations and rules
- the types of regulations and rules contained in the system
- the nature of collective bargaining and bargaining power
- the unitarist and pluralist views about the basis of the relationship between management and trade unions in particular or employees in general
- individualism and collectivism as approaches to employee relations
- the voluntarist approach to industrial relations and its decline
- human resource management (HRM) as a new paradigm for employee relations

The chapter continues with a review of developments in industrial relations and a summary of the current industrial relations scene and the context for employee relations. The legal framework to industrial relations is then summarised and the chapter concludes with a description of the various parties to industrial relations and the institutions, agencies and offices which are involved.

## The elements of employee relations

The elements of employee relations consist of:

- The formal and informal policies and practices of organization.

- The development, negotiation and application of formal systems, rules and procedures for collective bargaining, handling disputes and regulating employment. These serve to determine the reward for effort and other conditions of employment, to protect the interests of both employees and their employers, and to regulate the ways in which employers treat their employees and how the latter are expected to behave at work.
- The framework provided by legislation and case law.
- The informal as well as formal processes which take the form of continuous interactions between managers and team leaders or supervisors on the one hand and employee representatives and individuals on the other. These may happen within the framework of formal agreements but are often governed by custom and practice and the climate of relationships that have been built up over the years.
- The philosophies and policies of the major players in the industrial relations scene: the government of the day, management and the trade unions.
- A number of parties, each with different roles. These consist of the state, management, employers' organizations, the trade unions, individual managers and supervisors, personnel managers, employee representatives and employees.
- A number of institutions such as The Advisory, Conciliation and Arbitration Service (ACAS) and the industrial tribunals.
- The bargaining structures, recognition and procedural agreements and practices which have evolved to enable the formal system to operate.
- Policies and practices for employee involvement and communications.

## Industrial relations as a system of rules

Industrial relations can be regarded as a system or web of rules regulating employment and the ways in which people behave at work. The systems theory of industrial relations, as propounded by Dunlop (1958), states that the role of the system is to produce the regulations and procedural rules which govern how much is distributed in the bargaining process and how the parties involved, or the 'actors' in the industrial relations scene, relate to one another. According to Dunlop, the output of the system takes the form of:

The regulations and policies of the management hierarchy; the laws of any worker hierarchy; the regulations, degrees, decisions, awards or orders of governmental agencies; the rules and decisions of specialized agencies created by the management and worker hierarchies; collective bargaining arrangements and the customs and traditions of the workplace and work community.

The system is expressed in many more or less formal or informal guises: in legislation and statutory orders, in trade union regulations, in collective agreements and arbitration awards, in social conventions, in managerial decisions, and in accepted 'custom and practice'. The 'rules' may be defined and coherent, or ill-defined and incoherent. Within a plant the rules may mainly be concerned with doing no more than defining the *status quo* which both parties recognize as the norm from which deviations may be made only by agreement. In this sense, therefore, an industrial relations system is a normative system where a norm can be seen as a rule, a standard, or a pattern for action which is generally accepted or agreed as the basis upon which the parties concerned should operate.

Systems theory, however, does not sufficiently take into account the distribution of power between management and trade unions nor the impact of the State. Nor does it adequately explain the role of the individual in industrial relations.

## Types of regulations and rules

Job regulation aims to provide a framework of minimum rights and rules. Internal regulation is concerned with procedures for dealing with grievances, redundancies, or disciplinary problems and rules concerning the operation of the pay system and the rights of shop stewards. External regulation is carried out by means of employment legislation, the rules of trade unions and employers' associations, and the regulative content of procedural or substantive rules and agreements.

Procedural rules are intended to regulate conflict between the parties to collective bargaining, and when their importance is emphasized, a premium is being placed on industrial peace. Substantive rules settle the rights and obligations attached to jobs. It is interesting to note that in the UK, the parties to collective agreements have tended to concentrate more on procedural than on substantive rules. In the US, where there is greater emphasis on fixed-term agreements, the tendency has been to rely more on substantive rules.

## Collective bargaining

The industrial relations system is regulated by the process of collective bargaining, defined by Flanders (1970) as a social process that 'continually turns disagreements into agreements in an orderly fashion'. Collective bargaining aims to establish by negotiation and discussion agreed rules and decisions on matters of mutual concern to employers and unions as well as methods of regulating the conditions governing employment.

It therefore provides a framework within which the views of management and unions about disputed matters that could lead to industrial disorder can be considered with the aim of eliminating the causes of the disorder. Collective bargaining is a joint regulating process, dealing with the regulation of management in its relationships with work people as well as the regulation of conditions of employment. It has a political as well as an economic basis — both sides are interested in the distribution of power between them as well as the distribution of income.

Collective bargaining can be regarded as an exchange relationship in which wage-work bargains take place between employers and employees through the agency of a trade union. Traditionally, the role of trade unions as bargaining agents has been perceived as being to offset the inequalities of individual bargaining power between employers and employees in the labour market.

Collective bargaining can also be seen as a political relationship in which trade unions, as Chamberlain and Kuhn (1965) noted, share industrial sovereignty or power over those who are governed, the employees. The sovereignty is held jointly by management and union in the collective bargaining process.

Above all, collective bargaining is a power relationship which takes the form of a measure of power-sharing between management and trade unions (although recently the balance of power has shifted markedly in the direction of management).

### Bargaining power

The extent to which industrial sovereignty is shared by management with its trade unions (if at all) depends upon the relative bargaining powers of the two parties. Bargaining power can be defined as the ability to induce the other side to make a decision that it would otherwise not make. As Fox and Flanders (1969) commented: 'Power is the crucial variable which determines the outcome of collective bargaining'. It has been suggested by Hawkins (1979) that a crucial test of bargaining power is 'whether the cost to one side in accepting a proposal from the other is higher than the cost of not accepting it'.

Singh (1989) has pointed out that bargaining power is not static but varies over time. He also notes that:

> Bargaining power is inherent in any situation where differences have to be reconciled. It is, however, not an end in itself and negotiations must not rely solely on bargaining power. One side may have enormous bargaining power, but to use it to the point where the other side feels that it is impossible to deal with such a party is to defeat the purpose of negotiations.

Atkinson (1989) asserts that:

● What creates bargaining power can be appraised in terms of subjective assessments by individuals involved in the bargaining process.
● Each side can guess the bargaining preferences and bargaining power of the other side.
● There are normally a number of elements creating bargaining power.

## Forms of collective bargaining

Collective bargaining takes two basic forms, as identified by Chamberlain and Kuhn (1965):

1. *Conjunctive bargaining,* which 'arises from the absolute requirement that some agreement — any agreement — may be reached so that the operations on which both are dependent may continue', and results in a 'working relationship in which each party agrees, explicitly or implicitly, to provide certain requisite services, to recognize certain seats of authority, and to accept certain responsibilities in respect of each other'.
2. *Cooperative bargaining,* in which it is recognized that each party is dependent on the other and can achieve its objectives more effectively if it wins the support of the other.

A similar distinction was made by Walton and McKersie (1965), who referred to *distributive bargaining* as the 'complex system of activities instrumental to the attainment of one party's goals when they are in basic conflict with those of the other party', and to *integrative bargaining* as the 'system of activities which are not in fundamental conflict with those of the other party and which therefore can be integrated to some degree'. Such objectives are said to define an area of common concern, a purpose.

## The unitary and pluralist views

There are two basic views as expressed by Fox (1966) about the basis of the relationship between management and trade unions in particular or employees in general: the unitary and the pluralist perspectives.

*The unitary view* is typically held by managements who see their function as that of directing and controlling the workforce to achieve economic and growth objectives. To this end, management believes that it is the rule-making authority. Management tends to view the enterprise as a unitary system with one source of authority — itself — and one focus of loyalty — the company. It extols the virtue of team-work, where everyone strives jointly to a common objective, everyone pulls their weight to the best of their ability, and everyone accepts their place and function gladly, following the leadership of the appointed manager or supervisor. These are admirable sentiments, but they sometimes lead to what McClelland (1963) has referred to as an orgy of 'avuncular pontification' on the part of the leaders of industry. This unitary view, which is essentially autocratic and authoritarian, has sometimes been expressed in agreements as 'management's right to manage'. The philosophy of HRM with its emphasis on commitment and mutuality is essentially based on the unitary perspective.

In contrast, the *pluralist view* is that an industrial organization is a plural society, containing many related but separate interests and objectives which must be maintained in some kind of equilibrium. In place of a corporate unity reflected in a single focus of authority and loyalty, management has to accept the existence of rival sources of leadership and attachment. It has to face the fact that in Drucker's (1951) phrase, a business enterprise has a triple personality: it is at once an economic, a political and a social institution. In the first, it produces and distributes incomes. In the second, it embodies a system of government in which managers collectively exercise authority over the managed, but are also themselves involved in an intricate pattern of political relationships. Its third personality is revealed in the plant community which evolves from below out of face-to-face relations based on shared interests, sentiments, beliefs and values among various groups of employees.

Pluralism conventionally regards the workforce as being represented, by 'an opposition that does not seek to govern' Clegg (1976). Pluralism, as described by Cave (1994), involved 'a balance of power between two organized interests and a sufficient degree of trust within the relationship (usually) for each side to respect the other's legitimate and, on occasions, separate interests, and for both sides to refrain from pushing their interest separately to the point where it became impossible to keep the show on the road'. It has been noted by Guest (1995) that: 'the tradition of bargaining at plant or even company level has reinforced a pluralistic concept'.

The pluralist view has tended sometimes to take a Manichean view of employee relations, dividing everything into black and white: there are two sides in industry, and that is that. But it can be argued, following Heraclitus of Ephesus (500 BC), that the future may well be dependent upon the sustained differentiation of opposites but, because of the underlying unity, apparent opposites are really aspects of the same thing. The 1980s principle of mutuality — that management and employees in organizations are interdependent and both parties benefit from this interdependence — can be seen as an updated version of the Heraclitus doctrine.

## Individualism and collectivism

Purcell (1987) argues that the distinction between pluralist and unitary frames of management has 'provided a powerful impetus to the debate about management style, but the mutually exclusive nature of these categories has limited further development'. Moreover, wide variations can be found within both the unitary and the pluralist approach. He therefore suggests an alternative distinction between 'individualism' — policies focusing on individual employees and 'collectivism' — the extent to which groups of workers have an independent voice and participate in decision-making with managers. He believes that companies can and do operate in both these dimensions of management style.

## Voluntarism and its decline

The essence of the systems theory of industrial relations is that the rules are jointly agreed by the representatives of the parties to employment relations; an arrangement which, it is believed, makes for readier acceptance than if they were imposed by a third party such as the State.

This concept of voluntarism was defined by Kahn-Freund (1972) as 'the policy of the law to allow the two sides by agreement and practice to develop their own norms and their own sanctions and to abstain from legal compulsion in their collective relationship'. It was, in essence, voluntarism which came under attack by government legislation from 1974 onwards, including the principle of 'immunities' for industrial action and the closed shop.

# The HRM approach to employee relations

## *The HRM model*

The philosophy of HRM as described in Chapter 8 has been translated into the following prescriptions which constitute the HRM model for employee relations:

- a drive for commitment — winning the 'hearts and minds' of employees to get them to identify with the company, to exert themselves more on its behalf and to remain with the organization, thus ensuring a return on their training and development
- an emphasis on mutuality — getting the message across that 'we are all in this together' and that the interests of management and employees coincide (ie a unitarist approach)
- the organization of complementary forms of communication, such as team briefing, alongside traditional collective bargaining — ie approaching employees directly as individuals or in groups rather than through their representatives
- the use of employee involvement techniques such as quality circles or improvement groups
- continuous pressure on quality — total quality management
- increased flexibility in working arrangements including multi-skilling, to provide for the more effective use of human resources, sometimes accompanied by an agreement to provide secure employment for the 'core' workers
- emphasis on teamwork
- harmonization of terms and conditions for all employees.

The key contrasting dimensions of traditional industrial relations and HRM have been presented by Guest (1995) as follows:

## The Employee Relations Framework

| Dimension | Industrial Relations | HRM |
|---|---|---|
| Psychological contract | Compliance | Commitment |
| Behaviour references | Norms, custom and practice | Values/mission |
| Relations | Low trust, pluralist, collective | High trust, unitarist, individual |
| Organization design | Formal roles, hierarchy, division of labour, managerial control | Flexible roles, flat structure, teamwork/autonomy, self control |

Guest notes that this model aims to support the achievement of the three main sources of competitive advantage identified by Porter (1980), namely, innovation, quality and cost leadership. Innovation and quality strategies require employee commitment while cost leadership strategies are believed by many managements to be only achievable without a union. 'The logic of a market-driven HRM strategy is that where high organizational commitment is sought, unions are irrelevant. Where cost advantage is the goal, unions and industrial relations systems appear to carry higher costs'.

An HRM approach is still possible if trade unions are recognized by the company. In this case, the strategy might be to marginalize or at least side-step them by dealing direct with employees through involvement and communications processes.

But to what extent has this HRM model been taken up?

## Take-up of HRM

On the basis of the evidence provided by the 1990 Workshop Industrial Relations Survey (WIRS), Millward (1994) suggests that HRM practices did not greatly increase between 1984 and 1990, and in any event are more likely to be found in establishments which recognize trade unions than in non-union workplaces. However, evidence from the WIRS studies shows that the incidence of team briefings increased from 30 per cent of workplaces in industry and commerce in 1984 to 44 per cent in 1990. Team briefing, the method of communication which showed the fastest increase over the period 1984 to 1990 was quite common in the union sector but were hardly used at all in the non-union sector.

## HRM and the trade unions

The conclusion from this survey is that there is no correlation between human resource management and anti-unionism. Indeed, as Monks (1994) has put it 'the more anti-union the employer, the less likely it is that HRM techniques will be used'. He believes that although there has been a decline in the coverage of collective bargaining since 1984, no alternative 'HRM' model has replaced the trade union channel for employee representation. He comments on the evidence provided by the 1990 WIRS survey which showed a clear relationship between size and HRM as follows:

> Large employers are not only more likely to recognize trade unions but are also more likely to use a wide range of communication methods, offer financial participation and single status, and avoid low pay. This can be no coincidence, and it should be remembered that the vast majority of the FT top 50 companies recognize trade unions. World-class employers fully understand the importance of information, consultations and employee involvement.

## How systematic is HRM?

Monks noted that the WIRS survey revealed that relatively few employers were implementing the HRM agenda in a systematic way. He suggested that a 'pick and mix' approach to the HRM menu was frequently adopted, with one or two items being considered without any consideration being given to the wider implications for the company. He also commented that:

> From the trade union side there may be a tendency to overestimate the coherence of what British managers are doing. In part this may be because the literature and the reviews of the 'quality gurus' emphasize that anything less than a systematic approach is doomed to fail.

The view that HRM has to be either all or nothing is quite widespread, but, as was pointed out in Chapter 8 there is no reason why the HRM agenda should be adopted as a total package by any organization. Organizations must 'pick and mix', as John Monks put it, those ingredients which are most relevant to their needs and circumstances. Of course, the aim should still be to ensure that whatever mix is selected is coherent in the sense that the ingredients blend together satisfactorily. Thus it is necessary to consider the implications of each ingredient and the part it will play in achieving the overall industrial relations strategy. But, as Storey (1993) observed on the basis of his research in a number of large organizations, even those with unions which had developed HRM practices had not successfully integrated their HR and industrial relations strategies.

## The context of employee relations

Industrial relations are conducted within the external context of the national political and economic environment, the international context and the internal context of the organization.

### *The political context*

The political context is formed by the Government of the day. The Conservative administrations from 1979 onwards set out to curb the power of the trade unions. The Conservatives believed that the unions were largely responsible for wage inflation, supported practices which prevented increases in productivity, usurped managerial authority and restricted individual freedom. Indeed, as Kessler and Bayliss (1995) said, the Government's position was that the very existence of trade unions was at odds with an efficient labour market. It therefore wanted employers without unions to resist granting recognition and managements of new plants to avoid unions or to limit the degree of recognition. These views were translated into the trade union legislation summarized at the end of this chapter.

### *The economic context*

The economic context over the last 15 years has been one of recessions and recovery from recessions accompanied by marked fluctuations in productivity. Unemployment also fluctuated, being particularly high in 1986 and 1993 (the peak of the two recessions). Employment in manufacturing declined by 3 million or over 40 per cent between 1979 and 1993, while employment in services rose by 1.9 million or 15 per cent in the same period. Inflation has been brought under control.

Perhaps the most significant feature of the changing economic environment from the industrial relations viewpoint has been the drastic cutbacks in manufacturing industry where unions had traditionally been strongly organized.

## The international context

Employee relations in the UK are affected by European Union regulations and initiatives. A number of Articles in the original treaty of Rome referred to the promotion of improvements in working conditions and the need to develop dialogue between the two sides of industry. The Social Charter covers such matters as prior rights to information and consultation and collective bargaining rights. Although the Social Chapter agreed at Maastricht provided for the UK to 'opt out' of the Social Charter, it is certain that a Labour Government would 'opt in'. It seems likely that the conduct of employee relations in Britain will be increasingly affected by EU directives. Already, the European Works Council directive is affecting British firms operating in other EU countries.

Another significant feature which will continue to affect employee relations is the growth of international competition in product markets which has resulted in employers concentrating on cost reductions.

## The organizational context

The need to 'take cost out of the business' referred to above has meant that employers have focused on the cost of labour — usually the highest and most easily reduced cost. Hence 'the lean organization' movement and large-scale redundancies, especially in manufacturing. There has been pressure for greater flexibility and increased management control of operations which has had a direct impact on employee relations policies and union agreements.

The widespread introduction of new technology and information technology has aimed to increase productivity by achieving higher levels of efficiency and reducing labour costs. Organizations are relying more on a core of key full-time employees, leaving the peripheral work to be undertaken by sub-contractors and the increasing numbers of part-timers — women *and* men. This has reduced the number of employees who wish to join unions or remain trade union members.

## Developments in industrial relations

Developments in the practice of industrial relations since the 1950s can be divided into the following phases:

1. The traditional system existing prior to the 1970s.

2. The Donovan analysis of 1968.
3. The interventionist and employment protection measures of the 1970s.
4. The 1980s programme for curbing what were perceived by the Conservative government to be the excesses of rampant trade unionism.

## The traditional system — to 1971

Relations prior to 1971 and indeed for most of the 1970s could be described as a system of collective representation designed to contain conflict. Voluntary collective bargaining between employees and employers' associations was the central feature of the system, and this process of joint regulation was largely concerned with pay and basic conditions of employment, especially hours of work. During this period and, in fact, for most of the century, the British system of industrial relations was characterized by a tradition of voluntarism.

## The Donovan analysis

The high incidence of disputes and strikes, the perceived power of the trade unions and some well-publicized examples of shop steward militancy (although the majority were quite amenable) contributed to the pressure for the reform of industrial relations which led to the setting up of the Donovan Commission. This concluded in 1968 that the formal system of industry-wide bargaining was breaking down. Its key findings were that at plant level, bargaining is highly fragmented and ill-organized, based on informality and custom and practice. The Commission's prescription was for a continuation of voluntarism, reinforced by organized collective bargaining arrangements locally, thus relieving trade unions and employers' associations of the 'policing role', which they so often failed to carry out. This solution involved the creation of new, orderly and systematic frameworks for collective bargaining at plant level by means of formal negotiation and pro-cedural agreements.

Since Donovan, comprehensive policies, structures and procedures to deal with pay and conditions, shop steward facilities, discipline, health and safety, etc have been developed at plant level to a sub-stantial extent. The support provided by Donovan to the voluntary system of industrial relations was, however, underpinned by a powerful minority note of reservation penned by Andrew Shonfield in the 1968 report of the Royal Commission. He advocated a more interventionist approach which began to feature in government policies in the 1970s.

## Interventionism in the 1970s

The received wisdom in the 1960s which as reflected in the majority Donovan report was that industrial relations could not be controlled by legislation. But the Industrial Relations Act introduced by the Conservative government in 1971 ignored this belief and drew heavily on Shonfield's minority report. It introduced a strongly interventionist legal framework to replace the voluntary regulation of industrial relations systems. Trade unions lost their general immunity from legal action and had to register under the Act if they wanted any rights at all. Collective agreements were to become legally binding contracts and a number of 'unfair industrial practices' were proscribed. Individual workers were given the right to belong or not belong to a trade union but an attempt was made to outlaw the closed shop. The Act did, however, introduce the important general right of employees 'not to be unfairly dismissed'.

But the Act failed to make any impact; being ignored or side-stepped by both trade unions and employers.

The Labour government of 1974 promptly repealed the 1971 Industrial Relations Act and entered into a 'social contract' with the trade unions which incorporated an agreement that the TUC would support the introduction of a number of positive union rights. These included a statutory recognition procedure and in effect meant that the unions expressed their commitment to legal enforcement as a means of restricting management's prerogatives.

Statutory rights were also provided for minimum notice periods, statements of terms and conditions, redundancy payments and unfair dismissal.

## The 1980s — curbing the trade unions

The strike-ridden 'winter of discontent' in 1978 and the return of a Conservative government in 1979 paved the way for the ensuing step-by-step legislation which continued throughout the 1980s and into the early 1990s.

The ethos of the Conservative governments in the 1980s was summed up by Phelps Brown (1990) as follows:

People are no longer seen as dependent on society and bound by reciprocal relationship to it; indeed the very notion of society is rejected. Individuals are expected to shift for themselves and those who get into difficulties are thought to have only themselves to blame. Self-reliance, acquisitive individualism, the curtailment of public expenditure, the play of market forces instead of the restraints and directives of public policy, the prerogatives of management instead of the power of the unions, centralisation of power instead of pluralism.

The legislation on trade unions followed this ethos and was guided by an ideological analysis expressed in the 1981 Green Paper on *Trade Union Immunities* as follows:

Industrial relations cannot operate fairly and efficiently or to the benefit of the nation as a whole if either employers or employees collectively are given predominant power — that is, the capacity effectively to dictate the behaviour of others.

The government described industrial relations as 'the fundamental cause of weakness in the British economy', with strikes and restrictive practices inhibiting the country's ability to compete in international markets. The balance of bargaining power was perceived to have moved decisively in favour of trade unions which were described as 'irresponsible, undemocratic and intimidatory', while the closed shop was described as being destructive of the rights of the individual worker.

The ensuing legislation provided for unions to be sued for unlawful industrial action, outlawed the closed shop and gave additional protection to the rights of union members.

## The current industrial relations scene

The current industrial relations scene has been analysed and described by: The 1990 Workplace Industrial Relations Survey, the 1992 Second Company Level Industrial Relations Survey and various other commentators.

### The 1990 Workplace Industrial Relations Survey

The 1990 Workplace Industrial Relations Survey as analysed by Millward *et al* (1992) covered 2,061 workplaces employing over 1,140,000 people. It is the latest and most comprehensive survey of industrial practices in the UK available in 1995.

The main findings of the survey were as follows:

*General*

- There were major and probably irreversible changes in employee relations during the 1980s, so much so that 'the distinctive system of British industrial relations based on collective bargaining is no longer characteristic of the economy as a whole'.
- The decline of traditional industrial relations has not, however, led to the emergence of any new pattern of employee representation. Where new forms of employee relations were adopted they were usually complementary to trade union representation, rather than substitutes filling the gaps left by union decline.

*Trade union recognition*

- The proportion of workplaces recognizing one or more trade unions fell from 52 per cent in 1984 to 40 per cent in 1990. This, according to the survey, was the strongest evidence of the decline of collective bargaining as an institution. The fall was 'stark, substantial and incontrovertible'.
- Analysis of a matched panel of 537 trading sector workplaces which were included in the 1984 survey revealed that nearly a fifth of those that reported recognized unions in 1984 reported no recognized unions in 1990. However, nearly a tenth of workplaces with recognized unions in 1990 had none in 1984.
- There was little evidence of single union deals.

*Union membership*

- The proportion of employees in union membership — 'union density' — fell from 58 per cent to 48 per cent between 1984 and 1990.

*Coverage of collective bargaining*

- 54 per cent of employees were covered by collective bargaining in 1990 compared with 71 per cent in 1984.
- In 1990 only 54 per cent of employees covered by the surveys had their pay at least partly determined by management/trade union negotiations — down from 71 per cent in 1984.
- In workplaces where pay was determined by collective bargaining, multi-employer bargaining remained the single most popular method of pay determination.

*HRM practices*

- Collective bargaining has not been replaced by new-style human resource management practices, defined as changes in methods of communication and consultation which indicated that management was making efforts to gain the greater commitment of employees through greater participation and involvement, the harmonization of conditions of employment, and changes in the starting and finishing times of employees.

*Conclusions*

On the basis of his analysis of the survey findings, Millward (1994) came to the conclusion that non-managerial employees in British industry and commerce are increasingly being treated as 'factors of production'. This assertion is based on his view that while trade union recognition is in decline, no alternative methods of employee representation have emerged to deal either with 'conflicts between employers and employees' or to channel employees' contribution 'to the operation of their workplace in the broader context than that of their own job'.

Millward also comments that the combination of a decline in 'traditional' industrial relations, and the lack of a significant increase in 'new' forms of employee representation or communication, particularly in non-union workshops, means that where there should be orderly employee relations, there is now a vacuum in British workplaces.

## The Second Company Level Industrial Relations Survey (CLIRS)

This survey, as reported by Marginson *et al* (1993), covered 176 companies with 1,000 or more employees, produced somewhat different findings to the WIRS survey. The latter established that the proportion of workplace recognized trade unions was 40 per cent in 1990 compared with 52 per cent in 1984. But the CLIRS found that 69 per cent recognized trade unions for the largest group employed in the workplace. The CLIRS also found that among the 80 per cent of organizations which had opened new sites in the previous five years, union recognition was granted to the largest group in the organization in 41 per cent of the cases. In contrast, the WIRS found that only 29 per cent of workplaces established since 1984 had recognized trade unions.

## Other commentators

The key points emerging from the research conducted by Storey (1993) and colleagues were:

- the marginalization of trade unions and industrial relations
- the scope of issues covered by collective bargaining had narrowed considerably and it tended to become similar to joint consultation
- there was a notable shift towards individualized contracts and performance related pay
- the numbers and influence of shop stewards had been reduced
- there had been few outright assaults on trade unions but equally, there had been little attempt to involve them in the planning and implementation of change
- there had been a widespread move to decentralize collective bargaining
- trade union leaders both at national and workplace level were left on the sidelines of most of the managerial initiatives during this period
- the message from management to trade unions was that we 'are in the driving seat' — trade unions and industrial relations are relatively secondary and incidental to meeting market priorities, and secondary also to the newly rediscovered alternative ways of managing the labour (human) resource
- but there was a general failure to work out a coherent policy which embraces HRM *and* industrial relations.

Kessler and Bayliss (1995) comment that 'the needs of employers have increasingly been towards enterprise orientated rather than occupationally orientated trade unions'. They also note that:

> It is clear that the significance of industrial relations in many firms has diminished. It is part of a management controlled operation — a branch of human resource management. It is no longer a high profile problem-ridden part of personnel management as it so often was in the 1970s.

Guest (1995) notes that the industrial relations system may continue as a largely symbolic 'empty shell', insufficiently important for management to confront and eliminate, but retaining the outward appearance of health to the casual observer: 'Management sets the agenda, which is market-driven, while industrial relations issues are relatively low on the list of concerns'.

Cave's (1994) examination of 'whatever happened to industrial relations?' produced the following key points:

- In the early and mid-1980s the structure of the traditional industrial relations system still held. By 1990 it did not. 'It is now wrong to depict the UK scene as one in which traditional, union-based industrial relations is the norm: such a system covers at most 40 per cent of the economy'.
- 'The break with the voluntarist or "abstentionist" tradition is absolute — and almost certainly irreversible. The conduct of industrial relations is now tightly regulated by legislative requirements'.
- Employers have become more free to decide the basis 'on which they are to conduct their employee relations — whether with or without unions. They can largely inoculate themselves from any agreements, rules and procedures which have been drawn up outside their gates'.
- Employers have gradually adjusted their behaviour in order to take advantage of the leverage that the new legislative framework gives them. The use of injunctions, for example, has become part of the tactical armoury of employers to influence the course of disputes (hopefully to pre-empt them altogether), rather than to engage in acts of retribution against unions.
- Trade unions now have to operate within a regulatory environment which is arguably tighter than any other group in society.
- Trade unions have no legal scope to act on issues that fall outside the immediate 'bread and butter' concerns of the members' workplace.
- 'From the government's point of view, their programme has worked; the behaviour of trade unions and the balance of power between them and employers has shifted decisively'.

## The parties to industrial relations

The parties to industrial relations are:

- the trade unions
- the Trade Union Congress (the TUC)
- management
- employers' organizations
- the Confederation of British Industry.

The role of each of these parties is summarized in the next five sections of this chapter.

# The trade unions

## Role

Traditionally the fundamental purpose of trade unions is to promote and protect the interests of their members. They are there to redress the balance of power between employers and employees. The basis of the employment relationship is the contract of employment. But this is not a contract between equals. Employers are almost always in a stronger position to dictate the terms of the contract than individual employees. Trade unions, as indicated by Freeman and Medoff (1984) provide workers with a 'collective voice' to make their wishes known to management and thus bring actual and desired conditions closer together. This applies not only to terms of employment such as pay, working hours and holidays, but also to the way in which individuals are treated in such aspects of employment as the redress of grievances, discipline and redundancy. Trade unions also exist to let management know that there will be, from time to time, an alternative view on key issues affecting employees. More broadly, unions may see their role as that of participating with management on decision-making on matters affecting their members' interests.

Within this overall role, trade unions have a number of specific roles, namely to:

- secure, through collective bargaining, improved terms and conditions for their members
- provide protection, support and advice to members as individuals.

An additional role, that of providing legal, financial and other services to their members, has come into prominence more recently.

## Trade union structure

Trade unions are run by full time central and, usually, district officials. There may be local committees of members. National officials may conduct industry-wide or major employer pay negotiations while local officials may not be involved in plant negotiations unless there is a 'failure to agree' and the second stage of a negotiating procedure is invoked. Major employers who want to introduce significant changes in agreements or working arrangements may deal direct with national officials.

The trade union movement is now dominated by the large general unions and the recently merged craft and public service unions.

## Shop stewards

Shop stewards or trade union representatives may initially be responsible for plant negotiations, probably with the advice of full-time officials. They will certainly be involved in settling disputes and resolving collective grievances and in representing individual employees with grievances or over disciplinary matters. They may be members of joint consultative committees which could be wholly or partly composed of trade union representatives.

It was established by the WIRS 3 — the third Workshop Industrial Relations Survey (Millward, 1994) — that 70 per cent of workplaces in industry and commerce with recognized unions had a workplace representative. The remainder relied on local full-time officials or representatives from other establishments of the same employer. The decentralization of pay bargaining as discussed in the next chapter may have enhanced the negotiating role of trade union representatives at plant level.

At one time, shop stewards were the ogres of the industrial relations scene. Undoubtedly there were cases of militant shop stewards, but where there are recognized trade unions managements have generally recognized the value of shop stewards as points of contact and channels of communication. This is certainly the experience of the writer who, in some 15 years' experience of dealing directly with union representatives, found that it was possible, and invaluable, to maintain a climate of peaceful and cooperative coexistence by making regular informal contacts with plant shop stewards.

## Decline of the trade unions

The decline of the trade unions in the 1980s and 1990s is illustrated by the following figures:

- total trade union membership fell from 13 million in 1979 to 8.5 million in 1992
- the total membership as a proportion of the civilian workforce in employment (union density) fell from 53 per cent in 1979 to 37 per cent in 1990

- the proportion of the workforce covered by collective agreements fell from 50 per cent in 1983 to 35 per cent in 1992.

The problem, as defined by Basset and Cave (1993), is that there has been 'quite simply a collapse in demand for the core product that unions have offered to their twin markets (employees and employers) — collectivism enshrined most obviously in collective bargaining'.

The reasons for this decline are not primarily disenchantment with the trade unions, or the impact of trade union legislation, or large scale derecognitions. The real causes are structural and economic, namely:

- a shift in the economy away from large scale manufacturing industries (traditionally heavily unionized) to the service industries (traditionally non-unionized)
- the trend to decentralize organizations
- a decline in the number of workplaces employing large numbers of people
- growing numbers of women, white collar workers, and part-time workers
- the impact of unemployment.

The actions taken by the unions to counteract this trend have included mergers to increase their perceived power and enable them to operate more cost-effectively, recruitment drives in non-unionized sectors (not very successfully), and what is sometimes referred to as 'enterprise trade unionism'. The latter approach emphasizes the valuable role that unions can play as partners in the workplace, helping to manage change and improving productivity. This has worked in some instances, but most employers have remained unconvinced that the unions can play such a positive role.

## The Trades Union Congress (TUC)

The TUC acts as the collective voice of the unions. Its roles are to:

- represent the British trade union movement in the UK and internationally
- conduct research and develop policies on trade union, industrial, economic and social matters and to campaign actively for them
- regulate relationships between unions
- help unions in dispute
- provide various services (eg research) to affiliated unions.

But the TUC has effectively been marginalized by successive Conservative governments and is but a shadow of its former self, especially since its interventionary role concerning union disputes over membership (the Bridlington rules) has now effectively been abolished by legislation.

## International union organizations

The two main international union organizations are the European Trade Union Confederation and the International Confederation of Free Trade Unions. At present neither of these makes much impact on the UK but this could change.

## Staff associations

Staff associations may sometimes have negotiating and/or representational rights but they seldom have anything like the real power possessed by a well-organized and supported trade union. They are often suspected by employees as being no more than management's poodle. Managements have sometimes encouraged the development of staff associations as an alternative to trade unions but this strategy has not always worked. In fact, in some organizations the existence of an unsatisfactory staff association has provided an opportunity for a trade union to gain membership and recognition. Staff associations have their uses as channels of communication and representatives can play a role in consultative processes and representing colleagues who want to take up grievances or who are being subject to disciplinary proceedings.

## The role of management

The balance of power has undoubtedly shifted to managements who now have more choice over how they conduct relationships with their employees. But the evidence from the WIRS3 is that there has been no concerted drive by managements to derecognize unions. As Kessler and Bayliss (1995) point out: 'If managers in large establishments and companies wanted to make changes they looked at ways of doing so within the existing arrangements and if they could produce the goods they used them. Because managers found that the unions did not stand in their way they saw no reason for getting rid of them'. They argued that management's industrial relations objectives are now generally to:

- control the work process
- secure cost effectiveness
- re-assert managerial authority
- move towards a more unitary and individualistic approach.

As Storey (1992a) found in most of the cases he studied there was a tendency for managements to adopt HRM approaches to employee relations while still co-existing with the unions. But they gave increasing weight to systems of employee involvement, in particular communication, which by-pass trade unions.

The WIRS3 (Millward 1994) established that there were no obstacles to management's freedom to organize work in 72 per cent of the workplaces covered by the survey with recognized unions. Where there was a single negotiating group no constraints were present in 85 percent of workplaces, while if there were two or more negotiating groups the percentage of workplaces without constraints fell to 55 per cent.

## Employers' organizations

Traditionally, employers' organizations have bargained collectively for their members with trade unions and have in general aimed to protect the interests of those members in their dealings with unions. Multi-employers or industry-wide bargaining, it was believed, allowed companies to compete in product markets without undercutting their competitors' employment costs and prevented the trade unions 'picking off' individual employers in a dispute.

The trend towards decentralizing bargaining to plant level has reduced the extent to which employers' organizations fulfil this traditional role although some industries such as buildings and electrical contracting with large numbers of small companies in competitive markets have retained their central bargaining function, setting a floor of terms and conditions for the industry.

## The Confederation of British Industry (CBI)

The CBI is a management organization which is only indirectly concerned with industrial relations. It provides a means for its members to influence economic policy and it provides advice and services to them, supported by research.

## Institutions, agencies and officers

There are a number of bodies and people with a role in employee relations as described below.

### *The Advisory Conciliation and Arbitration Service (ACAS)*

ACAS was created by the Government but functions independently. It has three main statutory duties:

- to resolve disputes
- to provide conciliatory services for individuals in, for example, unfair dismissal cases
- to give advice, help and information on industrial relations and employment issues.

ACAS helps to resolve disputes in three ways: collective conciliation, arbitration and mediation. These are described in Chapter 40.

During the 1980s and early 1990s the use of ACAS's collective conciliation and arbitration services declined considerably. But the individual conciliation case load has been very heavy and the ACAS advisory work has flourished. In 1993 ACAS completed 517 'advisory mediation' projects. These are aimed at encouraging non-adversarial approaches to preventing and resolving problems at work by facilitating joint working groups of employers, employees and their representatives.

### *The Central Arbitration Committee (CAC)*

The CAC is an independent arbitration body which deals with disputes. It arbitrates at the request of one party but with the agreement of the other. It does not handle many arbitrations but it deals more frequently with claims by trade unions for disclosure of information for collective bargaining purposes.

### *Industrial tribunals*

Industrial tribunals are independent judicial bodies which deal with disputes on employment matters such as unfair dismissal, equal pay, sex and race discrimination and employment protection provisions. They have a legally qualified chair and two other members, one an employer, the other a trade unionist.

## The Employment Appeal Tribunal (EAT)

The EAT hears appeals from the decisions of industrial tribunals on questions of law only.

## The Certification Officer

The Certification Officer:

- ensures that the statutory provisions for union political funds and union amalgamations are complied with
- maintains lists of trade unions and employers' associations and ensures that their accounts are audited
- reimburses the expenses incurred by independent unions in conducting secret ballots
- deals with complaints by members that a union has failed to comply with the provisions for certain union elections.

## The Commissioner for the Rights of Trade Union Members

The Commissioner has two duties:

- to assist union members wanting to take legal action against a union arising from an alleged or threatened breach of a member's statutory union membership rights
- to assist members who complain that a union has failed to observe the requirements of its own rule book.

# 40

# Employee Relations — Processes and Outcomes

Employee relations processes consist of the approaches and methods adopted by employers to deal with employees either through their trade unions and/or directly. They will be based on the organization's articulated or implied employee relations policies, objectives and strategies as examined in the first three sections of this chapter. The way in which they are developed and how they function will be influenced by, and will influence, the employee relations climate, the concept of which is examined in the third section of the chapter.

Industrial relations processes, ie those aspects of employee relations which are concerned with the dealings between employers and trade unions consist of:

- approaches to recognizing or derecognizing trade unions
- formal methods of collective bargaining
- the informal day-to-day contacts on employment issues which take place in the workplace between management and trade union representatives or officials
- features of the industrial relations scene such as union membership in the work place, the check-off and strikes.

These processes are considered later in this chapter. Negotiating techniques and skills as an aspect of collective bargaining are dealt with separately in the next chapter.

In addition there are the employee relations processes of involvement, participation and communication which are discussed in Chapter 42.

The outcomes of these processes are various forms of procedural and substantive agreements and employment procedures, including harmonization of terms and conditions, and the approaches used by organizations to manage with and without trade unions. These are described in the last three sections of this chapter.

## Employee relations policies

### *Nature and purpose*

Employee relations policies express the philosophy of the organization on what sort of relationships between management and employees and their unions are wanted, and how they should be handled. The overall aim of the policies should be to develop and maintain a positive, productive, cooperative and trusting climate of employee relations.

When they are articulated, policies provide guidelines for action on employee relations issues and can help to ensure that these issues are dealt with consistently. They provide the basis for defining management's intentions (its industrial relations strategy) on key matters such as union recognition and collective bargaining.

### *Policy areas*

The specific areas covered by employee relations policies are:

- *trade union recognition* — whether trade unions should be recognized or derecognized, which unions or unions the organization would prefer to deal with, and whether or not it is desirable to recognize only one union for collective bargaining and/or employee representational purposes
- *collective bargaining* — the extent to which it should be centralized or decentralized and the scope of areas to be covered by collective bargaining
- *employee relations procedures* — the nature and scope of procedures for redundancy, grievance handling and discipline
- *the employment relationship* — the extent to which terms and conditions of employment should be governed by collective agreements or based on individual contracts of employment (ie collectivism *versus* individualism)
- *harmonization* of terms and conditions of employment for staff and manual workers

- *working arrangements* — the degree to which management has the prerogative to determine working arrangements without reference to trade unions or employees (this includes job-based or functional flexibility).

When formulating policies in these areas organizations may be consciously or unconsciously deciding on the extent to which they want to adopt the HRM approach to employee relations. As described in Chapter 39, this emphasizes commitment, mutuality and forms of involvement and participation which mean that management approaches and communicates with employees directly rather than through their representatives.

## Policy choices

There is, of course, no such thing as a model employee relations policy. Every organization develops its own policies. In a mature business these will be in accordance with established custom and practice, its core values and management style and the actual or perceived balance of power between management and unions. In younger organizations or those being established on a green field site, the policies will depend on the assumptions and beliefs of management and, where relevant, the existing philosophy and policies of the parent company. In both these cases policies will be affected by the type of people employed by the organization, its business strategies, technology, the industry or sector in which it operates, and its structure (for example, the extent to which it is centralized or decentralized).

The following four policy options for organizations on industrial relations and HRM have been described by Guest (1995):

1. *The new realism — a high emphasis on HRM and industrial relations.* The aim is to integrate HRM and industrial relations. This is the policy of such organizations as Rover, Nissan and Toshiba. A review of new collaborative arrangements in the shape of single-table bargaining (IRS, 1993) found that they were almost always the result of employer initiatives, but that both employers and unions seem satisfied with them. They have facilitated greater flexibility, more multiskilling, the removal of demarcations and improvements in quality. They can also extend consultation processes and accelerate moves towards single status.

2. *Traditional collectivism — priority to industrial relations without HRM.* This involves retaining the traditional pluralist industrial relations

arrangements within an eventually unchanged industrial relations system. Management may take the view in these circumstances that it is easier to continue to operate with a union, since it provides a useful, well-established channel for communication and for the handling of grievance, discipline and safety issues.

3. *Individualized HRM — high priority to HRM with no industrial relations.* According to Guest, this approach is not very common, except, as established by the WIRS3, in North American-owned firms. It is, he believes, 'essentially piecemeal and opportunistic'.

4. *The black hole — no industrial relations.* This option is becoming more prevalent in organizations in which HRM is not a policy priority for managements but where they do not see that there is a compelling reason to operate within a traditional industrial relations system. When such companies are facing a decision on whether or not to recognise a union, they are increasingly deciding not to do so. And, as shown by Millward (1994), non-union firms are not replacing the unions with an HRM strategy. Marginson *et al* (1993) similarly found no support for a non-union HRM strategy.

## Policy formulation

Employee relations policies usually evolve in the light of the circumstances of the firm, traditional practices, management's values and style and the power of trade unions to exert influence. They will change as new situations emerge and these may include competitive pressure, new management, a takeover, different views amongst employees about the value of trade unions, or new trade union policies. Sometimes these changes will be deliberate. Management may decide that it no longer has any use for trade unions and will therefore derecognise them. On other occasions the changes will simply emerge from the situation in which management finds itself.

The evolutionary and emergent nature of employee relations policies is the most typical case. But there is much to be said for managements occasionally to sit back and think through their policies in order to establish the extent to which they are still appropriate. This review should be based on an analysis of current policies and their relevance to the changing environment of the organization. This analysis could be extended to discussions with union representatives within the firm and local or even national officials to obtain their views. Employees could also be consulted so that their views could be obtained and acted upon, thus making it more likely that they will accept and be committed to policy changes. If there is a staff association, its role as a representative body should be reconsidered. Alternatively, the case for setting up a staff association should be reviewed. The outcome of attitude surveys designed to elicit the opinions of employees on matters of general concern to them can provide additional information on which to base policy decisions.

The result of such a review might, for example, be a decision not to make a frontal assault on the union, but simply to diminish its power by restricting the scope of collective bargaining and by-passing it and its shop stewards through more direct approaches to individual employees. As recent surveys such as the WIRS3 have shown, this, rather than outright derecognition, has been the typical policy of unionised firms. And it is probable in most of these cases that the policy evolved over time rather than being formulated after a systematic review.

Alternatively, processes of consultation with trade unions and employees may lead to the development of a more positive policy of partnership with the trade union which recognises the mutual advantages of working together.

## Expressing policy

Most organizations seem reluctant to commit their employee relations policies to writing. And this is understandable in the light of their fluid nature and, in some cases, the reluctance of managements to admit publicly that they are anti-union.

Policies which are deeply embedded as part of the managerial philosophy and values of the organization do not need to be expressed in writing. They will be fully understood by management and will therefore be acted upon consistently, especially when they are in effect broad expressions of the views of management rather than specific action guidelines.

The argument for having written policies is that everyone — line managers, team leaders and employees generally — will be clear about where they stand and how they are expected to act. Firms may also want to publish their employee relations policies to support a 'mutual commitment' strategy as described in Chapter 17. But this presupposes the involvement of employees in formulating the policies.

### Employee relations objectives

Employee relations objectives define what the organization means to achieve in the application of its employee relations policies. The objectives could refer to such matters as:

- improving the employee relations climate
- decentralizing collective bargaining arrangements
- introducing single table bargaining
- derecognizing trade unions
- developing HRM type approaches of involvement and communication to increase mutuality.

## Employee relations strategies

### Nature and purpose

Employee relations strategies set out how objectives such as those mentioned above are to be achieved. They define the intentions of the organization about what needs to be done and what needs to be changed in the ways in which the organization manages its relationships with employees and their trade unions. Like all other aspects of personnel or HR strategy, employee relations strategies will flow from the business strategy but will also aim to support it. For example, if the business strategy is to concentrate on achieving competitive edge through innovation and the delivery of quality to its customers, the employee relations strategy may emphasise processes of involvement and participation, including the implementation of programmes for continuous improvement and total quality management. If however, the strategy for competitive advantage, or even survival, is cost reduction, the employee relations strategy may concentrate on how this can be achieved by maximising cooperation with the unions and employees and by minimising detrimental effects on those employees and disruption to the organization.

Employee relations strategies should be distinguished from employee relations policies. Strategies are dynamic. They provide a sense of direction, and give an answer to the question 'how are we going to get from here to there?' Employee relations policies are more about the here and now. They express 'the way things are done around here' as far as dealing with unions and employees is concerned. Of course they will evolve but this may not be a result of a strategic choice. It is when a deliberate decision is made to change policies that a strategy for achieving this change has to be formulated. Thus if the policy is to increase commitment the strategy could consider how this might be achieved by involvement and participation processes.

## Strategic directions

The intentions expressed by employee relations strategies may direct the organization towards any of the following:

- changing forms of recognition, including single union recognition, or derecognition
- changes in the form and content of procedural agreements
- new bargaining structures, including decentralisation or single-table bargaining
- the achievement of increased levels of commitment through involvement or participation
- deliberately by-passing trade union representatives to communicate directly with employees
- increasing the extent to which management controls operations in such areas as flexibility
- generally improving the employee relations climate in order to produce more harmonious and cooperative relationships
- developing a 'partnership' with trade unions, recognising that employees are stakeholders and that it is to the advantage of both parties to work together (this could be described as a unitarist strategy aiming at increasing mutual commitment).

## Formulating strategies

Like other business and HR strategies, those concerned with employee relations can, in Mintzberg's (1987) words, 'emerge in response to an evolving situation'. But it is still useful to spend time deliberately formulating strategies and the aim should be to create a shared agenda which will communicate a common perspective on what needs to be done. This can be expressed in writing but it can also be clarified through involvement and communication processes.

## Employee relations climate

The employee relations climate of an organization represents the perceptions of management, employees and their representatives about the ways in which employee relations are conducted and how the various parties (managers, employees and trade unions) behave when dealing with one another. An employee relations climate can be good, bad or indifferent according to perceptions about the extent to which:

- management and employees trust one another
- management treats employees fairly and with consideration
- management is open about its actions and intentions — employee relations policies and procedures are transparent
- harmonious relationships are generally maintained on a day-to-day basis which result in willing cooperation rather than grudging submission
- conflict, when it does arise, is resolved without resort to industrial action and resolution is achieved by integrative processes which result in a 'win-win' solution
- employees are generally committed to the interests of the organization and, equally, management treat them as stakeholders whose interests should be protected as far as possible.

## Improving the climate

Improvements to the climate can be attained by developing fair employee relations policies and procedures and implementing them consistently. Line managers and team leaders who are largely responsible for the day-to-day conduct of employee relations need to be educated and trained on the approaches they should adopt. Transparency should be achieved by communicating policies to employees, and commitment increased by involvement and participation processes. Problems which need to be resolved can be identified by simply talking to employees, their representatives and their trade union officials. A quality of working life (QWL) strategy as described in Chapter 21 can be developed. Importantly, as discussed below, the organization can address its obligations to the employees as stakeholders and take steps to build trust.

## An ethical approach

Businesses aim to achieve prosperity, growth and survival. Ideally, success should benefit all the stakeholders in the organization — owners, management, employees, customers and suppliers. But the single-minded pursuit of business objectives can act to the detriment of employees' well-being and security. There may be a tension between accomplishing business purposes and the social and ethical obligations of an organization to its employees. But the chances of attaining a good climate of employee relations are slight if no attempt is made to recognize and act on an organization's duties to its members.

An ethical approach may be based on quality of working life considerations. It will also be transparent and, although the concept of a 'job for life' may no longer be valid in many organizations, at least an attempt will be made to maintain 'full employment' policies. Rover Group, for example, concluded a 'new deal' agreement with its unions in 1992 which incorporated a security of employment clause stating that 'employees who want to work for Rover will be able to stay with Rover'.

## Building trust

The Institute of Personnel and Development's (IPD) statement *People make the Difference* (1994) makes the point that much has been done in recent years to introduce a sense of reality into employee relations. But, according to the IPD,

> Managers should not kid themselves that acquiescence is the same thing as enthusiastic involvement. The pace of life and changing work patterns in the future will put a strain on the best of relationships between employees and managers.

The IPD suggests that building trust is the only basis on which commitment can be generated and these tensions contained. For these reasons, attaining or sustaining world class levels of performance will be increasingly unlikely in organizations which do not treat their employees in ways which are consistent with their status as the key business resource with this aim:

- employees cannot just be treated as a factor of production
- organizations must translate these values into specific and practical action. In too many organizations inconsistency between what is said and what is done undermines trust, generates employee cynicism and provides evidence of contradictions in management thinking.

# Union recognition and derecognition

## Recognition

An employer fully recognizes a union for the purposes of collective bargaining when pay and conditions of employment are jointly agreed between management and trade unions. Partial recognition takes place when employers restrict trade unions to representing their members on issues arising from employment. Full recognition therefore confers negotiating (and representational) rights on unions. Partial recognition only gives unions representational rights. The following discussion of union recognition is only concerned with the much more common practice of full recognition.

The WIRS3 (Millward, 1994) revealed that the proportion of workplaces which fully recognised trade unions fell from 52 per cent in 1984 to 40 per cent in 1990. Younger workplaces established since 1984 were less likely to recognise unions (29 per cent compared with the 40 per cent for all workplaces in 1990). However, it seems that many businesses with well-established unions are likely to retain them, possibly because they do not regard recognition as an issue.

## Derecognition

The WIRS3 (Millward *et al* 1992) matched panel analysis revealed that one-fifth of the firms had derecognized their union in the period 1984 to 1990. Derecognition is far more widely spread than is generally assumed, as a study by Gall (1993) showed. Once largely restricted to national newspapers, ports and shipping, it is slowly spreading to other industrial sectors.

## Single union recognition

The existence of a number of unions within one organization was frequently criticised in the 1980s because of the supposed increase in the complexity of bargaining arrangements and the danger of inter-union demarcation disputes (who does what). The answer to this problem was thought to be single union representation through single union deals. These had a number of characteristics which were considered to be advantageous to management (the features of such agreements are described on page 747 in this chapter).

The WIRS3 (Millward, 1994) established that the proportion of organizations with single union representation was higher than generally supposed. In all workplaces in industry and commerce, the presence of union members, as reported by the management respondents was as follows:

- 49 per cent had no union members
- 27 per cent had members of a single union
- 23 had members of two or more unions.

Among workplaces with union members, 54 per cent had members of a single union. As might be expected, multi-unionism is more common in larger establishments. Workplaces with single unions had one or more of the following characteristics in that they were:

- in the private sector
- head offices
- workplaces with a high proportion of part-time employees
- in the service sector
- younger workplaces
- a feature of particular industries such as banking and finance, textiles and transport.

## Factors influencing recognition or derecognition

Employers are in a strong position now to choose whether they recognise a union or not, which union they want to recognise and the terms on which they would grant recognition, for example a single union and a no-strike agreement.

When setting up on greenfield sites employers may refuse to recognize unions. Alternatively they hold 'beauty contests' to select the union they prefer to work with which will be prepared to reach an agreement in line with what management wants.

An organization deciding whether or not to recognise a union will take some or all of the following factors into account:

- the perceived value or lack of value of having a process for regulating collective bargaining
- if there is an existing union, the extent to which management has freedom to manage; for example to change working arrangements and introduce flexible working or multiskilling
- the history of relationships with the union
- the proportion of employees who are union members and the degree to which they believe they need the protection their union provides (employee opinion can now be overridden but the business has to decide whether the advantages of derecognition outweigh the disadvantages of upsetting the *status quo*)
- any preferences as to a particular union, because of its reputation or the extent to which it is believed a satisfactory relationship can be maintained.

In considering recognition arrangements employers may also consider entering into a 'single union deal' as described below.

## Collective bargaining arrangements

Collective bargaining arrangements are those set up by agreements between managements, employers' associations, or joint employer negotiating bodies and trade unions to determine specified terms and conditions of employment for groups of employees. Collective bargaining processes are usually governed by procedural agreements (see page 755) and result in substantive agreements and agreed employee relations procedures (see page 757).

Collective bargaining arrangements should aim to provide the basis for maintaining a good employee relations climate and harmonious relationships with trade unions and employees generally.

The considerations to be taken into account in agreeing arrangements are:

- the level at which bargaining should take place
- single-table bargaining where a number of unions are recognized in one workplace
- dispute resolution.

### Bargaining levels

A clear trend away from multi-employer bargaining was witnessed throughout the 1980s. The 1990 WIRS authors (Millward *et al* 1992) commented that:

> Government policy, both through its dealings with its own employees and through persuasion and advocacy to offer employers, encouraged a move away from national multi-employer settlements towards more locally determined ones which were more sensitive to local labour markets and the circumstances of the employer.

Multi-employer bargaining nevertheless remained the predominant form of collective bargaining for the whole of the economy in 1990, but this takes account of the public sector where such arrangements still predominate except, now, in the National Health Service. They are much less common in the private sector.

The 1990 WIRS established that there was no increase in plant-level bargaining in the private sector although the decentralization of pay negotiations had been presented by many commentators as a significant trend in the 1980s. What actually happened in a number of cases was that the move away from multi-employer bargaining was accompanied by an increase in negotiating structures at corporate or company level.

## Single table bargaining

Single table brings together all the unions in a company as a single bargaining unit. The reasons companies advance for wanting this arrangement are:

- A concern that existing multi-unit bargaining arrangements not only are inefficient in terms of time and management resources but are also a potential source of conflict.
- The desire to achieve major changes in working practices, with or without new technology, which can be achieved only through single table bargaining.
- A belief in the necessity of introducing harmonized or single status conditions.

Marginson and Sisson (1990), however, identified a number of critical issues which need to be resolved if single table bargaining is to be introduced successfully. These comprise:

- the commitment of management to the concept
- the need to maintain levels of negotiation which are specific to particular groups below the single bargaining table
- the need to allay the fears of managers that they will not be able to react flexibly to changes in the demand for particular groups of workers
- the willingness of management to discuss a wider range of issues with union representatives — this is because single table bargaining adds to existing arrangements a top tier in which matters affecting all employees, such as training, development, working time and fringe benefits can be discussed
- the need to persuade representatives from the various unions to forget their previous rivalries, sink their differences and work together
- the need to allay the fears of trade unions that they may lose representation rights and members, and of shop stewards that they will lose the ability to represent members effectively.

These are formidable requirements to satisfy, and however desirable single table bargaining may be, it will never be easy to introduce or to operate.

## *Dispute resolution*

The aim of collective bargaining is, of course, to reach agreement, preferably to the satisfaction of both parties. Negotiating procedures as described in the next section of this chapter provide for various stages of 'failure to agree' and often include a clause providing for some form of dispute resolution in the event of the procedure being exhausted. The processes of dispute resolution are conciliation, arbitration and mediation.

### *Conciliation*
Conciliation is the process of reconciling disagreeing parties. It is carried out by a third party, often an ACAS conciliation officer, who acts in effect as a go-between, attempting to get the employer and trade union representatives to agree on terms. Conciliators can only help the parties to come to an agreement. They do not make recommendations on what that agreement should be. That is the role of an arbitrator.

The incentives to seek conciliation are the hope that the conciliator can rebuild bridges and the belief that a determined, if last minute, search for agreement is better than confrontation, even if both parties have to compromise.

### *Arbitration*
Arbitration is the process of settling disputes by getting a third party, the arbitrator, to review and discuss the negotiating stances of the disagreeing parties and make a recommendation on the terms of settlement which is binding on both parties. The arbitrator is impartial and the role is often undertaken by ACAS officials, although industrial relations academics are sometimes asked to act in this capacity. Arbitration is the means of last resort for reaching a settlement, where disputes cannot be resolved in any other way.

Procedure agreements may provide for either side unilaterally to invoke arbitration, in which case the decision of the arbitrator is not binding on both parties. The process of arbitration in its fullest sense, however, only takes place at the request of both parties who agree in advance to accept the arbitrator's findings. ACAS will only act as an arbitrator if the content of both parties is obtained, conciliation is considered, any agreed procedures have been used to the full and a failure to agree has been recorded.

The number of arbitration cases referred to ACAS declined significantly during the 1980s and early 1990s. The decline in arbitration is attributed by Kessler and Bayliss (1995) to management dominance which has meant that arbitration was seen as pointless because managements were confident that their final offer would be accepted. In the prevailing climate, unions, if dissatisfied and denied arbitration, would in most cases be unwilling to take industrial action.

*Pendulum arbitration*

Pendulum or final offer arbitration increases the rigidity of the arbitration process by allowing an arbitrator no choice but to recommend either the union's or the employer's final offer — there is no middle ground. The aim of pendulum arbitration is to get the parties to avoid adopting extreme positions. As defined by Millward (1994) the features of pendulum arbitration are that the procedure has to be written and agreed by management and the union or unions, and it has to provide for arbitration which is:

- independent
- is equally accessible to both parties
- is binding on both parties, and
- involves finding wholly in favour of one party or the other.

The adoption of pendulum arbitration can be viewed as a concession by management, since it means giving up the power to impose a settlement on employees. But the evidence from the WIRS3 was that the full version of pendulum arbitration as defined above was extremely rare. In workplaces with a sole union agreement, less than 1 per cent had pendulum arbitration. In multi-union workplaces 2 per cent of cases reported it.

*Mediation*

Mediation is a watered down form of arbitration although it is stronger than conciliation. It takes place when a third party (often ACAS) helps the employer and the union by making recommendations which, however, they are not bound to accept.

## Informal employee relations processes

The formal processes of union recognition, collective bargaining and dispute resolution described earlier in this chapter provide the framework for industrial relations in so far as this is concerned with agreeing terms and conditions of employment and working arrangements and settling disputes. But within or outside that framework informal employee relations processes are taking place continuously.

Informal employee relationships take place whenever a line manager or team leader is handling an issue in contact with a shop steward, an employee representative, an individual employee or a group of employees. The issue may concern methods of work, allocation of work and overtime, working conditions, health and safety, achieving output and quality targets and standards, discipline or pay (especially if a payment-by-results scheme is in operation which can generate continuous arguments about times, standards, re-timings, payments for waiting time or when carrying out new tasks, and fluctuations or reductions in earnings because of alleged managerial inefficiency).

Line managers and supervisors handle day-to-day grievances arising from any of these issues and are expected to resolve them to the satisfaction of all parties without involving a formal grievance procedure. The thrust for devolving responsibility to line managers for personnel matters has increased the onus on them to handle employee relations effectively. A good team leader will establish a working relationship with the shop steward representing his or her staff which will enable issues arising on the shop floor or with individual employees to be settled amicably before they become a problem.

Creating and maintaining a good employee relations climate in an organization may be the ultimate responsibility of top management, advised by personnel specialists. But the climate will be strongly influenced by the behaviour of line managers and team leaders. The personnel function can help to improve the effectiveness of this behaviour by identifying and defining the competences required, advising on the selection of supervisors, ensuring that they are properly trained, encouraging the development of performance management processes which provide for the assessment of the level of competence achieved by line managers and team leaders in handling employee relations or by providing unobtrusive help and guidance as required.

## Other features of the industrial relations scene

There are three features of the industrial relations scene which are important besides the formal and informal processes discussed above. These features are union membership arrangements within the organization, the 'check off' system and strikes and other forms of industrial action (which should more realistically be called industrial inaction if it involves a 'go slow' or 'work to rule').

## Union membership within organizations

The closed shop which enforced union membership within organizations has been made illegal. But many managers prefer that all their employees should be in the union because on the whole it makes their life easier to have one channel of representation to deal with industrial relations issues and also because it prevented conflict between members and non-members of the union.

## The 'check-off' system

The 'check-off' is a system which involves management in deducting the subscriptions of trade union members on behalf of the union. It is popular with unions because it helps to maintain membership and provides a reasonably well guaranteed source of income. Managements have generally been willing to cooperate as a gesture of good faith to their trade union. They may support a check-off system because it enables them to find out how many employees are union members. Employers also know that they can exert pressure in the face of industrial action by threatening to end the check-off. However, the Trade Union Reform and Employment Rights Act 1993 provides that if an employer is lawfully to make check-off deductions from a worker's pay there must be prior written consent from the worker and renewed consent at least every three years. This three year renewal provision may inhibit the maintenance of the system.

## Strikes

Strikes are the most politically charged of all the features of industrial relations. The Conservative government in the 1980s believed that 'strikes are too often a weapon of first rather than last resort'. However those involved in negotiation — as well as trade unions — have recognized that a strike is a legitimate last resort if all else fails. It is a factor in the balance of power between the parties in a negotiation and has to be taken into account by both parties.

Unlike other Western European countries, there is no legal right in Britain for workers or their unions to take strike action. What has been built up through common law is a system of legal liability which suspended union liability for civil wrongs or 'torts' as long as industrial action falls within the legal definition of a trade dispute and takes place 'in contemplation of furtherance of a trade dispute'. A trade dispute is defined in law as any dispute between workers and their employer which relates 'wholly or mainly' to:

- terms and conditions of employment
- engagement or non-engagement of workers or termination or suspension of employment
- allocation of work or the duties of employment
- matters of discipline
- facilities for trade union officials
- machinery for negotiations, consultation and trade union recognition.

The Conservative government's 1980s and 1990s legislation has limited this legal immunity to situations where a properly conducted ballot has been conducted by the union authorising or endorsing the action and where the action is between an employer and their direct employees, with all secondary or sympathy action being unlawful. Immunity is also removed if industrial action is taken to impose or enforce a closed shop or where the action is unofficial and is not repudiated in writing by the union. The impact of this law is to deter the calling of strikes without careful consideration of where the line of legal immunity is now drawn and of the likely result of a secret ballot. But the secret ballot can in effect legitimise strike action.

The number of strikes and the proportion of days lost through strike action has diminished significantly in the UK since the 1970s. This reduction has been caused more by economic pressures than by the legislation. Unions have had to choose between taking strike action which could lead to closure, or survival on the terms dictated by employers with fewer jobs. In addition unions in manufacturing found that their members who remained in jobs did well out of local productivity bargaining and threatened strike action.

## Employee relations outcomes

The formal outcomes of the employee relations processes described in this chapter are procedural agreements, substantive agreements, employee relations procedures and, possibly the development of harmonized terms and conditions of employment.

## Procedural agreements

Procedural agreements set out the methods to be used and the procedures or rules to be followed in the processes of collective bargaining and the settlement of industrial disputes. Their purpose is to regulate the behaviour of the parties to the agreement, but they are not legally enforceable and the degree to which they are followed depends on the goodwill of both parties or the balance of power between them. Procedural and substantive agreements are seldom broken and if so, never lightly — the basic presumption of collective bargaining is that both parties will honour agreements that have been made freely between them. An attempt to make collective agreements legally enforceable in the 1971 Industrial Relations Act failed because employers generally did not seek to enforce its provisions. They readily accepted union requests for a clause in agreements to the effect that: 'This is not a legally enforceable agreement', popularly known as a TINALEA clause.

A typical procedure agreement traditionally contained the following sections:

- a preamble defining the objectives of the agreement
- a statement that the union is recognized as a representative body with negotiating rights
- a statement of general principles, which may include a commitment to use the procedure (a no-strike clause) and/or a *status quo* clause which restricts the ability of management to introduce changes outside negotiated or customary practice
- a statement of the facilities granted to unions, including the rights of shop stewards and the right to hold meetings
- provision for joint negotiating committees (in some agreements)
- the negotiating or disputes procedure
- provision for terminating the agreement.

The scope and content of such agreements can, however, vary widely. Some companies have limited recognition to the provision of representational rights only, others have taken an entirely different line in concluding single-union deals which, when they first emerged in the 1980s, were sometimes dubbed 'new style agreements', or referred to as the 'new realism'. However, these terms are not used so much nowadays, although there is a distinct trend towards single table bargaining.

## Single-union deals

Single-union deals have the following typical features:

- a single union representing all employees, with constraints put on the role of union full-time officials
- flexible working practices — agreement to the flexible use of labour across traditional demarcation lines
- single status for all employees — the harmonization of terms and conditions between manual and non-manual employees
- an expressed commitment by the company to involvement and the disclosure of information in the form of an open communications system and, often, a company council
- the resolution of disputes by means of devices such as pendulum arbitration, a commitment to continuity of production and a 'no-strike' provision. (Pendulum arbitration allows an arbitrator no choice but to recommend either the union's or the employer's final offer — there is no middle ground and the aim is to get the parties to abandon extreme positions).

Single-union deals have generally been concluded on green field sites, often by Japanese firms such as Nissan, Sanyo, Matshushsita and Toyota. A 'beauty contest' may be held by the employer to select a union from a number of contenders. Thus, the initiative is taken by the employer who can lay down radical terms for the agreement.

It has been estimated (Cave, 1994) that no more than about 50,000 people are currently covered by single-union deals. Millward (1994) analysed the deals agreements identified in the 1990 Workshop Industrial Relations Survey and established the limited extent to which the following arrangements were incorporated:

- *complete flexibility* — nearly three-quarters
- *single status* — one in eight
- *company council* — 17 per cent
- *pendulum arbitration* — less than half of one per cent

It seems to be difficult, if not impossible, for employers who have established recognition agreements with a number of different unions to negotiate a single-union deal.

## Substantive agreements

Substantive agreements are the outcome of collective bargaining. They set out agreed terms and conditions of employment covering pay and working hours and other aspects such as holidays, overtime regulations, flexibility arrangements and allowances. Again, they are not legally enforceable. A substantive agreement may detail the operational rules for a payment-by-results scheme which could include arrangements for timing or re-timing and for payments during waiting time or on new, untimed, work.

## Employee relations procedures

Employee relations procedures are those agreed by management and trade unions to regulate the ways in which management handles certain industrial relations and employment processes and issues. The main employee relations procedures as described in Chapter 45 are those concerned with grievances, discipline and redundancy. Disputes procedures are usually contained within an overall procedural agreement. In addition, agreements are sometimes reached on health and safety procedures.

# Harmonization

Harmonization is the process of introducing the same conditions of employment for all employees. It is distinguished by Roberts (1990) from single status and staff status as follows:

- Single status is the removal of differences in basic conditions of employment to give all employees equal status. Some organizations take this further by putting all employees into the same pay and grading structure.
- Staff status is a process whereby manual and craft employees gradually receive staff terms and conditions of employment, usually upon reaching some qualifying standard, for example, length of service.
- Harmonization means the reduction of differences in the pay structure and other employment conditions between categories of employee, usually manual and staff employees. The essence of harmonization is the adoption of a common approach and criteria to pay and conditions for all employees. It differs from staff status in that, in the process of harmonization, some staff employees may have to accept some of the conditions of employment of manual workers.

According to Duncan (1989), the pressure towards harmonization has arisen for the following reasons:

- *New technology* — status differentials can obstruct efficient labour utilization, and concessions on harmonization are invariably given in exchange for an agreement on flexibility. Moreover, technology, by deskilling many white-collar jobs and enhancing the skills of former blue-collar workers, has made differential treatment harder to defend.
- *Legislation* — equal pay, the banning of sex and racial discrimination, and employment protection legislation have extended rights to manual workers previously the preserve of staff. The concept of equal value has been a major challenge to differentiation between staff and manual workers.
- *Improving productivity* by the more flexible use of labour.
- *Simplifying personnel administration* and thereby reducing costs.
- *Changing employee attitudes*, thus improving commitment, motivation and morale.

In Roberts' view, questions of morality are probably of least importance.

ACAS (1982) has suggested that organizations, before pursuing a programme of harmonization, should seek answers to the following questions:

- What differences in the treatment of groups of employees are a rational result of differences in the work or the job requirements?
- Is it possible to estimate the direct costs of removing these differences?
- What differences in status are explicitly recognized as part of the 'reward package' for different groups in the labour force?
- What would be the possible repercussive effects of harmonization?
- How do the existing differences affect industrial relations in the organization?

## Managing with trade unions

Ideally, managements and trade unions learn to live together, often on a give and take basis, the presumption being that neither would benefit from a climate of hostility or by generating constant confrontation. It would be assumed in this ideal situation that mutual advantage would come from acting in accordance with the spirit as well as the letter of agreed joint regulatory procedures. However, both parties would probably adopt a realistic pluralist viewpoint, recognising the inevitability of differences of opinion, even disputes, but believing that with goodwill on both sides they could be settled without resource to industrial action.

Of course, the reality in the 1960s and 1970s was often different. In certain businesses, for example in the motor and shipbuilding industries, hostility and confrontation were rife. And newspaper proprietors tended to let their unions walk all over them in the interests of peace and profit.

Times have changed. As noted earlier, trade union power has diminished and managements have tended to seize the initiative. They may be content to live with trade unions but they give industrial relations lower priority. They may feel that it is easier to continue to operate with a union because it provides a useful, well-established channel for communication and for the handling of grievance, discipline and safety issues. In the absence of a union, management would need to develop its own alternatives, which would be costly and difficult to operate effectively. The trade union and the shop stewards remain a useful lubricant. Alternatively, as Smith and Morton (1993) suggest, the management perspective may be that it is safer to marginalize the unions than formally to derecognize them and risk provoking a confrontation: 'Better to let them wither on the vine than receive a reviving fertilizer'. However the alternative view was advanced by Purcell (1979) who argued that management will have greater success in achieving its objectives by working with trade unions, in particular by encouraging union membership and participation in union affairs. More recently, The Industrial Participation Association 1995 report recognized the high degree of common interests shared by employers and unions, and stressed the need to accept the legitimacy of representative institutions, although it did not seek to deny differences of opinions and goals.

The pattern varies considerably but there is general agreement based on surveys such as the WIRS3 that employers have been able to assert their prerogative — 'management must manage' in the workplace. They seem generally to have regained control over how they organise work, especially with regard to the flexible use of labour and multiskilling. The 'status quo' clause, typical of many agreements in the engineering industry, whereby management could not change working arrangements without union agreement, has virtually disappeared.

Although there is no evidence from the WIRS3 and other studies that many businesses are consciously developing and applying comprehensive HRM policies, there have been a lot of attempts to introduce involvement processes as a means of increasing employee commitment. Managements who still feel that it is beneficial to work with unions rather than against them have developed HRM approaches such as involvement in partnership with their unions rather than in opposition. Working with unions in the 1990s has often involved a dual approach of individualism (communicating direct with employees) and collectivism (working with the union to obtain agreement to change as well as to negotiate terms and conditions of employment).

Four types of industrial relations managements have been identified by Purcell and Sisson (1987):

1. *Traditionalists* who have unitary beliefs and are anti-union with forceful management.
2. *Sophisticated paternalists* who are essentially unitary but they do not take it for granted that their employees accept the company's objectives or automatically legitimise management decision-making. They spend considerable time and resources in ensuring that their employees adopt the right approach.
3. *Sophisticated moderns* who are either:

   - **constitutionalists**, where the limits of collective bargaining are codified in an agreement but management is free to take decisions on matters which are not the subject of such an agreement; or
   - **consultors**, who accept collective bargaining but do not want to codify everything in a collective agreement, and instead aim to minimize the amount of joint regulation and emphasise joint consultation with 'problems' having to be solved rather than 'disputes' settled.

4. *Standard moderns* who are pragmatic or opportunist. Trade unions are recognized, but industrial relations are seen as primarily fire-fighting and are assumed to be non-problematic unless events prove otherwise. This is by far the most typical approach.

But working with unions can mean adopting a more positive partnership approach, in the words of John Monks (1994) 'finding the common ground on issues that are best tackled through joint action'. Where collective agreements are being made, a cooperative or integrative bargaining philosophy can be adopted which is based on perceptions about the mutual interdependence of management and employees and the recognition by both parties that this is a means to achieve more for themselves.

## Managing without trade unions

Most organizations do, in fact, manage without trade unions. The WIRS3 found that the majority of the establishments covered by the survey (60 per cent) do not recognise them. In younger workplaces (those established since 1984) 71 per cent did not recognize unions.

An analysis of the WIRS3 by Millward *et al* (1992) established that the characteristics of union-free employee relations were as follows:

- Employee relations were generally seen by managers as better in the non-union sector than in the union sector.
- Strikes were almost unheard of.
- Labour turnover was high but absenteeism was no worse.
- Pay levels were generally set unilaterally by management.
- The dispersion of pay was higher, it was more market related and there was more performance related pay. There was also a greater incidence of low pay.
- In general, no alternative methods of employee representation existed as a substitute for trade union representation.
- Employee relations were generally conducted with a much higher degree of informality than in the union sector. In a quarter of non-union workplaces there were no grievance procedures and about a fifth had no formal disciplinary procedures.
- Managers generally felt unconstrained in the way in which they organized work.
- There was more flexibility in the use of labour than in the union sector which included the greater use of freelance and temporary workers.
- Employees in the non-union sector are two and a half times as likely to be dismissed as those in unionized firms and the incidence of compulsory redundancies is higher.

The survey concluded that many of the differences which exist between unionised and non-unionised workplaces could be explained by the generally smaller size of the non-union firms and the fact that many such workplaces were independent, rather than being part of a larger enterprise.

Another characteristic not mentioned by the survey is the use by non-unionised firms of personal contracts as an alternative to collective bargaining. In theory, employees are free to negotiate such contracts but as an Anglia Polytechnic University (1995) study found little bargaining activity takes place in the 500 workplaces they surveyed. The conclusion was that the personal contract 'reflects inherent inequality of bargaining power' and this suggests that there is a continuing role for trade unions.

This does not paint a very satisfactory picture of employee relations from the worker's point of view, but it is probably typical of smaller, independent firms. Some of the latter may be what Marchington (1995b) describes as the traditional sweatshop employer. The pressure on the firm could be to control costs and increase flexibility and responsiveness to customer demands. These are objectives which management may feel could only be achieved without union interference.

Some larger organizations, for example IBM and Marks & Spencer manage without unions by, in effect adopting a 'union substitution' policy. This offers a complete employment package which can be seen by employees as an attractive alternative to trade union membership. The package is likely to include highly competitive pay with harmonized employment conditions, recruitment tests designed to select people who match organizational norms, a focus on employee communications and information-sharing, induction programmes which aim to get employees to accept the organization's ethos, an emphasis on training and career development and a commitment to providing secure and satisfying work. Such businesses may broadly adhere to the HRM model (although they would not describe it as such, and this is the approach they used before HRM was invented).

HRM techniques for increasing commitment through involvement and communication processes provide a route which some organizations without unions follow in order to maintain a satisfactory employee relations climate. But it is not easy. Unless HRM fits the core values of the organization and is in accord with its management style, and unless a coherent and integrated approach is adopted to introducing HRM processes, it is unlikely to succeed.

# 41

# Negotiating and Bargaining

Collective bargaining requires the exercise of negotiating skills. Bargaining skills are also necessary during the process of negotiating collective substantive agreements on terms and conditions of employment. Negotiating skills are required in many other aspects of personnel and development, including, for example, agreeing individual contracts of employment and outsourcing contracts but this chapter concentrates on those used in collective bargaining. This chapter covers the nature and process of negotiation and bargaining, bargaining conventions, the stages of negotiation and, in summary, the skills required.

## The nature of negotiating and bargaining

To negotiate is to confer with a view to finding terms of agreement. To bargain is to go through the steps required to come to terms on a transaction. Collective bargaining is essentially a process of negotiation — of conferring and, it is hoped, reaching agreement without resorting to force (although hard words may be exchanged on the way).

Within this negotiating process bargaining takes place. This means coming to terms on a settlement, which in a pay negotiation, may be somewhere between the union's opening demand of, say, a six per cent increase and the employer's first response of, say, three per cent. The point at which a settlement is achieved between these figures will depend on the relative bargaining power of the two parties, the realism of the offer or response, the level of bargaining skills the parties can deploy and the sheer determination of either party to press its point or not to concede (this may be a function of bargaining power).

## Negotiations

Negotiations take place when two parties meet to reach an agreement. This can be a convergent process (in commercial terms this is sometimes referred to as a 'willing buyer — willing seller' situation) where both parties are equally keen to reach a win-win agreement. Clearly, if this can be achieved rather than a win-lose outcome, the future relationships between the parties are more likely to be harmonious. Certainly, the primary aim of any negotiator should be to proceed on this basis.

But some negotiations can be described as 'divergent' in which one or both of the parties aim to win as much as they can from the other while giving away as little as possible. In these circumstances, negotiating can be a war game. It is a battle in the sense that the bargainers are pitting their wits against each other while also bringing in the heavy artillery in the shape of sanctions or threatened sanctions. As with other battles, the negotiation process can produce a pyrrhic victory in which both sides, including the apparent winner, retire to mourn their losses and lick their wounds. It is a game in the sense that both sides are trying to win, but there are various conventions or rules which the parties tacitly adopt or recognize, although they may break them in the heat of the battle.

Negotiations can normally be broken down into four stages:

1. preparing for negotiation: setting objectives, defining strategy and assembling data
2. opening
3. bargaining
4. closing.

Before analysing these stages in detail it may be helpful to consider the process of bargaining and list the typical conventions that operate when bargaining takes place.

### The process of bargaining

The process of bargaining consists of three distinct, though related, functions. First, bargainers state their bargaining position to their opposite numbers. Second, they probe weaknesses in the bargaining position of their opposite numbers and try to convince them that they must move, by stages if this is inevitable, from their present position to a position closer to what the bargainer wants. Third, they adjust or confirm their original estimate of their own bargaining position in the light of information gleaned and reactions from their opposite numbers, in order that, if the time comes to put an estimate of bargaining position to the test, the ground chosen will be as favourable as possible.

The essence of the bargaining process was described by Peters (1968):

> In skilful hands the bargaining position performs a double function. It conceals and it reveals. The bargaining position is used to indicate — to unfold gradually, step by step — the maximum expectation of the negotiator, while at the same time concealing, for as long as necessary, his minimum expectation. By indirect means, such as the manner and timing of the changes in your bargaining position, you, as a negotiator, try to convince the other side that your maximum expectation is really your minimum breaking-off point. Since you have taken an appropriate bargaining position at the start of negotiations, each change in your position should give ever-clearer indications of your maximum expectation. Also, each change should be designed to encourage or pressure the other side to reciprocate with as much information as you give them, if not more.

## Bargaining conventions

There are certain conventions in collective bargaining which most experienced and responsible negotiators understand and accept, although they are never stated and, indeed, may be broken in the heat of the moment, or by a tyro in the bargaining game. These conventions help to create an atmosphere of trust and understanding which is essential to the maintenance of the type of stable bargaining relationship that benefits both sides. Some of the most generally accepted conventions are listed below:

- whatever happens during the bargaining, both parties are using the bargaining process in the hope of coming to a settlement
- while it is preferable to conduct negotiations in a civilized and friendly manner, attacks, hard words, threats, and (controlled) losses of temper are sometimes used by negotiators to underline determination to get their way and to shake their opponent's confidence and self-possession — but these should be treated by both sides as legitimate tactics and should not be allowed to shake the basic belief in each other's integrity or desire to settle without taking drastic action
- off-the-record discussions are mutually beneficial as a means of

probing attitudes and intentions and smoothing the way to a settlement, but they should not be referred to specifically in formal bargaining sessions unless both sides agree in advance

- each side should normally be prepared to move from its original position
- it is normal, although not inevitable, for the negotiation to proceed by alternate offers and counter-offers from each side which lead steadily towards a settlement
- concessions, once made, cannot be withdrawn
- firm offers must not be withdrawn, although it is legitimate to make and withdraw conditional offers
- third parties should not be brought in until both parties are agreed that no further progress would be made without them
- the final agreement should mean exactly what it says — there should be no trickery, and the terms agreed should be implemented without amendment
- so far as possible, the final settlement should be framed in such a way as to reduce the extent to which the other party obviously loses face or credibility.

## Preparing for negotiation

Negotiations take place in an atmosphere of uncertainty. Neither side knows how strong the other side's bargaining position is or what it really wants and will be prepared to accept. They do not know how much the other party will be prepared to concede or the strength of its convictions.

In a typical pay negotiation unions or representative bodies making the claim will define three things:

- the target they would like to achieve
- the minimum they will accept
- the opening claim which they believe will be most likely to help achieve the target.

Employers define three related things:

- the target settlement they would like to achieve
- the maximum they would be prepared to concede
- the opening offer they will make which would provide them with sufficient room to manoeuvre in reaching their target.

The difference between the union's claim and the employer's offer is the negotiating range. If your maximum exceeds their minimum, this will indicate the settlement range. This is illustrated in Figure 41.1. In this example the chance of settlement without too much trouble is fairly high. It is when their maximum is less than their minimum, as in Figure 41.2, that the trouble starts. Over a period of time a negotiation where a settlement range exists proceeds in the way demonstrated in Figure 41.3.

## Objectives

The objectives in the form of a target settlement and initial and minimum/maximum offers and agreements will be conditioned by:

- the perceptions of both parties about the relative strengths of their cases
- the relative power of the two parties
- the amount of room for negotiation the parties want to allow;
- the employer's ability to pay
- the going rate elsewhere

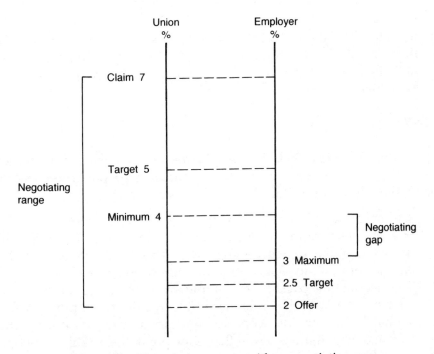

**Figure 41.1** Negotiating range with a negotiating gap

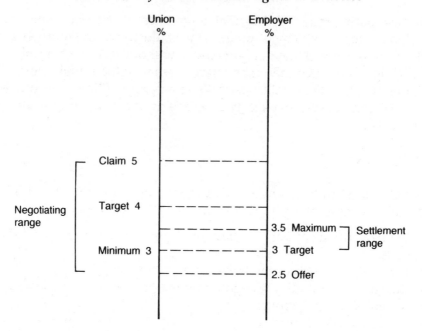

**Figure 41.2** Negotiating range with settlement range

● the rate of inflation — although employers are reluctant to concede that it is their job to protect their employees from inflation, the cost of living is often one of the chief arguments advanced by a union for an increase.

## Strategy

Negotiating strategy should clearly be designed to achieve the target settlement, with the maximum the negotiator is prepared to concede being the fall-back position. Two decisions are required:

1. The stages to follow in moving from, in the union's case. the opening claim to the final agreement, and in the employer's case from the initial to the closing offer. This is dependent on the amount of room for negotiation that has been allowed.

2. The negotiating package the employer wants to use in reply to whatever package the union has put forward. The employer's aim should be to provide scope for trading concessions during the course of negotiations. From their viewpoint, there is also much to be said for having in reserve various conditions which they can ask

**Figure 41.3** Stages of a negotiation

the unions to accept in return for any concessions they may be prepared to make. Employers might, for example, ask for an extended period before the next settlement in return for an increase in their offer.

## Preparation steps

Negotiators must prepare carefully for negotiations so that they do not, in Aneurin Bevan's phrase, 'go naked to the conference table'. The following steps should be taken:

- list the arguments to be used in supporting their case
- list the likely arguments or counter-arguments that the other party is likely to use
- list the counter-arguments to the arguments of the other side
- obtain the data you need to support your case

- select the negotiating team — this should never have fewer than two members, and for major negotiations should have three or more: one to take the lead and do most of the talking, one to take notes and feed the negotiator with any supporting information required, and the others to observe opposite numbers and play a specific part in negotiations in accordance with their brief
- brief the members of the negotiating team on their roles and the negotiating strategy and tactics that are to be adopted — if appropriate, prepared statements or arguments should be issued at this stage to be used as required by the strategic plan
- rehearse the members of the team in their roles; they can be asked to repeat their points to other members and deal with responses from them; or someone can act as devil's advocate and force the leader or other members of the team to handle awkward points or negotiating ploys

At this stage it may be possible to meet one or more members of the other side informally to sound out their position, while they sound out yours. This 'early warning' system can be used to condition either side to modify their likely initial demands or responses by convincing them either of the strength of your own position or their determination to persist with the claim or to resist.

## Opening

Opening tactics can be as follows:

- open realistically and move moderately
- challenge the other side's position as it stands; do not destroy their ability to move
- explore attitudes, ask questions, observe behaviour and, above all, listen in order to assess the other side's strengths and weaknesses, their tactics and the extent to which they may be bluffing
- make no concessions of any kind at this stage
- be non-committal about proposals and explanations (do not talk too much).

## Bargaining

After the opening moves, the main bargaining phase takes place in which the gap is narrowed between the initial positions and the parties attempt to persuade each other that their case is strong enough to force the other side to close at a less advantageous point than they had planned. The following tactics can be employed:

- always make conditional proposals: 'If you will do this, then I will consider doing that' — the words to remember are: if ... then...
- never make one-sided concessions: always trade off against a concession from the other party: 'If I concede x, then I expect you to concede y'
- negotiate on the whole package: negotiators should not allow the other side to pick off item by item
- keep the issues open to extract the maximum benefit from potential trade-offs.

## Closing

When and how negotiators should close is a matter of judgement, and depends on an assessment of the strength of the other side's case and their determination to see it through. There are various closing techniques:

- making a concession from the package, preferably a minor one which is traded off against an agreement to settle — the concession can be offered more positively than in the bargaining stage: 'If you will agree to settle at x, then I will concede y'
- doing a deal: splitting the difference, or bringing in something new, such as extending the settlement time-scale, agreeing to back-payments, phasing increases, or making a joint declaration of intent to do something in the future (eg introducing a productivity plan)
- summarizing what has happened to date, emphasizing the concessions that have been made and the extent to which movement has been made and stating that the final position has been reached
- applying pressure through a threat of the dire consequences which will follow if a 'final' claim is not agreed or a 'final' offer is not accepted
- giving the other side a choice between two courses of action.

Employers should not make a final offer unless they mean it. If it is not really their final offer and the union calls their bluff they may have to make further concessions and their credibility will be undermined. Each party will, of course, attempt to force the other side into revealing the extent to which they have reached their final position. But negotiators should not allow themselves to be pressurised. If negotiators want to avoid committing themselves and thus devaluing the word 'final', they should state as positively as they can that this is as far as they are prepared to go. But bargaining conventions accept that further moves may still be made on a *quid pro quo* basis from this 'final position'.

## Negotiating and bargaining skills

### Negotiating skills

The main negotiating skills are:

- *analytical ability* — the capacity to assess the key factors which will affect the negotiating stance and tactics of both sides, and to use this assessment to ensure that all the facts and arguments that can be used to support the negotiator's case or prejudice the other party's case are marshalled
- *empathy* — the ability to put oneself in the other party's shoes to understand not only what they are hoping to achieve but also why they have these expectations and the extent to which they are determined to fulfil them
- *planning ability* — to develop and implement negotiating strategies and tactics but to be prepared to be flexible about the tactics in the light of developments during negotiations
- *interactive skills* — the capacity to relate well with other people, to be persuasive without being domineering, to make a point without using it as an opportunity to make the other side lose face, to show respect to the other side's arguments and points if they are valid while questioning them if they are dubious, to respond quickly to changing moods and reactions so that the opportunity can be seized to make progress towards consensus (and the achievement of consensus is the ultimate aim)
- *communicating skills* — the ability to convey information and arguments clearly, positively and logically while also being prepared to listen to the other side and to respond appropriately.

### Bargaining skills

The basic bargaining skills are:

- the ability to sense the extent to which the other side wants or indeed expects to achieve its claim or sustain its offer

- the reciprocal ability not to give real wants away (bargaining, as was mentioned earlier, is about concealing as well as revealing) — in the market place it is always easier for sellers to drive a hard bargain with buyers who have revealed somehow that they covet the article
- flexible realism — the capacity to make realistic moves during the bargaining process to reduce the claim or increase the offer which will demonstrate that the bargainer is seeking a reasonable settlement and is prepared to respond appropriately to movements made by the other side
- respect — the ability to demonstrate to the other party that the negotiator respects their views and takes them seriously even if he or she disagree with them
- sensitivity — the ability to sense changes in moods and directions or weaknesses in arguments and respond quickly to press home a point.

## Acquiring the skills

Negotiating and bargaining skills are developed through experience. To a certain extent they can be taught in the classroom through role plays and simulations but these can never replace the reality of sitting down with the other side and discussing claims and counter-offers, making points, handling confrontation and working out and applying the tactics required to reach a satisfactory settlement. It is useful to be aware of the need to apply the skills listed above but they only become meaningful during actual negotiation.

The best way to learn is by being a subsidiary member of a team with the scope to observe and comment on the tactics, approaches and skills used by both sides and, increasingly, to make planned contributions. A good team leader will nurse the tyro negotiator and will review the nature of each negotiating session to assess what went right or wrong, and why. This is how the writer learnt his negotiating skills and it served him in good stead when faced with the task of leading negotiating teams at plant, local and national level in the stimulating, exciting but sometimes frustrating process of negotiation.

# 42

# Involvement, Participation and Communications

The decline in the significance of trade unions referred to in chapter 40 has meant that in many organizations more attention has been paid to forms of involvement and participation other than collective bargaining. This interest has been enhanced by the HRM rhetoric advocating the development of mutual commitment, empowerment and direct communication. Tom Peters (1988) has suggested that employers should 'involve everyone in everything' with the result that 'productivity gains of several hundred per cent should ensue'.

In this chapter:

- involvement and participation are defined and distinguished, as far as the latter is possible — there are a number of different definitions
- the forms and levels of employee involvement and participation processes and the reasons for introducing them are identified
- the main involvement processes of attitude surveys, quality circles and suggestion schemes are described (communication methods such as team briefing are discussed in the next chapter)
- the main participation methods of joint consultative committees, work councils (especially European Works Councils) and worker directors are examined
- the incidence of involvement and participation processes and the benefits they provide are assessed
- approaches to introducing involvement and participation are considered
- methods of communicating to employees are described.

## Definitions

The terms 'involvement' and 'participation' are sometimes used synonymously to cover all forms of individual and representative information, consultation and participation. Collective bargaining may be excluded from this definition. They can refer to any processes in organizations which are introduced by management to convey information to employees on business initiatives, decisions and results. Used interchangeably, they can also cover procedures, mechanisms and processes which are set up by management unilaterally or in agreement with trade unions, thus enabling employees through their union(s) or another representative body to exert influence on and to share in decision-taking on matters affecting their interests.

The IPD in its code for Employee Involvement and Participation, for example, uses 'participation' to cover both involvement and participation. Many commentators, however, distinguish between employee involvement and participation, although there are many different interpretations of what they mean, as set out below.

### Employee involvement

As defined by Marchington and Goodman (1992) employee involvement consists of 'those practices which are initiated principally by management, and are designed to increase employee information about, and commitment to, the organization'. They suggest that the phrase is 'redolent of employer initiative'. The employer gives employees the opportunity to become involved in their work and their organization 'beyond simple performance of the wage/work bargain'.

According to Brian Stevens, Director of the Involvement and Participation Society (1990) 'Involvement assumes a recognition that employees have a great untapped potential but that managers retain the right to manage'.

Marchington and Goodman (1992) suggest that employee involvement differs from collective bargaining and industrial democracy, ' both of which are explicitly forms of power sharing and joint decision-making between management and employees — via their representatives'. They believe that 'involvement has perhaps a less specific, milder and more general connotation than participation'.

### Participation

Participation is defined by Guest and Fatchett (1974) as 'any process through which a person or group of persons determines (that is, intentionally affects) what another person or group of persons will do'. Stevens (1990) believes that 'participation is about employees playing a greater part in the decision-making process'. Marchington *et al* use the term participation to cover 'employee influence which may be exercised through bargaining and negotiation over a wide range of issues associated with the organisation and conduct of work and the terms and conditions of employment'.

## Industrial democracy

The term 'industrial democracy' was much used in the late 1970s to refer to forms of power sharing in industry, with trade unions having a significant influence over how it might operate. The aim of industrial democracy is to increase the rights of employees or their representatives to participate in decision-making, often by appointing 'worker directors' onto boards. This was the era of the Bullock Committee (The Committee of Inquiry on Industrial Democracy) which reported in 1977 on *how* rather than *whether* employees (through their trade unions) should be represented on the boards of directors of private companies. The Bullock report was totally rejected and industrial democracy is not much discussed in the UK nowadays.

## The distinction between employee involvement and participation

To summarise, *employee involvement* is a process usually initiated by management to increase the information given to employees and thus enhance their commitment. Involvement processes tend to treat employees as individuals, that is, they address them directly, face-to-face, rather than through their representatives.

In contrast, *participation* refers to collective rather than individual processes which enable employees through their representatives to influence decision-making. The term participation can be extended to forms of financial participation such as profit-sharing.

## Aims of employee involvement and participation

The IPD in its *Code on Employee Involvement and Participation in the United Kingdom* (1993) states that the involvement of, and participation by, employees in any organization, should aim to:

- generate commitment of all employees to the success of the organization
- enable the organization better to meet the needs of its customers and adapt to changing market requirements, and hence to maximize its future prospects and the prospects of those who work in it
- help the organization to improve performance and productivity and adopt new methods of working to match new technology drawing on the resources of knowledge and practical skills of all its employees
- improve the satisfaction employees get from their work
- provide all employees with the opportunity to influence and be involved in decisions which are likely to affect their interests.

In 1988 the CBI made a statement to the effect that the CBI believes that employee involvement:

- is a range of processes designed to engage the support, understanding and optimum contribution of all employees in an organization and their commitment to its objectives;
- assists an organization to give the best possible service to customers and clients in the most cost-effective way;
- entails providing employees with the opportunity to influence and where appropriate take part in decision-making on matters which affect them;
- is an intrinsic part of good management practice and is therefore not confined to relationships with employee representatives;
- can only be developed voluntarily in ways suited to the activities, structure and history of an organization.

According to the CBI, involvement promotes business success by:

- fostering trust and a shared commitment to an organization's objectives;
- demonstrating respect for individual employees and drawing on a full range of their abilities;
- enabling employees to derive the maximum possible job satisfaction.

As Kessler and Bayliss (1995) comment, the CBI's approach is individualistic and unitary, and some employers would regard their involvement policies as having failed if employees still attached importance to collective action through trade unions.

# Forms of employee involvement and participation

Marchington (1995b) has identified five forms of employee involvement and participation:

## Downward communications

Downward communications (team briefing and meetings) take place from managers to employees in order to inform and 'educate' staff so that they accept management plans. They were the most popular form of employee involvement in the UK in the early 1990s.

## Upward problem-solving

Upward problem-solving is designed to tap into employee knowledge and opinion, either at an individual level or in small groups. The aims are to increase the stock of ideas in an organization, to encourage cooperative relationships at work, and to legitimize change. Attitude surveys, quality circles, suggestion schemes as discussed below and, possibly, total quality management/customer care committees come into this category.

## Task participation

Task participation and job redesign processes engage employees in extending the range and type of tasks they undertake. Approaches to job design such as horizontal job redesign (extending the range of tasks undertaken at the same level) job enrichment, vertical role integration (taking greater responsibility for supervisory duties) and teamworking (where the team organizes its own work so that it becomes 'self-managed') may be used.

## Consultation and representative participation

Consultation and representative participation enables employees to take part through their representatives in management decision-making. One of the aims of management in encouraging this form of participation is to use it as a safety valve — an alternative to formal disputes — by means of which more deep-seated employee grievances can be addressed. Joint consultation has been introduced by management in some businesses to hinder trade union recognition or, it is said, even to undermine their activities. This type of participation takes place in the form of joint consultative committees as described later in this chapter. The appointment of worker directors also falls into this category.

## Financial involvement/participation

Financial involvement or participation takes the form of such schemes as profit-sharing and employee share ownership. Gainsharing is also used by some companies as a means of involvement. Information on company performance is provided to employees as part of the scheme and they are encouraged to discuss with their managers or team leaders the reasons for success or failure and methods of improving performance. The aim of such schemes is to educate employees and gain their commitment.

# Varieties of employee involvement and participation

Employee involvement and participation can vary according to the level at which it takes place, the degree to which decision making is shared, and the extent to which the mechanisms are formal or informal.

## Levels

Involvement and participation takes various forms at different levels in an enterprise as defined by the Industrial Society (1974). These levels are described below.

The *job level* involves team leaders and their teams, and the processes include the communication of information about work and interchange of ideas about how the work should be done. These processes are essentially informal.

The *management level* can involve sharing information and decision making about issues which affect the way in which work is planned and carried out, and working arrangements and conditions. There are limits. Management as a whole, and individual managers, must retain authority to do what their function requires. Involvement does not imply anarchy. But it does require some degree of willingness on the part of management to share its decision-making powers. At this level, involvement and participation may become more formalized, through consultative committees, briefing groups or works councils involving management and employees or their representatives.

At the *policy-making level*, where the direction in which the business is going is determined, total participation would imply sharing the power to make key decisions. This is not much practised in the UK, although there may be processes for communicating information on proposed plans (which would almost certainly not reveal proposals for acquisitions or disinvestments or anything else where commercial security is vital) and discussing the implications of those plans.

At the *ownership level*, participation implies a share in the equity, which is not meaningful unless the workers have sufficient control through voting rights to determine the composition of the board. This is not a feature of the British employee relations scene.

## The degree to which decision-making is shared

At the one end of the scale, management makes decisions unilaterally; at the other end, in theory, but never in practice except in a worker's cooperative (almost non-existent in the UK), workers decide unilaterally. Between these extremes there is a range of intermediate points which can be expressed (Figure 42.1) as a scale.

The point on this scale at which participation should or can take place at any level in an organization depends on the attitudes, willingness and enthusiasm of both management and employees. Management may be reluctant to give up too much of its authority except under pressure from the unions (which is unlikely today), or from European Community directives on worker consultation.

## Mechanisms for involvement and participation

At the job level, involvement and participation should be as informal as possible. Teams may be called together on an *ad hoc* basis to consider a particular problem, but formal committees should be avoided. Team briefing (see Chapter 42) can be used to provide for informal two-way communications.

At the next higher level, more formality may be appropriate in larger organizations. There is scope for the use of consultative committees or departmental councils with carefully defined terms of reference on the matters they can discuss. At the enterprise level, company or works councils can be set up.

At the policy-forming level company or works councils may be given the chance to discuss policy issues, but if the final decision on any

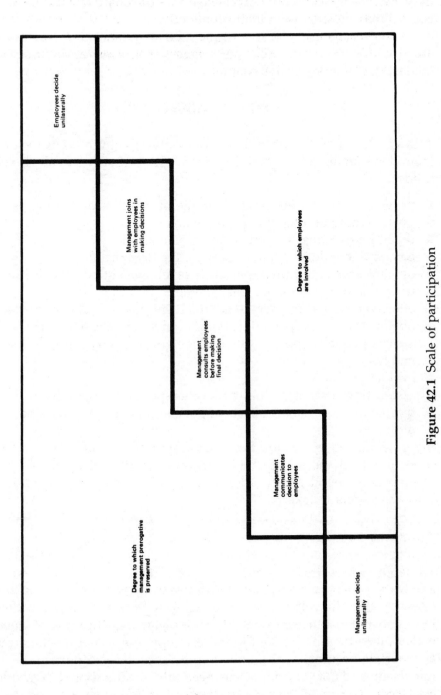

**Figure 42.1** Scale of participation

matter which is clearly not negotiable is made at board level, the works council may be seen as an ineffectual body.

Further mechanisms for involvement on an organization-wide basis are provided by quality circles and suggestion schemes as discussed in the last two sections of this chapter.

## Attitude surveys

Attitude surveys are a valuable way of involving employees by seeking their views on matters that concern them. Attitude surveys can also be used to:

- provide particular information on the preferences of employees
- give warning on potential problem areas
- diagnose the cause of particular problems
- compare morale in different parts of the organization
- obtain views about processes such as job evaluation, pay determination and performance management in order to assess their effectiveness and the degree to which employees feel they are fair
- obtain views about personnel policies and how they operate in such areas as equal opportunity, employee development, involvement and health and safety
- evaluate training
- assess how organizational and other policy changes have been received to observe the effects of policies and actions over a period of time
- provide a basis for additional communication and involvement, especially if the survey includes, as it should, discussions with employees on their attitudes and what actions they would like management to take.

### Approach

The approach is first to identify the individual's needs and then to assess the extent to which these needs are being met. This means first asking people how they feel about various things for any job they might do, not just their present job. Thus, against the heading of 'good wages', they would be asked to indicate how they feel by ticking the appropriate heading — absolutely top priority, very important, fairly important, and not very important. Secondly, the questionnaire would ask them to express their feelings about different aspects of their present job, for example, indicating against 'pay' whether their feelings about it are very good, good, neither good nor bad, bad, or very bad.

## Methods of conducting attitude surveys

There are four methods of conducting attitude surveys:

1. *By the use of structured questionnaires* issued to all or a sample of employees. The questionnaires may be standardized ones, such as the Brayfield and Rothe Index of Job Satisfaction, or they may be developed specially for the organization. The advantage of using standardized questionnaires is that they have been thoroughly tested and in many cases norms are available against which results can be compared. Additional questions specially relevant to the company can be added to the standard list. A tailor-made questionnaire can be used to highlight particular issues, but it may be advisable to obtain professional help from an experienced psychologist, who can carry out the skilled work of drafting and pilot-testing the questionnaire and interpreting the results. Questionnaires have the advantage of being relatively cheap to administer and analyse, especially when there are large numbers involved.

2. *By the use of interviews.* These may be 'open-ended' or depth interviews in which the discussion is allowed to range quite freely. Or they may be semi-structured in that there is a check-list of points to be covered, although the aim of the interviewer should be to allow discussion to flow around the points so that the frank and open views of the individual are obtained. Alternatively, and more rarely, interviews can be highly structured so that they become no more than the spoken application of a questionnaire. Individual interviews are to be preferred because they are more likely to be revealing. But they are expensive and time-consuming and not so easy to analyse. Discussions through 'focus groups' (ie groups of employees convened to focus their attention on particular issues) are a quicker way of reaching a large number of people, but the results are not so easy to quantify and some people may have difficulty in expressing their views in public.

3. *By a combination of questionnaire and interview.* This is the ideal approach because it combines the quantitative data from the questionnaire with the qualitative data from the interviews. It is always advisable to accompany questionnaires with some depth

interviews, even if time permits only a limited sample. An alternative approach is to administer the questionnaire to a group of people and then discuss the reactions to each question with the group. This ensures that a quantified analysis is possible but enables the group, or at least some members of it, to express their feelings more fully.

4. *By the use of focus groups.* A focus group is a representative sample of employees whose attitudes and opinions are sought on issues concerning the organization and their work. The essential features of a focus group are that it is structured, informed, constructive and confidential.

## *Assessing results*

It is an interesting fact that when people are asked directly if they are satisfied with their job, most of them (70 to 90 per cent) will say they are. This is regardless of the work being done and often in spite of strongly held grievances. The probable reason for this phenomenon is that while most people are willing to admit to having grievances — in fact, if invited to complain, they will complain — they may be reluctant to admit, even to themselves, to being dissatisfied with a job which they have no immediate intention of leaving. Many employees have become reconciled to their work, even if they do not like some aspects of it, and have no real desire to do anything else. So they are, in a sense, satisfied enough to continue, even if they have complaints. Finally, many people are satisfied with their job overall, although they grumbled about many aspects of it.

Overall measures of satisfaction do not, therefore, always reveal anything interesting. It is more important to look at particular aspects of satisfaction or dissatisfaction to decide whether or not anything needs to be done. In these circumstances, the questionnaire will indicate only a line to be followed up. It will not provide the answers. Hence the advantage of individual meetings or focus group discussions to explore in depth any issue raised.

## Quality circles

It can be argued that one of the greatest failings which result from the 'top-down' type of management prevailing in the UK and many other Western countries is that it ignores the knowledge that exists at the other levels in the organization. Quality circles, sometimes called improvement groups, can be used to overcome this problem. They are often associated with a total quality/continuous improvement programme.

Quality circles are small groups of volunteers who are engaged in related work and who meet regularly to discuss and propose ways of improving working methods or arrangements under a trained leader.

## Aims

The aims of quality circles are to:

- give those doing the job more scope to use their experience and know-how
- provide opportunities to tap the knowledge of employees, who may know more about work problems which are hidden from more remote managers and team leaders
- improve productivity and quality
- improve employee relations
- win commitment to the organization.

## Essential features

The essential features of quality circles are that they:

- consist of volunteers
- have a trained leader, usually but not always a team leader
- hold regular meetings which are strictly limited in duration — often one hour
- have five to ten members
- usually select which problems to tackle but may be steered away from problems which are clearly beyond their scope or are already being dealt with
- use systematic analytical techniques or brainstorming methods in which they have been trained to define and solve problems
- present their results to management
- implement accepted proposals.

## Pre-requisites for success

The first pre-requisite is that top management believes in the value of quality circles and is committed to their success. Middle management and team leaders must also be involved in their introduction. They are the people who are most likely to have reservations about quality circles because they can see them as a threat to their authority and reputation. Without management support, quality circles 'wither on the vine', as they often do.

Trade unions should also be informed of the plan to introduce quality circles. Some unions are hostile because they feel that quality circles can reduce their influence and power, and that management is deliberately introducing them for this purpose.

The introduction and maintenance of a quality circle needs a 'facilitator' who trains, encourages and guides quality circle members, ensures that they are given the resources they need, and sets up presentation sessions. The facilitator is often a line manager rather than a personnel specialist or a trainer. This vital role also involves encouraging the circles and ensuring that top management backing continues by keeping them informed of the benefits provided by quality circles — publicity on their achievements is important. The facilitator can also deal with any problems quality circles meet in getting information or in dealing with management.

Training is an important part of the quality circles. Team leaders need an initial two to three-day training course in the analytical techniques they will use and in team building and presentation skills. They also need refresher training from time to time. Team leaders, with the help of facilitators, also train the members of their team. This training effort is a valuable spin-off from a quality circle programme. Instruction in leadership, problem solving and analytical skills is a useful way of developing existing or potential team leaders. Membership of a quality circle is also a means of developing skills as well as getting more involved.

These requirements are demanding and although the essential concept of quality circles is valid they too often fail to survive after an initial spurt. But they can be replaced by more informal and *ad hoc* improvement groups or by regular team meetings held by team leaders (or organized by the team itself in a self-managed team) in which work problems and areas for innovation and improvement are discussed and agreed.

## Suggestion schemes

Suggestion schemes can provide a valuable means for employees to participate in improving the efficiency of the company. Properly organized, they can help to reduce the feelings of frustration endemic in all concerns where people think they have good ideas but cannot get them considered because there are no recognized channels of communication. Normally, only those ideas outside the usual scope of employees' duties are considered, and this should be made clear, as well as the categories of those eligible for the scheme — senior managers are often excluded.

The basis of a successful suggestion scheme should be an established procedure for submitting and evaluating ideas, with tangible recognition for those which have merit and an effective system for explaining to employees without discouraging them that their ideas cannot be accepted.

The most common arrangement is to use suggestion boxes with, possibly, a special form for entering a suggestion. Alternatively, or additionally, employees can be given the name of an individual or a committee to whom suggestions should be submitted. Managers and team leaders must be stimulated to encourage their staff to submit suggestions, and publicity in the shape of posters, leaflets and articles in the company magazine should be used to promote the scheme. The publicity should give prominence to the successful suggestions and how they are being implemented.

One person should be made responsible for administering the scheme. He or she should have the authority to reject facetious suggestions, but should be given clear guidance on the routing of suggestions by subject matter to departments or individuals for their comments. The administrator deals with all communications and, if necessary, may go back to the individual who submitted the suggestion to get more details of, for example, the savings in cost or improvements in output that should result from the idea.

It is desirable to have a suggestion committee consisting of management and employee representatives to review suggestions in the light of the comments of any specialist functions or executives who have evaluated them. This committee should be given the final power to accept or reject suggestions but could, if necessary, call for additional information or opinion before making its decision. The committee could also decide on the size of any award within established guidelines, such as a proportion of savings during the first year. There should be a standard procedure for recording the decisions of the committee and informing those who made suggestions of the outcome — with reasons for rejection if appropriate.

## Joint consultation

Joint consultation is the most familiar method of participation although, as noted later in this chapter, it is in decline. It is essentially a means for management and employees to get together in consultative committees to discuss and determine matters affecting their joint or respective interests.

### Aims of joint consultation

The aim of joint consultation is to provide a means of jointly examining and discussing problems which concern both management and employees. It should mean that mutually acceptable solutions can be sought through the exchange of views and information. Joint consultation allows management to inform employees of proposed changes which affect them and employees to express their views about those changes. It also provides a means for employees to contribute their own views on such matters as how work is organized (for example, flexibility), working conditions, the operation of personnel policies and procedures and health and safety. As noted earlier, joint consultation can act as a safety valve, relieving the pressure from grievances which, if not settled by some process of discussion, could escalate to a dispute.

### Topics for joint consultation

Joint consultation does not mean power-sharing, involving employees in strategic policy decisions on such matters as investments and dis-investments, product-market development plans and mergers or takeovers. Those would only be the subject of joint decision-making in the rare circumstances in which full participation at board level takes place.

The WIRS3 reported that 30 per cent of consultative committees were also concerned with negotiation. The majority of such committees, however, concentrate on non-negotiable matters such as working methods and organization, health and safety, working conditions and arrangements, employee facilities (restaurants, car parking, welfare etc) and works rules. Managements may upgrade consultation to cover important topics such as new products and investment plans so that negotiation becomes less meaningful or necessary. They may see consultation as simply another form of downward communications.

Joint consultation may be perceived as being meaningless or of marginal importance by either or both parties and in these circumstances will of course be ineffective. But, as Kessler and Bayliss (1995) note: 'Where trade unionism is strong and well-developed, consultation may be seen as a valuable adjunct to collective bargaining. Here the two processes are kept separate, although the representatives of each committee will be largely the same people.'

An argument which can be advanced for separating consultation and negotiation in a unionized plant is that this recognizes the distinction between cooperative or integrative bargaining and conjunctive or distributive bargaining referred to in Chapter 39. Cooperative bargaining recognizes the interdependence of management and employees and can take place in consultative committees without the power-plays and stress that frequently accompany pay negotiations.

## Membership of joint consultative committees

Depending on the degree to which the organization is unionized (if at all) joint consultative committees can be formed exclusively of trade union representatives nominated by union members, or consist of a mix of nominated trade union representatives and other non-union employees (the latter usually elected) or be entirely composed of elected representatives who might or might not be trade union members.

Consultative committees often exclude managers or team leaders and, if they are left out, this can be contentious because they may well feel that they are being bypassed.

## Structure

There may be one consultative committee or works council covering the whole organization but larger companies often have separate committees for each major division or unit.

## Constitution

The constitution of a consultative committee normally covers the following points:

- objectives
- terms of reference

- composition
- election procedures
- arrangements for chairing and holding meetings (in some organizations the chair is held by management and employee representatives alternately).

## Works councils

Works councils covering the whole organization often have broadly the same functions as company-wide consultative committees — only the name is different. But some works councils have wider membership, including managers, team leaders and professional, technical and office staff, thus covering everyone in the company. And as a result of the EU directive, European Works Councils are becoming significant for any UK company operating in Europe, even though the UK has opted out.

The aim of the Directive is 'to improve the right to information and to consultation of employees in Community-scale undertakings and Community-scale groups of undertakings'. The Directive states that it is necessary 'if economic activities are to develop in a harmonious fashion'. The subjects for discussion at a European Works Council include the general economic and financial situation of the business, and specific matters with a major impact on employees, such as relocations, closures, mergers, collective dismissals and the introduction of new technology. A Council must be set up in organizations with 1000 employees or more and it is required to be an employee-only body and it must comprise three to 30 employees elected or appointed by employee representatives or, in their absence, the whole workforce.

## Worker directors

The concept of worker directors on the board came to the fore in the 1970s as part of the campaign for industrial democracy. The idea was that employee representatives could get closer to the point at which strategic decisions are made. But the Bullock Committee's recommendations on this subject were totally rejected.

Experience with worker directors is very rare in the private sector and it has been argued that the few schemes which were introduced were used, as Marchington (1985) comments, 'to strengthen or reassert management control rather than to redistribute that control'.

Worker directors were appointed in public sector organizations —

British Steel and the Post Office. But studies on how they functioned quoted by Marchington found that management representatives tended to conduct any sensitive or confidential business away from the Board, while union members found themselves in the difficult position of attempting to defend member interests yet contributing to management decisions which may have negative implications for the workforce. For these reasons and because of the continuing hostility of managements to worker directors it seems unlikely that they will ever become a common feature of the employee relations scene.

## Incidence of involvement and participation

The WIRS 3, as analysed by Millward (1994) established that 84 per cent of the establishments covered by the survey had some form of communication channel between management and employees. The most popular form was the management chain of communication (59 per cent). The least popular channel was a consultative committee (18 per cent). The highest growth area was regular meetings with junior management (from 30 per cent in 1984 to 44 per cent in 1990).

In private manufacturing the WIRS 3 showed a marked decline in the percentage of workplaces with joint consultative committees (from 36 per cent in 1980 to 23 per cent in 1990). WIRS 3 concluded that the fall in the number of committees was primarily due to the changing composition of workplaces. It was not due to a tendency for workplaces to abandon committees, but to a fall in the number of larger more unionized workplaces which were more likely to have committees.

## Requirements for successful employee involvement and participation

According to the Department of Employment (1994) the overall success of employee involvement depends fundamentally on:

- building trust
- eliminating status differentials
- committing the organization to vigorous training and development
- breaking down barriers to change the organization's culture.

It is generally accepted that the ten basic requirements for success are:

1. The objectives of participation must be defined, discussed and agreed by all concerned.

2. The objectives must be related to tangible and significant aspects of the job, the process of management or the formulation of policies that affect the interests of employees. They must not relate to peripheral matters such as welfare or social amenities.

3. Management must believe in and must be seen to believe in involving employees. Actions speak better than words and management must demonstrate that it will put into effect the joint decisions made during discussions.

4. The unions must believe in participation as a genuine means of advancing the interests of their members and not simply as a way of getting more power. They should show by their actions that they are prepared to support unpopular decisions to which they have been a party.

5. Joint consultation machinery should be in line with any existing systems of negotiation and representation. It should not be supported by management as a possible way of reducing the powers of the union. If this naive approach is taken, it will fail — it always does. Joint consultation should be regarded as a process of integrative bargaining complementary to the distributive bargaining that takes place in joint negotiating committees.

6. If management does introduce joint consultation in a non-union environment, it should be prepared to widen the terms of reference as much as possible to cover issues concerning company employment policies and plans and working arrangements and conditions (eg, health and safety matters). It is rare, however, for such committees or councils to be involved in negotiations on terms and conditions of employment.

7. Consultative committees should always relate to a defined working unit, should never meet unless there is something specific to discuss, and should always conclude their meetings with agreed points which are implemented quickly.

8. Employee and management representatives should be properly briefed and trained and have all the information they require.

9. Managers and team leaders should be kept in the picture and, as appropriate, involved in the consultation process — it is clearly highly undesirable for them to feel that they have been left out.

10. Consultation should take place before decisions are made.

## Planning for involvement and participation

The form of involvement and participation appropriate for an organization depends upon the attitudes and relative strengths of management and unions, its past experience of negotiation and consultation, and the current climate of employee relations. It is essential to take into account the requirements for successful participation listed earlier in this chapter and to plan its introduction or development in the following stages:

- analyse and evaluate the existing systems of involvement, consultation, communication and other formal and informal means of participation
- identify the influences within and without the company which affect the climate of employee relations and suggest the most appropriate form in which participation should take place
- develop a plan for improving or extending employee involvement in whatever form is appropriate to the organization
- discuss the plan in depth with management, team leaders, work people and unions — the introduction of improved participation should itself be a participative process
- brief and train those concerned with employee involvement in their duties and how they should be carried out
- introduce new schemes on a pilot-scheme basis — do not expect immediate results and be prepared to modify them in the light of experience
- keep the whole process under continuous review as it develops to ensure that it is operating effectively.

## Communications

Organizations function by means of the collective action of people, yet each individual is capable of taking independent action which may not be in line with policy or instructions, or may not be reported properly to other people who ought to know about it. Good communications are required to achieve coordinated results.

Organizations are subject to the influence of continuous change which affects the work employees do, their well-being and their security. Change can be managed only by ensuring that the reasons for the implications of change are communicated to those affected in terms which they can understand and accept.

Individuals are motivated by the extrinsic reward system and the intrinsic rewards coming from the work itself. But the degree to which they are motivated depends upon the amount of responsibility and scope for achievement provided by their job, and upon their expectations that the rewards they will get will be the ones they want, and will follow from the efforts they make. Feelings about work and the associated rewards depend very much on the effectiveness of communications from their managers or team leaders and within the company.

Above all, good two-way communications are required so that management can keep employees informed of the policies and plans affecting them, and employees can react promptly with their views about management's proposals and actions. Change cannot be managed properly without an understanding of the feelings of those affected by it, and an efficient system of communications is needed to understand and influence these feelings.

But the extent to which good communications create satisfactory relationships rather than simply reducing unsatisfactory ones, can be exaggerated. A feature of management practices during this century is the way in which different management theories become fashionable or influential for a while and then decline in favour. Among these has been the 'good communications' theory of management. This approach to dealing with management problems is based upon the following assumptions:

1.  The needs and aims of both employees and management are, in the long run, the same in any organization. Managers' and employees' ideas and objectives can all be fitted together to form a single conceptual framework.
2.  Any differences in opinion between management and employees are due to misunderstandings which have arisen because communications are not good enough.
3.  The solution to industrial strife is to improve communications.

This theory is attractive and has some validity. Its weakness is that the assumptions are too sweeping, particularly the belief that the ultimate objectives of management and workers are necessarily identical. The good communications theory, like paternalism, seems to imply that a company can develop loyalty by keeping people informed and treating them well. But people working in organizations have other and, to them, more important loyalties elsewhere — and why not?

The existence of different loyalties and points of view in an organization does not mean that communication is unimportant. If anything, the need for a good communications system becomes even greater when differences and conflict exist. But it can only alleviate those differences and pave the way to better cooperation. It cannot solve them.

It is therefore necessary to bear in mind that the group with which we identify — the reference group — influences our attitudes and feelings. 'Management' and 'the union' as well as our family, our ethnic background, our political party and our religious beliefs (if any) constitute a reference group and colour our reactions to information. What each group 'hears' depends on its own interests. Shared experiences and common frames of reference have much more influence than exhortations from management. Employees may feel they have nothing to do with them because it conflicts with what they already believe.

However, although there may be limitations on the extent to which communication strategies can enhance mutuality and commitment, there is no doubt that it is essential for managements to keep people informed on matters that affect them and to provide channels for them to express their views. This is particularly necessary when new employment initiatives are taking place and effective change management is very much about communicating management's intentions to people and making sure that they understand how they will be affected.

## Communication areas and objectives

The main communication areas and their associated objectives are set out in Table 42.1.

Employee relations are mainly affected by managerial and internal communications, although external communications are an additional channel of information. The strategy for managerial communications is concerned with planning and control procedures, management information systems and techniques of delegating and giving instructions. These matters are outside the scope of this book, except in so far as the procedures and skills can be developed by training programmes.

## Communications strategy

The strategy for internal communications should be based on analyses of:

- what management wants to say
- what employees want to hear
- the problems being met in conveying or receiving information.

795

**Table 42.1** Communication areas and objectives

| | Communication Area | Objectives |
|---|---|---|
| **I. MANAGERIAL** | 1. The communication downwards and sideways of corporate or functional objectives, policies, plans and budgets to those who have to implement them. | To ensure that managers and supervisors receive clear, accurate and prompt information on what they are expected to achieve to further the company's objectives. |
| | 2. The communication downwards of direct instructions from a manager to a subordinate on what the latter has to do. | To ensure that the instructions are clear and precise and provide the necessary motivation to get people into action. |
| | 3. The communication upwards and sideways of proposals, suggestions and comments on corporate or functional objectives, policies and budgets from those who have to implement them. | To ensure that managers and supervisors have adequate scope to influence corporate and functional decisions on matters about which they have specific expertise and knowledge. |
| | 4. The communication upwards and sideways of management information on performance and results. | To enable management to monitor and control performance in order that, as necessary, opportunities can be exploited or swift corrective action taken. |
| **II. INTERNAL RELATIONS** | 5. The communication downwards of information on company plans, policies or performance. | To ensure that (i) employees are kept informed of matters that affect them, especially changes to working conditions, and factors influencing their prosperity and security; (ii) employees are encouraged to identify themselves more completely with the company. |
| | 6. The communication upwards of the comments and reactions of employees to what is proposed will happen or what is actually happening in matters that affect them. | To ensure that employees are given an opportunity to voice their suggestions and fears and that the company is in a position to amend its plans in the light of these comments. |
| **III. EXTERNAL RELATIONS** | 7. The receipt and analysis of information from outside which affects the company's interests. | To ensure that the company is fully aware of all the information on legislation and on marketing, commercial, financial and technological matters that affect its interests. |
| | 8. The presentation of information about the company and its products to the government, customers and the public at large. | To exert influence in the interests of the company, to present a good image of the company, and to persuade customers to buy its products or services. |

These analyses can be used to indicate the systems of communication that need to be developed and the education and training programmes required to make them work. They should also provide guidance on how communications should be managed and timed. Bad management and poor timing are frequently the fundamental causes of ineffective communication.

## What management wants to say

What management wants to say depends upon an assessment of what employees need to know, which, in turn, is affected by what they want to hear.

Management usually aims to achieve three things: first, to get employees to understand and accept what management proposes to do in areas that affect them; second, to obtain the commitment of employees to the objectives, plans and values of the organization; and, third, to help employees to appreciate more clearly the contribution they can make to organizational success and how it will benefit them.

Communications from management should be about values, plans, intentions and proposals (with the opportunity for discussion with and feedback from employees) as well as about achievements and results. Exhortations should not be used: no one listens to them. It is better to concentrate on specific requirements rather than resorting to general appeals for abstract things such as improved quality or productivity. The requirements should be phrased in a way which emphasizes how all concerned will actually work together and the mutual benefits that should result.

## What employees want to hear

Clearly, employees want to hear about and to comment upon the matters that affect their interests. These will include changes in working methods and conditions, changes in the arrangements for overtime and shift working, company plans which may affect pay or security, and changes in terms and conditions of employment. It is management's job to understand what employees want to hear and plan its communications strategy accordingly. Understanding can be obtained by conducting 'focus group' discussions which bring together groups of employees to focus on particular issues that concern them, by means of attitude surveys, by asking employee representatives, by informally listening to what employees say, and by analysing grievances to see if improved communications could modify them.

## *Analysing communication problems*

Specific examples of employee relations problems where communication failures have been the cause or a contributory factor should be analysed to determine exactly what went wrong and what needs to be done to put it right. The problems may be any of those listed earlier in this chapter, including lack of appropriate channels of communication, lack of appreciation of the need to communicate, and lack of skill in overcoming the many formidable barriers to communication. Problems with channels of communication can be dealt with by introducing new or improved communications systems. Lack of skill is a matter for education and training.

## Communication systems

Communication systems can be divided into those using the written word such as magazines, newsletters, bulletins and notice-boards, and those using oral methods such as meetings, briefing groups and public address systems. The aim should be to make judicious use of a number of channels to make sure that the message gets across.

## *Magazines*

Glossy magazines or house journals are an obvious way to keep employees informed about the company and are often used for public relations purposes as well. They can extol and explain the achievements of the company and may thus help to increase identification and even loyalty. If employees are encouraged to contribute (although this is difficult), the magazine can become more human. The biggest danger of this sort of magazine is that it becomes a public relations exercise which is seen by employees as having little relevance to their everyday affairs.

## *Newsletters*

Newsletters aim to appear more frequently and to angle their contents more to the immediate concerns of employees than the glossier form of house magazine. To be effective, they should include articles specifically aimed at explaining what management is planning to do and how this affects everyone. They can also include more chatty 'human interest' material about the doings of employees to capture the attention of readers. Correspondence columns can provide an avenue for the expression of employees' views and replies from management, but no attempt should be made to censor letters (except those that are purely abusive) or to pull punches in reply. Anonymous letters should be published if the writer gives his name to the editor.

The key factor in the success of a newsletter or any form of house magazine is the editor, who should be someone who knows the company and its employees and can be trusted by everyone to be frank and fair. Professional expertise is obviously desirable, but it is not the first consideration, as long as the editor can write reasonably well and has access to expert help in putting the paper together. It is often a good idea to have an editorial board consisting of management and employee representatives to advise and assist the editor.

Organizations often publish a newsletter in addition to a house magazine, treating the latter mainly as a public relations exercise and relying on the newsletter as the prime means of communicating with employees.

## Bulletins

Bulletins can be used to give immediate information to employees which cannot wait for the next issue of a newsletter; or they can be a substitute for a formal publication if the company does not feel that the expense is justified. Bulletins are useful only if they are distributed quickly and are seen by all interested employees. They can simply be posted on notice-boards or, more effectively, given to individual employees and used as a starting point for a briefing session if they contain information of sufficient interest to merit a face-to-face discussion.

## Notice-boards

Notice-boards are an obvious but frequently misused medium for communications. The biggest danger is allowing boards to be cluttered up with uninteresting or out-of-date material. It is essential to control what goes on to the boards and to appoint responsible people to service them by removing out-of-date or unauthorized notices.

A more impressive show can be made of notices and other material if an information centre is set up in the restaurant or some other suitable place where the information can be displayed in a more attractive and compelling manner than on a typical notice-board.

## Employee involvement

Employee involvement through such means as consultative committees provides a channel for two-way communication. Sometimes,
however, they are not particularly effective, either because their
thunder has been stolen by union negotiation committees, or because
their proceedings are over-formalized and restricted and fail to address
the real issues. It is essential to disseminate the information revealed at
committees around the offices and works, but it is impossible to rely on
committee members to do this. Minutes can be posted on notice-
boards, but they are seldom read, usually because they contain too
much redundant material.

## Videos

Specially made videos can be a cost-effective method of getting across
personal messages (eg from the chief executives) or information about
how the company is doing. They can, however be regarded by
employees as too impersonal and/or too slick to have any real
meaning.

## Team briefing

The concept of team briefing (previously called briefing groups), as
originally developed by the Industrial Society, is a device to overcome
the restricted nature of joint consultative committees by involving
everyone in an organization, level by level, in face-to-face meetings to
present, receive and discuss information. Team briefing aims to overcome the gaps and inadequacies of casual briefings by injecting some
order into the system.

Team briefing should operate as follows:

1. *Organization:*

   - cover all levels in an organization
   - fewest possible steps between the top and bottom
   - between 4 and 18 in each group
   - run by the immediate leader of each group at each level (who
     must be properly trained and briefed).

2. *Subjects:*

   - policies — explanations of new or changed policies;

- plans — as they affect the organization as a whole and the immediate group
- progress — how the organization and the group is getting on
- people — new appointments, points about personnel matters (pay, security, procedures).

3.  *Sequence* — the briefing groups should work to a brief prepared by the board on key issues. This briefing is written up and cascaded down the organization. The briefing group meetings should, however, allow for discussion of the brief, and the system should cater for any reactions or comments to be fed back to the top. This provides for two-way communication.

4.  *Timing and duration*:

    - a minimum of once a month for those in charge of others and once every two months for every individual in the organization — but meet only if there is something to say;
    - duration not longer than 20–30 minutes.

The merit of team briefing is that it enables face-to-face communications to be planned and, to a reasonable degree, formalized. It is easy, however, for it to start on a wave of enthusiasm and then to wither away because of lack of sufficient drive and enthusiasm from the top downward, inadequately trained and motivated managers and team leaders, reluctance of management to allow subjects of real importance to be discussed throughout the system, and insufficient feedback upwards through each level.

A team briefing system must be led and controlled effectively from the top, but it does require a senior manager with specific responsibility to advise on the subject matter and the preparation of briefs (it is important to have well-prepared material to ensure that briefing is carried out consistently and thoroughly at each level), to train managers and team leaders, and to monitor the system by checking on the effectiveness and frequency of meetings.

# Part IX
# Health, Safety and Welfare

*This part deals with the services provided by the personnel department in order to help the organization meet its legal and social responsibilities to ensure a healthy and safe place of work, to help employees cope with their personal problems, to help elderly and retired employees and, in some cases, to make recreational facilities available.*

# 43

# Occupational Health and Safety

Occupational health and safety policies and programmes are concerned with protecting employees — and other people affected by what the company produces and does — against the hazards arising from their employment or their links with the company.

Occupational health programmes deal with the prevention of ill-health arising from working conditions. They consist of two elements:

- *occupational medicine*, which is a specialized branch of preventive medicine concerned with the diagnosis and prevention of health hazards at work and dealing with any ill health or stress which has occurred in spite of preventive actions
- *occupational hygiene*, which is the province of the chemist and the engineer or ergonomist engaged in the measurement and control of environmental hazards.

Safety programmes deal with the prevention of accidents and with minimizing the resulting loss and damage to persons and property. They relate more to systems of work than the working environment, but both health and safety programmes are concerned with protection against hazards, and their aims and methods are clearly interlinked.

Health and safety programmes need to be considered against the background of the factors that affect health and safety at work, and this chapter therefore begins with an analysis of these factors and a discussion of the principles that influence policies and procedures. This is followed by a description of the elements of the overall health and safety programme, and the chapter then deals with each of these elements, namely:

- the identification and analysis of health and safety hazards and problems

- health and safety policies
- the organization of health and safety
- occupational health programmes and procedures
- accident prevention programmes and procedures
- the measurement and control of health and safety performance.

## Factors affecting health and safety

The work and writings of a number of distinguished practitioners and researchers in health and safety have resulted in a range of basic principle, concepts and approaches which need to be understood by everyone concerned with the development and implementation of health and safety programmes.

The first and most influential of the practitioners was Heinrich (1959), who developed his axioms of industrial safety to underline his thesis that the conventional approach to prevention, by concentrating on injuries that had happened rather than on accidental occurrences which might be predicted, looked at only a fraction of the problem and looked at it backwards. From this analysis a considerable body of literature has developed advocating the techniques of 'damage control' and 'total loss control'. The basic message of these approaches is that the employer who wants to prevent injuries in the future, to reduce loss and damage, and to increase efficiency must look systematically at the total pattern of accidental happenings — whether or not they caused injury or damage. The employer must then plan a comprehensive system of prevention rather than rely on the *ad hoc* patching-up of deficiencies which injury-causing accidents have brought to light.

## Principles of health and safety management

There are five basic principles which should determine the approach to be used in health and safety management:

1. Industrial disease and accidents result from a multiplicity of factors, but these have to be traced to their root causes, which are usually faults in the management system arising from poor leadership from the top, inadequate supervision, insufficient attention to the design of health and safety into the system, an unsystematic approach to the identification, analysis and elimination of hazards, and poor education and training facilities.

2. The most important function of health and safety programmes is to identify potential hazards, provide effective safety facilities and equipment, and take prompt remedial action. This is only possible if they are:

- comprehensive and effective systems for reporting all accidents causing damage or injury
- adequate accident records and statistics
- systematic procedures for carrying out safety checks, inspections and investigations
- methods of ensuring that safety equipment is properly maintained and used
- proper means for persuading managers, team leaders and employees generally to pay more attention to health and safety matters.

3. The health and safety policies of the organization should be determined by top management, who must be continuously involved in monitoring health and safety performance and in ensuring that corrective action is taken when necessary.
4. Managers and team leaders must be made fully accountable for health and safety performance in the working areas they control.
5. All employees should be given thorough training in safe methods of work and should receive continuing education and guidance on eliminating health and safety hazards and on the prevention of accidents.

These principles are underpinned by the Health and Safety at Work Act and the Control of Substances Hazardous to Health Act.

## Occupational health and safety programmes

The essential elements of an occupational health and safety programme are:

- *analysis* — of health and safety performance, problems and potential hazards
- *development* — of policies, organization, procedures and training systems
- *implementation* — of the programme by means of training, inspections, investigations and audits
- *evaluation* — of control information and reports and of the effec-

tiveness of the organization and training. This evaluation should provide feedback to be used for improving performance.

The constituents of the health and safety programme are shown in Figure 43.1.

Health and safety programmes are the responsibility of top management but they have to enlist the support of middle management, team leaders and other employees in conducting the initial analysis and in developing and implementing the programme. Assistance and guidance can be provided internally by specialist health and safety advisers. External help and advice can be provided by the government inspectorate (in the UK, the Health and Safety Executive), bodies concerned with health and safety such as the Royal Society for the Prevention of Accidents, or employer's associations. But advisory services do not detract from the ultimate responsibility of management for health and safety performance.

## Analysis of health and safety performance

Health and safety programmes must be based on an analysis of the facts about the organization of health and safety as it exists, and concerning the procedures and results obtained.

The facts should be analysed under the following headings:

- *policies* — the extent to which health and safety policies are defined and implemented
- *organization* — the role and effectiveness of management, team leaders, workpeople, health and safety staff and safety committees
- *systems and procedures* — for carrying out inspections and investigations, reporting and recording accidents, ensuring at the design or development stage that equipment, plant, facilities, processes

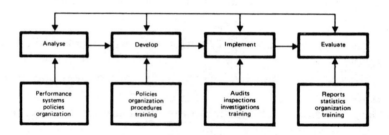

**Figure 43.1** Health and safety programme

and substances are not dangerous, providing safety equipment and educating and training employees

● *performance* — the health and safety record of the organization as shown by statistics, reports, special investigations and audits and sample checks.

Such an analysis involves discussions with managers, team leaders, workpeople, employee representatives, health and safety inspectors and insurers, as well as a review of standard procedures and an examination of safety records.

## Occupational health and safety policies

Written health and safety policies are required to demonstrate that top management is concerned about the protection of the organization's employees from hazards at work and to indicate how this protection will be provided. They are, therefore, first a declaration of intent, second, a definition of the means by which that intent will be realized and third, a statement of the guidelines which should be followed by everyone concerned — which means all employees — in implementing the policy. The policies should provide a base for organization, action and control, as illustrated in Figure 43.2.

The policy statement should consist of three parts:

● the general policy statement
● the description of the organization for health and safety
● details of arrangements for implementing the policy.

### *The general policy statement*

The general policy statement should be a declaration of the intention of

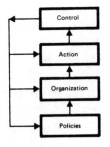

**Figure 43.2** The role of health and safety policies

the employer to safeguard the health and safety of employees. It should emphasize four fundamental points:

- that the safety of employees and the public is of paramount importance
- that safety takes precedence over expediency
- that every effort will be made to involve all managers, team leaders and employees in the development and implementation of health and safety procedures
- that health and safety legislation will be complied with in the spirit as well as the letter of the law.

## Organization

This section of the policy statement should describe the health and safety organization of the company through which high standards are set and achieved by people at all levels in the organization.

This statement should underline the ultimate responsibility of top management for the health and safety performance of the organization. It should then indicate how key management personnel are held accountable for performance in their areas. The role of safety representatives and safety committees should be defined, and the duties of specialists such as the safety adviser and the medical officer should be summarized.

## Occupational health and safety arrangements

The description of the occupational health and safety arrangements should indicate how the general policy statements to be put into effect. It should cover:

- procedures for reporting accidents, illness and safety hazards, fire precautions and first aid
- the precautions to be taken in handling or processing dangerous substances especially any process or substance where there is even a remote risk of a fire or explosion
- arrangements for monitoring the atmosphere and maintaining high standards of hygiene with regard to potentially harmful substances
- the precautions such as ergonomic design of workstations that will be taken to minimize the potential incidence of repetitive strain injury (RSI)
- arrangements for instructing the workforce in safe working

methods and for educating and training employees in health and safety precautions

- good housekeeping requirements covering storage facilities, adequate space for machinery and plant and the provision of gangways
- general rules on safe working habits
- special rules for work done at a height, in confined spaces, on certain electrical equipment
- the steps to be taken to ensure that safety is designed into the system of work
- the maintenance of equipment and the provision of proper testing and inspection arrangements
- special rules for internal transport drivers
- arrangements for checking new machinery and materials
- safety inspections
- the provision of personal protective equipment, and rules as to its use.

## Health and safety organization

Health and safety concerns everyone in an establishment, although the main responsibility lies with management and team leaders for formulating and implementing health and safety policies and procedures.

### The role of management

The role of management is to develop health and safety policies and procedures with the help of its medical and safety advisers. Top management must make departmental managers and team leaders accountable for health and safety performance in their areas. But the onus is on management to provide the required education, training and continuing help and guidance. Management must also set up the necessary information and control systems.

It is essential to have a director with specified responsibility for health and safety matters. It is his or her role to advise on policies and see that they are carried out. In larger organizations there should be a specialized health and safety adviser. Smaller companies should at least allocate the responsibility to a suitable line manager who should be given special training in his or her duties.

## The role of team leaders

Team leaders can exert the greatest influence on health and safety. They are in immediate control and it is up to them to keep a constant watch for unsafe conditions or practices. It is essential to emphasize their accountability for health and safety and that it must take priority over output and cost considerations. They need all the help and guidance on these responsibilities that they can get.

## The role of the medical adviser

Medical advisers have two functions: preventive and clinical. The preventive function is by far the most important and this will be particularly concerned with occupational health matters. To this end they advise on health precautions, carry out inspections and investigations and conduct medical examinations.

Their clinical function is to deal with industrial accidents and diseases and to advise on the steps necessary to recover from injury or illness arising from work. They do not usurp the role of the family doctor on non-work related illnesses.

Even if the organization is not large enough to have a full-time medical officer, it should still be able to call on the part-time advice of a local doctor.

## The role of the safety adviser

The role of the safety adviser or manager responsible for training is to:

- advise on health and safety policies and procedures
- advise on the health and safety aspects of the design and operation of plant and equipment and the use of dangerous substances and processes
- advise on the use of safety equipment and protective clothing
- conduct safety audits and inspections
- conduct investigations into accidents
- maintain health and safety records and statistics
- provide health and safety training
- liaise continually with managers and team leaders
- liaise with the health and safety inspectorate.

## *The role of the safety committee*

Safety committees should be concerned with reviewing unsafe practices and conditions and making suggestions on improving health and safety performance.

# Occupational health programmes

The IPD (1995) believes that:

> The effective management of the health of people at work provides a major contribution to improving performance and gaining competitive advantage. It offers a way of reducing unacceptable losses associated with ill-health and of realizing the opportunities for improving the development and productivity of people.

The control of occupational health and hygiene problems can be achieved by:

- eliminating the hazard at source by means of design and process engineering
- isolating hazardous processes and substances so that workers do not come into contact with them
- changing the processes or substances used to promote better protection or eliminate the risk
- providing protective equipment, but only if changes to the design, process or specification cannot completely remove the hazard
- training workers to avoid risk
- maintaining plant and equipment to eliminate the possibility of harmful emissions, controlling the use of toxic substances and eliminating radiation hazards
- good housekeeping to keep premises and machinery clean and free from toxic substances
- regular inspections to ensure that potential health risks are identified in good time
- pre-employment medical examinations and regular checks on those exposed to risk
- ensuring that ergonomic considerations (ie those concerning the design and use of equipment, machines, processes and workstations) are taken into account in design specifications, establishing work routines and training — this is particularly important as a means of minimizing the incidence of repetitive strain injury (RSI)

- maintaining preventive medicine programmes which develop health standards for each job and involves regular audits of potential health hazards and regular examinations for anyone at risk.

Particular attention needs to be exercised on the control of noise, fatigue and stress. Control of stress should be regarded as a major part of any occupational health programme.

## Managing stress

There are four main reasons why organizations should take account of stress and do something about it; first, because they have the social responsibility to provide a good quality of working life, second, because excessive stress causes illness, third, because it can result in inability to cope with the demands of the job which, of course, creates more stress and finally because excessive stress can reduce employee effectiveness and therefore organizational performance.

The ways in which stress can be managed by an organization include:

- *job design* — clarifying roles, reducing the danger of role ambiguity and conflict and giving people more autonomy within a defined structure to manage their responsibilities
- *placement* — taking care to place people in jobs which are within their capabilities
- *career development* — planning careers and promoting staff in accordance with their capabilities, taking care not to over- or under-promote
- *performance management processes,* which allow a dialogue to take place between managers and individuals about the latter's work problems and ambitions
- *counselling* — giving individuals the opportunity to talk about their problems with a member of the personnel department or the company medical officer, or through an employee assistance programme (see Chapter 44)
- *management training* in performance review and counselling techniques and in what managers can do to alleviate their own stress and reduce it in others.

## Accident prevention

The prevention of accidents is achieved by:

- identifying the causes of accidents and the conditions under which they are most likely to occur
- taking account of safety factors at the design stage — building safety into the system
- designing safety equipment and protective devices and providing protective clothing
- carrying out regular audits, inspections and checks and taking action to eliminate risks
- investigating all accidents resulting in damage to establish the cause and to initiate corrective action
- maintaining good records and statistics in order to identify problem areas and unsatisfactory trends
- conducting a continuous programme of education and training on safe working habits and methods of avoiding accidents
- leadership and motivation — encouraging methods of leadership and motivation which do not place excessive demands on people.

### Identifying the causes of accidents

Fundamentally, it is the system of work to which people are exposed that is the cause of accidents. The immediate cause may be carelessness, fatigue, inexperience, inadequate training or poor supervision, but all these factors are related to the system of work.

*Immediate factors*
The immediate factors causing accidents are:

- using unsafe equipment
- using equipment unsafely — deliberately or through fatigue
- unsafe loading and placing of materials or parts on machines or transport systems
- operating without sufficient clearance
- operating at an unsafe speed
- making safety devices inoperative to reduce interference and speed up work
- distractions from other people or noise
- failure to use protective clothing or devices.

*System of work factors*

System of work factors include:

- unsafely designed machinery, plant or processes
- congested layouts
- unguarded or inadequately guarded machinery
- defective plant, materials or working conditions
- poor housekeeping
- overloading of machines
- poor lighting or glare
- inadequate ventilation or means of extracting fumes in a toxic environment
- lack of protective clothing or devices.

## Building safety into the system

The prevention of accidents should be a major consideration with plant or work processes. It is much better to build safety into the system at the design stage rather than adding makeshift safety devices later.

## Safety inspections

The purpose of safety inspections is to locate and define the faults in the system and the operational errors which allow accidents to occur. A systematic approach involves first allocating the responsibility for managers and team leaders to carry out checks, it should not be left to safety advisers, although they will clearly be heavily involved. The following steps are then necessary:

- define the points to be covered in the form of a check-list
- divide the plant into areas and list the points to which attention needs to be given
- use check-lists to carry out safety audits on a regular basis — a form for recording results is illustrated in Figure 43.3, (these should be carried out daily by supervisors or team leaders using a form such as the one shown in Figure 43.4)
- carry out sample or spot checks on a random basis or to investigate special problems, such as the failure to use protective clothing, recording the results on a form like the one shown in Figure 43.5.
- set up a reporting system.

| Audit area | | Audited by | | Date | |
|---|---|---|---|---|---|
| Points to be checked | Symptoms | Causes | Action recommended | Responsibility for action | Date for completion |
| | | | | | |

**Figure 43.3** Safety audit form

## Accident reports

A standard system for reporting accidents should be used which classifies all accidents under appropriate headings, indicates the likely cause and suggests any remedial action which should be taken. An example of a report form is given in Figure 43.6.

More serious accidents should be investigated by the safety adviser or the manager responsible for safety.

## Measuring safety performance

A commonly used measure in the UK is the 'incidence rate' which is the number of reportable injuries per 1000 employees. Another measure is the 'severity rate', which is the days lost through accidents per 1,000,000 hours worked.

It is also necessary to adopt a 'total loss control' approach which covers the cost of accidents to the company under such headings as pay

| Area | Check carried out by | | | Date |
|---|---|---|---|---|
| | Number of observations | | | |
| Unsafe act or condition | Department A | Department B | Department C | Department D |
| | | | | |

**Figure 43.4** Safety sample inspection form

| Department | Supervisor | | Date | |
|---|---|---|---|---|
| Item | Condition | Immediate action taken | Future action proposed | |
| | | | | |

**Figure 43.5** Team leader's daily check list

| Department | | |
|---|---|---|
| **Name of injured** | **Date of injury** | |
| | **Date/time of return to work** | |
| **Where and how did the accident occur?** | | |
| **Nature of injury** | | |
| **Name(s) of witnesses** | | |
| **Classification of accident** | | |
| Type of accident | Location of accident | Severity of injury |
| | | |
| **Measures taken and proposed to avoid repetition** | | |
| *Signed* _____ *Date* _____ | | |

**Figure 43.6** Accident report form

to people off work, damage to plant or equipment and loss of production. A cost severity rate can then be calculated which is the total cost of accidents per 1,000,000 hours worked.

## Health and safety training

Health and safety training needs should be identified by an analysis of the hazards generally present at work and any particular hazards associated with the organization and individual jobs.

Managers, team leaders and health and safety representatives should be trained in the techniques of identifying potential hazards, conducting inspections and investigations, analysing health and safety performance data and communicating with people on what they should do to avoid risk. Employees should be provided with induction training as well as the hazards present in specific occupations.

### Induction training

Induction training should aim to give new employees a general understanding of what they must do to avoid risks and how the health and safety policies and facilities of the business can help them to avoid occupational illnesses and accidents. The points that should be covered are:

- health and safety policies
- the duties of employees to work safely
- the main hazards they may face and what to do about them
- methods of working to minimize risks to health and safety covering such matters as lifting, posture and working with VDUs
- the unsafe practices to avoid
- the use of protective clothing and safety equipment
- safety rules and procedures, including reporting accidents
- evacuation procedures
- first-aid facilities.

### Job safety training

Job safety training should be based on an analysis of the special hazards presented by a job. The job should be broken down into its constituent parts and the safety points to which the individual must pay attention should be defined for each part.

## Conclusions

Inspections, investigations, reports and statistics are all necessary to improve health and safety performance. However, they depend for their effectiveness on the determination of top management, managers and team leaders to minimize hazards and the risk of accidents before they occur and to take instant remedial action, if in spite of all their precautions there is a health problem or an accident. Training is also important.

# 44

# Welfare Services

---

Welfare services may be provided for matters concerning employees which are not immediately connected with their jobs although they may be connected generally with their place of work. These matters will include individual services relating to employees' welfare such as private help with or counselling on personal problems, assistance with problems of health or sickness and special services for retired employees. Group services may include the provision of social and sporting activities and restaurants. Child care facilities may be provided for individual employees but on a collective basis.

## Why provide welfare services?

There are arguments against the provision of welfare services. They imply do-gooding and the personnel management fraternity has spent many years trying to shake off its association with what it, and others, like to think of as at best peripheral and at worst redundant welfare activities. Welfare is provided for by the state services — why should industrial, commercial or public sector organizations duplicate what is already there? The private affairs of employees and their out-of-work interests should not be the concern of their employers. It is selfish to maintain large playing fields and erect huge sports pavilions if they are going to be used by a minute proportion of staff for a very limited period of time — the space and facilities could be better used by the community. The argument that the provision of employee welfare services increases the loyalty and motivation of employees has long been exploded. If such services are used at all, they are taken for granted. Gratitude, even if it exists, is not a motivating factor.

The case against employee welfare services is formidable; the last point is particularly telling and there is some truth in each of the others — although there are limitations to their validity. State welfare services are, in theory, available to all, but the ability of social workers to give individual advice, especially on problems arising from work, is limited in terms both of time and knowledge. It is all too easy for people to fall into the cracks existing in the decaying edifice of the welfare state.

The case for providing employee services rests mainly on the abstract grounds of the social responsibility of organizations for those who work in them. This is not paternalism in the Victorian sense — turkeys at Christmas — nor in the traditional Japanese sense, where the worker's whole life centres on the employer. Rather, it is simply the realization that in exchange for offering their services, employees are entitled to rather more than their pay, benefits and healthy and safe systems of work. They are also entitled to consideration as human beings, especially when it is remembered that many of their personal problems arise in the context of work and are best dealt with there. People's worries and the resulting stress may well arise from work and their concerns about security, money, health, and relationships with others. But they also bring their personal problems to work; and many of these cannot be solved without reference to the situation there — they may require time off to deal with aged parents or sick wives, or advice on how to solve their problems and so minimize interference with their work.

The argument for employee welfare services at work was well put by Martin (1957):

> Staff spend at least half their waking time at work or in getting to it or leaving it. They know they contribute to the organization when they are reasonably free from worry, and they feel, perhaps inarticulately, that when they are in trouble they are due to get something back from the organization. People are entitled to be treated as full human beings with personal needs, hopes and anxieties; they are employed as people; they bring themselves to work, not just their hands, and they cannot readily leave their troubles at home.

The social argument for employee welfare services is the most compelling one, but there is also an economic argument. Increases in morale or loyalty may not result in commensurate or, indeed, in any increases in productivity, but undue anxiety can result in reduced effectiveness. Even if welfare services cannot increase individual productivity, they can help to minimize decreases. Herzberg's two-factor model, in effect, placed welfare among the hygiene factors, but he did not underestimate the importance of 'hygiene' as a means of eliminating or at least reducing causes of anxiety or dissatisfaction.

A further practical argument in favour of employee welfare services is that a reputation for showing concern helps to improve the image of the firm as a good employer and thus assists in recruitment. Welfare may not directly increase productivity, but it may increase commitment and help in the retention of key employees.

A strong case for employee welfare services therefore exists, and the real question is not 'Why welfare?' but 'What sort of welfare?' This question needs to be answered in general terms before discussing the type of welfare services that can be provided and how they should be organized.

## What sort of welfare services?

Welfare services fall into two categories:

1. Individual or personal services in connection with sickness, bereavement, domestic problems, employment problems, and elderly and retired employees.
2. Group services, which consist of sports and social activities, clubs for retired staff and benevolent organizations.

### *Principles of personal casework*

Individual services require personal casework, and the most important principle to adopt is that this work should aim to help individuals to help themselves. The employer, manager, or personnel specialist should not try to stand between individuals and their problems by taking them out of their hands. Emergency action may sometimes have to be taken on behalf of individuals, but, if so, it should be taken in such a way that they can later cope with their own difficulties. Welfare action must start on the basis that disengagement will take place at the earliest possible moment when individuals can, figuratively, stand on their own two feet. This does not mean that follow-up action is unnecessary, but it is only to check that things are going according to plan, not to provide additional help unless something is seriously wrong.

Personal services should be provided when a need is established, and a welfare need exists where it is clear that help is required, that it cannot be given more effectively from another source, and that the individual is likely to benefit from the services that can be offered.

In an organizational setting, an essential element in personal case-work services is confidentiality. There is no point in offering help or advice to people if they think that their personal problems are going to be revealed to others, possibly to the detriment of their future careers. This is the argument for having specialized welfare officers in organizations large enough to be able to afford them. They can be detached in a way that line managers and even personnel managers cannot be.

## Principles for providing group services

Group services, such as sports or social clubs, should not be laid on because they are 'good for morale'. There is no evidence that they are. They are costly and should be provided only if there is a real need and demand for them, arising from a very strong community spirit in a company or lack of local facilities. In the latter case, the facilities should be shared in an agreed and controlled way with the local community.

## Individual services

### Sickness

These services aim to provide help and advice to employees absent from work for long periods because of illness. The practical reason for providing them is that they should help to speed the return of the employee to work, although it is not part of the employee services function to check up on possible malingerers. The social reason is to provide employees with support and counsel where a need exists. In this context, a need exists where employees cannot help themselves without support and where such aid is not forthcoming from the state medical or welfare services or the employees' own families.

Needs can be established by keeping in touch with an absent employee. This should be done by rushing round as soon as anyone has been absent for more than, say, ten days or has exhausted sickness benefit from work. It is generally better to write to sick absentees, expressing general concern and good wishes for a speedy recovery and reminding them that the firm can provide help if they wish, or simply asking them if they would like someone to visit them — with a stamped, addressed envelope for their reply. Such letters should preferably be sent by the employee's line manager.

There will be some cases where the employee is reluctant to request help or a visit, and the company may have to decide whether a visit should be made to establish if help is required. This will be a matter of judgement based on the known facts about employees and their circumstances.

Visits can be made by the line manager, a personnel officer, or a specialized full- or part-time sick visitor. Some organizations use retired employees for this purpose. Alternatively, arrangements can be made for a colleague to pay the visit. The aims of the visit should be, first, to show employees that their firm and colleagues are concerned about their welfare, second, to alleviate any loneliness they may feel; and, third, to provide practical advice or help. The latter may consist of putting them in touch with suitable organizations or ensuring that such organizations are informed and take action. Or more immediate help may be provided to deal with pressing domestic problems.

## Bereavement

Bereavement is a time when many people need all the help and advice they can get. The state welfare services may not be able to assist and families are often non-existent or unhelpful. Established welfare organizations in industry, commerce or the public sector attach a lot of importance to this service. The advice may often be no more than putting the bereaved employee or the widow or widower of an employee in touch with the right organizations, but it is often extended to help with funeral arrangements and dealing with will and probate matters.

## Domestic problems

Domestic problems seem the least likely area for employee welfare services. Why should the company intervene, even when asked, in purely private matters? If, for example, employees get into debt, that is surely their own affair. What business is it of the company?

These are fair questions. But employers who have any real interest in the wellbeing of their staff cannot ignore appeals for help. The assistance should not consist of bailing people out of debt whenever they get into trouble, or acting as an amateur marriage guidance or family casework officer. But, in accordance with the basic principle of personal casework already mentioned, employees can be counselled on how to help themselves or where to go for expert advice. A counselling service could be provided by company staff or through an employee assistance programme (see page 828). It can do an immense amount of good simply by providing an opportunity for employees to talk through their problems with a disinterested person. The help can be provided either through internal counselling services or by means of employee assistance programmes as described later in this chapter.

There is indeed a limit to how much can or should be done in the way of allowing employees to pour out their troubles but, used with discretion, it is a valuable service.

## Employment problems

Employment problems should normally be solved by discussion between the individual and his or her manager or team leader, or through the company's grievance procedure. There may be times, however, when employees have problems over interpersonal relations, or feelings of inadequacy, about which they want to talk to a third party. Such counselling talks, as a means of relieving feelings and helping people to work through their problems for themselves, can do a lot of good, but extreme caution must be displayed by any company officials who are involved. They must not cut across line management authority, but, at the same time, they must preserve the confidentiality of the discussion. It is a delicate business, and where it affects relationships between individuals and their managers, it is one in which the giving of advice can be dangerous. The most that can be done is to provide a counselling service which gives employees an opportunity to talk about their problems and allows the counsellor to suggest actions the employee can take to put things right. Counsellors must not comment on the actions of anyone else who is involved. They can comment only on what the employee who seeks their help is doing or might do.

## Elderly and retired employees

Employee services for elderly employees is primarily a matter of preparing them for retirement and dealing with any problems they have in coping with their work. Preparation for retirement is a valuable service that many firms offer. This may be limited to advising on the classes and facilities local authorities provide for people prior to retirement, or when they have retired, or it may be extended to running special pre-retirement courses held during working hours.

Some companies have made special provision for elderly employees by setting aside jobs or work areas for them. This has its dangers. Treating employees as special cases ahead of their time may make them over-aware of their condition or too dependent on the services provided for them. There is much to be said for treating elderly employees as normal workers, even though the health and safety services may take particular care to ensure that the age of the worker does not increase the danger of accident or industrial disease.

Retired employees, particularly those with long service, deserve the continuing interest of their former employer. The interest need not be oppressive, but continuing sick visiting can be carried out, and social occasions can be provided for them.

## Group welfare services

Group employee services mainly consist of restaurants, sports and social clubs, and nursery facilities although some companies still support various benevolent societies which provide additional help and finance in times of need.

Company restaurant facilities are obviously desirable in any reasonably sized establishment where there is relatively little choice of facilities in the vicinity. Alternatively, luncheon vouchers can be provided.

A massive investment in sports facilities is usually of doubtful value unless there is nothing else in the neighbourhood and, in accordance with the principles mentioned earlier, the company is prepared to share its facilities with the local community. In a large company in a large town, it is very difficult to develop feelings of loyalty towards the company teams or to encourage people to use the sports club. Why should they support an obscure side when their loyalties have always been directed to the local club? Why should they travel miles when they have perfectly adequate facilities near at hand? Such clubs are usually supported by small cliques who have little or no influence over the feelings of other employees, who leave the enthusiasts to get on with whatever they are doing.

The same argument applies to social clubs, especially those run by paternalistic companies. It is different when they arise spontaneously from the needs of employees. If they want to club together, then the company should say good luck to them and provide them with a reasonable amount of support. The subsidy, however, should not be complete. The clubs should generate their own funds as well as their own enthusiasm. Facilities can be provided within the firm's premises if they are needed and readily available. An investment in special facilities should be made only if there is a real likelihood of their being used regularly by a large proportion of employees. This is an area where prior consultation, before setting up the facility, and self-government, when it has been established, are essential.

Child care or nursery facilities (creches) have obvious value as a means of attracting and retaining parents who would not otherwise be able to work on a full or part-time basis.

## Provision of employee welfare services

It seems obvious that the personnel department should provide employee welfare services. Inevitably, personnel staff will be dealing with cases and providing advice because they are in constant contact with employees and may be seen to be disinterested. It is to be hoped that they will also have some expertise in counselling.

Increasingly, however, it is being recognized that employee welfare is the responsibility of line management and supervision. If the latter take on their proper role as team leaders rather than their traditional autocratic and directive role, they should be close enough to each member of their team to be aware of any personal problems affecting their work. They should be trained in identifying symptoms and at least be able to refer people for counselling if it is clear that they need more help than the team leader can provide.

Employee welfare services can be provided for either internally by means of a counselling service or externally through an agency which runs employee assistance programmes (EAPs).

## Internal counselling services

Internal counselling services can be provided by full-time staff or volunteers who may work on a part-time basis. No specific academic qualifications are required for this work, but those carrying it out should be carefully assessed for suitability and relevant experience and they should have undergone extended training in counselling methods.

## Employee assistance programmes

Employee assistance programmes (EAPs) originated in the US in the 1960s. The idea was slow to catch on in the UK, but it is now subscribed to by more than 100 organizations.

There are a number of external agencies which provide EAP services.

They offer, on a contractual basis, a 24-hour phone service giving employees and their families access to counselling on a range of problems including stress, alcohol and drug abuse, marital breakdown and financial and legal problems. Most services identify the problem and arrange for a relevant specialist to phone back, although face-to-face counselling may also be offered, either at local offices or at surgeries on company premises. In addition, employers may refer employees direct to the service. Where long-term treatment relating to alcohol and drug problems or psychological problems is needed, employees are referred to state services.

Confidentiality is guaranteed by all EAPs to users, although employers are usually provided with a periodic statistical report on take-up of the service, which may be broken down by sex, seniority, department or type of problem. Advocates of the programmes argue that the anonymity they offer makes them particularly suitable for use in this country since it helps overcome the traditional British reluctance to discuss personal matters. Larger EAP providers offer clients the option of reports on average statistics based on work for comparable companies. Additional services include workplace seminars on problems identified as particularly prevalent, training of managers and personnel staff and related literature. The service may be charged for at a per capita rate or according to take-up, which can be as much as 25 per cent of the workforce.

# Part X
# Employment and
# Personnel Services

---

*This handbook emphasizes the importance of strategic considerations in formulating personnel policies and planning personnel programmes to achieve defined objectives. The fact remains, however, that much of personnel management is about managing the employment relationship and dealing with the problems that will always arise when people work together. This also includes the various employment procedures and approaches needed to ensure that both employees and the organization feel that their needs are being satisfied. These are dealt with in Chapter 45.*

*Organizations also need to maintain a comprehensive personnel information system, not only to maintain employee records but also, and importantly, to build a computerized database which will assist in strategic decision-taking. This is covered in Chapter 46.*

# 45

# Employment Practices and Procedures

---

Employment practices and procedures need to be defined in the following areas as described in this chapter:

- terms and conditions and contracts of employment
- grievances
- transfers
- promotions
- attendance management
- equal opportunities and ethnic monitoring
- managing diversity
- age and employment
- sexual harassment
- smoking
- substance abuse at work
- AIDS.

Administrative procedures for dealing with the legal requirements for maternity leave and pay and sick pay will also have to be developed. Redundancy and disciplinary procedures are considered in Chapter 25.

## Terms and conditions and contracts of employment

Terms and conditions of employment which apply generally or to groups of employees need to be defined in the areas included in the contract of employment as described below.

Individual contracts of employment must satisfy the provisions of contracts of employment legislation. They include a statement of the capacity in which the person is employed and the name or job title of the individual to whom he or she is responsible. They also include details of pay, allowances, hours, holidays, leave and pension arrangements and refer to relevant company policies, procedures and rules. Increasing use is being made of fixed-term contracts.

The basic information that should be included in a written contract of employment varies according to the level of job, but the following check-list sets out the typical headings:

- job title
- duties, preferably including a flexibility clause such as: 'The employee will perform such duties and will be responsible to such person, as the company may from time to time require,' and, in certain cases: 'The employee will work at different locations as required by the company'
- the date when continuous employment starts and basis for calculating service
- the rate of pay, allowances, overtime and shift rates, method and timing of payment
- hours of work including lunch break and overtime and shift arrangements
- holiday arrangements

  — days paid holiday per year
  — calculation of holiday pay
  — qualifying period
  — accrual of holidays and holiday pay
  — details of holiday year
  — dates when holidays can be taken
  — maximum holiday that can be taken at any one time
  — carry-over of holiday entitlement
  — public holidays

- sickness

  — pay for time lost
  — duration of sickness payments
  — deductions of national insurance benefits
  — termination due to continued illness
  — notification of illness (medical certificate)

- length of notice due to and from employee

- grievance procedure (or reference to it)
- disciplinary procedure (or reference to it)
- works rules (or reference to them)
- arrangements for terminating employment
- arrangements for union membership (if applicable)
- special terms relating to rights to patents and designs, confidential information and restraints on trade after termination of employment
- employer's right to vary terms of the contract subject to proper notification being given.

## Mobility clauses

Case law has established that employers can invoke mobility clauses which specify that the employee must work in any location as required by the employer as long as that discretion is exercised reasonably and not in such a way as to prevent the employee being able to carry out his or her part of the contract. A mobility clause could, however, be held to discriminate against women, who may not be in a position to move (*Meade-Hill and another vs British Council*, 1995). The acid test is whether or not the employer acts reasonably.

## Grievances

It is often said that the best way to settle grievances is to get the facts and then settle on an equitable solution. This is easier said than done. The problem is frequently hedged round with matters of opinion and prejudice, and it is essential to attempt to penetrate the facade — the ostensible problem or grievance — and reach the real feelings. In any case, facts are always subject to interpretation and feelings are, by definition, subjective. It is not possible to reach behind the facade or achieve the cooperation of the individual in solving the problem if an autocratic or directive approach is adopted — ie telling someone what the problem is and telling them what to do about it. More cooperation and more information will be obtained if the following non-directive counselling approach is used:

- Listen with intelligence and sympathy. People in difficulty cannot fail to benefit if they are allowed to discuss their problems with a sympathetic listener: attentive silence is often the interviewer's best contribution.
- Define the problem. Ideally, individuals should be encouraged to

define the problems for themselves with the aid of sympathetic listening and brief, well-directed questions. It is essential to get the problem clearly stated and accepted as a problem by the person with a grievance as well as interviewers. A considerable amount of listening and questioning may be necessary before the point becomes clear since strong emotions and clarity of expression seldom go together. When you think you understand the individual's viewpoint, it is often helpful to ask a summarizing or reflecting question — 'Is that what you mean?' or 'What I understand you're telling me is that you feel...' — without making any moral judgement at this stage.

- Stay alert and flexible. Plan the meeting in advance to decide broadly how you will tackle it, but be prepared to change direction in the light of new information.
- Observe behaviour. While listening to the words being spoken, take note of body language (gestures, manner), tone and inflexion, pauses and other ways of responding.
- Conclude the meeting. Try to get the individual to summarize his or her problem and suggest a possible solution. If this response is not forthcoming, help them either by a summarizing question or a crystallizing statement, such as 'Am I right in thinking that your problem boils down to this...?'

The aim should be to get to the root of the matter and, if there is no justification for being aggrieved, let individuals work it out for themselves with prompting from you as necessary. If there is something in the complaint, time and trouble should be taken to identify causes rather than just dwelling on symptoms.

Individuals should be given the right to appeal if they feel that their complaint has not been adequately dealt with. A grievance procedure should allow people to take their case through higher levels of authority to the chief executive of the organization if they want. An example of a grievance procedure is given in Appendix E.

## Transfer procedures

Flexibility and redeployment in response to changing or seasonal demands for labour is a necessary feature in any large enterprise. The clumsy handling of transfers by management, however, can do as much long-lasting harm to the climate of employee relations as ill-considered managerial actions in any other sphere of personnel practice.

Management may be compelled to move people in the interests of production. But in making the move, managers should be aware of the fears of those affected in order that they can be alleviated as much as possible.

The basic fear will be of change itself — a fear of the unknown and of the disruption of a well-established situation: work, pay, environment, colleagues and workmates, and travelling arrangements. There will be immediate fears that the new work will make additional and unpalatable demands for extra skill or effort. There will be concern about loss of earnings because new jobs have to be tackled or because of different pay scales or bonus systems. Loss of overtime opportunities or the danger of shift or night work may also arouse concern.

Transfer policies should establish the circumstances when employees can be transferred and the arrangements for pay, resettlement and retraining. If the transfer is at the company's request and to suit the convenience of the company, it is normal to pay the employee's present rate or the rate for the new job, whichever is higher. This policy is easiest to apply in temporary transfers. It may have to be modified in the case of long-term or permanent transfers to eliminate the possibility of a multi-tiered pay structure emerging in the new location, which must cause serious dissatisfaction among those already employed there.

When transfers are made to avoid redundancy in the present location, the rate for the job in the new department should be paid. Employees affected in this way would, of course, be given the choice between being made redundant or accepting a lower-paid job.

The policies should also provide guidelines on how requests from employees for transfer should be treated. The normal approach should be to give a sympathetic hearing to such requests from long-serving employees, especially if the transfer is wanted for health or family reasons. But the transferred employees would have to accept the rate for the job in their new department.

The procedures for handling transfers may have to include joint consultation or discussions with workers' representatives on any major transfer programme. If regular transfers take place because of seasonal changes, it is best to establish a standard procedure for making transfers which would include payment arrangements. Individual transfers would be managed by departmental supervisors, but they should be made aware of company policies and procedures and the need to treat the human problems involved with care and consideration.

## Promotion procedures

The aims of the promotion procedures of a company should be, first, to enable management to obtain the best talent available within the company to fill more senior posts and, second, to provide employees with the opportunity to advance their careers within the company, in accordance with the opportunities available (taking into account equal opportunity policies) and their own abilities.

In any organization where there are frequent promotional moves and where promotion arrangements cause problems, it is advisable to have a promotion policy and procedure which is known to both management and employees and this procedure should take full account of equal opportunity policies (it is often incorporated in equal opportunity policy statements). The basic points that should be included in such a procedure are:

- promotion vacancies should be notified to the personnel department
- vacancies should be advertised internally
- departmental managers should not be allowed to refuse promotions within a reasonable time unless the individual has been in the department for less than, say, one year, or the department has recently suffered heavy losses through promotions or transfers
- promotion opportunities should be open to all, irrespective of race, creed, sex or marital status.

An example of a promotion procedure is given in Appendix E.

## Attendance management

Attendance management is the process of minimizing lateness and absenteeism. The traditional method was to require hourly paid wage earners to clock on, and to deduct pay for lateness or unauthorized absence. There is now an increasing tendency to harmonize conditions of employment by granting full staff terms and conditions to manual workers, which includes payment when absent from work. Some 'single-status' organizations require all employees to clock on; others, have abolished clocking on altogether. Whether or not harmonization has taken place or clocking on is in operation, it is still necessary to control lateness and absenteeism.

### Timekeeping

The best approach to the control of timekeeping is to give team leaders the responsibility for maintaining good timekeeping. They maintain the records (which might be computerized) and take whatever action is required if the trust bestowed on employees is abused. In serious cases this could mean pay deductions and, ultimately, more stringent disciplinary action. But it is the responsibility of the team leader to exercise leadership and develop the team spirit which will minimize such actions.

A policy on timekeeping may be negotiated with the union along the lines of the agreement made between Continental Can and its unions, as described by Wickens (1987). This included the following statement:

> The company trusts its employees to act responsibly and to be at work on time. In the event of this trust being abused and the Company being dissatisfied with an employee's timekeeping record, he or she will be liable to be stopped pay and may be required to comply with a more rigorous form of timekeeping. He or she will also be liable to disciplinary action. The company and the union recognize that it is in the interests of all parties to minimize lateness and will work together in whatever way necessary to this end.

## Absenteeism

Absenteeism can be disruptive and costly. It needs to be controlled. The steps required to achieve effective absence control are:

- *commitment* on the part of management to reduce the cost of absenteeism
- *trust* — the control of absenteeism is also best carried out on the basis that employees are to be trusted — companies who are operating on this basis provide sickness benefit for all workers and rely upon the commitment and motivation of their employees (which they work hard at achieving) to minimize abuse, but they reserve the right to review sickness benefit if the level of sickness absence is unacceptable
- *information* — sadly, a trusting approach will not necessarily work and hard, accurate information on absence is required — this can be provided by computerized systems
- *a documented attendance policy* which spells out the organization's views on absenteeism and the rules for sick pay
- *regular training for managers and team leaders* which ensures that they are aware of their responsibilities for controlling absenteeism and indicates the actions they can take

- *communications* which inform employees why absence control is important
- *counselling* for employees at return to work interviews which provides advice on any attendance problems they may and creates trust
- *disciplinary procedure* — this must be operated fairly and consistently.

## Equal opportunity

Equal opportunity policies were considered in Chapter 10. To get them into action the following are the key steps as set out in the Institute of Personnel and Development's code of conduct:

1. *The recruitment process:*

   — have accurate, up-to-date job descriptions which are not sex biased
   — avoid over-inflated job criteria in person specifications
   — check that job requirements are really necessary to the job and are not a reflection of traditional biased practices
   — guard against sex/race stereotyping in advertisements and recruitment literature.

2. *The interview* — to reduce interview bias:

   — provide training to all who conduct selection interviews
   — ensure that only trained interviewers conduct preliminary interviews
   — avoid discriminatory questions, although interviewers can discuss with applicants any domestic or personal circumstances which might have an adverse effect on job performance as long as this is done without making assumptions based on the sex of the applicant.

3. *Training:*

   — check that women and men have equal opportunities to participate in training and development programmes
   — take late entrants into training schemes
   — ensure that selection criteria for training do not discriminate against women
   — consider using positive training provisions for women and ethnic minorities.

4.  *Promotion*:

    — improve performance review procedures to minimize bias
    — avoid perpetuating the effects of past discriminatory practices in selection for promotion
    — do not presume that women or minorities do not want promotion.

# Ethnic monitoring

The Commission for Racial Equality's (CRE) guide on ethnic monitoring recommends that analyses of the workforce should be conducted in sufficient detail to show whether there is under-representation in more skilled jobs and grades, as well as whether there are general concentrations of ethnic minority employees in certain jobs, levels or departments in the organization. The Institute of Personnel and Development Equal Opportunities Code states that the most important processes to monitor are recruitment and selection since these are easily influenced by prejudice or indirect discrimination. But the proportion of ethnic minorities at different levels in the organization should also be checked regularly.

The CRE has suggested that ethnic monitoring should collect employment information under the following ethnic classifications:

- white
- black-Caribbean
- black-African
- black-other
- Indian
- Pakistani
- Bangladeshi
- Chinese
- other (those describing themselves in this category should be invited to provide further information).

The results of ethnic monitoring should be used to establish whether:

- in comparison with the workforce as a whole, or in comparison with the local labour market, ethnic minority workers are significantly under- or over-represented in any area
- representative numbers of ethnic minorities apply for and are accepted for jobs

- higher or lower proportions of employees from ethnic minorities leave the organization
- there are any disparities in the proportion of members of ethnic minorities.

If necessary, positive affirmative action, as recommended by the CRE, can be taken along the following lines:

- job advertisements designed to reach members of under-represented groups
- the use of employment agencies and careers offices in areas where these groups are concentrated
- recruitment and training for school leavers designed to reach members of these groups
- encouragement to employees from these groups to apply for promotion or transfer opportunities
- training for promotion or skill training for employees of these groups who lack particular expertise but show potential.

## Managing diversity

As described by Kandola and Fullerton (1994):

> The basic concept of managing diversity accepts that the workforce consists of a diverse population of people. The diversity consists of visible and non-visible differences which will include factors such as sex, age, background, race, disability, personality and workstyle. It is founded on the premise that harnessing these differences will create a productive environment in which everybody feels valued, where their talents are being fully utilised and in which organizational goals are met.

Managing diversity is about ensuring that all people maximize their potential and their contribution to the organization. It means valuing diversity, that is, valuing the differences between people and the different qualities they bring to their jobs which can lead to the development of a more rewarding and productive environment.

The International Distillers and Vintners statement on managing diversity as quoted by Kandola and Fullerton explains that:

> Managing diversity is about managing people who are not like you, and who do not necessarily aspire to be like you. It is about having management skill to allow their different perspectives and views to improve the quality of your decisions.

Kandola and Fullerton also quote the following ten most successful initiatives adopted by organizations who are pursuing diversity policies:

1. Introducing equal rights and benefits for part-time workers (compared with full-time workers).
2. Allowing flexibility in uniform/dress requirements.
3. Allowing time off for caring for dependents beyond that required by law eg extended maternity/paternity leave.
4. Benefits provided for employees' partners are equally available to same-sex and different-sex partners.
5. Buying specialized equipment eg braille keyboards
6. Employing helpers/signers for those who need them.
7. Training trainers in equal opportunities.
8. Eliminating age criteria from selection decisions.
9. Providing assistance with child care.
10. Allowing staff to take career breaks.

## Age and employment

Recruitment, employment and training practices should take into account the following key facts about age and age discrimination as listed by the Institute of Personnel and Development:

- Age is a poor predictor of job performance.
- It is misleading to equate physical and mental ability with age.
- More of the population than ever before are living active, healthy lives as they get older.
- There is an increasing number of older workers in the labour market.
- Age is rarely a genuine employment requirement.
- Society's attitudes may encourage compliance with outmoded personnel practices regarding recruitment, promotion, training, redundancy and retirement.
- Reduced self-confidence, self-esteem, and motivation, together with loss or reduction of financial independence for individuals and their dependants, are some of the harmful effects of age discrimination.

## Sexual harassment

Sadly, sexual harassment has always been a feature of life at work. Perhaps it is not always quite so blatant today as it has been in the past, but it is still there, in more or less subtle forms, and it is just as unpleasant.

Persons subject to harassment can take legal action but, of course, it must be the policy of the company to make it clear that it will not be tolerated.

## Problems of dealing with harassment

The first problem always met in stamping out sexual harassment is that it can be difficult to make a clear-cut case. An accusation of harassment can be hard to prove unless there are witnesses. And those who indulge in this practice usually take care to carry it out on a one-to-one basis. In this situation, it may be a case of one person's word against another's. The harasser, almost inevitably a man, resorts to two defences: one, that it did not take place ('it was all in her mind'); and two, that if anything did take place, it was provoked by the behaviour of the female. In these situations, whoever deals with the case has to exercise judgement and attempt, difficult though it may be, to remove any prejudice in favour of the word of the man, the woman, the boss or the subordinate.

The second problem is that victims of sexual harassment are often unwilling to take action and in practice seldom do so. This is because of the actual or perceived difficulty of proving their case. But they may also feel that they will not get a fair hearing and are worried about the effect making such accusations will have on how they are treated by their boss or their colleagues in future — whether or not they will have substantiated their accusation.

The third and possibly the most deep-rooted and difficult problem of all, is that sexual harassment can be part of the culture of the organization — a way of life, a 'norm', practised at all levels.

## Solutions

There are no easy solutions to these problems. It may be very hard to eradicate sexual harassment completely. But an effort must be made to deal with it and the following approaches should be considered:

1.  Issue a clear statement by the chief executive that sexual harassment will not be tolerated. The absolute requirement to treat all people equally, irrespective of sex, role, creed, sexual orientation or disability, should be one of the fundamental values of the

organization. This should be reinforced by the explicit condemnation of harassment as a direct and unacceptable contravention of that value.

2. Back up the value statement with a policy directive on sexual harassment which spells out in more detail how the company deplores it, why it is not acceptable and what people who believe they are being subjected to harassment can do about it.

3. Reinforce the value and policy statements by behaviour at senior level which demonstrates that they are not simply words but that these exhortations have meaning.

4. Ensure that the company's policy on harassment is stated clearly in induction courses and is conveyed to everyone in the form of a strong reminder on promotion.

5. Make arrangements for employees subjected to sexual harassment to be able to seek advice, support and counselling in total confidence without any obligation to take a complaint further. A counsellor can be designated to provide advice and assistance covering such functions as:

   - offering guidance on handling sexual harassment problems
   - assisting in resolving problems informally by seeking, with the consent of the complainant, a confidential and voluntary interview with the person complained against in order to pursue a solution without resource to the formal disciplinary or grievance procedure
   - assisting in submitting a grievance if the employee wishes to complain formally
   - securing an undertaking, where appropriate, by the person who is the subject of the complaint to stop the behaviour which has caused offence
   - counselling the parties as to their future conduct where a problem has been resolved without resource to formal procedures.

6. Create a special procedure for hearing complaints about sexual harassment — the normal grievance procedure may not be suitable because the sexual harasser could be the employee's line manager. The procedure should provide for employees to bring their complaint to someone of their own sex, should they so choose.

7. Handle investigations of complaints with sensitivity and due respect for the rights of both the complainant and the accused.

Ensure that hearings are conducted fairly, both parties being given an equal opportunity to put their case. The principles of natural justice mentioned earlier in this chapter should prevail. Care should be taken to ensure that the careers and reputations of neither party are unjustly affected.

8. Where sexual harassment has taken place, crack down on it. It should be stated in the policy that it is regarded as gross industrial misconduct and, if it is proved, makes the individual liable to instant dismissal. Less severe penalties may be reserved for minor cases but there should always be a warning that repetition will result in dismissal.

9. Ensure that everyone is aware that the organization does take action when required to punish those who indulge in sexual harassment.

10. Provide training to managers and team leaders to ensure that the policy is properly implemented and to make them aware of their direct responsibility to prevent harassment taking place and to take action if it does.

## Smoking

Smoking policies at work are designed to provide employees with a healthy and efficient workplace and to avoid conflict. A smoking policy should be developed in consultation with employees and may involve the use of an opinion survey. Most smokers agree to the right of non-smokers to work in air free from tobacco smoke. Smoking policies can involve a total ban on all smoking except, usually, in a smoking-permitted area away from the workplace. Remember that smokers do have some rights and that a ban in all areas may be oppressive. Sometimes, by agreement, there is a partial ban with separate working areas for those who wish to smoke. Kitchens and lifts are always non-smoking areas and rest rooms generally are.

It is sometimes appropriate to introduce smoking bans in stages, starting by restricting smoking in meeting rooms, corridors and canteens before extending the restriction to other communal and work areas.

## Substance abuse at work

Substance abuse is the use of alcohol, drugs or other substances which cause difficulties at work such as absenteeism, low perfor-

mance standards and interpersonal problems, for example, unpredictable reactions to criticism, paranoia, irritability, avoiding colleagues, borrowing money or physical or verbal abuse of colleagues.
A policy on how to deal with incidents of substance abuse is necessary because:

- many employers have some employees with a drink problem and
  possibly a drug problem
- substance abuse may be a result of work pressures, for which
  employers must take some responsibility
- employers are required to maintain a safe and healthy work
  environment.

The Institute of Personnel and Development has produced guidelines
for a substance-abuse policy which suggest that the following issues
are the ones most likely to be covered:

- an assurance that employees identified as having abuse problems
  will be offered advice and other necessary assistance
- any reasonable absence from work necessary to receive treatment
  will be granted under the organization's sickness scheme provided
  that there is full cooperation from the employee
- an opportunity to discuss the matter once it has become evident or
  suspected that work performance is being affected by substance-
  related problems
- the right to be accompanied at any discussion by a friend or
  employee representative
- the right to full confidentiality
- the provision of agencies to whom an employee can be referred for
  help or a commitment to provide the same expertise where
  employers operate their own treatment or counselling services
- the safeguarding of all employment rights during any reasonable
  period of treatment, including the right, if proven capable, of
  returning to the same job or to suitable alternative employment
- the links between substance-abuse policy and the disciplinary
  procedure
- the policy to deal with subsequent recurrences (recurrences will be
  given due consideration and evaluated on their merits)
- the procedure for monitoring, evaluating and reviewing the policy
- the designation of responsibilities for ensuring that the policy is
  carried out, and the selection of the person primarily responsible for
  its implementation

- a commitment to an employee education programme, and a training programme for designated staff to provide them with the skills and knowledge necessary to carry out their duties under the policy.

## AIDS

There are no logical reasons why AIDS should be treated differently from any other diseases which employees may be carrying, many of which are contagious and some of which are fatal. However, AIDS is a new, frightening and threatening disease which has received enormous publicity, not all of which has been accurate. Because of this fact it is necessary to develop a company policy, which might include the following points:

- The risks of infection through workplace contact are negligible.
- Where the occupation does involve blood contact as in laboratories, hospitals, and doctors' surgeries, the special precautions advised by the Health and Safety Commission will be implemented.
- Employees who know that they are infected with HIV will not be obliged to disclose the fact to the company, but if they do, the fact will remain completely confidential.
- There will be no discrimination against anyone with, or at risk of acquiring, AIDS.
- Employees infected by HIV or suffering from AIDS will be treated no differently from anyone else suffering from a serious illness.

# 46

# Personnel Information and Record Systems

## Introduction

The quality of decisions made about people and the quality of the services provided by the personnel department are largely dependent on the quality of information and records available. In this connection it is useful to distinguish between data, information and knowledge:

- *data* consists of the basic building blocks
- *information* is data arranged into meaningful patterns — as Drucker (1988) wrote, 'information is data endowed with meaning and purpose'
- *knowledge* is the application and productive use of information.

Knowledge is the key. It provides personnel specialists with the ability not only to administrate their functions effectively but also to contribute to strategic decision-taking on matters affecting people. It enables the responsibility for personnel to be increasingly devolved to line managers who, with the knowledge acquired through a computerized personnel information system (CPIS), can be empowered to make decisions related to their team management responsibilities. As Richard Wheeler (1995) expressed it: a 'Computerized human resource information system functions as a repository of critical information and an enabler of change'.... The key to obtaining knowledge and understanding of human resources is being able to access and manipulate information'.

The basis for the acquisition of this knowledge and to the provision of decision-making and administrative support is information technology (IT). This chapter therefore starts with an analysis of the potential benefits of IT as applied in a CPIS and then reviews the considerations affecting IT strategy for personnel information. Examples of CPIS applications and methods of developing a system are then examined.

Personnel information systems will, however, usually incorporate some form of manual information storage (dossiers) and many smaller companies still rely entirely on manual records. The final section of this chapter describes briefly the elements of manual record systems.

## Benefits of a computerized personnel information system (CPIS)

A CPIS can:

- enable the function to provide better services to line management
- provide a conduit to link personnel policies and processes throughout the organization, thus facilitating the development of an integrated and coherent approach to personnel management
- provide essential data for strategic personnel decision-taking enabling personnel people to access and analyze information quickly to put their ideas and plans to the test — it helps in the identification of the benefits of personnel strategies in terms that the business can recognize as adding value, not just cutting costs
- help in the process of empowering line managers to manage their own personnel affairs which, as Wheeler (1995) suggests supports 'the devolution of HR management to the line, not only ensuring that HR policies are complied with thorough validation procedures but also by providing line managers with on-line advice and guidance'
- reduce the workload of the personnel function, eliminating low-value tasks while still enabling the function to provide efficient administrative services.

These benefits will only be achieved in full if a strategic and corporate view is taken of personnel information requirements. If the CPIS is simply used to automate certain aspects of personnel administration such as record keeping it will not realize its full potential.

## Information technology strategy for a CPIS

The IT strategy of an organization in relation to personnel information is concerned first with the use of computerized information for strategic decision-making, second with the range of applications which should be included in the system and finally with the provision to line managers of the facility to have direct access to any personnel data they need to manage their own teams in a devolved organization.

## Strategic decision-taking

The strategic areas in which computerized information and the knowledge gained from analysing that information include macro concerns about organization, human resource requirements, the utilization of human resources, employee development and organizational health.

Specifically the information may focus on areas such as:

- organization development — how the structure may need to adapt to future needs and how IT can enable structural change, for example, high performance team structures
- human resource plans, especially those concerned with 'mapping' future competence requirements and enlarging the skills base
- determination of future development and training needs
- determination of the performance and personality characteristics of the people who will be successful in the organization
- assessment of the 'health' of the organization measured by attitude surveys and turnover and absence statistics, leading to the development of motivation, retention and absence control strategies
- analysis of productivity levels as the basis for productivity improvement programmes
- analysis of the scope for cutting down the number of employees — taking unnecessary costs out of the business.

## Range of applications

There is an immense range of applications to choose from, starting from basic employee records and extending to highly sophisticated 'expert' systems which focus on fundamental personnel decision areas.

The 1994 Computers in Personnel Survey (Richards-Carpenter, 1994) established that the applications which were regarded as most helpful were (percentage of respondents in brackets):

- employee records (86)
- payroll (86)
- absence and holiday recording (43)
- sick and maternity pay records (35)

A smaller proportion of respondents to the survey (13 to 17 per cent) regarded the following activities as being highly important: competency information, recruitment, job/skill matching and training administration.

A fully developed personnel system as marketed by the Hoskyns Group may cover the following areas:

- basic employee data
- appraisal analysis
- training
- manpower planning
- applicant tracking and recruitment
- employee communications
- absence control
- holiday control
- performance tracking
- compensations and benefits
- salary structuring and analysis
- job evaluation
- occupational health.

On the basis of the truism that information is only useful if it is used, the basis for deciding on which applications to select will depend on an analysis of which are the priority areas — the aspects of personnel management where information is most likely to help in reducing administrative work, cutting costs, speeding up the provision of information and helping to make strategic decisions. The strategy may well be to start with the basic administrative support applications and, having set up a database, expand its use progressively through other applications.

## Involving line managers

With the universal availability of personal computers (PCs) and the development of distributed data processing in local area networks (LANS) and wide area networks (WANS), it is possible for data for use by line managers to be down loaded from the centre (a mainframe, mini computer or a UNIX system). Managers can also maintain their own data and manipulate the figures by the use of spreadsheets, for example, considering alternative ways of distributing their budget for a payroll increase amongst their staff. All this will, of course, be subjected to intensive security so that information goes only to authorized people and some data may be on a 'read only' basis.

The strategy for extending the CPIS to line managers will clearly be entirely dependent on the organization's policies for devolving personnel decisions to them. But if this is the policy, its implementation will be much more likely to take place if the information required by line managers is made available.

# Developing a CPIS

## *Overall approach*

Wheeler (1995) states that the following are the typical stages in the development of a CPIS:

- Establish the current and future needs of the business and how these impinge on HR, and the implications for information systems
- Prepare a high level statement of requirement.
- Identify the options available to meet the HR business requirements.
- Prepare a recommendation on how to proceed for executive approval and buy-in. This must be supported both by a financial evaluation and by an analysis of the benefits to the business and any associated changes in business practices. A transition plan will be required which sets out the sequence of activities that would allow the organization to move swiftly and efficiently to any new system with the minimum of disruption.

## *Preferred characteristics of a CPIS*

As suggested by Richards-Carpenter (1993) today's CPISs must emphasize:

- direct input of data at source
- easy access by line managers to a networked system (with proper provisions for the security of personal data)
- systems which can be used by the 'occasional user', not just a dedicated expert
- systems able to deal with administrative processes, not simply a management information system which can be programmed to perform the occasional process
- systems which provide the information needed by line managers in an easily understood format.

The range of applications will be defined by the IT strategy. It will be vital to ensure that the hardware is appropriate to the organizational requirements in that PCs and terminals are provided where needed and are linked together in a network as required.

It is equally essential to ensure that the system is designed in such a way as to hold all the base data needed to provide management information. The system should be user-friendly, bearing in mind that the task which demands most time in using a CPIS is data entry and that the enquiry system for obtaining information must be as easy to learn and use as possible.

The detailed points to be considered when developing a system are:

- the choice of hardware
- the choice of software
- database management
- the degree to which the system is integrated with the payroll
- the development programme.

## Choice of hardware

There may be no choice of hardware — a large proportion of CPISs (39 per cent of the 1994 Computers in Personnel survey companies) are still linked to a mainframe computer. But 39 per cent of systems are linked to a minicomputer and the number of networked PC systems using either mini or microcomputers is increasing, either because this is happening generally within organizations or because of the special advantages of having a distributed and easily accessible system for a personnel application. The numbers of UNIX systems is still small but is growing as manufacturers promote this approach (UNIX is a shared multitasking operating system developed initially for minicomputers but now being used more for workstations which fall somewhere between microcomputers and minicomputers).

## Database management

The system should be founded on a database — a self-describing collection of integrated personnel records. Particular attention has to be paid to the data base management system (DBMS), the program or set of programs that develops and uses the database and database applications. Careful attention has also to be given to the design of database forms: data entry forms which are custom developed, video displays used to enter and change data, queries using standard query language (SQL) and report forms which are the hard copy output of database data. The base data is likely to be of much better quality if it is used in such day-to-day processes as recruitment, training administration and job evaluation.

## Integration

Although many organizations have separated the payroll and purely personnel applications (the former usually being controlled by the accounts department) there is a lot to be said for having an integrated system. This makes economic use of one comprehensive database and facilitates such processes as flexible payment (cafeteria) systems.

## Software

There is a massive and almost bewildering choice of software packages for application programs to provide information and generate reports. The software houses are constantly innovating and developing their products and between them provide something for everyone. However, if the organization has its own systems analysis and programming resources there are advantages in developing tailor-made software. But great care will need to be taken to debug the system, especially if a distributed system involving line managers is being created.

## The development programme

The ten steps required to develop and implement a CPIS are:

1. Determine objectives — are they to save administrative costs, speed up processing, provide advanced decision support, or a combination of any of these?
2. Carry out a feasibility study to consider applications and their likely costs and benefits. This study could be carried out in-house or with the help of outside consultants or software houses who provide a consultancy service. The feasibility study will broadly analyse and define user requirements and ensure that all concerned are aware of what is being planned, how they will benefit from it and the contribution they will be expected to make to the development and application of the system. The information the

system will be required to store and process and the uses to which the information will be put should be specified. Account should be taken of the provisions of the Data Protection Act.

3. Prepare a requirements specification which will set out in detail what the system is expected to do and how the company would like to use it. This specification can be used to brief hardware and software suppliers before selecting the system.

4. Select the system in the form of the hardware and the software required. This may involve decisions on the extent to which existing hardware or systems (eg payroll systems) will be used. The need and scope for networking, that is, linking users by means of terminals, and the employment of word processors will also need to be considered.

5. Plan the implementation programme to ensure that the objectives will be achieved within a given time-scale and in line with the cost budget.

6. Involve users to ensure that everyone who will benefit from the system (line managers as well as members of the personnel department) can contribute their ideas and thus feel that it is their system rather than one imposed upon them.

7. Control the project against the implementation programme to ensure that it delivers what is required, on time and within the budget.

8. Provide training to all users to ensure that they can operate and get the most out of the system.

9. Monitor performance to ensure that the system lives up to expectations.

10. Continually develop the basic system to extend its use in decision support.

## Examples of CPIS applications

### Personnel records

These can include personal details, job details, employment contracts, salary details, performance appraisal, contacts and addresses and employee transactional data. The latter includes all the special items of information a company may need for its employees including qualifications, special skills and competences, training, absence, medical history and discipline.

## Human resource planning

A CPIS can be used to model the effects on groups of people within the organization of change over time in the numbers and structure of each group and movements into, through and out of each group. Such a model looks as the organization, using a manpower system consisting of grades and flows. The user has considerable freedom in defining the number and type of flows required whether into, through, or out of each level of the system, ie:

- flows in — recruitment, transfers in;
- flows out — transfers out, retirement, resignation (uncontrolled losses), early retirement (controlled losses).

## Employee turnover monitoring and control

Computer models can monitor and help in the control of employee turnover. They can therefore provide a critical input to other areas of human resource decision making such as policies on recruitment, promotion, redeployment, training and career planning.

## Employee scheduling

A CPIS can be used to provide an integral system for matching the numbers of employees to business needs. The process of scheduling human resources to meet output in processing targets is becoming increasingly complex with the availability of more flexible ways of deploying people. They include multiskilling (employees who are capable of carrying out different tasks and are not subject to trade-union-imposed constraints in doing so), the use of contract workers, the use of outworkers (people working at home or in another centre, a process which is facilitated by computer networking and electronic mailing), twilight shifts, more part-timers, job sharing, etc.

Human resource planning is an interactive process which is always using output from one part of the process to influence another part of the process. Thus, assessments of the demand and supply of people, scheduling policies and possibilities, and the scope for flexing work-loads and the use of people all influence the human resource supply policies adopted by the organization.

## Employee profiling

Profiling is a particular aspect of employee scheduling concerned with the matching of staff to workloads and ensuring that the right number of people are available to meet fluctuations in activity levels over time. Profiling techniques are used where there are measurable volumes of work that can be costed and forecast with reasonable accuracy. Profiling can be linked with employee budgeting control in the sense that the use of people is both constrained and influenced by the cash budget and performance and employee establishment targets.

Profiling models can be used to:

- monitor and analyse employee utilization
- test the effects of moving some activities to different times of the year and analyse their predicted impact on the employment profile
- monitor movements in expenditure on pay and other employee benefits and carry out sensitivity tests on the impact of different pay assumptions
- forecast future employee requirements
- synchronize the recruitment of permanent and temporary employees with forecast workloads
- flex employee budgets on the basis of revised activity level forecasts
- control employee budgets.

## Skills inventories and audits

Many organizations need to store detailed information about the skills, competences and experience of the individuals they employ. A separate skills inventory can be linked to a personnel database in order that any individual changes in experience or additional training can be fed through automatically to it.

Periodical audits can be carried out by the CPIS of the skills and competences available in the organization. These can be compared with estimates of current and future requirements to identify areas where recruitment or training action is required.

## Competence modelling

Competence modelling brings together organization planning and performance management data to establish the skills or competences required to do particular jobs. This assists in appointment, promotion and training decisions. Competence analysis looks both at what tasks have to be carried out and at the and the competences required. Profiles can then be developed by the computer and matched to assessments of current job holders or job applicants.

## Recruitment

A CPIS recruitment system can carry out four basic administrative tasks:

- storage of applicant's details
- retrieval and amendment of those details
- letter writing (linking the system to word-processing facilities) — acknowledgements, invitations to interview, offers and rejections
- management reports, analysis of response by media and monitoring recruitment costs.

Computerized recruitment control packages not only automate recruitment correspondence (coupling the CPIS with word processors) but also enable users to determine instantly who has applied for which post, track progress in recruiting for a specific post and match and process internal candidates.

The CPIS database can be used in more advanced applications to assist in establishing selection profiles which the standards against which potential job holders can be assessed in order that the right people can be appointed to or promoted into jobs.

## Reward management

A CPIS can be used for pay modelling and to carry out a number of reward administration activities. It can also be used in job evaluation as described later.

Pay models provide the answers to 'what if?' questions such as, 'How much would it cost if we gave x per cent to this part of the company, y per cent to another part of the company, and implemented the following special package across these job functions?'

A CPIS can also:

- analyse and report on average pay or pay distributions by job, grade, age or length of service
- calculate compa-ratios to show how average pay in a range differs from the target pay
- calculate the effects of attrition
- assist in job evaluation
- forecast future pay roll costs on the basis of assumptions about numbers, promotions and pay levels
- administer pay reviews, producing review forms, analysing

proposals against the budgets and calculating the cost of performance-related pay awards in accordance with different assumptions about amounts and the distribution of awards within a budget
- provide information to line managers which will guide them on their pay decisions
- generate instructions to adjust pay as well as letters to individuals informing them of their increases.

## Performance management

A CPIS can help to operate performance management, generating forms, analysing and reporting on the result of performance reviews showing the distribution of people with different degrees of potential or performing at different levels, and highlighting individuals with particular skills or special promise. This system can be linked to others to provide an integrated basis for creating and implementing human resource management policies.

## Training administration (computer-managed learning)

A CPIS can be used for training administration by:
- storing competence-based training modules on the database which enables trainers to select an appropriate module or mix of modules to meet a specified learning need
- analysing the training recommendations contained in performance review reports to identify collective and individual training needs
- identifying suitable training courses to meet training needs
- making arrangements for off-the-job courses
- informing employees about the arrangements for courses
- handling correspondence about training courses
- storing data on standard or individually tailored induction, continuation or development training programmes, including syllabi, routings, responsibilities for giving training, test procedures and progress reporting
- generating instructions and notes for guidance for all concerned with providing or undergoing on-the-job training programmes
- storing progress reports and monitoring achievements against training objectives
- producing reports summarizing current and projected training activities and calculating the output of training programmes — this

can be linked to human resource planning models including those designed to determine the input of trainees required for training schemes
- recording and monitoring training expenditure against budget.

Computers can also be used as training aids (see Appendix D).

## Career management

A CPIS can help in the implementation of career management policies and procedures which embrace both career planning and management development. The system does this by analysing the progression of individuals and comparing the results of that analysis, first, with assessments of organizational requirements as generated by the human resource planning models and, secondly, with the outputs of the performance management system.

## Absence control

Absence control can be carried out with the help of computerized time recording and attendance systems which:

- record clocking-on or -out time and the hours actually worked
- enable employees to record the time spent on particular jobs
- get employees to explain the reason for late arrival, early departure, or any other absence
- can be linked to the payroll system for pay and bonus calculation purposes and to a flexible working hours system
- provide team leaders with a statement showing the length and reasons for absence.

Advanced systems link information obtained from clocking-on or -out direct to a screen in team leaders' offices so that they can have instant information on how many people are at work and on the incidence of lateness.

## Equal opportunity monitoring

The CPIS can store records of the ethnic composition of the workforce. This information can be analysed to produce data on the distribution of ethnic minorities by occupation, job grade, age, service and location. The analysis could show the overall proportion of ethnic minority employees compared with the proportion in each job grade. Similar statistics can be produced for men and women. The analysis can be extended to cover career progression, splitting the results of the overall analysis into comparisons of the rate at which women and men of different ethnic groups progress.

## Expert systems

Knowledge-based software or expert systems are computer programs which contain knowledge about particular fields of human activity and experience, which, through linkages and rules built into the system design, can help solve human resource management problems. Unlike a database system which stores, sorts, manipulates, and presents bits of information — ie data — expert systems store, sort, manipulate and present managers with ready-to-use knowledge of management practice, written in a language that management understands, as opposed to computerese.

Expert systems are developed through a process of knowledge engineering which starts from a knowledge base containing facts and a body of expertise ('heuristics', or rules of thumb) about the use of those facts. These 'rules' enable decisions to be made on the basis of factual information presented to the computer. Thus, a fact may be information on employee turnover during the last three years, and the rule of thumb may be the method by which turnover could be predicted over the next three years. These facts and rules are processed by what is termed the 'inference engine', which solves problems or makes predictions, and the results of this process are presented to the user in the 'user interface'.

An expert system can produce a list of suitable candidates for promotion by using information from the database. If more information were required, it would ask the user to answer questions. It would also respond to users' questions about why particular candidates had been identified, by giving details of qualifications, performance appraisal results and so on.

Expert systems are also used in job evaluation applications where they make use of a database of job analyses and evaluations in order to make consistent judgements about evaluation scores. The expert system does this by:

● defining the evaluation rules relating to the weighting of factors, the points, levels or degrees attached to each factor and the

assessment standards which guide evaluators to the correct weighing of jobs — these may take the form of benchmark jobs and/or level definitions
- programming the computer to ask appropriate questions concerning each factor in a job to enable it to apply the evaluation rules — this involves the analysis of structured questionnaires which have been specially designed to facilitate the systematic collection and analysis of data
- applying the rules consistently and determining the factor score for the job
- grading the job
- sorting the job into position in the rank order
- storing the information entered in the form of a factor analysis into the computer's memory so that it can be called to the screen or printed at any time.

## Manual records

A comprehensive system of records covers all the information required about individual employees or needed for personnel decision making. As discussed earlier in this chapter, most companies now have computerized personnel records which means that the only manual records required will be the dossier containing the employee's application form, contract of employment and any other documents related to his or her employment.

If records are not computerized it will be necessary to have some form of manual record system. Such a system would contain the records required concerning individual employees and collective data on all employees as the basis for reports or returns.

### Individual data

Individual information should include:

- the application form, giving personal particulars, including qualifications
- interview and test record
- job history after joining the organization, including details of transfers, promotions and changes in occupation
- current pay details and changes in salary or pay
- inventory of skills and competences possessed by the job holder

- education and training record with details of courses attended and results obtained
- details of performance assessments and reports from appraisal or counselling sessions
- absence, lateness, accident, medical and disciplinary records with details of formal warnings and suspensions
- holiday entitlement
- pensions data
- termination record, with details of exit interview and suitability for re-engagement.

## Collective data

Collective information may include:

- numbers, grades and occupations of employees
- skills audit data — analyses of the skills available
- absenteeism, labour turnover and lateness statistics
- accident rates
- age and length of service distributions
- wage rates and salary levels
- employee costs
- overtime statistics
- records of grievances and disputes
- training records.

## Designing the system

The type and complexity of the personnel records and information system must obviously depend upon the company and its needs. Small companies may need only a basic card index system for individual employees and a simple set of forms for recording information on numbers employed, labour turnover and absenteeism. But a larger company will almost certainly need a more complex system because more information has to be handled, many more decisions have to be made, and the data change more often. Card indexes are not enough, because supplementary records may be needed to give more detailed information about individual employees. The benefits of a computerizing record in these circumstances are considerable.

Examples of forms and records are given in Appendix C.

# Appendices

# Appendix A

# Personnel Job Descriptions

### Job description — personnel director

*Overall purpose*

To advise on personnel strategies and policies and ensure that the personnel function provides the support required to implement them and that 'world class' personnel processes are functioning effectively.

*Principal accountabilities*

1. Participate as a member of the Board in formulating corporate strategies, policies, plans and budgets and in monitoring the company's performance so as to ensure that the corporate mission and goals are achieved.
2. Advise the Chief Executive and colleagues on the personnel and employee relations policies required by the company in all areas of personnel management in order to uphold core values and fulfil social responsibilities.
3. Formulate and implement personnel strategies which are fully integrated with business strategies and cohere over all aspects of personnel management.
4. Develop plans to implement the strategies to ensure that the number of people with the right skills and competences are available to enable the company to achieve its business strategies and goals.
5. Advise on the development of organizational structures and processes and on the management of change in order to maximize organizational effectiveness.
6. Plan and direct employee development, performance management and career management processes and programmes designed to improve individual and organizational effectiveness and to give employees the best opportunities to develop their abilities and careers in the company.
7. Develop reward management and remuneration (including pensions) policies, processes and procedures which attract, retain and motivate employees, are internally equitable as well as externally competitive, and operate cost-effectively.
8. Advise on employee relations and communication strategies and policies designed to maximize involvement and commitment while minimizing conflict.

9. Direct and control the operations of the personnel function to ensure that it provides cost-effective services throughout the organization.
10. Ensure through advice and monitoring that personnel policies are implemented consistently, and that the core values of the company concerning people are upheld, especially those concerned with fairness, equal opportunity and the management of diversity.
11. Keep up to date with the latest developments in good personnel practice by benchmarking and other means and introduce innovations as appropriate.

## Personnel manager

### Overall responsibility

To provide advice and cost-effective personnel services which enable the company to achieve its goals and meet its responsibilities to the people it employs.

### Key result areas

1. Advise on personnel strategies, policies and practices which support the achievement of the company's business objectives while fulfilling its obligations to employees.
2. Prepare demand and supply forecasts of people requirements in terms of numbers, skills and competences and plans for the recruitment and retention of employees to meet business requirements.
3. Provide a recruitment and selection service to meet the company's needs.
4. Provide advice on all employment and health and safety matters, including issues arising in connection with employment legislation, to ensure that the company meets its legal and social obligations and avoids legal actions.
5. Develop and help to maintain performance management processes which are owned by line managers and employees and make a significant contribution to employee motivation, performance and development.
6. Plan and implement employee development programmes to meet identified needs and satisfy the company's requirements for an effective and multiskilled work-force.
7. Advise on reward management systems and the operation of the company's pay structure and performance pay schemes which obtain, retain and motivate employees.
8. Advise on employee relations issues and coordinate the company's involvement and communication processes in order to develop and maintain a cooperative and peaceful climate of employee relations in the company.
9. Develop and maintain an effective computerized personnel information system.

### Performance standards

Performance will be up to standard when:

1. A proactive approach is consistently adopted in making proposals to management on the development of personnel policies and practices which will improve business performance and add value.

2. Realistic plans are made to anticipate future employee requirements which avoid skill shortages or unmanageable employee surpluses.

3. Systematic recruitment and selection procedures are maintained which provide a wholly acceptable service to line managers. An acceptable service being one that includes:

   - a prompt (within one working day) response to requests for advice or help in recruitment;
   - the delivery of accurate and acceptable job descriptions, person specifications, draft advertisements and media plans within three working days
   - the use of psychometric tests which have been properly evaluated, are administered by trained staff and provide valuable insights for selection purposes
   - the delivery of a short list of candidates by an agreed deadline who meet the specification, supported by helpful profiles.

4. Helpful advice is given on employment and health and safety matters which is based on a thorough understanding of the relevant legislation and company policies and procedures. The advice is such that the company is not involved in any tribunal or other form of legal action.

5. Performance management is introduced by the end of the year, the pilot tests having shown that the approach is acceptable to managers and employees and full preliminary briefing and training programmes having taken place.

6. Employee development programmes are based on a systematic analysis of needs and meet success criteria as established by programme and course evaluations.

7. Reward management policies and practices are developed which ensure that rewards are both competitive and equitable, help the company to acquire and keep high quality employees and provide a sound and cost-effective basis for improving motivation, commitment and performance. Reward reviews are conducted efficiently (ie on time and accurately) and managers are provided with practical and helpful advice on their responsibilities for managing rewards in their departments.

8. A good climate of employee relations is maintained as indicated by the outcomes of employee attitude surveys and the absence of disputes or references to the grievance procedure.

9. The computerized personnel information system is used to maintain accurate records and to generate information as a basis for decision-making on key personnel issues.

## Job description, role definition, person specification and factor analysis — Personnel Officer

## Job description

**Job title:** Personnel Officer

**Responsible to:** Personnel Manager

**Responsible to job holder:** Secretary (half-time)

### *Overall purpose*

To provide personnel services (recruitment, job evaluation and general advice) for all office and junior professional staff in the London office.

### *Main tasks*

1. Provide advice and services on the recruitment and selection of clerical, secretarial, administrative and junior professional staff.
2. Organize induction training programmes in conjunction with the Training Manager.
3. Act as secretary to the job evaluation panel.
4. Analyse jobs and prepares job descriptions for evaluation purposes.
5. Advise on handling disciplinary matters up to the stage of a formal written warning.
6. Advises on other employment matters, including equal opportunity, maternity leave and the handling of grievances.
7. Counsels junior staff on work-related problems.
8. Provide administrative support in conducting the annual salary review.
9. Ensure that data on personnel are input to the company computerized personnel record system.

### *Role definition*

*Context, nature and scope*

The Personnel Officer is based in the London office of the company where approximately 400 staff are employed in the marketing, sales, advertising and public relations functions. The job holder is responsible to the Personnel Manager based at the headquarters of the company in Birmingham. The Personnel Officer is concerned with the recruitment of clerical, secretarial, administrative and junior professional staff, of whom there are about 320. The Personnel Manager deals with more senior staff. Labour turnover is high (20 per cent), and 60 to 70 selections are handled each year. The Personnel Officer prepares job descriptions, agrees salaries, advertises, sifts applicants, administers psychometric tests (OPQ) and carries out initial interviews. The job holder can reject unsuitable candidates, but the final selection is always made by the manager. There is a detailed personnel manual and salary grading scheme which has to be followed. In conjunction with the Training Manager, the job holder organizes induction programmes for new staff.

# Appendix A

In addition to recruitment, the job holder is secretary of the job evaluation panel, which is chaired by the Personnel Manager (a points evaluation scheme is used). The Personnel Officer conducts the job analyses for clerical, administrative and junior professional staff. The job holder also takes part in the evaluation of these staff.

The job holder's other duties include advising on disciplinary cases to ensure that the proper procedure is carried out. He/she drafts written warnings (two last year) and agrees that they should be issued, but does not deal with dismissals — these are dealt with by the Personnel Manager. The Personnel Officer advises on handling equal opportunity and maternity issues and grievances (about 12 cases a year) and is also available to counsel junior staff on work-related problems (one or two cases a week). Inevitably, the job holder is also involved in personal problems.

The Personnel Officer provides administrative support to the annual salary review but is not involved in deciding increases. The job holder ensures that personnel data is input to the computerized record system.

*Role*
The Personnel Officer has four main roles:

- interacting with line managers on recruitment and various personnel issues — this requires the ability to use interpersonal skills in dealing with people who can be difficult and demanding, and political sensitivity in handling inter-departmental issues
- interacting with individual members of staff to deal with work-related and, sometimes personal problems — this also requires interpersonal skills together with an awareness of the culture of the organization
- the application of personnel techniques and procedures which requires competence in such areas as job evaluation and psychometric testing as well as an understanding of the computerized personnel system
- as an administrator, who has to manage considerable flows of paperwork to do with recruitment, job evaluation and salary reviews.

The job requires a flexible approach and the ability to switch into a number of different modes of operation. There is a fair degree of stress arising from the demands of both managers and staff and conflicting priorities.

## Person specification (for recruitment purposes)

1. *Qualifications:*

   - essential — 2–3 A levels plus relevant experience in personnel management which ensures that an acceptable standard of competence has been achieved in each of the main work-related areas of competence
   - ideal — full Member of the Institute of Personnel and Development

2. *Work-based competences:*

   - essential in:

     - all aspects of recruitment including test administration
     - interviewing techniques
     - job analysis

    — inputting data to computers

    — administrating fairly complex paperwork processes

- desirable in:

    — administering OPQ test

    — job evaluation

    — counselling techniques

    — conducting training sessions

3. *Behavioral competences*:

- able to relate well to others and use interpersonal skills to achieve desired objectives
- able to influence the behaviour and decisions of people on matters concerning recruitment and other personnel or individual issues
- able to cope with change, to be flexible and to handle uncertainty
- able to make sense of issues, identify and solve problems and 'think on one's feet'
- focus on achieving results
- able to maintain appropriately directed energy and stamina, to exercise self-control and to learn new behaviours
- able to communicate well, orally and on paper.

## Job analysis (for job evaluation purposes)

*Knowledge and skills*

Needs to understand fully the company's selection and job evaluation procedures. Should have a good working knowledge of employment legislation, particularly that concerned with discipline, equal opportunities and maternity leave.

The skills needed include interviewing, drafting job advertisements, job analysis, counselling and instructing. Also needs to be able to handle the computerized record system.

Ideally, the Personnel Officer should be a member of the Institute of Personnel Management, having taken either a full-time, one-year course or a part-time course extending over three to four years. But the necessary knowledge and skills could be obtained by a combination of work experience and training, although it is unlikely that the maturity and skills would be acquired by anyone with less than five years' experience in administration involving extensive dealings with people.

*Responsibility*

The job holder can make a quite significant impact on the effectiveness of the London office by his/her contribution to maintaining morale and obtaining high-quality staff. Errors can have a damaging effect on efficiency or staff relations, but they are fairly easy to detect. The job holder controls a secretary (part-time) but no other resource of any significance.

*Decisions*

The job holder operates in a separate unit and reports to the Personnel Manager who is based 100 miles away. The Personnel Officer frequently has to make instant decisions within an agreed range of responsibility. The job holder is working within well-defined guide lines (administrative and legal), but, because people issues are being handled, discretion has often to be used in interpreting how a particular guideline should apply. It should be remembered, however, that the ultimate decision on personnel matters rests with the Personnel Manager, although the Personnel Officer is responsible for providing firm advice if a legal or policy issue is involved and, at his/her discretion, can refer the matter to the Personnel Manager.

*Complexity*

The complexity of the job arises from the constant stream of people the job holder has to see and the variety of problems (recruitment, job evaluation, employment) he/she has to deal with during the day. However, the job holder is exercising on a consistent basis a fairly limited range of skills (interpersonal and administrative).

*Contacts*

The job holder is constantly dealing with management at all levels and is expected to provide advice as well as services. He/she is also involved in counselling staff, often on sensitive issues. External contacts include employment agencies and the advertising agency of the company.

# Appendix B

# Generic Role Definitions

---

### Generic role definition for managers

*Managing operations*

1. Set clear objectives, introduce appropriate changes and improvements, and maintain quality services by:

- identifying needs and establishing user requirements
- identifying opportunities to improve the service
- assessing benefits or disadvantages of proposed changes
- negotiating and agreeing areas of change
- ensuring appropriate resources are available
- monitoring the service provided against objectives and quality standards.

*Managing finance*

2. Secure resources for effective management of the services and ensure that these resources are properly used:

- negotiating and controlling expenditure against budgets
- ensuring minimal waste of resources and securing value for money
- monitoring and controlling expenditure against budgets.

*Managing people*

3. Manage people effectively by:

- developing positive relationships with colleagues and members of teams
- establishing and maintaining the trust and support of colleagues, managers and teams
- identifying future staffing needs
- maintaining established standards for recruitment, selection, management of performance, disciplinary and grievance issues
- ensuring the appropriate training and development of individuals and teams

- encouraging self-development and self-motivation
- promoting good working practices and procedures
- regularly reviewing individual and team needs, and endeavouring to meet such needs
- offering support/guidance to individuals as required.

## Managing information

4. Provide an efficient service and communication network (both internally and externally) by:

- obtaining, evaluating and processing information to enable appropriate decisions to be made
- forecasting trends and developments to enable objectives to be met
- ensuring accurate storage and prompt retrieval of information
- leading meetings and group discussions to prepare plans, solve problems and make decisions
- ensuring individuals, teams, colleagues, managers and service users are advised of appropriate information
- promoting good verbal and written dialogue with internal and external contacts/ users.

### Generic role definition for team leaders

*Overall purpose of role:*
To lead teams in order to attain team goals and further the achievement of the organization's objectives.

*Key result areas*

1. Agree targets and standards with team members which support the achievement of the organization's objectives.
2. Plan with team members work schedules and resource requirements which will ensure that team targets will be reached, indeed exceeded.
3. Agree performance measures and quality assurance processes with team members.
4. Agree with team members the allocation of tasks, rotating responsibilities as appropriate to achieve flexibility and the best use of the skills and capabilities of team members.
5. Coordinate the work of the team to ensure that team goals are achieved.
6. Ensure that the team members collectively monitor the team's performance in terms of achieving output, speed of response and quality targets and standards.
7. Agree with team members any corrective action required to ensure that team goals are achieved.
8. Conduct team reviews of performance to agree improvement plans.
9. Conduct individual reviews of performance to agree areas for improvement and personal development plans.
10. Recommend appropriate team performance rewards and individual rewards related to the acquisition and effective use of skills and capabilities.

*Capabilities:*

- Builds effective team relationships, ensuring that team members are committed to the common purpose.
- Encourages self-direction amongst team members but provides guidance and clear direction as required.
- Shares information with team members.
- Trusts team members to get on with things — not continually checking.
- Treats team members fairly and consistently.
- Supports and guides team members to make the best use of their capabilities.
- Encourages self-development by example.
- Actively offers constructive feedback to team members and positively seeks and is open to constructive feedback from them.
- Contributes to the development of team members, encouraging the acquisition of additional skills and providingopportunities for them to be used effectively.

# Appendix C

# Personnel Forms

---

## C1 Application Form

---

# Application Form

# A, B, C & Co Ltd

---

| SURNAME | FIRST NAMES |
|---|---|
| ADDRESS | MAIDEN NAME (IF APPLICABLE) |
| | DATE OF BIRTH |
| | COUNTRY OF BIRTH |
| TELEPHONE (HOME) | MARITAL STATUS |
| TELEPHONE (WORK) | NUMBER OF CHILDREN |
| POSITION APPLIED FOR | |
| WHERE DID YOU LEARN OF THIS VACANCY? | |

# EDUCATION AND TRAINING
## QUALIFICATIONS

What academic and/or professional qualifications do you hold?
(Use initials to indicate this eg CSE, 'O' Level, BSc, ACA etc)

## SECONDARY EDUCATION

| Dates | | Name of school or college | Give details of major subjects studied, examinations taken and results |
|-------|-------|---|---|
| From | To | | |
| | | | |

## EDUCATION BEYOND SECONDARY LEVEL

| Dates | | Name of college/university or other institution (Indicate if part-time or by home study) | Give details of major subjects studied, examinations taken and results |
|-------|-------|---|---|
| From | To | | |
| | | | |

## TRAINING

Give details of any specialized training received and/or courses attended

## OTHER SKILLS

Other qualifications and skills (including languages, current driving licence, keyboard skills, etc)

# EMPLOYMENT HISTORY

Give details here of all positions held since completing your full-time education. Start with your present or most recent position and work back.

| Dates | | Name of employer, address and nature of business. Include any service with the Armed Forces. | Position and duties | Starting and leaving salary and any other benefits | Reason for leaving or wanting to leave |
|-------|-----|----|----|----|----|
| from | to | | | | |
| | | | | | |

# INTERESTS

Please describe your leisure interests.

## ADDITIONAL INFORMATION AND COMMENTS

Do you have any permanent or persistent health problems? Please give details.

Have you ever worked for A, B, C & Co Ltd? Please give details.

Please state salary required.

When would you be able to start work, if you were offered a position?

Please give the names and addresses of *two* persons who are in a position to comment on your professional/work ability. (References will not be taken up without your knowledge.)

Name _____     Name _____

Address _____     Address _____

_____     _____

_____ Telephone no. _____     _____ Telephone no. _____

Position _____     Position _____

Add any comments you wish to make to support your application.

I confirm that the information given on this application form is correct.

Signature of applicant _____     Date _____

*Appendix C*

## C2 Performance Management Forms

| PERFORMANCE MANAGEMENT – PERSONAL PREPARATION FORM | |
|---|---|
| Name | Job title |
| Department | Date |

1. Please list what you consider to be the key tasks for which you are responsible.

2. Please write down what you believe are the main things you are trying to achieve (your objectives) in carrying out your key tasks.

3. What do you think have been your main achievements since the last review? Have you met any problems in carrying out your work? If so, what sort of problems and what do you think should be done about them?

4. Do you believe that the best use is being made of your skills and abilities? If not, what needs to be done?

5. Where would you like to go from here, ie what further experience or additional responsibilities would you like and what direction would you like your future career to take?

6. What further development or training would you like to help you to do even better in your job and/or to advance your career?

*Appendix C*

| PERFORMANCE MANAGEMENT – MANAGER'S PREPARATION FORM | |
|---|---|
| Name of job holder to be assessed | Job title |
| Name of manager | Date |

1. What are the key tasks of the job holder, the performance of which you want to discuss with him/her?

2. Consider and list the objectives you would like to discuss with the job holder with regard to each of the key tasks. Indicate also your views on how the job holder's achievements can be measured or assessed (performance criteria).

3. Consider the results achieved by the job holder since the last review. Identify any areas where there have been notable achievements or where performance has been sub-standard. How do you explain these outcomes?

4. Think about the job holder's skills and abilities. Are you satisfied that the best use is being made of them?

5. What is the job holder's potential for promotion or to take on higher levels of responsibility?

6. What sort of development or training does the individual need to fit him/her for promotion and/or to improve performance?

## PERFORMANCE MANAGEMENT FORM

| Job holder | Department |
|---|---|
| Manager | Period of review |

### PERFORMANCE REVIEW

**ACHIEVEMENT OF OBJECTIVES**
Comment on whether objectives were achieved, partly achieved or not achieved
and the factors which are agreed to have affected performance.

| Objectives | Achievements | Factors affecting |
|---|---|---|
| | | |
| | | |
| | | |
| | | |
| | | |
| | | |
| | | |
| | | |

**ACTION PLANS**
Comment on progress made in completing agreed action plans.

| Action plans | Achievements | Factors affecting |
|---|---|---|
| | | |
| | | |
| | | |
| | | |

**MEETING DEVELOPMENT NEEDS**
Comment on the development and training programmes completed during
the period and their effectiveness.

| PERFORMANCE AGREEMENT | |
|---|---|
| **Agreed objectives** | **Agreed performance criteria** |
| | |
| | |
| | |
| | |
| | |
| | |
| | |
| **Agreed action plans** | **Agreed critical success factors** |
| | |
| | |
| | |
| | |

Agreed development and training needs

| COMMENTS | | |
|---|---|---|
| By manager | | |
| | Signed | Date |
| By job holder | | |
| | Signed | Date |
| By manager's manager | | |
| | Signed | Date |

*Appendix C*

| PERFORMANCE AND DEVELOPMENT PLAN | | |
|---|---|---|
| Job holder | Job title | |
| Department | Period of plan | |
| Agreed objectives | How they will be achieved | Progress during the year |
|  |  |  |
|  |  |  |
|  |  |  |
|  |  |  |
|  |  |  |
|  |  |  |
|  |  |  |
| Agreed action plans | How they will be achieved | Progress during the year |
|  |  |  |
|  |  |  |
|  |  |  |
|  |  |  |
| Agreed development needs | How they will be achieved | Progress during the year |
|  |  |  |
|  |  |  |
|  |  |  |
|  |  |  |

## C3 Personnel Record Forms

| Name | | Date joined |
|---|---|---|
| Date of birth | Marital status | No. of children |
| Address | | Home telephone no. |
| | | |
| Qualifications | | |
| Languages | | |

| Previous employment | | |
|---|---|---|
| Company | Position | Dates |
| | | |

| Present employment | | |
|---|---|---|
| Department | Position | Dates |
| | | |
| Date left | Reason for leaving | |

*Front*

| Salary — Performance — Potential Record | | | |
|---|---|---|---|
| Date | Salary | Performance rating | Potential rating |
| | | | |

| Training received | |
|---|---|
| Date | Course |
| | |

*Reverse*

Basic personnel record card

## MONTHLY ANALYSIS OF LEAVERS

| Month of | 19 | Department | Occupation(s) |
|---|---|---|---|

### Reasons for Leaving

| Length of service | Sex | Discharge Unsuitable | Discharge Discipline | Redundancy | Personal betterment | Dissatisfaction with: Pay | Work | Working conditions | Hours | Management | Other factors | Domestic reasons | Retirement | Death | Unknown | Total |
|---|---|---|---|---|---|---|---|---|---|---|---|---|---|---|---|---|
| Less than 1 month | M | | | | | | | | | | | | | | | |
| | F | | | | | | | | | | | | | | | |
| 1–3 months | M | | | | | | | | | | | | | | | |
| | F | | | | | | | | | | | | | | | |
| 4–12 months | M | | | | | | | | | | | | | | | |
| | F | | | | | | | | | | | | | | | |
| 1–5 years | M | | | | | | | | | | | | | | | |
| | F | | | | | | | | | | | | | | | |
| Over 6 years | M | | | | | | | | | | | | | | | |
| | F | | | | | | | | | | | | | | | |
| Total | M | | | | | | | | | | | | | | | |
| | F | | | | | | | | | | | | | | | |

### Labour turnover rate expressed as an annual rate%*

| | This month | Last month | Same month last year |
|---|---|---|---|
| Male | | | |
| Female | | | |
| Total | | | |

* Monthly labour turnover rate expressed as an annual rate%.

$$\text{Monthly labour turnover rate} = \left( \frac{\text{Number of leavers during month}}{\text{Average number employed during month}} \right) \times 100 \times 12$$

Monthly analysis of leavers

## MONTHLY/ANNUAL SUMMARY OF ABSENCE

**Year:**

**Department/company:**

**Occupation(s):**

| Month | Hours of absence | | | | Total absence (including lateness) | Total planned hours (including overtime) | % lost of planned hours (including overtime) |
|---|---|---|---|---|---|---|---|
| | Sickness or accident | | Other absence | | | | |
| | Certified | Uncertified | Authorized | Unauthorized (inc. lateness) | | | |
| January | | | | | | | |
| February | | | | | | | |
| March | | | | | | | |
| April | | | | | | | |
| May | | | | | | | |
| June | | | | | | | |
| July | | | | | | | |
| August | | | | | | | |
| September | | | | | | | |
| October | | | | | | | |
| November | | | | | | | |
| December | | | | | | | |
| Total for year | | | | | | | |

Monthly/annual summary of absence

| QUARTERLY RETURN — EMPLOYMENT, LABOUR TURNOVER, AND EARNINGS | | | | | | | | | | | *Quarter ending* |
|---|---|---|---|---|---|---|---|---|---|---|---|
| Occupation | Number on payroll | | | Labour turnover annual rate % | | | Average weekly earnings | | | |
| | This quarter | Increase(+) or decrease(-) since: | | This quarter | Increase(+) or decrease(-) since: | | This quarter | Increase(+) or decrease(-) since: | | |
| | | Last quarter | Same quarter last year | | Last quarter | Same quarter last year | | Last quarter | Same quarter last year | |
| | | | | | | | | | | |
| Total | | | | | | | | | | |

Quarterly return — employment, labour turnover and earnings

# Appendix D

# Training Techniques

The training techniques analysed in this appendix are classified into three groups according to where they are generally used:

1. *On-the-job techniques* — demonstration, coaching, mentoring, job rotation/planned experience.
2. *On-the-job or off-the-job techniques* — action learning, job (skill) instruction, question and answer, assignments, projects, guided reading, computer-based training, video, interactive video, multimedia training.
3. *Off-the-job techniques* — lecture, talk, discussion, case study, role-playing, simulation, group exercises, group dynamics, T-groups, inter-active skills training, assertiveness training, distance learning, outdoor learning.

## On-the-job training techniques

### Demonstration

Demonstration is the technique of telling or showing trainees how to do a job and then allowing them to get on with it. It is the most commonly used — and abused — training method. It is direct and the trainee is actively engaged. Reinforcement or feedback can be good, if the supervisor, trainer, or colleague (that well-known character, Nellie, by whom the trainee sits) does it properly by clearly defining what results have been achieved and how they can be improved. But demonstration in its typically crude form does not provide a structured learning system where trainees understand the sequence of training they are following and can proceed by deliberate steps along the learning curve. This is more likely to happen if job (skill) instruction techniques are used, as described later.

### Coaching

Coaching is a person to person technique designed to develop individual skills, knowledge and attitudes.

Coaching is most effective if it can take place informally as part of the normal process of management or team leadership. This type of coaching consists of:

- helping people to become aware of how well they are doing and what they need to learn
- controlled delegation
- using whatever situations arise as learning opportunities
- providing guidance on how to carry out specific tasks as necessary, but always on the basis of helping individuals to learn rather than force-feeding them with instructions on what to do and how to do it.

## Mentoring

Mentoring is the process of using specially selected and trained individuals to provide guidance and advice which will help to develop the careers of the 'protégés' allocated to them.

Mentoring is aimed at complementing learning on the job, which must always be the best way of acquiring the particular skills and knowledge the job holder needs. Mentoring also complements formal training by providing those who benefit from it with individual guidance from experienced managers who are 'wise in the ways of the organization'.

Mentors provide for the person or persons allocated to them (their 'protégés'):

- advice in drawing up self-development programmes or learning contracts
- general help with learning programmes
- guidance on how to acquire the necessary knowledge and skills to do a new job;
- advice on dealing with any administrative, technical or people problems individuals meet, especially in the early stages of their careers
- information on 'the way things are done around here' — the corporate culture and its manifestations in the shape of core values and organizational behaviour (management style)
- coaching in specific skills
- help in tackling projects — not by doing it for protégés but by pointing them in the right direction, that is — helping people to help themselves
- a parental figure with whom protégés can discuss their aspirations and concerns and who will lend a sympathetic ear to their problems.

There are no standard mentoring procedures. Typically, however, a mentor is allocated one or more protégés and given a very general brief to carry out the functions described above.

## Job rotation/planned experience

Job rotation aims to broaden experience by moving people from job to job or department to department. It can be an inefficient and frustrating method of acquiring additional knowledge and skills unless it is carefully planned and controlled. What has sometimes been referred to as the 'Cook's tour' method of moving trainees from department to department has incurred much justified criticism because of the time wasted by them in locations where no one knew what to do with them or cared.

It is better to use the term 'planned sequence of experience' rather than 'job rotation' to emphasize that the experience should be programmed to satisfy a learning specification for acquiring knowledge and skills in different departments and occupations.

Success in using this method depends on designing a programme which sets down what trainees are expected to learn in each department or job in which they gain experience. There must also be a suitable person available to see that trainees are given the right experience or opportunity to learn, and arrangements must be made to check progress. A good way of stimulating trainees to find out for themselves is to provide them with a list of questions to answer. It is essential, however, to follow up each segment of experience to check what has been learnt and, if necessary, modify the programme.

## On- or off-the-job training techniques

### Action learning

Action learning, as developed by Revans (1971), is a method of helping managers develop their talents by exposing them to real problems. They are required to analyse them, formulate recommendations, and then, instead of being satisfied with a report, take action. It accords with the belief that managers learn best by doing rather than being taught.

The concept of action learning is based on six assumptions:

1. Experienced managers have a huge curiosity to know how other managers work.
2. We learn not as much when we are motivated to learn, as when we are motivated to learn something.
3. Learning about oneself is threatening and is resisted if it tends to change one's self-image. However, it is possible to reduce the external threat to a level which no longer acts as a total barrier to learning about oneself.
4. People learn only when they do something, and they learn more the more responsible they feel the task to be.
5. Learning is deepest when it involves the whole person — mind, values, body, emotions.
6. The learner knows better than anyone else what he or she has learned. Nobody else has much chance of knowing.

A typical action learning programme brings together a group, or 'set', of four or five managers to solve the problem. They help and learn from each other, but an external consultant, or 'set adviser', sits in with them regularly. The project may last several months, and the set meets frequently, possibly one day a week. The adviser helps the members of the set to learn from one another and clarifies the process of action learning. This process involves change embedded in the web of relationships called 'the client system'. The web comprises at least three separate networks; the power network, the information network, and the motivational network (this is what Revans means by 'who can, who knows, and who cares'). The forces for change are already there within the client system and it is the adviser's role to point out the dynamics of this system as the work of diagnosis and implementation proceeds.

The group or set has to manage the project like any other project, deciding on objectives, planning resources, initiating action and monitoring progress. But all the time, with the help of their adviser, they are learning about the management processes involved as they actually happen.

# Appendix D

## Job instruction

Job instruction techniques should be based on skills analysis and learning theory as discussed in Chapters 20 and 32. The sequence of instruction should follow four stages:

1. preparation
2. presentation — explanation and demonstration
3. practice and testing
4. follow-up.

Preparation for each instruction period means that the trainer must have a plan for presenting the subject matter and using appropriate teaching methods, visual aids and demonstration aids. It also means preparing trainees for the instruction that is to follow. They should want to learn. They must perceive that the learning will be relevant and useful to them personally. They should be encouraged to take pride in their job and to appreciate the satisfaction that comes from skilled performance.

Presentation should consist of a combination of telling and showing — explanation and demonstration.

Explanation should be as simple and direct as possible: the trainer explains briefly the ground to be covered and what to look for. He or she makes the maximum use of films, charts, diagrams, and other visual aids. The aim should be to teach first things first and then proceed from the known to the unknown, the simple to the complex, the concrete to the abstract, the general to the particular, the observation to reasoning, and the whole to the parts and back to the whole again.

Demonstration is an essential stage in instruction, especially when the skill to be learned is mainly a doing skill. Demonstration takes place in three stages:

1. The complete operation is shown at normal speed to show the trainee how the task should be carried out eventually.
2. The operation is demonstrated slowly and in correct sequence, element by element, to indicate clearly what is done and the order in which each task is carried out.
3. The operation is demonstrated again slowly, at least two or three times, to stress the how, when and why of successive movements.

Practice consists of the learner's imitating the instructor and then constantly repeating the operation under guidance. The aim is to reach the target level of performance for each element of the total task, but the instructor must constantly strive to develop coordinated and integrated performance; that is, the smooth combination of the separate elements of the task into a whole job pattern.

Follow up continues during the training period for all the time required by the learner to reach a level of performance equal to that of the normal experienced worker in terms of quality, speed, and attention to safety. During the follow-up stage, the learner will continue to need help with particularly difficult tasks or to overcome temporary set-backs which result in a deterioration of performance. The instructor may have to repeat the presentation for the elements and supervise practice more closely until the trainee regains confidence or masters the task.

## Assignments

Assignments are a specific task or investigation which trainees do at the request of their trainer or manager. The assignment may be used as a test at the end of a training session, and, as long as it is realistic, it should help to transfer learning to the work situation. The trainer may still have to provide some guidance to trainees to ensure that the latter do not lose confidence if they meet difficulties in completing the task.

Assignments may also be given by managers to their staff as a means of extending their experience. They should be linked to a coaching programme in order that the lessons from the assignment are fully absorbed.

## Projects

Projects are broader studies or tasks which trainees are asked to complete, often with only very generalized guidelines from their trainer or manager. They encourage initiative in seeking and analysing information, in originating ideas, and in preparing and presenting the results of the project. For apprentices, especially students and graduates, the project can be a practical exercise in which the trainees are required to design, manufacture, and test a piece of equipment. Projects for managers may consist of an investigation into a company policy issue or an operating problem.

Like assignments, projects give trainees or managers an opportunity to test their learning and extend their experience, although the scope of the study is likely to be wider, and the project is often carried out by a group of people.

## Guided reading

Knowledge can be increased by giving trainees books, hand-outs, or company literature and asking them to read and comment on them. Guided reading may take place before a course when the members are asked to read 'pre-course' literature. They seldom do. Or it may be given during a training course and used as reinforcement. The beautiful hand-outs that lecturers prepare are often allowed to gather dust when the course is over. They can be far more effective if they are distributed at appropriate points during or immediately after the lecture and those attending are required to discuss specific questions arising from them.

Reading as part of a development programme may be a valuable way of broadening knowledge as long as the material is seen by the trainee as relevant and there is follow-up to ensure that learning has taken place. The best way is to ask trainees to read a handbook or one or two chapters from a longer text and then come back to the trainer or their manager to discuss the relevance of the material and how they can use their knowledge.

## Computer-based training

Computer-based training (CBT) is a form of individualized learning and, as such, is a manifestation of educational technology. It uses the power of the computer to assist in the constant need to train and retrain people in new processes and procedures. It also plays an important part in 'distance learning' in the fields of occupational training and higher education for institutions such as the Open University.

CBT starts with the process of instructional systems design (ISD). Each individual lesson is planned on the basis of careful analysis, sequencing and testing. CBT enables instructors to build into their sessions the adaptability that a truly interactive process of learning should provide. Using a computer, the author can devise an interactive sequence in which the responses the students make will determine their route through the training unit or programme — a route which will be unique to them.

Most CBT systems get trainees to study text on a visual display unit (VDU). They respond to problems which appear on the screen by typing an answer on a keyboard. More advanced systems use interactive video.

Computers can be used for training in the following ways:

1. To simulate actual situations in order that trainees can 'learn by doing'. For example, technicians can be trained in troubleshooting and repairing electronic circuitry by looking at circuit diagrams displayed on the screen and using a light pen to measure voltage at different points in the circuit. When faults are diagnosed, 'repairs' are effected by means of a light pen, this time employed as a soldering iron.

2. To provide diagrammatic and pictorial displays in colour and to allow interaction between the trainee and the information presented on the screen.

3. To provide a database for information which trainees can access through a computer terminal.

4. To measure the performances of trainees against predefined criteria.

5. To provide tests or exercises for trainees. The technique of adaptive testing uses a program containing a large number of items designed to test trainees' comprehension of certain principles. But it is not necessary for them to work through all of them or even to satisfy them sequentially in order to demonstrate their understanding. Their responses to a limited number of questions will show whether or not they have grasped the appropriate concepts. The process of testing can thus be speeded up considerably and prove less frustrating for the trainee.

## *Video*

While the printed word is often limited as a medium, the ability of video to present information visually is an obvious aid to training where there is a shortage of good trainers to get the message across. They are most effective if they are backed up by a trainer's guide which ensures that the passive nature of screen-watching is followed up by active learning.

With the help of cameras, video can provide instant feedback when training is taking place in such interactive skills as interviewing, counselling, selling, running meetings, and instructing.

## *Interactive video*

Interactive video is based on the fusion of two powerful training technologies — computer-based training and video — combined such that the sum is greater than the parts.

Computer-based training (CBT) is individualized and interactive. It is able to accommodate each trainee's needs and pace with the software. Video is effective when realistic sound and pictures are essential and a moving camera angle can compensate for the flatness of the screen, helping to portray three-dimensional reality. But video is limited as a training medium. It cannot be individualized. Watching video is a passive activity and the sequence of instruction is always linear.

Interactive video offers the trainer the best of both worlds. It is individualistic, interactive, and random-access, like CBT, but interactive video can also present, like video, realistic still or moving pictures without sound. It is expensive, but its benefits are considerable in a number of different applications, such as:

- Distance learning — where trainees are widely scattered.
- When trainees have learning difficulties — many people, especially those without much formal education, find it difficult to absorb information from large blocks of text. As long as the interactive video programme is carefully constructed on the basis of a thorough task and skills analysis, and is designed to meet the requirements of learning theory, it will be an effective way of helping people to take in and use complex instructions.
- Where there is a scarce training resource — this might include skilled trainers or the real equipment that a trainee must operate, such as a robot system or an aircraft.
- Where interpersonal skills are important — interactive video is much better than print or CBT in improving interpersonal skills such as interviewing, dealing with customers, counselling, or handling people problems.
- When training time is at a premium — interactive video can cut the time required to achieve learning objectives.

## Multimedia training

Multimedia training uses a variety of media including audio, video, text, graphics, photography and animation which are combined together to create an interactive programme that is delivered on a PC. A multimedia programme will therefore be rich in presentation, making use of a variety of learning approaches which reinforce one another. Trainees receive rapid feedback and can work at their own speed, thus enhancing concentration and information retention. Multimedia training is well suited to procedural-driven or process training where simulations, drills and practice are part of the educational requirement. It is also appropriate for the 'soft skills' of managing people and handling interpersonal relations where scenarios and role plays can be used to practise and develop the skills required.

## Off-the-job training techniques

### Lecture

A lecture is a talk with little or no participation except a question-and-answer session at the end. It is used to transfer information to an audience with controlled content and timing. When the audience is large, there may be no alternative to a 'straight lecture' if there is no scope to break it up into discussion groups.

The effectiveness of a lecture depends on the ability of the speaker to present material with the judicious use of visual aids. But there are several limits on the amount an inert audience can absorb. However effective the speaker, it is unlikely that more than 20 per cent of what was said will be remembered at the end of the day. And after a week, all will be forgotten unless the listeners have put some of their learning into practice. For maximum effectiveness, the lecture must never be longer than 30 or 40 minutes; it must not contain too much information (if the speaker can convey three new ideas which more than one-half of the audience understands and remembers, the lecture will have been successful); it must reinforce learning with appropriate visual aids (but not too many); and it must clearly indicate the action that should be taken to make use of the material.

## Talk

A talk is a less formal lecture for a small group of not more than 20 people, with plenty of time for discussion. The encouragement of participation and interest means that more learning is likely to be retained than in a lecture, but the discussion may be dominated by the more articulate and confident members of the group unless carefully controlled.

## Discussion

The objectives of using discussion techniques are to:

- get the audience to participate actively in learning
- give people an opportunity of learning from the experience of others
- help people to gain understanding of other points of view
- develop powers of self-expression.

The aim of the trainer should be to guide the group's thinking. He or she may, therefore, be more concerned with shaping attitudes than imparting new knowledge. The trainer has unobtrusively to stimulate people to talk, guide the discussion along predetermined lines (there must be a plan and an ultimate objective), and provide interim summaries and a final summary.

The following techniques should be used to get active participation:

- Ask for contributions by direct questions.
- Use open-ended questions which will stimulate thought.
- Check understanding; make sure that everyone is following the argument.
- Encourage participation by providing support rather than criticism.
- Prevent domination by individual members of the group by bringing in other people and asking cross-reference questions.
- Avoid dominating the group yourself. The leader's job is to guide the discussion, maintain control and summarize from time to time. If necessary, 'reflect' opinions expressed by individuals back to the group to make sure they find the answer for themselves. The leader's job is to help them reach a conclusion, not to do it for them.
- Maintain control — ensure that the discussion is progressing along the right lines towards a firm conclusion.

## Case study

A case study is a history or description of an event or set of circumstances which is analysed by trainees in order to diagnose the causes of a problem and work out how to solve it. Case studies are mainly used in courses for managers and team leaders because they are based on the belief that managerial competence and understanding can best be achieved through the study and discussion of real events.

Case studies should aim to promote enquiry, the exchange of ideas, and the analysis of experience in order that the trainees can discover underlying principles which the case study is designed to illustrate. They are not light relief. Nor are they a means of lightening the load on the instructor. Trainers have to work hard to define the learning points that must come out of each case, and they must work even harder to ensure that these points do emerge.

The danger of case studies is that they are often perceived by trainees to be irrelevant to their needs, even if based on fact. Consequently, the analysis is superficial and the situation is unrealistic. It is the trainer's job to avoid these dangers by ensuring that the participants are not allowed to get away with half-baked comments. Trainers have to challenge assumptions and force people to justify their reasoning. Above all, they have to seize every chance to draw out the principles they want to illustrate from the discussion and to get the group to see how these are relevant to their own working situation.

### Role-playing

In role-playing, the participants act out a situation by assuming the roles of the characters involved. The situation will be one in which there is interaction between two people or within a group. It should be specially prepared with briefs written for each participant explaining the situation and, broadly, their role in it. Alternatively, role-playing could emerge naturally from a case study when the trainees are asked to test their solution by playing the parts of those concerned.

Role-playing is used to give managers, team leaders or sales representatives practice in dealing with face-to-face situations such as interviewing, conducting a performance review meeting, counselling, coaching, dealing with a grievance, selling, leading a group or running a meeting. It develops interactive skills and gives people insight into the way in which people behave and feel.

The technique of 'role reversal', in which a pair playing, say, a manager and a team leader run through the case and then exchange roles and repeat it, gives extra insight into the feelings involved and the skills required.

Role-playing enables trainees to get expert advice and constructive criticism from the trainer and their colleagues in a protected training situation. It can help to increase confidence as well as developing skills in handling people. The main difficulties are either that trainees are embarrassed or that they do not take the exercise seriously and overplay their parts.

### Simulation

Simulation is a training technique which combines case studies and role playing to obtain the maximum amount of realism in classroom training. The aim is to facilitate the transfer of what has been learned off the job to on-the-job behaviour by reproducing, in the training room, situations which are as close as possible to real life. Trainees are thus given the opportunity to practise behaviour in conditions identical to or at least very similar to those they will meet when they complete the course.

### Group exercises

In a group exercise the trainees examine problems and develop solutions to them as a group. The problem may be a case study or it could be a problem entirely unrelated to

# Appendix D

everyday work. The aims of an exercise of this kind are to give members practice in working together and to obtain insight into the way in which groups behave in tackling problems and arriving at decisions.

Group exercises can be used as part of a team-building programme and to develop interactive skills. They can be combined with other techniques such as the discovery method to enable participants to work out for themselves the techniques and skills they need to use.

## Group dynamics

Group dynamics training is largely based on the work of Kurt Lewin and the Research Centre for Group Dynamics at MIT in 1946. It has three interconnected and often overlapping aims: first, to improve the effectiveness with which groups operate (team building), second, to increase self-understanding and awareness of social processes and, third, to develop interactive skills which will enable people to function more effectively in groups. Group training can also help in modifying individual attitudes and values.

Group dynamics programmes may emphasize one of these aims more than the others, and they come in a number of forms. The basic variety is 'T-group' or 'sensitivity' training as described below, but this approach can be modified for use in courses primarily designed to improve interactive skills. There are also various packaged group dynamics courses, of which the best known are Blake's Managerial Grid and Coverdale Training.

## T-group training

'T-group' stands for 'training group', which is not a very helpful description. It is also referred to as 'sensitivity training', 'group dynamics', and 'group relations training'. T-group training has three aims:

1. To increase sensitivity — the ability to perceive accurately how others are reacting to one's behaviour.

2. To increase diagnostic ability — the ability to perceive accurately the state of relationships between others.

3. To increase action skill — the ability to carry out skilfully the behaviour required by the situation.

In a T-group, trainers explain the aims of the programme and may encourage discussion and contribute their own reactions. But they do not take a strong lead, and the group is largely left to its own devices to develop a structure which takes account of the goals of both the members of the group and the trainer, and provides a climate in which the group are sufficiently trusting of one another to discuss their own behaviour. They do this by giving feedback or expressing their reactions to one another. Members may not always accept comments about themselves, but as the T-group develops they will increasingly understand how some aspects of their behaviour are hidden from them, and they will, therefore, be well on the way to an increase in sensitivity, diagnostic ability, and action skill.

The design of a T-group 'laboratory' may include short inputs from trainers to clarify problems of group behaviour, intergroup exercises to extent T-group learning to problems of representation, negotiation, and conflict management, and application groups in which members get together to decide how they can best transfer what they have learned to their actual job behaviour. As much opportunity as possible is given to members to test out and develop their own behavioural (interactive) skills — seeking or giving information, enlisting support, persuading, and commanding.

T-group laboratories in their purest form are unlikely ever to become a major part of company training programmes, but the group dynamics approach has valid uses in the modified forms described below.

## Interactive skills training

Interactive skills training is defined by Rackham *et al* (1967) as: 'any form of training which aims to increase the effectiveness of an individual's interaction with others'. It has the following features:

- It is based on the assumption that the primary limitation on or managerial effectiveness lies not within each job boundary, but on the interface between jobs.
- There are no preconceived rules about how people should interact. It is assumed that the way interaction happens is dependent upon the situation and the people in it — this is what has to be analysed and used as a basis for the programme.
- The training takes place through groups, enabling people to practise interactive skills — such skills can only be acquired through practice.
- Participants have to receive controlled and systematic feedback on their performance — this is achieved by using specially developed techniques of behaviour analysis.

A typical interactive skills programme consists of three stages:

1. The diagnostic stage, in which the groups undertake a wide range of activities. These are designed to provide reliable behaviour samples which the trainer records and analyses.
2. The formal feedback stage, in which the trainer gives groups and individuals feedback on their interactive performance during the diagnostic phase.
3. The practice, monitoring, feedback stage, in which the group undertakes further activities to develop and practise new behaviour patterns and receives feedback from the trainer to gauge the success of attempts at behaviour change.

## Assertiveness training

Assertiveness training is designed to help people to become more effective by expressing their opinions, beliefs, wants and feelings in direct, honest and appropriate ways. It is mainly about interpersonal skills and relies largely on role plays and simulations. Self-report questionnaires (ie questionnaires completed by the trainee) may be used to help people to understand their behaviour in situations where it is necessary to be assertive — fighting their corner and standing up for their rights in such a way that they do not violate other people's rights.

## Workshops

A workshop is a specially assembled group of people who, with the help of a facilitator, jointly examine organization issues and/or review their effectiveness as a team in order to develop agreed courses of action to which they will be fully committed.

## Distance learning

Distance learning enables trainees to learn, often in their own time and at home, from instructional material prepared and sometimes presented elsewhere.

The most familiar method of distance learning is the correspondence course. This is normally conducted by post and thus suffers from a time lag between the student's sending in work and receiving it back marked by the tutor. These delays could be protracted, which is a disadvantage when what is really required to enable learning to take place is a dialogue between pupil and teacher. Success in taking a correspondence course relies on the tenacity of the student as well as the quality of instruction and the speed with which correspondence is turned round.

In the UK, the Open University provides a highly developed form of distance learning with some elements of the correspondence course, but a lot is added to this basic approach by the use of television, radio, and video as well as highly sophisticated teaching texts which often rely on the discovery method or a form of programmed learning. Computer-based training techniques are also used, and there is the opportunity to be exposed directly to the Open University tutors at summer schools.

## Outdoor learning

Outdoor learning involves exposing individuals to various 'Outward Bound' type activities: sailing, mountain walking, rock climbing, canoeing, caving etc. It means placing participants, operating in teams, under pressure to carry out physical activities which are completely unfamiliar to them. The rationale is that these tests are paradigms of the sort of challenges people have to meet at work, but their unfamiliar nature means that they can learn more about how they act under pressure as team leaders or team members. Outdoor learning involves a facilitator helping participants to learn individually and collectively from their experiences.

# Appendix E

# Personnel Procedures

---

### Grievance procedure

*Policy*

1. It is the policy of the company that employees should:

    - be given a fair hearing by their immediate supervisor or manager concerning any grievances they may wish to raise
    - have the right to appeal to a more senior manager against a decision made by their supervisor or manager
    - have the right to be accompanied by a fellow employee of their own choice, when raising a grievance or appealing against a decision.

The aim of the procedure is to settle the grievance as nearly as possible to its point of origin.

*Procedure*

The main stages through which a grievance may be raised are as follows:

1. The employee raises the matter with his or her immediate team leader or manager and may be accompanied by a fellow employee of his or her own choice.
2. If the employee is not satisfied with the decision, the employee requests a meeting with a member of management who is more senior than the team leader or manager who initially heard the grievance. This meeting takes place within five working days of the request and is attended by the manager, the manager responsible for personnel, the employee appealing against the decision, and, if desired, his or her representative. The manager responsible for personnel records the result of the meeting in writing and issues copies to all concerned.
3. If the employee is still not satisfied with the decision, he or she may appeal to the appropriate director. The meeting to hear this appeal is held within five working days of the request and is attended by the director, the manager responsible for personnel, the employee making the appeal, and, if desired, his

or her representative. The manager responsible for personnel records the result of this meeting in writing and issues copies to all concerned.

## Disciplinary procedure

### *Policy*

It is the policy of the company that if disciplinary action has to be taken against employees it should:

- be undertaken only in cases where good reason and clear evidence exists
- be appropriate to the nature of the offence that has been committed
- be demonstrably fair and consistent with previous action in similar circumstances
- take place only when employees are aware of the standards that are expected of them or the rules with which they are required to conform
- allow employees the right to be represented by a representative or colleague during any formal proceedings
- allow employees the right to answer any charges made against them
- allow employees the right of appeal against any disciplinary action.

### *Rules*

The company is responsible for ensuring that up-to-date rules are published and available to all employees.

### *Procedure*

The procedure is carried out in the following stages:

1. *Informal warning.* A verbal or informal warning is given to the employee in the first instance or instances of minor offences. The warning is administered by the employee's immediate team leader or manager.
2. *Formal warning.* A written formal warning is given to the employee in the first instance of more serious offences or after repeated instances of minor offences. The warning is administered by the employee's immediate team leader or manager — it states the exact nature of the offence and indicates any future disciplinary action which will be taken against the employee if the offence is repeated within a specified time limit. A copy of the written warning is placed in the employee's personnel record file but is destroyed 12 months after the date on which it was given, if the intervening service has been satisfactory. The employee is required to read and sign the formal warning and has the right to appeal to higher management if he or she thinks the warning is unjustified. The personnel manager should be asked to advise on the text of the written warning.
3. *Further disciplinary action.* If, despite previous warnings, an employee still fails to reach the required standards in a reasonable period of time, it may become necessary to consider further disciplinary action. The action taken may be up to three days' suspension without pay, or dismissal. In either case the departmental manager should discuss the matter with the personnel manager before taking action. Staff below the rank of departmental manager may only recommend

disciplinary action to higher management, except when their manager is not present (for example, on night-shift), when they may suspend the employee for up to one day pending an inquiry on the following day. Disciplinary action should not be confirmed until the appeal procedure has been carried out.

## Summary dismissal

An employee may be summarily dismissed (ie given instant dismissal without notice) only in the event of gross misconduct, as defined in company rules. Only departmental managers and above can recommend summary dismissal, and the action should not be finalized until the case has been discussed with the personnel manager and the appeal procedure has been carried out.

## Appeals

In all circumstances, an employee may appeal against suspension, dismissal with notice, or summary dismissal. The appeal is conducted by a member of management who is more senior than the manager who initially administered the disciplinary action. The personnel manager should also be present at the hearing. If he or she wishes, the employee may be represented at the appeal by a fellow employee of his or her own choice. Appeal against summary dismissal or suspension should be heard immediately. Appeals against dismissal with notice should be held within two days. No disciplinary action which is subject to appeal is confirmed until the outcome of the appeal.

If an appeal against dismissal (but not suspension) is rejected at this level, the employee has the right to appeal to the chief executive. The manager responsible for personnel and, if required, the employee's representative should be present at this appeal.

## Redundancy procedure

### Definition

Redundancy is defined as the situation in which management decides that an employee or employees are surplus to requirements in a particular occupation and cannot be offered suitable alternative work.

Employees may be surplus to requirements because changes in the economic circumstances of the company mean that fewer employees are required, or because changes in methods of working mean that a job no longer exists in its previous form. An employee who is given notice because he or she is unsuitable or inefficient is not regarded as redundant and would be dealt with in accordance with the usual disciplinary procedure.

### Objectives

The objectives of the procedure are to ensure that:

- employees who may be affected by the discontinuance of their work are given fair and equitable treatment

- the minimum disruption is caused to employees and the company
- as far as possible, changes are effected with the understanding and agreement of the unions and employees concerned.

## *Principles*

The principles governing the procedure are as follows:

- The trade unions concerned will be informed as soon as the possibility of redundancy occurs.
- Every attempt will be made to:

  — absorb redundancy by the natural wastage of employees
  — find suitable alternative employment within the company for employees who might be affected, and provide training if this is necessary
  — give individuals reasonable warning of pending redundancy in addition to the statutory period of notice.

- If alternative employment in the company is not available and more than one individual is affected, the factors to be taken into consideration in deciding who should be made redundant will include:

  — length of service with the company
  — age (especially those who could be retired early)
  — value to the company
  — opportunities for alternative employment elsewhere.

The first three of these factors should normally be regarded as the most important; other things being equal, however, length of service should be the determining factor.

## *Procedure*

The procedure for dealing with employees who are surplus to requirements is set out below.

### *Review of employee requirements*
Management will continuously keep under review possible future developments which might affect the number of employees required, and will prepare overall plans for dealing with possible redundancies.

### *Measures to avoid redundancies*
If the likelihood of redundancy is foreseen, the company will inform the union(s), explaining the reasons, and in consultation with the union(s) will give consideration to taking appropriate measures to prevent redundancy.

Departmental managers will be warned by the management of future developments which might affect them in order that detailed plans can be made for running down staff, retraining, or transfers.

Departmental managers will be expected to keep under review the work situation in their departments in order that contingency plans can be prepared and the manager responsible for personnel warned of any likely surpluses.

*Consultation on redundancies*
If all measures to avoid redundancy fail, the company will consult the union(s) at the earliest opportunity in order to reach agreement.

*Selection of redundant employees*
In the event of impending redundancy, the individuals who might be surplus to requirements should be selected by the departmental manager with the advice of the manager responsible for personnel on the principles that should be adopted.

The manager responsible for personnel should explore the possibilities of transferring affected staff to alternative work.

The manager responsible for personnel should inform management of proposed action (either redundancy or transfer) to obtain approval.

The union(s) will be informed of the numbers affected but not of individual names.

The departmental manager and the manager responsible for personnel will jointly interview the employees affected either to offer a transfer or, if a suitable alternative is not available, to inform them they will be redundant. At this interview, full information should be available to give to the employee on, as appropriate:

- the reasons for being surplus
- the alternative jobs that are available
- the date when the employee will become surplus (that is, the period of notice)
- the entitlement to redundancy pay
- the employee's right to appeal to an appropriate director
- the help the company will provide.

An appropriate director will hear any appeals with the manager responsible for personnel.

The manager responsible for personnel will ensure that all the required administrative arrangements are made.

If the union(s) have any points to raise about the selection of employees or the actions taken by the company, these should be discussed in the first place with the manager responsible for personnel. If the results of these discussions are unsatisfactory, a meeting will be arranged with an appropriate director.

*Alternative work within the company*
If an employee is offered and accepts suitable alternative work within the company, it will take affect without a break from the previous employment and will be confirmed in writing. If the offer is refused, the employee may forfeit his or her redundancy payment. Employees will receive appropriate training and will be entitled to a four week trial period to see if the work is suitable. This trial period may be extended by mutual agreement to provide additional training. During this period, employees are free to terminate their employment and if they do, would be treated as if they had been made redundant on the day the old job ended. They would then receive any redundancy pay to which they are entitled.

*Alternative employment*
Employees for whom no suitable work is available in the company will be given reasonable opportunities to look for alternative employment.

## Appendix E

### Promotion policy and procedure

*Policy*

The promotion policy of the company is based on three main principles:

- all employees will be given an equal opportunity for promotion which will not be affected by race, creed, sex or marital status
- all vacancies will be advertised internally
- whenever possible, vacancies will be filled by the most effective people available from within the company, subject to the right of the company to recruit from outside if there are no suitable internal candidates
- the excellence of an employee's performance in his or her present job in the company or the absence of a suitable replacement shall not be a valid reason for refusing promotion to a suitable post, provided that the procedure set out below is complied with.

*Procedure*

When a vacancy arises, the head of the department concerned will obtain the necessary authority, according to company regulations to obtain a replacement.

Following the agreement of the person specification with the line manager, the personnel department will be responsible for placing an internal advertisement and, if necessary, an external advertisement submitting suitable candidates. The personnel department will conduct initial interviews but the departmental manager has the final decision in accepting or rejecting a candidate.

Line managers cannot block the promotion of one of their staff although they can request a short delay (no more than one month) while alternative arrangements are made.

# References

ACAS (1982) *Developments in Harmonization: Discussion Paper No 1*, London.

ACAS (1991) *Effective Organizations: The People Factor, ACAS Advisory Booklet No 6*, ACAS, London.

Adair, J (1973) *The Action-Centred Leader*, McGraw-Hill, London.

Adams, J S (1965) 'Injustice in social exchange', in L Berkowitz (ed) *Advances in Experimental Psychology*, vol 2, Academic Press, New York.

Adams, K (1991) 'Externalisation vs specialisation: what is happening to personnel?' *Human Resource Management Journal*, 14, pp 40–54.

Akinnusi, D K (1991) 'Personnel management in Africa: a comparative analysis of Ghana, Kenya and Nigeria', in C Brewster and S Tyson (eds) *International Human Resource Management*, Pitman, London.

Alderfer, C (1972) *Existence, Relatedness and Growth*, The Free Press, New York.

Allport, G (1954) 'The historical background of modern social psychology', in G Lindzey (ed) *Theoretical Models and Personality*, Addison-Wesley, Cambridge, Mass.

Allport, G (1960) 'The open system in personality theory', *Journal of Abnormal and Social Psychology*, 61, pp 301–311.

Anglia Polytechnic University (1995) *Collectivism or Individualism in Employee Contracts*, Employment Relations, Research and Development Centre, Chelmsford.

Annet, J and Duncan, K (1971) *Task Analysis*, HMSO, London.

Argyle, M (1989) *The Social Psychology of Work*, Penguin, Harmondsworth.

Argyris, C (1957) *Personality and Organization*, Harper & Row, New York.

Argyris, C (1970) *Intervention Theory and Method*, Addison-Wesley, Reading, Mass.

Armstrong, M (1987) 'Human resource management: a case of the emperor's new clothes', *Personnel Management*, August, pp 30–35.

Armstrong, M (1989) *Personnel and the Bottom Line*, Institute of Personnel Management, London.

Armstrong, M and Baron, A (1995) *The Job Evaluation Handbook*, Institute of Personnel and Development, London.

Armstrong, M and Long, P (1994) *The Reality of Strategic HRM*, Institute of Personnel and Development, London.

Armstrong, M and Murlis, H (1994) *Reward Management* (3rd edition), Kogan Page, London.

Armstrong, M and Ryden, O (1996) *The IPD Policy Guide to Team Reward*, Institute of Personnel and Development, London.

# References

Atkinson, G (1989) *The Effective Negotiator*, Negotiating Systems Publications, Newbury.

Atkinson, J (1984) 'Manpower strategies for flexible organizations,' *Personnel Management*, August, pp 28–31.

Atkinson, J and Meager N, (1986) *Changing Patterns of Work*, IMS/OECD, London.

Baillie, J (1995) *The Changing Nature of Work and the Psychological Contract*, IPD (unpublished).

Bales, R F (1950) *Interaction Process Analysis*, Addison-Wesley, Reading, Mass.

Bandura, A (1977) *Social Learning Theory*, Prentice-Hall, Englewood Cliffs, NJ.

Bandura, A (1982) 'Self-efficacy mechanism in human agency', *American Psychologist*, vol 37, pp 122–147.

Bandura, A (1986) *Social Boundaries of Thought and Action*, Prentice-Hall, Englewood Cliffs, NJ.

Barnard, C (1938) *The Functions of an Executive*, Harvard University Press, Boston Mass.

Bass, B M and Vaughan, J A (1966) *Training in Industry: The Management of Learning*, Tavistock, London.

Basset, P and Cave, A (1993) *All for One: The Future of Trade Unions*, Fabian Society, London.

Beard, D (1993) 'Learning to change organizations', *Personnel Management*, January, pp 32–35.

Beardwell, I and Holden, R (1994) *Human Resource Management*, Pitman, London.

Beckhard, R (1969) *Organization Development: Strategy and Models*, Addison-Wesley, Reading, Mass.

Beer, M (1981) 'Performance appraisal — dilemmas and possibilities,' *Organization Dynamics*, Winter, pp 24–36.

Beer, M, Eisenstat, R and Spector, B (1990) 'Why change programs don't produce change,' *Harvard Business Review*, November-December, pp 158–166.

Beer, M and Spector, B (1985) 'Corporate transformations in human resource management', in R Walton and P Lawrence (eds) *HRM Trends and Challenges*, Harvard University Press, Boston, Mass.

Beer, M, Spector, B, Lawrence, P, Quinn Mills, D and Walton, R (1984) *Managing Human Assets*, The Free Press, New York.

Belbin, M (1981) *Management Teams: Why They Succeed or Fail*, Heinemann, London.

Bell, W and Hanson, C (1987) *Profit Sharing and Profitability*, London, Kogan Page.

Bennis, W (1960) *Organizational Development*, Addison-Wesley, Reading, Mass.

Bennis, W and Nanus, B (1985) *Leaders*, Harper & Row, New York.

Berlet, K and Cravens, D (1991) *Performance Pay as a Competitive Weapon*, Wiley, New York.

Berridge, J (1992) 'Human resource management in Britain', *Employee Relations*, vol 14 no 5, pp 62–85.

Bevan, S and Thompson, M (1991) 'Performance management at the cross roads,' *Personnel Management*, November, pp 36–39.

Blackburn, R M and Mann, R (1979) *The Working Class in the Labour Market*, Macmillan, London.

Blake, R and Mouton, J (1964) *The Managerial Grid*, Gulf Publishing, Houston.

Blake, R, Shepart, H and Mouton, J (1964) 'Breakthrough in Organizational Development', *Harvard Business Review*, vol 42, pp 237–258.

Blyton, P and Turnbull, P (eds) (1992) *Reassessing Human Resource Management*, Sage Publications, London.

Boudreau, J W (1988) 'Utility analysis', in L Dyer (ed) *Human Resource Management: Evolving Roles and Responsibilities*, Bureau of National Affairs, Washington, DC.

Bower, J L (1982) 'Business policy in the 1980s', *Academy of Management Review*, vol 7 no 4, pp 630–638.

Boxall, P F (1992) 'Strategic HRM: a beginning, a new theoretical direction', *Human Resource Management Journal*, vol 2 no 3, pp 61–79.

Boxall, P F (1993) 'The significance of human resource management: a reconsideration of the evidence', *The International Journal of Human Resource Management*, vol 4 no 3, pp 645–665.

Boxall, P (1994) 'Placing HR strategy at the heart of the business', *Personnel Management*, July, pp 32–35.

Boyatzis, R (1982) *The Competent Manager*, Wiley, New York.

Brayfield, A H and Crockett, W H (1955) 'Employee attitudes and employee performance', *Psychological Bulletin*, vol 52, pp 346–424.

Brehm, J W (1966) *A Theory of Psychological Reactance*, Academic Press, New York.

Brewster, C and Holt Larsen, H (1992) 'Human resource management in Europe: evidence from ten countries', *International Journal of Human Resource Management*, vol 3 no 3, pp 409–434.

Brewster, C (1993) 'Developing a "European" model of human resource management', *The International Journal of Human Resource Management*, vol 4 no 4, pp 765–784.

Brooklyn Derr, C. Wood, J D, Jones, C and Dupres, C (1993) *The Emerging Role of the Personnel/HR Manager: A United Kingdom and Irish Perspective*, Institute of Personnel Management, London.

Brown, J A C (1954) *The Social Psychology of Industry*, Penguin Books, Harmondsworth.

Brown, W B D (1962) *Piecework Abandoned: the Effect of Wage Incentive Systems on Managerial Authority*, Heinemann, London.

Buchanan, D (1987) 'Job enrichment is dead: long live high performance work design!', *Personnel Management*, May, pp 40–43.

Buchanan, D and Huczynski, A (1985) *Organizational Behaviour*, Prentice-Hall, Englewood Cliffs, NJ.

Burdett, J O (1991) 'What is empowerment anyway?', *Journal of European Industrial Training*, vol 15 no 6, pp 23–30.

Burgess, S and Rees, H (1996) 'Job tenure in Britain 1973–92', *Economic Journal*, March, pp 334–344.

Burgoyne, J (1988a) *Competency Approaches to Management Development*, Centre for the Study of Management Learning, University of Lancaster.

Burgoyne, J (1988b) 'Management development for the individual *and* the organization', *Personnel Management*, June, pp 40–44.

Burgoyne, J (1994) As reported in *Personnel Management Plus*, May, p 7.

Burns, J (1979) *Leadership*, Harper & Row, New York.

Burns, T and Stalker, G (1961) *The Management of Innovation*, Tavistock, London.

Burt, C (1954) 'The Differentiation of Intellectual Ability', *British Journal of Educational Psychology*, vol 24.

Cannell, M and Wood, S (1992) *Incentive Pay: Impact and Evolution*, Institute of Personnel Management, London.

Capelli, P and Singh, H (1992) 'Integrating strategic human resources and strategic management', *Research Frontiers in Industrial Relations and Human Resources*, Industrial Relations Research Association Series.

# References

Casson, J (1978) *Re-evaluating Company Manpower Planning in the Light of Some Practical Experiences*, Institute of Manpower Studies, Brighton.

Cattell, R B (1963) *The Sixteen Personality Factor Questionnaire*, Institute for Personality and Ability Training, Illinois.

Cave, A (1994) *Organizational Change in the Workplace*, Kogan Page, London.

CBI (1990) *Employment and Training*, Mercury Books, London.

CBI/Wyatt (1993) *Variable Pay*, CBI, London.

CBI/HAY Management Consultants (1996) *Trends in Pay and Benefits Systems*, CBI, London.

Chamberlain, N W and Kuhn, J (1965) *Collective Bargaining*, McGraw-Hill, New York.

Chandler, A D (1962) *Strategy and Structure*, The MIT Press, Cambridge, Mass.

Chell, E (1985) *Participation and Organisation*, Macmillan, London.

Chell, E (1987) *The Psychology of Behaviour in Organisations*, Macmillan, London.

Child, J (1977) *Organization: A Guide to Problems and Practice*, Harper & Row, London.

Clegg, H (1976) *The System of Industrial Relations in Great Britain*, Blackwell, Oxford.

Collard, R (1993) *Total Quality: Success Through People*, IPM, London.

Collard, R (1992) 'Total quality: the role of human resources', In M Armstrong (ed.), *Strategies for Human Resource Management*, Kogan Page, London.

Coombe, A (1996) *Competency-based Pay in the NHS*, NHS Personnel, Sheffield.

Cooper, R (1973) 'Task characteristics and intrinsic motivation', *Human Relations*, August 1973, pp 387–408.

Coopers & Lybrand (1985) *A Challenge to Complacency: Changing Attitudes to Training*, Manpower Services Commission, Sheffield.

Coopey, J and Hartley, J (1991) 'Reconsidering the case for organizational commitment', *Human Resource Management Journal*, vol 3 Spring, pp 18–31.

Coyle, D (1996) 'Flexible jobs seen as future face of labour', *The Independent*, 8 March, p 4.

Cross, M (1991) 'Monitoring multiskilling: the way to guarantee long-term change,' *Personnel Management*, March, pp 44–49.

Cyert, R M and March, J G (1963) *A Behavioural Theory of the Firm*, Prentice-Hall, Englewood Cliffs, NJ.

Davis, L E (1966) 'The design of jobs', *Industrial Relations*, vol 6.

Deming, W E (1982) *Quality, Productivity and Competitive Position*, MIT Centre for Advanced Engineering Study, Cambridge, Mass.

Department of Employment (1994) *People and Companies — Employee Involvement in Britain*, HMSO, London.

Diehl, M and Stroebe, W (1987) 'Productivity loss in brainstorming groups: towards the solution of a riddle', *Journal of Personality and Psychology*, 53, pp 407–509.

Digman, L A (1990) *Strategic Management — Concepts, Decisions, Cases*, Irwin, Georgetown, Ontario.

Drucker, P (1951) *The New Society*, Heinemann, London.

Drucker, P (1955) *The Practice of Management*, Heinemann, London.

Drucker, P (1967) *The Effective Executive*, Heinemann, London.

Drucker, P (1988) 'The coming of the new organization', *Harvard Business Review*, January–February, pp 45–53.

Drucker, P (1995) 'The information executives truly need', *Harvard Business Review*, January-February, pp 54–62.

Dulewicz, V (1989) 'Assessment centres as the route to competence', *Personnel Management*, November, pp 56–59.

Duncan, C (1989) 'Pay and payment systems' in B Towers (ed) *A Handbook of Industrial Relations Practice*, Kogan Page, London.

Dunlop, J T (1958) *Industrial Relations Systems*, Holt, New York.

Dyer, L and Holder, G W (1988) 'Strategic human resource management and planning', in L Dyer (ed), *Human Resource Management: Evolving Roles and Responsibilities*, Bureau of National Affairs, Washington DC.

Eagleton, T (1983) *Literary Theory*, Blackwell, Oxford.

Egan, G (1990) *The Skilled Helper: A Systematic Approach to Effective Helping*, Brooks Cole, London.

Eggert, M (1991) *Outplacement: A Guide to Management and Delivery*, Institute of Personnel Management, London.

Elliot, L (1996) 'Dealing with the dirty end of jobs for life', *The Guardian*, April 22, p 14.

Elliott, R F (1991) *Labour Economics*, McGraw-Hill, Maidenhead.

Emery, F F (1980) 'Designing socio-technical systems for greenfield sites', *Journal of Occupational Behaviour*, vol 1, no 1, pp 19–27.

Erez, M (1977) 'Feedback: a necessary condition for the goal-setting performance relationship', *Journal of Occupational Psychology*, vol 62 no 5, pp 624–627.

Erez, M and Zidon, I (1984) 'Effect of good acceptance on the relationship of goal difficulty on performance', *Journal of Applied Psychology*, vol 69 no 1, pp 69–78.

Eysenck, H J (1953) *The Structure of Human Personality*, Methuen, London.

Fayol, H (1916) *Administration Industrielle et General*, Translated by C Storrs as General and Industrial Management, Pitman, London, 1949.

Fein, M (1970) *Approaches to Motivation*, Hillsdale, NJ.

Fernie, S, Metcalf, D and Woodland, S (1994) *What Has Human Resource Management Achieved in the Workplace?* Employment Policy Institute, London.

Fiedler, F (1967) *A Theory of Leadership Effectiveness*, McGraw-Hill, New York.

Flanders, A (1970) *Management and Unions: The Theory and Reform of Industrial Relations*, Faber and Faber, London.

Fletcher, C (1984) 'What's new in performance appraisal', *Personnel Management*, February, pp 20–22.

Fletcher, C (1993) *Appraisal: Routes to Improved Performance*, Institute of Personnel Management, London.

Fletcher, C and Williams, R (1992) 'The route to performance management', *Personnel Management*, October, pp 42–47.

Fletcher, S (1991) *NVQs, Standards and Competence*, Kogan Page, London.

Fletcher, S (1992) *Competence-Based Assessment Techniques*, Kogan Page, London.

Follett, M P (1924) *Creative Experience*, Longmans Green, New York.

Fombrun, C J, Tichy, N M and Devanna, M A (1984) *Strategic Human Resource Management*, Wiley, New York.

Fonda, N (1989) 'Management development: the missing link in sustained business performance', *Personnel Management*, December, pp 50–53.

Fowler, A (1987) 'When chief executives discover HRM', *Personnel Management*, January, p 3.

Fowler, A (1991a) 'An even-handed approach to graphology' *Personnel Management*, March, pp 40–43.

Fowler, A (1991b) 'How to conduct interviews effectively', *Personnel Management Plus*, August, pp 20–21.

# References

Fowler, A (1993) 'Implement a customer care scheme', *Personnel Management Plus*, January, pp 23–24.

Fowler, A (1994) 'How to obtain an Investors in People Award', *Personnel Management Plus*, June, pp 31–32.

Fox, A (1966) 'Industrial sociology and industrial relations', *Royal Commission on Trade Unions and Employers' Associations Research Paper No. 3*, HMSO, London.

Fox, A and Flanders, A (1969) 'Collective bargaining: from Donovan to Durkheim', in A Flanders (ed) *Management and Unions*, Faber and Faber, London.

Freeman, R and Medoff, J (1984) *What do Unions do?* Basic Books, New York.

French, W R, Kast, F E and Rosenzweig, J E (1985) *Understanding Human Behaviour in Organizations*, Harper & Row, New York.

Furnham, A (1990) 'A question of competency', *Personnel Management*, June, p 37.

Gagne, R M (1965) *Conditions of Learning*, Holt, Rhinehart and Winston, New York.

Gall, G (1993) *New Trade Union Recognition Agreements in Britain*, University of Stirling.

Gannon, M (1995) 'Personal development planning', in M Walters (ed) *The Performance Management Handbook*, Institute of Personnel and Development, London.

Garratt, R (1990) *Creating a Learning Organization*, Institute of Directors, London.

Garvin, D A (1993) 'Building a learning organization', *Harvard Business Review*, July–August, pp 78–91.

Ghoshal, S and Bartlett, C A 'Changing the role of top management: beyond structure to process', *Harvard Business Review*, Jan–Feb 1995, pp 86–96.

Giles, E and Williams, R (1991) 'Can the personnel department survive quality management?' *Personnel Management*, April, pp 28–33.

Glaze, T (1989) 'Cadbury's dictionary of competence', *Personnel Management*, July, pp 44–48.

Gluckman, M (1964) *Closed Systems and Open Minds*, Oliver and Boyd, London.

Goldthorpe, J H, Lockwood, D C, Bechofer, F and Platt, J (1968) *The Affluent Worker: Industrial Attitudes and Behaviour*, Cambridge University Press, Cambridge.

Goold, M and Campbell, A (1986) *Strategies and Styles: The Role of the Centre in Managing Diversified Corporations*, Blackwell, Oxford.

Guest, D E (1984) 'What's new in motivation', *Personnel Management*, May, pp 30–33.

Guest, D E (1987) 'Human resource management and industrial relations', *Journal of Management Studies*, vol 14 no 5, pp 503–521.

Guest, D E (1989a) 'Human resource management: its implications for industrial relations', in J Storey (ed), *New Perspectives in Human Resource Management*, Routledge, London.

Guest, D E (1989b) 'Personnel and HRM: can you tell the difference?' *Personnel Management*, January, pp 48–51.

Guest, D E (1990) 'Human resource management and the American dream', *Journal of Management Studies*, vol 27 no 4, pp 378–397.

Guest, D E (1991) 'Personnel management: the end of orthodoxy', *British Journal of Industrial Relations*, vol 29 no 2, pp 149–176.

Guest, D E (1992a) 'Human resource management in the UK', In B Towers, (ed) *The Handbook of Human Resource Management*, Blackwell, Oxford.

Guest, D E (1992b) *Motivation After Herzberg*, Unpublished paper delivered at the Compensation Forum, London.

Guest, D E (1994) Presentation at the Institute of Personnel and Development's annual conference, October (unpublished).

Guest, D E (1995) 'Human resource management: trade unions and industrial relations', in J Storey (ed) *Human Resource Management: A Critical Text*, Routledge, London.

Guest, D E and Fatchett, D (1974) *Worker Participation: Industrial Control and Performance*, Institute of Personnel Management, London.

Guest, D E and Hoque, K (1994) 'Yes, personnel management does make the difference' *Personnel Management*, November, pp 40–44.

Guest, D E and Hoque, K (1995) 'An assessment and further analysis of the 1990 Workshop Industrial Relations Survey' in Guest, D E, Tyson, S, Doherty, N, Hoque, K and Viney, K (eds) *The Contribution of Personnel Management to Organizational Performance*, Institute of Personnel and Development, London.

Guest, D E and Horwood, R (1981) 'Characteristics of the successful personnel manager', *Personnel Management*, May, pp 18–23.

Guest, D E and Peccei, R (1994) 'The nature and causes of effective human resource management', *British Journal of Industrial Relations*, June, pp 219–242.

Guilford, J P (1967) *The Nature of Human Intelligence*, McGraw-Hill, New York.

Gunnigle, P and Moore, S (1994) 'Linking business strategy and human resource management: issues and implications', *Personnel Review*, vol 23 no 1, pp 63–83.

Guzzo, R A and Noonan, K A (1994) 'Human resource practices as communication and the psychological contract', *Human Resource Management*, Fall, pp 447–462.

Hackman, J R and Oldham, G R (1974) 'Motivation through the design of work: test of a theory', *Organizational Behaviour and Human Performance*, vol 16 no 2, pp 250–279.

Hall, R (1992) 'The strategic analysis of intangible resources', *Strategic Management Journal*, 13, pp 135–144.

Hall, P and Norris, P (1992) 'Development centres: making the learning organization happen', *Human Resources*, Autumn, pp 126–128.

Halpin, A and Winer, B A (1957) *Factorial Study of the Leader Behaviour Description*, Ohio State University.

Hamblin, A C (1974) *Evaluation and Control of Training*, McGraw-Hill, Maidenhead.

Hamel, G and Prahalad C K (1989) 'Strategic intent', *Harvard Business Review*, May–June, pp 63–76.

Handy, C (1981) *Understanding Organizations*, Penguin Books, Harmondsworth.

Handy, C (1984) *The Future of Work*, Blackwell, Oxford.

Handy, C (1989) *The Age of Unreason*, Business Books, London.

Handy, C (1994) *The Empty Raincoat*, Hutchinson, London.

Harre, R (1979) *Social Being*, Blackwell, Oxford.

Harrison, R (1992) *Employee Development*, Institute of Personnel Management, London.

Harvey-Jones, J (1989) *Making it Happen*, Collins, Glasgow.

Hawkins, K A (1979) *A Handbook of Industrial Relations Practice*, Kogan Page, London.

Hayes Committee on Personnel Management (1972) *Training for the Management of Human Resources*, Department of Employment, HMSO, London.

Heider, F (1958) *The Psychology of Interpersonal Relationships*, Wiley, New York.

Heinrich, H W (1959) *Industrial Accident Prevention*, McGraw-Hill, New York.

Hendry, C and Pettigrew, A (1986) 'The practice of strategic human resource management', *Personnel Review*, 15, pp 2–8.

Hendry, C and Pettigrew, A (1990) 'Human resource management: an agenda for the 1990s', *International Journal of Human Resource Management*, vol 1 no 3, pp 17–43.

Herriot, P (1996) 'An alternative view on HRM', *Human Resources*, January.

# References

Herzberg, F (1968) 'One more time: how do you motivate employees?' *Harvard Business Review*, Jan–Feb, pp 109–120.

Herzberg, F W, Mausner, B and Snyderman, B (1957) *The Motivation to Work*. Wiley, New York.

Heskett, J (1986) *Managing in the Service Economy*, Harvard Business School Press, Boston, Mass.

Holbeche, L (1994) *Career Development in Flatter Structures*, Roffey Park Management Institute, Horsham.

Holmes, L (1992) 'Taking the lead on professional standards', *Personnel Management*, November, pp 36–39.

Honey, P and Mumford, A (1986) *The Manual of Learning Styles*, Peter Honey, Maidenhead.

Hulin, C L and Blood, M R (1968) 'Job enlargement, individual differences and worker responses', *Psychological Bulletin*, vol 69, no 1.

Hull, C (1951) *Essentials of behaviour*, Yale University Press, New Haven CT.

Humble, J (1963) 'Programmitis and crown princes', *The Manager*, December.

Hunter, J E and Hunter, R F (1984) 'Validity and utility of alternative predictors of job performance', *Psychological Bulletin*, vol 96 no 1.

Hutchinson, S and Wood, S (1995) *Personnel and the Line: Developing the Employment Relationship*, IPD, London.

Hutton, W (1995) *The State We're In*, Cape, London.

IBM/Towers Perrin (1992) *Priorities for Competitive Advantage*, Towers Perrin, New York.

Industrial Data Services (1993) 'Managers, teams and reward', *IDS Management Pay Review*, August, pp 20–23.

Industrial Participation Association (1995) *Towards Industrial Partnership*, IPA, London.

The Industrial Society (1974) *Practical Policies for Participation*, The Industrial Society, London.

Institute of Personnel Management (1992a) *Performance Management in the UK: an Analysis of the Issues*, IPM, London.

Institute of Personnel Management (1992b) *Statement on Counselling in the Workplace*, IPM, London.

Institute of Personnel and Development (1993a) *Code of Professional Conduct*, Institute of Personnel and Development, London.

Institute of Personnel and Development (1993b) *Quality: People Management Matters*, Institute of Personnel and Development, London.

Institute of Personnel and Development (1995) *The IPD Guide to Occupational Health and Organizational Effectiveness*, London.

Institute of Personnel and Development (1995) *The Development of the New Psychological Contract* (unpublished).

*IRS Employee Development Bulletin* no 54 (1994) 'Management development', June, pp 10–12.

Jackson, L (1989) 'Transforming management performance: a competency approach', in Proceedings of Institute of Personnel Management annual conference, October (unpublished).

Jaques, E (1961) *Equitable Payment*, Heinemann, London.

Janis, I (1972) *Victims of Groupthink*, Houghton Mifflin, Boston, Mass.

Johnston, J (1991) 'An empirical study of repatriation of managers in UK multi-nationals', *Human Resource Management Journal*, vol 1 no 4, pp 102–108.

Kahn-Freund, O (1972) *Labour and the Law*, Stevens, London.

Kakabadse, A (1983) *The Politics of Management*, Gower, Aldershot.

Kalleberg, A L and Loscocco, K A (1983) 'Aging, values and rewards: explaining age differences in job satisfaction', *American Sociological Review*, 48.

Kandola, R and Fullerton, J (1994) *Managing the Mosaic: Diversity in Action*, Institute of Personnel and Development, London.

Kanter, M R (1989) 'Becoming PALS: pooling, allying and linking across companies', *Academy of Management Executive*, vol 3 no 3, pp 183–193.

Kanter, R M (1984) *The Change Masters*, Allen & Unwin, London.

Kanter, R M (1989) *When Giants Learn to Dance*, Simon & Schuster, London.

Kaplan, R S and Norton, D P (1992) 'The balanced scorecard — measures that drive performance', *Harvard Business Review*, January–February, pp 71–79.

Katz, D and Kahn, R (1964) *The Social Psychology of Organizations*, John Wiley, New York.

Katzenbach, J and Smith, D (1993) *The Magic of Teams*, Harvard Business School Press, Boston, Mass.

Kay, J (1993a) *Functions of Corporate Success*, Oxford University Press, Oxford.

Kay, J (1993b) 'The structure of strategy', *Business Strategy Review*, vol 4 no 2, pp 17–37.

Keenoy, T and Anthony, P (1992) 'HRM: metaphor, meaning and morality', in P Blyton and P Turnbull (eds), *Reassessing Human Resource Management*, Sage Publications, London.

Kelley, H H (1967) 'Attribution theory in social psychology', in D Levine (ed), *Nebraska Symposium on Motivation*, University of Nebraska Press, Lincoln, NB,

Kelly, G (1955) *The Psychology of Personal Constructs*, Norton, New York.

Kenney, J and Reid, M (1994) *Training Interventions*, 4th ed, Institute of Personnel and Development, London.

Kessler, S and Bayliss, F. (1995) *Contemporary British Industrial Relations*, Macmillan, London.

Kirkbride, P S , Durcan, J and Obeng, E D (1994) 'Change in a chaotic post-modern world', *Journal of Strategic Change*, vol 3, pp 151–163.

Kirkpatrick, I, Davies, A and Oliver, N (1992) 'Decentralisation: friend or foe of HRM?, in P Blyton and P Turnbull (eds) *Reassessing Human Resource Management*, Sage, London.

Kissler, G D (1994) 'The new employment contract', *Human Resource Management*, Fall, vol 33 no 3, pp 335–352.

Kochan, T A and Dyer, L (1993) 'HRM: an American view', in J Storey (ed), *Human Resource Management: A Critical Text*, Routledge, London.

Kolb, D A, Rubin, I M and McIntyre, J M (1974) *Organizational Psychology: An Experimental Approach*, Prentice-Hall, Englewood Cliffs, New Jersey.

Kotter, J (1990) 'What leaders really do', *Harvard Business Review*, May–June, pp 103–111.

Landy, F and Farr, J (1980) 'Performance ratings', *Psychological Bulletin*, 87, pp 72–107.

Latham, G P and Locke, E A (1979) 'Goal setting — a motivational technique that works', *Organizational Dynamics*, Autumn, pp 68–80.

Latham, G P, Saari, L M, Pursell, E D and Campion, M A (1980) 'The situational interview', *The Journal of Applied Psychology*, 65, pp 442–447.

Laurent, A (1986) 'The cultural diversity of western conceptions of management', *International Studies of Management and Organization*, vol 13 no 1–2, pp 75–96.

# References

Lawler, E E (1969) 'Job design and employee motivation', *Personnel Psychology*, vol 22, pp 426–435.

Lawler, E E (1986) 'What's wrong with point-factor job evaluation?', *Compensation and Benefits Review*, March–April, pp 20–28.

Lawler, E E (1990) *Strategic Pay*, Jossey-Bass, San Francisco.

Lawler, E E (1995) 'The new pay: a strategic approach', *Compensation and Benefits Review*, July–August, pp 14–22.

Lawrence, P R and Lorsch, J W (1969) *Developing Organizations*, Addison-Wiley, Reading, Mass.

Lawrence, P and Lorsch, J (1976) *Organization and Environment*, Harvard University Press, Cambridge, Mass.

Leavitt, H J (1951) 'Some effects of certain communication patterns on group performance', *Journal of Abnormal Psychology*.

Legge, K (1978) *Power, Innovation and Problem Solving in Personnel Management*, McGraw-Hill, Maidenhead.

Legge, K (1989) 'Human resource management: a critical analysis', in J Storey (ed), *New Perspectives in Human Resource Management*, Routledge, London.

Legg, K (1995) 'HRM: rhetoric, reality and hidden agenda' in J Storey (ed.) *Human Resource Management: A Critical Text*, Routledge, London.

Lengnick-Hall, C A and Lengnick-Hall, M L (1990) *Interactive Human Resource Management and Strategic Planning*, Quorum Books, Westport.

Levinson, D (1978) *The Seasons of Man's Life*, Knopf, New York.

Levitt, T (1983) *The Marketing Imagination*, Free Press, New York.

Lewin, K (1947) 'Frontiers in group dynamics', *Human Relations*, vol 1 no 1, pp 5–42.

Lewin, K (1951) *Field Theory in Social Science*, Harper & Row, New York.

Likert, R (1961) *New Patterns of Management*, Harper & Row, New York.

Likert, R (1967) *The Human Organization*, McGraw-Hill, New York.

Litwin, G H and Stringer, R A (1968) *Motivation and Organizational Climate*, Harvard University Press, Boston, Mass.

Locke, E A (1984) 'Effect of self-efficacy, goals and task strategies on task performance', *Journal of Applied Psychology*, vol 69 no 2, pp 241–251.

Lorenz, K (1966) *On Aggression*, Methuen, London.

Lowry, P (1990) as reported in *Personnel Management Plus*, December, p. 8.

Lupton, T (1975) 'Best fit in the design of organizations', *Personnel Review*, 4, 1, 1975, pp 15–22.

Luthans, F and Kreitner, R (1975) *Organizational Behaviour Modification*, Scott-Foresman, Glenview, Ill.

Mackay, L and Torrington, D (1986) *The Changing Nature of Personnel Management*, Institute of Personnel Management, London.

MacLachlan, R (1994) 'Robust research — or just headline-seeking analysis?' *Personnel Management Plus*, June, p 9.

Macneil, R (1985) 'Relational contract: what we do and do not know', *Wisconsin Law Review*, pp 483–525.

Maier, N (1958) *The Appraisal Interview*, Wiley, New York.

Mangham, L L (1979) *The Politics of Organizational Change*, Associated Business Press, London.

Manpower Services Commission (1981) *Glossary of Training Terms*, 3rd ed, HMSO, London.

Mant, A (1970) *The Experienced Manager*, British Institute of Management, London.

Marchington, M (1985) *Joint Consultations Revisited*, Glasgow University, Glasgow.

Marchington, M (1995a) 'Fairy tales and magic wands: new employment practices in perspective', *Employee Relations*, Spring, pp 51–66.

Marchington, M (1995b) 'Employee relations', in S Tyson (ed.) *Strategic Prospects for HRM*, Institute of Personnel and Development, London.

Marchingon M and Goodman, J (1992) *New Developments in Employee Involvement*, Employment Department, Sheffield.

Marckham, C (1987) *Practical Consulting*, Institute of Chartered Accountants, London.

Margerison, C (1976) 'A constructive approach to appraisal', *Personnel Management*. July, pp 30–33.

Margerison, C and McCann, R (1986) The Margerison/McCann team management resource: theory and application', *International Journal of Manpower*, vol 7 no 2, pp 1–32.

Marginson, P, Armstrong, P, Edwards P and Purcell, J (1993) 'The control of industrial relations in large companies: an initial analysis of the Second Company Level Industrial Relations Survey', *Warwick Papers in Industrial Relations No. 45*, University of Warwick, Coventry.

Marginson, P and Sisson, K (1990) 'Single table talk', *Personnel Management*, May, pp 46–49.

Marsh, A (1981) *Employee Relations Policy and Decision Making*, Gower, Aldershot.

Martin, A O (1967) *Welfare at Work*, Batsford, London.

Maslow, A (1954) *Motivation and Personality*, Harper & Row, New York.

Mayo, A (1992) 'A framework for career management', *Personnel Management*, February, pp 36–39.

Mayo, E (1933) *Human Problems of an Industrial Civilisation*, Macmillan, London.

Mayo, A and Lank, E (1994) *The Power of Learning*, Institute of Personnel and Development, London.

McClelland, D (1975) *Power, The Inner Experience*, Irvington, New York.

McClelland, G (1963) *British Journal of Industrial Relations*, June, p 278.

McCormick, E J, Jeanneret, P R and Mecham, R C (1972) 'A study of job characteristics and job dimensions based on the Position Analysis Questionnaire (PAQ)', *Journal of Applied Psychology*, vol 56, pp 347–368.

McGregor, D (1960) *The Human Side of Enterprise*, McGraw-Hill, New York.

McLean, A (1981) 'Organization Development: A Case of the Emperor's New Clothes?' *Personnel Review*, vol. 4, no 1, pp 38–46.

Mendenhall, M and Oddou, G (1985) 'The dimensions of expatriate accumulation: a review', *Academy of Management Review*, vol 10, pp 39–47.

Miller, E and Rice, A (1967) *Systems of Organization*, Tavistock, London.

Miller, P (1989) 'Strategic human resource management: what it is and what it isn't', *Personnel Management*, February, pp 46–51.

Miller, P (1991) 'Strategic human resource management: an assessment of progress', *Human Resource Management Journal*, vol 1 no 4, pp 23–39.

Millward, N, Stevens, M, Smart, D and Hawes, W R (1992) *Workplace Industrial Relations in Transition*, Dartmouth Publishing, Hampshire.

Millward, N (1994) *The New Industrial Relations?* Policy Studies Institute, Poole.

Mintzberg, H (1973) *The Nature of Managerial Work*, Harper & Row, New York.

Mintzberg, H (1978) 'Patterns in strategy formation', *Management Science*, May, pp 934–948.

# References

Mintzberg, H (1981) 'Organization Design: Fashion or Fit,' *Harvard Business Review*, January–February, pp 103–116.

Mintzberg, H (1983a) *Power in and Around Organizations*, Prentice-Hall, Englewood Cliffs, NJ.

Mintzberg, H (1983b) *Structure in Fives*, Prentice-Hall, Englewood Cliffs, NJ.

Mintzberg, H (1987) 'Crafting strategy', *Harvard Business Review*, July–August, pp 66–74.

Mintzberg, H, Quinn, J B and James, R M (1988) *The Strategy Process: Concepts, Contexts and Cases*, Prentice-Hall, Englewood Cliffs, NJ.

Mischel, W (1968) *Personality and Assessment*, Wiley, New York.

Mischel, W (1981) *Introduction to Personality*, Holt, Rinehart and Winston, New York.

Monks, J (1994) 'The union response to HRM: fraud or opportunity?' *Personnel Management*, September, pp 42–47.

Monks, K (1992) 'Models of personnel management: a means of understanding the diversity of personnel practices? *Human Resource Management Journal*, vol 3 no 2, pp 29–41.

Moorby, E (1991) *How to Succeed in Employee Development*, McGraw Hill, Maidenhead.

Mowday, R, Porter, L and Steers, R (1982) *Employee–Organization Linkages: The Psychology of Commitment, Absenteeism and Turnover*, Academic Press, London.

Mullen, B and Cooper, C (1994) 'The relation between group cohesiveness and performance: an integration', *Psychological Bulletin*, 115, pp 210–227.

Mumford, A (1993) 'How managers can become developers', *Personnel Management*, June, pp 42–45.

Mumford, A (1994) *Management Development: Strategies for Action*, Institute of Personnel Management, London.

Munro Fraser, J (1954) *A Handbook of Employment Interviewing*, Macdonald and Evans, London.

Murlis, H and Fitt, D (1991) 'Job evaluation in a changing world', *Personnel Management*, May, pp 39–43.

Murphy, J (1993) 'Developing performance through competency frameworks', From proceedings of the annual Hay Management Consultants' conference (unpublished).

Nadler, D A and Tushman, M L (1980) 'A congruence model for diagnosing organizational behaviour', in R H Miles (ed), *Resource Book in Macro-Organizational Behaviour*, Goodyear Publishing, Santa Monica, CA.

Neathey, F (1994) *Job Evaluation in the 1990s*, Industrial Relations Services, London.

Noon, M (1992) 'HRM: a map, model or theory?' in P Blyton, and P Turnbull, (eds), *Reassessing Human Resource Management*, Sage Publications, London.

Ouchi, W G (1981) *Theory Z*, Addison-Wesley, Reading, Mass.

Opsahl, R and Dunnette, M (1966) 'The role of financial compensation in industrial motivation', *Psychological Bulletin*, 66, pp 94–118.

Partridge, B (1989) 'The problem of supervision', in K Sisson, (ed) *Personnel Management in Britain*, Blackwell, Oxford.

Pascale, R (1990) *Managing on the Edge*, Viking, London.

Pascale, R and Athos, A (1981) *The Art of Japanese Management*, Simon & Schuster, New York.

Pearce, J A and Robinson, R B (1988) *Strategic Management: Strategy Formulation and Implementation*, Irwin, Georgetown, Ontario.

Pearn, K and Kandola, R (1993) *Job Analysis*, Institute of Personnel Management, London.

Pedler, M, Boydell, T and Burgoyne, J (1989) 'Towards the learning company', *Management Education and Development*, vol 20.1, pp 1–8.

Perrow, C (1970) *Organizational Analysis. A Sociological View*, Tavistock, London.

Perrow, C (1980) 'The Short and Glorious History of Organizational Theory', R H Miles (ed), *Resource Book in Macro-Organizational Behaviour*, Goodyear Publishing, Santa Monica, CA.

Personnel Standards Lead Body (1993) *A Perspective on Personnel*, London.

Peters, J (1968) *Strategies and Tactics in Labour Negotiations*, McGraw-Hill, New York.

Peters, T (1988) *Thriving on Chaos*, Macmillan, London.

Peters, T and Austin, N (1985) *A Passion for Excellence*, Collins, Glasgow.

Peters, T and Waterman, R (1982) *In Search of Excellence*, Harper & Row, New York.

Pettigrew, A and Whipp, R (1991) *Managing Change for Competitive Success*, Blackwell, Oxford.

Phelps Brown, H (1990) 'The counter revolution of our time', *Industrial Relations*, vol 29 no 1.

Pickard, J (1995) 'Prepare to make a moral judgement' *People Management*.

Porter, L W (1961). 'A study of perceived need satisfaction in bottom and middle management jobs'. *Journal of Applied Psychology*, 45, pp 1–10.

Porter, L W and Lawler, E E (1968) *Managerial Attitudes and Performance*, Irwin-Dorsey, Homewood, Illinois.

Porter, L W, Steers, R, Mowday, R and Boulian, P (1974) 'Organizational commitment, job satisfaction and turnover amongst psychiatric technicians', *Journal of Applied Psychology*, vol 59, pp 603–609.

Porter, M (1980) *Competitive Strategy*, The Free Press, New York.

Porter, M (1985) *Competitive Advantage: Creating and Sustaining Superior Performance*, The Free Press, New York.

Prahalad, C K and Hamel, G (1990) 'The core competences of the corporation', *Harvard Business Review*, May–June, pp 79–91.

Pritchard, D and Murlis, H (1992) *Jobs, Roles and People*, Nicholas Brearley, London.

Purcell, J (1979) 'A strategy for management control in industrial relations', in J Purcell and R Smith (eds) *The Control of Work*, Macmillan, London, 4 May, pp 22–25.

Purcell, J (1987) 'Mapping management styles in employee relations' *Journal of Management Studies*, September.

Purcell, J (1989) 'The impact of corporate strategy on human resource management', in J Storey (ed) *New Perspectives on Human Resource Management*, Routledge, London.

Purcell, J (1993) 'The challenge of human resource management for industrial relations research and practice', *The International Journal of Human Resource Management*, vol 4 no 3, pp 511–527.

Purcell, J (1994) 'Personnel earns a place on the board', *Personnel Management*, February, pp 26–29.

Purcell, J and Sisson, K (1983) 'Strategies and practice in the management of industrial relations', in G Bain (ed) *Industrial Relations in Britain*, Blackwell, Oxford.

Quinn Mills, D (1983) 'Planning with people in mind', *Harvard Business Review*, November–December.

Rackham, N, Honey, P and Colbert, M (1967) *Developing Interactive Skills*, Wellens Publishing, Northampton.

Reay, D G (1994) *Understanding How People Learn*, Kogan Page, London.

# References

Recruitment and Development Report (1991) 'New ways of managing your human resources: a survey of top employers', *Industrial Relations Review*, March.

*Report of the Royal Commission on Trade Unions and Employer's Associations* (1968) HMSO, London.

Revans, R W (1971) *Developing Effective Managers*, Longman, Harlow.

Revans, R W (1989) *Action Learning*, Blond and Briggs, London.

Richards-Carpenter, C (1993) 'Preparing for the next leap forward', *Personnel Management*, April, p 69.

Richards-Carpenter, C (1994) 'Another year of growth', *Personnel Management*, May, pp 19–20.

Richardson, W (1993) 'The visionary leader', *Administator*, September, pp 3–7.

Roberts, C (1990) *Harmonization: Whys and Wherefores*, Institute of Personnel Management, London.

Robertson, I T and Cooper, C L (1983) *Human Behaviour in Organizations*, Macdonald & Evans, Plymouth.

Robertson, I T and Smith, M (1985) *Motivation and Job Design*, Institute of Personnel Management, London.

Robertson, I T, Smith, M and Cooper, C L (1992) *Motivation*, Institute of Personnel Management, London.

Rodger, A (1952) *The Seven-Point Plan*, National Institute of Industrial Psychology, London.

Roethlisberger, F and Dickson, W (1939) *Management and the Worker*, Harvard University Press, Cambridge, Mass.

Rousseau, D M and Wade-Benzoni, K A (1994) 'Linking strategy and human resource practices: how employee and customer contracts are created', *Human Resource Management*, Fall, vol 33 no 3, pp 463–489.

Rousseau, D M and Greller, M M (1994) 'Human resource practices: administrative contract makers', *Human Resource Management*, vol 33 no 3, pp 385–401.

Salancik, G R (1977) 'Commitment and the control of organizational behaviour and belief', in B M Staw and G R Salancik (eds), *New Directions in Organizational Behaviour*, St Clair Press, Chicago.

Saville, P and Sik, G (1992) 'Personality questionnaires: current issues and controversies', *Human Resources Management Yearbook*, A P Services, London, pp 28–32.

Schein, E H (1965) *Organizational Psychology*, Prentice-Hall, Englewood Cliffs, NJ.

Schein, E H (1969) *Process Consultation: Its Role in Organizational Development*, Addison-Wesley, Reading, Mass.

Schein, E H (1977) *Career Dynamics*, Addison-Wesley, Reading, Mass.

Schein, E H (1984) 'Coming to a new awareness of culture', *Sloan Management Review*, Winter.

Schein, E H (1987) *Organization Culture and Leadership*, Jossey Bass, New York.

Schmitt, N, Gooding, R Z, Noe, R A and Kirsch, M (1984) 'Meta-analysis of validity studies published between 1964 and 1982 and the investigation of study characteristics', *Personnel Psychology*, vol 37, no 3, pp 407–422.

Schumacher, E F (1973) *Small is Beautiful*, Blond and Briggs, London.

Schumacher, E F (1976/1977) 'Structuring Work', *Industrial Participation*, Winter, pp 4–7.

Schuster, J R and Zingheim, P K (1992) *The New Pay*, Lexington Books, New York.

Scullion, H (1991) 'Why companies prefer to use expatriates', *Personnel Management*, November.

Scullion, H (1995) 'International HRM', in J Storey (ed) *Human Resource Management: A Critical Text*, Routledge, London.

Selznick, P (1957) *Leadership and Administration,*. Row, Evanston, Il.

Senge, P (1990) *The Fifth Discipline: The Art and Practice of the Learning Organization*, Random Century, New York.

Sheard, A (1992) 'Learning to improve performance', *Personnel Management*, November, pp 40–45.

Sheehy, G (1976) *Passages: Predictable Crises of Adult Life*, Dutton, New York.

Silverman, D (1970) *The Theory of Organizations: A Sociological Framework*, Heinemann, London.

Sims, R R (1994) 'Human resource management's role in clarifying the new psychological contract', *Human Resource Management*, vol 33 no 3, pp 373–382.

Singh, R (1989) 'Negotiations', in B Towers (ed) *A Handbook of Industrial Relations Practice*, Kogan Page, London.

Sisson, K (1990) 'Introducing the Human Resource Management Journal', *Human Resource Management Journal*, vol 1 no 1, pp 1–11.

Sisson, K (1995) 'Human resource management and the personnel function', in J Storey (ed.) *Human Resource Management: A Critical Text*, Routledge, London.

Skinner, B F (1974) *About Behaviourism*, Knopf, New York.

Sloan, A P (1963) *My Years With General Motors*, Doubleday, New York.

Smith, M (1988) 'Calculating the sterling values of selection', *Guidance and Assessment Review*, 4.1, pp 6–8.

Smith, M (1984) *Survey Item Blank*, MCB Publications, Bradford.

Smith, P and Morton, G (1993) 'Union exclusion and decollectivisation of industrial relations in contemporary Britain', *British Journal of Industrial Relations*, vol 31 no 1, pp 97–114.

Spencer, L, McClelland, D and Spencer, S (1990) *Competency Assessment Methods*, Hay/McBer Research Press, Boston.

Spindler, G S (1994) 'Psychological contracts in the workplace: a lawyer's view', *Human Resource Management*, vol 33 no 3, pp 325–333.

Stacey, R D (1993) 'Strategy as order emerging from chaos', *Long Range Planning*, 26(1), pp 10–17.

Stanton, M (1992) 'Organization and human resource management', in M Armstrong (ed) *Strategies for Human Resource Management*, Kogan Page, London.

Stevens, B (1990) Quoted at conference of the Institute of Personnel Management (unpublished).

Stevens, J (1995) 'People management in transition', *Human Resources Management Yearbook*, AP Information Services, London.

Storey, J (1987) 'Developments in the management of human resources: an interim report', *Warwick Papers on Industrial Relations*, No 17, University of Warwick.

Storey, J (1989) 'From personnel management to human resource management', in Storey, J (ed) *New Perspectives on Human Resource Management*, Routledge, London.

Storey, J (1992a) *New Developments in the Management of Human Resources*, Blackwell, Oxford.

Storey, J (1992b) 'HRM in action: the truth is out at last', *Personnel Management*, April, pp 28–31.

# References

Storey, J (1993) 'The take-up of human resource management by mainstream companies: key lessons from research', *The International Journal of Human Resource Management*, vol 4 no 3, pp 529–557.

Storey, J (1995) 'Human resource management: still marching on or marching out?' in J Storey (ed) *Human Resource Management: A Critical Text*, Routledge, London.

Storey, J and Sisson, K (1990) 'Limits to transformation: human resource management in the British context', *Industrial Relations Journal*, vol 21 no 1, pp 60–65.

Strauss, G and Sayles, L R (1972) *Personnel: The Human Problems of Management*, Prentice-Hall, Eaglewood Cliffs, NJ.

Tannenbaum, S I, Beard, R L and Sales, E (1992) 'Team building and its influence on team effectiveness: an examination of conceptual and empirical developments', in K Kelley (ed) *Issues, Theory and Research in Industrial/Organizational Psychology*, North Holland, London.

Taylor, F W (1911) *Principles of Scientific Management*, New York, Harper.

Thurley, K (1979) *Supervision: A Reappraisal*, Heinemann, London.

Thurley, K (1981) 'Personnel management: a case for urgent treatment', *Personnel Management*, August, pp 24–29.

Thurstone, L L (1940) 'Current issues in factor analysis', *Psychological Bulletin*, vol 30.

Toplis, J, Dulewicz, V and Fletcher, C (1991) *Psychological Testing*, Institute of Personnel Management, London.

Torrington, D P (1989) 'Human resource management and the personnel function', in J Storey (ed), *New Perspectives on Human Resource Management*, Routledge, London.

Torrington, D P (1994) *International Personnel Management*, Prentice Hall, Hemel Hempstead.

Torrington, D P and Cooper, C L (1977) 'The management of stress in organisations and the personnel initiative', *Personnel Review*, Summer, pp 48–54.

Torrington, D and Hall, L (1995) *Personnel Management: A New Approach*, Prentice-Hall, Englewood Cliffs, NJ.

Townley, B (1989) 'Selection and appraisal: reconstructing social relations?' in J Storey (ed) *New Perspectives in Human Resource Management*, Routledge, London.

Training Agency (1988) *Competence and Assessment*, Standards Methodology Unit, Sheffield.

Training Agency (1988–90) *The Development of Assessable Standards of Occupational Competence*, Training Agency, Sheffield.

Trist, E L, Higgin G W, Murray, H and Pollack, A B (1963) *Organizational Choice*, Tavistock, London.

Tsui, A S and Gomez-Mejia, L R (1988) 'Evaluating human resource effectiveness', in L Dyer (ed), *Human Resource Management: Evolving Roles and Responsibilities*, Bureau of National Affairs, Washington DC.

Tuckman, B (1965) 'Development sequences in small groups', *Psychological Bulletin*, 63.

Turner, A N and Lawrence, P R (1965) *Industrial Jobs and the Worker: An Investigation of Response to Task Attributes*, Harvard University Graduate School of Business Administration, Boston, Mass.

Tyler, T R and Bies, R J (1990) 'Beyond formal procedures: the interpersonal context of procedural justice', in J S Carrol (ed), *Applied Social Psychology and Organizational Settings*, Lawrence Earlbaum, Hillsdale, NJ.

Tyson, S (1985) 'Is this the very model of a modern personnel manager', *Personnel Management*, 26, pp 35–39.

Tyson, S (1987) 'The management of the personnel function', *Journal of Management Studies*, September, pp 523–532.

Tyson, S and Fell, A (1986) *Evaluating the Personnel Function*, Hutchinson, London.

Tyson, S and Witcher, M (1994) 'Getting in gear: post-recession HR management', *Personnel Management*, August, pp 20–23.

Urwick, L F (1947) *Dynamic Administration*, Pitman, London.

Vernon, P E (1961) *The Structure of Human Abilities*, Methuen, London.

Von Bertalanffy, L (1952) 'Theoretical models in biology and psychology', in G Lindzay (ed), *Handbook of Social Psychology*, Addison-Wesley, Cambridge, Mass.

Vroom, V (1964) *Work and Motivation*, Wiley, New York.

Walker, J W (1992) *Human Resource Strategy*, McGraw-Hill, New York.

Walton, R E (1969) *Interpersonal Peacemaking: Confrontations and Third Party Peacemaking*, Addison-Wesley, Reading, Mass.

Walton, R E (1985a) 'From control to commitment in the workplace', *Harvard Business Review*, 63, pp 76–84.

Walton, R E (1985b) 'Towards a strategy of eliciting employee commitment based on principles of mutuality', in R E Walton and P R Lawrence (eds), *HRM Trends and Challenges*, Harvard Business School Press, Boston, Mass.

Walton, R E and McKersie, R B (1965) *Behavioural Theory of Labour Negotiations*, McGraw-Hill, New York.

Ward, P (1995) 'A 360-degree turn for the better', *People Management*, February, pp 20–22.

Ware, J and Barnes, L (1991) 'Managing interpersonal conflict,' in J Gabarro, (ed), *Managing People and Organizations*, Harvard Business School Publications, Boston, Mass.

Waterman, R (1988) *The Renewal Factor*, Bantam, New York.

Watson, A (1977) *The Personnel Managers*, Routledge and Kegan Paul, London.

Weber, M (1946) *From Max Weber*, H H Gerth and C W Mills (eds), Oxford University Press, Oxford.

Wedderburn, Lord (1989) 'Freedom of association and philosophies of labour law', *Industrial Law Journal*, 18, p 28.

Weiner, B (1974) *Achievement Motivation and Attribution Theory*, General Learning Press, New Jersey.

Welch, J (1991) Quoted in *Managing People and Organizations*, J Gabarro (ed), Harvard Business School Publications, Boston, Mass.

West, M A and Slater J A (1995) 'Teamwork: myths, reality and research', *Occupational Psychologist*, April, pp 24–29.

Wheatley, M (1994) 'Is nothing sacred', *Human Resources*, Spring, pp 8–12.

Wheeler, R (1995) 'Developing IT strategies for human resources', *Human Resource Management Yearbook*, APS, London.

Whipp, R (1992) 'HRM: competition and strategy', in P Blyton and P. Turnbull (eds), *Reassessing Human Resource Management*, Sage Publications, London.

Whittington, R (1991) *What is Strategy and Does it Matter?*, Routledge, London.

Wickens, P (1987) *The Road to Nissan*, Macmillan, London.

Wick, C W and Leon, L S (1995) 'From ideas to action: creating a learning organization', *Human Resource Management*, vol 34 no 2, pp 299–311.

Williamson, E E and Ouchi, W C (1983) 'The markets and hierarchical programmes of research, origins, implications and prospects', in Francis, A, Turk, J and Willmar, P, (eds), *Power, Efficiency and Institutions,*. Heinemann, London.

# References

Wilson, N A B (1973) *On the Quality of Working Life*, HMSO, London.

Wood, S (1996) 'High commitment management and organization in the UK', *The International Journal of Human Resource Management*, February, pp 41–58.

Woodruffe, C (1990) *Assessment Centres*, Institute of Personnel Management, London.

Woodruffe, C (1991) 'Competent by any other name', *Personnel Management*, September, pp 30–33.

Woodward, J (1965) *Industrial Organization*, Oxford University Press, Oxford.

Woodward, J (1968) 'Resistance to change,' *Management International Review*, Vol. 8.

Wooldridge, B and Floyd, S W (1990) 'The strategy process, middle management involvement and organizational performance', *Strategic Management Journal*, 11, pp 231–241.

Wright, V (1991) 'Performance-related pay', in F Neale (ed), *The Handbook of Performance Management*, Institute of Personnel Management, London.

Wright, V and Brading, L (1992) 'A balanced performance', *Total Quality Magazine*, October, pp 275–278.

Wright, P M and Snell, S A (1989) 'Towards an integrative view of strategic human resource management', *Human Resource Management Review*, vol 1 no 3, pp 203–225.

Wright, D S and Taylor, A (1970) *Introducing Psychology*, Penguin, Harmondsworth.

# Subject Index

abilities, use of 382
ability 265–6, 307
absence control – use of computers 861
absenteeism 499–500, 839–40
ACAS *see* Advisory, Conciliation and
    Arbitration Service
accident prevention
    accident reports 817
    achievement of 815
    building safety into the system 816
    identifying causes 815–16
    safety inspections 816
accident reports 817
achievement bonuses 661
achievement motivation 202
achievement needs 304
action learning 545, 894
action research 394
accountabilities 228–9
activity-based costing 70
adaptive behaviour 277
added value
    contribution of the personnel function to
        108–9
    defined 108
    and gainsharing 679
    per £ of employment costs 487
adhocracies 340
advertising
    analysing requirements 453–4
    copy writing 454–6
    designing the advertisement 456
    evaluate response 457
    media planning 456
    objectives 453
    using an advertising agency 454
Advisory, Conciliation and Arbitration Service
    (ACAS) 43, 389, 630, 712, 735, 750–1, 758

affiliation needs 304
affirmative action 182
affluent workers 279
age and employment 182, 843
age as a predictor of performance 479
age distribution, analysis of 417
ageing 273
agency theory 596–7
aggression 276
AIDS policy 182
Alderfer's ERG theory of motivation 303–4
allocation of work 376
allowances and other payments 592, 685–6
ambiguities in the personnel contribution 90–2
Anglia Polytechnic University 762
annual hours 440
annuity approach to pay progression 595
appeals, job evaluation 629
application forms 461
appraisal 234–5
    *see also* performance management
apprenticeship 547
aptitude tests 474
arbitration 751–2
artifacts 364
assertiveness training 902
assessment *see* performance management and
        performance review
assessment centres 202, 463–4
assets, human resources as 141
assignments 895–6
attachment to the organization 319
attainment tests 475
attendance management 838–40
attitude surveys
    approach 782–3
    assessing results 784
    and attitudes 283

methods 783–4
use of 88, 782
attitudes 276, 282–3
attributes 205
attribution theory 274–5, 282, 311
attrition 699
auditing the reward system 697
authority 330
autonomous work groups 384

balanced score card 104–5
Bales analysis 394
bargaining
collective 55, 714, 726, 748–9, 726
conjunctive 715
conventions 765–6
cooperative 715
distributive 715
integrative 716–17
nature of 763
power 714–15
process of 764–5, 770–1
skills 772–3
base/basic pay
additions to 591–2
defined 590–1
behaviour and competence 190
behaviour at work
aggression 276
attitudes 276
factors affecting 275–6
frustration 276
stress 277
and values 242
behavioural
analysis 205
commitment 296, 316
competences 190
dimensions 189
interview 468, 469
modification 317–18
scientists 33
theory of motivation 310, 312
behavioural science
movement 34
and organizational development 334, 391
school of organization theory 332–5,
behaviourally anchored rating scales (BARS)
255–6
behaviourally-based interviews 202, 469
Belbin's team roles 352–3
benchmark jobs 215, 623
benchmarking
defined 522
and personnel management 34, 80, 127–8
and productivity 26, 430
and world class performance 40

bereavement 825
best fit 39, 45, 80, 185–6, 373
best practice 34, 39, 80, 98, 185–6
Binet-type intelligence tests 472
biodata 461–2
blockages and barriers to personnel
management
from employees 86
within management 85–6
bonuses
achievement 661
defined 591, 659
executive 666–7, 694
group 677
and incentives 659–60
for sales staff 690
Boots the Chemist 106
bottom line 58, 108
BP 197–8
Brayfield and Rothe Index of Job Satisfaction
783
briefing groups *see* team briefing
British Psychological Society 476
British Rates and Data (BRAD) 456
British Standards Institution (BSI) 669–70
broad-banded pay structures
advantages and disadvantages 647–8
characteristics of 645–6
defining bands 646–7
pay progression in 647
*Bromley and Others v H & J Quick (1988)* 622,
630
budgets, pay 696–7
bulletins 799
Bullock Committee 776, 790
bureaucracy 335
bureaucratic organization 335–6
bureaucratic structure 339
business manager model of personnel
management 60
business partner, personnel director as 100
business plans 508
business process re-engineering 41, 81
business strategy 160, 172, 410

Cadbury Report 94, 692–3
Cadbury Schweppes 198
CADCAM 548
cafeteria system 682
call-out allowances 686
career analysis 572
career counselling 585
career development 434–5
Career Development and Outplacement
Association 495
career dynamics 488–9, 572, 574
career expectations 286

career management
  aims 571
  defined 29, 571
  demand and supply forecasts 578–9
  in delayered organizations 586
  policies 576–7
  process of 572–5
  use of computers 861
career planning
  for core managers 583–4
  defined 571
  for individuals 584–5
  modelling a 'career prospectus' 426
  process of 582
  techniques 585
career progression 583
careers
  and age 273
  and the future of work 285
case study 899–900
CBI *see* Confederation of British Industry
Central Arbitration Committee 735
Certification Officer 736
chain of command 342
change
  and organizational culture 344
  management of 344
  models 395–9
  resistance to 277–8, 362
  significance of 343–4
  types of change 345
change agents 111
change management
  contribution of personnel function 111–12
  and culture management 368
  guidelines 399–400
  and organizational development 390
  requirements 344
change models
  Bandura's 397–8
  Beckhard's 396
  Beer *et al*'s 398–9
  Lewin's 395
  Thurley's 396–7
check list – job analysis 211
check-off system 753
chief executives 80
child care facilities 828
Civil Service 45, 198
classical school of organization theory 330–1
climate *see* organizational climate
closed questions 470
closed shop 753
coaching 892–3
code of ethics 94–5
Code of Professional Conduct, IPD 93
cognitive learning 514

cognitive learning theory 306–10, 517
coherence
  achievement of 76–8, 177–8
  through competence frameworks 201
  defined 76
  and horizontal integration 76
  and human resource management 163
  and performance management 232
  and personnel strategies 177–8
  and strategic HRM 162, 167–8
collective bargaining
  arrangements 748–9
  bargaining levels 748–9
  bargaining power 714–15
  conjunctive bargaining 715
  cooperative bargaining 715
  coverage 726
  decentralization of 55
  decline of 726
  defined 714
  dispute resolution 750–1
  distributive 715
  integrative 716–17
  as a joint regulating process 714
  multi-employer 726, 748
  nature of 714
  plant-level 748
  policy 738
  single-table bargaining 749
collectivism 707, 717, 739–40
command and control 355
commission payments 591, 689
Commission for Racial Equality (CRE) 841–2
Commissioner for the Rights of Trade Union
      Members 736
commitment
  attachment to the organization 319
  to change 396
  and communications 325
  and compliance 147, 355
  and control 320
  and culture 362
  defined 319
  drive for 718
  and education 325
  and employee involvement 776
  high commitment management 328
  and human resource management 144, 762
  impact of 323–4
  increasing 435
  Japanese model 320
  meaning of 319
  model of organization 341
  and motivation 323
  and mutual commitment firms 327–8
  mutual commitment strategy 328
  and mutuality 143, 327

and ownership 326
and performance 323
and performance management 326
as a policy goal 144
problems with the concept 149, 321–2
and reward management 327
and a sense of excitement in the job 326
significance of 319–21
strategy 320–1, 324–7
and training 325–6
communications
analysing communication problems 798
areas 795, 796
downwards 778
importance of 666
nature of 793–4
need for 794–5
objectives 795, 796
and organizations 346
strategy 795, 796
systems 798–801
what employees want to hear 797
what management wants to say 797
communicating to employees on reward
generally 704–5
individually 705
Company Level Industrial Relations Survey
(CLIRS) 727
compa-ratio analysis 698–9
compensation management 588
see also employee reward
competence(s)
applications 200–3
areas of 193–4
behavioural competences 190
and career progression 583
clusters of competences 196
and coherence 77–8
competence definition, example of 198–9
concept of competence 188, 189, 270
constituents of competence 194–5
core competences 190–1
criterion referenced competences 190
criterion validated competences 190
definition of competence 189–90, 539, 583
describing competences 196
and development centres 569
differentiating competences 191–2, 199–200
and employee development 202–3
and employee reward 203
forecasting requirements 415
frameworks 77, 196, 203
generic competences 190–1, 202
and integrated personnel management 201
lists 196–8
maps 100, 101, 136, 203
meaning of competence 192

modelling 858
and NVQs 190, 192, 203
occupational competences 190
and pay progression 674
personal competences 190
in personnel management 100–2
and performance management 29, 202
profiles 77, 111, 196
and recruitment and selection 201–2, 446–7,
449–50
specific competences 190–1
threshold competences 191
types of competences 190–2
using the concept of competence 195
work based competences 190
competence analysis
approaches to 219
choice of approach 225
critical incident technique 222–3
defined 205, 219
expert opinion method 219
functional analysis 222
repertory grid 224–5
and role analysis 216
structured interview method 219–20
and training specifications 539
workshop method 220–2
competence-based job evaluation 617, 650
competence-based management development
568–9
competence-related pay
approach 674
defined 592, 674
competence-related personnel management
188
competency 193
competitive advantage
achievement of 164
causes of 106, 109, 110
contribution of personnel function to
109–10
impact on personnel strategy 176
and HRM 114, 719
as a key concept of strategic management
159
and raising the skills base 510
competitive pressures 39–42
compliance
and commitment 147
in groups 274
computer-based training 896–7
computer integrated manufacturing (CIM) 415
computer-managed learning 860–1
computerized personnel information systems
(CPIS)
applications 856–63
benefits of 850

choice of hardware 854
database management 854–5
developing a CPIS 853–6
development programme 855–6
IT strategy for CPIS 850–3
and line managers 850, 852–3
preferred characteristics of a CPIS 853–4
software 855
strategic decision-taking 851
computerized personnel information systems
    (CPIS) – applications
absence control 861
career management 861
competence modelling 858
computer-managed learning 860–1
employee profiling 857–8
employee scheduling 857
employee turnover modelling and control
    857
equal opportunity monitoring 861–2
expert systems 862–3
human resource planning 856
job evaluation 629, 862–3
performance management 860
personnel records 856
recruitment 859
reward management 859–60
training administration 860–1
skills inventories and audits 858
conciliation 750
conditioning 317
Confederation of British Industry (CBI) 51, 591,
    603, 662, 734, 777
conflict 357, 435–6
conflict in the personnel contribution 92–3
conflict resolution 92–3, 400–2
conformist innovators 59
conjunctive bargaining 715
constructs 224
consultation *see* joint consultation
content theory of motivation 301
contingency approach
    to leadership 354–5
    to organization design 373
    to personnel management 53–4
contingency school of organization theory
    337–9
contingency theory 37–9
continuing professional development (IPD)
    103
continuous development
    conditions for continuous development
        524–5
    as a lever for change 111
    and performance management 244
    philosophy 524
    and training 533

continuous improvement
    concept 113
    and employee development 507
    and quality 115, 116
continuous learning, management of 236
contracts
    psychological 287, 288–93
    relational 287
    transactional 287
contracts of employment
    fixed/short-term 285
    flexible 427–8
    information required 834–5
    legal requirements 833–4
    mobility clauses 835
    and recruitment 483
contribution, paying for 659
contribution of personnel function to
        organizational success
    areas of contribution 110
    contribution to added value 108–9
    contribution to change management
        111–12
    contribution to competitive advantage
        109–10
    contribution to continuous improvement
        112–13
    contribution to quality management 113–16
    extent of contribution 106–8
    organizational success defined 104
cooperative bargaining 715, 760
coordination 320
core competences 190–1
core workers 341, 345, 359, 437, 438, 722
corporate culture *see* organizational culture
corporate governance 692
corporate strategy 160–1, 173–4, 177
cost leadership 76
counselling 835–6
counselling services 828
craft training 547–8
criterion behaviour 540, 553
criterion-referenced assessment 270
criterion-referenced competences 190
criterion-validated competences 190
critical-incident technique 222–3
critical success factors 160
culture *see* organizational culture
culture management
    aims of 368–9
    approaches to 369–70
    and culture change 368
    defined 368
    programmes 371
    and reward management 371
    and strategy 176
    strategies 370–1

# Subject Index

CVs 461, 495
cybernetic theory of learning 517

damage control 806
data 849
database management 854–5
Data Protection Act 856
day rates 653
decentralization 377
decentralized organizations 358–9
deficiency model of training 536
defined benefit pension scheme 685
defined contribution pension scheme 685
degeneration of incentive schemes 670–1
delayered organizations and careers 586
delayering 377
demand and supply forecasting models 424–7
demand forecasting
    basis of 411
    defined 410, 411
    managerial judgement method 413
    methods 412–15
    modelling 415
    planning data 411–12
    ratio-trend analysis 413–14
    work study techniques 414–15
'demographic time bomb' 410
demographics 410, 431
demonstration 892
demotivation 434
Department of Employment 791
dependency culture 89
derecognition, union 738, 741, 746, 747
development
    defined 508
    and learning 513
    model of 272–3
    self-development 559
    stages of 272
development centres 203, 569–70, 585
development of people over time
    ageing 273
    maturation 271–2
    process of development 272–3
deviant innovators 59
diaries 214
differentials, pay 639, 642, 698
differentiating competences 191–2, 199–200
differentiation in organizations 338, 376
directors' and senior executives' rewards
    base salary 693–4
    benefits 695
    bonus schemes 694
    service contracts 695
    share option schemes 694
    share ownership schemes 695

discipline
    approach to handling disciplinary problems 500
    incapability 498
    natural justice 500
    policy 182
    poor timekeeping 499–500
    procedure 500, 905–6
    professional approach to 488
    unfair dismissal 496–7
discussion 899
dismissal
    for absenteeism or poor timekeeping 499–500
    definition of 495–6
    fair dismissal 496
    for incapability 498
    legal framework 495–500
    reasonable in the circumstances 497
    unfair dismissal 496–7
dispute resolution 750–1
dissatisfaction 435–6
dissatisfiers 305
distance learning 903
distributive bargaining 715
diversity, management of 130, 183, 842–3
divisionalized organizations 358
domestic problems 825–6
dominant coalition 186
Donovan Commission 723–4
downsizing 285, 411, 441, 486, 488, 489
drivers of organizational performance 111

earnings drift 667
earnings, total 592
economic management 42
education defined 508
efficiency wage theory 595–6
effort bargain 653
elderly and retired employees 826–7
electronic CVs 461
employee assistance programmes 828–9
employee benefits
    choice 682–3
    defined 592, 681
    objectives 681
    taxation 682
    types 681–2
employee contracts
    fixed/short-term 285
    flexible 427–8
    information required 834–5
    legal requirements 833–4
    mobility clauses 835
    and recruitment 483
employee development
    activities 507–8

aims 507
context 510–11
defined 29, 505, 507
evaluating the employee development
    contribution 512
international 134–6
marketing of 511–12
philosophy 510
policy 184
strategy 508–10
employee handbooks 293
employee involvement
    aims 776–7
    attitude surveys 782–4
    contribution to business success 777
    defined 29, 775, 777
    and employee participation 776
    and empowerment 387
    financial 779
    in job evaluation 623
    joint consultation 778–9
    levels 779–80, 781
    mechanisms 780, 782
    quality circles 784–6
    requirements for success 791–2
    in reward system design and management
        666
    suggestion schemes 786–7
employee participation
    aims 776–7
    defined 775–6
    and employee involvement 776
    financial 779
    levels 779–80, 781
    mechanisms 780, 782
    planning 792–3
    requirements for success 791–2
    shared decision-making 780
employee profiling 857–8
employee relations
    climate 709, 752
    context 721–2
    defined 29, 707–8, 737
    economic context 721
    elements of 711–12
    and HRM 762
    and industrial relations 707–8
    informal processes 751–2
    international context 722
    objectives 741–2
    organizational context 722
    policy 738–41
    political context 721
    procedures 757
    role of management 733–4
    strategy 742–3
    *see also* industrial relations

employee relations climate
    building trust 745
    defined 743–4
    an ethical approach 744–5
    improving and maintaining the climate 744,
        752
employee relations policies
    areas 738–9
    choices 739–40
    expression of 741
    formulation 740–1
    nature 738
    purpose 738
employee relations strategies
    formulation of 743
    nature 742
    purpose 742
    strategic directions 743
employee resourcing
    defined 403
    policies 406
    strategy 409–11
employee reward
    achieving the aims 598–9
    aims 597–8
    and competence-related pay 203, 588
    defined 29, 588, 589
    developments 603–4
    elements of 590–3
    employee reward system 589–90
    overall aim 597
    specific aims 598–9
    strategy 598, 600–1
employee satisfaction measures 126
employee services *see* welfare
employee scheduling 857
employee share option plan (ESOP) 680
employee turnover or wastage
    analysis of reasons for 502
    choice of measurement 422
    half-life index 422
    length of service analysis 419
    monitoring 857
    reason for analysis 417
    retention plan 433–6
    stability index 419
    survival rate 419–21
    turnover or wastage index 418
employees
    blockages and barriers 86
    gaining support and commitment 87–8
employer's associations 734
employment
    contracts 833
    international 131–3
    policies 181–2
    problems 826

terms and conditions 833–5
Employment Act (1982) 480
Employment Appeal Tribunal (EAT) 736
employment legislation 42–3
Employment Protection (Consolidation) Act
    (1978) 480
employment relationship
    and agency theory 596–7
    contractual basis 287
    and employee relations 707, 738
    in Europe 48
    management of 293–4
    nature of 286–7
    power basis 287
    and the psychological contract 287, 289
empowerment
    defined 79, 384, 385
    and line managers 80
    management style 387
    process of 386–7
    reasons for 386
    structural empowerment 386–7
environmental factors 37
equal opportunity
    code of conduct 840–1
    monitoring 861
    policy 181, 182–3
Equal Opportunity Commission (EOC) 43, 630
Equal Pay Act 1970 630
equal pay for work of equal value
    and analytical job evaluation 622
    and job families 649
    legislation 629–30
equity
    and personnel policy 180
    policy on 601
    theory 309–10
    types of 309
ERG theory of motivation 303–4
esteem needs 302
ethical approach to employee relations 744–5
ethical considerations in organizational release
    488
ethical framework for recruitment and
    selection 480–1
ethical standards in the firm 94–5
ethics in personnel and development 93–5
ethics training and development programme
    95
ethnic monitoring 181, 841–2
European approach to personnel management
    50
European Commission 47
European Court of Justice 47
European diversity 48–50
European Union
    directives 46–7

legislation 177, 186
    Social Chapter 46, 722
    Social Charter 46, 722
    social policies 46
    Social Protocol 46, 48
European Works Council Directive (1994) 50,
    790
evaluating the employee development
    contribution 512
evaluating the personnel function contribution
    achievement of specified goals 122–3
    approaches to 117–18, 128
    benchmarking 127–8
    employee behaviour criteria 121
    employee satisfaction measures 126
    evaluation criteria 119
    factors 116
    individual evaluation 126
    methods 118–19, 120–8
    output criteria 118
    performance measures 119
    personnel department service-level criteria
        121–2
    process criteria 118
    quantitative criteria 120–1
    service level agreements 123–4
    subjective evaluation 124–5
    surveys 117
    user reaction 125
    utility analysis 126–7
evaluating the recruitment process 479–80
evaluating the reward system 697–9
evaluation of training 553–5
exemplar role of state as employer 45
existence needs 303
exit interviews 433, 501–2
ExecuGROW 579
executive bonus and incentive schemes 666–7
executive search consultants 458
expatriates
    management of 136–8
    pay 690–2
expectancy theory of motivation 306–8
expectations 275, 312
experienced worker's standard (EWS) 270, 514
experiential learning 517, 568
expert systems
    and career management 579
    defined 862
    development of 862
    use in job evaluation 629, 862–3
external environment 37, 176, 367, 374
external labour market 405–6
external relativities 590, 638–9, 698
extrinsic motivation 299, 306

factor analysis 230

factor plan, job evaluation 610–11, 614
factor rating scales 512
factor weighting 613–14
factors, job evaluation
  choice of 611–12
  defined 611
  examples 612, 613
  number of 611
faults analysis 218
federal firm/organization 341–2
feedback
  and learning 516
  and motivation 308
  and performance management 249
  360–degree feedback 251
  to poor performers 247
felt-fair principle 315
field force analysis 395
final offer arbitration 751
final salary pension scheme 685
financial flexibility 345
financial incentives 314–15, 659
financial involvement 779
financial rewards 659
five-fold grading system 449
fixation 276
fixed-term contracts 285
flat rates 653
flexibility
  contract-based 427–8
  developments in 285
  financial 345
  functional 345, 428–9
  HRM approach 144
  job-based 428–9
  multiskilling 429–30
  numerical 345
  organization-based 430
  organizational 376–7
  plan 436–40
  as a policy goal of HRM 144
  skill-based 429–30
  time-based 428
flexible firm 40, 345
flexible hours 439–40
flexible labour force 341
flexible manufacturing system (FMS) 548
flexible organizations 359
focus groups 88, 783, 784
follow-up (selection) 485
forced distribution 254
forecasting (human resource planning)
  demand forecasting 412–15
  models 424–7
  supply forecasting 416–25
formal groups 347
formal organization 331, 333

frustration 276
full employment policies 745
functional analysis 190, 193
functional flexibility 428–9

gaining support and commitment to
    personnel
  from employees 87–8
  from line management 87
  from top management 86–7
gainsharing 679
GE Plastics 647
General Motors 241
generic competences 190–1, 196, 197
generic role definitions, examples of 874–6
generic roles 231
global
  competition 39, 50, 290
  context 50–1
  markets 51
  strategy 51
  trends 51
goal directed behaviour 296
goal theory of motivation 308
goals 296, 527–8
  see also objectives
Gordon Personal Profile and Inventory 269
governance, corporate 692
government agencies 43
government, role of in setting personnel
    agenda 42–5
government services 43
grade definitions and job classification 609
grade drift 644
graded pay structures
  advantages and disadvantages 643–5
  broad-banded 645–8
  defined 640
  differentials 642
  design of 644–5
  features of 640–3
  job grades 641
  and job ranking 609
  overlap 642
  pay ranges 642–3
  progression through ranges 642–3
  reference point 642
grading jobs 645, 701
graphology 478
Greenbury Report 693
grievances
  handling 835–6
  policy 182
  procedure 904
group
  behaviour 345–50
  cohesion 435

# Subject Index

development 349–50
formal groups 347
identification 350
ideology 349
informal groups 347
interaction 348–9
norms 274
pressure 274
processes 347–8
reference group 795
group dynamics 394, 901
group exercises 900–1
group think 349
growth needs 303–4
guided reading 896

half-life index 422
halo effect 472
harassment *see* sexual harassment
hard competences 190
hard HRM 147
Hardy Spicer 429
harmonization 738, 757–8
Hawthorne studies 331–2
Hay Management Consultants 227, 603
Hayes Committee 95
head hunters 458
health and safety
    accident prevention 815–17
    defined 805
    factors affecting 806
    organization 811–13
    performance analysis 808–9
    performance measurement 817, 819
    policies 809–11
    principles 806–7
    programmes 807–8
    training 819
Health and Safety at Work Act 43
Health and Safety Executive 43
hedonism of the past 297
Herzberg's two-factor model of motivation
    304–6
heuristics 862
Hewlett-Packard 367
hierarchical task analysis 214
hierarchy, organizational 330
hierarchy of needs 302–3
high commitment management 328
high day rates 654
home-based pay for expatriates 690–2
homeostasis 298
horizontal integration 76–8
horns effect 472
host-based pay for expatriates 692
HRM *see* human resource management
human capital theory 596

human relations 34
human resource development (HRD) *see*
    employee development
human resource development plan 432
human resource management (HRM)
    approach 34–5
    as a business-orientated approach 142
    characteristics of 147–8
    coherence 147
    and collectivism 149
    and commitment 144, 147, 320
    concept of 139–40, 141–2
    conditions for success 762
    contradictions in 149
    defined 141
    definitions, common themes of 145
    degree to which HRM is systematic 720–1
    development of the concept 33, 142–3
    devolution to the line 146
    driving force for 144
    emphasis of 141–2
    and employee relations 718–21, 739, 740
    and the employment relationship 146
    features of 145
    flaws in 149–50
    and flexibility 144
    hard and soft HRM 147
    the Harvard framework 142–3
    HRM model 718
    'hyped' 139
    and individualism 149
    individualistic values of 144
    and industrial relations 149, 719
    and innovation 78
    and integration 141, 144
    and line management 142, 146, 147
    management-orientated nature 145, 146
    matching model of HRM 141
    meaningful version of (Storey) 146–7
    morality of 150–1
    and mutuality 143, 327
    normative nature of 145
    and personnel management 152–3
    philosophy 42, 155, 718
    policy goals of 144
    practicality of 151
    and quality 144
    and recruitment 478–9
    reservations about 148–51
    as a resource centred approach 155
    rhetoric 139, 145, 149, 774
    shift from collectivism to individualism 146
    simplistic nature of 149
    and strategic integration 144
    strategic nature of 153
    take up of 154–5, 719
    themes 145

as a theory 148
and trade unions 33, 720–1
trends 33–4
UK versions of the HRM model 144–7
unitary perspective of 144
values – unitarist and individualistic 144
human resource management and personnel
   management
  debate on 91
  differences 153–4
  relationship 152
  similarities 152–3
human resource planning
  achieving the aims 407–9
  action planning 431–41
  aims 406
  and business plans 508
  computerized systems 424–7, 857
  control 441–2
  defined 28, 404, 405
  demand forecasting 411–15
  downsizing plan 441
  employee turnover analysis 417–22
  employment costs analysis 431
  flexibility plan 427–30, 436–40
  forecasting human resource requirements 424
  forecasting skill and competence
    requirements 415
  human resource development plan 432
  modelling 424–6
  productivity plan 430, 440–1
  recruitment plan 432–3
  retention plan 433–6
  stocks and flows analysis 425–6
  strategies 409–10
  supply forecasting 416–24
human resource strategy *see* personnel
  strategies and strategic HRM
humanistic approach to personnel
  management 58, 91
humanistic values 98, 390–1
hygiene factors 305, 314

IBM 51, 110, 367
impression management 79
incapability 498
incentives 591, 659
incentive alignment 597
incentive schemes
  degeneration of 670–1
  executive 666–7
  shop floor 667–70
incidence rate 817
incremental pay 652
individual contributors 618
individual differences 265–70, 281–2
individual job ranges 648

individual piecework 668
individualism 707, 717
induction 293, 483–5
industrial democracy 776
Industrial Participation Society 759
industrial relations
  collective bargaining 714–16, 748–9
  collectivism 717
  defined 29
  developments in 722–5
  Donovan analysis 723–4
  employers' organizations 734
  the HRM model 718–21
  individualism 717
  interventionism 724
  legal framework 712, 754
  managements 760
  parties involved 729
  pluralist view 716
  procedural agreements 755
  regulations 713
  role of management 733–4
  role of trade unions 739–42
  single-table bargaining 749
  single-union deals 756
  strategy, employee relations 742–3
  substantive rules 713
  as a system of rules 712–13
  trade union recognition 726
  traditional system 723
  unitary view 716
  voluntarism 717–18
  *see also* employee relations
Industrial Society 779
industrial tribunals 735
informal groups 347
informal organization 331
information 849
information systems, personnel *see* personnel
  information systems
information technology 849, 850–1
information theory of learning 517
innovation
  in personnel management 78–80
  and personnel strategies 75
  planning 76
input-process-output model 614
Institute of Business Ethics 94
Institute of Employment Studies 426–7
Institute of Personnel and Development (IPD)
  41–2, 93, 96, 102–3, 105, 405, 489, 495,
  524–5, 556, 745, 775, 776–7, 813, 840–1,
  847–8
Institute of Personnel Management *see* Institute
  of Personnel and Development
instrumentality theory of motivation 300–1
integrated pay structures 655

integrated personnel management 201
integrating the personnel and development
  contribution 74–5
integration (organizational)
  contingency model of integration 338
  and differentiation 376
  and supportive relationships 332
  and theory Y (McGregor) 332
integration of personnel strategies, policies and
  practices
  achieving horizontal integration 76–8
  achieving vertical integration 75–6
  through competence-related personnel
    management 195, 201
  of HR and business strategies 141
  HRM as an integrating approach 144
  through performance management 77–8,
    232, 233–4
  strategic 108
integrative bargaining 715–16, 760
intelligence 266–7, 474
intelligence quotient (IQ) 473
intelligence tests 473–4
interaction 346, 348–9
interactionism 275
interactive skills training 902
interactive video 897–8
internal benchmarking 610
internal consultancy
  conducting projects 67–8
  development of role for personnel specialists
    34
  and interventions 80–1
  methods of operation 67
  and process consulting 392
  role of personnel practitioner 54, 65–6
  skills 68
internal differentials 639
internal environment 37, 374–5
internal equity 598
internal labour market 406
internal relativities 590, 638, 698
international pay 690–2
international personnel management
  challenge of 129–30
  characteristics of 130
  defined 129
  employment and development strategies
    131–2
  expatriates, management of 136–8
  and the global context 51
  international employee development 134–5
  recruitment across international boundaries
    133–4
interpersonal relationships 278
interventions, organization development 401
interventions, personnel management 80–2

interviewing
  dos and don'ts 471
  ethical considerations 481
  preparation 457
  redundancy 493
  sequence 468
  starting and finishing 468
  questioning techniques 469–71
  techniques 469–71
  timing 468
interviews
  advantages and disadvantages 471
  aim 466
  arrangements 464–5
  attitude surveys 783
  behavioural event 202, 469
  behaviourally-based 469
  individual interviews 462
  inviting candidates 460
  job analysis 208–11
  nature of 466–7
  number to hold in a day 459
  panels 462
  purpose 465–6
  selection boards 463
  structured 468–9
  time allowed 459–60
  types of 462
intrinsic motivation
  defined 299
  and extrinsic motivation 299
  and Herzberg's two-factor model 306
  and job design 380
  and job enrichment 306
inventories, job analysis 211
Investors in People (IIP) 44–5
involvement *see* employee involvement

Japanese management
  *kaizen* 112
  model of commitment 320
job analysis
  approach to 207
  check list 211, 215
  choice of method 215
  critical-incident technique 222–3
  data collection 208–9
  defined 204
  diaries and logs 214
  faults analysis 218
  functional analysis 222
  hierarchical task analysis 214, 215
  information provided 206–7
  interviews 208–11, 215
  inventories 211–12, 215
  job learning analysis 218–19
  observation 213

questionnaires 211, 215
repertory grid 224–5
self-description 213–14, 215
task analysis 217–18
for training needs 538–9
job breakdown method of job analysis 216–17
job classification 609–10
job description
defined 205–6
examples 867–73
and flexibility 226
format 226–7
for job evaluation purposes 227
purpose 225
for training purposes 227, 538–9
use of 226
writing a job description 227–30
job design
aims 379
approaches to 382–4
defined 28, 379
factors affecting 380
horizontal 778
job enlargement 383
job enrichment 384–5
job rotation 383
motivating characteristics of jobs 381
and motivation strategy 316
process 379–80
redesign 778
self-managing teams 388
task structure 381
vertical role integration 778
job enlargement 383
job enrichment
aim 384
defined 384
impact of 384–5
job evaluation
analytical schemes 608
appeals 629
benchmark jobs 623
briefing employees 627–8
choice of scheme 621–3
competence-based evaluation 617
and computers 629
conducting job evaluation exercises 625–9
defined 29, 605
developing a point-factor scheme 622–9
equal value 629
factor plan 614
features of 606
informing employees 623
internal benchmarking 610
introducing 620–2
involving employees 623
job-centred evaluation 618

job classification 609–10
job ranking 609
jobs and people, significance of 607
management consultant's schemes 608
market pricing 617–18
methodology 607
nature of 606
non-analytical schemes 608
number of schemes 621
panels 626–9
people-focused schemes 622
point-factor rating 610–16
programme 623–4
proprietary brands 608, 621
pros and cons 618–20
purpose 605–6
schemes 607–8
skill-based 616–617
tailor-made schemes 521
trade union attitudes 623
use of expert systems (computers) 862–3
job family
and career planning 575
competences 196
defined 196
pay curve 651
pay structures 648–9
job grades 641
job hierarchies 607, 650
job instruction 895
job-for-life 34, 745
job ladders 575
job learning analysis 218–19
job matching 631–2
job ranking 609
job regulation 713
job rotation 383
job satisfaction 34, 313
job sharing 438
job shops 494
job specification *see* person specification
joint consultation
aims 788
constitution 789–90
defined 778–9
membership of joint consultative
    committees 789
structure 789
topics 788–9
works councils 790
just-in-time (JIT) 81

*kaizen* 112
key result areas
knowledge 539, 849
knowledge-based pay 592
    *see also* skill-based pay

knowledge workers 410
Kolb's learning cycle 518, 519
Kolb's learning styles 518–19
Kumatsu 478

labour market
  defined 405
  external labour market 405–6
  impact on pay levels 593, 595
  internal labour market 406
labour market analysis
  local 423
  national 424
labour turnover/wastage *see* employee
  turnover
law of effect 297, 301
leaders
  function of 353
  qualities 354
  roles 353–4
leadership
  behavioural dimensions 354
  effectiveness 355
  situational aspects 355
  skills 316
  styles 355
lean organization 40
learning
  as an active process 520
  agreements 524, 526
  approaches to 510
  conditions for effective learning 520–1
  contracts 524, 526
  curve 514–15
  cycle (Kolb) 518, 519
  defined 507
  and development 605
  by doing 516
  experiential 517
  levels of 521
  motivation to learn 515, 520
  and personal development plans 525
  process of 514
  psychology 515–16
  reflective 517
  reinforcement 516–17
  retrospective 517
  self-managed 525–6
  specification 206
  styles 518–20
  theory 516–20
  transfer of 542
learning agreement or contract 526
learning curve 514–15
learning organization
  concept of 510–11
  defined 521

model of 523
  and performance management 244
learning psychology 515–16
learning theory
  cybernetic 517
  experiential learning 517
  Kolb's learning cycle 518–19
  learning styles 519–20
  and motivation 520
  reinforcement 516–17
  self-efficacy 518
  stimulus-response 517–18
lecture 898–9
legal framework (industrial relations) 43, 712,
  725, 753, 754
length of service analysis 419
levels of pay 590–1
levers for change, provided by personnel 111
life-long careers 286, 489
line jobs 330
line managers
  competence in personnel management 90
  and computerised personnel information
    systems 850, 852–3
  conflict with personnel managers 92
  devolution of responsibility for personnel
    management to 85, 89–90, 92, 703, 752
  discretion to make PRP awards 663
  division of responsibility for personnel 90
  and employee relations 752
  gaining support from 87
  and innovations in personnel management
    80, 87
  and personnel specialists 88–90
  responsibility for reward 703–4
line and staff organizations 330, 358
line of sight 660
location allowances 686
logs 213
London Borough of Richmond on Thames 183
loyalty 319
Lucas Aerospace 94

macho-management 78
magazines 798
main tasks – definition of 228–9
management by objectives 234, 308
Management Charter Initiative (MCI) 191
management consultants
  legal implications 74
  use of 71–4
management development
  activities 558
  analysis of needs 558
  approaches to 565–6
  assessment of skills and competences 558–9
  basis of 564–5

as a business-led process 556–7
competence-based 568–9
defined 556
formal approaches 566–7
impact of 557–8
informal approaches 567
integrated approach 567–8
international 132–3
meeting assessed needs 559
nature of 559–60
objectives of 556
and organization development 390
philosophy of 566
processes of 558
responsibility for 560, 561
role of personnel/management
    development specialists 564
strategy 560
management prerogative 734, 759
management style 334, 365, 387
management succession planning
aim 580
defined 571
demand and supply forecasts 422
performance and potential assessment 580–2
use of computerized personnel information
    system 861
management training 545–6
managing change see change management
managing diversity 130, 183, 842–3
managing employee reward see reward
    management procedures
managing under-performers 247–8
managing with trade unions 758–61
managing without trade unions 761–2
manpower planning see human resource
    planning
Manpower Services Commission 536
manual skills analysis 217
manual workers' pay
effort bargain 653
high day rates 654
incentive schemes 667–71
pay structures 653
plus rates 654–5
rates of pay 653
spot rate structures 652
time rates 653–4
manufacturing requirements planning (MRP2)
    415
Margerison and McCann's Team Management
    System 353
market clearing wage 595
market-driven organizations 638–9
market equilibrium wage 595
market groups 649
market premium 639

market pricing 617–18
market rate anchors 646
market rate surveys
advertisements 634
club surveys 634
information required 631
job matching 631–2
presentation of data 632
published surveys 633
purpose 630–1
sources of information 632–3
special surveys 633–4
using survey data 634–5
market rates
and broadbanding 646
concept of 631
differentials 639
market stance 638
marketing employee development 511–12
marketing the personnel function 82–3
Marks and Spencer 367
Maslow's hierarchy of needs 302–3
matrix organizations 359
maturation 271–2
maturity curves 649
McLelland's achievement, affiliation and
    power needs 304
measured day work 671–2
mechanistic organizations 337
mediation 751
medical adviser, role of 812
mentors/mentoring 583
merit rating 234
methods time measurement (MTM) 669
midpoint, pay range 642, 646
mission statements 370
mobility clauses, contracts of employment 835
models, human resource planning 415, 578–9
models of personnel management
Karen Legge 59
Kathleen Monks 62–3
John Storey 63
Shaun Tyson 59–60
Shaun Tyson and Allen Fell 60–1
money and motivation 314–15
money purchase pension schemes 685
motivation
Alderfer's ERG theory 303–4
approaches to 318
attribution theory 311, 313
behavioural theory 310
and commitment 323
content theory 301–4
defined 296
equity theory 309–10
expectancy theory 306–8
extrinsic 299, 306, 312

goal theory 308
Herzberg's two-factor model 304–6
homeostasis 298
instrumentality theory 300–1
intrinsic 299, 306, 312
key messages 311
Maslow's hierarchy of needs 302–3
McClelland's theory of needs 304
measuring 315–16
model 296–7
and money 314–15
motivating characteristics of jobs 381
needs 312
needs theory 301–4
open system theory 298–9
orientation theory 283, 313
and performance 313
process of 296
process theory 306–10
and quality of working life 299
reactance theory 308–9, 313
reinforcement 297–8, 301
role modelling 311, 313
self-efficacy theory 310
social learning theory 310–11, 312
strategies 315–18
theory 295
wants 296, 312
worker motivation 385
multimedia training 898
multinational firms 51
multiskilling 429–30
multi-rater assessment *see* 360–degree
     feedback
multi-source assessment *see* 360–degree
     feedback
mutual commitment firms 327–8
mutual commitment strategy 328, 741
mutuality
     and commitment 327
     concept of 143
     and HRM 143, 150, 327, 718
     principle of 180
     as a unitarist concept 327
Myers-Brigg Type Indicator 268

National Vocational Education and Training
     Framework 43–4
National Vocational Qualifications (NVQs) 44,
     190, 192, 194, 202, 225, 270, 547, 673
natural justice, principles of 500
nature and scope of jobs 229–30
NatWest 94
needs
     achievement needs 304
     affiliation needs 304
     Alderfer's ERG theory 303–4

Herzberg's two-factor model 304–5
Maslow's hierarchy of needs 302–3
need for power 304
and the process of motivation 296
self-fulfilment needs 302
and wants 296
theory 301–4
negotiating
     skills 772, 773
     strategy 768–9
negotiations
     bargaining 770–1
     closing 771–2
     nature of 764
     opening 770
     preparing for 766–7, 769–70
networking 87, 99, 346
new pay, the 599–600
new realism in employee relations 739
new style union agreements 755
new technology
     home- and tele-working 438–9
     impact on organizations 340
     introduction of 76
     policy 184–5
     and redundancy 486–7
     and trade unions 722
newsletters 798–9
Nissan 113, 478
non-directive counselling 835–6
non-financial rewards 592
normative approach to change management
     396
norms
     defined 274, 363
     examples 363–4
     group 274
notice boards 799
numerical flexibility 345, 359
NVQs *see* National Vocational Qualifications

objectives
     agreement of 238
     corporate 238
     defined 238
     defining work objectives 239–40
     departmental/functional 238
     developmental 240
     good work objectives 239
     individual 238–9
     learning 240
     operational 238
     personal 240
     qualitative 239
     standing objectives 239
     target-related objectives 239
     team 238

types of 238
updating 245–6
work objectives 238, 239–40
observation, job analysis 213
occupational health
  occupational hygiene 805
  occupational medicine 805
  programmes 805, 813–14
  stress management 814
occupational pension schemes
  approved scheme 684
  benefits statements 685
  contracting out 685
  contributions 684
  defined 683
  operation 683–4
  retiring age and sex discrimination 684–5
  types of schemes 685
Occupational Personality Questionnaire (OPQ)
  269
OD see organizational development
offers of employment 481, 483
office staff training 550
open-system theory 298–9
operant conditioning 317
organic organizations 337
organization
  analysis 374–5
  authority in 330
  behavioural science school 332–5
  bureaucratic 335–6
  classical school 330–1
  contingency school 337–9
  coordination 330
  decentralized 358
  divisionalized 358
  federal 341
  flexible 359
  formal 331, 333
  guidelines 376–7
  human relations school 331–2
  informal 331
  and interest group coalitions 321
  lean 40
  line and staff 330
  matrix 358
  mechanistic 337
  the new organizational paradigm 341
  organic 337
  of personnel function 62–4
  planning 377–8
  political processes 321
  processes 343–57
  shamrock 341
  socio-technical model 37, 336–7
  specialisation 320
  structure 330, 333, 340, 342–3

as a system 37
systems school 336–7
types 340
organization-based flexibility 376–7
organization charts 342–3
organization design
  activity analysis 375
  aim 373–4
  defined 28
  guidelines 376–8
  organization reviews 374
  responsibility for 378
organization planning 377–8
organization reviews 374
organization structure
  analysis of 375
  defined 342
  formal and informal structures 330, 331
  and integration 338–9
  nature of 330
  need for 333, 342
organizational behaviour 263
organizational climate
  defined 362, 364
  and motivation 316
  perceptions of 364–5
organizational culture
  analysis of 370
  artifacts 364
  and change 362, 370
  components of 362–7
  defined 361
  development of 366–7
  and the formulation of policy 186
  implications 388
  importance of 361–2
  management of 368–71
  management style 365
  norms 363–4
  organization climate 364–5
  and process 366
  reinforcement of 369–70
  and strategy 365
  strong cultures 367
  and structures 366
  and systems 366
  values 362–3
  varieties of 367
organizational development (OD)
  analysis 393–4
  basis of 390–1
  and change management 395–400
  and conflict resolution 400–1
  decline of 402
  defined 81, 390
  diagnosis 393
  educational activities 401

as a lever for change 111
and management development 390
methods 391–2
philosophy 390–1
planning OD programmes 394–5
process consulting 67, 71, 81, 392–3
role of OD practitioner 401
organizational effectiveness 28
organizational processes 360
change 343–6
command and control 355
communications 346
conflict 357
flexibility 345–6
group behaviour 346–50
interaction 346
leadership 353–5
networking 346
politics 356–7
power 355–6
teamworking 350–3
organizational release see release from the
organization
organizational success
contribution of personnel function 106–16
definition of a successful organization 104
managerial factors contributing to success
105
people factors contributing to organizational
success 105–6
organizations
as a coalition of interest groups 321
decentralized 358–9
divisionalized 358
flexible 359
line and staff 358
matrix 359
process-based 359–60
as systems 329, 372
organizing
aim 373–4
contingent approach 373
process of 372
orientation theory 283
orientation to work 278–80
outdoor learning 552, 903
outplacement 491, 493–5
outsourcing
case for 69
decisions on 69–70
managerial and legal implications 70–1
and the personnel function 62, 63, 64, 66
selecting service providers 70
overtime 440
overtime payments 686

panels, job evaluation 626–8

part-time workers 438
participation
defined 775–6
and employee involvement 776
forms of 778–9
incidence of 791
mechanisms for 780–1
planning for 792–3
task participation 778
pay
additions to base pay 591
base pay 590
problems and solutions 433
at risk pay 591
variable pay 591
pay curves 649–51
pay determination 649
pay levels
and base pay 590–1
defined 593
economic factors affecting pay levels 593,
595–7
and market rate surveys 630
pay policy 184
pay practices 598
pay progression
annuity approach to 595
incremental systems 595
through pay curves 650
through pay ranges 642–3, 647
pay ranges
definition of 641
differentials 642
and market rates 641
number of 641
overlap 642
progression through 642–3
reference points 642
size of 641–2
span 642
pay reviews
budgets 663, 697
general reviews 699–700
individual reviews 700
pay spines 652–3
pay/market stance 635, 638
pay structures
basis of 638–9
broad-banded 645–8
choice of 655–6
criteria for 637
defined 593, 636
graded 640–5
individual job range 648
integrated 655
job family 648–9
for manual workers 653–5

number of 637–8
pay curves 649–51
pay spines 652–3
purpose 636–7
rate for age 655
spot rate 652
pay surveys *see* market rate surveys
pay zones 646
paying for performance
   advantages and disadvantages 657–8
   criteria for success 660
   defined 29, 657
   executive bonus schemes 666–7
   incentive or reward 659
   incentives and bonuses 659
   performance-related pay 661–6
   related to organizational performance
      679–80
   shop floor incentive schemes 667–72
   types 660
payment-by-results *see* shop floor incentive
   schemes
pendulum arbitration 751
pension schemes *see* occupational pension
   schemes
performance 313, 487
performance agreements 235–6, 237
performance appraisal 234–5
   *see also* performance management
performance improvement plans 240
performance management
   activities 237
   background to 234–5
   basis of 232
   and career counselling 585
   and competences 29, 241–2
   and continuous learning 246
   as a continuous process 244–5
   coverage 259
   cycle 235–6
   defined 29, 232–3
   documentation (forms) 257–8, 881–7
   evaluation of 260–1
   as an integrating process 78
   introduction of 258–60
   managing performance throughout the year
      243–4
   managing under-performers 247–8
   monitoring 260
   objectives 238–40
   performance agreements 235–6, 237
   performance plans 242–3
   performance measures 240–1
   performance review discussions/meetings
      248–51
   principles of 235
   process of 235–6

as a process of management 233
   purpose 232–3
   and self-managed learning 525–6
   updating objectives and work plans 245–6
   use of computers 860
   and values 242
performance measures 240–1
performance pay *see* paying for performance
performance problems, dealing with 247–8
performance rating
   achieving consistency 253–6
   arguments for and against 252–3
   behaviourally anchored rating scales (BARS)
      255–6
   methodology 252
   and performance-related pay 256–7
   scales 252
performance-related pay (PRP)
   arguments for and against 665–6
   conditions for success 666
   defined 661
   individual 591
   as a lever for change 111
   matrix 664
   and motivation 314
   operation of 661–2
   and rating 256–7
   size of increases 662
   and the State 45
performance reviews
   basis of 249
   conducting discussions 250–1
   focus of 250
   purpose 248
   360–degree feedback 251–2
   and training specifications 539
performance standards 539
peripheral workers 345, 359, 437, 438, 722
person specification 206, 446
personal characteristics 275
personal construct 224
personal development plans
   content 563
   defined 526
   preparation of 527–8
   purpose 526–7
   and self-managed learning 525
personality 267–70, 475
personality tests 475–6
personality traits 475
personnel activities 28–30
personnel budgets 84–5
personnel competence map 101
personnel and development function
   activities 52
   aim 53
   changes to the role 55–7

contribution to added value 108–9
contribution to change management 111–12
contribution to competitive advantage 109–10
contribution to continuous improvement 112–13
contribution to organizational success 106–16
contribution to quality management 113–16
evaluation of 117–18
externalization of activities 56
marketing of 82–3
organization 62–4
outsourcing personnel work 69–71
overall role 52–3
re-engineering of 70–4
role in employee relations 708–9
role in managing organizational release 487–8
using management consultants 71–4
variations in practice 58–9
personnel and development management
  activities 28–30
  aims 102
  ambiguous nature of 90–1
  blockages and barriers 85–6
  competence in 100–2
  concerns 27–8
  conflict 92–3
  defined 25
  ethical considerations 93–5
  European approach to 50
  evolution of 32–4
  gaining support and commitment 85–8
  and human resource management 152–5
  integrated personnel management 201
  key requirements 30, 32
  and line management 87–90
  models of 60–2
  purpose 27
  values 93–4
  workforce centred 155
personnel and development management, context of
  competitive pressures 39–42
  contingency theory 37–9
  the European context 46
  external environment 37
  the global context 50–1
  government, role of in setting agenda 42–6
  internal environment 37
  technology 39
personnel and development practice
  ambiguities in the personnel contribution 90–1, 96
  blockages and barriers 85–6
  conflict in the personnel contribution 92–3

ethics in 93–5
gaining support and commitment 85–7
innovations in 78–80
interventions 80–2
respective roles of line managers and personnel specialists 88–90
personnel budgets 84–5
personnel and development practitioners/professionals
  as business partners 54
  as change agents 54, 65, 111–12
  competences 100–2
  ethical standards 93–5
  how to be effective 97–9
  as influencers 85
  as innovators 78–80
  as internal consultants 54, 65–8
  as interventionists 80–2
  IPD Code of Professional Conduct 93
  and line managers 87, 87–90
  as part of management 93–4
  professionalism 95–7
  responsibility for redundancy policy and practice 489–90
  roles of 53–5, 65–6
  as service providers 65
  as strategists 65
  values 93–4
personnel director
  as a business partner 172
  requirements for 99–100
  as an internal consultant 68
  job description 867–8
personnel forms
  application form 877–80
  employment, labour turnover and earnings – quarterly return 891
  monthly analysis of leavers 889
  monthly/annual summary of absence 890
  performance management 881–7
  personnel record card 888
personnel function *see* personnel and development function
personnel information systems
  importance of 849
  manual records 863–4
  *see also* computerized personnel information systems
personnel managers
  as 'architects' 60–1
  as business managers 60
  as 'clerks of works' 60
  as conformist innovators 59
  as 'contracts managers' 60
  as deviant innovators 59
  job description 868–9
  roles of 53–5, 65–6

*see also* personnel and development
    practitioners
personnel officer, job and role description 870–3
personnel policies
    AIDS 848
    areas 179
    career management 576–8
    defined 178
    distinction between policies, strategies and
        procedures 171
    employee development 184
    employee relations 184, 738–41
    employment 181–2
    equal opportunity 181, 182–3
    formalization of 179
    formulation of 185–7
    grievances 182
    health and safety 182, 809–10
    managing diversity 183
    new technology 184
    overall policy 179–80
    pay 184
    personnel policy dilemmas 180–1
    promotion 909
    redundancy 182
    resourcing 406
    sexual harassment 182, 185, 844–6
    smoking 182, 185
    substance abuse 182, 846–8
    training 533
    transfer 837
personnel procedures
    defined 171
    disciplinary 905–6
    distinction between procedures, policies and
        strategies 171
    grievance 904–5
    promotion 838, 909
    reason for 187
    redundancy 906–8
    transfer 836
personnel records 856, 863–4
personnel specialists/professionals *see*
    personnel and development practitioners
personnel specification *see* person specification
Personnel Standards Lead Body (PSLB) 27–8,
    30, 53, 100, 102
personnel strategies
    and coherence achievement 77
    content 171
    development/formulation of 172–8
    distinction between strategies, policies and
        procedures 171
    employee development 508–10
    employee relations 742–3
    employee resourcing 409–11
    key issues 176–7

    nature 171
    quality of working life 388–9
    relationship to business strategy 172
    relationship to strategic HRM 171–2
    resourcing 409–11
    reward 600–1
    training 531–2
Peter Principle 575
philosophy
    continuous development 524
    employee development 510
    employee relations 738
    HRM 89, 707, 718
    management development 566
    organizational development 390–1
    performance management 244
    training 531–3
physiological needs 302
piece work 668
Pilkington Optronics 120
planned experience 893–4
planned training 534–6
plateaued managers 578
pluralism 717
pluralist concept of organizations 321
pluralist view of industrial relations 716–17
plus rates 654–5
point-factor rating job evaluation
    advantages and disadvantages 614–16
    choice of factors 611–12
    defined 610
    developing a point-factor scheme 622–5
    factor plan 614
    factor rating scales 612–13
    factor weighting 613–14
policies *see* personnel policies
politics 356–7
portfolio career 489
Position Analysis Questionnaire 212–13
positive reinforcement 249
potential assessment 580, 582
power
    need for 304
    in organizations 355–6
    and organization development 390
    sources of 356
predetermined motion time system 669
principal agent theory 596–7
procedural agreements 755
procedural rules 713
procedures *see* personnel procedures
process
    -based organization 359–60
    defined 366
    focus on 341
    group 347–8
    and organization 360

organizational 80–1
and organizational culture 366
process consulting 67, 71, 392–3
process theory (motivation) 306–10
processes, organizational 360
productivity 430, 487, 722
productivity planning 76, 440
product-market considerations 160
product-market development 174
professional considerations in redundancy 488
professionalism in personnel and development
    management 95–7
profit-related pay 679–80
profit sharing 678–9
progression curves 649
progression, pay 642–3, 647
progressive parts method of training 515
projects 896
promotion
  increases 702
  policies 181
  procedure 838, 909
  and supply forecasting 422
psychological contract
  basic nature 289–90
  changing nature 290–1
  defined 288
  development of 291–2
  and the employment relationship 287, 293
  and realistic job previews 466
  significance of 292–3
psychometric tests
  purpose 472–3
  types 473
  use of 477

quality circles
  aims 785
  defined 785
  features 785
  prerequisites for success 785–6
  and trade unions 80
quality management
  defined 113
  importance of 113
  role of personnel function 114–16
  strategy 75, 389
  total quality 113
quality of working life (QWL)
  aim 388
  ethical obligation to provide 745
  and motivation 299
  policy 180
  strategy 388–9
questions, interview
  behavioural event 469
  closed 470

hypothetical 470
leading 470
open-ended 469
play-back 470
probing 470
questionnaires
  attitude surveys 783
  job analysis 211
  organization climate 364–5

Race Commission 43
Race Relations Act (1976) 480
rate for age scales 655
rating performance *see* performance rating
ratio-trend analysis 413–14
reactance theory of motivation 308–9
realistic job previews 293, 466
reciprocal determinism 310
recognition, union 726, 727, 738, 745–7
recruitment across international boundaries
  133–4
recruitment consultants 457–8
Recruitment and Development Report (1991)
  56, 58
recruitment plan 432–3
recruitment and selection
  advantages and disadvantages of interviews
    472
  advertising 453–7
  aim 443
  analysis of recruitment strengths and
    weaknesses 452
  application forms 461
  assessment centres 463–4
  attracting candidates 451
  behavioural event interviews 202
  biodata 461–2
  and competence analyses/profiles 201–2
  contracts of employment 483
  defined 28
  defining requirements 446
  electronic CVs 461
  ethical framework 480–1
  evaluating the recruitment process 479–80
  executive search consultants 458
  five-fold grading system 449
  follow-up 485
  graphology 478
  HRM approach 478
  improving effectiveness of 478–9
  inadequacy of interview 479
  induction 483–5
  interviewing 462–72
  the legal framework 480
  offers of employment 481, 483
  person specifications 446, 448
  realistic job previews 293, 466

recruitment consultants 457–8
references 481–2
selection tests 472–8
seven point plan 448–9
sifting applications 459–60
sources of candidates 452–3
use of computers 859
use of tests 477
using executive search consultants 458
using recruitment agencies 457
using recruitment consultants 457–8
red circling 645
redundancy
   avoidance of 490
   causes of 486–7
   defined 906
   ethical approach to 94
   handling redundancy 492–3
   outplacement 491, 493–5
   payment arrangements 492
   planning for 490
   policy 182
   procedure 491–2, 906–8
   professional approach to 488
   responsibilities of personnel professionals 489–90
   selection for 491, 492
   voluntary 490–1
reference group 795
reference point (pay structure) 642
references 481–3
reinforcement
   and behavioural theory 310
   and expectations 307
   and learning theory 516–17
   positive reinforcement 249
   theory 297–8
relatedness needs 303
relating rewards to organizational performance
   gainsharing 679
   profit-related pay 679–80
   profit sharing 678–9
relativities 590, 638–9
release from the organization
   career dynamics 488–9
   dismissal 495–500
   ethical considerations 488
   general considerations 486–9
   managing organizational release 487–8
   outplacement 491, 493–5
   redundancy 486–7, 489–91
   references 502–3
   retirement 503
   voluntary leavers 501–2
   voluntary redundancy 490–1
reliability, in tests 473

repertory grid 224–5
repetitive strain injury (RSI) 668, 810
resistance to change 277–8, 400
resource capability 160
resourcing policies 406
resourcing strategy 409–11
retention plan 433–6
retirement 503
review meetings *see* performance review meetings
reward management 588 *see* employee reward
reward management procedures
   attrition 699
   auditing the reward system 697
   budgeting 696–7
   communicating to employees generally 704–5
   communicating to individual employees 705
   compa-ratio analysis 698–9
   control 700–1
   dealing with anomalies 702–3
   evaluating the reward system 697–8
   fixing rates of pay 701–2
   grading jobs 701
   monitoring the reward system 696
   pay reviews 699–700
   payroll budgets 696
   promotion increases 702
   responsibility for reward 703–4
   review budgets 697
   use of computers 859–60
reward policies 601–2
reward strategy
   content 601
   development of 598, 600–1
   effectiveness 600
   purpose 600
reward system 593, 594
rewarding special groups
   directors and senior executives 692–5
   expatriates (international pay) 690–2
   sales staff 687–90
rightsizing 486
role
   ambiguity 281
   clarification 377
   conflict 281
   definition 206, 280
   flexibility 226
   incompatibility 281
   and job 280
   modelling 311
   perceptions 308
   set 280
   theory 283

role analysis
  defined 205
  methodology 216
role definitions
  defined 205
  examples of 870–1, 874–6
  and flexibility 226
  generic 231
  preparation of 231
role of government in setting personnel agenda 42–5
role-playing 900
Rover Group 113, 120, 745

safety
  accident prevention 815–17
  adviser, role of 812
  committee, role of 813
  measuring safety performance 817–19
  programmes 807–8
  see also health and safety
safety needs 302
sales staff rewards
  basic salary 688
  bonus schemes 690
  choice of approach 690
  commission 689
sales training 546–7
satisfaction and performance 313
satisfiers 305
Saville and Holdsworth Occupational Personality Questionnaire 269
scientific management 331
Scottish National Vocational Qualifications (SNVQs) 44
Second Company Level Industrial Relations Survey 727
selection tests
  aptitude 474
  attainment tests 475
  characteristics of a good test 473
  choosing tests 476–7
  intelligence tests 473–4
  personality tests 475–6
  purpose 472–3
  test battery 477
  use of 477
  validation 474, 477
self-actualization 271, 302
self-description, job analysis 213–14
self-development 559
self-efficacy theory 310, 518
self-fulfilment 302
self-managed learning 525–6
self-managing teams 384, 388
self-report questionnaires 902
service contracts 695

service level agreements 85, 123–4
service providers 70
service provision, personnel management 65
service-related pay 591
seven point plan 448–9
severity rate 817
Sex Discrimination Acts (1975 and 1986) 480
sexual harassment
  policy 182
  problems of dealing with 844
  solutions 844–7
shamrock organization 341
share options 694
share ownership 680, 695
shift payments 686
shift-working 440
shop floor incentive schemes
  defined 667
  degeneration of 670–1
  fall-back rate 667
  individual piecework 668
  measured daywork 671–2
  ratio of base rate to incentive 667
  work-measured schemes 668–70
shop stewards 731, 752
short-term contracts 285
short-term employment 285
sickness 824–5
Siemans 51
simulation 900
single table bargaining 749
single union deals 746, 747
single union recognition 746–7
situation-act model 280
Sixteen Personality Factor Questionnaire (16PF personality test) 268
skill-based job evaluation 616–17
skill-based pay
  defined 592, 672–3
  operation 673–4
skilled performance 270, 282
skills
  categorization of 527
  defined 539
  transferable 527
skills analysis
  defined 216
  faults analysis 218
  job breakdown 216–17
  job learning analysis 218–19
  manual skills analysis 217
  task analysis 217–18
skills audits 858
skills base 510
skills inventories 858
Smith, W H 198
smoking policy 182, 846

# Subject Index

Social Chapter (EU) 46, 722
Social Charter (EU) 46, 722
social group *see* groups
social influences on people 273–4, 282
social learning theory 310–11
social needs 302
Social Policy (EU) 46
Social Protocol (EU) 46
socio-technical model of organization 329, 336–7
socio-technical systems 384, 388, 389
soft HRM 147
soft skills (competences) 190
specialization 330
spot rate pay structures 652
stability index 419
staff associations 733
staff organization 330
stakeholders
    and employee development strategy 508
    and employee relations 745
    perspective in evaluating personnel effectiveness 119
    and personnel practitioners 55
    recognition of interests by HRM 143
    responsibility of organization to 104
stand-by payments 686
State Earnings Related Pension Scheme (SERPS) 685
the State as employer 45
*status quo* 759
'sticky' wages 595
stimulus-response theory of learning 517–18
straight piecework 668
strategic alliances 51
strategic fit 75–6
strategic human resource management (SHRM)
    aims 158
    and coherence 167–8
    defined 157, 172
    as discussed by Beer *et al* 142–3
    as defined by Fombrun *et al* 161–2
    development processes 166–7
    difficulties 164–6
    fundamental concepts of 168, 178
    holistic nature of 167–8
    and human resource planning 407–8
    integration 108, 163–6, 172
    meaning of 162–3
    origins of concept 161–2
    and personnel practitioners 65
    and personnel strategies 171–2
    rationale for 162
    requirements for 168
    significance of 153
    *see also* personnel strategies

strategic fit 166–7
strategic integration 108, 163–6
strategic management
    defined 158–9
    key concepts 159–60
    purpose 159
strategy
    and culture 365
    defined 159
    formulation of 160–1, 164
    information technology 850–1
    *see also* personnel strategy and strategic HRM
stress
    causes of 277
    coping with 277
    interviews 481
    management of 814
strikes 753–5
structured interview 468–9
subcontracting 285, 439
subsistence allowances 686
substance abuse policy 182, 846–8
substantive agreements 756–7
substantive rules 713
succession planning
    aim 571, 580
    computerized approaches to 580
    information for 580
    methods 580
suggestion schemes 786–7
supply and demand factors influencing pay levels 595
supply forecasting
    age analysis 416–17
    analysing existing resources 416–17
    analysing sources of supply 423–4
    changes in conditions of work 423
    defined 410
    effect of absenteeism 423
    employee turnover analysis 417–22
    forecasting requirements 424
    length of service analysis 417
    promotions and transfers analysis 422
supply-side planning 410
supportive relationships 332
survival rate 419
synergy 160
system theory 37
systematic training 533–4
systems 366
systems approach to planned training 536
systems school of organization theory 329, 336–7
systems theory of industrial relations 712

talk 899
target rates of pay 646

952

task
  alignment 398
  analysis 217–18
  definition of 228–9
Tavistock Institute 351
team briefing 800–1
team building training 550–1
team effectiveness 351–2
team leader training 545–6
Team Management Systems (Margerison and
    McCann) 353
team pay
  introduction of 677–8
  requirements for 677
  schemes 677
team rewards
  basis of 676
  defined 675
  purpose 675–6
  types of teams 676
team roles (Belbin) 352–3
teams
  characteristics of 350–1
  defined 350
  disadvantages of 351
  effectiveness of 351–2
  high-performance 351
  and performance 351
  self-managing teams 384
teamwork 376
teamworking 226
technical training 547
technology 39
teleworking 438–9
temporary workers 437–8
terminal behaviour 540, 553–4
tests *see* selection tests
theory Y 332, 335, 391
threshold competences 191
timekeeping 499–500, 838–9
time rates 653–4
360–degree appraisal *see* 360–degree
    feedback
360–degree feedback 251–2
T–group training 901–2
top management 86–7
Toshiba 51
total earnings 592
total loss control 806, 817
total quality management (TQM) 81, 113
total remuneration 592 , 683
Towers Perrin 110
Toyota 756
Trade Union Congress 732–3
trade union legislation 43, 725, 753, 754
Trade Union Reform and Employment Rights
    Act (1993) 480, 753

trade unions
  and the check-off system 753
  decline of 731–2
  derecognition 738, 741, 746, 747
  and HRM 720
  and innovation 80
  international union organizations 733
  managing with unions 758–61
  managing without unions 761–2
  membership 726
  procedural agreements 755
  recognition 726, 727, 738, 745–7
  role of 730
  single union deals 756
  structure 713, 730–1
  substantive agreements 756–7
training
  action-orientated training 532
  administration 860–1
  aim 529–30
  benefits 530
  and continuous development 533
  craft 547
  deficiency model approach 536
  defined 508, 529
  ethics training and development programme
    95
  evaluation of 553–5
  gap 536–7
  health and safety 819
  and human resource planning 434
  identifying learning and training needs
    536–40
  management training 545–6
  modules 547
  objectives 540
  office staff 550
  outdoor 552, 903
  performance-related 533
  philosophy 531–3
  policies 533
  planned training 534–5
  problem-based training 532
  programmes 540–3
  project 896
  relevant training 532
  responsibility for 544, 552–3
  sales 546–7
  skill 547–50
  for special groups 552
  specification 539
  strategic approach to 531–2
  surveys 540
  systematic training 533–4
  systems approach 536
  team building 550–2
  team leader training 545–6

technical 547
transfer of learning 540
Training and Enterprise Councils (TECs) 44
training for special groups 552
training needs analysis
  aims 536–7
  areas 537–8
  job analysis 538–9
  methods 538–40
  surveys 540
training programmes
  conducting 544–5
  content 541
  external 542–3
  in-company 541–2
  length 541
  objectives 540
  off-the-job 542
  on-the-job 541–2
  Training Services Agency 44
training specification 206, 539
training techniques
  action learning 894
  assertiveness 902
  assignments 895–6
  case study 899–900
  coaching 892–3
  computer-based training 896–7
  demonstration 892
  discussion 899
  distance learning 903
  group dynamics 901
  group exercises 900–1
  guided reading 896
  interactive skills training 902
  interactive video 897–8
  job instruction 895
  job rotation 893–4
  lecture 898–9
  mentoring 893
  multimedia 898
  off-the-job 543
  on-the-job 543
  on- or off-the job techniques 543–4
  outdoor learning 903
  planned experience 893–4
  projects 896
  role-playing 900
  simulation 901
  talk 899
  T–group training 901–2
  video 897
  workshops 902–3
traits 268–9
transferable skills 527
transfers
  and supply forecasting 422

procedures 836–7
transparency 294
trust 328, 744
trust, building of 745
two-factor model motivation (Herzberg) 304–6
two-tier workforces 438

unemployment 285–6
unfair dismissal 496–7
unitarist philosophy of HRM 144
unitary frame of reference of commitment strategies 321–2, 327
unitary view of industrial relations 716
utility analysis 126–7

valency 306
validity in tests 473
value statements 370
values
  areas 362–3
  and culture 362–3
  defined 362
  and organizational development 390, 393–4
  and performance management 242
  in personnel and development management 93–4
valuing employees 316
variable pay 591, 662
variable progression 662
vertical integration 75–6
vertical role integration 778
video 897
virtual corporation 40
vision 77
visionary leadership
vocational education and training 43–5
voluntarism 717–18
voluntary leavers
  analysing reasons for turnover 502
  exit interviews 501–2
voluntary redundancy 487, 490–1
voluntary release 487

wage drift 667
wants 296, 312
wastage rate 418
welfare
  defined 821
  employee assistance programmes 828–9
  group services 824
  individual services 824–7
  personal case work 823–4
  what sort? 823
  why provide? 821–3
world class performance 40
work 284–5

work councils 790
work-measured incentive schemes 668–70
work study techniques of human resource
    planning 414–15
worker directors 790–1
working groups *see* teams
Workplace Industrial Relations Survey (WIRS
    3, 1990) findings
  on the coverage of collective bargaining 726
  on the personnel function 57–8
  on HRM 719, 727
  on joint consultation 788
  main findings 725–7
  on involvement and participation 791

on management prerogative 734, 759
on multi-employer bargaining 748–9
on plant-level bargaining 748–9
scope of personnel function 55–6
on shop stewards 731
on single union recognition 746–7
on single-union deals 756
on trade union recognition and
    derecognition 726, 733, 746, 761
works councils 790
workshops 220–1, 902–3
world class performance 40, 113

xero-based budgeting 84–5

# Author Index

Adair, J 354
Adams, J S 309
Akinussi, D K 134
Alderfer, C 300, 301, 303–4
Allport, G 297, 298
Annet, J 214
Anthony, P 151
Argyle, M 266
Argyris, C 34, 271, 333, 401
Armstrong, G 149–50
Armstrong, M 81, 106, 117, 120, 152, 155, 168, 173, 603, 606, 675
Athos, A 34, 321
Atkinson, G 715
Atkinson, J 345
Austin, N 321

Baillie, J 290
Bales, R F 352, 394
Bandura, A 310, 397–8, 518
Barnard, C 331
Baron, A 603, 606
Bartlett, C A 360
Bass, B M 507
Basset, P 732
Bayliss, F 728, 733, 751, 777
Beardwell, I 154
Beckett, Samuel 516
Beckhard, R 34, 393–4, 396
Beer, M 34, 142, 398–9
Belbin, M 352–3
Bennis, W 34, 390–1
Berridge, J 32
Bies, R J 310
Blackburn, R M 279–80
Blake R 334, 400
Blinkorn, S 476
Blood, M R 385
Boudreau, J W 127

Bower, J L 161
Boxall, P F 142, 143, 158, 174
Boyatzis, R 189, 191
Brayfield, A H 389
Brehm, J W 308 , 309
Brooklyn Derr, C 110
Buchanan, D 323
Burdett, J O 385
Burgoyne, J 189, 192–3, 523
Burns, T 336, 337–8
Burt, C 266

Campbell, A 358–9, 367
Cappelli, P 106
Casson, J 407
Cattell, R B 268, 269
Cave, A 386, 717, 729, 732, 756
Chamberlain, N W 714, 715
Chandler, A D 173, 365
Chell, E 268, 274, 280
Child, J 331, 342
Clegg, H 717
Coombe, A 196
Cooper, C 351
Cooper, C L 277, 310–11
Cooper, R 383
Coopey, J 321–2
Coyle, D 285
Crockett, W H 389
Cross, M 429–30
Cyert, R M 186, 321

Devanna, M A 34, 142, 159, 161–2, 163
Dickson, W 331–2
Digman, L A 161
Drucker, P 79, 104, 118, 340, 562, 716
Dulewicz, V 197, 266, 270
Duncan, C 214, 758
Dunlop, J T 712–13

# Author Index

Dyer, L 174–6, 327, 328

Eisenstat, R 34
Elliott, L 286, 405
Emery, F F 388
Erez, M 308
Eysenck, H J 269

Fayol, H 330
Fein, M 385
Fell, A 60–1, 96
Fernie, S 107
Fiedler, F 355
Flanders, A 714–15
Fletcher, C 266, 270
Fletcher, S 194
Follett, M P 92
Fombrun, C J 34, 142, 159, 161–2,163
Fonda, N 557–8
Fowler, A 148, 149, 150, 467, 468, 478
Fox, A 714–15, 716
Freeman, R 730
French, W R 364
Fullerton, J 183, 523, 842–3
Furnham, A 189, 193

Gagne, R M 517–18
Gall, G 746
Gannon, M 527–8
Garratt, R 523
Gall, G 746
Garvin, D A 521–2
Ghoshal, S 360
Giles, E
Gluckman, M 37
Goldthorpe, J H 279, 314
Gomez-Mejia, L R 118
Goodman, J 775
Goold, M 358–9, 367
Greller M M 288
Guest, D E 85, 96–7, 107–8, 119, 128, 144, 152,
    155, 163, 166, 279, 306, 311, 318, 323, 518, 717,
    718–19, 728, 739–40, 775–6
Guilford, J P 267
Gunnigle, P 158
Guzzo, R A 287

Hackman, J R 382
Hall, L 155
Hall, P 570
Hall, R 106
Halpin, A 334
Hamblin, A C 553, 554–5
Hamel, G 160
Handy, C 284–5, 341–2, 348, 355, 359
Harrison, R 526, 558
Hartley, J 321–2

Hawkins, K A 715
Heider, F 274
Heinrich, H W 806
Hendry, C 145, 153, 162–3, 164–5, 172
Heraclitus of Ephesus 343, 717
Herriot, P 151, 334
Herzberg, F 34, 300, 304–6, 314, 384, 386, 388,
    389
Holbeche, L 586
Holden, R 154
Holder, G W 174–6
Holmes, L 194
Honey, P 519–20
Hoque, K 85, 107–8
Horwood, R 96–7
Huczynski, A 323
Hulin, C L 385
Hull, C 297
Humble, J 562
Hunter, J E 479
Hutton, W 285–6

Jaques, E 315
Janis, I 349
Johnson, C 476
Johnston, J 138

Kahn, R 288, 336
Kahn-Freund, O 718
Kakabadse, A 357
Kandola, R 183, 218, 523, 842–3
Kanter, M R 129–30
Kanter, R M 159, 568
Kaplan, R S 104–5
Katz, D 288, 336
Katzenbach, J 350–1
Kay, J 161
Keenoy, T 141
Kelley, H H 274–5
Kelly, G 224
Kenney, J 534–5
Kessler, S 728, 733, 751, 777
Kirkpatrick, I 151
Kissler, G D 290–1
Kochan, T A 327, 328
Kolb, D A 518–19
Kreitner, R 317–18
Kuhn, J 714

Latham, G P 308, 469
Lawler, E E 307–8, 382, 599, 616, 620, 660, 662
Lawrence P R 34, 142, 298, 299, 337, 338–9, 383
Lawrent, A 48–9
Leavitt, H J 348
Legge, K 53, 59, 145, 149, 150, 153, 322, 369
Lengnick-Hall, C A 162
Leon, L S 521, 523–4

Levinson, D 272–3
Levitt, T 82
Lewin, K 394, 395, 901
Likert, R 34, 332–3
Litwin, G H 364–5
Locke, E A 308
Long, P , 106, 117, 120, 155, 168, 173
Lorsch, J W 298, 298, 337, 338–9
Lorenz, K 276
Loscocco,K A 273
Lupton, T 331
Luthans, F 317–18

Macneil, R 287
Mangham, L L 321
Mann, R 279–80
Mant, A 545
March, J G 186, 321
Marchingon M 78–9, 762, 775, 778–9, 790, 791
Margerison, C 353
Marginson, P 727, 740, 749
Martin, A O 822
Maslow, A 34, 300, 301, 302–3, 386
Mayo, A 510
Mayo, E 34
McCann, R 353
McClelland, D 300, 301, 304
McClelland, G 716
McCormick, E J 212
McGregor, D 332, 335, 391, 562, 563
McKersie, R B 715–16
Medoff, J 730
Mendenhall, M 137
Metcalf, D 107
Miller, E 329, 336
Miller, P 158, 160, 163, 164
Millward, N 719, 731, 734, 740, 746, 748, 756, 762, 791
Mintzberg, H 161, 165, 321, 339–40, 743
Mischel, W 269, 275
Monks, J 720
Monks, K 61–2, 760
Moorby, E 511
Moore, S 158
Morton, G 759
Mouton, J 400
Mullern, B 351
Mumford, A 519–20, 525, 559–60
Munro Fraser, J 448
Murlis, H 575

Nadler, D A 263
Neathey, F 608
Noonan, K A 287
Noon, M 148
Norris, P 570
Norton, D P 104–5

Oldham, G R 382
Ouchi, W G 321
Oddou, G 137

Pascale, R 34, 321, 339, 341
Pearn, K 218
Peccei, R 119, 128
Pedler, M 513, 521
Perrow, C 335, 339
Peters, J 765
Peters, T 34, 69, 180, 321, 367, 774
Pettigrew, A 145, 153, 162–3, 164–5, 172, 344
Phelps Brown, H 724–5
Pichard, J 94–5
Porter, L W 307–8
Porter, M 109, 159, 719
Prahalad, C K 160
Pritchard, D 575
Purcell, J 145, 173, 717, 759, 760

Quinn Mills, D 34, 142, 166

Reay, D G 514, 515–16
Reid, M 534–5
Revans, R W 545, 894
Rice, A 329, 336
Richards-Carpenter, C 851, 853
Roberts, C 757, 758
Robertson, I T 273, 307, 310–11, 382–3
Robinson, R B 158
Rodger, A 448
Roethlisberger, F 331–2
Rousseau, D M 287, 288
Ryden, O 675

Salancik, G R 319
Saville, P 475
Schein, E H 34, 288, 369–70, 392
Schmitt, N 475
Schumacher, E F 387
Schuster, J R 598, 600
Scullion, H 132, 137
Selznick, P 180
Senge, P 523
Sheehy, G 272
Shepart, H 400
Sik, G 475
Silverman, D 38
Singh, H 106
Singh, R 715
Sisson, K 55, 56–7, 146, 749, 760
Skinner, B F 288, 310
Slater, J A 351
Sloan, A P 358
Smith, D 350–1
Smith, M 273, 382–3, 475–6
Smith, P 759

# Author Index

Snell, S A 158
Spector, B 34
Spencer, L 189
Spindler, G S 291, 292
Stalker, G 336, 337–8
Stanton, M 135
Stevens, B 775, 776
Stevens, J 76–7
Storey, J 59, 62, 141, 146–7, 154–5, 166, 728, 734
Stringer, R A 364–5

Tannenbaum, S I 351
Taylor, A 266
Taylor, F W , 300, 301, 330
Thurley, K 90–1, 92, 396–7
Thurstone, L L 266, 267
Tichy, N M 34, 142, 159, 161–2, 163
Toplis, J 266, 270
Torrington, D P 51, 130–1, 152, 155, 277
Townley, B 473
Trist, E L 329, 351
Tsui, A S 118
Tuckman, B 349–50
Turner, A N 383
Tushman, N L 263
Tyler, T R 310
Tyson, S 55, 59, 60–1, 96, 106, 120, 163, 168, 172, 173

Urwick, L F 330

Vaughan, J A 507
Vernon, P E 266
Von Bertalanffy, L 298
Vroom, V 288, 306–7, 389

Wade-Benzoni, K A 287, 288
Walker, J W 158, 164, 166–7
Walton, R E 34, 142, 143, 323, 327, 401, 715–16
Waterman, R 34, 180, 321, 367
Watson, A 96
Weber, M 335
Weiner, B 275
West, M A 351
Wheeler, R 849, 850, 853
Whipp, R 344
Wick, C W 521, 523–4
Wickens, P 478–9, 839
Wilson, N A B 388
Winer, B A 354
Witcher, M 163, 168, 172, 173
Wood, S 328
Woodland, S 107
Woodruffe, C 189, 191, 193–4
Woodward, J 278, 337, 338
Wright, P M 158
Wright, D S 266
Wright, V 658

Zidon, I 307
Zingheim, P K 598, 600